DAVID O. MCKAY LIBRARY

3 1404 00721 5582

P9-CKV-122

**SECOND EDITION**

# Learning and Teaching
## *Research-Based Methods*

SEP 16 2002

**Donald P. Kauchak**
*University of Utah*

**Paul D. Eggen**
*University of North Florida*

WITHDRAWN

MAY 07 2024

DAVID O. McKAY LIBRARY
BYU-IDAHO

ALLYN AND BACON

Boston London Toronto Sydney Tokyo Singapore

PROPER
DAVID O. McKAY LIBRARY
BYU-IDAHO
REXBURG ID 83460-0405

*Editor-in-Chief, Education:* Nancy Forsyth
*Series Editor:* Virginia C. Lanigan
*Series Editorial Assistant:* Nicole DePalma
*Production Administrator:* Annette Joseph
*Production Coordinator:* Holly Crawford
*Editorial-Production Service:* Laura Cleveland, WordCrafters Editorial Services, Inc.
*Cover Administrator:* Linda K. Dickinson
*Cover Designer:* Susan Paradise
*Manufacturing Buyer:* Louise Richardson

Copyright © 1993, 1989 by Allyn and Bacon
A Division of Simon & Schuster, Inc.
160 Gould Street
Needham Heights, MA 02194

All rights reserved. No part of the material protected by this copyright notice may be reproduced or utilized in any form or by any means, electronic or mechanical, including photocopying, recording, or by any information storage and retrieval system, without the written permission of the copyright owner.

**Library of Congress Cataloging-in-Publication Data**

Kauchak, Donald P.
 Learning and teaching : research-based methods / Donald P.
Kauchak, Paul D. Eggen. — 2nd ed.
  p.    cm.
 Includes bibliographical references and index.
 ISBN 0-205-14634-1
 1. Teaching.  I. Eggen, Paul D.   II. Title.
LB1025.3.K38  1993
371.1′02 — dc20                           92–1613
                                          CIP

Printed in the United States of America

10  9  8  7  6  5  4  3  2  1    97  96  95  94  93  92

Photos by Frank Siteman.

*Text credit:* p. 337, from *The First Year of Teaching: Real World Stories from American Teachers.* Copyright © 1991 by Pearl Rock Kane. Reprinted with permission from Walker and Company.

# Contents

## CHAPTER 3    Teacher Planning: Research and Reality    56

# CHAPTER 4        Effective Teaching: A General Instructional Model        97

# CHAPTER 5        Involving Students in Learning        136

## CHAPTER 6    Adapting Instruction for Different Goals: Teaching Facts, Concepts, and Generalizations    179

## CHAPTER 7    Organized Bodies of Knowledge: Integrating Facts, Concepts, and Generalizations    218

## CHAPTER 8    Skills Instruction    253

## CHAPTER 9   Teaching Thinking Skills      281

## CHAPTER 10  Alternatives to Direct Instruction     312

## CHAPTER 11    Classroom Management                    353

# Preface

The preface to the first edition of this text began this way:

> Recent research has highlighted the centrality of the teacher in determining the quality of instruction in the classroom, and the quality of instruction with the amount that students learn. Teachers *do* make a difference in determining how much students learn, and this difference is influenced by the ways that teachers teach. The goal of this book is to translate the results of research on effective teaching into methods that preservice and in-service teachers can use in their classrooms.

We share this with you in our preface to the second edition because we believe this optimistic view of teaching is equally appropriate today. Teachers indeed exert a powerful influence on both student achievement and motivation, and these influences are even more convincingly documented in the research literature than they were in 1989. In addition, we are still convinced that knowledge of research findings can make teachers more effective professionals both inside and outside the classroom.

But change has occurred. The role that cognitive psychology, anthropology, linguistics, and research on teachers' thinking play in helping teachers learn to teach is better understood than it was in the late 1980s, and these influences are reflected in this edition. Studies from these areas form a powerful body of research that can help teachers understand how learning can be enhanced in the classroom.

This book brings together two areas of educational literature. One is the research on effective teaching, which refers to the broad spectrum of studies conducted since about 1970 on how teachers influence learning. The search for effective teaching strategies that produce student learning is central to these studies. In addition to the core of effective teaching literature, however, we also consider such diverse topics as teacher and student cognition, teacher expectations, classroom management, and planning.

Teaching methodology is the second major area directly addressed in this book. Methods texts historically have stressed those teaching procedures viewed as desirable based on the state of the art at the time. The emphasis in these texts has been on practical application in classrooms, with less emphasis on research.

This text combines the best of the two areas. In doing so, we attempt to apply the research on effective teaching to strategies that are practical, usable, and, at the same time, theoretically sound. This interpretation of the literature has been enriched by our work in the schools; teachers and students have helped us make these applications realistic and true to the complexities of real schools and today's students.

We have two goals in combining the two areas: to change how teachers think about teaching and to change how they actually teach. Changing thinking is difficult enough; altering actual teaching practice is even harder. Teaching is a highly personal and idiosyncratic enterprise; no two teachers think alike or teach alike. This is as it should be. The personal energies and insights each of us brings to teaching provide the creativity that is one of the major rewards of teaching. However, to translate these personal beliefs into a framework for thinking about and structuring their experience, teachers need knowledge and concepts. Research on effective teaching can provide powerful ways to analyze and think about our teaching.

In addition to helping teachers analyze their own teaching, we have tried to provide the means for translating this thinking into practice. Here is where a combination of the literature and our own experience comes into play. Without the literature to provide a conceptual foundation, methods become mechanical applications of rules implemented without understanding. Conversely, in the absence of feasible suggestions for teaching practice, the research literature remains abstract, if not irrelevant. We hope to avoid both pitfalls by emphasizing the conceptual underpinnings of the research and the implications of this research for actual classroom practice.

In translating these research findings into methods for teaching, we have organized the text around three major themes. The first theme is the central role the teacher plays in promoting student learning, and the importance of the teacher–student relationship. The second area is the research that documents and explains this role. The third theme—teacher judgment and decision making—connects the other two. Teachers must exercise professional judgment in the interpretation of research findings and the application of teaching strategies. Teachers using this book should understand where this research came from and its strengths and limitations. The decisions they make will be based on this understanding.

As we used the first edition in our own classrooms and listened to the suggestions of our colleagues, we added coverage of the following topics to the second edition:

- Student diversity
- Teaching exceptional students
- Multicultural education
- Teaching at-risk students
- Task analysis as a planning tool
- Teaching thinking skills
- Expanded coverage of cooperative learning.

These changes reflect the changing realities of modern classrooms, as well as the new responsibilities being given to today's teachers. We hope the addition of these topics helps teachers prepare for the challenges of teaching in the twenty-first century.

We would like to thank the following reviewers for their comments and suggestions on the manuscript: Rosemarie Deering, Kansas State University; David Petkosh, Pennsylvania State University; and Sandra Winecoff, University of South Carolina.

D.K.
P.E.

# CHAPTER 1

# Research and Teaching

................................................

## OVERVIEW

This chapter introduces you to the content of your text. We begin to discuss research in effective teaching, and we state our theme that teachers are the most important factor in student learning next to the pupils themselves. The preeminence of teachers and of the decisions they make, together with their knowledge of the research literature, are the threads that bind this text together. Chapter 1 introduces the concept of effective teaching, briefly outlines its history, and illustrates how research can be used to improve student learning.

Chapter 1 also describes the different components of learning to teach. Knowledge of subject matter enables teachers to present topics in accurate and understandable ways. Pedagogical knowledge describes the research-based connections between teaching and learning. Teaching strategies translate this research into classroom-oriented plans for action. These three components are tied together by teacher decision making, which integrates them into purposeful teacher actions.

## MAIN IDEAS

### Effective Teaching

*Effective teaching* involves the ability to apply research findings to classroom practice.

Effective teaching combines human relations skills, judgment, intuition, knowledge of subject matter, and understanding of learning into one unified act, resulting in improved learning for students.

### History of Effective Teaching

Initial studies were based more on the views of prominent thinkers than on research.

Studies of teacher traits marked the next step in teaching research.

The search for an ideal methodology attempted to discover the one best way to teach.

School-level research focused on global variables.

Studies linking teacher behaviors and student achievement evolved into the body of knowledge called *teacher effectiveness research*.

### Learning to Teach

*Knowledge of subject matter* allows teachers to present topics accurately and understandably.

*Pedagogical knowledge* translates research into connections between teaching and learning.

*Teaching strategies* are prescriptive, research-based methods designed to achieve specific goals.

*Teacher decision making* integrates the other components of learning to teach into logical and coherent plans of action.

. . . . . . . . . . . . . . . . . . . . . . . . . . . . . . . .

Three junior high teachers were eating lunch together on their 40-minute break between classes. After weather and local politics, the conversation turned to teaching, or, more specifically, to students.

"How are your seventh graders this year?" Stan Williams asked. "I can't seem to get them motivated. I've got three basic math classes, and I've spent the first 2 months reviewing stuff they're supposed to know already. They don't seem to want to think," he concluded, turning to the others with an exasperated look.

"Mine aren't so bad," Leona Foster replied. "In fact, the other day we had a great discussion on individual rights. We were discussing the Bill of Rights, and some of them actually got excited about it. And it was even one of my slower classes. I was impressed with some of their comments."

"But how am I going to get them to think if they don't even know how to multiply or divide?" Stan answered in frustration.

"I know what you're talking about, Stan," Paul Escabar interjected. "I'm supposed to teach them to write, but they don't even know basic grammar. How am I supposed to teach them subject–verb agreement when they don't know what a noun or verb is?"

"Exactly!" Stan answered. "We've got to teach them basics before we can teach them all the other stuff, like problem solving and thinking skills."

"I'm not so sure about that," Paul replied. "I had a real eye opener the other day. . . . Let me tell you about it. I've been going to workshops on using writing teams to teach composition. I tried it out, putting high- and low-ability students on the same team. They were supposed to write a critical review of a short story we had read, using Siskel and Ebert as a model. We talked a little about basic concepts like plot and action, watched a short clip of Siskel and Ebert, and then I turned them loose. I couldn't believe it—some of the kids that never participate actually got excited."

"That's all fine and good for English classes, but I'm a math teacher. What am I supposed to do, have them critique math problems? Oh, I give this math problem two thumbs up! Besides, these are supposed to be junior high students. I shouldn't have to sugar coat the content. They should come ready to learn. My job is to teach; theirs is to learn. It's as simple as that."

Or is it? Teaching has always been a challenging profession, but changes both within and outside the classroom have made it more complex. Schools are being asked to teach thinking and problem-solving skills at the same time that the students they teach come from increasingly diverse and challenging backgrounds. Definitions of good or effective teaching are becoming not only more crucial but also more complicated.

What is effective teaching? How does effective teaching relate to learning? What responsibilities do teachers have to motivate their students? Are "basics" the best path to thinking skills, or should thinking skills be used as a vehicle to teach basics?

These are important considerations for anyone in education because they center around the question "What is good teaching?" These concerns are particularly important to developing teachers because their answers will influence the kind of teacher you become. As you ponder these questions, thinking about yourself and the classrooms you've experienced, each of you will form a personal definition of effective teaching. This response is as it should be: Each teacher is as unique as each student. But beyond this individual uniqueness, some strands exist that pull these questions together.

Pursue the issue further. Does your definition of effective teaching generalize to all levels? That is, what similarities or differences would you expect to see in effective kindergarten and high school teachers? What about different students? Would your definition apply equally well to low- and high-ability classes? What difference does subject matter make? That is, do effective history teachers teach the same way as English (or art) teachers? Finally, how does time influence your definition? Do effective teachers teach the same way at the beginning of the school year and at its close; at the beginning of a unit and at the end; or even at the beginning of a lesson and at its completion?

Each of you will have answered these questions, either implicitly or explicitly, by the time you enter the classroom as a teacher. The purpose of this book is to help you resolve these questions based on the best information available to the profession.

Currently, the field of teaching is at a particularly exciting time in its history. Education has always been one of the most rewarding professions; but, at the same time, it continues to be one of the most difficult in which to perform well. An effective teacher combines the best of human relations, intuition, sound judgment, knowledge of subject matter, and knowledge of how people learn—all in one simultaneous act. This task is extremely complex, and one of the factors making it particularly difficult has been the lack of a clear and documented body of knowledge on which to base professional decisions.

Now the situation has changed. For the first time in its history, education has a significant body of research that can be used to help guide both teaching practice and the training of teachers. That is what this text is all about: It is a book about teaching practice that is founded in and based on research. As you read the material, you will be introduced to the research findings and you will learn how these findings can be applied in the classroom to help increase student learning.

We developed this text around a series of themes that will be introduced in this chapter. As your study continues, you will see the growing usefulness of education research to teachers. This research, as with all research, is not perfect, and we take care to identify its limitations and possible misinterpretations as we describe it. However, having this research as a base is a giant step forward, and despite some weaknesses and even some controversy, this research marks a major advance in education. This research is already finding its way into tests used to certify teachers (e.g., Florida and Georgia), into inservice programs for experienced teachers (e.g., Madeline Hunter, 1984), and into the field of educational psychology (Gage and Berliner, 1992; Glover, Ronning, and Bruning, 1990). Your study of this material will provide you with the best information available to the profession at this time.

# RESEARCH IN TEACHING: A HISTORICAL PERSPECTIVE

Historically, teaching has been a profession in search of research to inform classroom practice. In the past, much development in the field of education and educational reforms has been based on the views and intuition of prominent thinkers in the field rather than on hard research evidence (Slavin, 1989). Because of the stature of these people and the power and eloquence of their positions, their assertions often were translated into practice. While this process is not necessarily bad, often little evidence existed either to support or to change the practice.

For example, the post-Sputnik years spawned a national wave of curriculum revision in math and science during the sixties and early seventies. The view held by prominent scientists and mathematicians was that the content in those areas was inappropriate because it did not accurately reflect the beauty and structure of the disciplines. Curricular revision was aimed at correcting these deficiencies. The changes sounded good, and enormous amounts of money, time, and effort were pumped into the revision effort. While the programs enjoyed modest popularity, they were clearly not as successful as the original developers had hoped nor as the millions of dollars poured into them promised.

One of the reasons for this lack of success was that the programs were developed without a coherent body of knowledge on which to base the curricular decisions, such as considerations of the intellectual development of the learners who would study the materials, of the extent to which the materials would be motivating for the students, and of whether they were usable by teachers (Berman and McLaughlin, 1978). Many of the new strategies required skills not possessed by teachers and materials not readily found in the classroom. These factors, together with the lack of a research base, were primary reasons for the demise of these curriculum projects.

Other examples of trends in education without a sufficient research base could be cited. In pointing to these examples, we do not want to imply that, historically, education has not been systematically studied or that educational research has begun only recently. To the contrary, an enormous number of studies have been conducted in an attempt to identify variables that make a difference in student learning. Unfortunately, until quite recently these studies were largely unsuccessful, as the following section shows.

## Studies of Teacher Characteristics

All research begins with a question, and one reason for the spotty results of previous educational research on effective teaching stems from the type of research questions asked. The initial wave of research into teaching focused on teacher characteristics like neatness, sense of humor, or cognitive flexibility, rather than on teachers' actions in the classroom, such as how they grouped students, the kind and amount of seatwork they assigned, or the type of questions they asked (Rosenshine, 1979). Initial research questions asked whether teachers' possession of these desirable traits resulted in increased learning. For example, do students taught by a teacher with a good sense of humor learn better and/or have a better attitude than those taught by a more sober teacher? Hindsight affords us an opportunity here to criticize this overly simplified question; magnificent teachers of many different personalities can be found. Variety is one of the attractive qualities of the human species.

In addition to problems with initial focus, the research had problems with methodology. Notable among these deficiencies was the fact that researchers seldom entered classrooms to see if teachers rated high in a certain trait taught any differently from those rated low in the trait. They merely assumed that a difference existed. Unfortunately, this line of research led nowhere. Gage (1960), a prominent researcher in the field, reviewed over 10,000 studies in this area and concluded that few, if any, generalizations could be made about the kinds of things teachers could do to produce consistent student learning.

In hindsight, the research on teacher characteristics was not completely misguided. Two dimensions, teacher experience and understanding of subject matter, have proved to be powerful variables influencing how teachers understand events in the classroom and explain content (Berliner, 1987; Carter and Doyle, 1987; Shulman, 1987). Experienced teachers are able to call on previous years in the classroom to interpret the complex events that occur in classrooms and to make the hundreds (if not thousands) of split-second decisions needed daily. In a similar way, subject-matter expertise allows effective teachers to frame and explain ideas in ways that make sense to students. We will return to both of these ideas later.

## The Search for the Right Method

During the sixties, the next wave of research focused on global methods and attempted to link certain teaching techniques or orientations, such as inquiry or discovery, with student outcomes, such as scores on standardized tests of achievement or measures of student attitude (Dunkin and Biddle, 1974; Medley, 1979). This research was characterized by a belief that a particular type of teaching, such as discussion or problem solving, was better than an alternative, such as lecture, or drill and practice. To investigate this question, teachers were trained in a particular technique and then were asked to teach their students by this method. The performance of their students was compared to the performance of students taught by an alternate method.

Like the previous research, these studies were flawed. The methods themselves were often either poorly defined or poorly taught to the teachers; few classroom observations were made to determine if the methods actually were used; and there often was no sound relationship between the teaching methods and the tests used to measure learning differences. For instance, a research study might ask if the discussion method was superior to lecture, but the criterion measure designed to measure student learning employed a paper and pencil test of recall. Tests such as these ignore the more probable benefits of a discussion, such as increased human relations skills or the development of higher level thinking skills, areas not readily measured by fill-in-the-blank, factual-information test items. As you would expect from this description, this line of research also proved unproductive.

## School-Level Research

A third line of research focused on larger variables like school size, training level of teachers, and aptitude or socioeconomic status of the students, and tried to determine their effect on student achievement or attitude. The most notable study of this type was the famous Coleman Report (1966), which involved 4,000 schools and 654,000 students. The study analyzed data at the school level rather than the classroom level—thus masking individual teacher differences—and concluded that teachers made little difference in how much students learned. Understandably, this research had a dampening effect on efforts to identify effective teacher practices; this study concluded that factors outside teachers' influence, such as the background of the students and the curriculum, were more important than the teacher.

Subsequent researchers questioned some assumptions and procedures involved in these schoolwide studies and, as a consequence, their results as well. For example, in these studies, standardized test scores of student achievement for each individual class were averaged with those of the other classes in a school to get a schoolwide score. These averages masked results that would provide valuable information about an *individual* teacher within the school. As we all know, individual teachers within a school can vary considerably in terms of their teaching effectiveness. Prominent researchers pointed out these problems (Alexander and McDill, 1976; Good, Biddle, and Brophy, 1975), and a new wave of research based on the previous studies was launched.

## Teacher Effectiveness Research: Teachers Do Make a Difference

As a consequence of the results, or more accurately, the *non*results of earlier efforts, teaching research finally focused on teachers' actions in the classroom in an attempt to find a link between these actions and student learning. Notice the word *action*; we use this term rather than *behavior*, because some of the actions, such as grouping students or eliciting student involvement during seatwork, are larger, more global strategies that go beyond a specific behavior. In other cases, the actions are specific teacher behaviors, such as conducting a lesson-ending review or asking a question to encourage students to relate two ideas.

These studies marked a new paradigm, or way of thinking about research in education. Unlike previous work, this research focused on the teacher and the kinds of interactions teachers had with students (Good, 1983). The researchers did this by identifying samples of teachers whose students scored higher than would be expected on standardized tests and other samples whose students scored as expected or below expectations for their age and ability level. They then went into teachers' classrooms, took literally hundreds of hours of videotapes and tried to determine if any patterns existed between the teachers in the different samples. These studies were labeled *process–product research* because they attempted to find a link between teacher actions or behaviors and student learning outcomes — primarily scores on standardized achievement tests. The teacher behaviors were the processes and the student outcomes were the products (Gage, 1985). Finally, researchers were focusing on what teachers *did* that made a difference in what students learned.

Initially, the process–product research was correlational; that is, teacher actions and student outcomes were related, but the researchers did not know if the results were actually *caused* by the teacher actions. Gage and Giaconia (1981) illustrated this idea with the problem of teacher disapproval. Researchers found an inverse relationship between teacher disapproval and student achievement; teachers who were more negative in their classrooms had students who achieved at lower levels than teachers who were more positive (see Figure 1.1). However, it was unclear whether the expression of disapproval *caused* or was the *result* of low achievement, or whether it was related to a completely different variable such as classroom management problems. (Any conjectures?) The point here is that correlational findings may *suggest* cause-and-effect relationships but do not in themselves *prove* them. To address this problem directly, the next wave of research was experimental and designed to find causal links, if they existed, between teacher actions and student outcomes (Gage and Giaconia, 1981).

These experimental studies had three important characteristics. First, teachers were trained to display the specific behaviors identified in the correlational studies (e.g., waiting a period of time after asking a question before calling on a student to respond). Second, unlike earlier researchers, investigators observed the trained teachers' classes to determine whether the teachers were actually implementing the desired behavior in the classroom. Finally, classes of trained and untrained teachers were compared. Much of the content of this text is grounded in this type of research; a brief illustration might be helpful to provide you with a frame of reference.

**FIGURE 1.1**   Teacher Disapproval and Student Learning

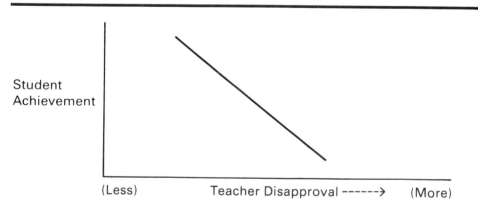

Stallings (1980) focused on a concept called *student-engaged time*, which refers to the amount of time students spend actively studying a subject, rather than talking to each other, walking to seats, passing papers, or waiting for class to begin. Previous research had shown significant positive correlations between the amounts of time students spent actively engaged in a content area and achievement in that area (Karweit, 1984, 1985). The teachers in Stallings's study taught secondary basic reading classes. They were trained in techniques designed to increase student engagement, such as discussion groups focusing on the content read, and teacher feedback to student responses. The researchers then went into the classrooms to see if the trained teachers exhibited these behaviors and whether student engaged time had indeed increased; that is, did the teacher training work? The students then were tested and compared to a control group of students taught by untrained teachers. The investigators found that the experimental students not only were more actively engaged in their work but also learned more than counterparts in the control group.

The results of these lines of research are what make this an exciting time to study education. Researchers are uncovering a number of links between teacher behaviors and student achievement and verifying these through experimentation. Because of this research and other research employing more qualitative or observational teaching techniques (e.g., Erickson, 1986), there are significant implications for teaching practice and the training of teachers. Our goal in preparing this text is to communicate these findings and their implications to prospective teachers and teachers in the classroom.

# LEARNING TO TEACH

This book is written to help you in the life-long process of learning to teach. Becoming an expert teacher is a complex, multifaceted process that continues throughout an individual's professional lifetime. It requires intelligence, sensitivity, experience, and hard work. It also requires several different kinds of knowledge—thorough knowledge of subject matter, such as history, literature, biology, or algebra; knowledge about schools and classrooms within them; knowledge of students, their motivation, and how they learn; and an understanding of how teachers can help in this process. All this takes time, and your experiences will become richer and more meaningful as you progress in this profession. Our hope is that your study of this text contributes to your growth in this process.

Let's turn now to a closer look at the different kinds of knowledge it takes to become an expert teacher.

## Knowledge of Subject Matter

To teach something, we must know something. This simple statement seems self-evident, and it is well documented by a number of studies linking what teachers know and how they teach (Shulman, 1986; Wilson, Shulman, and Richert, 1987). To teach effectively about the American Revolution, for example, a social studies teacher must know not only basic facts about the event but also the historical context in which it occurred and its implications for later events. Elementary teachers teaching the distinction between adjectives and adverbs must not only understand these concepts themselves but must also understand their relationship to other parts of speech and why the distinction between the two is important.

This knowledge—no matter how complete—is not enough, however. An effective teacher must also translate that information into a form that learners will understand. For example, consider the concept of *mammal*, which is typically taught in different ways to students at different levels. At the elementary level, the teacher might use pictures and concrete examples (e.g., a gerbil or guinea pig) to emphasize characteristics like "covered with hair" and "warm blooded." At the junior high level, teachers build on this foundation by emphasizing additional characteristics like "live birth" and "four-chambered heart." Finally, at the high school level, biology teachers can discuss characteristics like mammals' ability to adapt to their surroundings, different classes of mammals, and what it means to be a primitive compared to an advanced mammal. The same concept is taught in different ways at each of these levels to accommodate the background, interests, and capabilities of students.

When teachers plan, one of their most important challenges is to figure out ways of translating abstract concepts into understandable ideas. Let's examine one teacher's thinking as he wrestles with teaching the concept of *theme* to a high school English class. As he plans, he first defines it for himself as "an idea or thought that a story explores or treats." He realizes that this definition is abstract, and if the students are to understand it, he will need to illustrate it with concrete examples.

I'm trying to think of an everyday example so as to "get into it," with the students. . . . What things are repeated in your life—but are never the same each time? Seasons, school, sunrises, meals, etc., . . . for example: A baseball game has a pattern that we can anticipate—9, 3-out innings. However, it is how that pattern is varied in each of its nine repetitions that gives a game meaning; that tells us who wins or loses. We know that a school year has a planned pattern of 2 semesters and four grading periods. But it is the variation within that pattern that gives the school year meaning for you or for me. What is in those semesters, those quarters? The people, the classes. (Wilson et al., 1987, pp. 115–116)

He unsuccessfully teaches the lesson, and students do not grasp the parallels between a baseball game and a theme, nor are they able to identify one in a piece of literature. So he plans again.

Anyway, my frustrations led me to look for a better image, a better metaphor that I could give the guys for tracing and understanding theme. What I came up with was the trailing of a wounded animal by a hunter. Here the hunter discards all or most of the information the scene before him presents. He concentrates only on that which pertains to the animal he is searching for. Now some of the clues might be from the animal itself—blood or hair—just as the word or words of a theme might appear outright in any given passage. But also a hunter must see the broken grass, the hoofprint, the things that are indicators. (Wilson et al., 1987, pp. 116–117)

Throughout the transformation of content from an abstract idea to the analogy of trailing a wounded animal, the teacher tried to help his students understand the process of finding a theme in literature. Effective teachers use their knowledge of content to help students make connections like this every day.

## Pedagogical Knowledge

Learning to teach not only involves learning content and how to translate that subject matter into an understandable form, but it also requires knowledge about the process of teaching itself. **Pedagogical knowledge** is the information we gather from research and the experience of expert teachers that helps us understand connections between teaching and learning. To understand this idea, let's look at a teacher who has taught her students the process for adding fractions and is now reviewing this process with them.

"Class, look at this fraction on the board. What do we call the number on the bottom? Celena?"
"Uh . . . denominator."
"Good, Celena. And what do we call the number on the top, Carl?"
" . . ."
"We talked about this yesterday, Carl. Remember, it tells us the number of parts in the fraction. Think about the term that is derived from, *number*."
"Oh yeah, numerator."
"Excellent, Carl. Now, look closely at this addition problem. It says to add 1/2 and 1/3. What do we have to do first? Think for a moment, because this is important. Look up at the pies that I've drawn on the board to represent these different fractions."

The teacher was trying to help her students do several things in this review. First, she wanted them to remember the names for the top and bottom number in a fraction—two concepts that she had already taught. When Carl could not answer, the teacher provided a prompt that helped him respond correctly. After students recalled the terms *numerator* and *denominator*, the teacher referred them to a problem on the board. She illustrated the abstract problem with a concrete example to promote their understanding of the process. Finally, she told them to pause for a moment—an idea called "wait-time"—encouraging them to take some time to think about why changing the denominator was important.

*Review*, *concept*, *prompting*, *concrete example*, and *wait-time* are all pedagogical concepts. As such, they are part of a professional body of knowledge that helps us analyze and understand the process of teaching. Your teacher education program is designed to help you understand these and many other pedagogical concepts, which will help you recognize and appreciate effective teaching when you observe it and ultimately help you plan and implement effective lessons in your own classroom.

## Teaching Strategies

Research on effective teaching has established links between a number of teacher behaviors and student learning. We can consider these links to be probabilistic if–then statements. *If* the teacher does so and so, *then* particular outcomes are predicted to follow. Using the preceding example, research on wait-time indicates that giving students time to think about a question not only increases the quality of their immediate responses but also results in long-term improvements in achievement (Tobin, 1987). Research also tells us that providing students with concrete examples to illustrate abstract ideas improves students' ability to understand those ideas (Eggen and Kauchak, 1992). An expert teacher is one who understands what research suggests about the relationship between teacher actions and student learning and can implement these behaviors with students.

In our work with teachers, we have found that sharing research with them is not enough; mere discussion of research is unlikely to change the way they teach. The research results must be translated into teaching strategies directly related to classroom practice, and teachers must be given an opportunity to practice the strategies and receive feedback about their efforts. Teaching strategies are a third component of learning to teach. A **teaching strategy** is an interconnected set of teaching behaviors designed to accomplish specific goals. Teaching strategies can be thought of as research translated into teacher actions.

To illustrate the idea of a teaching strategy, let's return to the teacher wrestling with the concept of *theme* and look at one way to teach this abstract idea.

"Class, today we're going to learn about the idea of *theme.* It's an idea that will help us understand and appreciate the literature we read. Look up at the overhead and read the definition there.

'A theme is an idea that reoccurs or repeats itself throughout a story.'

"Let's see if we can understand how theme relates to a story, Hemingway's *The Old Man and the Sea*, which we've just finished. One of the major themes in that book was the struggle of man against nature. Hemingway introduced this theme at the beginning when he told us about the old man's struggles to make a living catching fish. He worked hard every day but went for weeks without catching a decent fish. That's one place where this theme — man against nature — occurred. The fisherman represented man, and the sea that wouldn't let him catch fish was nature. Who can give me a second example of this theme where man struggled with nature? Deena?"

"Well, like when the old man hooked the fish and had to fight with it for a long time."

"Good, Deena. Go ahead and explain how that illustrates the idea of this theme."

"Hmm . . . I'm not sure, but I'll try. The theme . . . the theme is man's struggle against nature and the fish is nature, so he's struggling with it."

"Excellent answer, Deena. Note, everyone, how the same idea — man against nature — is repeated in the story. That's why it's a theme. Who can think of another place where this theme reoccurred or repeated itself? Eddie?"

". . . How about the shark attack?"

"Go on."

". . . Well, after he caught the fish, he tried to bring it back to sell it, but the sharks wouldn't let him. So he . . ."

"What was he struggling with—besides the sharks?"

"Oh, okay, nature. He was struggling with nature."

How does this illustrate a teaching strategy? A teaching strategy consists of coordinated teacher actions designed to reach a particular goal—in this case, helping students understand the concept of *theme*. The teaching strategy used by this teacher involved three basic steps:

- Defining the concept
- Illustrating the abstract idea with specific examples taken from the story
- Questioning to promote students' active involvement in learning.

Research indicates that this is an effective strategy when we want students to understand abstract concepts (Eggen and Kauchak, 1992). Defining the idea provides a frame of reference for the rest of the lesson, the examples illustrate the concept and give it meaning, and the interactive questioning actively involves students in the learning process. In this text, we describe a number of teaching strategies ranging from lecture recitation and skills instruction to discussions and peer tutoring. Each has a specific set of research-based procedures designed to accomplish specific goals.

## Teacher Decision Making

Teachers must know the content they teach and know how to transform this content into a form students can understand. They must also understand how teachers can help students learn and how to translate this knowledge into teacher actions. We call these three components of learning to teach knowledge of subject matter, pedagogical knowledge, and teaching strategies. But learning to teach involves even more than a thorough understanding of these components. Expert teachers not only have a repertoire of knowledge and strategies but also understand when certain teacher actions are appropriate and why. They know that different goals require different teacher actions. For example, the teacher-centered approach to teaching concepts described earlier, which results in increased understanding of concepts, may not be appropriate for teaching other important goals, such as improved race relations or social interaction skills. These alternate goals need alternate approaches that require student interaction and encourage student initiative (Slavin, 1990). Understanding how to implement pedagogical knowledge and when and how different teacher strategies are appropriate is an important dimension of effective teaching, and it requires a great deal of teacher expertise. This dimension is called professional decision making, a process which helps govern and guide the other three components.

**Decision making** involves the application of professional judgment in deciding when, where, how, and why to use the other components of teaching. As shown in

Figure 1.2, decision making is an executive function that governs the application of the other teaching components.

Professional decision making can be thought of as a filter which helps determine when and where research findings should be used. Educational research needs to be applied selectively and strategically, with the goals of teaching and with students' well-being continually in mind; this is the essence of professional decision making. The following examples illustrate this idea:

> A kindergarten teacher has just distributed the materials for an art project and is now surveying the room to see if everyone has started. She notices that Jimmy is staring out the window with his thumb in his mouth and tears in his eyes. It is the beginning of the school year, and Jimmy still isn't used to the idea of being away from home. Should the teacher wait a minute and see if the art materials will do the trick, or should she intervene?

> A junior high teacher is getting more and more frustrated. Mary is obviously more interested in her friends than in English, and the teacher can't keep her from talking. He calls on her; she doesn't hear the question. Should he reprimand her, repeat the question, or go on to another student?

> A high school teacher has just distributed an assignment. She goes over the work in some depth, explaining its importance and how it should be done. She concludes by reminding the class that the grade for the assignment counts as one fourth of the semester grade. A barely audible "who cares?" follows. Should the teacher ignore it and go on, or should she respond?

We all remember our educational psychology texts' admonitions about the different effects on behavior of positive and negative reinforcement (as well as punishment). These are documented research findings. But what do the findings tell the

**FIGURE 1.2** Components of Learning to Teach

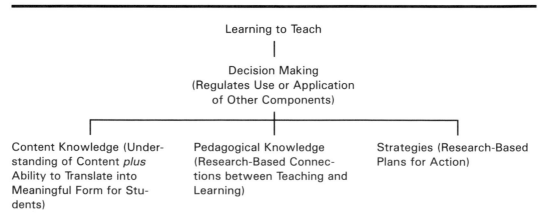

classroom teachers in the preceding examples? In each case, direct intervention might cause as many problems as it solves. Ignoring the problem raises similar issues. To make the situation more complex, these decisions must be made immediately.

The number of decisions—conscious or otherwise—that teachers must make daily is staggering. Jackson (1968), in his observational study of elementary classrooms, fixed the figure at 800; Murray (1986) estimated the number at 1,500. Taking the conservative figure, that translates into more than 130 decisions per hour in a 6-hour teaching day!

Before you get discouraged, remember that effective teachers not only make these decisions but also make them well. Research also shows that expert teachers structure their classrooms to run efficiently, so their time and energy can be devoted to important decisions—decisions that affect learning (Doyle, 1986; Leinhardt and Greeno, 1986).

## Using This Book to Learn to Teach

This book can help you in your efforts to become an expert teacher in several ways. Perhaps most importantly, it describes research findings that connect teaching and learning. Much of this research is described in terms of concepts that are highlighted in **boldface** type to identify them as important ideas. Other research findings appear as teaching strategies designed to accomplish specific goals. Our intent in presenting this information is to provide you with the conceptual tools you need to analyze your own and others' teaching and to implement effective lessons in your own classroom.

Case studies are used throughout this book in an attempt to bridge theory and practice. These case studies serve several functions. First, they illustrate abstract ideas. We used brief case studies in the previous section to illustrate *teacher decision making*—an abstract and potentially difficult to understand concept. In addition to being useful illustrations, case studies show how important ideas can be applied in classrooms. These cases are based on our experiences in real schools and are an attempt to provide you with a realistic slice of classroom life.

Exercises at the end of each chapter (except for Chapter 1) ask you to apply the knowledge gained in that chapter to real-life teaching situations. Most of the exercises use a case study format so you can use concepts taught in the chapter to solve realistic classroom problems. Answers to these exercises are found at the back of the book.

Discussion questions are also found at the end of each chapter. They invite you to go beyond the content, to look for relationships in the material, and to integrate the material in a personal way. The answers to some of these discussion questions can be found within the text, while others are more open ended, asking you to use your own experience and judgment. Hopefully, they will stimulate your growth in professional decision making.

The third set of exercises, "Applying It in the Schools," is designed to assist you in applying research findings in actual classrooms, through assignments that demonstrate the implications of abstract ideas for classroom practice. These exercises appear in three forms. Some ask you to interview teachers, to discover how expert teachers examine and solve real-world problems. Research suggests that studying the thoughts and actions of expert teachers is a productive way to learn about teaching (Berliner, 1988). A second kind of exercise asks you to observe teachers in action, based on information you've studied in this book. You'll be asked to watch teachers teach and to analyze the strategies they use to help students learn. The third kind of exercise invites you to try these ideas for yourself. It involves structured teaching experiences designed to help you apply concepts and strategies in real classrooms with real students. If at all possible, we recommend that you use these to make the content of this text personally meaningful.

# THE ORGANIZATION OF THIS BOOK

## Section One: Pedagogical Knowledge

We have organized this book to facilitate the process of learning to teach. The book is organized into three major sections, the first of which describes general research findings about teaching. This first section provides you with essential pedagogical knowledge to help you analyze your teaching and others'. In the first chapter of this section, we've talked about the central role of research in teaching and how different types of knowledge contribute to the process of learning to teach.

The second chapter, "Student Diversity," was placed at the beginning of the book for two reasons. First, it serves as a reminder that students are the reason we teach and that each student comes to us as a unique individual with potential and promise. Second, research shows that dealing with student diversity presents major challenges to both beginning teachers (Veennan, 1984) and veterans (Good and Brophy, 1991). Hopefully, this chapter will provide a foundation for adapting the content of later chapters to the needs of different learners.

Student diversity is an important consideration during the planning process, in which teachers identify goals and strategies to help students meet these goals. Planning also includes organizing content into understandable segments and sequencing the steps logically. We discuss planning in Chapter 3.

In Chapter 4, we analyze time and explore its impact on student learning. In this chapter we also examine the effects of teacher characteristics such as attitudes, expectations, organization, and clear communication on achievement and motivation. Chapter 4 closes with the description of a general instructional model that is used to frame the specific teaching strategies described in later chapters.

Chapter 5 focuses on involving students in learning. The use of student collaboration and teacher questioning skills as devices to promote involvement are emphasized.

## Section Two: Teaching Strategies

The second section of the text offers strategies for teaching specific kinds of content. The appropriateness of each strategy for specific content goals and student characteristics is carefully analyzed. We emphasize the selection and design of lessons based on the best that we know about how students learn.

Chapter 6 discusses the teaching of facts, concepts, and generalizations. Inductive and deductive approaches to teaching concepts and generalizations stress the importance of positive and negative examples. The chapter integrates principles of learning from educational psychology with teacher effectiveness research and the classroom experience of expert teachers.

In Chapter 7 we discuss ways of teaching larger, organized bodies of information. As with concepts and generalizations, inductive and deductive approaches are used. Emphasis is on building long-term retention and helping students see relationships among facts and abstractions.

The problems involved in teaching specific skills are the focus of Chapter 8. A general approach to teaching cognitive and psychomotor skills is explained in terms of modeling, examples, guided practice, and corrective feedback. Building on the foundation in Chapter 8, Chapter 9 discusses how to teach thinking skills in various content areas and at different grade levels. The chapter begins by defining the concept of *thinking skills* and then describes how thinking skills can be integrated into different academic subjects.

In Chapter 10 we consider alternatives to teacher-centered direct instruction. Peer tutoring and cooperative learning are discussed as two ways to use students as resources in the classroom. Alternatives are analyzed in terms of both short- and long-term goals. Finally, we consider how technology can be used to enhance learning.

## Section Three: Classroom Management and Assessment

In the final section of this book, we consider two processes central to teaching and learning—classroom management and assessment.

Chapter 11 discusses classroom management. The effects of the most thorough planning and energetic presentation of material are minimized, if not destroyed, if classrooms are not well managed. The picture that emerges from the research literature is that management is an integral part of effective teaching (Doyle, 1986). Classroom management begins with teacher planning and continues with communicating positive behavioral and achievement expectations to students. All students should understand that the teacher expects them to learn and to operate within the constraints of the classroom's rule structures. But beyond that, effective teaching requires that teachers translate these positive expectations into prescriptions for actual student behaviors and that they constantly monitor students for active involvement in learning.

Research also documents the powerful role that assessment plays in learning (Crooks, 1988). Classroom assessment is the topic of Chapter 12. Measuring and evaluating, and ways of using these processes to enhance learning, are described. Grades and grading, homework and seatwork, and methods of communicating assessment results to both students and parents are discussed as part of the total assessment system.

## SUMMARY

The central role of research in informing teaching practice is this chapter's theme. Historically, the role of research has been minor because of its failure to address the real-life concerns of teachers.

Initially, research on teaching focused on teacher characteristics and later moved to a search for one effective method. Both lines of research failed to link teacher behaviors to student learning. School-level research, focusing on out-of-classroom variables, also ignored the role of teacher actions in promoting student learning.

More recently, research has focused on teacher thoughts and actions and their relation to learning. This research attempts to link the way teachers think, plan, and actually teach to what students learn. This research comes to teachers in several forms. Pedagogical knowledge describes research-based concepts that can be used to analyze and reflect on our own as well as other teachers' practices. Teaching strategies attempt to integrate research findings into comprehensive plans for action. Teacher decision making encourages teachers to use these findings judiciously in working in real classrooms with live students. The process of learning to teach involves combining these three components with content knowledge in an individual and personal way.

## ADDITIONAL READINGS FOR PROFESSIONAL GROWTH

Bullough, R. (1989). *First-year teacher: A case study*. New York: Teachers College Press. A readable case study of a teacher's struggle with the sometimes bewildering first year of teaching.

Jackson, P. (1968). *Life in classrooms*. New York: Holt, Rinehart & Winston. This was one of the first books that documented the complexities of classroom life. Though written in 1968, it still captures current realities of living and teaching with children.

Kane, P. (Ed.). (1991). *The first year of teaching: Real world stories from America's teachers*. New York: Walker & Co. Kane has collected a number of interesting anecdotal accounts of teachers' experiences during their first year of teaching.

Richardson–Kolhler, V. (Ed.). (1987). *Educator's handbook: A research perspective*. New York: Longman. This book contains a collection of chapters written by experts in different areas of teaching, ranging from instruction to classroom management.

## DISCUSSION QUESTIONS

1. Reread the episode at the beginning of this chapter (p. 3). What is the teacher's responsibility in terms of motivation? Do you agree with Stan Williams? What about the question regarding basic skills versus thinking strategies: Do basic skills need to precede thinking skills?

2. In terms of defining effective teaching, research suggests that content mastery is an essential component. Is this component equally important at all grade levels? In all subject-matter areas?

3. How does your definition of good teaching vary in terms of high- and low-ability students? Are there more similarities or differences between the two groups? What would you do with one group that would be different from the other?

4. How would you have responded to the incidents on page 14? Why did you choose that course of action? What alternatives did you consider? What additional information would have been helpful in making a decision?

5. Student time on task, or the extent to which students are attending to the lesson, was listed as one general characteristic of effective teaching. What are some things that a teacher can do to encourage high engagement rates? What are some behaviors that teachers use to infer engagement? Lack of engagement?

6. Given what we know about the latest round of teacher effectiveness research, what should the researchers investigating teacher traits, like sense of humor, have done?

7. Research has shown a correlation between teacher enthusiasm and student learning. Explain this correlation in two ways; then design an experiment to test one of these explanations.

8. Think about the teaching strategies that you have encountered as a student. How many of these can you list? Rank order these in terms of their effectiveness for the grade level or subject matter that you'll be teaching. What factors influenced your decisions?

9. One of the problems in learning to teach is that good teaching often appears effortless. Think back to some of the good teachers that you've had. What specific things did they do that made them effective? Compare these behaviors with other, less effective teachers.

## APPLYING IT IN THE SCHOOLS

1. *Effective Teaching: The Teacher's Perspective.* How do experienced teachers think about effective teaching? Interview two teachers and ask the following questions:

   What is effective teaching?
   How do they know when it is occurring in their classrooms?
   What are some ways to measure effective teaching?
   What factors (e.g., students) influence the definition of good teaching?

   Compare the responses of the two teachers with your own ideas about effective teaching.

2. *Effective Teaching: The District's Perspective.* How does the district evaluate its teachers? In your interview with the teachers in exercise 1, find out how they are evaluated. If a form or instrument is used, ask to see it.

What criteria are used?

How is the form used? That is, how many times is the teacher observed with it? What does the teacher think of the process?

3. *Effective Teaching: The Student's Perspective.* The bottom line in our teaching is its effect on students. This exercise is designed to make you more sensitive to the learning process from a student's perspective.

Identify six students to observe; three should be male and three should be female. Also, one should be a high achiever in the class, one a medium, and one a low. If you are using another teacher's classroom, an ideal way to do this is to have the teacher select the students but not identify their status. This provides you with an opportunity to infer classifications from behavior and responses.

Position yourself at the side of the classroom and toward the front so you can see the students' faces. Observe the six students as they enter the class, at the beginning of the lesson, during the major part of the lesson, and during any seatwork.

Which students are most attentive?

Which students take notes?

Which students participate the most in the lesson?

Is there any relationship between teacher behaviors (e.g., questioning) and student engagement rates?

4. *Measuring Learning: How Do We Do It?* Examine a test (standardized or teacher-made) used in the classroom in which you are working. (A teacher's manual, if available, would be helpful in interpreting the standardized test.) What kinds of knowledge and skills are addressed? What areas are ignored? How are the results communicated to students and parents? How do the results influence learning?

# CHAPTER 2
# Student Diversity

## OVERVIEW

When we walk into classrooms across the country, one fact is obvious: There is amazing variation in the students we teach. This variation is evidenced, for example, by the differences between kindergartners and sixth graders or even between ninth and twelfth graders.

We see diversity even within grade levels, not only in physical appearance but also in the way students respond to instruction. In a single grade we have learners who are mature for their age and others who are slower in developing. Some students will be poised and self-confident, while others will be shy and hesitant. Many will have traveled extensively, while others will have spent most or all of their lives in one small neighborhood. All of these differences influence our students' ability to profit from schooling.

In this chapter we discuss different dimensions of student diversity and examine ways that teachers can adapt their instruction to best meet the needs of all their students. In the process, we look at the influence that intelligence, culture, socioeconomic status, and learner exceptionalities have on learning. We focus especially on the ways teachers can most effectively work with at-risk students.

## MAIN IDEAS

Student diversity makes teaching today more challenging.

A *positive classroom climate* is a prerequisite for teaching all students.

*Caring*, the human dimension of teaching, communicates concern for the welfare of all students.

An *orderly classroom climate* allows learning to occur.

*Positive expectations* communicate that all students can and will learn.

### Learning Ability

In every classroom, students will vary in their *ability to learn*.

*Intelligence*, or the ability to profit from instruction, is a multifaceted quantity.

Strategies to deal with different learning abilities include varying the amount of time available for learning, grouping, strategy instruction, peer tutoring, and cooperative learning.

### Exceptional Students

*Exceptional students* require special help to reach their full potential.

*Mildly handicapped* students learn well enough to remain in the regular classroom but have learning problems that require special help.

Classroom teachers aid exceptional students through identification, developing acceptance, and modifying instruction.

## Teaching Students from Different Cultures

The *cultural deficit theory* suggests that students from minority cultures come to school lacking critical cultural experiences.

*Negative teacher expectations* adversely affect the learning of minority students.

The *cultural difference theory* attributes learning problems to differences or discontinuities between home and school.

Strategies to deal with cultural diversity include understanding the cultures of our students, communicating positive attitudes about diversity, and employing a variety of instructional approaches.

## At-Risk Students: Teaching the Children of Poverty

*At-risk students* are less likely to profit from educational opportunities and more likely to leave our schools with skills that are inadequate for survival in a modern, technological society.

Effective teaching practices for at-risk students provide extra instructional structure and support to ensure that learning takes place.

. . . . . . . . . . . . . . . . . . . . . . . . . . . . . . . .

Shannon Jackson watched as her first graders streamed into the room on the first day of school. Though she had read the class rolls as she planned, she couldn't believe the different shapes, colors, and sizes before her eyes. Some were tall—looking almost like second graders—while others were tiny. A few were husky and well developed, while others were almost skinny. "I wonder if all their parents know about the free breakfast program," she asked herself. And the names—she hoped she'd be able to remember them and pronounce them all correctly. There were Joneses and Lees and Wongs and Hassads and Trangs and Jamals. This was going to be an interesting class.

As Shannon got to know her students, she also noticed differences in the way they acted. Some came to class bright and eager, while others looked like they hadn't gotten enough sleep. Several knew how to print and read their names; others acted as if they had never held a book. A few used their fingers to count and even add, and others began sucking on them when they became tired or discouraged. "They're lovable," Shannon thought and smiled to herself, "but how am I ever going to get them all to learn?"

How indeed? One of the facts of modern teaching is the increasing diversity of our students. They not only come in different sizes and levels of maturity, as they always have, but now they come to our classes speaking different languages and bring with them different cultural values and background experiences.

As we saw in Chapter 1, research can be a powerful tool in helping teachers become more effective, and it can also help us deal with these differences in our students. It does this by identifying general patterns of teaching that are effective with *all* learners and by suggesting ways to adapt our teaching to meet the needs of specific groups of students.

In the first part of this chapter, we examine teaching patterns that are effective with all learners. We begin with a discussion of classroom climate.

# POSITIVE CLASSROOM CLIMATE: PREREQUISITE TO LEARNING

Think back to some of your experiences in elementary and secondary school. In which were you most comfortable? Which classes did you look forward to? In which did you learn the most? Now think about the other kind of classroom. Were there some that you disliked or even dreaded? Were there classes that made you uncomfortable and insecure? Were there some that you felt were a waste of time and in which you watched the clock as the time dragged by?

These comparisons illustrate the concept of classroom climate. **Classroom climate** is the sum of students' attitudes, feelings, and beliefs about a learning environment (Hamachek, 1987). When the climate is positive, students feel good about entering the room, knowing that they are cared about as human beings and believing that they will learn something valuable. In contrast, when the classroom climate is negative, students are apprehensive in class and doubtful about taking something valuable away from the experiences.

Positive classroom climate is the foundation of all subsequent learning and results from the interaction of three components. These are shown in Figure 2.1 and consist of the following:

- A teacher who sincerely cares about the welfare of students
- An orderly environment in which students feel safe and secure
- Positive teacher expectations which communicate that all students can and will learn

When these components exist and interact, teachers create the potential for learning for all students, regardless of their diversity. Let's examine these different components now and see how they contribute to learning.

**FIGURE 2.1**  Components of Positive Classroom Climate

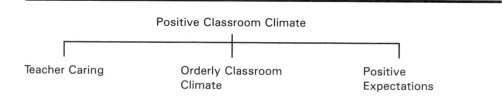

Positive Classroom Climate

Teacher Caring    Orderly Classroom Climate    Positive Expectations

## Caring: The Human Dimension of Teaching

Sean Williams surveyed his eighth graders as he passed out his unit exam. The desks were spread apart, and there was a feeling of anticipation in the air as the students began the test. As Sean moved around the room, he noted with satisfaction that most of his students had plunged into the test and were working diligently—except for Tony, who was sitting at his desk and staring out the window.

Sean watched Tony, not saying anything initially, but when Tony still hadn't started the test five minutes later, Sean went over to him, bent down, and quietly said, "Tony, you still haven't started the test. Is something wrong?" Tony said nothing, turning away and looking out the window to avoid looking at Sean. Sean thought for a moment and then asked Tony to come out in the hall with him.

When they got there, Sean could see that Tony was close to crying—something that rough-and-tough Tony was not noted for. Tony reluctantly told of a fight between his parents the night before, which had ended with Tony's dad storming out. As Tony described the incident, tears came to his eyes and Sean realized that the test wouldn't do Tony any good at this time. He told Tony to go and wash his face and that he'd bring his books out to the hall so Tony could go to the next class. When he met Tony in the hall a couple of minutes later, Sean asked if Tony wanted to talk about it. Tony shook his head but managed a weak smile when Sean put his hand on Tony's shoulder. They arranged for Tony to make up the test the next day after school.

What does *caring* mean? Admittedly, it is a difficult idea to define. Like love, it has many different meanings and dimensions, but common to all of them is a core concern about the well-being of our students as human beings. Sean Williams demonstrated sensitivity and caring when he noticed that Tony wasn't working on his exam. Further evidence of caring and concern was Sean's willingness to spend *time* with Tony, both during the test, to find out what was wrong, and the next day, to let Tony make up the test. Think about your own personal experiences. We all react well when people, and particularly people in positions of power or authority, are willing to spend time with us. In contrast, we react badly to being "brushed off" or dismissed after being helped briefly.

One researcher tried to describe this caring dimension systematically. In an article titled, "Showing Them That I Want Them to Learn and That I Care about Who They Are," she described her year in a rural southern secondary school in which she focused on a Mr. Appleby, who was considered to be outstanding (Dillon, 1989). In an attempt to understand this teaching effectiveness, the author asked Mr. Appleby to describe his philosophy of teaching. His description was as follows:

They need to know that when they walk into your classroom that you'll say something nice to them or that they can talk to you if things are bad 'cause there's nobody else they can go to. . . . Kids need to feel they can open up and share some of their feelings which they may not ever do, because they may be in a family situation where they get slapped for it or put down for it. . . . Education isn't worth a hill of beans if the kid doesn't feel good about it or the kid doesn't feel good about himself or isn't going to do anything with his life. (Dillon, 1989, p. 238)

How did his students, mostly black and in remedial reading classes, respond to this approach? Here's what some of his students said.

*Melinda:* I act differently in his [Appleby's] class—I guess because of the type of teacher he is. . . . He is hisself—he acts natural—not tryin' to be what somebody wants him to be . . . he makes sure that nobody makes fun of anybody if they mess up when they read out loud.

*Bernard:* [I like him] just by the way he'd talk, he were good to you . . . he don't be afraid to tell you how he feels—he don't talk mean to you, he just speak right to you . . . some teachers only likes the smart people—and Coach Appleby don't do that.

*LaVonne:* Appleby's fun, he helps you when you feel bad, he'll talk to you. . . . He makes me want to work, he makes me want to give and do something. . . . He shows me that I can do it. (1989, pp. 241–242)

Something is happening in this classroom that transcends or goes beyond mere good teaching. It is the teacher as a human being sincerely expressing genuine concern for his students, both as people and as learners. Caring is at the core of it, and this caring lays a foundation for learning and growth.

## Classroom Management: Creating an Orderly Learning Environment

The teacher says, "We have a little filmstrip on weather." And she quickly overviews the content on the filmstrip, which is called "The Weather Is Poetry." As the teacher arranges the filmstrip in the machine, she says, "Before we start this, we're going to turn out the lights, but you can finish your work anyway. We're going to pick it up afterwards." Greg says, "Miss, I can't see to finish." The teacher says, "Yes, you can. Your eyes will adjust." Andrew is yelling, "lights off, lights off" four times. Finally, the teacher starts the filmstrip, which is a sound filmstrip. Someone turns the lights off. Everyone starts yelling, "I can't see. It's dark in here." The teacher assures everyone that their eyes will adjust. As the film is running, the students talk, move around. Apparently, two of them go outside to work, although the observer did not notice until later. Some move desks. Observer notes that no one can hear the movie. Joe comes in from the hall and stands at the front of the room to watch. The class finally settles a little. About half are watching the film, and half are working on the assignment in the dark. The teacher walks out of the room. And then she walks about the room. She says, "In a few minutes, you're going to see the part about the mud. That's my favorite part. They describe the sound of people walking in the mud." Greg says, "Turn on the lights." The teacher ignores him. During the filmstrip there is a steady exchange of students with restroom passes. Susan comes in, Joe goes not. The teacher goes out. Robert calls after her sarcastically, "You missed the mud." (Carter, 1986, pp. 33–34)

This was a description of an actual junior high classroom. Consider for a moment what it would be like to learn in this kind of environment.

Positive classroom environments require teachers to care, to think about students not just as customers or clients but as people. But classroom environments conducive to learning require more than just caring. Classrooms can be potentially chaotic places, and if they are, learning is discouraged. The presence of 30 or more students in a relatively small space requires a **safe and orderly learning environment.** Students can't learn if they can't see, can't hear, or the noise level is too high to think. A safe and orderly learning environment is the second essential component of a positive classroom climate.

Research indicates that an essential precondition for teaching all kinds of students—fast, slow, white, minority, poor, or well-to-do—is an orderly classroom where students know what to expect and what is expected of them (Doyle, 1986). This dimension is so crucial to teaching effectiveness that we devote all of Chapter 11 to the topic.

## Positive Expectations

Mary Willis looked around the room as her fourth graders put away their math books and took out their language arts workbooks. When she saw that all books were out, she said, "Class, can I have everyone's eyes up here. . . . Good. Today we're going to learn a new skill, how to alphabetize. This is an important skill that you will use again and again, not only this year, but every year of your life. If you don't know the meaning of a word, it will help you find it in the dictionary. I know that all of you will learn how to do this, and we'll practice until we're all good at it. Now let's turn to page 47 in our workbooks and see how we begin."

As the class opened their books, Mary noticed Will leaning forward to poke Steve with his pencil. She walked down the aisle, looked Will in the eye, and asked, "Will, have you found the page yet? Quickly now. This is too important for you to be wasting time monkeying around."

The lesson continued with Mrs. Willis explaining and modeling the skill at the board and then asking students to come to practice with new lists of words. With each she asked for a show of hands to see who was performing the skill correctly. When she was confident that most students understood, she gave an assignment that all students were to complete before free reading. As they worked on the lists, Mrs. Willis moved around the room checking papers and answering questions.

Effective teachers clearly communicate their expectations for learning. They *tell* students that something is important. They explain *why* it's important. They openly communicate that they expect *all* students to learn, as Mrs. Willis did when she said, "I know that all of you will learn how to do this, and we'll practice until we're all good at it."

Sometimes their communication is more subtle. They monitor the class for misbehavior, communicating that it is unacceptable because it interferes with learning, as Mrs. Willis did when she said, "Quickly now. This is too important for you to be wasting time monkeying around." They provide practice that allows all students to practice new skills and receive feedback. Finally, they communicate positive expectations by holding all students accountable for learning.

**Positive teacher expectations** is the third essential component of a positive classroom climate. When students come into our classrooms, they must literally feel our desire for them to learn. Each and every student must know that we expect them to learn and that we will do everything we can to help them learn. As with *caring* and *order, positive expectations* provide a foundation teachers build on to promote learning in *all* their students. We'll return to positive expectations again in Chapter 4, when we discuss specific ways to use them to increase learning.

In this section, we've discussed the elements of a positive learning environment and we've emphasized that a positive environment is critical for all learners. We now turn to different dimensions of learner diversity and suggest ways teachers can accommodate these differences in their classrooms.

# TEACHING STUDENTS WITH DIFFERENT LEARNING ABILITIES

Melanie Parker, an intern from a nearby university, was ready to teach her first math lesson in Mrs. Jenkins's second-grade class. She had preplanned with Mrs. Jenkins, who had suggested a review of place value, such as identifying 3 tens and 2 ones in a number like 32. Though nervous at the beginning, everything went smoothly as Melanie explained the concept and used interlocking cubes to illustrate it. As she passed out practice worksheets, Mrs. Jenkins walked over to Melanie and whispered, "You're doing great. I need to run down to the office. I'll be right back." The children, accustomed to having interns and preinterns in the class, didn't react as Mrs. Jenkins left and quickly got to work.

Melanie's nervousness calmed as she circulated among the students, periodically making comments. She noticed that some were galloping through the assignment, others needed minor help, and a few were totally confused. As she worked with the students, she noticed that the quiet of the classroom was turning into a low buzz.

"Joel, why aren't you working?" Melanie asked as she turned to a student near her.

"I'm done."

"Hmm?" she thought as she looked around the room.

"Beth, finish your assignment and stop talking," Melanie said, turning to another student visiting with her neighbor.

"I can't do this stuff!"

Melanie looked at the clock and saw that there were still ten minutes until recess. From the fidgeting and talking, it appeared that several of the students had completed their assignment, while others had barely begun. Panic! What to do?

Just then, Mrs. Jenkins walked in the room, surveyed the class, and looked at the clock as she walked over to Melanie. "How is it going?"

"Fine, but half of them are done and the other half need extra help."

Mrs. Jenkins then turned to the class and said in an authoritative voice, "Class, if you're done with your work, put it in your folders. Then you can either do math games—*quietly*—in the back of the room or take out your reading book. Let's get busy now."

As Melanie quickly learned, the students we teach differ in their ability to profit from our instruction. As one of our colleagues jokingly estimates, "In any lesson, probably a third already know it, another third are really learning it, and the rest don't know what you're talking about." Although this is probably overstated, there is truth in what she says. The students in most classes vary considerably in their ability to learn, and this has important implications for instruction.

What does this variability mean? One way experts study it is to use students' reading ability. In a typical second-grade classroom, for example, students will range in reading level from below first grade to beyond the fourth, meaning that some will still be working on beginning reading skills like sounding out words, while others will be ready to work on complex comprehension skills (Elwall and Shanker, 1989). In the sixth grade, the range is even greater, with some students reading at the second-grade level while others are past the ninth-grade level.

The amount of time it takes students to master new content is another way of thinking about variability. Melanie Parker found this out when she taught the same lesson to all students in her class; some learned it quickly, while others really struggled. In an average class, it can take slower students six or seven times longer to master a topic than the fastest students (Bloom, 1981).

While reading ability and time needed to learn are ways of describing learner variability, it is still most commonly described in terms of *intelligence* or intellectual ability. For example, estimates suggest that you're likely to have students with intelligence test scores ranging from 60 or 70 to 130 or 140 in an average, heterogeneously grouped classroom (Hardman, Drew, Egan, and Wolf, 1990). This range is so great that students at the lower end would be classified as mildly handicapped and would be eligible for special help, while students at the upper end might also be considered exceptional—gifted and/or talented. In the next section, we examine the concepts of intelligence and discuss how it influences teaching.

## Intelligence: What Does It Mean?

We all have a concept of **intelligence**. In everyday language, it's how "smart" or "sharp" people are, how quickly they learn, the insights they have, or even the wide range of—sometimes trivial—knowledge they possess. More formally, intelligence is measured by standardized tests that produce the well-known IQ or intelligence test score. The two most popular intelligence tests used today are the Wechsler Intelligence Scale for Children (WISC) and the Stanford–Binet.

What do these tests actually measure, or perhaps more appropriately, what is intelligence? When a thousand experts were asked the second question, they identified three characteristics:

- Abstract thinking and reasoning
- Problem-solving ability
- Capacity to acquire knowledge (Snyderman and Rothman, 1987)

When we examine these dimensions, we can see why intelligence is an important concept for educators and why scores on intelligence tests correlate moderately well (.50 to .70) with school performance.

Despite this correlation, the concept of intelligence is controversial, with the controversy often focusing on three issues. First is the "nature–nurture" controversy, with some authorities arguing that intelligence is genetically determined and essentially fixed at birth (Jensen, 1987)—the nature position. Others contend that intelligence can be influenced both indirectly (e.g., diet, medical care) and directly through educational interventions (Sternberg, 1986). This issue has important implications for how we view our students. Do they come to us with their intellectual ability fixed and unchangeable, or are there things that teachers can do to improve students' intelligence? An optimistic view of education, called the interactionist position, holds that students come to our classrooms with genetic potential and that we as teachers can do much to help that potential grow and develop.

Closely related to the nature–nurture controversy is the issue of cultural bias. Current thinking suggests that intelligence tests *are* culturally embedded and are heavily influenced by both language and the past experiences of the test-taker (Anastasi, 1988). This issue has important implications for the use of the tests with minority populations. One study found that an overreliance on intelligence tests with non-English-speaking populations resulted in a disproportionate number of these students being classified as mentally retarded (Mercer, 1973; Smith, 1987).

The third controversy relates to the concept of single versus multiple dimensions to intelligence. Historically, intelligence tests produced a single score which indicated a general measure of intellectual functioning; later, tests such as the WISC provided two scores, one verbal and the other performance; and now there is considerable interest in the concept of "multiple intelligences" (Gardner, 1983; Sternberg, 1986). Theories of multiple intelligences suggest that there are several kinds of "smarts" rather than just one. For example, Gardner's theory of multiple intelligences breaks intelligence into seven different areas: *linguistic, logical-mathematical, musical, spatial, bodily-kinesthetic, interpersonal,* and *intrapersonal.*

Gardner's work is intuitively sensible. We all know people who don't seem particularly "sharp," but they have a special ability to get along well with others, or they appear to have insights into their own strengths and weaknesses. Gardner would describe these people as being high in interpersonal and intrapersonal intelligence. In other cases, we see people who excel in English but do less well in math—linguistic versus logical-mathematical intelligence—and we've all seen examples of gifted musicians and gifted athletes who don't excel in the other areas.

Multiple views of intelligence suggest that teachers should create learning environments in which different kinds of students can prosper. One way to do this is to provide students with choices as they learn new content. For example, a middle school English teacher breaks assignments down into required and optional. Seventy percent of the assignments are required for everyone; the other thirty percent provide students with choices about what to read and do, and students negotiate with the teacher on the specific assignments. Other ways of providing students with learning options are discussed in the next section.

In summary, we see that students *do* differ in terms of intelligence or intellectual ability, and these differences influence their ability to profit from instruction. But what implications does knowing this have for our teaching? We answer this question in the next section.

## Intellectual Diversity: Implications for Teaching

Intellectual diversity is a fact of teaching life. We will all encounter a range of learning abilities in our classrooms. In responding to this diversity, a teacher has several options:

1. Make time requirements flexible. Adjusting time requirements allows slower students more time to complete assignments.
2. Group students according to their ability. This allows teachers to teach to a particular ability level but carries with it other problems.
3. Provide strategy instruction for slower students. Strategy instruction attempts to increase students' capability by teaching them more efficient ways of performing academic tasks.
4. Provide peer tutoring and cooperative learning experiences. Peer tutoring and cooperative learning use more able students as resources to help other students.

Let's examine these options now.

**Flexible Time Requirements**   In a heterogeneous class when the amount of time allowed to learn something is kept constant, some students are going to learn faster than others (Bloom, 1981). When the amount of time available for learning is the same for all students, the gap between the faster students and the slower students grows wider and wider. One way to accommodate these differences is to provide extra time for slower students to master content before introducing new topics.

But what about the faster students? For this strategy to work, the classroom must be set up so enrichment activities are available to students who complete their assignments quickly. Mrs. Jenkins did this by having her students do math games and free reading when they completed their assignments early. Other enrichment options are described in Table 2.1.

Each of the options in Table 2.1 provides learning activities for students completing their assignments early. They can also be used to provide learning options for different students.

**TABLE 2.1** Enrichment Options for Faster Students

| Enrichment Option | Description |
| --- | --- |
| 1. Free reading | A shelf of books or magazines (e.g., *Ranger Rick, National Geographic World*) are kept in the back of the room for students to use. |
| 2. Games | A part of the room is sectioned off where students can play academic games on the floor. |
| 3. Computers | A menu of computer software games and simulations provides student choice (see Chapter 10). |
| 4. Learning centers | Learning materials with objectives, directions, and learning activities guide students. |
| 5. Individual research projects | Students choose long-term projects to investigate; teachers assist by helping to gather individual books and other resources. |
| 6. Peer tutoring | Structured learning activities help students assist each other (see Chapter 10). |

## Ability Grouping

Adrienne Foster sat back and thought as she finished checking her third-grade students' math quiz. The scores were bimodal; half of her class understood multiplication with carrying and half were still struggling. If she continued with multiplication, half the class would be bored; if she went ahead with division, the other half would be lost. What to do?

The next day she began her math class by explaining that some students were ready for division and some needed some more work on multiplication. She gathered the students still working on multiplication around her in one corner of the room and gave them a sheet with some additional problems on it. She told them that they would get back together as soon as she introduced division to the other group. As she worked with the division group, she kept one eye on them and the other on the group doing their multiplication. Some hands went up, but she had to tell them to wait a few minutes until she was done with the division group. It wasn't an easy juggling act, but she didn't know what her alternatives were.

Grouping is a common instructional response to student diversity, especially at the elementary level, and it can take several forms (Good and Brophy, 1991). **Between-class ability grouping** divides a class of 75 third graders, for example, into three classes; one high, one medium, and one low. Grouping across grade levels, also called the Joplin Plan, mixes, for example, third-, fourth-, and fifth-grade students of similar reading ability in the same reading class. These students would then return to their own classrooms for the other subjects. **Within-class grouping** breaks students in an individual class into different groups for specific subjects. Adrienne Foster did this in her third-grade class.

Despite its popularity, grouping has several problems:

- Teachers have inappropriately lowered expectations for students in lower groups, and instruction in these groups is often poorer than that for high-ability groups (Good and Brophy, 1991). As a result, low groups fall farther and farther behind.
- Students in low groups often develop affective problems, such as lowered self-concept and motivation.
- Ability tracks tend to stabilize, which permanently labels students as "slow" not only within a grade level but over the years (Rist, 1970).
- Teaching multiple groups is very demanding, and off-task behavior is a common problem for students who are not in direct contact with the teacher.

Sometimes, however, as Adrienne Foster concluded, groups are necessary. This often occurs in subjects that are organized hierarchically, such as reading and math, where later skills build on prerequisite ones. When grouping is used, experts recommend the following precautions.

1. Only use grouping when necessary; avoid grouping in subjects that are not hierarchical (e.g., music, art, science, social studies).
2. Keep groups flexible and reassign students when their learning progress warrants it.
3. Make sure that the quality of instruction provided to low-ability students is comparable (or better) than that provided to high-ability students.
4. Constantly be aware of the potential negative consequences of grouping (Hallihan, 1984).

**Strategy Instruction**    Research indicates that a major difference between high- and low-ability students is their knowledge and use of learning strategies. High-ability students have a richer content background than do their lower ability peers, and they are also more efficient at learning new information. For example, consider the strategic thinking of a high-ability student faced with the task of learning a list of 10 spelling words for a quiz.

> Hmm, ten words for the quiz on Friday. That shouldn't be too hard. I have 3 days to learn them.
>
> Let's see. These are all about airports and stuff. Which of these do I already know—airplane, taxi, apron, and jet. No problem. Hmm. Some of these aren't so easy like causeway and tarmac. I don't even know what "tarmac" is. I better spend more time on them. I'll cover them up and try to write them down and then check 'em. Tonight I can get Mom to give me a quiz and then I'll know which ones to study extra tomorrow. (Eggen and Kauchak, 1992, p. 241)

This student's actions were strategic in several ways. He assessed the nature of the learning task and adapted his studying to match it; he allocated extra time and effort to the words he didn't know; and he monitored his learning progress through quiz-like exercises. Low-ability students, in contrast, passively approach the task, reading the list with no thought to initial competency or ways of improving. They spend time on words they already know and make little effort to test themselves to receive feedback.

This suggests that effort to teach learning strategies to our students would be productive, and this suggestion is confirmed by research. The results of strategy training have been promising (Graham and Harris, 1989; Palincsar and Brown, 1987). This includes talking about the strategy, modeling it while thinking out loud, and providing opportunities for practice. For example, a teacher trying to teach the spelling memorization strategy could have all students take a pretest and talk about the words they know and don't know. Then she might suggest different ways of practicing, like self-quizzes, peer quizzes, and flash cards. Finally, she could do long-term follow-up by reminding students from time to time when strategies are appropriate. Some examples of strategies in different areas are found in Table 2.2.

**Peer Tutoring and Cooperative Learning**    A final way to deal with intellectual diversity in your classroom is to use the students themselves to help each other. Peer tutoring places students in one-to-one pairs and supplies them with structured learning materials for practice and feedback. Cooperative learning strategies place students of differing abilities on the same team and use group rewards to encourage cooperative learning. The research on both of these practices is so promising (Slavin, 1990; Top and Osguthorpe, 1987) that we'll return to them in Chapter 10 and discuss ways to implement them in your classroom.

# EXCEPTIONAL STUDENTS

Jim Kessler circulated around the room while his sixth-grade students worked on their unit test. Most were working smoothly, writing an answer and then looking up to think. Others were obviously struggling, and Jim could only shake his head in both understanding and frustration. It was like this during regular class time, too.

There was quiet Samantha—barely said a word in class—shy, slow; she seemed to struggle in every subject. Gosh, she was a sweet girl. Never complained; tried her hardest. Next to her was Jake. Even now his feet were shuf-

**TABLE 2.2**    Learning Strategies in Different Content Areas

| Strategy Area | Examples |
| --- | --- |
| Memorization tasks | Selective rehearsal; categorization; grouping; imaging |
| Reading | Summarization; outlining; underlining |
| Math | Identifying givens in word problems; selective rehearsal of math facts |
| Writing | Outlining; considering the audience; illustrating ideas with facts; making coherent transitions |

fling and his pencil beat a rhythm on his desk. He was energy looking for a destination. Though he did all right in math, he struggled in any subject in which he had to read. Jim had to cajole and coerce him just to pick up a book. Next to Jake was Steven, the playground terror. Steven did all right in the classroom, when other students let him alone, but he had a temper with a short fuse that seemed to ignite at just the slightest provocation. Once Jim got him settled down again, he'd do fine, but it took some doing.

What a collection! If Jim didn't have the resource teacher to help him, he didn't know what he'd do.

Samantha, Jake, and Steven are exceptional students. **Exceptional students** are those who require special help to reach their full potential, and you will almost certainly have some of them in your classes (Hardman et al., 1990). This is the result of Public Law 94-142, passed in 1975 with the goal of providing a quality education for all exceptional students. A major provision of this law, the **least restrictive learning environment,** requires that students be placed in a learning setting that is as normal as possible while still meeting a student's needs. This provision often results in the process of **mainstreaming,** or the integration of special education students into the regular classroom with special assistance from resource or special education teachers.

Mainstreaming has increased the classroom teacher's role in working with these students. This role begins with identification. The classroom teacher is probably in the best position to identify students needing special help and can do much to help them gain acceptance and friendship from other students. In addition, the classroom teacher will team with specially trained special education teachers to adapt instruction to meet these students' unique academic needs. Samantha, Jake, and Steven were mainstreamed in Jim Kessler's class, and a resource teacher helped Jim adjust his teaching to meet their needs.

How common are students like Samantha, Jake, and Steven? Approximately 11 percent of the school-age population is classified as exceptional, and the majority of these (about 70 percent) are taught either in the regular classroom or in a regular classroom with assistance from a resource room (U.S. Department of Education, 1990). If your class is typical, you will have two or three exceptional students needing extra help.

## Students with Mild Disabilities

Of these students, the vast majority have mild disabilities. Students with mild disabilities learn well enough to remain in the regular classroom but have enough problems with learning to warrant special help. The three major subcategories of mild disabilities are mentally retarded, learning disabled, and behaviorally disordered. Let's look at these now.

Students with intellectual disabilities have limited intellectual ability, resulting in problems in adapting to classroom tasks. The majority of these students are mildly or educable mentally retarded and have IQs ranging from 50 to 70 (an average

IQ is around 100). This lower level of intellectual functioning means that classroom requirements need to be adapted to match the learner's capabilities.

In contrast, students with learning disabilities have normal intellectual capabilities but have problems with specific classroom tasks such as listening, reading, writing, spelling, or math operations. This category is the largest group of students with disabilities, constituting almost 45 percent of the total exceptional student population. Behavior patterns include hyperactivity and fidgeting, problems with attention, disorganization and lack of follow-through, and uneven performance in different school subjects.

Students with **behavior disorders, emotional disturbances,** or **emotional disabilities** display persistent behaviors that interfere with their classroom work and interpersonal relations. Students with behavioral disorders fall into two general categories—the acting-out child, and the quiet, withdrawn child. The acting-out child can be physically aggressive and display uncooperative, defiant, and even cruel behaviors. The quiet, withdrawn child is much less visible and is often timid, shy, and depressed and lacks self-confidence. Experts warn that virtually all students act like behaviorally disordered students sometime in their school years; the key characteristic is that the behavior pattern is chronic and persistent.

In addition to the students we have just discussed, you may have learners in your classes with impaired sight, hearing, or speech. If you see indicators of these disabilities in any of your students, immediately bring them to the attention of your principal, school nurse, school psychologist, or guidance counselor, who can have the student tested.

## Exceptional Students: Instructional Implications

Toni Morrison had been working with her class of second graders for a week trying to get them into reading and math groups that matched their abilities. Marisse, a transfer student, was hard to place. She seemed to understand the material but lost attention during different parts of lessons. When Toni worked with her one-on-one, she did fine, but Toni often noticed her staring out the window.

One day as Toni watched the class work in small groups, she noticed that Marisse held her head to one side when she talked to the other side. Toni wondered. . . . She spoke to the principal, who recommended that Marisse be referred to the school psychologist for possible testing.

Two weeks later, the school psychologist came by to discuss her findings. Marisse had a hearing problem in one ear that would require a hearing aid as well as special help from Toni.

In a few days, Marisse came to school with her hearing aid. She obviously felt funny about it and wasn't sure if this was a good idea. Toni moved her to the front of the room so she could hear better, made sure to give directions while standing in front of Marisse's desk, and double-checked after an assignment was given to ensure that the directions were clear to her.

After a couple of days, Toni took Marisse aside to talk about her new hearing aid. Marisse *could* hear better, but she still felt a little strange with it. Some of the kids looked at her funny, and that made her uneasy. Toni had an inspiration: Why not discuss the hearing aid in class and let the others try it? This was a risky strategy, but Marisse reluctantly agreed to it.

It worked. During show-and-tell, Marisse explained about her new hearing aid and gave the class a chance to try it out themselves. The strange and different became understandable, and Marisse's hearing aid became a normal part of the classroom. (Eggen and Kauchak, 1992, pp. 204–205)

In working with exceptional students, teachers have three major roles: **identification, acceptance,** and **instruction.** Because teachers are able to observe students on a day-to-day basis, teachers are in the best position to identify learning problems in their students. When this occurs, the teacher can begin the process of remediation by referring the student to a special educator or school psychologist for formal evaluation.

A second role that teachers perform in working with exceptional children is acceptance. Perhaps the most difficult obstacles exceptional students face are the negative attitudes of other students and the impact these attitudes have on their own confidence and self-esteem (Chapman, 1988). Having a disability and being different is often not well understood or accepted by other students, and just placing students together in mainstreamed classrooms is often not sufficient to bring about attitude change and acceptance. The teacher's active efforts are necessary to change attitudes and bring about acceptance.

Teachers can help by modeling acceptance, by actively teaching about diversity, and by making every possible effort to ensure that these students experience success and feel needed and wanted. Toni Morrison did this by adapting her classroom to meet Marisse's special learning needs. This may be the most important contribution a classroom teacher makes for these students. Teachers also help by helping other students understand the nature of the learning disability. Toni did this when she had Marisse explain her hearing aid to other students.

Research supports this approach. In one experimental program, teachers used direct and indirect experiences to help elementary students understand physical handicaps (Jones, Sowell, Jones, and Butler, 1981). In addition to seeing films and having discussions about different disabilities, students had opportunities to talk with deaf and blind students about their disabilities. They were taught about the manual alphabet, experienced the use of Braille, performed routine activities while blindfolded, and experienced what it was like to use wheelchairs and crutches. This combination of experiences and information resulted in more positive attitudes toward the disabled.

## Teaching Exceptional Students

Probably the most extensive role that teachers will play in working with exceptional students is instruction. The practice of mainstreaming places exceptional students in the regular classroom, and the classroom teacher is expected to help in meeting the needs of exceptional students. Fortunately, the classroom teacher will not be alone in working with these students.

Assistance for the classroom teacher comes in several forms. Specially trained special educators and school psychologists will meet with classroom teachers to help adapt instruction. If warranted, exceptional students will receive extra assistance in a pull-out resource room where students may visit for an hour or two each day. In addition, mainstream assistance teams (Fuchs et al., 1990) bring special educators into the regular classroom to help the classroom teacher in the following ways:

- Meet with the classroom teacher to identify and define any learning problems.
- Observe a student's classroom behavior.
- Collect work samples from the classroom.
- Cooperatively design specific instructional changes with the teacher.

A major outcome of these meetings is the construction of an Individualized Education Program (IEP). Mandated by law, the purpose of an IEP is to outline an individualized instructional plan of action for each exceptional student. Each IEP must contain the following components:

- The child's present levels of educational performance
- Annual goals and short-term instructional objectives
- Specific educational services to be provided
- The extent to which the child will participate in regular education
- Projected date for initiation of services
- Expected duration of those services
- Objective criteria and evaluation procedures (Smith and Luckason, 1992).

The classroom teacher's input during the planning process is essential to the program's success.

## Adapting Instruction for Exceptional Students

Many classroom teachers are apprehensive when faced with the prospect of adapting instruction to meet the needs of exceptional students. Probably the label "exceptional students" has much to do with this apprehension. This is unfortunate, because research shows that many of the basic strategies that work with regular teachers also work with mainstreamed students (Larrivee, 1985). These include:

- Warm academic climate
- Effective use of time
- Effective classroom management
- High success rates
- Effective feedback.

The biggest challenge facing classroom teachers attempting to implement instructional strategies with nonmainstreamed students will be adapting instruction to ensure high success rates. One way to do this is to teach topics at a slower pace, providing more opportunities for practice and feedback. (Recall the earlier discussion of adapting instruction for different learning abilities.) Other adaptations include giving shorter assignments (e.g., 10 versus 20 problems) or breaking assignments into smaller parts (e.g., 20 problems into four groups of five) so the teacher, another student, or the students themselves can check answers more frequently.

Reading assignments pose special problems for mainstreamed students because available texts are often inappropriate for their reading level. Some ways of adapting regular reading materials include the following:

- Setting goals at the beginning of an assignment
- Using advance organizers that structure or summarize the passage
- Introducing key concepts and terms before students read the text
- Creating study guides with questions that focus attention on important information
- Asking students to summarize information in the text (Graham and Johnson, 1989).

These adaptations also work with regular students; their use with exceptional students provides extra structure and support to help ensure success.

# TEACHING STUDENTS FROM DIFFERENT CULTURES

Nola Collins sat back on the bus and breathed a sigh of relief—26 students there and 26 students back. There were moments at the zoo when she had wondered if she would get them all back on the bus, but now that the head counting was over, she could relax.

Was it worth all the trouble, she wondered? It *was* a fun trip, and many of her second graders had never been to the zoo. It also gave Nola a chance to see her students in action in a different setting. She couldn't believe how different they were.

It wasn't just how different they looked. Nola knew when she signed her contract to teach in this large, inner-city school district that her students would be diverse, but she wasn't prepared for this—11 different cultures and six different languages. She jokingly referred to her class as her "Little United Nations." They not only responded differently in class but also on this field trip. Some were active and assertive and led the way in exploring the zoo, while others hung back, clinging to her for moral and physical support. Some asked questions eagerly while others listened shyly. She knew some of these differences were due to what they were used to at home, but she hadn't quite figured out how to use these differences productively in the classroom.

Another source of diversity in the classrooms of today's school is the cultural background of the students we teach. The United States has always been a nation of immigrants, and this immigration has produced a country of many different cultures. This diversity has been hailed as one of this country's strengths, bringing new ideas and energy. But this diversity also poses challenges to teachers as they attempt to teach children with different attitudes, values, and even languages. In this section, we discuss cultural diversity and examine ways that student culture can be used to enhance learning in the classroom.

## Multicultural Education: The Challenge

**Culture** refers to the attitudes, values, beliefs, and ways of acting and interacting that characterize a social group. It includes the foods we eat, how we dress, how we play, the music we listen to, and the kinds of churches we attend. It also includes the attitudes and beliefs we have about learning and the views we have about schools and classrooms.

**Multicultural education** examines ways that culture influences learning and attempts to find ways that students' cultures can be used to complement and enhance learning. It attempts to help teachers become more aware of and sensitive to the subtle and not so subtle ways that students' culture can affect the way they approach learning in the classroom.

The need for teachers to be knowledgeable about multicultural issues increased recently due to both demographic and economic changes in the United States. Demographically, our country is becoming more ethnically diverse. During the 1970s and 1980s, over 7 million people immigrated each decade from other countries. Between 1980 and 1990, the minority population increased by over 9 percent. The fastest-growing minority groups were Asian American (up almost 100 percent) and Hispanic (up 53 percent). Currently, ethnic minorities compose over 20 percent of the school-age population in the United States, and experts estimate that this number will increase to 40 percent by the year 2000 (Villegas, 1991a). The odds are overwhelming that you will teach students from other cultures in your classroom, and your understanding of multicultural principles will significantly affect your instructional effectiveness.

Economic changes in our country also point to the need for effective multicultural education. In earlier times, many immigrants and members of minority groups easily found jobs in factories and jobs requiring minimal levels of education. These types of jobs are rapidly declining in our technological society, and the skills of reading, writing, and computing are becoming increasingly important to economic survival. Students who exit our schools without these minimal skills are considered at risk, a topic we'll return to later in this chapter.

## Theories of Minority Achievement

The data on minority student achievement in the schools is clear: The schools have not done an effective job of educating and integrating minority students into the mainstream of American life. Whether the measures are achievement test scores or drop-out rates, statistics indicate that minority students underperform in schools (Ballantine, 1989). Why is this so?

**The Cultural Deficit Theory**    According to the cultural deficit theory, the linguistic, social, and cultural backgrounds of minority children prevent them from performing well in the classroom (Villegas, 1991b). Minority children come to school lacking "cultural capital," which represents the accumulation of experiences in the early years that schools use and build on. Minority students do poorly in school — according to the deficit theory — because what they bring to school is inadequate compared to the majority population.

There are two major problems with this theory (Villegas, 1991b). The first is that it points the finger of blame at minority children, absolving the schools from responsibility for their success. In one sense it's as foolish as saying, "I taught them; they just didn't learn." If they don't learn, then we didn't teach them. In the same way, it is our professional responsibility to take students, regardless of their backgrounds, and teach them as much as possible.

The second problem with the deficit theory is that, theoretically, once these students get to school, the school should be able to "fix" the deficit, patching up and altering areas where the students are deficient. Through spending increased periods of time in the schools, minority students should gradually "catch up." Unfortunately (both for the theory and these students), just the opposite occurs. As the number of years in school increases, the gap in achievement grows wider and wider.

**The Teacher Expectations Theory**    A second theory used to explain lower minority achievement in the schools focuses on lowered teacher expectations. As we saw earlier in this chapter, positive teacher expectations form a powerful foundation for learning. Teachers' beliefs that all students can learn exert a powerful and positive influence on learning. Unfortunately, the opposite is also true.

Negative expectations affect learning in both explicit and implicit ways. Explicitly, they influence minorities through tracking and grouping practices that diminish learning, as we saw in our discussion of grouping earlier in this chapter. Research indicates that, in addition to the negative features of grouping that we discussed earlier, a disproportionately high percentage of minorities find themselves in lower groups (Good and Brophy, 1991). When minorities find themselves in lower groups in the lower grades, this often results in a one-way street to an inferior educational experience.

The teacher expectations theory also has problems, however. As with the cultural deficit theory, it focuses on blame, but in this case the blame is directed at teachers.

Teachers must be aware of the expectations that they have for students and must continually monitor their actions to ensure that positive expectations are communicated to all students. We will examine ways to do this in Chapter 4. But what else can teachers do to help students from different cultures learn?

**The Cultural Difference Theory**

A second-grade class in Albuquerque, New Mexico, was reading "The Box Car Children" and was about to start a new chapter. The teacher said, "Look at the illustration at the beginning of the chapter and tell me what you think is going to happen."

A few students raised their hands. The teacher called on a boy in the back row.

He said, "I think the boy is going to meet his grandfather."

The teacher asked, "Based on what you know, how does the boy feel about meeting his grandfather?"

Trying to involve the whole class, the teacher called on another student — one of four Native Americans in the group — even though she had not raised her hand. When she didn't answer, the teacher tried rephrasing the question, but again the students sat in silence.

Feeling exasperated, the teacher wondered if there was something in the way the lesson was being conducted that made it difficult for the students to respond. She sensed that the student she had called on understood the story and was enjoying it. Why, then, wouldn't she answer what appeared to be a simple question?

The teacher recalled that this was not the first time this had happened, and that, in fact, the other Native American students in the class rarely answered questions in class discussions. She wanted to involve them, wanted them to participate in class, but could not think of ways to get them to talk. (Villegas, 1991b, p. 3)

Why didn't Native Americans eagerly respond to the teacher's questions? Are they interested in the same kinds of topics and issues as other students? Do they feel that answering questions in class is important? Could the questions have been asked differently to encourage their participation? The cultural difference theory provides answers to these and other related questions about the influences of culture on learning.

The cultural difference theory of learning attributes academic problems of minority students to cultural differences or discontinuities between home and school. Probably the most important of these is in the way that language is used in the home and school. When home language patterns are congruent with school patterns, learning is enhanced; when home language patterns differ, then conflict occurs. Let's see how this works by analyzing the language patterns in two "cultures" — school and Native American families.

Language use patterns in schools are amazingly homogeneous, not only over time but across grade levels and different parts of the country (Cazden, 1986; Cuban, 1984).

[T]he dominant form of interaction is the teacher-directed lesson in which the instructor is in control, determining the topics of discussion, allocating turns at speaking, and deciding what qualifies as a correct response. Verbal participation is required of students. Implicitly, teaching and learning are equated with talking, and silence is interpreted as the absence of knowledge. Students are questioned in public and bid for the floor by raising their hands. They are expected to wait until the teacher awards the floor to one of them before answering. Speaking in turn is the rule, unless the teacher specifically asks for choral responses. Display questions prevail. Individual competition is preferred to group cooperation. Topics are normally introduced in small and carefully sequenced steps, with the overall picture emerging only at the end of the teaching sequence. (Villegas, 1991a, p. 20)

Contrast this pattern with one uncovered by an anthropologist working in the Warm Springs Indian Reservation in Oregon (Philips, 1972). Philips found that Indian children grew up being supervised by older children rather than adults. What they did learn from adults was learned by observation rather than direct verbal instruction. Question and answer sessions were rare or virtually nonexistent. Children would learn by observing adults and then trying things out on their own, receiving praise and feedback not from adults but from other children.

When we contrast the "culture" of the classroom with the culture of their home, we can see why these students were reticent to ask and answer questions in front of the whole class. Over time, they became less and less involved in classroom activities and fell further and further behind in achievement. Sensitized to these differences, teachers found that when these students were placed in peer learning situations, like group projects or peer tutoring, they spoke freely with their peers and participated in classroom activities. This was something they were used to doing.

A similar problem of cultural language discontinuity was discovered by Shirley Heath (1983) in her study of rural black students in the Piedmont area of the Carolinas. Like the Native Americans from Oregon, these children struggled with the question and answer format found in most classrooms. Both teachers and parents were perplexed and frustrated about why black students failed to participate in school. As Heath studied the language patterns found in black homes, she discovered why.

Heath found that although black children were immersed in the language of the home, they were spoken to differently than in school. Black parents did not regard children as legitimate conversational partners until they were older, tending to give directives rather than questions. When questions were used, they were "real" questions asking for "real" information (e.g., "Where have you been?") rather than testing the child's knowledge, or they were a more "open-ended story-starter" type (e.g., "What you been doin' today?") that did not have a single answer. This was in sharp contrast to the schools, where teachers ask questions all the time, testing students' knowledge and providing practice and feedback. When these students went to school, they were unprepared to participate in the active give and take of convergent question and answer sessions.

When teachers were made aware of these cultural differences, they incorporated more open-ended questions in their lessons. For example, in an elementary social studies unit on "our community," teachers would show the class photographs of different sections of local communities and ask questions like, "What's happening here?", "Have you ever been here?", and "What did you do when you were here?" This not only fit black students' home language patterns more closely but also provided safe, nonrestrictive opportunities for students to tell what they knew about a topic. Teachers also helped black children become more comfortable with, and competent at, answering factual questions. Effective bridges were built between black students' natural learning styles and the schools.

## Mutual Accommodation: Culturally Responsive Teaching

What does this suggest to us about our teaching? Should minority students be made to fit in with schools as they exist today? A pragmatic response to this question is that it hasn't happened yet and isn't likely to occur in the foreseeable future. Should schools be completely overhauled to match the learning patterns of a cultural group? This is an intriguing idea but one that is unlikely to work in today's schools. In most classrooms, we find a combination of different cultural groups. One study in the Los Angeles School District found 81 different cultures in the district, with as many as 20 different native languages spoken in one classroom (Nazario, 1989). While these figures are extreme, we will often teach several different cultural groups in one classroom. Logistics alone preclude the use of any one particular strategy or adaptation.

What *is* required is a general approach of acceptance and valuing, the same basic components of a positive classroom climate discussed at the beginning of this chapter. In addition, teachers in multicultural classrooms need to understand the cultures of the students they teach, communicate positive attitudes about cultural diversity, and employ a variety of instructional approaches that accommodate cultural diversity (Villegas, 1991b). These strategies are listed in Table 2.3 and are discussed next.

**Learning about the Cultures of Our Students**   Culture affects learning, and one of the most effective ways of dealing with culture in our classrooms is to find out about the cultures of the students we teach. One principal did this and reported these interesting results. As principal, she was invited to a special ceremony at a local church attended by Pacific Islanders, a significant minority in her school. She arrived a few minutes early and was seated on the stage as a guest of honor. She settled down and waited for the ceremony to begin—and waited and waited—until it finally began nearly an hour late. She didn't quite know what to make of this.

The ceremony itself was warm and loving and showcased each child, who was applauded by the group. After the ceremony, the children returned to their seats for the remainder of the meeting, which involved adult concerns. For a while, they were fine; then they got bored and started fidgeting. The principal describes the rest:

**TABLE 2.3**   Strategies for Working in Multicultural Classrooms

| Strategy | Examples |
| --- | --- |
| 1. Get to know the cultural resources of your students. | Visit homes and talk to parents. Observe students in school and out of school. Read literature by writers of other cultures. Talk to teachers from other cultures. |
| 2. Communicate positive attitudes about student diversity. | Emphasize mutual respect for all types of diversity. Acknowledge cultural differences in class, emphasizing positive aspects of diversity. Encourage students to share their cultures with each other. |
| 3. Employ instructional strategies that accommodate diversity. | Actively teach about different student cultures, both directly and indirectly. Use a variety of strategies that accommodate different cultural styles (e.g., peer tutoring, group work, cooperative learning). Deemphasize instructional grading practices that emphasize differences and competition. |

Fidgeting and whispering turned into poking, prodding, and open chatting. I became a little anxious at the disruption, but none of the other adults appeared to even notice, so I ignored it, too. Pretty soon several of the children were up and out of their seats, strolling about the back and sides of the auditorium. All adult faces continued looking serenely up at the speaker on the stage. Then the kids started playing tag, running circles around the seating area and yelling gleefully. No adult response—I was amazed, and struggled to resist the urge to quiet the children. Then some of the kids got up onto the stage, running around the speaker, flicking the lights on and off, and opening and closing the curtain! Still nothing from the Islander parents! It was not my place, and I shouldn't have done it, but I was so beyond my comfort zone that with eye contact and a pantomimed shush, I got the kids to settle down.

I suddenly realized then that when these children, say, come to school late, it doesn't mean that they or their parents don't care about learning or that they're a little bit lazy—that's just how all the adults in their world operate. When they squirm under desks and run around the classroom, they aren't trying to be disrespectful or defiant, they're just doing what they do everywhere else. (Winitzky, 1991, pp. 137–138)

One implication of the cultural difference theory is that we must get to know our students if we expect to teach them effectively. They bring with them sets of attitudes, values, and ways of acting that may or may not be conducive to learning in a unidimensional classroom. We saw this in the examples of language conflict, and we can see it in the example with the Pacific Island students. Teachers of multicultural classrooms need to make an active effort to enter into students' communities and get to know those communities' values and ways of acting and behaving.

## Communicating Positive Attitudes about Diversity

In one third grade classroom with a predominately Central American student population, youngsters are greeted most mornings with the sound of salsa music in the background, instruction takes place in both English and Spanish, magazines and games in both languages are available throughout the classroom, maps of both the United States and Latin America line one wall, with pins noting each student's origin, and every afternoon there is a Spanish reading lesson to ensure that students learn to read and write in Spanish as well as English. Here the teacher argues very clearly that a positive instructional environment for these students must be tailored to the home cultures ("These kids have music in their homes all the time, so we have it here in the classroom"). (Shields and Shaver, 1990, p. 9)

Our students need to know that we understand their home cultures and that we value the diversity that they bring to our classrooms. We do this by openly discussing the topic of cultural diversity in our classrooms, emphasizing the positive aspects of diversity not only in the classroom but in society as a whole. We also communicate positive attitudes about diversity by encouraging students to bring their cultures into the classroom. Music, dress, and the recognition and celebration of different holi-days like Martin Luther King Day, Mexican Independence Day, and the Jewish holi-days communicate that students' cultures are important. We also teach positive attitudes by emphasizing mutual respect for all cultures and ensuring that all cultural groups are treated with respect in our classrooms.

### Instructional Strategies to Accommodate Diversity

A Japanese-American teacher takes pains to make her classroom quiet and comfortable for her predominately Asian immigrant children, who often find the hustle and bustle of the school building overwhelming. At the same time, she has set up a series of learning activities designed to help the students adapt to the culture of schools in the United States. Her lessons are filled with activities that require students to take more control of the learning environment, to get up and address their peers and teacher in a loud voice, and to move about the classroom. The teacher argues that these students, because of their home cul-ture, are very deferential to adults and so remain quiet in class. Although the teacher respects these characteristics, she designs activities that help the stu-dents learn new methods of relating to peers and adults. (Shields and Shaver, 1990, pp. 9–10)

Effective multicultural teachers need not only to be aware of cultural differ-ences in their students and how these differences influence learning, but also how classrooms can be adapted to meet their learning needs. As we saw earlier, teacher-led whole group instruction featuring question and answer may not be the most ef-fective way for all students to learn.

What alternatives exist? Many of the enrichment options listed in Table 2.1 provide alternatives to teacher-led instruction. Games, computers, learning centers, and individual research projects all provide different learning options. In addition, cooperative learning, where students help each other learn, has been found to be an effective alternative to whole-group instruction. We describe different cooperative learning strategies in detail in Chapter 10.

# AT-RISK STUDENTS: TEACHING THE CHILDREN OF POVERTY

Today's students are different in yet another way. Never before have schools at-tempted to teach so many students who are physically and mentally ill-prepared to learn. A combination of economic and social forces threaten the ability of many students to profit from their educational opportunities.

Consider these statistics:

- One fourth of U.S. children currently live below the poverty level, the highest percentage in 20 years. Fifteen million children are being raised by single mothers, whose family income averaged $11,400 in 1988 dollars.

- On any given night, between 50,000 and 200,000 children have no place called home; 40 percent of shelter users are families with children.
- Fourteen percent of the children in the United States have teenage mothers.
- Between one fourth and one third of today's children have no adult at home when they return home from school.
- Twenty percent of America's preschoolers have not been vaccinated against polio (Hodgkinson, 1991; Kellog, 1988).

When we compare these figures with life in middle-class America, they paint a picture of a different kind of diversity—a diversity in terms of economic and social opportunity. These children often come to school underfed and without proper care. They aren't eager to learn because their emotional needs for safety and security have not been met. These children are at risk.

**At-risk students** are those in danger of failing to complete their education with the skills necessary to survive in a modern technological society (Slavin, Karweit, and Madden, 1989). Economic and social ills combine to produce the following educational problems:

- Poor attendance
- High dropout rates
- Low achievement
- Low motivation
- Management problems
- Dissatisfaction with and disinterest in school
- Less involvement in extracurricular activities
- High rates of drug use
- High criminal activity rates (Vito and Connell, 1988).

At-risk students are not easy to teach and pose serious educational problems for teachers. To deal with these problems, we need to understand how economic and social factors interact to affect learning.

## At-Risk Students: Understanding the Problem

How does poverty, and the myriad of ills that go with it, result in decreased learning and motivation? Sociologists offer us one way to understand the connection. They use **socioeconomic status (SES)** as a concept to describe a family's relative position in the community. Socioeconomic status is determined by a combination of parents' income, occupation, and level of education and consistently predicts not only performance on intelligence tests but also classroom performance, achievement test scores, grades, truancy, and dropout and suspension rates (Ballantine, 1989). Children of wealthier parents, children of parents who have white-collar versus blue-collar jobs, and children of parents with higher levels of education generally perform better on all of these school-related measures. Interestingly, of the three, the best predictor of a student's academic performance is the level of school attained by the parents. We'll see why shortly.

Socioeconomic status influences learning in a number of ways. At the most basic level, SES affects learning through basic growth needs such as nutrition and medical care; students who do not receive adequate food and medical and dental care come to school with physical deficits that are hard to overcome. Free school lunch programs for low-income families are one government response to this problem. Many teachers in low-income neighborhoods will keep a box of crackers in the desk for students who come to school without breakfast.

Socioeconomic status also influences the kinds of experiences students bring with them to school. High SES students are more likely to travel extensively, to visit museums and zoos, and to talk about these experiences with their parents. When they come to school, they are more likely to know concepts like big and small, up and down, and left and right. Why are these concepts important? Think for a moment about teaching the differences between the letters *d* and *b, p* and *q,* and a capital *C* and a small *c* without these concepts. All learning is cumulative, building on previous experiences. Low SES students' early years often fail to provide the experiences and concepts needed to succeed in school.

The impact of SES is also transmitted through parental attitudes and values. Is learning important? Are schools essential for learning? How do hard work and effort contribute to learning? What about homework? How important is it? These attitudes and values are learned in subtle and not-so-subtle ways.

Learning to read is a classic example. High SES homes have books, magazines, and newspapers around the house, and parents model the importance of reading by reading themselves and reading to their children. They develop "print awareness" in their young children by showing their children the writing on cereal boxes, pointing to stop signs, and putting the child's name on the door to his or her bedroom. When their children enter school, they not only know about the power of the printed word, they are eager to read.

The opposite is also true. The homes of poverty are less likely to have books and magazines lying around. The television set plays continually, competing with quiet reading time as well as homework time. The parents are less likely to read, and when the young child comes to school, reading is more a mystery than an exciting challenge.

In reviewing differences between high and low SES students, one researcher reached these conclusions:

> High socioeconomic status students are likely to be confident, eager to participate, and responsive to challenge. They typically want respect and require feedback, but do not require a great deal of encouragement or praise. They tend to thrive in an atmosphere that is academically stimulating and somewhat demanding. In contrast, low socioeconomic status students are more likely to require warmth and support in addition to good instruction from their teachers, and to need more encouragement for their efforts and more praise for their successes. It appears to be especially important to teach them to respond overtly rather than to remain passive when asked a question, and to be accepting of their relevant call-outs and other academic initiations when they do occur. (Brophy, 1986, p. IV-146)

## Teaching At-Risk Students

Teaching at-risk students is not easy, but fortunately research provides us with some directions for action. At-risk students need greater structure and support both instructionally and motivationally. They need to experience success in learning and need to understand how their efforts resulted in this learning. Let's see how this works in a first-grade classroom.

### Instructional Adaptations for At-Risk Students

Keith Wilson began this math lesson by having students from each row come up to distribute the baggies of beans. When all the students had these, he began.

"Class, I need to have everyone's eyes up here. Good. Today we're going to learn a new idea in math. It's called subtraction. Can everyone say subtraction? Good! Subtraction is when you take away. Let's look up here at the felt board. Kareem had four cookies in his lunch. He sat down next to his friend, Jared. Jared didn't have any, so Kareem gave him two of his. How many are left? Let's do that up here. Hmm, four cookies—see how they're round—take away two cookies, leaves how many cookies? Let's count them. Four minus two equals two. That's subtraction.

"Now I want each of you to take out four beans from your bag and do the same."

As the students did this, Keith moved around the room to make sure they were doing it correctly.

"Excellent, everyone. Now I have another problem for you. Let's pretend the beans are pieces of candy. Who likes candy? [All hands go up.] Cassie had three pieces of candy. Everyone take out the right number of beans to show how much candy she had."

Keith circulated again to make sure every student had three beans out.

"Cassie's two friends came along, and each of them wanted a piece, so Cassie gave one to each. Can you take away two beans, one for each of her friends? Now who can tell me how many pieces of candy Cassie had left?"

Teaching at-risk students is not fundamentally different from teaching students in general. It utilizes general principles of effective teaching and refines these to ensure greater structure and support during learning. The increased structure and support appear in several forms, as we see in Table 2.4 (Brophy, 1986; Peterson, 1986).

Let's see how Keith Wilson's lesson contained each of these elements of effective instruction. Active teaching means that the teacher assumes responsibility for explaining and modeling the idea to be learned. Keith did this when he called the class together and told them that they were learning a new skill today and then explained the skill at the feltboard.

Keith used manipulatives and active student involvement to help his first graders learn the abstract process of subtraction. Note that he didn't just write numbers on the board like $4 - 2 = 2$. Instead, he illustrated the process with real-life exam-

**TABLE 2.4** Effective Instruction for At-Risk Students

| At-Risk Strategy | Description |
| --- | --- |
| Active teaching | The teacher needs to explain concepts and skills through interactive teaching. |
| Use of manipulatives and examples | Abstract ideas need to be illustrated with examples and concrete manipulatives. |
| Interactive teaching | Students need to be actively engaged and doing something while learning. |
| Practice and feedback | Students need opportunities to practice the concept or skill they're learning. |
| High success rates | Students need to be successful as they practice a skill. |

ples using cookies and candy—examples that six-year-olds could understand and identify with. In addition, he actively involved students, having all students do the physical operation at their own desks.

Interactive learning involves all students through question and answers. This not only allows all students to participate but also provides the teacher with an informal opportunity to check the students' comprehension. Keith used interactive teaching in several ways. For example,

- He asked students to say "subtraction."
- He asked who liked candy.
- He asked how many pieces of candy Cassie had left.

These questions both encouraged student involvement and helped Keith diagnose his students' attention and understanding.

Effective teaching also allows students opportunities to try out their ideas. To be effective, opportunities for practice and feedback should be available to all students. For example, all of Keith's students had beans to manipulate, and he moved around the room to make sure all students were involved and on-task.

Student success is critical in the process. Because they lack a history of successful experiences, lack of success can result in frustration for at-risk students and can further detract from motivation that is already low. Keith Wilson ensured high success rates by taking small instructional steps and monitoring learning progress as the lesson proceeded.

By now you might be saying to yourself, "Wait a minute. Aren't those effective instructional procedures for at-risk students just good teaching?" You're absolutely correct. Effective instructional practices for at-risk students are not qualitatively different from those for "regular" students. The same principles of good teaching that work in the regular classroom also work with at-risk students. However, it is all the more critical that they be applied conscientiously and thoroughly with at-risk students. Collectively, these practices provide an instructional safety net that minimizes the possibility for frustration and failure, two factors that are especially damaging for at-risk students.

# SUMMARY

Students in today's classroom are more diverse than they have ever been in the history of our society, and this diversity poses special challenges for the classroom teacher. The diversity comes in many different forms, but the most important, from an instructional perspective, are differences in learning ability, cultural background, and socioeconomic status. A positive classroom climate is essential for teaching all types of students.

There are three dimensions to a positive classroom climate: teacher caring, an orderly classroom environment, and positive teacher expectations. Teachers demonstrate their caring in their willingness to spend time with students and, in the process, displaying respect for the students as people and as learners. A positive climate also requires that a classroom be orderly so learning can take place. Positive teacher expectations communicate to students that all can and will learn.

Intellectual ability is one form of diversity. Current views hold that intelligence is alterable, culture-embedded, and multifaceted. Flexible time frames, grouping, strategy instruction, peer tutoring, and cooperative learning activities are all ways teachers adapt their instruction for students of different abilities.

Exceptional students require special help to reach their full potential. Teachers help exceptional students through identification, fostering acceptance, and modifying instruction to meet their special needs.

The cultural backgrounds of our students also affect their ability to profit from instruction. This impact is explained in different ways; cultural deficit, teacher expectations, and cultural differences are three of the most prominent. Teachers can deal with cultural diversity in their classrooms by getting to know the cultural resources of their students, by communicating positive attitudes about student diversity, and by employing instructional strategies that accommodate diversity.

At-risk students are in danger of failing to complete their education with the skills necessary to survive in a modern technological society. Economic and social problems combine to produce conditions that detract from learning. These include nutritional and health problems and experiential differences that fail to provide a firm foundation for learning. Effective teaching for at-risk students is not fundamentally different from good teaching in general; the importance of effective teaching is just more crucial because without it learning is less likely to take place.

# ADDITIONAL READINGS FOR PROFESSIONAL GROWTH

Banks, J., & Banks, C. (Eds.). (1989). *Multicultural education: Issues & perspectives*. An excellent overview of the issues involved in teaching students from different cultures.

Dealing with diversity: At-risk students (1989, February). *Educational Leadership*. This entire issue describes research-oriented ways to deal with diversity in the classroom.

Hallahan, D., & Kauffman, J. (1989). *Exceptional Children* (5th ed.). Englewood Cliffs, NJ: Prentice Hall. This book provides an overview of the major dimensions of exceptionality and how to adapt instruction to meet this diversity.

Kirk, S., & Gallagher, J. (1989). *Educating exceptional children* (6th ed.). An excellent overview of the field of special education.

Villegas, A. (1991). *Culturally responsive teaching*. Educational Testing Service: Princeton, NJ. This readable and up-to-date treatment of multicultural education can be obtained by writing to Educational Testing Service.

## EXERCISES

(The answers to these and all other exercises are found in the "Exercise Feedback" section at the end of this book.)

1. Reread the episode at the beginning of the section titled "Positive Expectations." Identify how Mary Willis demonstrated the following aspects of positive expectations.

   **a.** Emphasizing the importance of a topic _____

   _____

   **b.** Communicating that all are expected to learn _____

   _____

   **c.** Monitoring _____

   _____

   **d.** Opportunities for practice and feedback _____

   _____

   **e.** Accountability _____

   _____

2. Reexamine the episode involving Jim Kessler at the beginning of the section titled "Exceptional Students." Based on the information in the episode, what mild learning disabilities do the following students have? Substantiate your answer with specific information from the episode and the text.

   **a.** Samantha _____

   _____

   **b.** Jake _____

   _____

c. Steven _____

_____

3. Reread the episode involving the second-grade classroom in Albuquerque, New Mexico at the beginning of the section titled "The Cultural Difference Theory." How does the lesson correspond to the dominant pattern of interaction found in most classrooms on the following dimensions? (Use information from the episode to answer this question.)

   a. Teacher directed _____

   _____

   b. Public questioning _____

   _____

   c. Ordered turn-taking _____

   _____

   d. Competition for turns _____

   _____

## DISCUSSION QUESTIONS

1. Of the three elements of positive classroom climate, which do you think is most crucial? Least? Why? Can you support your answer with an example from your own past experience? How would your answer change with the following:

   a. Grade level?

   b. Type of student (e.g., basic or remedial versus college bound)?

   c. Experience level of teacher (e.g., beginning versus veteran)?

2. Analyze the description of Mr. Appleby and the reactions of his students to uncover some of the subcomponents of caring. Which of these do you think is most important? Least? Would your answer change if he were teaching a different type of student?

3. Reread the description of the teacher showing the filmstrip in her class. What might she have done differently to produce a more orderly classroom?

4. Think about the dimensions of intelligence identified by experts: (a) abstract thinking and reasoning, (b) problem-solving ability, and (c) capacity to acquire knowledge. Which do you think is more important in today's world? Least? Why?

5. Of the four strategies listed to accommodate diversity—flexible time, grouping,

strategy instruction, and peer tutoring and cooperative learning—which have the most positive long-term potential for students? Least? Why?

6. How are the three mildly disabled conditions—mentally retarded, learning disabled, and behaviorally disordered—similar? Different?

7. What cultural groups live in the areas where you will be teaching? What do you know about these cultures? How do their cultural beliefs and attitudes influence learning?

8. What important differences exist between the cultural difference theory and the other two theories? Why are these differences important for teachers and students?

9. How were the interaction patterns of the Warm Springs Indians similar to those of rural blacks in the Carolinas? Different? What implications do these similarities and differences have for instruction?

10. How are at-risk students similar to culturally different students? Different? What implications does this have for instruction?

11. At-risk students used to be called underachievers or potential dropouts. Why is *at-risk* a more appropriate term, and how does the use of this term signal changes in society?

12. What is the SES of the students you will likely be teaching? What indicators did you use to reach this conclusion?

## APPLYING IT IN THE SCHOOLS

1. *Differences in Learning Ability.* Observe a class working on an in-class assignment. As you do this, circulate around the room so you can observe the work progress of different students. As you do so, note the following:

   a. Beginning Times—Do all students get immediately to work, or do some take their time starting?

   b. On-Task Behaviors—What percentage of the class stays on task throughout the assignment?

   c. Teacher Monitoring—What does the teacher do during the seatwork? How do students signal that they need help?

   d. Options—What options are there for students who complete their assignments early?

2. *Differences in Learning Ability.* Interview a teacher to investigate the teacher's use of the following strategies to deal with differences in learning ability: (a) flexible time requirements, (b) grouping, (c) strategy instruction, (d) peer tutoring and cooperative learning. Ask these questions:

   a. Is different learning ability a problem for the teacher? Why or how?

   b. Does the teacher use any of the strategies mentioned in this book? Which ones work and why? Have any been tried that didn't work?

    **c.** Does the teacher employ any other strategy for dealing with differences in learning ability?

**3.** *Exceptional Students.* Interview a teacher about exceptional students in the classroom. Ask the following questions:

    **a.** Which students are classified as exceptional? What behaviors led to this classification? What role did the teacher play in identification?

    **b.** In working with exceptional students, what assistance does the classroom teacher receive from the following people?

        **(1)** Special education teacher

        **(2)** School psychologist or school counselor

        **(3)** Principal

    **c.** What does an IEP look like? How helpful is it in working with exceptional students in the classroom?

**4.** *Interaction Patterns.* Observe the classroom interaction patterns in an interactive teaching segment. To what extent does the session display the following characteristics?

    **a.** Teacher directed

    **b.** Public questioning

    **c.** Ordered turn-taking

    **d.** Competition for turns

**5.** *Teaching Multicultural Students.* In observing this same classroom, analyze the class for any differential participation rates by minority students. To do this, identify a comparable number of minority and nonminority students to observe (three or four of each is optimal). Observe them during the lesson, noting the following:

    **a.** How do their attending rates compare (i.e., are they participating in the lesson and listening to the interaction)?

    **b.** How often do students from each group raise their hands to answer a teacher question?

    **c.** How often do students from each group get called on?

**6.** *Teaching At-Risk Students.* Identify a class with considerable numbers of at-risk students. Observe a lesson in that class and analyze it in terms of the following strategies:

    **a.** Active teaching

    **b.** Use of manipulatives and examples

    **c.** Active student involvement

    **d.** Interactive teaching

    **e.** Practice and feedback

    **f.** High success rates

# CHAPTER 3

# Teacher Planning: Research and Reality

# OVERVIEW

Why do teachers plan? How do they actually plan? How does it help them in their professional decision making? Planning plays a vital role in teachers' security and confidence and in the way they conduct their classes. In this chapter, you will study topics such as preparing year-long, unit, and lesson plans together with their components and consider how planning influences teaching and learning. You will also examine different planning models such as the historically revered linear planning model and the widely popular Hunter model.

# MAIN IDEAS

## Why Teachers Plan

Planning provides a form of *security* and bolsters *confidence*.

Planning provides a classroom *script* to follow as lessons are conducted.

The environment is simplified through planning by reducing the *number of decisions* that need to be made.

## Variables Affecting Planning

*Teachers* committed to helping students plan more carefully than those demanding less of themselves.

Planning is affected by students, content, and the *learning context*, which includes state and district guidelines, teacher autonomy, and requirements of administrators.

Teachers plan more carefully when given extra *time*.

## Planning Models

The *linear rational model* provides for objectives, selection and organization of activities, and specified evaluation procedures.

Objectives from the cognitive, affective, and psychomotor domains provide for a broad spectrum of learning.

Task analysis helps teachers break complex content and skills into teachable and learnable parts.

Teachers typically begin plans with *learning activities* or *content*.

Plans are made for the entire *year*, specified *units*, or individual *lessons*.

A basic *lesson plan* includes a unit title, goal and objective, rationale, content and procedures, materials, and evaluation.

The *Hunter planning model* includes anticipatory set, objectives, input and modeling, checking for understanding, and practice.

The intercom breaks into the middle of teachers' classes and blares, "Teachers, don't forget to turn in your plans for next week before you leave this afternoon."

A teacher, responding to another's question about her summer, replies, "I'm going to be writing curriculum for the district the first two weeks, and then I'm going to rest, rest, rest!"

Two friends discuss their plans for the weekend.

In the broadest sense, each of these examples involves some element of planning. Planning is a human endeavor that spans a broad spectrum of activities; its basic function is to simplify the environment and allow for strategic, goal-oriented activity. The importance of planning in teaching cannot be overemphasized.

To introduce the topic of teacher planning, consider the following examples of teachers involved in classroom planning.

Peggy Stone, a student intern in a large middle school, was preparing to teach a lesson under the watchful eye of her university supervisor. While understandably a bit apprehensive at the prospect of being evaluated, she nevertheless approached the experience with confidence because she had carefully planned her lesson the night before in anticipation of the visit.

As the students filed in the room, she handed her visitor a copy of her lesson plan. It appeared as follows:

**Unit Title: Mathematical Operations**

**Instructional Goal:**

To have students understand the order of mathematical operations and how they are used in math.

**Performance Objective:**

Students will understand the order of arithmetic operations, so when given a series of problems involving the four operations, they will solve each correctly.

**Rationale:**

Students need to understand the order of operations so they can properly simplify and solve algebraic expressions.

**Content:**

Arithmetic operations are completed in the following sequential order:

1. Multiply and divide (left to right).
2. Add and subtract (left to right).

**Procedures:**

1. Show the students the following problem:

$$14/7 \times 2 + 5 - 6$$

Ask what the right answer is. Encourage multiple answers.

2. Explain to the students that we're beginning the topic "Order of Opera-tions."
3. Ask the students to explain what *operation* means. Clarify if necessary.
4. Present the rules for order of operations. Write on board.
5. Demonstrate a solution to the problem, referring the students to rules for order of operations as the demonstration proceeds.
6. Show the students the following problem:

$$6 + 9 \times 4/3 - 7$$

7. Solve the problem with the help of the students, calling on individuals to describe each step verbally.
8. Present several other problems and solve them as a group.
9. Present the students with the attached worksheet and guide them through the first two problems.
10. Have the students work the remaining problems on the sheet as I monitor the class.
11. Give the homework assignment, p. 194; all odd-numbered problems.

**Evaluation Procedures:**

Present the students with problems involving order of operations, and have them solve the problems.

**Materials and Aids:**

Sample problems, worksheet, text.

Now, let's look at a second teacher.

Jim Hartley, a veteran of 10 years' experience teaching secondary American history, walked into his room early, as he always did, and pulled out his planning book. He looked to see what he had written in anticipation of the day's work, nodded to himself, and headed off to the media center. His plan appeared as follows:

**British Exploration**

Religious freedom, secular, nongovernment sponsored

**Spanish Exploration**

3 Gs—gold, God, glory
More integration with natives, slave labor
(Film on Spanish and Mexican fiesta)

Were these two teachers' lessons well planned? Was Peggy Stone's class better planned than Jim Hartley's? Do their plans alone or together represent the scope of teacher planning? What does teacher *planning* mean? We will attempt to answer these questions in the paragraphs that follow.

We will answer the last question first. Concepts of planning range from the simple products that appear on paper or in a planning book, such as those of Peggy and Jim, to complex psychological processes in which a teacher "visualizes the future, inventories means and ends, and constructs a framework to guide his or her future action" (Clark and Peterson, 1986, p. 260). The future might be as long as a year or as short as the next day. In both cases, teachers consider content, goals, materials, and learning activities. With year-long planning, the thinking will be global and somewhat abstract, while daily lesson planning will be more specific and concrete.

Beginning education students often think of planning simply as writing an objective and preparing a lesson plan. It is much more than that, and it is much more than the information that appeared in Peggy Stone's and Jim Hartley's respective plans. For example, Jim planned to use the film to encourage a comparison of Spanish and Mexican fiestas and ultimately lead to questions about cultural similarities and differences between the two groups. He wanted the students to conjecture why there were differences in light of the fact that the origins of the two groups were similar. He then planned to compare the integration of the Spanish and English settlers with the native Americans. As we see, Jim had much more in mind in terms of content, sequence, and method than appeared on paper. He is a typical veteran teacher, and his actual plans were much more complex than his written ones (Morine–Dershimer, 1979). In contrast, Peggy was much more detailed in her written plans. This is typical of a beginning teacher; inexperienced teachers need to structure their lessons in greater detail and write more things down (Neale, Pace, and Case, 1983).

Planning includes *all the decisions teachers make that affect their instruction.* Content, activities, student grouping, major projects, grading practices, and classroom management are all considered in this process. We discuss the process of planning in three different chapters of this text. We discuss planning for management in Chapter 11 and describe the central role that rules, procedures, and routines play in this process. This chapter is devoted to instructional planning, which considers questions of what content and skills should be included in the teacher's curriculum and how they should be taught. The role planning plays in evaluating student progress is described in Chapter 12.

Every teacher plans, be it short, garbled personal notes or elaborate lesson plans. The widespread use of teacher planning can be explained from a number of perspectives. These uses are the focus of the next section.

## PLANNING: A FUNCTIONAL ANALYSIS

Why do teachers plan? The answers to this question are the focus of this section. No two teachers teach in the same way; similarly, no two teachers plan in exactly the same way. Teaching is a highly personal and idiosyncratic process, and planning lets teachers personalize the curriculum, in a sense, to make it their own. This is its primary function. It also provides a form of emotional or psychological security, which bolsters teachers' confidence and helps reduce the normal anxiety associated with teaching (Clark and Yinger, 1979; McCutcheon, 1982).

Planning also serves two practical functions. It allows teachers to anticipate instructional needs in advance so materials can be gathered and organized, and it provides a "script" that directs classroom interactions with students. Teaching is a complex activity, and careful advance planning helps simplify the process. Planning plays a major role in guiding the decisions teachers make as they work with students (Clark and Peterson, 1986). Let us look at these functions in practice.

Mrs. Evans is a new faculty member in a math department at a magnet school designed to attract high-ability students from throughout the city. Because her transcript revealed a few computer courses, she was assigned to teach a second-year programming course for which she has minimal background. She is experiencing considerable anxiety, both because she is new and because she lacks confidence in her understanding of the material. She spends hours every day in study but is quite dissatisfied with her preparation as she enters the classroom.

One day she comes into the teachers' lounge with an extra bounce in her step; her conversation is more animated, and her manner is more enthusiastic.

"You're in a good mood today," remarks another rookie who has become her confidant.

"I've found the secret," she replies. "It's transparencies. When I have to present new material, I just write my outline down on the transparency. I use it to remind me where I am, and then I can keep the flow of my lecture going."

She added with a grin. "It takes nine transparencies to make it through the class."

Consider another example.

Mrs. Arnold is an elementary teacher planning a lesson on invertebrates.

"The kids don't like science," she thinks. "I heard two of them saying how boring it is. What am I going to do?"

She then seized on the idea of bringing in some real animals to class. On her way home from school that evening, she stopped in at a fish market and bought a crab, a clam, and a small fish. The next day she took all three, plus her daughter's hamster, into class. During the lesson, students examined and compared the four animals, analyzing similarities and differences between vertebrates and invertebrates, with the chart shown in Figure 3.1. Her students were excited, touching the animals and comparing their similarities and differences.

"That's the best science lesson I ever did," she concluded to herself afterward. After that experience, Mrs. Evans tried to bring something interesting to class and to involve students actively in each science lesson.

Consider how each of the planning functions manifested themselves in these two scenarios. We said that planning serves as a means of organizing instruction and helps teachers feel more confident and secure. Mrs. Evans's experience illustrates these functions. Through structuring the math content on her transparencies, she was able to personalize it, deleting some topics and emphasizing others. In addition,

**FIGURE 3.1** Instructional Chart Comparing Vertebrates and Invertebrates

| | Examples | Similarities | Differences |
|---|---|---|---|
| Vertebrates | | | |
| Invertebrates | | | |

the transparencies provided a script for her interactions with students; she no longer had to keep all the information in her head. Finally, the transparencies bolstered her confidence and helped ease her anxiety because she was well prepared.

We have all been in situations where we feel nervous or uncertain in anticipating a future teaching situation. Perhaps the content is unfamiliar, we are unsure of our audience, or we have had a bad experience in the past. The tendency in these cases is to plan in more detail and to write more information on paper. This also helps explain why Peggy Stone had more extensive written plans than did Jim Hartley; she was an intern, in contrast to his 10 years' experience.

Our second example is quite different from the first. While Mrs. Evans used her planning time to identify and sequence topics that helped her both organizationally and emotionally, Mrs. Arnold used her planning time to consider the motivation and involvement of the students.

Does planning actually affect teacher behavior? The literature suggests that it does. Researchers have found a positive correlation between the number of planning statements teachers made about content and their tendency to remain focused on the topic they were teaching (Peterson, Marx, and Clark, 1978). They further found that written statements about teaching procedures were related to the way teachers interacted with their students. Planning *is* functional, and teachers carry out their plans once they are made, but what factors influence the shape these plans take? This question is the focus of the next section.

# VARIABLES IN INSTRUCTIONAL PLANNING

A number of variables—including teachers and their individuality, the students we teach, the content, the instructional context, resources, and available time—affect the planning process. We will look at these elements in the sections that follow.

## The Teacher

The most significant variable in the planning process is the teachers themselves. Their beliefs about the role of schools and what children should learn, their own capacity to help students, and their general philosophical approach to living all affect the decisions they make. This philosophical stand, while seemingly remote and abstract, is important for learning. Teachers who feel a sense of mission in guiding student learning and believe all students are capable of learning are more active in their role, have higher expectations, and work harder to help students achieve (Dembo and Gibson, 1985). Teachers with philosophical commitments to excellence take more personal responsibility for student failures and increase their efforts to help underachieving students. Less committed teachers are more likely to attribute lack of achievement to student shortcomings (Ames, 1982). Effective teachers believe that all students can learn and that teachers play an important role in the process (Good, 1983). This belief is translated into positive action that affects the teachers' efforts, the amount of content covered, and the depth of their goals. They are more enthusiastic, have higher expectations, and are better models. Views such as these have an impact on planning. If teachers believe students can learn, they plan to teach more content or skills and they consciously plan for student thinking and interaction.

Teachers' content background also affects the planning process. Research on teachers' understanding of the content they teach reveals that content background is an important variable influencing lesson organization and clarity as well as the type of questions asked in the lesson (Carlsen, 1987; Shulman, 1986). Teachers unfamiliar with lesson content asked lower level questions, stuck closer to the text, and discouraged students from asking questions. The implications of this research are clear: Your understanding of the content of your teaching is an essential planning component. Take the time while you are planning to familiarize yourself with the content.

## Students

> Karen Passey, a kindergarten teacher, sat down to plan her next week's lessons. "Hmm, let's see, figures and shapes. I better plan on something active and fun for my afternoon group, or they'll get bored and go bonkers after five minutes."

> Pam Shepard looked at her planning book to refresh her memory about next month's topics. "Hmm. Shakespeare. My college prep classes should be able to handle it without any problems, but I'll have to really plan it carefully with my third period class."

As we saw in Chapter 2, students exert a powerful influence on our instructional decisions. Many of these decisions occur during the planning process. The age of our students, their background knowledge, motivational level, and interests all affect decisions we make as we plan for instruction.

The age of our students is one of the most powerful variables affecting planning. Age is closely related to attention spans, which determine the length of any individual activity within a lesson. One teaching adage recommends, "Don't plan any single learning activity longer than the age of your students." Karen Passey, in planning for her kindergartners, would make sure that any quiet listening time wouldn't exceed 5 minutes. A junior high teacher might be able to stretch this to 12 or 15 minutes, but our experience is that this would be pushing it.

Students' background knowledge is another factor influencing planning. What students know and understand affects future learning. For example, a lesson on writing paragraphs is heavily dependent on a number of prerequisite skills like writing sentences, capitalization, and punctuation. In a later section, we'll describe how task analysis can be used to determine prerequisite knowledge.

A third student variable influencing the planning process is student interests. Experienced teachers are able to use student interests as a springboard to propel students into lessons. For example, elementary teachers use children's fascination with Halloween to teach writing, poetry, art, and music. In a similar way, junior high and high school science teachers capitalize on teenagers' fascination with their changing bodies to teach biology and health concepts.

A fourth student variable influencing planning is students' motivational level. Motivation is the second greatest concern of beginning teachers, exceeded only by management (Veenman, 1984). Experienced teachers continue to wrestle with motivation long after management concerns disappear.

Student motivation occurs at two levels: global and lesson specific (Eggen and Kauchak, 1992). At a more global level, it represents the cumulative effects of all past learning experiences. If these have been successful, students come to us confident, alert, and eager for new learning; the opposite is also true, unfortunately.

The second type of motivation, occurring at the lesson level, is more malleable and more readily influenced by the teacher. Arousing students' curiosity at the beginning of a lesson can draw them into the lesson and keep them there. One way to do this is through an open-ended or rhetorical question. For example, a lesson on dinosaurs might begin with, "Consider the dinosaur—the largest and most fearsome of all land animals, some as big as a house. Suddenly they became extinct. Why?" In a similar way, a lesson might begin with a physical discrepant event—an event that is puzzling to students. For example, a home economics lesson on baking might begin with two loaves of bread, one perfect and the other flat. The teacher would then begin the lesson by saying, "These two loaves started out the same way and had the same ingredients. One turned out like this; the other like this. Why? We'll find out in this lesson." Curiosity can be a powerful motivator for pulling students into the lesson. Teachers take student motivation into account when they plan high-interest activities at the beginning of a lesson.

## Content

The type of content we're teaching also influences the planning process. For example, if we're planning to teach a concept, we'll need to gather positive and negative examples to illustrate the abstraction. In a similar way, if we're teaching a skill like solving math word problems involving addition, we'll need to find or construct a number of these problems so students can practice on them. We'll return to this idea in Chapters 6 through 10, when we discuss alternative teaching strategies.

## Learning Context

Another powerful factor influencing planning is the learning context. The learning context includes state and district guidelines, school policy, and leadership. For instance, McCutcheon (1982) described two school districts in Virginia; both had adopted the same basic text, but the first encouraged teachers to adapt freely, and the second required teachers to cover all the content in the book before turning to supplementary materials. Teacher autonomy and initiative had quite different meanings in the two districts. Planning is also influenced by district guidelines where teachers are held accountable for their students' achievement in terms of specific goals as measured by yearly standardized tests (Bullough, Goldstein, and Holt, 1984; Floden, Porter, Schmidt, Freeman, and Schuille, 1981). When teachers feel pressured to cover certain content and topics because the information will show up on a test, their planning is affected.

The school principal also affects the planning process. In her study of elementary teachers' planning, McCutcheon (1982) found that even though all the principals she studied required written plans, their plans varied greatly in detail, format, and length of time. Some inspected plans weekly, others monthly, and still others at random intervals.

One principal sent out the following memo:

> Each teacher is expected to keep *daily* lesson plans of classroom activities. Good teacher planning is essential for effective teaching. In case of teacher absence, lesson plans are to be available in the top desk drawer for the substitute teacher. This is a must. Detailed lesson plans should be kept a week in advance.
>
> Lesson plans should be kept in a looseleaf notebook. These notebooks will be checked from time to time by the principal. (McCutcheon, 1982, p. 263)

Clearly, the plans written at this principal's school will be quite different from those in a school where planning is considered to be a personally functional, professional activity.

## Materials and Resources

Materials and other resources also have a major impact on teacher planning. Textbooks are first among them. Beginning teachers depend heavily on text materials to help them decide the topics to be taught, sequencing, depth, and even the test items they give their students. As teachers acquire experience, they become more independent, adding and deleting topics and generally personalizing their curriculum. However, even veterans rely heavily on available materials and often voice frustration when topics covered by district or state objectives do not appear in their textbooks (Clark and Elmore, 1981).

Other materials also influence planning. If the film had not existed, Jim Hartley's approach to his lesson comparing Mexican and Spanish customs would necessarily have been quite different. Reaching his goal would have been difficult;

the goal might even have been revised. In fact, some research indicates that teachers first consider activities when they plan (Clark and Peterson, 1986), and their activities are usually based on materials. Pragmatically, if the materials do not exist, the activity cannot be conducted.

## Time

Time is related to planning in several ways. First, planning consumes considerable teacher time—as much as 10 to 20 hours a week in some cases (Clark and Yinger, 1979; McDaniel–Hine and Willower, 1988). This is a considerable expenditure of effort, especially for beginning teachers trying to survive their first years of teaching. Time also interacts with other variables; teachers of young children spend much of their planning time gathering and arranging the physical materials that students will use in activities (Hill, Yinger, and Robbins, 1981). In general, teachers spend most of their planning time organizing activities and gathering available materials (Institute of Research on Teaching, 1978). This relates to the organizing and scripting functions discussed earlier.

Time interacts with the planning process in a second way: It provides both a goal and frame of reference for the planning process. As a goal, classroom time is often thought of as an empty vessel to be filled (Wiley and Harnishefeger, 1974). One researcher in this area even developed the idea of "sponges," interim activities to be used to fill up unused time (Stallings, 1983). To take advantage of 5-minute segments before lunch or recess, elementary students brainstorm lists from categories like farm animals or fruits and vegetables, while secondary students would list the capitals of states or presidents in order. Hmmmm? What do *you* think of the idea?

Time also serves as a frame of reference, helping teachers structure their planning. The school year is divided into months, the months into weeks, and courses are divided into units framed in terms of these months and weeks. Breaking time down into manageable chunks and framing these chunks into units makes the seemingly overwhelming task of planning manageable. We will discuss this process later in this chapter.

# MODELS OF PLANNING

As we said earlier, no two teachers teach or plan exactly alike. But some similarities exist in terms of the processes that teachers go through as they plan and the products they produce. These similarities are summarized in terms of planning models, discussed in this section. To introduce this topic, consider the following:

Objective: You will understand process/product research so that given an article containing this type of research you will identify the process/product variables in the study and explain their relationship.

**Reading**

Group 1:  Read pp. 57–63. Discuss ? in TG p. 187. Workbook pp. 12–13 suffixes. Boardwork—suffixes, TG p. 188–189.

**Social Studies**

Map reading. Dittos of Magellan's and da Gama's voyages. Groups put on project maps or project globe. Discuss oceans and continents. (McCutcheon, 1982, p. 262)

The first of these two excerpts is an objective that might have accompanied Chapter 1 of this text. As such, it is an integral part of the *rational model* of teacher planning that we discuss in this section. The reading and social studies examples are taken from an actual teacher's plan book. They represent what typically occurs in classrooms across the country. The similarities and differences between these two approaches are the topic of this section of the chapter.

## The Linear Rational Model

A central component of most teacher training programs is typically devoted to teacher planning, with the preparation of written objectives and daily lesson plans being the primary focus. Textbooks used for these courses also allow considerable space for discussions of objectives and lesson planning (Borich, 1988; Jacobson, Eggen, and Kauchak, 1989).

This approach to planning is part of a model created by Ralph Tyler and presented in his book *Basic Principles of Curriculum and Instruction*, first published in 1949. This small text, originally created as a course syllabus, is a classic, having exerted more influence on the way teachers are taught to plan and organize instruction than any other single work.

Tyler suggested that planning should proceed in a series of four sequential steps: (1) Specify objectives, (2) select learning activities, (3) organize the learning activities, and (4) specify evaluation procedures. This model was so influential that it was not studied critically for nearly 20 years, and literally hundreds of thousands of teachers and educational leaders were trained in its use. It was not until the 1970s that researchers began to investigate teacher planning and compare the actual practice to the prescription suggested in the Tyler model. We will examine this research in a subsequent section, but first let us look at the components of the model in more detail.

## Behavioral Objectives

The Tyler model begins with the statement of objectives. Because of the impact of Tyler's model, objectives, their form, and the ability to express them have been major components of teacher preparation courses, and much time and energy is devoted to developing preservice teachers' skills in preparing objectives. Tyler suggested that the most useful form for stating objectives was "to express them in terms which identify both the kind of behavior to be developed in the student and the content or area of life in which this behavior is to operate" (p. 46). Thus, behavioral objectives were born.

When objectives first came into widespread use, they were enormously controversial. The debate raged from state departments of education, through universities, and all the way to the classroom teacher. Many of their early proponents implied that because they translated sometimes vague learning activities into specifically defined learning outcomes, they would be an educational panacea, and their zeal further fueled the controversy. Opponents were equally adamant; their complaint centered on the argument that truly meaningful education could not be broken down into a number of specific objectives. For example, how could you operationalize, or put into concrete terms, goals like aesthetic appreciation of art or growth in self-concept or self-confidence? While some debate continues today, the issue is insignificant compared to the past, and the use of objectives is widespread in materials such as county curriculum guides and state-level curriculum frameworks.

Another powerful teacher training influence followed Tyler's in 1962 when Robert Mager published *Preparing Instructional Objectives*. In this highly readable book, he suggested that an objective ought to describe "what the student will be doing when demonstrating his achievement and how you will know he is doing it" (p. 53). In addition, a good objective should have three parts: (1) an observable behavior, (2) the conditions under which the behavior will occur, and (3) criteria for acceptable performance. The following are examples of objectives written according to Mager's format:

1. Given a ruler and compass, geometry students will construct the bisector of an angle within one degree of error.
2. Given a list of sentences, language arts students will identify 90 percent of the prepositional phrases in the sentences.
3. Given a written argument, the advanced composition student will outline the logic of the presentation, identifying all assumptions and conclusions.

In the examples, the conditions respectively are as follows: (1) Given a ruler and compass; (2) given a list of sentences; and (3) given a written argument. The observable performances are as follows: (1) will construct, (2) will identify, and (3) will outline; the respective criteria are (1) within one degree of error, (2) 90 percent, and (3) all assumptions and conclusions.

Peggy Stone used Mager's approach in stating her objective. She modified it slightly to include a general goal as well, but the essence of a Mager objective was illustrated in her plan.

An alternate and very popular approach to preparing objectives was suggested by Norman Gronlund (1985b). He believes objectives should first be stated in terms of general goals such as "understand," "appreciate," "know," "evaluate," or "apply," which are then followed by observable behaviors specifying evidence that the learner has met the objective. Using the same content as illustrated in the Mager examples, Gronlund's objectives would appear as follows:

| *General Objective:* | Applies rules of geometric constructions |
| *Specific Behavior:* | 1. Constructs bisectors |
| | 2. Constructs prescribed shapes |

| *General Objective:* | Understands prepositional phrases |
| *Specific Behavior:* | 1. Provides examples of prepositions |
| | 2. Identifies prepositional phrases in sentences |
| | 3. Writes sentences including prepositional phrases |

| *General Objective:* | Can evaluate persuasive communications |
| *Specific Behavior:* | 1. Outlines logic |
| | 2. Identifies assumptions |
| | 3. Identifies conclusions |

In comparing the two approaches, we see that, in addition to including a general goal statement, Gronlund's objectives do not include conditions and criteria. He directly addresses the issue by saying conditions and criteria "are especially useful for programmed instruction and for mastery testing in simple training programs. When used for regular classroom instruction, however, they result in long cumbersome lists that restrict the freedom of the teacher" (Gronlund 1985b, p. 5). We, and the thousands of teachers who have tried to use Mager's format to plan for day-to-day instruction, agree; it *can* be cumbersome and time-consuming.

Other approaches to preparing objectives exist (e.g., Eisner, 1969; McAshan, 1974; Popham and Baker, 1970), but Mager's and Gronlund's approaches are the most widely used today. Mager is significant because of his historical impact, but most of the written curriculum guides you will encounter use Gronlund's approach or a modification of it.

## Kinds of Objectives: The Three Domains

Three physical education teachers were comparing their objectives for a unit on exercise. Carol commented, "I'm trying to develop muscle tone, strength, and flexibility so that no matter how they use their bodies in other activities, they'll have a good foundation." "I'm interested in that, too," added Sharon, a second-year teacher, "but I'm more concerned that they know about the different kinds of exercise. They need to know the difference between aerobic and anaerobic exercise and how each affects their bodies." "Both of those are important," acknowledged Tanya, "but I'm concerned about what happens after they leave school. We've got too many couch potatoes out there already. I'm trying to get them turned on to exercise so that they'll exercise for the rest of their lives."

Which of these goals is most important? What kinds of learning should schools focus on? How will your particular class contribute to the overall growth of your students? Questions like these are not easy to answer. Part of the reason for this difficulty is that schools attempt to accomplish a broad spectrum of goals, and individual teachers must select from this broad array in writing and selecting objectives for their classrooms.

Two conceptual tools help teachers think about their objectives in the planning process. The first of these divides objectives into areas or domains—cognitive, affective, and psychomotor—that correspond to the kinds of learning intended. Each of the physical education teachers had one of these domains in mind when she talked about her goals for the exercise unit. Within each domain, objectives can be classified further into levels that correspond to the specific kind of performance outcome intended. Let's see how this works with the cognitive domain, probably the most common area of learning in the schools today.

**Cognitive Domain**   The **cognitive domain** deals with the acquisition of knowledge and skills. Sharon's unit was focused on the cognitive domain because it targeted students' knowledge about different kinds of exercise. Recently, other cognitive skills like study skills, problem-solving skills, analytical skills have received increased attention because of their increased importance in a technological society. One way to differentiate these kinds of cognitive goals is in terms of the cognitive taxonomy (Bloom, 1956), which divides this area into the following six levels:

*Knowledge:* At the knowledge level, the student can recognize, define, or recall specific information. This might include important names, dates, capitals, or even the equation for a formula.

*Comprehension:* This level targets whether students understand content. Ways of demonstrating comprehension include summarizing, translating, or providing examples of a concept.

*Application:* This level focuses on whether students can use information to solve problems. Examples of application-level goals include having students solve math word problems and using punctuation properly in written communication.

*Analysis:* This level involves asking students to break something down to reveal its organization and structure. Students perform analysis when they discuss why a short story works or when they identify the component parts of a science experiment.

*Synthesis:* Students employ synthesis when they use creativity to create a unique product. This might include writing a poem, painting a picture, or creating a computer program.

*Evaluation:* In the highest level of the taxonomy, students judge the value or worth of something by comparing it to some standard or criteria. We ask students to evaluate when they critique a plan to solve a pollution problem or when we ask students to judge a writing sample.

Teachers have found the taxonomy to be a useful planning tool as they think about their objectives. It serves as a reminder that knowledge is only one of several important goals, supplies them with alternate goals, and provides them with a tool to analyze the plans they make. We'll discuss the cognitive taxonomy again when we discuss questioning strategies in Chapter 5.

**Affective Taxonomy**  As Tanya suggested, schools exist for more than just making students smarter. We also want students to develop into happy individuals with healthy views about themselves and others. The **affective domain** (Krathwohl, Bloom, and Masia, 1964) focuses on the development of attitudes and values and divides this process into five levels that correspond to the degree to which attitudes and values are internalized by the individual:

*Receiving:*  At this level, the student is willing to listen passively to or attend to some message. Students who listen to a speaker on drugs without "tuning him out" are acting at this level.

*Responding:*  Beyond just receiving a message, students must also react to it. Students can do this by obeying, discussing, or responding to the attitude or value.

*Valuing:*  When students respond at this level, they show their preference for an idea by voluntarily displaying it. For example, a health class has been talking about nutrition. A student turns to his friend in the cafeteria and says, "Those french fries aren't good for you. They've got too much fat."

*Organization:*  This level occurs when students take an attitude or value and incorporate it into a larger value system. In the health example, this would occur when the student looks at his own diet and examines implications for himself.

*Characterization:*  At the highest level of the affective domain, students not only reorganize their own thinking but also act consistently with their beliefs. A student who actually changes the way he or she eats over a long period of time would be operating at this level.

As with the cognitive taxonomy, the affective taxonomy provides teachers with a conceptual tool to analyze their planning. If respect for the rights of others is one of our goals, do we just want students to nod when we talk about the importance of respect, or do we want to create a classroom where everyone feels secure in responding, knowing they won't be interrupted or laughed at? In a larger sense, the affective taxonomy provides some interesting answers to the question, "What are schools for?"

**Psychomotor Domain**  A third area that serves as a source of goals for our teaching is the **psychomotor domain**, which involves the development of muscles and coordination. Though we typically associate the psychomotor domain with physical education, other areas (like typing, music, art, industrial arts, and home economics) are also involved. In addition, preschool, kindergarten, and the lower primary grades focus on the psychomotor domain through activities like cutting and pasting, coloring, printing, and writing. Like the other areas, the psychomotor taxonomy (Harrow, 1972), shown in Table 3.1, proceeds from simplex to complex and from externally to internally controlled.

**TABLE 3.1**   The Psychomotor Taxonomy

| Level | Description |
|---|---|
| 1. Reflex movements | Behaviors outside the conscious control of the learner |
| 2. Basic fundamental movements | Behaviors learned at an early age (e.g., grasping, walking) that form the foundation for later growth |
| 3. Perceptual abilities | Allow the coordination of muscular movements with the outside world through feedback with the sense organs |
| 4. Physical abilities | The development of strength, endurance, flexibility, and agility |
| 5. Skilled movements | Complex physical skills (e.g., skipping rope, shooting a basket) that utilize the first four levels |
| 6. Nondiscursive communication | The use of our bodies to express feelings or ideas |

In the linear rational model, objectives form a logical starting point for the planning process. Taxonomies in the three domains serve not only as a source of goals but also as a means of preparing and sequencing learning activities, the next steps in Tyler's model.

## Preparing and Organizing Learning Activities

The second and third steps in the linear rational model involve the preparation and organization of learning activities. For instance, Peggy Stone planned to make an oral presentation of the rules for order of operations, which would be followed by modeling a solution to sample problems, guided practice, and independent practice. Her plan specified both the activities and the sequence in which they would occur. It nicely illustrates the second and third steps of Tyler's rational model.

In contrast, Jim Hartley's plan was merely an outline of the topics to be taught together with a note to himself to get a film on Spanish and Mexican fiestas. The suggestion of a sequence of activities was there, but from this brief description of his plans we cannot be sure if the planning model used was Tyler's.

## Task Analysis:   A Planning Tool to Organize Activities

How should learning activities be sequenced? Which activities come before others? What will students need to know to participate successfully in a lesson? Answers to these questions can be found in the process of task analysis.

**Task analysis** is the process of breaking down a topic or skill into its prerequisite skills or parts. For example, a task analysis for the skill of changing a tire could be broken down into the subskills of jacking up the car, loosening the wheel nuts, taking off the flat, replacing it with the spare, replacing the wheel nuts, and lowering the car. Breaking a complex skill into simpler subskills helps the teacher plan for instruction.

Task analysis involves the following four steps:

- Specify terminal behavior.
- Identify prerequisite skills.
- Sequence subskills.
- Diagnose students.

Task analysis begins with specification of the terminal behavior. Objectives stated in behavioral terms are especially valuable here. In identifying prerequisite skills, the planner is attempting to specify the subskills that lead to the terminal behavior. Sequencing helps the teacher by providing an order for teaching and provides learners with structure for learning. In the final phase of task analysis, diagnosis, the teacher attempts to find out which of these subskills are already mastered by students. Let's see how these steps help a teacher in the planning process.

> Jerilyn McIntire stared at the stack of writing assignments on her desk and didn't know where to begin. Her seventh-grade English students weren't afraid to write, but it seemed like half of them had never heard of punctuation. There were sentence fragments, run-on sentences, sentences without periods, and commas and semicolons were virtually nonexistent. Where to start?

In considering all of the possible starting points for her attack on punctuation, Jerilyn came up with one specific starting point—punctuating simple sentences. As she thought about this, she identified the following terminal behavior:

> Students will be able to write simple sentences with correct end-of-sentence punctuation.

Continuing to think about this target goal, Jerilyn wrote down some skills that were prerequisite to the terminal behavior:

- Being able to differentiate between complete sentences and sentence fragments
- Knowing the difference between declarative, interrogatory, and imperative sentences
- Knowing whether periods, question marks, or exclamation marks go with each type of sentence
- Correctly using these marks to punctuate different kinds of sentences.

As she wrestled with the problem of ordering these, Jerilyn decided that the sequence of subskills as written made instructional sense. First students had to understand what sentences were. Then she could work on helping them understand the different kinds of sentences and how they were punctuated. Finally, she wanted them to write and punctuate their own sentences.

A final problem confronted Jerilyn: How many (and which) students already knew how to do these? In attempting to diagnose her students, Jerilyn came up with a simple quiz that she would administer the next day. In the first part, students would have to differentiate between sentences and sentence fragments. In the second part, they'd have to punctuate different kinds of sentences, and in the third part they'd have to write their own sentences and punctuate them.

Task analysis works for several reasons. First, it encourages us to examine our goals and state them in behavioral terms. Like the process of writing objectives in general, this helps clarify our thinking. Task analysis also encourages us to break complex skills into smaller, more teachable subskills. Finally, task analysis shifts our attention from abstract concepts and skills to our students and encourages us to ask, "What do they already know and where should I begin teaching them?" Each of these steps is helpful in preparing and organizing learning activities.

## Evaluation

The final phase of the Tyler model calls for specifying evaluation procedures. Again, Peggy Stone adhered to the model by stating in advance how students' understanding of the lesson would be measured. Notice, also, that the objective specified the evaluation at the outset, and the objective, procedure, and description of evaluation were all congruent. Tyler would enthusiastically endorse Peggy Stone's lesson plan as an excellent illustration of his rational approach to planning. In contrast, Jim Hartley did not mention evaluation in his plan, and from the written plan, no insight is given into the way students' understanding of the lesson's content would be measured.

We have discussed and illustrated the linear rational model with a single lesson designed to cover one class period. It can be applied equally well to a unit or larger block of study, as we will see later. Here, the scope would be greater, but the process is essentially the same. We turn now to research related to this model.

# RESEARCH ON TEACHER PLANNING

*The great tragedy of science — the betraying of theory by an ugly fact.*
T. H. Huxley

The logic behind the linear rational model is compelling. It makes sense to start the planning process with an objective, proceed to instructional activities designed to meet the objective, and end with the construction of evaluation items to measure students' attainment of the objective. In fact, this approach was so attractive that it was widely accepted for nearly 20 years, and it still heavily influences teacher education programs and educational methods textbooks. Once research on how teachers actually plan began to appear in the literature, however, some interesting patterns emerged.

## Planning Research: Results

The results of the research on teacher planning highlight an interesting paradox. Time and effort in teacher training programs are being spent on processes experienced teachers apparently do not use. The accumulating evidence suggests that experienced teachers do not prepare written objectives and detailed lesson plans

(Morine–Dershimer and Vallance, 1976; Peterson et al., 1978; Zahorik, 1975), and our experience in the schools supports these findings. Further, teachers believe the systematic model is primarily useful for inexperienced teachers, and student teachers use the model only when required to do so by their university supervisors (Neale et al., 1983). Other researchers found that only the least experienced teachers planned according to the Tyler model (Sardo, 1982), and many teachers prepare written plans of any kind only because of administrator demands (McCutcheon, 1982). Finally, Taylor (1970) found little focus on evaluation during the process of instructional planning. The only elements of the Tyler model that show up in writing in the plans of experienced teachers are the identification and organization of learning activities. The evidence is clear and consistent. The linear rational model, so revered by teacher trainers, does not appear in the written plans of experienced teachers in the real world.

Why do teachers not write out objectives when they plan? Elementary teachers in McCutcheon's 1982 study had several good reasons. First, objectives already exist in most curriculum guides and texts. To write them again would be redundant and a waste of time. Second, objectives for an activity are often embedded in the activity itself. For example, a kindergarten lesson on geometric shapes would have as an implicit goal the children's ability to identify the different shapes. Similarly, the goal for lessons on single-digit addition could be inferred from the problems used in the activity. Third, objectives are often embedded in criterion-referenced math and reading tests. One teacher had this comment: "It seems ludicrous to list objectives. They wouldn't be doing the work unless it was aimed at an objective, because the test is all objectives based" (McCutcheon, 1982, p. 263).

Other possible reasons that teachers do not write objectives might simply be that it is just too difficult or it requires too much work. Attempting to write an objective at the beginning of the planning process may be an overwhelming task. It requires teachers to wrestle with not only content selection, but also the problem of evaluation at the same time. Juggling both of these components while still trying to articulate a goal or specific outcome for an activity may be overwhelming at this juncture.

From a time perspective, writing out objectives might be too labor intensive. If teachers wrote specific objectives for each lesson they taught over the course of a year, the time demands would be overwhelming. In this regard, we need to remember that planning is a means toward an end. The end result is student learning. If teachers can plan effectively for instruction without writing out formal objectives, more time and energy are left for interactive teaching, providing students with feedback, and a myriad of other professional activities.

**Why Learn to Write Objectives?**    What should we conclude from all this? Because teachers do not write objectives and are unlikely to change, should they be abandoned? Probably not. First, while written objectives are not often the starting point for teacher planning, it does not mean they are ignored completely. Zahorik (1975) and Peterson et al. (1978) found that teachers use objectives, but they come later in the process rather than first, as dictated by the Tyler model. Our experience supports this result. Even though objectives are unwritten, effective teachers know exactly what they want their students to know or understand. When asked, they are able to state precisely what their goal is. The issue seems to be more one of *writing the objective down* than it is thinking about objectives. Second, understanding objectives is important because of their widespread use in state and district curriculum materials, textbooks, and achievement tests. For instance, consider the following example, taken from minimum standards in elementary science for the state of Florida.

| *Standards* | *Basic Skills—The Student Will:* |
|---|---|
| The student will know basic physical concepts. | Identify some properties of air and water. |
| | Identify the forms of matter as solid, liquid, and gas. |
| | Define matter. |
| | (Florida State Office of Education, 1985, p. 31) |

We see that this standard fits Gronlund's format for preparing objectives. The evaluation procedures to assess the objectives are also tied directly to them and are designed according to the principles of the linear rational model.

Teachers are expected to be able to take objectives like these and translate them into classroom learning activities. Further, in addition to being consumers of objectives, teachers are often asked to participate in curriculum-development projects in which objectives are a major product. This might be at the grade level, where team planning is involved; at the school level, where intergrade articulation of a curriculum is concerned; or even at the district or state level, where curriculum guides are produced. Also, with the continuing emphasis on educational accountability, teachers are being required to tie learning activities, objectives, and competency tests to performance. In addition, objectives can be a useful communication tool for talking with other teachers as well as students and parents. In sum, an understanding of them should be a part of every teacher's professional repertoire.

If objectives are not the starting point for teacher planning, what is? A number of studies (Morine–Dersheimer and Vallance, 1976; Peterson et al., 1978; Zahorik, 1975) suggest that consideration of content sometimes serves an initial framing function. The selection of learning activities is another common beginning point in planning (Clark and Peterson, 1986; Sardo, 1982).

As teachers plan and record these activities, they often do so in a shorthand, cryptic fashion in plan books much like the examples earlier in this chapter (e.g., "third reading group, pp. 13–20, questions 1–10"). The brevity of these directions belies the thought and energy that goes into the plans. McCutcheon (1982) likened them to shopping lists; the items on a shopping list represent considerable implicit planning and coordination for different menus. This planning and coordination are not evident from a brief inspection of the shopping list. In a similar way, the brief description of activities in a plan book do not do justice to the considerable amount of mental planning that precedes them.

The literature suggests that, contrary to the Tyler model, the planning process is not discrete and linear but rather a continual, nested process. It begins sometime before the school year starts and continues throughout the year. Yinger (1977) described this as a cyclical process in which general ideas undergo progressive elaboration. The germ of an idea for a lesson or unit, encountered in the summer, becomes elaborated over time. As the time to teach a particular class grows closer, teachers fill in more and more detail, using not only feedback that they have gathered from the present year's students but also information from previous years (Kauchak and Peterson, 1987).

Finally, planning for instruction is not a uniform, standard process. Instead, it is quite variable and subject to influences from a number of sources; the strongest of these is experience (Sardo, 1982). Experienced teachers have last year's curriculum to call on, and the planning process may be more adaptation or modification than construction from the ground up. As one teacher put it, "We go with ideas that worked well in the past. We *know* what those are like" (McCutcheon, 1982, p. 264). When we asked a group of experienced elementary teachers to estimate the amount of overlap of this year's curriculum with last year's, they generally agreed it was 70 to 80 percent. Teachers retain the best ideas that worked, adding new ones to replace those that did not. This ability to call on past experiences is a major difference between experienced and beginning teachers (Sabers, Cushing, and Berliner, 1991). Because experienced teachers have a wealth of past experiences to rely on (not to mention dittos and tests), their work load is reduced. Beginning teachers, in contrast, start from scratch as attested to by the countless hours spent planning during student teaching and the first year on the job (Bullough, 1989).

Another factor working to make planning a variable process is the content area itself. Elementary teachers report that 85 to 95 percent of the activities in math are adapted from teacher guides (McCutcheon, 1982). This adaption process is not a passive one; teachers screen these activities with dual criteria: (1) Had the activity worked in the past? and (2) Would it work with this group? In contrast, planning in other elementary content areas such as science and social studies is much more individualized and teacher centered. Teachers chose isolated units, and interest and availability of materials were primary factors for inclusion of a topic.

Within the framework of state and county curriculum guidelines, teachers teach what they like and know. The weaker the teacher's content background and the more inexperienced the teacher, the more the published curriculum in the form of texts and teachers' guides influences curriculum. Beginning teachers should not feel guilty about using these aids; as they become more experienced, they will begin to personalize the curriculum, making it their own. Finally, logistical considerations such as the availability of lab materials, videotapes, and movies have major influences on how a course is taught.

One major conclusion from this research is that planning is not a uniform process and is instead dependent on a number of related factors (e.g., experience, content, and the availability of curriculum materials). Also, research underscores the functional nature of teacher planning—teachers plan as they do to get the job done, to maximize student learning given the constraints of the situation.

Given these influences and constraints on the planning process, what suggestions are there for people undertaking this complex task? We discuss these in the next section.

# SYNTHESIS OF RESEARCH AND EXPERIENCE: A PLANNING MODEL

In the previous sections, we discussed the nature of planning, the function it serves, and what research tells us about the ways teachers plan. We now want to use this information to describe a comprehensive model of planning that is realistic and practical. This planning model occurs in three stages. In the first stage, called *long-term*, teachers survey available resources, including texts and state and district curriculum guides, and outline a year's or semester's instruction in terms of time frames. During *unit planning*, the second phase of the process, teachers translate these broad outlines into interrelated lessons focused on a central topic or theme. Finally, during *lesson planning*, specific activities for a given day are considered. The broad ideas considered earlier are translated into specific plans of action. Let us examine how this works.

## Long-Term Planning

**Long-term planning** typically involves preparing for a year or semester and serves primarily as a framework for later planning efforts. Yearly planning serves the following purposes: (1) adapts the curriculum to fit the teacher's knowledge and priorities, (2) helps the teacher learn the structure and content of the new curricula, and (3) develops a practical schedule for instruction (Clark and Elmore, 1981). Note how these functions are similar to the general functions of planning discussed earlier.

Long-term planning also serves to establish routines, or establish procedures for how the school year will run. In instructional planning, the structure provided by routines "played such a major role in the teacher's planning behavior that planning could be characterized as decision making about the selection, organization, and sequencing of routines" (Yinger, 1977, p. 165). One example of a routine in the elementary classroom that was found to be effective in producing math achievement is the following:

> Monday starts with a longer than usual review to compensate for the long weekend. Each subsequent day begins with homework checking and then proceeds to presentation of new material, and then group and individual practice. Friday's session wraps up the week with further review and a quiz. Students know what to expect each day as math begins, and there is a natural rhythm to the tempo of the classroom during the week. (Good, Grouws, and Ebmeier, 1983, p. 44)

Establishing routines at this stage in planning provides a content-free superstructure that helps guide the school year.

Much of the initial effort at this stage is covert mental activity. It is also continual and may occur at strange times and places, such as late in the evening or while driving to school or watching a football game on television (McCutcheon, 1982). As one teacher described it, "The subconscious does a lot of sorting for you. You can think of many things almost simultaneously. The sorting is rapid, not logical or sequenced, and is different for different reasons" (McCutcheon, 1982, p. 265).

To aid this covert, subconscious process, teachers turn to a number of sources including curriculum guides, textbooks, teachers' guides, notes from college courses, and other teachers' experience. They often do a lot of scribbling, sketching, and note taking, making lists of topics, sequencing them, and then adjusting the sequence. Secondary teachers focus primarily on content when they plan, and content decisions are typically the ones made first (Peterson et al., 1978; Sardo, 1982). If clear guidelines from the state or district exist, they become a valuable resource. Let's see how all this might work.

A third-grade teacher starts her beginning-of-the-year science planning by browsing through some materials. She notes that the state curriculum guide has identified plants as one of the topics to be covered during the school year. More specifically, the guide outlines the following objectives as desirable learning outcomes:

| *Plants* | Grade | | | | |
|---|---|---|---|---|---|
| 57. Identify the parts of a plant: root, stem and leaf. | 3 | | | | |
| 58. Identify environmental conditions necessary for plant growth. | 3 | | | | |
| 59. Identify the stages of growth of a plant as seed, seedling, and mature plant. | 3 | | | | |

(Minimum Student Performance Standards for Florida Schools, p. 25)

With that information the teacher then turns to the third-grade science text and finds that "Seeds and Plants" compose two chapters in the text. (This is more than coincidence; state curriculum writers target their objectives on content covered in state-adopted texts, and text writers are sensitive to the kinds of content in state curriculum guides.)

A quick check of the contents of these chapters reveals the following topics:

| | |
|---|---|
| seeds | roots |
| embryo | stems |
| germination | leaves |
| seedlings | flowers |
| seed plants | plant life cycle |

(Adapted from Sund, Adams, Hackett, and Moyer, 1985)

The text will be a definite resource. Now on to the Teacher's Edition. Here she found a number of aids, including the following:

1. Classroom activities (e.g., planting seeds, measuring plant growth)
2. Lab activities, including materials needed
3. Ditto masters for worksheets
4. Enrichment activities, including out-of-class projects
5. Test items
6. Additional books to read (for both the teacher and students)

Satisfied with the topic, the direction she is headed, and the availability of resources, the teacher jots down, "Plants and Seeds, September and one half of October" and moves on to the next general topic.

As we can see from this example, long-term planning is only concrete enough to provide a framework for more specific short-range planning. Specific day-to-day learning activities usually are not considered at this point, nor is extensive study to refresh content background. Too much specificity at this point can be counterproductive, as two teachers observed:

> If I plan too far ahead, it's not flexible enough to incorporate children's interests and the needs I see while teaching.
> I have to do so much reteaching because kids are absent or gone for band or something that it gets in the way of long-range planning. It interrupts the flow. (McCutcheon, 1982, p. 267)

**Products of Long-Term Planning**  As teachers proceed with long-term planning, they produce lists in different content areas that are framed in terms of time dimensions. These lists are refinements of the scribblings and random thinking that occur in the beginning of the long-term planning process. For example, the products of a seventh-grade geography teacher's long-term planning might appear as follows:

**World Geography (First Semester)**
1. Basic concepts (September/October)
Maps, landforms, water and waterways, elements of climate, population patterns
2. Cultural change and development (November 1–15)
3. Anglo-America (Canada and United States) (November 15–December 15)
4. Latin America (Mexico, Central America, South America) (December 15–January 15)

While brief, the outline serves the important function of simplifying subsequent planning efforts by reducing the number of decisions that must be made later. At this point, the teacher thinks of potential content, some possible objectives, and some long-range gathering of resources, such as ordering films that require advance scheduling. Otherwise, teachers typically wait until the topic approaches before unit planning, which entails consideration of objectives, details of the content, specific learning activities involved, and measurement and evaluation. The topic list helps the teacher by providing initial structure. Later, the teacher merely refers to it and notes,

"Ah, yes. I'll be starting Anglo-America next week, so I need to get ready." The specifics of getting ready are a function of unit planning.

## Unit Planning

Once a general framework is established in long-term planning, teachers find it useful to convert this framework into specific units. A **unit** is a series of interconnected lessons focusing on a general topic. It can last anywhere from a week or two to a month or more depending on the topic itself and the age level of the students. Some examples of unit topics in different content areas are as follows:

| Art | Home Economics | Physical Education | Music |
|-----|----------------|--------------------|-------|
| Watercolors | Nutrition | Aerobic exercise | Rhythm |
| Perspective | Fabrics | Tennis | Jazz |
| Pottery | Money | Body | Wind instruments |
| Print making | management | conditioning | Classical era |
| | Baking | Swimming | |

Unit plans are useful to teachers because they help bridge the gap between long-term and day-to-day lesson planning. Units are functional for students because the components—including objectives, content, and activities—are tied together in a logical, coherent manner, providing structure for the new material to be learned.

Unit planning, like all aspects of planning, is a personal process, and no two teachers will construct units that are exactly alike. We propose the system shown in Table 3.2 as a starting point for this process and encourage you to experiment and adapt as you gain experience.

Although these components are listed sequentially, our experience, as well as the research discussed earlier, indicate that the process is not necessarily linear or sequential. Teachers sometimes start with content, other times with objectives or activities. These various components interact continually in the refinement process.

Let us see what these various components look like in an elementary language arts unit on library skills.

**TABLE 3.2** Unit Components

| Component | Function |
|-----------|----------|
| Overview/general goal | Summarizes the general purpose of the unit |
| Rationale | Answers the question, "Why is this topic or skill important?" |
| Objectives | Describes the major outcomes from this unit |
| Content | What are the important ideas and how are they organized? |
| Instructional activities | What will students do to learn? |
| Evaluation | Describes how student learning will be measured |

### Overview/Goal

This unit is designed to develop fourth-grade students' library skills for working in the card catalog. This unit will focus on the development of skills with three different types of catalog cards: title card, author card, and subject card.

The overview or goal describes the general purpose of the unit. It can serve as a starting point for the unit-planning process in several ways. If the teacher's ideas are clear about where the unit is going, it can serve as a conceptual organizer for the rest of the process. If unit directions are still unclear, it can serve as a reference point to be returned to later and refined. It can also help communicate instructional intents to other professionals, including principals and substitute teachers.

### Rationale

A working knowledge of card catalogs and how they're organized is necessary for students using the library. They need to be able to locate desired materials from the collection to use in their research projects. With the building of library skills related to catalog work, the student will be able to work quite independently using this resource. Often, students using the school library have a vague idea about a subject area on which more information is needed or they have only limited information about a particular book in the collection. Upon completion of this unit, the student will be able to retrieve this needed information successfully to assist him or her in locating the appropriate materials in the collection.

The rationale can also be useful in several ways. Asking "Why?" encourages the teacher to be thoughtful and reflective during the planning process, linking learning activities to the goals of the unit. The rationale can also help to connect the new content to the course as a whole. Sharing the rationale with students helps them understand the importance of the new material in their lives, giving them a reason to learn the new content.

### Objectives

1. Students will be able to identify three different ways a book can be found in the card catalog, so when asked to write them from memory, they can do so with 100 percent accuracy.
2. Students will learn the basic differences between the title card, the author card, and the subject card, so when asked to make flash cards of each, they will include all the necessary information common to each type of card.
3. Students will be able to choose which of the three catalog cards they need to look for in the catalog when given limited information about a book, so when given certain information about a particular book, they can locate the appropriate catalog card each time.
4. Students will be able to locate names of authors, titles, and subjects in individual catalog drawers by using the outside guides, so when given a

list of these and a diagram of the outside guides on a catalog drawer, they can choose the correct guide letters for each.

5. Students will be able to locate any book available in the school library collection by using the card catalog, so when asked to locate five different book titles, subjects, or authors they have an interest in reading, they can locate them successfully in the card catalog and write the call number of each.

Sooner or later in the planning process, teachers need to grapple with the question, "What do I want students to learn?" As we saw earlier, sometimes planning begins with the objectives themselves, other times with content or activities. Activities serve as a useful starting point for the planning process when skills are involved, as in the present unit. This process, basically a form of task analysis, might sound like this in a teacher's mind:

Let's see now, I want them to be able to use the card catalog, so what do they need to know? Well, they need to know about each of the three catalogs and how they're different. Then they'll need to know how to look up a topic and find it in the catalog. What about alphabetization? . . .

A second starting point for objectives might be the content itself. Refer back to World Geography list cited earlier, which described one product of long-term planning in a geography class. A teacher might use this outline to ask these questions:

Hmmm, basic concepts. What ideas do students need to know to understand the rest of the material? Maps. What kind of maps? Topographic? No, too detailed. How will maps help later? . . . They'll need to be able to find major cities and waterways. . . .

From both of these examples, we can see that the planning process is not a clean, linear, sequential process. It proceeds in fits and starts as purpose, content, and activities interact. Out of these come objectives that help clarify the teacher's thinking. Sometimes these objectives are present in curriculum guides or the teacher's guide. When this happens, we encourage you to analyze these carefully, modifying some and rejecting others to fit *your* needs. This is your unit; no one else can teach it just like you. When objectives do not exist in curriculum guides, you will have to wrestle with them, at least in your mind.

**Content**   Another aid in the planning process is to try to organize the major ideas to find connections between concepts. Is there a logical order to the presentation? Do the ideas fit together? Are the interrelationships among the ideas made clear to student? If so, students have something meaningful and coherent to learn; if not, the logic as well as the structure of the unit comes across as garbled, disconnected ideas.

Schematic diagrams, hierarchies, and outlines are all powerful means of communicating lesson organization. The exact type of organizational scheme will depend on the type of content being taught. Outlines are especially useful when teaching large bodies of interrelated knowledge. Like hierarchies, outlines help communicate the major ideas of a lesson as well as the relationships among the ideas. For example, an outline for a high school social studies lesson covering the causes of the Civil War might appear as follows:

**Civil War**

1. Causes of the Civil War
   - A. Historical antecedents
     1. Westward expansion
     2. Missouri compromise
     3. Dred Scott decision
     4. John Brown's raid on Harper's Ferry
   - B. Conflicting philosophies
     1. Industrial versus agrarian
     2. State's rights versus federal rights
     3. Slavery
   - C. Election of 1860
   - D. Fort Sumter

The outline serves a dual purpose: It helps the teacher clarify his or her own thinking, and it communicates to students the relationship of ideas to be dealt within the lesson.

An outline for the unit on card catalogs might look like this:

**Card Catalogs**

1. Purposes
   - A. To find a specific book
   - B. To locate books by an author
   - C. To find out about a topic
2. Types
   - A. Title
   - B. Author
   - C. Subject
3. Using the card catalog, etc.

A second way of organizing the content of a unit is through conceptual hierarchies. For example, when discussing several concepts, conceptual hierarchies provide a powerful instructional tool (Eggen, Kauchak, and Kirk, 1978). In studying a lesson hierarchically, the teacher is attempting to communicate the relationship between major concepts or ideas. Hierarchies describe not only how concepts within the unit relate but also how the lesson content relates to a broader framework. For example, consider the hierarchy in Figure 3.2.

Organizing content in this way raises useful questions for instruction. For example,

**FIGURE 3.2**   Content Organizational Schemes

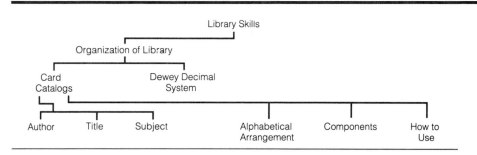

Should I deal with card catalogs and the Dewey Decimal System separately, or does it make more sense to integrate them? Or will integrating them overwhelm and confuse them? What about the alphabetical organization of the card catalogs? Students know how to use a dictionary; should I review that skill before plunging into the alphabetical organization of the card catalogs?

A third way to organize content is through task analysis, which we discussed earlier. Through task analysis, the teacher examines content and tries to determine which concepts are prerequisite to other ideas.

Content organization serves a dual purpose. It helps the teacher clarify his or her own thinking about the unit, and the product of this thinking can be shared with students to help them understand the structure of the content.

**Instructional Activities**   This component may be the most important part of the whole unit because it brings students into contact with the important ideas and skills contained in the unit. The connection between content and activities is so crucial that Chapters 5, 6, 7, 8, and 9 of this book are devoted to this topic. In those chapters, we will develop the idea that what you are trying to teach (your objectives) should influence how you teach it and how students should learn it. For example, contrast objectives 1 and 4 for the present unit (on library skills). Number 1 asks students to *know* something, the three different ways a book can be found in the card catalog; 4 asks students to be able to *do* something (locate names of authors, titles, subjects in the card catalog). This latter objective is a skill and requires modeling by the teacher and practice by students. The first objective, in contrast, requires memorization and understanding. We will discuss these important differences and the implications for instruction in Chapters 7 through 10.

**Evaluation**   Although it falls at the end of our list of unit components, the idea of evaluation is integrally connected to other parts. How you will measure student learning is dependent on what you wanted students to learn (your objectives) and the learning activities you involved them in. For example, contrast the following measurement items:

**A.** What are the three different kinds of card catalogs?

_____

_____

_____

**B.** Go to the card catalog and locate the author's name and call number for each title below.

| Title | Call Number | Author |
|-------|-------------|--------|
| _Ramona the Pest_ | | |
| _Where the Red Fern Grows_ | | |
| _The Little House on the Prairie_ | | |

The first type measures knowledge-level learning, while the second requires students to apply information. In the evaluation component of a unit, teachers test what they have taught. We will return to this important idea in Chapter 12 when we return to the topics of measurement and evaluation.

## Lesson Planning

Long-term planning helps organize the school year into manageable chunks. Unit planning is a vehicle through which sometimes vague and unconnected ideas are translated into concrete and interconnected learning experiences. Lesson planning focuses these efforts on specific instructional sessions. At the junior high and high school level, a lesson plan corresponds to a given period, while at the elementary level, in self-contained classrooms, lesson length may vary from 15 minutes to an hour or more, depending on the topic and maturity of students.

As with other dimensions of planning, each teacher approaches lesson planning in unique, personal ways. In addition, the process varies with the topic; if you are familiar with and confident about a subject, you will plan differently than if you are hesitant about it. Experience, too, makes a difference, not only in general terms (i.e., the difference between experienced and beginning teachers) but also in terms of whether you have taught the specific topic before.

With these ideas in mind, we will examine several models of lesson planning. As you think about them, we encourage you to adapt selectively from them to fit your individual needs.

**A Basic Lesson Plan Model** A lesson plan needs to be specific enough to provide structure to the lesson but general enough to provide flexibility when the situation warrants. Few lessons proceed exactly as planned. This fact makes teaching both challenging and potentially bewildering at times.

Writers in this area (Jacobson et al., 1993; Orlich et al., 1989) suggest the lesson plan of Table 3.3 as the optimal blend of structure and flexibility.

**TABLE 3.3**   Elements of a Basic Lesson Plan

| Component | Function |
|---|---|
| Unit title | How does this lesson relate to others in the unit? |
| Instructional goal | What broad goal does this lesson address? |
| Performance objective | What specifically should students learn? |
| Rationale | Why is this lesson important? |
| Content | What are the major ideas/skills in the lesson? |
| Instructional procedures | How will the teacher help students learn? |
| Evaluation procedures | How will student learning be measured? |
| Materials and aids | What equipment or supplies are needed? |

As we can see, this lesson plan begins by linking the individual lesson to the unit in which it is embedded. Goals are then stated, both in broad and performance terms, and a rationale is considered. This rationale is more specific than the unit rationale and can be used instructionally to introduce the lesson (e.g., "This lesson on punctuation will help us write sentences that are clear and understandable"). This is followed by the content, instructional procedures, and the evaluation procedures for this particular lesson. Finally, materials and aids are noted to serve as last-minute reminders for the teacher. We saw an example of this model in practice at the beginning of this chapter with Peggy Stone and her math lesson.

A shorter variation of the basic lesson-plan model can be seen in Table 3.4. This model eliminates the unit component, the goal statement, and the rationale, on the assumption that a teacher will keep these in mind during the planning process.

A third planning model has been suggested by Madeline Hunter, one of the more popular translators of the effectiveness research. As we can see from Table 3.5, the Hunter planning model differs from previous ones in several important ways. First, it is much more detailed and prescriptive in terms of instructional procedures, beginning with an anticipatory set which draws students into the lesson and ending with independent practice that is designed to reinforce new content.

**TABLE 3.4**   An Abbreviated Lesson-Plan Model

| Component | Function |
|---|---|
| Instructional objectives | What do you want students to learn? |
| Contents | What are the major ideas? |
| Procedure(s) | What will happen in the lesson? |
| Instructional materials and resources | What materials will be needed to teach the lesson? |
| Evaluation | Did the students learn the material, and what could I have done differently? |

*Source:* Kim and Kellough, 1983

**TABLE 3.5**   Madeline Hunter's Elements of Lesson Design

| Component | Function |
| --- | --- |
| Anticipatory set | How will students' attention be focused? |
| Objective and purpose | What will students learn and why? |
| Input | What new information will be discussed? |
| Modeling | How can the teacher illustrate the new skill or content? |
| Checking for understanding | How can the teacher ascertain whether students are learning the new material? |
| Guided practice | What opportunities are students given to practice the new material in class? |
| Independent practice | How can assignments and homework be used for long-term retention? |

*Source:* Hunter, 1984

Related to this prescriptiveness, the sequence of activities is preestablished, with initial teacher input, followed by modeling and student practice. Finally, the evaluation procedures are an integral part of the instructional sequence; teachers evaluate learning during the last three phrases of the lesson by observing student responses to practice exercises. This emphasis on student participation is based on research findings related to the importance of practice and feedback on success (Rosenshine and Stevens, 1986).

The prescriptiveness of this lesson plan model has both advantages and disadvantages. One major advantage is the structure it provides a teacher; we are reminded of important teaching behaviors at each point of the lesson. Also, the model is research based; each component can be justified in terms of research evidence. Finally, the emphasis on student involvement and success is valuable, especially for beginning teachers. A major problem encountered by beginning teachers is rushing through a lesson without providing adequate opportunities for student practice and feedback.

But these advantages come at a cost, and the price is narrowness. This format, which is quite appropriate for skill learning and many forms of teacher-centered instruction (such as lecturing and question and answer sessions), is inappropriate for others. For example, these seven steps would be inappropriate in a discussion-oriented session focusing on attitudes or values. Similarly, more inquiry-oriented lessons, beginning with a problem followed by student hypotheses and data gathering, also would not fit into this format (Shulman, 1987).

So where does this leave us with the Hunter planning model? As with other products of effectiveness research, teachers should exercise judgment in the application of this research. When the model is appropriate, use it; when not, select some other format that makes more sense.

**Lesson Plan Reality**   This chapter's title promised research and reality. In terms of the latter, we would be remiss (and our discussion of lesson planning incomplete) without considering the teacher plan book, a mainstay of classrooms throughout the country. In its basic form, these commercially prepared guides look like this:

| Date | Period 1 | Period 2 | Period 3 |
|---|---|---|---|
| Monday September 24 | | | |
| Tuesday September 25 | | | |
| Wednesday September 26 | | | |
| Thursday September 27 | | | |
| Friday September 28 | | | |

The date on the left identifies the day; the numbers at the top correspond to lessons or periods, depending on whether the form is being used in elementary or secondary classrooms. The boxes aren't very big; typically, they'll average one by two inches. There is room only for brief comments:

Collect homework
Ask for problems
Review trig functions
(Text, pp. 217–222)
Do problems 9–14 on board (p. 228)
Fri. Quiz, Chpt. 9
Homework, p. 228, #'s 15–30

Two questions are central here: Why is this planning format so popular, and how does it relate to the other formats we have discussed? The popularity question is a simple one to answer—this format is popular because it is functional. Teachers' days (and nights) are jam-packed with things to do. When they are not actively teaching, teachers plan, grade papers, and do a myriad of other professionally related things. A plan book provides teachers with a quick and efficient way of recording and keeping track of their planning thoughts. A teacher can plan on Friday, go home and enjoy the weekend, and return on Monday secure with the knowledge that the week is "under control."

But does the efficiency and practicality of this model negate the value of the others we discussed? No, for two important reasons. At the beginning of this chapter, we said that planning entails more than the written products of this process. Planning includes all the professional decisions teachers make over a broad time frame. The shortened notes placed in planning books are just summaries of a number of decisions made earlier. When they plan, professional teachers consider things like rationale and objectives and how a particular lesson relates to others. Because of time and energy, these deliberations do not show up on paper.

One value of these lengthier planning models relates to teachers' development as they first learn to plan; these models provide a structure to assist in the planning process. As teachers become more proficient, these conceptual reminders become unnecessary, and automaticity develops. As you sit down with a blank sheet of paper, you will automatically ask, "Now what do I want them to know? Why is this important? How will I evaluate whether they learned it or not?" Practice during the initial stages ensures the development of these skills.

Finally, from a practical perspective, the ability to put your planning decisions on paper and describe them to others is fast becoming a prerequisite to entrance to the teaching profession. In short, you will be asked to plan and execute lessons and justify your decisions not only to college professors and supervisors but also to cooperating teachers during student teaching and administrators supervising you during your first years on the job. The greater push toward accountability in education requires beginning teachers to be able to demonstrate their ability to make professional decisions. Effective lesson planning is a major dimension of professional decision making.

## SUMMARY

Planning to teach is much more complex than it might appear at a casual glance. In addition to the written products that provide the artifacts of planning, it involves a myriad of decisions about content, students, learning activities, and evaluation procedures, among others. Further, well-planned lessons might be detailed in writing, but they may also consist of a brief sketch outlining the topics to be covered in the lesson and a list of supporting instructional materials.

Planning serves a number of functions, ranging from providing psychological security to simplifying subsequent instructional decisions. In addition, a number of factors influence the planning process, including the time and resources available and the context within which the instruction is embedded.

Research on teacher planning reveals a number of interesting findings, all of which question the use of the linear rational model as a primary planning tool for experienced teachers. In addition to discovering that planning was not a discrete, sequential process, researchers found that written objectives often were not the starting point for planning activities, nor was evaluation a major concern prior to instruction.

Why don't teachers write objectives as a starting point for planning? Time, effort, and the fact that they often exist in curriculum materials or are embedded in learning activities are major reasons.

How do teachers begin to plan if not with objectives? Content and learning activities appear to provide alternative starting points for the planning process.

One major conclusion from this research is that planning is not a uniform process and is instead dependent on a number of related factors (e.g., teaching experience, content, and the availability of curriculum materials). Research underscores the functional nature of teacher planning: Teachers plan as they do to get the job done and to maximize student learning given the constraints of the situation.

Long-term planning represents teachers' first attempts to place planning decisions within a time framework. Typically done at the course or semester level, long-term planning frames content and objectives within broad outlines of time. Routines (recurring patterns in instructional activities) are another major product of long-term planning.

Unit planning bridges the gap between long-term planning and lesson planning. It takes a discrete amount of time (e.g., 2 or 3 weeks) and constructs learning activities that are organized and coherent. A unit plan begins with an overview or general goal that summarizes the general purpose of the unit. A rationale is an explanation of the unit's value and can be shared with students as a motivational tool. Objectives specify the major outcomes of the unit, and the content section outlines and organizes major ideas. Instructional activities translate content and objectives into learning and teaching strategies, and the evaluation component describes how learning will be assessed. Together, these components make up a tangible plan of action for the teacher to follow in the weeks to come.

Lesson planning is the final step in the planning process and generates specific plans of action for a specific class period. The form that specific lesson plans take will vary with the teacher and the situation, but all deal, either explicitly or implicitly, with the fundamental questions of what to teach, how to teach, and why. The thoughtful decision making of expert teachers is often masked by the ease with which they produce thoughtful plans for strategic action.

## ADDITIONAL READINGS FOR PROFESSIONAL GROWTH

Gronlund, N. (1985). *Stating objectives for classroom instruction* (3rd ed.). New York: Macmillan. Gronlund describes and illustrates his approach to stating objectives.

Mager, R. (1984). *Preparing instructional objectives* (2nd rev. ed.). Palo Alto, CA: D. S. Lake. This revised and updated book describes why objectives are important in the planning process and provides a thorough description of how to write them.

Posner, G., & Rudnitsky, A. (1986). *Course design: A guide to curriculum development for teachers* (3rd ed.). This book places the topic of planning in the larger framework of course and unit design.

## EXERCISES

1. *Behavioral Objectives*. Analyze the following objectives in terms of Mager's three components by enclosing each part in parentheses and labeling each part condition (C), performance (P), or criteria (Cr).

   **a.** When given a list of both facts and opinions, students will label 90 percent of these correctly.

   **b.** Given the names of composers of the Romantic period and their major works, students will match all the works with their composers.

    c. Given a clock with hands, the student will be able to tell the time within 1 minute of the correct time.

    d. Given a description of an experiment illustrating the basic steps of the scientific method, the student will label each step and explain the basis of his or her classification in writing.

    e. Given a bar graph, the student will describe the information in the graph in factual terms.

    f. Given a list of 10 words, the student will alphabetize these so the whole list is alphabetized correctly.

    g. Given the choice of topics and resources such as a dictionary, the student will write a 500-word expository essay that is grammatically correct, punctuated properly, corrected for spelling, and organized according to the format described in class.

2. *Gronlund's Format.* Gronlund, a popular worker in the area of objectives, believes that a general objective describing the goal should precede the specific instructional objective. For the objectives listed in exercise 1, supply a general goal statement.

    a.

    b.

    c.

    d.

    e.

    f.

    g.

3. Examine the following goals and decide whether they focus primarily on the affective (A), cognitive (C), or psychomotor (P) domain.

    a. Preschool students will be able to use scissors to cut out various geometric shapes.

    b. First-grade students will learn the names of the letters of the alphabet.

    c. Junior high social studies students will know the major economic products of South American countries.

    d. Fourth-grade students will follow assembly rules without being reminded.

    e. Elementary students will learn how to turn the computer on and off.

    f. High school science students will develop an appreciation for the value of scientific evidence.

    g. High school word processing students will be able to type at a rate of 45 words per minute.

    h. Kindergarten students will learn how to print their names in upper- and lower-case letters.

4. *Lesson Planning*. Match the following components of the basic lesson plan model with their function.

| | | |
|---|---|---|
| _____ **a.** Unit title | **A.** | Reminds the teacher of the major concepts, skills, or topics |
| _____ **b.** Instructional goal | **B.** | Describes how student learning will be measured |
| _____ **c.** Performance objective | **C.** | Specifies what students will be able to do after the lesson |
| _____ **d.** Rationale | **D.** | Links the lesson to broader topics |
| _____ **e.** Content | **E.** | Describes the purpose of the lesson in general terms |
| _____ **f.** Instructional procedures | **F.** | Explains the importance or significance of the lesson |
| _____ **g.** Evaluation procedures | **G.** | Provides a quick reference for any supplies or equipment needed |
| _____ **h.** Materials and aids | **H.** | Outlines teaching/learning strategies |

5. *Lesson Planning*. Now it is your turn to try your hand at lesson planning. Try a simple topic that everyone knows, like proper nouns (names a specific person, place, or thing). Using this topic, construct a lesson plan using the basic lesson plan model:

**a.** Unit

**b.** Instructional goal

**c.** Performance objective

**d.** Rationale

**e.** Content

**f.** Instructional procedures

**g.** Evaluation procedures

**h.** Materials and aids

# DISCUSSION QUESTIONS

1. A colleague of ours claims that teacher planning behaviors are heavily influenced by a teacher's personality. To get at this, he suggests asking two questions: How do you plan for a trip? How are your socks arranged in your drawers? He claims that people who make long travel planning lists and who sort their socks by color tend to be overplanners. How much does personality affect planning? What does your personality say about how you'll approach the planning process?

2. In the text, the potential influence on teachers' planning of curriculum guides and

texts, both student and teacher editions, was stressed. What advantages are there in using these? What disadvantages?

3. The following arguments have been raised against the practice of writing objectives in performance terms:

   **a.** Only trivial and nonmeaningful objectives can be written in performance terms.

   **b.** They stifle teacher flexibility and responsiveness to students.

   **c.** They encourage narrowness; that is, teachers will teach to the objects and students will study to the objectives.

   How valid are these criticisms? Are they more valid in some areas of the curriculum (e.g., art or literature) than others? What can teachers do to minimize these potential problems?

4. Are objectives easier to write in some areas of the curriculum than others? What about grade levels? Within a curriculum area, is it easier to write objectives for some types of goals? What can be done in areas where objectives are hard to write?

5. Some people have suggested that education could be improved if the planning process were a centralized process, occurring at the state or district level. Teachers would then be responsible for implementing preplanning units of study. This method would save teachers' time, ensure uniform content, and provide for coordination between teachers at different grade levels. Is this a good idea? What advantages does it have? What disadvantages?

6. You are a substitute teacher who has been called at the last minute to take over a class. How will the following influence your teaching?

   **a.** The teacher's long-term plans

   **b.** The teacher's unit plan

   **c.** The teacher's lesson plan

## APPLYING IT IN THE SCHOOLS

1. *Teaching Planning.* How do experienced teachers plan? Interview a teacher to find out how he or she plans. Some possible questions might include the following:

   **a.** Where do you begin?

   **b.** What help are state and district curriculum guides?

   **c.** Is there a teacher's edition, and, if so, how is it useful?

   **d.** Do you coordinate your planning activities with other teachers?

   **e.** What does your administrator expect of you in terms of lesson plans?

   **f.** What do the products of the planning process look like?

2. *Teacher Planning: Contextual Factors*. Analyze a teacher's syllabus or outline for a course or a unit within a course. In doing this, compare it with:

   a. State guidelines

   b. District guidelines

   c. The text being used

   d. Your college courses in this area (either subject matter, text, or special methods courses)

   What things are missing? What things are there that you wouldn't do? How would your syllabus look different?

3. *Curriculum Guides*. Analyze either a state or district curriculum guide in an area of the curriculum (or compare them).

   a. How recent is it?

   b. Who constructed it?

   c. How is it organized (e.g., chronologically, developmentally, topically, etc.)?

   d. How do the topics covered compare with a text for this area?

   e. How many objectives are listed for a particular course of study?

   f. How many objectives per week are implicitly suggested? Is it a realistic number?

   g. What types of learning (e.g., memory versus higher levels) are targeted?

4. *Teacher's Editions*. Examine a teacher's edition of a text. Does it explain how the text is organized? Does it contain the following aids?

   a. Chapter overview or summary

   b. Objectives

   c. Suggested learning activities

   d. Ditto or overhead masters

   e. Test items

   f. Enrichment activities

   g. Supplementary readings

   How helpful would these aids be to you as a teacher?

5. *Objectives*. Write an objective for a lesson you might want to teach. Share it with a fellow student. Is it clear? (Could he or she construct a complete lesson plan based on it?)

6. *Objectives and Measurement*. Take the objective you wrote in exercise 5 and construct a measurement item for it. How else might you evaluate your goal?

7. *Task Analysis*. Using the objective you wrote for exercise 5, do a task analysis on it. This should include the following:

   a. Prerequisite knowledge and skills

    **b.** A sequence for these prerequisites

    **c.** Some type of diagnostic instrument to let you find out what students know

**8.** *Lesson Planning.* Using one of the models discussed in this chapter, construct a complete lesson plan. Share it with a fellow student and ask him or her to critique it in terms of clarity. (Use the substitute teacher's test—if they had to come in and substitute teach for you, would they know what to do?)

**9.** *Planning and Microteaching.* Microteaching is a teaching technique that allows prospective teachers to focus on one aspect of their teaching at a time. This exercise focuses on planning. Take the lesson you constructed in exercise 8 and teach it for 10 to 15 minutes to either a small group of your peers or a small group of real students. Audiotape the lesson. Listen to the tape and answer these questions:

    **a.** Were you over- or underprepared?

    **b.** How well did the planning model you chose fit your personal needs?

    **c.** In hindsight, what should you have done differently in the planning process to improve your teaching?

# CHAPTER 4

# Effective Teaching: A General Instructional Model

## OVERVIEW

In Chapter 3 we examined the ways teachers plan and how planning affects the way they actually teach. We also looked at the types of planning that are most effective for promoting student learning.

We now turn to instruction. As a way of thinking about the content of this chapter, imagine entering a number of classrooms, sitting at the back of each room, and watching effective teachers at different grade levels and in different content areas work with their students. What would you expect to see? Are these teachers unique? What do they do that makes them effective?

Research helps us answer these questions. Analysis of research results indicates that regardless of grade level, content area, or topic, effective teachers display some common patterns of behavior. A discussion of these patterns is the focus of this chapter. In an effort to make the information more meaningful, we have organized the patterns into a general model of instruction that applies to virtually all classroom situations.

## MAIN IDEAS

### Effective Teaching and the Concept of Time

*Allocated time* reflects school and teacher priorities.

The portion of allocated time devoted directly to learning activities is called *instructional time*.

*Engaged time* is maximized when students are attentive and involved.

The amount of time students spend engaged and *successful* is termed *academic learning time*.

### Personal Characteristics of Effective Teachers

Effective teachers have *high expectations* for their students, they *model* desired behaviors, they teach *enthusiastically*, and they are *responsive* to the students.

The use of *precise language*, logical and connected presentations, clear *transition signals*, appropriate *emphasis*, and congruent *verbal* and *nonverbal* behavior is important in effective communication.

Organized teachers *start on time*, have *materials prepared in advance*, and have well-established *routines*.

### Lesson Beginnings

*Introductory reviews* provide a connection between old and new learning.

*Introductory focus* attracts students' attention and provides a context for the topic being taught.

## Lesson Development

Effective teachers *present content* with examples and applications.
 Learner *involvement* is critical to maximize learning.
 *Practice* and *feedback* reinforce learning and help students interrelate ideas.

## Lesson Endings

*Review* and *closure* help learners organize their understanding and provide a foundation for future learning.
 Classroom *assessment* helps determine the level of student learning.

. . . . . . . . . . . . . . . . . . . . . . . . . . . . . . . . .

Kathy Johnson is a fifth-grade teacher in an urban Midwestern city. About half of her 27 students are classified as at risk, and come from mostly low- to middle-income families. A veteran of 6 years, Kathy typically schedules her day as follows:

| | |
|---|---|
| 8:15– 9:15 | Math |
| 9:15–10:45 | Language Arts |
| 10:45–11:00 | Break |
| 11:00–11:30 | Social Studies |
| 11:30–12:00 | Lunch |
| 12:00– 1:25 | Reading |
| 1:25– 1:35 | Break |
| 1:35– 2:00 | Science |
| 2:00– 2:45 | Resource (art, music, PE, computer) |

In social studies, Kathy has begun a unit on the Northern and Southern Colonies prior to the Civil War.
 As the students file into the room after their break, they see a large chart displayed at the front of the room that appears as follows:

| | People | Land | Economy |
|---|---|---|---|
| Northern Colonies | Small towns<br>Religious<br>Valued education<br>Cooperative | Timber covered<br>Glacial remnants<br>Poor soil<br>Short growing season<br>Cold winters | Syrup<br>Rum<br>Lumber<br>Shipbuilding<br>Small farms |
| Southern | Aristocratic<br>Isolated<br>Social class distinction | Fertile soil<br>Hot weather<br>Large rivers<br>Long growing season | Large farms<br>Tobacco<br>Cotton<br>Unskilled workers<br>Servants and slaves |

Kathy is standing at the doorway as her students enter the room. She smiles and jokes with them as they pass by and reminds them of what they're about to do, with comments such as, "Look carefully at the chart at the front of the room," and "See if you can find anything about how the North and South were different."

At 11:02 the students have their social studies books on their desks. Kathy has moved to the front of the room. She begins, "We began talking about the Northern and Southern Colonies yesterday. Let's see what we remember. Where are they compared to where we live? Jo?"

"They're over here," Lorenda answers, motioning to the right.

"Yes, they're generally east of us," Kathy adds as she walks quickly and points to the map at the side of the room, identifying the general location of the colonies.

"And about how long ago are we talking about, a few years or a long time? Greg?"

"A long time. Like when our great, great, great, grandfathers and grandmothers might have lived."

"Yes, very good," Kathy smiles and nods. "We're talking about the time during the early and middle 1800s.

"We also talked about some important ideas, like 'economy,' " Kathy continues. "What do we mean by *economy*? Carol?"

"It's the way they make their money, like when we said that the economy here is based on manufacturing, like making cars and parts for cars and stuff," Carol responds uncertainly.

"Very good description, Carol," Kathy nods. "You identified auto manufacturing as an important part of our economy, and that's a good example."

"Now, look here," Kathy directs, pointing to the column marked *Economy*. "We see that the economy for the two groups of colonies is very different. Today we want to see what some of these specific differences are and why the two economies are so different. So, remember as we go through the lesson that we're talking about the way the colonies made their money, and we're trying to figure out why it is so different. . . . Everybody ready?" Kathy surveys the class. "Good. Let's go."

She then begins, "What are some of the differences we see in the economies for the two regions? Ann Marie?"

". . ."

"What do you notice about the farms in the two colonies?"

"The farms were much bigger in the Southern Colonies than they were in the Northern Colonies," Anne Marie offers.

"OK, good observation," Kathy nods energetically. "Now why might that have been the case? Jim?"

". . ."

"Would you like me to repeat the question?" Kathy asks, knowing that Jim has not heard her.

"Yes," Jim responds quickly, with a look of relief.

Kathy continues guiding the students' analysis of the information on the chart, in the process finding relationships between the geography, climate, and economy. When students are unable to answer, she rephrases her questions and provides cues to help them along. She then has them consider why the economy of their city might be the way it is. We return to her lesson now as it draws to a close.

"You have done very well, everyone," she smiles, pointing her finger in the air for emphasis. "Now, everyone, get with your partner, take two minutes and write two or three summary statements about what we've learned here today. . . . Quickly now, get started."

The students start buzzing, pointing at the chart, and one of the two in each pair begin writing. In some cases they stop, crumple their papers, and begin again. As they work, Kathy walks among them, offering encouragement and periodic suggestions.

At the end of the 2 minutes Kathy announces, "One more minute, and we're going to look at what you wrote."

After another minute she says, "OK, let's see what you've got. What did you and Linda say, David?"

"We said that the weather and the land had a lot to do with the way the different colonies made their money."

"Excellent! That's a good one. How about someone else. . . . Danielle, how about you and Tony?"

Kathy had several other pairs offer their summary statements; they further developed the statements as a whole group; and then Kathy collects the papers.

At 11:28 Kathy she announces, "Almost lunch time. Please put away your papers."

The students quickly away put their books, papers, and pencils, glance around their desks for any waste paper, and are sitting quietly at 11:30.

# EFFECTIVE TEACHING AND
# THE CONCEPT OF TIME

*Dost thou love life? Then do not squander time, for that is the stuff life is made of.*

Benjamin Franklin
*Poor Richard's Almanac*, 1775

*There has been a lot of talk about the importance of time in the determination of educational outcomes. . . . Certainly, we should take a look at how time is being used or misused in our schools. It may indeed turn out to be the culprit that critics claim it is. As we test this possibility, however, we must keep in mind that time itself is valueless. It acquires value chiefly because it marks the expenditure of a precious commodity—human life. . . . Let us not seize too quickly at remedies for our educational ailments that call for little more than adding days or hours to our present efforts. The real key lies in making better use of the time we already have.*

Phillip Jackson, 1977

In introducing this chapter, we suggested that you ask yourself what you would expect if you observed effective teachers in action, whether they teach kindergarten, fourth grade, seventh-grade life science, ninth-grade English, or eleventh-grade American History. We would quickly see that they use their time very efficiently.

Students in other industrialized countries typically spend more time in school than do American students, and these students score higher on standardized tests than do American youngsters. This has led to suggestions that the American school year and school day be lengthened.

These suggestions are overly simplistic, however, because the length of the school year or day is only one aspect of the way effective teachers use time. A more complete picture examines how teachers use their time and how this influences student learning. In analyzing use of classroom time, we'll focus on four dimensions:

- Allocated time
- Instructional time
- Engaged time (time-on-task)
- Academic learning time.

These dimensions can be illustrated as a series of concentric circles, as shown in Figure 4.1.

## Allocated Time: Priorities in the Curriculum

**Allocated time** is the amount of time a teacher or school designates for a particular topic. It is the area of the largest circle in Figure 4.1, and people who advocate

**FIGURE 4.1**  Different Dimensions of Time

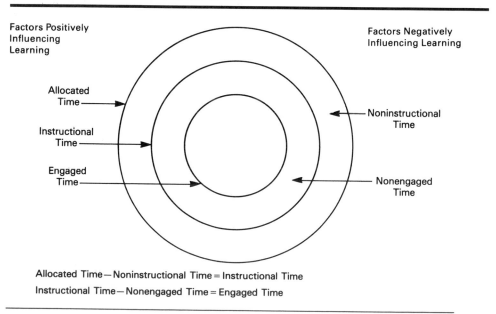

Allocated Time—Noninstructional Time = Instructional Time

Instructional Time—Nonengaged Time = Engaged Time

lengthening the school year or day are arguing for an increase in allocated time. If we look again at Kathy Johnson's schedule, we see that she has allocated an hour and a half for reading, almost as much for language arts, and an hour for math. In contrast, social studies gets only a half hour and science a mere 25 minutes. These allocations reflect the emphasis on basic skills that permeates the elementary school curriculum.

While it appears that elementary teachers have more control over time allocations than do middle or secondary teachers, this isn't necessarily the case. For instance, a middle school English teacher could choose to emphasize writing by spending a great deal of time on it, while another might devote that time to grammar instead.

What is the relationship between allocated time and learning? Research indicates a positive but weak correlation (Karweit, 1984). As a simple way of thinking about this relationship, imagine that we double the allocated time for a certain subject. While we would expect the students to learn more, they would not learn twice as much. In fact, they would only learn slightly more than they did with the previous allocation.

## Instructional Time: Time from a Teacher's Perspective

Consider the following example:

The bell had rung and Dennis Orr's eighth graders were filing into his class. Dennis was at the back of the room working on some equipment as the students moved to their seats.

In a few moments he moved to the front of the room and said, "Now, let's see who's here today." He glanced at the top of his desk, looking for his roll book. He didn't find it, and he looked in his desk drawer. "I let some of you look at your averages yesterday," he called out to the class. "Did you return my book?"

"We put it in your file cabinet," one of the boys responded.

"Ah, yes, here it is," Dennis said quietly as he looked in the drawer and saw the book.

When he finished taking roll, Dennis said to the class, "I'm going to show you a demonstration today. Get your books and notebooks out while I finish getting this set up."

The students did as he suggested as he began to take equipment from a nearby shelf and assemble it. A few minutes later he signaled the class.

"Okay, everyone, let's take a look at what we have here." He began the demonstration, having the students make observations about the equipment and the phenomenon taking place. Suddenly he said, "Oh, I almost forgot. All of you in the band will be released 10 minutes early today so you can gather your instruments for the trip to Seaside Jr. High."

Now, let's look at another eighth-grade teacher in essentially the same situation.

Steve Weiss, Mr. Orr's colleague across the hall, was sitting at his desk as his students walked in. As they sat down, they got their books and notebooks out of their backpacks and put them on their desks. Steve checked their names in his roll book as students milled toward their seats.

"I see Jim isn't here. Has he been absent all day?" Steve asked.

"He's sick," a classmate volunteered, and with that Steve signed the roll and hung it on the clip on his door. As he walked to the door, he pointed to an announcement on the board. "All you band students will be dismissed 10 minutes early so you can get your equipment ready for your trip to Seaside."

Walking back to the center of the room, Steve began, "We studied the concept of pressure yesterday, and today we want to look at how pressure changes under different conditions. I have a demonstration for you. Everyone take a look at the cart." With that, he rolled a cart to the center of the room. Some equipment was assembled on it. "What do you notice on the cart, Tony?" he asked as he began the lesson.

In comparing the two teachers, we see distinct differences. Dennis spent several minutes taking roll, searching for his grade book, preparing his demonstration, and making an announcement, while Steve took roll as the students came in the door, made his announcement as he hung up his roll slip, and had his demonstration prepared in advance. Dennis spent more time on noninstructional activities than did Steve.

**Instructional time** is the amount of time that teachers devote to active teaching. It's also the amount of time left for teaching after routine management and administrative tasks are completed. In visual terms, the area of the second circle in Figure 4.1 would be larger for Steve than it would be for Dennis. Steve produced more instructional time than did Dennis.

As illustrated in the case of Dennis Orr, significant portions of time are frequently lost to noninstructional activities (Karweit, 1984), often more than a third of the time available (Berliner, 1979; Leinhardt, Zigmond, and Cooley, 1981). Significantly, when these noninstructional lapses are decreased, student achievement increases (Stallings, 1980).

Sometimes lost instructional time is out of a teacher's control due to school activities (e.g., assemblies and pep rallies) and standardized testing. Berliner (1987) estimated that these interruptions may consume 20 percent or more of available time—essentially time lost to classroom instruction.

Further, some teachers seem to be unaware of time as a valuable resource, thinking of it as something to be filled, or even "killed," rather than a valuable opportunity to increase learning (Wiley and Harnischfeger, 1974). Because instructional time is so valuable, teachers must do everything they can to maximize it.

Instructional time is important for another, more subtle reason—its absence represents a vacuum in which management problems can occur. The research is clear on this point: Well-run classrooms with high rates of instructional time are places with fewer management problems (Emmer, Evertson, Sanford, Clements, and Worsham, 1989; Evertson, Emmer, Clements, Sanford, and Worsham, 1989).

## Engaged Time: Time from a Student's Perspective

Teacher planning results in allocated time; daily, weekly, and unit planning translate abstract goals into tangible blocks of time available for learning activities. Teachers take this allocated time and attempt to translate it into learning using instructional time, the portion of the class period devoted to learning. Effective teachers maximize instructional time, wrestling opportunities for teaching from the hectic teaching day.

Despite our best efforts, however, not all students pay attention all the time, so we have another area within instructional time called **engaged time** or **time-on-task**, which is the portion of instructional time students spend directly involved in learning activities (Berliner, 1984; Karweit, 1984; Rosenshine, 1983). It is the third circle in Figure 4.1, and its smaller size compared to instructional time is related to the amount of time lost to inattention and misbehavior. Researchers have found considerable variation in engagement rates in different classrooms, ranging from as low as 50 percent in some classrooms to as high as 90 percent in others (Berliner, 1987). In a study of second- and fifth-grade classrooms, researchers found engagement rates in these classrooms to be about 74 percent (Rosenshine, 1980). Significantly, when researchers compared engagement rates for more and less effective teachers (as defined by the achievement test scores of their students), they found significant differences at both levels. For example, at the fifth-grade level, effective teachers produced on-task rates of over 80 percent; in less effective classrooms, on-task rates dropped to almost 60 percent. Time-on-task is important because it is a tangible gauge of a teacher's impact on students; if students are not attending, the most diligently organized and emphatically well-presented presentation will fall on deaf ears.

Not surprisingly, when principals and other supervisors enter a classroom to evaluate a teacher, one of the first things they look for is student-engagement rates. How can we tell if students are engaged or on-task? Conversely, how can we tell when students are off-task? Or, more specifically, what kinds of things would you look for in determining whether *your* students are with you? Try eye contact—are they watching you during a teacher-led presentation, and during seatwork do their eye movements suggest that they are reading and actually responding to worksheets? Or do their eye movements flit back and forth between the window and clock or, worse yet, not move at all? Responding is another indicator—do they raise their hands to your questions, or are they unaware that you asked a question? You can probably add half a dozen other indicators to this list.

A comparison of high- and low-achieving students demonstrates the importance of engaged time. High-achieving students are typically engaged for 75 percent of the time or more, while low achievers have engagement rates that are often below 50 percent (Evertson, 1980; Fredrick, 1977).

Consider these figures for a moment: Students in low-achieving classes were off-task almost half the time, and even high achievers drifted away a quarter of the time. These lapses provide real challenges for the teacher (Evertson, 1980; Fredrick, 1977).

Other studies suggest that the link between on-task behaviors and achievement is more complex than at first glance. Two studies found that high- and low-ability students differ not only in *amounts* of engaged time but also in the patterns in which these behaviors occurred (Rusnock and Brandler, 1979; Smyth, 1979). High-ability students finished their academic tasks and *then* went off-task; low-ability students went off-task *while* they were working on academic tasks. A study of seatwork in first-grade classrooms (Anderson, Brubaker, Alleman–Brooks, and Duffy, 1985) partially explains this pattern. These researchers found that low-ability students were often given tasks that were beyond their abilities and, consequently, too difficult to complete. In response, they became frustrated and inattentive.

The issue, then, is not as simple as merely allocating more time to a particular subject; nor does increasing efficiency so instructional time is maximized solve the problem. A maximally efficient classroom that is well organized but that fails to engage students in learning activities is little better off than a disorganized one. In addition, engagement rates are complex phenomena that are influenced both by the type of student as well as by the learning task itself.

Just as with allocated and instructional time, teachers exert a powerful influence on engaged time. Kathy Johnson demonstrated several teaching behaviors that attracted and maintained students' attention, and we discuss these in the next section.

Our consideration of time has shifted in two important ways. The first is in terms of perspective: Initially, we focused on the teacher and have since turned our attention to what students are doing with their time. The second shift is from *quantity* to *quality*: Allocated time looks at how much time is devoted to a topic, while engaged time looks at how well instruction actively involves the learner. This leads us to the fourth time-related concept — academic learning time.

## Academic Learning Time: The Role of Success

As we saw, part of the reason that low achievers go off-task relates to frustration. The work they're assigned is often beyond their ability, making it impossible to complete. As a result, they give up and go off-task. The key in these cases is *success*. **Academic learning time** combines engagement and success; it is the amount of time students are *successful* while engaged.

The powerful connection between academic learning time and learning runs counter to past wisdom, which suggests that students need to be "challenged" because too much success results in boredom or unrealistic attitudes about school. A study of 250 classrooms showed that students in classes where success was the dominant pattern not only learned more but also felt better about themselves and the material they were learning (Fisher et al., 1980).

The following is an example of how one skillful teacher helped students be successful in a lesson on context clues in reading.

> *Teacher:* "Okay, let's try another one. 'When you did not come, Jerry was so miffed that he left in a rage.' You are reading and you come to that sentence. How are you going to figure out that word 'miffed'? Matt, what would you do first?"

*Student:* "I would look through the context. I see 'rage' and 'did not come.' "

*Teacher:* 'Did not come' is a clue. When the man didn't come, whatever it was he caused, it was because he didn't come. Now you are thinking about what you know about when people don't come and people are in rages. What do you suppose that means he was?"

*Student:* "He was angry or mad at the person."

*Teacher:* "So, do you have a one-word synonym that you could put there?"

*Student:* "Mad."

*Teacher:* "Check to see if that makes sense."

*Student:* "When he didn't come, Jerry was so mad that he left in a rage."

*Teacher:* "Does that sound reasonable? Did he use all the steps to get that meaning?"

(Duffy, Roehler, Meloth, & Vavrus, 1985, pp. 33–34)

From this example, we can see what a powerful influence the teacher has on promoting student success. This success is important for several reasons:

- It indicates that the new learning is building effectively on what a student already knows (Fisher et al., 1980).
- Success is reinforcing; it is much more rewarding to get questions and problems right than wrong.
- Success builds confidence, preparing students for future learning.

How high should success rates be? The answer depends on the situation. Research suggests that students in question and answer sessions should be about 80 percent successful (McGreal, 1985), and in homework assignments, where the potential for confusion and frustration is higher, success rates should be 90 percent or higher (Berliner, 1984, 1987).

Students themselves are a second factor. In general, younger students, low achievers, and students from lower socioeconomic backgrounds need higher rates of success than do their older, higher achieving, or more advantaged counterparts. These types of students often don't have a robust history of success in the classroom and tend to become frustrated or discouraged by low success rates.

Content is also a factor in considering optimal success rates. Topics that are sequential and that build on previous knowledge and skills, such as much of math and reading, require higher success rates than other less structured areas, such as Kathy Johnson's social studies lesson.

For example, a student who experiences problems in one-digit addition is going to experience further difficulty in two-digit addition and other math operations requiring addition, like multiplication with carrying. High success rates on prerequisite skills help build a strong foundation for future learning.

This doesn't mean, however, that teachers shouldn't be concerned about success in all areas. It should be an overriding goal that affects teaching at every level.

How can teachers increase student success rates? Rosenshine and Stevens (1986) offer these suggestions:

1. Break instruction into smaller steps, giving students time to master content before proceeding to the next step.
2. Be very explicit about the content, and provide demonstrations when skills are involved.
3. Use frequent questions to maintain attention and monitor student comprehension.
4. Provide students with teacher-monitored practice before having them work independently.
5. Provide sufficient practice so students overlearn content.
6. Reteach problem areas if necessary.

As we review the concept of time, we see that the issue is not as simple as merely allocating more time to a particular subject; nor does increasing efficiency so instructional time is maximized solve the problem. Our goal is a well-organized classroom that has students successfully engaged in meaningful learning activities. While this isn't easy, with effort it is attainable. We examine ways to accomplish this goal in the next section.

# A GENERAL INSTRUCTIONAL MODEL

In the last section, we discussed the way effective teachers use their time. The goal we're striving for is the largest amount of academic learning time possible, keeping in mind that the topics students learn should be meaningful and worthwhile.

The model outlined in Figure 4.2 summarizes teacher behaviors that can help students reach that goal, regardless of grade level, content area, or specific topic.

As we would intuitively expect, teacher characteristics such as attitudes, the way they communicate, and how they organize the classroom and learning activities influence the total continuum of a lesson — its beginning, development, and closure. This is why teacher characteristics are connected to each phase of the lesson in Figure 4.2. In the other three boxes we have divided effective teaching behaviors into those that occur at the beginning, middle, and end of a lesson. Let's see how these components interact to produce effective teaching.

## Teacher Attitudes

Looking again at Figure 4.2, we see that teachers' attitudes are listed first. Teachers' attitudes and beliefs about their ability to influence student learning have a powerful impact on their behavior, and this behavior influences learning (Dembo and Gibson, 1985; Good and Brophy, 1991). Effective teachers both believe that their students can learn and communicate this belief through their actions in the classroom.

These attitudes are demonstrated subtly but clearly. Let's look at an example.

**FIGURE 4.2**  A General Instructional Model

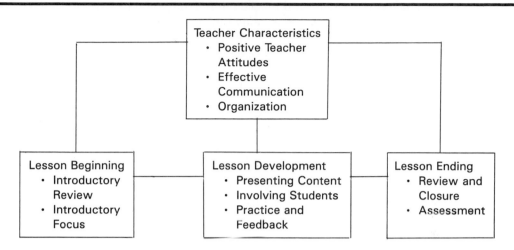

Donna Brewster, a veteran with 14 years of experience, teaches three sections of Advanced Placement American History and two sections with students of below-average to average ability. We look in on one of her average classes.

"We better get moving," Monica says to Jim as they approach the door of the classroom. "The bell is going to ring, and you know how Brewster is about this class."

"Yeh," Jim smiles wryly. "She thinks this stuff is sooo important."

"Did you finish your homework?"

"Are you kidding?" Monica returns. "You miss a homework assignment in this class and you're a dead duck."

"Right," Jim confirms. "Nobody messes with Brewster."

"I didn't know what she wanted, so I went to her help session after school yesterday, and she went over everything again," Monica continues. "She really tries to help you get it."

Why were Monica and Jim reacting so strongly to Donna Brewster and her teaching? What did Donna communicate to her students, and how did she do it?

From this short episode, we can infer a great deal about Donna and her attitude toward her students and teaching. These attitudes and beliefs consist of the following four elements:

- Positive expectations
- Modeling
- Enthusiasm
- Responsiveness to students.

**Teacher Expectations**    Consider the following scenario, based on an actual classroom incident.

Mrs. Cummings watched as her new fifth-grade class filed into her room. She noticed a girl named Nicole and recalled that she had had Nicole's brother Mike 2 years earlier. Mike had been an above-average student with excellent study habits, and he was a pleasure to work with in class. Their parents were very involved in the children's schoolwork, and the home environment was very positive.

Mrs. Cummings didn't know, however, that Nicole had few of her brother's study habits. She was a happy-go-lucky girl interested in socializing, and she was already developing an interest in boys. Schoolwork was not a high priority for her.

Mrs. Cummings greeted Nicole with a big smile, told her it was nice to have her in class, and that she was sure they would have a very good year.

Partway through the grading period, Mrs. Cummings was scoring some math papers and noticed that Nicole's was missing. In checking her book, she found to her surprise that two other assignments were also absent. Also, Nicole's first test score was a bit lower than Mrs. Cummings had anticipated, but she hadn't reacted at the time.

The next day, she called Nicole to her desk before class, put her arm around her, and said, "Honey, I can't imagine what happened to your homework papers. Please find them and turn them in. If you get them in tomorrow, you'll get credit."

To be on the safe side, she called Nicole's parents that evening. They had been unaware of the homework and commented that Nicole had been rather vague when they asked if she had any homework for the next day.

Nicole's parents took immediate action. They eliminated all TV and telephone conversations until they saw that her homework was completely finished, and they called Mrs. Cummings a week later—in response to Mrs. Cummings's request—to check on Nicole's progress. Mrs. Cummings reported that everything was fine and that Nicole had done very well on the last test.

Consider Mrs. Cummings's response to Nicole. Because of her experience with Mike, she had a set of *expectations* that influenced her reactions to Nicole. Mrs. Cummings greeted Nicole warmly, and when her behavior was less conscientious than her brother's had been, Mrs. Cummings quickly acted, and as a result Nicole "shaped up." In essence, the teacher expected Nicole to learn, and when this didn't occur the teacher acted accordingly.

Teacher expectations are the inferences teachers make about students' future academic achievement, behavior, or attitudes (Good and Brophy, 1991), and they exert a powerful influence on teachers' behavior.

What can we infer about Donna Brewster's expectations for her students based on Monica's and Jim's behavior? They wouldn't dare to go to class unprepared, because Donna had clearly communicated that she *expected* them to do their homework. More importantly, by word and action she communicated her belief that all the students could learn, and she was there to be sure that they did. Believing that students can and will learn (positive teacher expectations) is a key variable that separates teachers who produce good student gains from those who don't (Good, 1987).

Unfortunately, teachers tend to treat students they perceive as high achievers much better than those perceived as lower in ability. This differential treatment occurs in four areas: (1) emotional support, (2) teacher effort and demands, (3) questioning, and (4) feedback and evaluation. The differences are outlined in Table 4.1 (Eggen and Kauchak, 1992).

Do students sense this differential treatment? One study concluded, "After 10 seconds of seeing and/or hearing a teacher, even very young students could detect whether the teacher talked about, or to, an excellent or a weak student, and could determine the extent to which that student was loved by the teacher" (Babad, Bernieri, and Rosenthal, 1991, p. 230). Think about the cumulative effects of positive and negative expectations over the course of a school year.

Donna Brewster didn't fall into the trap of lowered expectations for students of average or below-average ability. Monica and Jim were in a standard class, yet Donna's expectations for their performance remained high, and she demonstrated a strong commitment to their learning.

**Implications for Practice**   We are not suggesting, nor does any of the literature indicate, that all children will learn at the same rate. In the real world, children bring different levels of ability to the classroom. They all are not going to achieve at the same level or at the same rate. Considerable teacher judgment is required to set appropriate levels of expectation for all students. The point is not that teachers should avoid forming expectations, that they should have unrealistic expectations for their students, or that they should expect all students to achieve equally. Rather, each child should have the opportunity to achieve to his or her highest possible level. Idealistic, you say. Unquestionably, yes, but not impossible.

At this point you might say, "I understand all this, but if expectations are unconscious, what am I to do, and how am I going to do it?" Fortunately, there are formal efforts that can be made. Kerman (1979) reports a program in which teachers were trained to treat students as equally as possible. Teachers attended workshops where they were made aware of the need for calling on all students equally, giving equivalent feedback, and maintaining positive verbal and nonverbal behavior. The results were dramatic. The researchers found that not only did the achievement level

**TABLE 4.1**   Characteristics of Effective Teacher Expectations

| *Characteristic* | *Teacher Behaviors Favoring Perceived High Achievers* |
| --- | --- |
| Emotional support | More interactions; interactions more positive; more smiles; more eye contact; stand closer; orient body more directly; seat students closer to teacher |
| Teacher effort and demands | Clearer and more thorough explanations; more enthusiastic instruction; more follow-up questions; require more complete and accurate student answers |
| Questioning | Call on more often; more time to answer; more encouragement; more prompting |
| Feedback and evaluation | More praise; less criticism; more complete and more lengthy feedback; more conceptual evaluations |

of the students go up, but the number of discipline referrals went down and the absentee rate was reduced. All these positive responses were a result of equal treatment in the classroom. The program involved 742 teachers from more than 30 districts and over 2,000 students equally distributed over all grade levels, making the results impressive indeed.

We close this section with some specific suggestions about establishing and maintaining positive expectations. Throughout the rest of the text, we discuss each of the suggestions in more detail. At the forefront is an awareness and sensitivity to the possibility of treating students discriminatorily and an honest effort to avoid doing so. The specific suggestions are as follows:

1. Make an effort to call on all students equally. This means calling on the low achievers as often as on those most able to answer.
2. When a student is unable to respond, rather than redirecting the question to someone else, prompt the student until an acceptable answer is given.
3. When a low achiever gives an incorrect answer, provide as much information about why the answer is incorrect as you would for a high achiever.
4. Make eye contact with all students, and orient your body directly toward individuals as you talk to them. Do not talk to low achievers "out of the corner of your mouth" or "over your shoulder."
5. Change the seating arrangement of the students in your class so everyone is periodically near the front. Move around so you are physically near all the students as much as possible.
6. Use the "2-minute intervention" (Wlodkowski, 1987) with low achievers. This means taking a minute or two to discuss something personal with them, such as a family question, special interest, or recent accomplishment. We all are pleased when someone pays individual attention to us, and school-aged children are no exception.
7. Above all, make a concerted and ongoing effort to treat all students with dignity and respect. The results of this stance will probably have more powerful and long-lasting effects on your students than any content you teach.

### Teacher Modeling

"I see you have David in class too," one teacher said to another. "He sure is a good kid, isn't he?"

"I'm not surprised," the second one responded. "Have you ever met his parents? They're both super people too—enthusiastic and supportive. David probably picks up his attitude from them."

As the kids lined up to return from their lunch break, a teacher commented with a smile, "I can't believe it. Now they've *all* got their shirt collars up."

**Modeling** is the direct imitation of behavior observed in others, and we see its effects in a myriad of examples. We have worn hair styles like those of figure skaters and princesses and clothing influenced by rock musicians, first ladies, and professional athletes, and we have exercised to celebrity workout videos. Students pick up attitudes and expressions from the thousands of hours of TV they watch. The examples could go on and on. A major way that students learn is by observing and imitating the behaviors of others.

The enormously powerful effects teachers have on students through their modeling are well documented in the research literature (Good and Brophy, 1991). However, the process is often subtle and nearly imperceptible, and the effects of modeling are often out of the conscious control of the sender. For example, if a teacher claims to encourage free thinking in her classroom but disapproves when students offer novel or occasional "off the wall" ideas, she will soon have students who say only what they think she wants to hear. If teachers are inconsistent in what they say and do, children imitate their behavior rather than their spoken words (Bryan and Walbeck, 1970).

Teachers also teach attitudes toward learning through their actions. For example, teachers who modeled persistence in attempting to solve problems had students who strongly persisted in their own efforts, while students who saw a teacher persist only minimally actually declined in persistence (Zimmerman and Blotner, 1979). Further, when teachers made statements of confidence about their ability as they persisted, their students had increased estimates of their own ability (Zimmerman and Ringle, 1981). Through modeling students learn attitudes and motivation as well as direct behaviors.

Monica's and Jim's conclusion that "Brewster thinks this stuff is sooo important" was the result of Donna's modeling. It wasn't anything in particular that she said; it was the way she behaved. Students who see their teachers study and examine—or even struggle with—ideas are learning powerful behaviors that they can apply to their own learning. They see that effort, and even struggle, are positive, desirable behaviors.

**Teacher Enthusiasm**    Enthusiasm is a highly regarded characteristic in teachers, other professionals, and people in general. We react well to enthusiastic people. We find them attractive, and we enjoy being around them. They seem to relish life and get more out of it than do their less enthusiastic counterparts. Enthusiasm is associated with energy, good health, and high self-esteem.

Are these perceptions valid? Can they be documented? What is enthusiasm? Fortunately, research provides us with some answers. Good and Brophy (1991) suggested that enthusiasm has two essential aspects:

- the ability to convey sincere interest in the subject
- vigor and dynamics.

Collins (1978) operationally defined teacher enthusiasm in more concrete terms. These behaviors are summarized in Table 4.2.

With effort, teachers can increase their enthusiasm by consciously planning to communicate interest in the subjects they teach (Bettencourt, Gillett, Gall, and Hull, 1983), and the result is increased learning (Driscoll, 1978; Otteson and Otteson, 1980).

**TABLE 4.2** Characteristics of Enthusiasm

| Characteristic | Description |
|---|---|
| Vocal delivery | Varies the pitch, loudness, and rate of delivery |
| Eyes | Makes eye contact; animated eyes |
| Gestures | Frequent gesturing with head and arms |
| Body movement | Moves from place to place; energetic manner; vitality, drive, and spirit |
| Language | Uses descriptive language; varies word selection |

*Source:* Adapted from Eggen and Kauchak, 1992.

***Enthusiasm and Student Motivation.*** While teacher enthusiasm is correlated with increased learning, it is linked more strongly to student motivation. Wlodkowski and Jaynes (1990) observed, "One of the characteristics of motivating teachers is enthusiasm. They care about what they teach and communicate to their students that what they are learning is important. Such teachers offer living proof of this and are apt models whose intensity beckons identification and inspiration" (p. 19). Since people tend to display the behaviors they observe in others, students are certainly more likely to be motivated by enthusiastic than by unenthusiastic teachers.

**Responsiveness to Students**   Another characteristic of effective teachers is their responsiveness to students. Responsiveness to students is teachers' constant awareness of their students' verbal and nonverbal behavior throughout learning activities. It is closely related to the concept of "withitness," which Kounin (1970) described as knowing what is going on in all parts of the classroom all the time. With effective teachers, responsiveness is automatic; they continually monitor their students as a matter of habit, and they quickly adapt when the students seem confused or "drift off" (Duffy, Roehler, Meloth, and Vavrus, 1985; O'Keefe and Johnston, 1987).

Kathy Johnson demonstrated responsiveness in her questioning in several ways. First, when Carol answered correctly but uncertainly, Kathy responded with an encouraging "Very good description, Carol." Kathy was also responsive when she helped Ann Marie answer through prompting. Finally, Kathy demonstrated responsiveness when she helped Jim off the hook when she realized he had been daydreaming and hadn't heard the question. The fact that Kathy didn't admonish Jim for his attentiveness also demonstrated a form of teacher support that promotes a positive classroom climate. This type of intervention as a pattern both increases engaged time and student motivation.

## Effective Communication

Language and thinking are so closely interrelated that the ability of the teacher to communicate clearly is an essential component of effective teaching. Just as time and positive attitudes are important in learning, regardless of grade level, content area, or specific teaching method, effective teachers at all levels communicate clearly. This section of the chapter examines the process of communication in teaching and discusses implications for the classroom.

> This mathematics lesson will enab . . . , will get you to understand number uh, number patterns. Before we get to the main idea of the, main idea of the lesson, you need to review four concepts . . . four prerequisite concepts. (Smith and Land, 1981, p. 38)

Does this example sound extreme? How often would your classroom presentations sound like this? The quote is an example of a **maze,** which is a brief description that does not make semantic sense. Mazes include false starts or halting speech, redundant words, and word jumbles or tangles. When researchers investigated mazes in classroom settings, they found an average of *four mazes per minute of teacher talk* (Smith and Land, 1981), a high rate for formal classroom presentations. (It is probably much higher for informal conversations.) Compare the preceding example with the following statement:

> The purpose of this lesson is to help you understand number patterns. Before we begin the number patterns themselves, however, there are four concepts we want to review. These concepts are. . . .

Here the purpose in the lesson is stated clearly and precisely, increasing the likelihood that students will know what the lesson is about and where it's going.

Teachers' language is one of the most widely researched variables in the history of the teacher effectiveness literature (Dunkin and Biddle, 1974; Rosenshine, 1971). As evidence has accumulated, a strong link between clarity of language and student achievement has been found (Cruickshank, 1985; Snyder et al., 1991), and effective communication is also linked to student satisfaction with instruction (Hines, Cruickshank, and Kennedy, 1985; Snyder et al., 1991). The clarity of teachers' presentations affects student attitude as well as achievement.

But what does clear communication mean? Researchers have identified five components:

- Precise terminology
- Connected discourse
- Transition signals
- Emphasis
- Congruent verbal and nonverbal behavior.

**Precise Terminology**  Precise terminology simply means that teachers eliminate vague and ambiguous words and phrases in their communications with their students. For example, researchers have found that vague terms such as *might, a little more, some, usually,* and *probably* adversely affect achievement (Smith and Cotten, 1980). Further, teachers who frequently interject vague terminology into their verbal communication are perceived by their students as disorganized, unprepared, and nervous (Smith and Land, 1981).

**Connected Discourse**   Connected discourse, a second element of teacher clarity, means that the teacher's presentation is logically connected and leads to a point. In contrast, *scrambled discourse* includes loosely connected ideas that occur when a teacher rambles, interrupts the direction of the lesson by including irrelevant material, or sequences the presentation inappropriately. For instance, examine the following:

We've been studying the countries on the Arabian peninsula as part of our unit on the Middle East and have continually stressed the importance of oil in this area of the country. As we know, these countries make most of their money on oil, which they use to buy goods and services from the Western economies. However, as precious as oil is, water looms as even a bigger problem. Most of the people live near water and overextend the available supplies, and, in some cases, even extracting and refining the oil has been hampered by the lack of water.

Compare this now with the following.

We've been studying the countries on the Arabian peninsula as part of our unit on the Middle East. As we know, these countries make most of their money on oil; they were the ones who were most responsible for the Arab embargo that pushed our gas prices up in the 1970s. Venezuela and other oil producers were involved too. That contributed to our inflation rate. These countries also have a problem with water. Most of the people live on the coast or near water, although the holy city of Mecca is inland. Three major religions, Islam, Judaism, and Christianity, have their roots there. The people tend to overextend their water supply, and often there isn't enough water to extract and refine the oil.

In the first example, the point is clear and focused; in the second, the point is uncertain. Is the major theme the water problem, religion, or the oil embargo? With the added information about Venezuela and the inflation rate, it isn't even clear whether or not the focus is on the Middle East. Though essentially free of mazes and vague terms, the presentation is still unclear, and the result is lowered achievement (Smith and Cotten, 1980).

**Transition Signals**   Teachers also contribute to the clarity of their presentations with clear transition signals during the progress of the lesson (Hines et al., 1985). A transition signal communicates that one idea is ending and another is beginning and explains the link between the two. Using our illustration with the countries of the Arabian peninsula, a teacher might say, "We've been discussing the problems these countries have with water. Now let's talk about the countries of North Africa and see if the situation is similar." Or "We're going to stop talking about the countries on the Arabian peninsula for now, and turn to those in North Africa." In either case, the teacher clearly indicates that a shift in the topic is being made. This sign posting allows students to structure the content in their minds as the lesson develops. Our chapter headings in this text serve the same purpose.

### Emphasis

When you're solving equations remember that whatever you do to one side of the equation, you must also do exactly the same thing to the other side.

Keep in mind as you read the contents of this chapter that we're looking at effective teaching behaviors that apply across grade levels, subject-matter areas, and specific teaching techniques.

We said that one of the characteristics of the Jackson era was the rise of the common man.

These three statements are examples of emphasis, which communicates that an idea or topic has special significance. It is a form of effective communication that helps students determine the relative importance of the topics they're covering.

Emphasis can be accomplished in four different ways, and teachers often combine these: verbal statements, nonverbal behaviors, repetition, and written signals. They are illustrated in Table 4.3.

Research indicates that each form of emphasis increases achievement (Maddox and Hoole, 1975; Mayer, 1983). If there is something in the lesson that is essential for students to learn, we ought to tell them it is important.

**Congruent Verbal and Nonverbal Behavior**   "It's not what you say; it's how you say it." We've all heard this maxim, and it refers to **nonverbal communication,** which is the part of our messages that we convey without spoken words. Nonverbal communication includes the tone, pitch, and loudness of our voice, our gestures, body orientation, facial expressions, and eye contact. It even includes our use of space, such as moving close to another person.

Nonverbal communication is very important as we interact with people in general and students in particular, because it is through these channels that people consciously (and unconsciously) evaluate our motives, intentions, and attitudes. Our perceptions of people and theirs of us are based primarily on nonverbal behavior. For example, four of the five characteristics of enthusiasm—vocal delivery, eyes, ges-

**TABLE 4.3**   Forms of Emphasis in the Classroom

| *Type* | *Example* |
| --- | --- |
| Verbal statements | "Be sure to get this," "Now remember . . ." |
| Nonverbal behaviors | Raised or louder voice Gestures or pointing to specific information |
| Repetition | "What did Heather say about our first example?" |
| Written signal | "As you'll see on the board, the three functions of the circulatory system . . ." |

tures, and body movement—outlined in Table 4.2 are nonverbal. In addition, the way we communicate, through modeling, our commitment to teaching, our expectations for students, and overall sincerity is primarily nonverbal. As we noted earlier in this chapter, even young children are capable of reading and judging the nonverbal messages of teachers (Babad et al., 1991).

It is literally impossible to communicate clearly if our verbal and nonverbal behavior are inconsistent. Steve's conviction that Donna Brewster "thinks this stuff is sooo important" and Monica's conclusion, "She really tries to help you get it," were based primarily on Donna's nonverbal behavior and not her words. There is little Donna could have said to convince the students that American history is important if her nonverbal messages were inconsistent with her words.

Researchers have quantified the credibility of messages sent through the different communication channels (Mehrabian and Ferris, 1967) . They found that a mere 7 percent of the message's credibility was communicated through the spoken words; 38 percent was delivered through tone, pitch, and variation in voice, and the remaining 55 percent through body language. This means that the nonverbal channels are nearly eight times more powerful in communicating the credibility of a message than is the verbal channel. Let's see how this works in the classroom.

Mr. Inez is helping Tyrone with a problem as the class is doing seatwork. Behind him, Steve and Tony are whispering loudly.

"You boys stop talking and get started on your problems," Mr. Inez says, glancing at the boys over his shoulder.

The boys slow their whispering briefly, but do not actually stop and are soon at it as loudly as ever.

"I thought I told you to stop talking," Mr. Inez repeats again over his shoulder.

This time Tony and Steve barely slow down. Mr. Inez, his back to the boys, doesn't seem to notice.

What message did Mr. Inez send? His words said stop, but his body language said that he didn't really mean it. He spoke over his shoulder, left his back turned to them, and he didn't follow through to be sure they actually stopped. Mr. Inez's communication was incongruent, and his words had little credibility. This pattern of behavior is quite common for teachers who have classroom management problems.

**Improving Communication: Suggestions for Teachers**   The research on language clarity has two important implications for teachers. First, we must thoroughly understand the content we teach, and if we are uncertain we must spend more time studying and preparing. Teachers with thorough content backgrounds use clearer language and form better explanations than those with weaker backgrounds (Carlsen, 1987; Cruickshank, 1985). This makes sense. Teachers who understand their content approach topics with confidence and certainty. They use precise language, their presentations flow logically, and they emphasize the appropriate points. They model confidence, and in turn their students feel more confident.

Second, we must literally listen to ourselves talk as we teach—monitor our own communication—to be as clear and concise as possible. This can be done easily by audiotaping a lesson and then listening to ourselves. Even veteran teachers are often surprised when they hear themselves on tape. Other processes, such as peer coaching, in which a colleague observes a portion of a lesson and provides feedback, can be very helpful (Glickman, 1990). Either way, the increase in clarity (and student learning) is worth the effort.

## Organization

The term *organization*, like time, is one that we use not only to talk about teaching but also to discuss our everyday lives: "I've got to get organized," "My new year's resolution is to be better organized this year," "He would be good at the job, but he is so disorganized." These are familiar-sounding statements, and we all struggle at times to improve our organizational schemes. We write lists; we arrange elaborate filing systems that we do not use; we pick up the same piece of paper several times before we do anything with it. Each example serves to underscore that while organization seems quite simple on the surface, in reality it can be a major stumbling block to efficiency. This is true in the classroom as well as life.

Earlier in the chapter, we found that Steve Weiss, an eighth-grade science teacher, utilized more of his available time for instruction than did his colleague, Dennis Orr. This was primarily due to his organization. A comparison reveals three important differences between the two, which are outlined in Table 4.4.

In examining Table 4.4, we see that each of these behaviors increases classroom instructional time; conversely, failure to apply one or more reduces instructional time and ultimately reduces learning (Emmer and Evertson, 1980; Evertson, 1980). These managerial functions are so important to the success of a classroom that we will return to them in Chapter 11 when we examine them in the total context of classroom management.

**TABLE 4.4**  Characteristics of Effective Organization

| Aspect of Organization | Example |
| --- | --- |
| Starting on time | Steve Weiss began class when the bell stopped ringing. |
| | Dennis Orr moved to the front of the room after several minutes. |
| Materials prepared in advance | Steve's demonstration was prepared in advance. |
| | Dennis finished preparing his demonstration while the students waited. |
| Established routines | Steve's students knew what to do when they came to class. |
| | Dennis had to tell his students how to get started. |

## The General Instructional Model: Beginning the Lesson

Earlier, we discussed teacher characteristics and skills that are important throughout the lesson. We turn now to the sequential phases of the general instructional model individually, to examine effective teaching behaviors in different parts of the lesson. We start with lesson beginnings.

An effective introduction to a lesson draws students into the lesson, focuses their attention on the new content to be learned, and relates that new material to content already learned. Let's see how this occurs.

**Introductory Review**  Introductory review examines information that has been covered in an earlier lesson, refreshing students' memories and setting the stage for new learning. Research examining the way learners process information helps us understand the value of reviews at the beginning of a lesson. When we learn new information, we interpret it in terms of what we already know, connecting it in our memory to other concepts and ideas. Resnick and Klopfer (1989) observed that "people are not recorders of information but builders of knowledge structures. To know something is not just to have received information but also to have interpreted and related it to other knowledge" (p. 4). Review helps learners establish what they already know, which then provides an anchor for the new information to come. Let's look at two examples.

> Ken Thomas has begun a unit on the Crusades and wants to examine their effects on the Western World. He begins his lesson by saying, "We've been discussing the Crusades. Let's think for a moment now about what we learned yesterday. First, identify some reasons the Crusades occurred in the first place. David?"

> Dorothy Williams's students have studied gerunds and participles, and now she wants to move to infinitives. She begins her lesson by saying, "We talked about gerunds and participles yesterday. Before we proceed with today's topic I'd like you to give me an example of each. Jeff?"

In both cases the teachers used prior learning as a point of departure for the day's lesson. Students can then connect the new learning to old—Dorothy's students related infinitives to gerunds and participles, for example—which makes both more meaningful.

**Introductory Focus**  Introductory focus is the process teachers use to introduce a learning activity. It provides two functions:

- To attract students' attention
- To provide a context for the topic being studied.

For instance, rather than merely saying something such as, "Today we're going to discuss the Northern and Southern Colonies," Kathy Johnson effectively introduced her lesson by referring to the chart and saying, "We see that the economy for the two groups of colonies is very different. . . . So, remember as we go through the lesson that we're talking about the way the colonies made their money, and we're trying to figure out why it is so different. . . ." By introducing her lesson in the form of a problem, she capitalized on both aspects of introductory focus.

Introductory focus can be accomplished in a variety of ways. The following are some additional examples.

> As an introduction to the topic of cities and where they are located, Jim Edwards, a fifth-grade teacher, passed out a map of a fictitious island. On it were physical features such as lakes, rivers, mountains, and bays. The map also included the latitude, prevailing winds, ocean currents, and rainfall for the island. He began, "We have been sent to this island to settle it. Based on the information we have here, we need to decide what would be the best place to start our first settlement."

> Susan Wood began a unit on heat and atmospheric pressure with her science students by putting a cup of water in an empty duplicating fluid can, heating the can with a hot plate, and capping it. As the students watched, the can collapsed, almost "magically." Susan then commented, "Now, keep what you saw in mind, and we'll be able to figure out why it happened as we study this unit."

> Jessie Andrews began his math lesson on percentages by asking, "Who's the best hitter in baseball today?" After a number of opinions had been offered by students, Jessie continued, "Do you want to learn one way to find out? Let's look at percentages and see how they can tell us who is the best hitter."

One of the most effective types of introductory focus employs some type of sensory device. A **sensory focus** provides students with something to see, hear, feel, smell, or even taste as they begin the lesson. The concept is borrowed from cognitive learning theory and is a type of orienting stimulus (Gage and Berliner, 1992). An orienting stimulus is any environmental factor that attracts and maintains an individual's attention.

The most common type of sensory focus is visual, but all forms have been used effectively. Any sensory reference point that is observable and explicit can serve as a suitable focus. For instance, a series of sentences on the chalkboard or equations on an overhead projector would work in an English or algebra class. In addition, outlines, hierarchies, or objectives are also effective.

Hunter (1984) used the term **anticipatory set** for introductory activities that focus student attention on the material to be presented, reminding them of what they already know and stimulating their interest in the subject. For example, a teacher introducing the book *Moby Dick* might say, "We know from our previous readings that the color white has historically symbolized goodness and purity. What a strange color for a whale that kills men and capsizes boats. What do you think Melville was trying to say to us?" A focusing event like this pulls students into the lesson, focuses their attention, and frames subsequent activities.

*Advanced Organizers.* David Ausubel (1968), a noted cognitive psychologist, also had distinct ideas about how to focus lessons. He advocated the use of **advance organizers**, introductory statements that framed new content and related it to content students already knew. For example, a lesson on the circulatory system might be introduced with the following statement:

> The circulatory system is like the sanitary system of a city. In both, there is a pumping station, pipelines with varying sized pipes to carry clean water, a filtration plan to clean dirty water, an exchange terminal and a capacity for disposal of waste. (Eggen and Kauchak, 1988, p. 294)

Advance organizers are effective for a number of reasons: They (1) focus students' attention on the topic at hand, (2) inform them where the lesson is going, (3) relate new material to content already understood, and (4) provide structure for the subsequent lesson.

Whatever the form the introductory focus takes, the fact that this information is written on the board or projected overhead provides better focus than the same information on individual sheets provided for the students. If students are looking down at their desks, the teacher cannot tell if they are looking at the sheet or are looking down because they are not paying attention. When the focus is at the front of the room, the teacher can monitor students' attention through eye contact, which is one of the major ways that researchers assess student engagement. If the teacher finds that students are not looking at whatever is being displayed for them, the teacher can adjust the lesson to regain their attention.

Some of the best focusing events use realistic objects to grab and hold the students' attention. This can be achieved by increasing the concreteness of the orienting stimulus. For example, colored pictures of animals provide a good focus for an elementary lesson on a topic such as mammals, but imagine the attention-getting power of bringing someone's guinea pig or hamster to class. It would be simple to do and carries a powerful motivational impact. Science and other areas of the curriculum involving real-world phenomena such as vocational or home economics classes have some inherent advantages over other subject-matter areas in that an enormous number of eye-catching demonstrations exist that can be used as the focal points for lessons.

Providing introductory focus in a lesson can be quite simple. For example, it is easy enough to write sentences or equations on the chalkboard, and it is not difficult to bring a guinea pig to class. Despite this simplicity, we have observed a surprising number of teachers having problems with students' inattention that can be traced directly to lack of focus at the beginning of a lesson; they did not lose students — they never *had* them. A significant percentage of the lessons we observe in the schools begin weakly, with little apparent attempt to attract the attention, if not the curiosity, of students. Unfortunately, all too often these lessons go downhill from there — students are lost because they were not there at the beginning. Good focus at the beginning of a lesson can be a powerful aid not only in increasing student engagement rates but also in improving learning.

## The General Instructional Model: Developing the Lesson

You have established a link to what the students already know with a beginning review, and you have provided context for the lesson with introductory focus. You are now ready to develop the lesson by presenting new content or skills.

**Presenting Content**   Presenting content, which Madeline Hunter (1984) called "input," is the point in the lesson where the teacher presents the new information or skills that the students are to learn. Kathy Johnson, for example, began this phase of her lesson as soon as she had finished her review and began her analysis of the chart by pointing out differences in the North's and South's economies and asking students to analyze these differences.

One of the most common methods of presenting content is the lecture. Lecture, a basically ineffective method of instruction, endures primarily because of its simplicity. Lectures place students in a passive role, allow inattention, and low levels of engaged time often result.

Research has identified a number of effective alternatives to teacher lectures. These include concept-teaching strategies, inductive methods, lecture recitation, skills instruction, discussions, and cooperative learning. Brief examples of each are presented in Table 4.5.

As we can see from Table 4.5, there are a number of alternatives available for presenting new content and skills. The particular lesson format that a teacher selects depends on the type of content being taught and the students themselves. For example, when teaching a concept, we must clearly define the abstraction and provide positive and negative examples. In a similar way, when teaching a skill we need to explain and model the skill and provide ample opportunities for students to practice it.

Students also influence the selection of a teaching strategy in powerful ways. As we saw in Chapter 2, students vary considerably in terms of their background knowledge and the skills and attitudes they bring to class. A skillful teacher is sensitive to these differences and selects a teaching strategy that matches needs and abilities. For example, a teacher working with a heterogeneous group of students can strategically team strong students with weaker students, encouraging the more advanced students to help the slower ones. In a similar way, an elementary teacher who recognizes that her students lack prerequisite experiences to understand abstract ideas will use hands-on experiences and concrete examples to compensate.

The selection and implementation of a number of teaching strategies is an essential skill for effective teaching. Chapters 6 through 10 discuss the most effective of these and how to implement them in your classroom.

**Active Student Involvement**   Regardless of students' ages, the topic, or specific teaching strategy, effective teachers maintain high levels of student involvement in their learning activities. To see how this is done, let's return once more to Kathy

**TABLE 4.5** Strategies for Presenting Content

| Strategy | Chapter | Example |
|---|---|---|
| Concept teaching | 6 | An elementary teacher shows his students equilateral, isosceles, right, and scalene triangles. The students identify the characteristics of each and then create their own with compasses and protractors. |
| Inductive methods | 6 and 7 | Kathy Johnson's lesson with her fifth graders. She presented information in a matrix and led her students to conclusions about the economies of the Northern and Southern Colonies. |
| Lecture recitation | 7 | An American History teacher presents film clips, songs, slides, and personal accounts of the Great Depression. From the information, the students form conclusions about different aspects of life in the United States during this time. |
| Skills instruction | 8 | An English class is working on essays in which they write thesis statements and paragraphs that support the theses. The teacher presents and explains sample essays, and the students then practice writing their own. |
| Cooperative learning | 10 | Math students are learning to add fractions with unlike denominators. After the teacher explains and illustrates the process, she breaks the students into teams to practice. Kathy Johnson did a modification of cooperative learning with her fifth graders. |
| Discussions | 10 | Following a playground incident, a teacher initiates a discussion of individual rights. She presents a hypothetical interpersonal problem and asks the students to suggest ways to solve it. |

Johnson's teaching. As soon as students were oriented to her lesson, Kathy made them active participants in the learning process first through her questioning and later as they worked in pairs. The need to place learners in active roles is well documented (Anderson, 1989; Carnine, 1990; Rosenshine, 1987), and Kathy's procedure is an application of this research. A number of teaching and learning strategies place students in active roles. These include the following:

- Teacher questioning (especially those questions that ask students to re-think or analyze information)
- Having students paraphrase information (rather than restate it as presented by the teacher or written materials)
- Building lessons around analysis of examples and applications (rather than around definitions)
- Problem solving
- Providing practice problems and homework
- Writing (themes, essays, term papers)
- "Hands-on" activities
- Tests and quizzes requiring more than rote memory. (Eggen and Kauchak, 1992, p. 335)

Common to each of these is the active engagement of the learner in working with the new content being learned. We illustrate these processes in detail in the chapters that follow.

**Practice and Feedback**   As students learn new content and skills, they need opportunities to try these out and interrelate them, with assistance from the teacher. Practice provides students opportunities to try out and test their grasp of new content on their own. Feedback is any information about current behavior that can be used to improve future performance. For example, a teacher has just introduced the skill of drawing in three-point perspective. Providing opportunities for students to practice the skill with feedback not only helps students learn the skill but also provides valuable information to the teacher about the progress of the lesson. The value of practice and feedback in improving learning is one of the most consistent findings from the teacher effectiveness literature (Good and Brophy, 1991; Rosenshine and Stevens, 1986). Through interactive practice and feedback, teachers give students opportunities to consolidate new learning, reinforce old, and eliminate errors and misconceptions. Interactive question and answer sessions typically have high student-engagement rates and provide teachers with the opportunity to gauge the level of learning, diagnose student problems, and motivate certain students through strategic selection of them to respond.

The form that these interactive practice and feedback sessions take depends on the type of content being taught. Skills-oriented lessons provide students with practice in performing the skill, while concept-related lessons focus on positive and negative examples of the concept. Lessons focusing on organized bodies of information use questions that ask students to relate different pieces of information. Common to all of these types is the active involvement of the learners in making sense of the new content.

Just as the type of practice can vary, so can feedback. In a careful analysis of teacher feedback, Zahorik (1968) identified 175 observable forms. They ranged from smiling faces on papers to verbal comments such as "Good answer" or "Fine." Common to all of these responses was an attempt on the teacher's part to provide students with information about how well they were learning.

Research indicates that effective feedback has four characteristics:

- It is immediate.
- It is specific.
- It provides corrective information.
- It has a positive emotional tone.

To illustrate these ideas, let's look at the following examples, each focusing on the same topic.

*Mr. Horn:*   What kind of triangle is shown on the board, Jo?

*Jo:*   A right triangle.

*Mr. Horn:*   Not quite. Help her out. Steve?

*Ms. West:*   What kind of triangle is shown on the board, Jo?

*Jo:*   A right triangle.

*Ms. West:*   No, it's an equilateral triangle. What kind of triangle is the next one, Don?

*Mr. Park:*   What kind of triangle is shown on the board, Jo?

*Jo:*   A right triangle.

*Mr. Park:*   No, remember we said that a right triangle must have a 90-degree angle. What do you notice about each of the angles in our triangle?

In comparing our three examples, we see that each is *immediate.* However, Mr. Horn's feedback gave Jo no information about her answer other than it was incorrect—it had none of the other attributes of effective feedback—and while Ms. West's feedback was *specific*, it gave Jo no *corrective* information. Mr. Park, in contrast, identified the essential feature of a right triangle and specifically directed Jo to the angles in the equilateral triangle. This type of feedback not only provides information about the quality of the response but gives additional information that can help both Jo and the rest of the class.

Research indicates that the informational quality of feedback affects not only short-term learning but also long-term motivation for learning (Schunk and Swartz, 1991). Feedback that helped students gauge their progress as learners developed their confidence to attack other types of learning.

Positive *emotional tone*, the fourth characteristic of effective feedback, means that teachers present their feedback in a supportive manner. This relates to the importance of establishing a positive learning environment discussed in Chapter 2. Harsh, critical, or sarcastic feedback is destructive to both learning and student motivation (Murphy, Weil, and McGreal, 1986).

*Teacher Praise.* Teacher praise, the most common form of positive feedback, appears on the surface to be a simple concept; teachers simply tell students when they've given a good answer or done good work. However, classroom research indicates some interesting patterns. For example, praise occurs less frequently than most teachers believe; praise for good answers typically occurs fewer than five times per hour. Praise for good behavior happens even less frequently, occurring once every two to ten hours in the early grades and even less later on (Brophy, 1981a, 1981b) . Also, praise appears to depend as much on the type of student (bright, attentive, and well behaved) as on the answer itself. As we saw earlier in this chapter, teacher expectations have a powerful influence on who and what gets rewarded (Brophy, 1981a).

Praise, when used effectively, can have an important effect on learning. From his review of the literature on teacher praise, Brophy (1981a) made a series of recommendations, which are summarized in Table 4.6.

Specific as compared to general praise is somewhat controversial. Some con-

**TABLE 4.6**   Recommendations for Effective Praise

| Recommendation | Explanation |
| --- | --- |
| Praise genuinely | Insincere praise lacks credibility, particularly with older students. |
| Praise strategically | Be sure the praise matches the achievement. Avoid overuse of effusive praise. Young and low-achieving students react better to praise than do their older, higher achieving counterparts (Stipek, 1988). |
| Praise efforts as well as accomplishment | Praise for effort communicates that perseverance is a valued personal characteristic. |
| Praise incidental accomplishment | Praising students for a new insight or good thought, even if it isn't directly relevant, promotes a positive learning climate. |
| Praise specifically | Specific praise provides information that enhances learning. |

tend that if each and every desired answer is to be praised specifically, the praise begins to sound stilted and artificial, and the flow of a lesson is disrupted.

A solution to this dilemma is to vary the praise with the answer (Rosenshine, 1987). Praise for student answers that are delivered with confidence should be simple and general, such as "Good," or "Good answer." In contrast, when students give correct but tentative answers, the praise should be specific and informational. Confident responses indicate that the students understand *why* their answers are correct, while uncertainty suggests that though the answer is right, they are not sure why. Specific praise helps eliminate the uncertainty.

The following example illustrates the difference between general and specific praise.

> *Mrs. Chu:* How does the direction of the ocean current off the coast of Chile affect the rainfall in the Chilean desert?
>
> *Tim:* The current comes from the south, so the water is cold. The air over the water is more dense than the air over the land, so the air that moves over the land is warmed up, and it doesn't rain. That's why a desert is there.
>
> *General Praise:* Yes, good answer.
>
> *Specific Praise:* Excellent answer! You identified the relationship between the direction of the ocean current, density of the air, and direction of the air flow. You have to understand these relationships to understand the weather. Well done!

Mrs. Chu's first response simply acknowledged Tim's response with a statement of general praise. In contrast, her second response gave the class in general, and Tim in particular, specific information as to why the answer was good. If a pattern of using this type of praise is established, students develop an understanding of the criteria for desirable answers, and the quality of answers over time is increased. In addition, logical connections between ideas are reinforced.

## The General Instructional Model: Lesson Endings

Just as effective lessons begin by drawing students into the activity and providing a reference frame for new material, effective lessons end by tying the different parts of the lesson together and assessing students' understanding. Review and closure help students summarize the major ideas in the lesson, and assessment tells both the teacher and students what has been learned and what needs further work.

### Review and Closure

We're near the end of the period, so we'll stop here and pick it up tomorrow.

That's all for now. Put your stuff away and get ready for lunch.

We have reviewed previous material, have provided an attention-getting lesson beginning, and have carefully developed the lesson with high levels of student involvement and appropriate feedback. The positive effects of these efforts are diminished, however, if we abruptly end the lesson, as we see in the two examples.

Closure is a form of review that occurs at the end of a lesson, when the topic is summarized and structured. This technique allows students to leave the class with a sense of the day's content and what they were supposed to have derived from it. It also provides a springboard for students' further study at home.

Closure is important because as learners we instinctively structure information into patterns that make sense to us (Carnine, 1990). If we leave a learning experience with uncertainties, the ideas we intuitively form may be invalid, and because new learning is built on old, these misconceptions detract from future learning. The notion of closure is common and intuitively sensible. Perhaps you have even used the term in a conversation, saying something such as, "Let's try and get to 'closure' on this."

Let's look at some specific examples of closure.

Mary Eng had developed the process for factoring the difference of two squares in her Algebra I class. She noted, "It's near the end of the period, so let's go over what we've covered so far. First, give me an example that is the difference of two squares. Wendy."

In finishing a lesson on "main idea," Harry Soo said, "Children, I want you now to tell me in your own words what the main idea of a story is. Define it for me."

Teresa Bon had finished a lesson relating the pitch of a sound to the length, thickness, and tension of the object producing the sound. She completed her lesson by saying, "Now let's write a statement that tells us in one sentence what we've found today."

Additional examples of concepts learned, a definition, or a summary can all be used to tie together lesson content. Research indicates that each of these forms of closure is a powerful aid in student learning (Rosenshine, 1983; Tennyson and Cocciarella, 1986). We discuss closure in more detail in the chapters devoted to specific teaching strategies.

### Assessment

> They seem to be able to solve percent increase problems, but I wonder if they really understand how these are different from percent decrease problems.

> Most of them are getting some ideas down on paper, but they don't seem to elaborate very well. I wonder if I should work more on that, or if I should start having them work a little harder now on the mechanics of their grammar?

> The lab homework looked good on solving the density problems, but how many of them just put the numbers in the formula without knowing what they were doing?

Questions like these occur continually when we teach. Teachers are constantly asking themselves if their students "really get it." They're gauging how fast they can cover the content, trying to identify problems and misconceptions that need to be remedied, and deciding whether or not they should go on to the next topic. Assessment helps teachers answer these questions.

**Assessment** is the process of gathering information and making instructional decisions based on the information. Its basic purpose is to gauge the learners' progress and provide feedback for both the teacher and students. It can take several different forms:

- Quizzes
- Tests
- Homework
- Writing assignments
- Projects
- Work samples.

We examine the assessment process in detail in Chapter 12.

This completes our examination of the general instructional model. The model is designed to serve as a framework — an advance organizer if you will — for the content of Chapters 5 through 10. Hopefully, the information presented here will serve as a foundation for your study of those chapters. Before turning to Chapter 5, however, please read the summary and complete the exercises that follow.

## SUMMARY

The essence of this chapter is captured with the question, *If we watch effective teachers teach, regardless of grade level, content area, or topic, what would we expect to see them doing?*

In answering the question, we find that they use their time well—they spend little time on noninstructional matters, and they employ learning activities in which students are successfully engaged.

Effective teachers also display the personal characteristics we associate with good teaching. They have high expectations for their students, they are enthusiastic and energetic, and they model the behaviors they expect in others.

Clear communication is also a characteristic of effective teachers. They use precise language, their presentations follow a clear theme, and their verbal and nonverbal behaviors are consistent.

Effective teachers are well organized. They begin learning activities promptly, have materials prepared in advance, and have well-established, time-saving routines.

They begin their lessons with a careful review of previous work, and they consciously plan their lesson beginnings to capture and maintain student attention. As their lessons are developed, they deliver the content with a wide variety of examples and applications while maintaining high levels of student involvement. They give the students feedback about their progress and provide practice to reinforce learning.

Effective teachers end their lessons with a thorough review to summarize the topics they've studied, and they have a well-developed assessment system to give them information about the progress of their students.

## ADDITIONAL READINGS FOR PROFESSIONAL GROWTH

Berliner, D., & Rosenshine, B. (Eds). (1988). *Talks to teachers.* New York: Random House. This edited book discusses a number of variables associated with effective teaching.

Good, T., & Brophy, J. (1991). *Looking in classrooms* (5th ed.). Good and Brophy do an excellent job of translating research into observational tools to help teachers analyze their practice.

Fisher, C., & Berliner, D. (Eds). (1985). *Perspectives on instructional time.* New York: Longman. This is a comprehensive overview of the issues involved in using time as a barometer of effective teaching.

## EXERCISES

1. Look at the band between allocated and instructional time in Figure 4.1. What does the area of this band represent? For which teacher, Dennis Orr or Steve Weiss in our example at the beginning of the section on instructional time, would the area of this band be greater? Explain why.

2. Based on our opening case study, how much instructional time did Kathy Johnson have in her social studies lesson?

3. Think about the engaged time in Kathy Johnson's lesson. Was it equal to, slightly greater than, or slightly less than the instructional time in her lesson? Defend your answer with information from the case study.

4. Identify an example in the case study where Kathy Johnson promoted academic learning time through her encouragement of student success.

5. Identify at least three examples of enthusiasm in Kathy Johnson's behavior in the case study. Cite examples directly from the case study.

6. Identify two examples from the case study suggesting that Kathy was responsive to her students. Then explain how these illustrate responsiveness to students.

7. Kathy said, "So remember that we're focusing on the economy of the colonies today," and we identified it as introductory focus. What element of effective communication does this statement also illustrate?

8. Describe how Kathy Johnson demonstrated each of the characteristics of effective organization in her class. Support your answer with information taken directly from the case study.

9. Describe Kathy Johnson's opening review.

10. Identify two ways in which Kathy Johnson promoted active student involvement in her lesson.

11. Describe Kathy Johnson's closure in her lesson.

12. To which aspect of time does teacher organization most closely relate?

13. Of the four different aspects of time, which two are most strongly influenced by active student involvement?

14. We emphasized the importance of enthusiasm in teachers. To which aspect of time does enthusiasm most directly relate?

15. To which aspect of time do opening reviews and lesson closure most closely relate?

## DISCUSSION QUESTIONS

1. Some authorities suggest lengthening the school day or school year, and they support their position by citing the relationship between allocated time and achievement. How would you respond to these people? What are some arguments for and against this approach to increasing learning?

2. In the text we stated that, when compared to other time measures, allocated time had one of the weakest relationships to learning. Why is this so? How do the aspects of time differ in this regard?

3. What are the major activities in a classroom that interfere with instructional time? How can they be minimized?

4. In research studies, engagement is often inferred from the expressions and actions of students. What are some behaviors that suggest student engagement? Lack of engagement? What are some problems involved in inferring attention from behavior?

5. The ideal engagement rate is, of course, 100 percent. What is a realistic engagement rate for students you work with? (Estimate a percentage.) How does this engagement rate vary with the type of students? time of day? different times within the same class period? What can be done to increase engagement rates? What factors outside the teacher's control will affect student engagement rates?

6. This chapter focused on enthusiasm from a teacher perspective. What are some indicators of students' enthusiasm? lack of enthusiasm? Are these low- or high-inference behaviors?

7. Describe in a paragraph or so two or three of the best teachers that you can recall from your experience in school. Analyze your description in terms of cognitive and affective behaviors. Were these high- or low-inference descriptors?

8. Are positive teacher attitudes more important at some grade levels than others? Why? In some curriculum areas and/or content areas? Why?

9. Review the findings on teacher expectations in terms of teacher effort and demands and questioning behaviors. What might be some explanations for why teachers treat high achievers and low achievers differently in terms of these two categories of behaviors?

10. Research suggests a link between enthusiasm and students' time-on-task. Describe one possible explanation for this link. Are there any alternate interpretations?

11. The model of teaching described in this chapter is strongly teacher centered. For what kinds of goals is a teacher-centered model most desirable? least desirable?

12. We identified some examples of introductory focus in this chapter. Are they also advance organizers? Why or why not?

13. Do all students respond the same way to feedback? Are there some types of feedback that are more effective than others for different groups? How does the type of feedback a teacher gives depend on his or her personality?

## APPLYING IT IN THE SCHOOLS

1. *Allocated Time.* Contact several teachers teaching at the same grade level or in the same content areas. If they are elementary teachers, ask them how much time they devote to different subject-matter areas, and if they are middle or secondary teachers, to topics within their content area. Ask them why they have decided on these allocations. Bring the information back to class. Compare the rationales these teachers offer to those uncovered by researchers (e.g., how much they like the area or topic, how much preparation it requires, and how difficult they perceive it to be for their students). Finally, describe what you personally believe to be an optimal time-allocation plan for the grade or subject, and justify your answer.

2. *Instructional Time.* Observe (or tape) a complete lesson and note the amount of time spent in each of the following categories.

| *Lesson Segment* | *Amount of Time Spent* |
| --- | --- |
| a.  Introductory management | |
| b.  Introduction to lesson | |
| c.  Development (main part of lesson) | |
| d.  Summary | |
| c.  Seatwork or practice | |
| f.  Total | |

3. *Student Engagement.* In this exercise, you will be measuring student engagement through a time-sampling technique. Select four students to observe, two high-achieving and two low-achieving (ask the teacher for help in selecting the students), and seat yourself so that you can observe their faces during the lesson. Focus on each student at 15-second intervals and decide whether the student was attending to the lesson. A *Y* indicates yes, an *N* indicates no, and a question mark indicates that you cannot tell. At the end of the 20-minute observation period, compute averages for each student and the group as a whole.

| *Student A* | *Student B* | *Student C* | *Student D* |
| --- | --- | --- | --- |
| Minute 1 | | | |
| Minute 2 | | | |
| Minute 3 | | | |
| . . . | | | |
| Minute 20 | | | |

a. Were the engagement rates similar for each student? If they varied, suggest a reason why.

b. Did the engagement rates vary during the course of the presentation? If so, why?

c. Were there any specific teacher behaviors that appeared to produce high or low engagement rates? Explain.

d. Were the engagement rates for the high- and low-achieving students different?

e. Observe the same students for 3 days and see if any patterns emerge.

f. Observe several classes (or subjects) taught by the same teacher and see if engagement rates are similar.

g. Select students who are physically close to where the teacher spends most of his or her time during lessons, and compare engagement rates with students farther away.

h. Does the type of activity influence student-engagement rates? Find out when the teacher is going to be using two different types of lessons and observe students during each.

i. Compare your responses with your classmates.

4. *Success Rates.* Observe (or tape) a lesson during an interactive teaching session and count the number of questions asked, the number answered correctly, correctly with prompting, and the number answered incorrectly or not at all. Comment on the success rate in terms of what you have learned in this chapter.

5. *Verbal and Nonverbal Behavior.* This exercise investigates the relative amounts of information gained from verbal and nonverbal channels. Have a class first observe a videotape of a teacher teaching a lesson with the sound off; then, turn the volume on and watch the tape again. As you listen to and watch the videotape, list the nonverbal behaviors that give you clues regarding the following characteristics:

a. Teacher warmth and empathy

b. Enthusiasm

c. Modeling

d. Expectations

Were there any instances when the two separate channels produced incongruent messages?

6. *Enthusiasm.* Identify an "enthusiastic" college teacher by asking your fellow students. Obtain permission to sit in on a class, situating yourself so that you can also observe students. Analyze the teacher's behavior using Collins's (1978) operational definitions, which follow. You will find that you are often inferring some dimension rather than directly observing precise behaviors. This reaction is characteristic of a concept like enthusiasm, which is a high-inference measure.

A. Varied vocal delivery _____

    Notes _____

    _____

B. Animated eyes, eyebrows, eye contact _____

    Notes _____

    _____

C. Head, arms, body gestures _____

    Notes _____

    _____

D. Body movement, position change _____

    Notes _____

    _____

E. Demonstrative facial expressions _____

    Notes _____

    _____

F. Descriptive word selection _____

Notes _____

_____

**G.** Vigorous acceptance of ideas _____

Notes _____

_____

7. *Effective Communication.* Make an audiotape of yourself teaching a lesson. Then, listen to the tape and note when vague, ambiguous terms, mazes, and other distracting speech mannerisms occur. Is there any pattern to their occurrence? Do more of them occur at the beginning or end of a lesson? Do transitions or interruptions affect these speech mannerisms? If possible, teach another lesson to the same group and try to eliminate these distractors.

8. *Student Involvement.* This exercise examines patterns of interaction in a classroom. Observe a class during an interactive teaching session after sketching a seating chart with boxes large enough to allow you to put numbers in them. Code the teacher's first interaction with a student with a 1 in that student's square. The second student called on gets a 2, the third a 3, and so on. You now have a running tally of who gets called on and in what order.

   Is there any pattern to the interactions? Do all students participate? Does location make a difference? Is there any pattern to the sequence of interactions? Discuss your analysis in terms of the teacher expectations research.

9. *Feedback.* Observe a class or make an audiotape of a lesson you have taught. Using the following instrument, note the kind of feedback that follows students' responses to questions for a 10-minute segment of interactive teaching. Then, answer the questions that follow.

| *Question* | *Student Answer* | *Teacher Response* |
|------------|------------------|--------------------|
| 1. | | |
| 2. | | |
| 3. | | |
| 4. | | |
| 5. | | |
| 6. | | |
| 7. | | |
| 8. | | |
| 9. | | |
| 10. | | |

**a.** What is the most common form of teacher response to a student answer?

**b.** Does the teacher verbally acknowledge every response? If not, what effect does this appear to have on students?

**c.** How does the teacher deal with either an incomplete or partial response?

# CHAPTER 5

# Involving Students in Learning

# OVERVIEW

In Chapter 4 we discussed a general instructional model that applies to virtually all learning situations regardless of grade level, content area, or topic. Among the model's components, we found that *student involvement* was an important part of the lesson development phase. That students should be actively involved in their own learning is both intuitively sensible and thoroughly documented by research. Think about some of your own experiences. In which do you learn more—classes in which you and the other students are often asked questions and perhaps given a chance to collaborate with a partner, or those in which the teacher typically gives long lectures? For the latter, many learners—including college students—become inattentive in a matter of minutes.

One of the most practical ways of involving students is through teacher questioning. In addition to promoting involvement, skilled teachers use questioning to reinforce basic skills, stimulate student thought, help students experience success, and enhance self-esteem. It is difficult to overstate the importance of questioning as a teaching skill.

Because active student involvement is so critical, we devote this chapter to strategies teachers can use to promote it in their students. In this process we focus on teacher questioning and student groupwork as mechanisms to promote involvement.

# MAIN IDEAS

## Promoting Student Involvement

*Student involvement* is critical both for learning and motivation.

Teachers can promote involvement by combining individual learning tasks with *student collaboration* and *teacher questioning*.

## Effective Questioning

The ability to question effectively is a critical teaching skill for promoting student involvement.

Questions perform diagnostic, instructional, and motivational functions.

To be effective, questions must be heard, understood, and responded to by *each* student.

Teachers who develop their lessons with questions have students who learn more than those who ask few questions.

*Effective teachers* have *clear goals*, and their questions lead students to the goal.

*Effective teachers* are sensitive to their students; they give students *time to think* about their answers, and they provide *cues* and *prompts* when students are unable to respond.

## Student Groupwork

*Student groupwork* promotes high levels of student involvement and reduces the energy that whole-class activities require of teachers.

*Effective groupwork* requires *clear tasks*, *specified time limits*, *written products*, and *teacher monitoring* to promote effective use of instructional time.

· · · · · · · · · · · · · · · · · · · · · · · · · · · · · · · ·

José Alvarez is a fourth-grade teacher with a class of 30 students ranging widely in ability. The class is labeled average and is composed primarily of lower- to lower-middle-class students. Keith, Don, Gretchen, Jason, and Ginny are the five lowest achievers in his group.

José typically teaches science for 30 minutes each day. In this lesson, he wanted his students to understand the relationship between heat, expansion, and the motion of molecules. The students had studied molecules in earlier lessons, so they were familiar with this concept. He began his activity by displaying two soft drink bottles, two balloons, and a coffee pot full of hot water, as shown in Figure 5.1.

"Now look at these bottles," he began as he held them up. "What can you tell me about them? Keith?"

"You drink out of them."

"Fine, Keith. Beverly?"

"They're sort of green."

"Yes, they are," José smiled. "What else, Elizabeth?"

"They look like they're the same size."

"Yes, indeed, they certainly do. Very good, Elizabeth."

**FIGURE 5.1** Initial Science Demonstration

"What's in the bottles, Nikki?" he went on.

"They're empty."

"Wave your hand in front of your face, Nikki," he smiled. "What do you feel?"

"Well, I feel the air on my face."

"Yes," he enthused. "So what do you think might be in the bottles?"

"Air?"

"Yes, indeed. Very good conclusion, Nikki. What was one of the characteristics of air that we've discussed, Christy?"

"It's all around us," Jason interjected.

"That's right. Air is all around us. Well done, Jason."

"Now look at these balloons," José went on, holding up two balloons for the students to see. "How would you compare the balloons, David?"

"One is red and the other is yellow."

"Yes. Good, David. What else, Rachel?"

"They look like they're made out of rubber."

"Yes, they are rubber balloons. How would you compare their sizes? Michael?"

"They look like they're the same size."

"Good, Michael. They do appear to be the same size. Now let me put the balloons on each of the bottles." With that, José put a balloon over the mouth of each bottle, as shown in Figure 5.2.

"Now look at the balloons and bottles, everyone," he continued. "What did Elizabeth say about the bottles themselves? Cliff?"

"We drink out of them."

"Yes we do," José smiled. "How do the sizes compare? Alfredo?"

**FIGURE 5.2**   Bottles with Balloons on Top

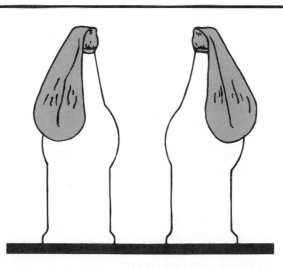

"They're the same."

"Good, Alfredo. We said they were the same size. And how about the balloons, Linda?"

"They were the same size, too?"

"And what is in the bottles, Steve?"

"Air," Steve responded.

"So, now what do we know about the amount of air in each system? Kathy?"

"It's the same."

"And how do we know, Dan?"

". . ."

"What did we say about the sizes of the balloons and bottles, Dan?"

". . ."

"What was one of the things we said about the bottles and balloons?"

"One balloon was red and the other was yellow."

"Good, Dan. Were the sizes the same or different?"

"Same."

"So what do we know about the amount of air in each?"

"It's the same."

"Yes, Dan. Good thinking."

"Now watch what I do." José then placed one of the bottles in the coffee pot and asked, "And what did we say about the amount of air in each of the systems, everyone?"

"IT IS THE SAME," everyone shouted in unison.

"Just watch now," he said with anticipation. As the students watched, the balloon began to rise slowly above the bottle placed in the hot water, as shown in Figure 5.3.

The students began to giggle and titter as they watched. As the balloon popped up, the students were laughing openly, and José laughed with them.

"Now," he said, taking advantage of their interest, "work with your partner, and make as many comparisons as you can of the two bottles. As always, write them down. Work quickly now. You have 3 minutes."

The students, all of whom were sitting next to their partners, turned to each other and immediately went to work. In seconds, a hum of activity could be heard throughout the room as the students began talking, pointing at the two bottles and balloons, and writing statements on their papers. José walked among them as they worked, periodically stopping to make brief comments to individual pairs.

"OK, everyone, all eyes up here," José directed at the end of exactly 3 minutes. He paused a few seconds as the groups stopped their writing and turned their attention to him.

"Good, everyone," he smiled. "Let's see what you came up with. Give us one of your comparisons. Judy?"

"The bottles are the same size."

"Yes, the size of the bottles hasn't changed," José responded, smiling. "And what else? Jim and Gretchen?"

**FIGURE 5.3**   Bottles with Expanded Balloon

"The red balloon is sticking up," Gretchen answered for the pair.

"And what else? Stacy and Albert?"

"We think that the amount of air has increased in the first bottle," Stacy answered.

"Good thought," José smiled. "Now, when you mean *amount* of air, do you mean volume or do you mean mass? . . . Think about it for a moment everyone. . . . OK, what do you think?"

"We think volume."

"Great! Super thinking," José enthused. "Outstanding work. . . . Now, how do the masses compare? What did you and David come up with there, Robin?"

"We think the masses are still the same."

"Excellent thinking again," José smiled and shook his head. "Boy, you people are sharp today."

"Now, let's look at some other things," he continued. "Jim and Gretchen said the red balloon was sticking up. Why do you suppose it is sticking up? Mike?"

"It was heated," Mike responded quickly.

"How do we know it was heated? Ginny?"

"I, er, I didn't hear the question," she answered sheepishly.

"What did I do with this bottle, Ginny?" he asked, holding up the bottle with the red balloon.

"You put it in the coffee pot."

"Yes I did, Ginny. Very good. And how do we know the coffee pot was hot? Rosemary?"

"I saw steam coming off from it."

"Very good observation, Rosemary," he smiled. "So, what can we say happened to the balloon? Jill?"

"It stuck up."

"What else might we say?" he continued, forming semicircles with his hands and spreading them apart. Hesitantly, Jill responded, "It got bigger."

"Yes, excellent, Jill. Now, everyone, I'm going to give you another word for gets bigger. It's called expand. Everyone say expand."

"EXPAND," they all shouted in unison.

"So what happens when we heat something? Deandra?"

"It expands," Deandra responded instantly.

"And what expanded in this case? Toni?"

"The balloon."

"And what else?"

". . ."

"What is in the bottles and balloons?"

"Air," Toni blurted out.

"Good. So, what is expanding in addition to the balloon?"

"The air!" Toni proclaimed.

"Yes! The air is expanding. And what did we say made that happen? Keith?"

"We heated the bottle?"

"So now let's make a statement about heat and expansion. Give it a try. Gary?"

". . ."

"What does heat do to things?"

"It makes them expand," Gary answered finally.

"Good! Now let's write that down." With that, José wrote the statement on the board as he had the class repeat it.

José then brought out two drawings (see Figure 5.4). He established with the students that the arrows in the drawings were there to help visualize air molecules, and the quotation marks around the arrows were there to help visualize the motion of the molecules. He also led students to conclude that the drawing on the left represented the bottle that had been put into the hot water. He reinforced these ideas with his questioning.

**FIGURE 5.4**   Drawings with Molecules

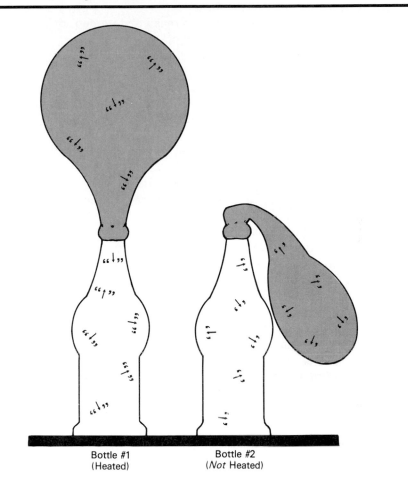

Bottle #1
(Heated)

Bottle #2
(*Not* Heated)

José continued, "Now work again with your partner. As you did with the actual bottles, again make as many comparisons as you can about the two drawings, and write them down. You have 2 minutes. Go ahead right now." Again, the students quickly began talking, pointing at the drawings, and writing on their papers, and José again walked among them as they worked.

At the end of the 2 minutes, José announced, "OK, stop. Everyone, eyes on me."

The students quickly stopped working and turned their attention to the front of the room. José began, "Good, now give us a comparison. Roy and Barbara?"

"The molecules in number one are moving faster than the ones in number two."

"Good! And what did we do to the air in number one? Della and Jim?"

"We heated it!" Della shouted.

"Excellent, Della. So now let's make a statement describing heat and the speed of molecules. Go ahead, Jason."

". . ."

"Do you want me to say that again?" José asked.

"Yes," Jason replied, obviously relieved.

"Let's try and make a statement relating heat and the speed of molecules," he repeated.

". . ."

"Look at these drawings, Jason. What did we say about the molecules in each?"

"They were moving," Jason responded.

"Yes, they were," José smiled patiently. "And which ones were moving faster?"

"Those," Jason responded, pointing to #1.

"Good, Jason," José smiled reassuringly. "And what did we do to the molecules in this one? Vicki?"

". . ."

"Is this the one we put in the hot water, or is it the one that we left out?"

"Put in the hot water."

"Yes. So what did heating the molecules do?"

"Made them move faster."

"Fine, Vicki. Yes! Heat makes molecules move faster," José said, and he wrote 'Heat makes molecules move faster' immediately below his statement, 'Heat makes materials expand.'

"What else did you notice about the molecules in number one and number two? Steve and Kim?"

"We thought the molecules in number one were farther apart than those in number two."

"Yes! Good, both of you. And why do you suppose they're farther apart?"

". . ."

"What did we do to these molecules?"

"We heated them," Kim said shyly after conferring briefly with Steve.

"Good. So what does heating molecules do to them? Kelly?"

"It makes them move farther apart."

"Yes! Now here's a tough one. What did we say *expand* meant? Ginny?"

"Gets bigger!" Ginny enthused after thinking for a few seconds.

"So what actually happens when something expands? David?"

". . ."

"What happens to the molecules in the material?"

"They move."

"Do they move apart or do they move together?"

"Apart."

"So what does *expand* mean, David?" José encouraged.

"The molecules move apart," David smiled as the realization struck him.

"Yes! Exactly! That's excellent thinking, everyone. Now let's review what we've found out today." He erased the first two statements on the board. He then proceeded to help students make these statements:

"Heat makes materials expand."
"*Expand* means the molecules move apart."
"Heat makes molecules move faster."

He saw it was 11:25, so he asked the children to tell him where in the room the air molecules would be moving the fastest. They concluded that over by the window would be the fastest, reasoning that it was the hottest over there. They further decided that the molecules would be farther apart at the ceiling than they would be at the floor. José praised them for their thinking and then finished the lesson.

# STUDENT INVOLVEMENT: A KEY TO LEARNING AND MOTIVATION

As we saw in the overview to this chapter, the need for student involvement is both intuitively sensible and well documented in the research literature. We know from our own experience that we are more motivated and we learn more in classes when the instructor involves us in the learning process. Research into the ways learners process information confirms this experience; they transfer information into their long-term memories more accurately and efficiently when they are put in an active role than they do when learning passively (Eggen and Kauchak, 1992).

Using the case study you have just read as a frame of reference, let's look now at specific strategies teachers can use for involving students in learning activities. In doing so, we focus specifically on two techniques—teacher questioning and student collaboration. While either can be used separately, they are totally compatible and are even more effective when used together, as José Alvarez demonstrated in his teaching. Involving an entire class of students with questioning alone can be done, but it is very demanding. Questioning combined with student collaboration in small groups actively involves more students, resulting in greater learning.

# CLASSROOM QUESTIONS: A STATUS REPORT

Classroom questions are the most widely used instructional strategy in the classroom (Hamilton and Brady, 1991). Research dating back as far as 1912 has highlighted the centrality of questions in classroom procedures. In his study of classrooms at the beginning of this century, Stevens (1912) estimated that 80 percent of classroom time was spent in question and answer recitation and that high school teachers asked an average of 395 questions per day. More recent work supports these figures. Floyd (1960) studied primary grade teachers and found that they asked an average of 348 questions in a typical school day. A study of elementary science activities revealed that teachers used 180 questions in the course of a lesson (Moyer, 1966). A similar investigation of fifth-grade social studies lessons revealed an average of 64 questions per 30 minutes of lesson, or a rate of more than two questions per minute (Schreiber, 1967).

The frequency of teacher questions correlates positively with achievement. Hamilton and Brady (1991) explained this finding in several ways (Good and Brophy, 1991). First, a high number of questions is one indicator of active teaching and of a well-organized and managed classroom. A second reason for the effectiveness of frequent questions is that a large number of verbal questions effectively supplements written materials, allowing students ample opportunity to practice and process new material. The concept of active participation is also relevant here (Pratton and Hales, 1986).

*Active participation* means that instructional activities provide students with the opportunity to learn and practice new content and skills. When actively engaged in learning, students encounter questions and problems and focus their attention on solving and answering these tasks. Question and answer sessions, in which teachers consciously involve all students in the process, are characterized by high involvement and active participation rates.

## FUNCTIONS OF TEACHER QUESTIONS

The pervasiveness of teacher questions in the classroom can also be explained by the specific functions they perform. These functions can be grouped into three broad areas: diagnostic, instructional, and motivational. At any one time, a single question may serve more than one of these functions, but an effective teacher typically has a particular function foremost in mind when he or she asks a question. Let's look at these functions more thoroughly.

As a diagnostic tool, classroom questions allow the teacher to glimpse into the minds of students to find out not only what they know or don't know but also *how* they think about a topic. Recent research on how students learn suggests that the structure of students' existing knowledge is a powerful determinant of how (and whether) new information will be learned, and that often student misconceptions and prior beliefs interfere with the learning of new material (Mayer, 1987; Neale, Smith, and Johnson, 1990). Through strategic questioning, the teacher can assess the current state of student thinking, identifying not only what students know but also gaps and misconceptions.

A second important function that questions perform is instructional. The instructional function focuses on the role that questions play in helping students learn new material and integrate old. For fact and skill learning, questions provide the practice and feedback essential for the development of automaticity. Questions also perform a cueing function, alerting students to the important information in a lesson. Questions are also valuable in the learning of larger organized bodies of knowledge. Toward this goal, questions can be used to review previously learned material to establish a knowledge base for the new material to be learned. In addition, as the new material is being developed, questions can be used to clarify relationships within the content and to make explicit the internal organization of the content being discussed. As we saw in Chapter 4, both question clarity and organization influence not only initial learning but also long-term retention (Cruickshank, 1985; Good and Brophy, 1991).

A third function that classroom questions perform is motivational (Brophy, 1983; Gall, 1984). Through questions, teachers can engage students actively in the lesson at hand, challenging their thinking and posing problems for them to consider. From a lesson perspective, a question at the beginning can be used to capture students' attention and provide a focus for the lesson. In addition, frequent and periodic questions can encourage active participation and provide opportunities in the lesson for continued student involvement. Research in this area shows that student on-task behaviors are highest during teacher-led questioning sessions (Doyle, 1986). Finally, at the individual level, questions can be used to draw wandering students back into the lesson or to provide an opportunity for one student to "shine."

## QUESTIONS: THE STUDENT'S PERSPECTIVE

To be effective, teachers' instructional strategies must have an impact on student thinking. The best planned and executed questioning sequence is worthless if it does not cause students to think.

In answering a teacher question, students engage in five separate operations (Gall, 1984). The first of these is attending: Questions draw students' attention away from the clock, window, and each other and invite them to participate in the lesson. Once attending, students must then decipher the meaning of the question. This task is not always easy; the intent of the question may be clear to the teacher, but unless the question is framed clearly and in consideration of the students' background, the specific information or skill being requested may be lost to students. Once understood, the question should elicit a *covert response* from each student in the class. Ideally, when a question is asked, all of the students in the class should be thinking about the response, and this response should approximate the one the teacher intended. This idea relates to success rates discussed in Chapter 4. Often, teachers' attempts to guide students through higher cognitive processes fail when students respond to a high-level question with a low-level response (Dillon, 1982; Mills, Rice, Berliner, and Rousseau, 1980). This reaction may be due to a lack of clarity in the teacher's question or a lack of experience in answering higher level questions, or both. Optimally, the generation of a covert response should be followed by an attempt to put that private response into words to be shared with others. The additional task of verbalizing an answer helps clarify the content in students' minds. Finally, students generate a revised response in terms of the teacher's reaction to the answer. A correct answer is reinforced; an incorrect answer is modified. This entire process occurs within the span of two or three seconds and is repeated hundreds of times a day in a typical classroom. Figure 5.5 summarizes these processes.

The sequence illustrated in Figure 5.5 is an optimal one. Ideally, all students attend to a question, understand its meaning, generate covert and overt responses,

**FIGURE 5.5**  Student Mental Operations Elicited by Effective Question

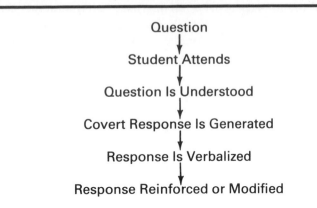

and incorporate the teacher's response into their answer. When this occurs, learning is maximized. However, the realities of the classroom suggest that this ideal is difficult, if not impossible, to approximate. But what kinds of things can teachers do to make their questions as effective as possible?

## Effective Questioning: What Are the Key Components?

Effective questioning depends on two key factors. The first is the teacher having a goal clearly and precisely in mind for the lesson. The difference between *good* and *effective* teachers is that effective teachers do the things good teachers have always done, but in addition, they teach with a specific goal in mind (Berliner, 1985). This goal may not always be written in a plan book, but if asked, the teacher is able to state it clearly and precisely. José knew exactly what he wanted from his students, and he used his questions to guide the students there.

Second, effective teachers adjust their questions to the needs of the students and requirements of the lesson (Duffy, Roehler, and Rackliffe, 1985; O'Keefe and Johnston, 1987). For instance, in virtually every instance when a student was unable to respond, José rephrased the original question or asked another one, as we examine in detail later in this chapter.

In another case, José reacted immediately to Ginny's inattention and called on her to encourage her reinvolvement:

"How do we know it was heated? Ginny?"

"I, er, I didn't hear the question," she answered sheepishly.

"What did I do with this bottle, Ginny?" he asked, holding up the bottle with the red balloon.

"You put it in the coffee pot."

"Yes I did. Very good. And how do we know the coffee pot was hot? Rosemary?"

When he caught Ginny "drifting," José called on her. The sound of her name caught her attention, and realizing that she had not heard the question, José simply rephrased it to guide her to the answer. He got Ginny back into the lesson without admonishing her for her inattention. When this teaching behavior is a pattern, it creates a positive and supportive climate for learners, especially low achievers.

As José demonstrated in his lesson, effective teachers are constantly monitoring their students, and they adapt their questions and intervene based on the students' behavior—both verbal and nonverbal.

Effective questioning is a highly sophisticated set of skills, and you won't become an expert overnight. However, the skills can be developed with practice, and if you persevere, research indicates that—just as aspiring athletes develop their skills—you can develop questioning expertise (Rowe, 1986).

In the following sections, we examine specific aspects of effective questioning:

- Questioning frequency
- Equitable distribution
- Prompting
- Repetition
- Wait-time.

## Questioning Frequency

**Questioning frequency** refers to the number of questions that teachers ask over a period of time, and research indicates that effective teachers ask more questions than do those who are less effective (Eggen and Kauchak, 1992; Hamilton and Brady, 1991; Pratton and Hales, 1986). This is intuitively sensible. Large numbers of questions result in high levels of student involvement, which in turn increases motivation and achievement. In addition, questions help keep students focused on the lesson, they communicate what is most important, and they allow teachers to informally assess student understanding.

## Equitable Distribution

**Equitable distribution** describes teacher-student interaction patterns in which all the students in the class are treated as equally as possible—in this case, called on equally (Kerman, 1979). In Chapter 4, we found that teachers tend to treat students differently based on their expectations of the students, which are demonstrated, in part, by a tendency to call on high-ability students more frequently than on low-ability students. Kerman found that changing these patterns, so all the students were called on equally, resulted not only in higher achievement but also in fewer discipline referrals and a lowered absentee rate.

Consider again the dialogue between José and his students. What do you notice about the distribution of his questions? Among other features, you see that he called on all the students in his class *equally* and by *name*. He had 30 students in the class, and they all responded at least once. (In the actual lesson we observed, each student answered several questions.)

José called on his students whether or not they had their hands up. In typical classroom practice, 65 percent of all teacher questions are undirected, meaning that students who volunteer answers are allowed to answer the questions, and those who don't are allowed to remain passive (McGreal, 1985). This practice correlates negatively with achievement (Anderson, Evertson, and Brophy, 1979; Brophy and Evertson, 1974). The reasons are simple. A pattern of not responding is established, the nonresponders become inattentive and uninvolved, and motivation and achievement suffer.

In contrast, students in José's class knew that they were certain to be called on, and as a result their attention significantly improved. When students "drifted off," José intervened immediately, as illustrated in the segment with Ginny when she was momentarily inattentive.

In a review of the literature in this area, Gage and Berliner (1992) concluded that teachers should call on volunteers infrequently — less than ten to fifteen percent of the time. Think about that figure. It suggests that 85 to 90 percent of all teacher questions should be directed to students who do not volunteer! Equitable distribution communicates that the teacher expects all the students to attend and that each student will be able to answer (or at least to make an attempt). If teachers practice equitable distribution as a pattern, student engagement rates can be increased dramatically, and learning will increase.

While it seems simple, establishing a pattern of calling on all the students in your classes requires effort; it's easier merely to let volunteers answer the questions. Because they've raised their hands, the likelihood of a correct response is higher, eliminating the need for subsequent prompting. However, if you persevere, the results, both in terms of learning and in classroom management, will more than repay your efforts.

**Implementing Equitable Distribution: Questions to Consider**   A number of decisions must be made as a teacher tries to implement equitable distribution. The first of these is sequencing; that is, should you call on a student first and then ask the question or vice versa? Then the issue of how to select a respondent arises; is it better to call on students randomly or use patterned turn-taking? Should "call-outs" be encouraged or discouraged? What about choral responding; does it have a place in the classroom at all? Finally, how do these decisions depend on the content being taught and the students themselves? Let's examine these issues.

*Sequencing: Name and Question.* In general, asking the question first and then identifying a student is preferable to the opposite sequence, and this is the pattern we saw in José's questioning. Asking the question, pausing, and then calling on a specific student communicates that the question is meant for all students and everyone is expected to pay attention and think about the answer. Exceptions to this rule occur for management or motivational reasons. For example, "John, what did we say yesterday about the relationship of Hemingway's early life to his later writing?" can communicate that John ought to refrain from his conversation with a classmate and rejoin the discussion, or that John made a comment yesterday that was especially pertinent to the topic. The fact that this sequence violates the teacher's regular one, as well as the inflection in the voice, communicates the intent of the message.

*Selecting Students.* How do we decide who to call on? As we saw earlier, teachers tend to call on students who volunteer, but this is less effective than calling on both volunteers and nonvolunteers.

The most desirable practice is to call on the students randomly, and expert teachers manage this process by mentally monitoring who they've called on as the lesson proceeds. As the activity develops, if you've lost track of who you've called on, simply ask, "Who have I not called on yet?" When students are in an environment where large numbers of questions are being asked, and the teacher supports the students in their efforts to answer, being called on is desirable, and students will admit it if they haven't been called on (or one of their classmates will point it out). Further, a simple, straightforward question such as "Who haven't I called on?" promotes a comfortable climate of open communication.

An exception to the random selection rule is often noted in the research literature. In studies at the lower elementary level, patterned questions (e.g., up and down rows) resulted in higher achievement than did a random arrangement (Anderson et al., 1979; Brophy and Evertson, 1976). However, the reasons for these differences were that equitable distribution was accomplished in the patterned sequence, while it was *not* in the random arrangement, and the patterned sequence made the class easier to manage.

If teachers are able to manage their classrooms and maintain equitable distribution, a random arrangement is more effective than patterned turns. An alternative to mentally monitoring who has been called on is to use a deck of cards with all of the students' names and to shuffle them at frequent intervals to prevent sequential patterns from occurring. This cumbersome way of distributing questions can be helpful for beginning teachers, but expert teachers rarely use the technique.

*Call-Outs.* A **call-out** is an answer given by a student before the student is recognized by the teacher. We have all been in classes where teachers have said, sometimes pleadingly, "Now, don't shout out answers," or "Don't answer until you're called on." These are efforts to eliminate call-outs.

In general, call-outs should be prevented. (This is accomplished most effectively by establishing and consistently enforcing a rule requiring students to be recognized before answering.) Allowing students to respond without being called on is undesirable because call-outs typically come from the higher achieving segment of the class. These students dominate the interaction, and slower or more reticent students are forced out of the game. In addition, call-outs increase management problems and decrease the amount of time other students have to think about an answer.

However, exceptions to these patterns have been found in studies of achievement with minority students and students from low socioeconomic backgrounds. With these students, who often lack confidence and are reluctant to respond, allowing at least some call-outs has been positively correlated with achievement (Brophy and Evertson, 1976). With high socioeconomic status students who are more motivated and aggressive, call-outs result in shorter thinking time after a question is asked and an unequal distribution of opportunities to respond, both circumstances that relate negatively to achievement.

So here, as with so many other decisions, teacher judgment is necessary. With lower ability and low socioeconomic status students, the teacher may decide to tolerate some call-outs while discouraging them in high socioeconomic status classes. In heterogeneous classes, the decision becomes even more complicated, with the specter of different behavior expectations for some students compared to others. Our suggestion is to minimize call-outs except in small, homogeneously arranged groups. The basic argument here relates to the teacher's sanity and the chaos involved with several students shouting out the answer at the same time. Such classes can be stressful and unpleasant.

*Choral Responses.*  The entire class answering a question at the same time is termed **choral responding.** Choral responses are effective for practicing skills, terms, and facts that should be overlearned and available for immediate recall. Choral responding is commonly used in foreign language classes when students need to repeat words and phrases in the new language. José appropriately called for a choral response when he taught his students the term *expand*, as illustrated in the following segment:

> "Yes, excellent, Jill. Now, everyone, I'm going to give you another word for gets bigger. It's called expand. Everyone say expand."
> "EXPAND," they all shouted in unison.

In this case José was teaching a new term and wanted everyone in the class to say it.

In contrast, choral responses are inappropriate for divergent or higher level questions. Imagine a choral response to a question such as, "Who do you think was our most effective President, and why do you think so?"

The disadvantages of choral responding relate to timing and participation; if all students don't answer at the same time, slower students can hesitate and parrot or mouth the answers of the quicker students. A solution to this problem is the use of a standard expression or signal, such as "Class," that follows a question and signals time for participation. Becker (1977), in his Distar program designed to teach basic reading skills, advocated a blend of choral and individual responding to provide opportunities for both wide participation and diagnosis of individual strengths and weaknesses.

*Open-Ended Questions.*  Look again at the questions José asked in the beginning of his lesson. Throughout the lesson he asked questions such as,

> "Now look at these bottles, . . . What can you tell me about them?"
> "What else?"
> "How would you compare the balloons?"
> "How would you compare their sizes?"

These are called divergent or **open-ended** questions because a wide variety of answers are acceptable. For instance, when José asked Keith to tell him about the bottles, Keith said, "You drink out of them," but he could have as appropriately said that they were the same height, they had writing on them, they were sort of greenish in color, they had a rounded shape, or a variety of other responses.

Open-ended questions exist in two basic types. The first and easiest form of open-ended question is simple **description,** which asks students to make an observation or recall information from a previous lesson. To do this the teacher can ask questions such as the following:

> "Tell me about this."
>> "What do you notice about . . . ?"
>> "What were some of the major ideas that we've discussed so far?"
>> "Let's review a few of the points we made yesterday."

Description questions are an excellent way to begin a lesson, whether it is the introduction to a new topic or the review of an old one, and this is the way José introduced his lesson.

The second type of open-ended questions are **comparisons,** or compare-and-contrast questions, as they are sometimes called. They let the teacher narrow the range of possible student responses while at the same time allowing a variety of acceptable answers. When José asked,

> "How would you compare the balloons?"
>> "How would you compare their sizes?"

he was involved in this process.

Asking questions that do not have specific answers may seem like a waste of time; why don't we merely tell the students or ask more direct questions? They are an excellent tool to promote motivation and involvement. Some other uses include the following:

- They can be asked and answered quickly and easily, making equitable distribution easy to accomplish. It is very difficult to call on all students in a large class without asking some open-ended questions.
- Because students "can't miss," open-ended questions virtually assure high levels of student success, which in turn make students feel safe in attempting to answer. Both safety and success are critical factors for promoting student motivation and involvement (Wlodkowski, 1984) Open-ended questions are particularly effective in working with cultural minorities, who sometimes lack confidence in fast-paced convergent question and answer sessions (Langer, Bartolome, Vasquez, and Lucas, 1990).
- Open-ended questions allow informal diagnosis of students' understanding. For example, suppose a class has recently studied adjectives. The teacher displays the sentence, "Teri moved quickly to remove the hot dish from the stove, and asks, "What can you tell me about the sentence?" If students have mas-

tered the concept, they will identify *hot* as an adjective in one of the first few responses. If they do not, it suggests that they are less aware of the concept than they should be.

- Responding to open-ended questions—particularly comparing and contrasting—is excellent practice in the development of student thinking skills. We discuss this process in more detail in Chapter 9.

The power of open-ended questioning as a tool is reinforced by our own demonstration teaching in the schools. We have seen students who were hostile and visibly refusing to respond at the beginning of a class period begin to volunteer responses to questions by the *end of the same class period*, all because they could see that each student was able to respond successfully. Open-ended questioning was the technique used to induce this change. What a powerful and exciting change in student behavior in a relatively short period of time! Imagine the impact of assured success on participation and motivation over an extended time frame.

Finally, open-ended questions address the objections of teachers who are reluctant to call on nonvolunteers because they are afraid to embarrass the students if they can't respond. Because students are virtually ensured of giving an acceptable response, they can be "put on the spot" without danger of embarrassment or anxiety. When students are put in a situation where they know they will be called on, but they are almost certain of being able to answer, their attention and motivation are sharply increased. We have observed the effectiveness of these techniques at all grade levels and curriculum areas.

There are no hard-and-fast rules that tell teachers how many open-ended questions they should ask. This is a case, again, for teacher judgment. We certainly do not suggest that each student be asked a description question before moving on to comparisons or that each should be asked a comparison question during the course of a lesson. Instead, we recommend that these questions be included strategically in a repertoire of skills, which can be employed according to a teacher's judgment to involve students effectively, to diagnose their background, and to enhance motivation.

In closing this section, let us share an actual experience. In an earlier paragraph we stated that open-ended questions virtually assure high levels of student success, but as you well know, anything can happen in a classroom. We were observing a first-grade teacher who was using open-ended questioning with her students. She held a shoe up for the students to observe, and she began, "Tell me about the shoe." "It's red," Mike responded. The shoe was black. There was no sign of red on it anywhere! As we all know, young children occasionally give "off-the-wall" responses, and the teacher handled this one very well. She simply smiled and said, "The shoe is actually black. Now, Mike, tell me something else about it." Quick thinking.

## Prompting

In the previous section we discussed equitable distribution and emphasized open-ended questioning as a tool for promoting student involvement. Open-ended questions are excellent for that purpose, but they can be used only to a certain point.

Because teachers have specific goals for the lesson, students must supply "right answers" as the lesson moves toward the goal. Their involvement and success is no less important at this point, however, than it is in the beginning, so teachers must have a tool for maintaining successful interaction. **Prompting**—cues teachers provide or other questions they ask when students are unable to answer the original question correctly—is that tool.

Research indicates that prompting in response to students' inability to give correct responses provides more benefit to learning than do other options (Anderson et al., 1979; Stallings, Needels, and Staybrook, 1979) . Our experience in classrooms strongly supports the results of these studies; in fact, prompting may be the most important skill in a teacher's total repertoire. It is hard to overstate the importance of prompting in guiding students toward lesson goals.

José's skill with prompting is illustrated in the following segment taken from our opening case study.

> "What's in the bottles, Nikki?" he went on.
> "They're empty."
> "Wave your hand in front of your face, Nikki," he smiled. "What do you feel?"
> "Well, I feel the air on my face."
> "Yes," he enthused. "So what do you think might be in the bottles?"
> "Air?"
> "Yes, indeed. Very good conclusion, Nikki. . . ."

Here, José asked a question for which only one answer—air— was acceptable. However, Nikki said the bottles were empty. He then provided a simple cue by asking her to wave her hand in front of her face, which led her to conclude that air was in the bottles. In the last example, José prompted with a cue. Now let's look at another segment where he prompted by asking additional questions to lead a student to an acceptable answer.

> "So, now what do we know about the amount of air in each system? Kathy?"
> "It's the same."
> "And how do we know, Dan?"
> ". . ."
> "What did we say about the sizes of the balloons and bottles, Dan?"
> ". . ."
> "What was one of the things we said about the bottles and balloons?"
> "One balloon was red and the other was yellow."
> "Good, Dan. Were the sizes the same or different?'
> "Same."
> "So what do we know about the amount of air in each?"
> "It's the same."
> "Yes, Dan. Good thinking."

When Dan was unable (or unwilling) to answer José's original question, he simply rephrased it by asking, "What do we know about the sizes of the bottles and balloons?" Usually, this prompt would be sufficient, since it was established earlier in the lesson that the sizes were the same. However, Dan still didn't respond, and when he didn't, José quickly moved to an open-ended question, "What was one of the things we said about the bottles and balloons?" When Dan commented on the colors, which was irrelevant to the goal, José merely refocused him by asking if the sizes were the same or different.

**Prompting and Lesson Goals**   The key to successful prompting is having clear lesson goals in mind. José knew exactly what he wanted his students to understand, and this goal guided him as he "thought up" his prompting questions. If lesson goals are clear in your own mind, and you practice, the process of prompting can become automatic over time.

**A Prompting Sequence**   Developing skill in prompting takes practice and effort, and you won't become an expert immediately. Every prompt is a response to a student answer, which means prompting can only be practiced in the context of a lesson, and you must be able to "think on your feet." However, as you acquire expertise, you will find it most rewarding. It's fun to help someone give an answer or form a conclusion that a moment earlier they were unable to give.

As you study this section, keep two ideas in mind. First, it is important to remember that you may not be able to prompt the student who didn't answer correctly all the way to the answer originally intended. A secondary but important affective goal is to get an *acceptable* and *appropriate* answer from the student. For instance, when José prompted Dan by asking, "What was one of the things we said about the bottles and balloons?" and Dan answered, "One balloon was red and the other was yellow," he could have turned to another student with his next question, since Dan had given an acceptable and appropriate answer.

In a prompting sequence, each question or cue is more leading than the previous one, and the thinking required by the students is reduced until they are finally put in a situation where they can't miss. This sequence is illustrated in Figure 5.6.

José illustrated each of the steps in the sequence as he prompted Dan. Let's look at them in a bit more detail now.

*The Alternate Question.*   The first option a teacher has when a student is unable to give an acceptable response is to ask the original question in a different way, ask another related question that is simpler, or give a directive that leads to a successful

**FIGURE 5.6**   A Prompting Sequence

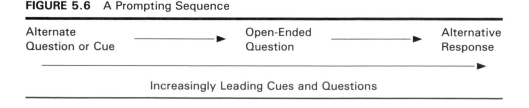

response. This is what José did when he told Nikki to wave her hand in front of her face, and this is again what he did when he asked Dan what he knew about the sizes of the balloons and bottles.

An alternative question helps in case the students misunderstand the original question. We all know what we want when we ask a question, but our intent may not be obvious to students. Research supports this contention (French and Maclure, 1981). The simplest solution is to rephrase the question in different terms. The following are examples:

*First Question:* How are plot and characterization related in this novel?

*Follow-Up:* How does the development of the story line help us understand the major actors in the story?

*First Question:* How does the carrying power of a river vary with the speed of its current?

*Follow-Up:* Will a fast river carry more or less silt than a slow one?

As in the second example, an effective prompt sometimes rephrases the question in more concrete terms. In addition, effective prompts often narrow the range of response options, as in the following examples:

| Original Question | Reformulation |
|---|---|
| What are these people doing? | What are they planting? |
| What kind of an elephant is this? | Was he happy or sad? |
| What else did you see? | Did you see any furniture? |
| How did they travel? | Did they go by air or water? |
| What color was it? | Was it a bright or subdued color? |

(Adapted from French and Maclure, 1981)

In each of these reformulations, the teacher attempted to help students by not only rephrasing the question but also making the question easier by making the answer more obvious. This tactic serves two functions. From the individual student's perspective, it takes the pressure off the nonresponding students by making the answering task easier. From a lesson perspective, it not only approaches the content in a slightly different way but also helps to maintain the continuity and thrust of the lesson.

As another example, consider the following segment, in which a teacher is guiding the students to an understanding of adjectives.

*Teacher:* Look at the following sentence: "The heavy-metal band made an overwhelming noise." What is an example of an adjective in that sentence?

*Student:* [No response.]

*Teacher:* What did the band do?

*Student:* It made a noise.

> *Teacher:* What kind of noise?
>
> *Student:* Overwhelming.
>
> *Teacher:* So what word describes noise?
>
> *Student:* Overwhelming.
>
> *Teacher:* So now what is an example of an adjective?
>
> *Student:* Overwhelming.

Obviously, prompting is contextual, and there is no single prompting sequence that is necessarily better than any other. You probably can think of other sequences of questions that would lead the students to the same conclusion, and you may think that they would be better than the one presented here. If so, excellent!

Notice also that the teacher could have turned to another student anytime after the student first said, "It made a noise," since this was an acceptable and appropriate response.

*Open-Ended Questions.* We saw in the segment with José and Dan that Dan still didn't respond when José asked an alternate question. He then asked Dan to identify something that they had originally said about the bottles and balloons, which was an open-ended question. In using open-ended questions as prompts, either simple descriptions or comparisons are excellent tools.

*Alternative Response.* A more extreme form of comparison question, called alternative response, gives students two options, one of which is better than the other. José used this technique when he asked Dan if the sizes were the same or different. This question put Dan in a virtual "can't miss" situation, so his success was assured.

In studying these illustrations, you may have thought, "Isn't some of this [José's extra effort to get acceptable answers from a student like Dan] a waste of time, and won't the rest of the students become bored?"

The answer is no, for two reasons. First, as we saw at the beginning of the case study, Dan is one of the lowest achievers in José's class, so helping him experience success is even more critical than it is with José's higher achievers. Students such as Dan are often very reluctant to respond and will rarely if ever volunteer. This pattern of nonresponding may have existed for years, and it is extremely difficult to break. One solution is to call on the students directly and to stay with them until they answer.

Second, the episode with Dan took little time; the entire prompting sequence was completed in less than 10 seconds. Ten seconds or less is a good rule of thumb, and this is the reason José quickly reverted to an open-ended question when Dan didn't respond to his first prompt.

**Alternatives to Student-Centered Prompting**  In the previous sections, we emphasized affective concerns and the importance of student involvement. However, when excessive prompting occurs, lesson pace and momentum may suffer. When this happens, the teacher can decide to insert supplementary information to steer the direction of the lesson. Consider the following excerpt, taken from an actual fifth-grade classroom.

> *Teacher:* "What we're going to talk about today is the punctuation that tells when someone is speaking. How do we know, when we are reading, that someone is speaking?"
>
> *Student:* "When it is has a . . . um . . . two parentheses around them."
>
> *Teacher:* "All right." The teacher draws a set of quotation marks on the chalkboard. "These are called. . . . Does anybody know what these are called?"
>
> *Student:* "Commas."
>
> *Teacher:* "Not commas. Not when they're up in the air like this."
>
> *Student:* "Brackets."
>
> *Teacher:* "Not brackets. These are brackets." The teacher draws a pair of brackets on the chalkboard.
>
> *Student:* "Parentheses."
>
> *Teacher:* "Not parentheses. These are up in the air above the words . . ."
>
> The teacher points to the words within the quotation marks.
>
> *Student:* "Oooh, ooh, oooh! Quotation marks!"
>
> *Teacher:* "Perfect. These are quotation marks. And quotation marks, when you run across them in a story, tell you that someone is speaking directly."
>
> (Duffy, Roehler, Meloth, and Vavrus, 1985, p. 10)

Note how the teacher's response builds on the student's answer, assessing areas of misunderstanding and clarifying areas of understanding. The way in which the teacher responds to a student answer not only provides feedback about the adequacy of the student's reply but can also set the direction for subsequent interactions.

For example, with a correct answer, the teacher not only can affirm the correctness of the answer but also can stress important aspects of the answer:

> *Teacher:* Can anyone give me an example of a mammal?
>
> *Student:* A dog's a mammal because it gives birth to its young live.
>
> *Teacher:* Good, Johnny, live birth is one of the essential characteristics of mammals. Let's talk about that one for a while. . . .

In addition to verifying that an answer is correct, the teacher can add more information, explain the response more fully, or frame the response in a larger context. All of these strategies improve the informational quality of the response (Duffy, Roehler, and Rackliffe, 1985; Gage, 1978). In a similar way, a teacher's response to an incorrect or partially correct answer provides the teacher with the opportunity to (1) ignore the incorrect part of the answer, (2) emphasize the correct part, and (3) prompt for the part of the answer that was not given.

The point is that teachers do not need to be afraid of steering the direction of the lesson through the interjection of comments or additional information as they prompt their students. The teacher knows where the lesson should go; responses to student answers provide one opportunity to steer the lesson in that direction.

## Repetition Questions

In Chapter 4, we discussed the concept of emphasis and identified repetition as one type. A very effective form of emphasis is a **repetition question,** which simply asks students to respond to a question that has been asked earlier in the lesson. Repetition questions have an advantage over typical statements of repetition provided by the teacher, because in addition to providing emphasis and academic focus, they help maintain interaction between teacher and students while providing the teacher with a quick estimate of whether they "got it" earlier. We have all had the experience of "getting lost" occasionally as a teacher develops a topic, and while this problem is impossible to avoid, it can be arrested with frequent repetition.

The following segment illustrates José's use of the technique.

"Now, look at the balloons and bottles, everyone," he continued. "What did Elizabeth say about the bottles themselves? Cliff?"

"We drink out of them."

"Yes, we do," José smiled. "How do the sizes compare? Alfredo?"

"They're the same."

At this point in the lesson José wanted to emphasize that the bottles were the same size, and he asked Cliff what Elizabeth had said about them. The need for repetition is illustrated by Cliff's response, "We drink out of them," suggesting that he had lost academic focus. Without the repetition, Cliff, and probably others, would have been uncertain about where the lesson was headed.

José used repetition extensively, and some might even conclude that he used it excessively. This, of course, is a matter of judgment, but it is clearly better to refocus students too often than not often enough. Our experience in working with teachers and public school students indicates that repetition is not merely a positive teacher action but is, in fact, critical in helping students follow the direction of complex lessons.

## Wait-Time

What's the square root of 256? Quick! Some of you probably answered the question immediately, while others fidgeted with a paper and pencil first. Still others may have seen the "Quick!" and given up immediately.

This problem is analogous to situations that occur in classrooms in all content areas and at all levels. Research indicates that teachers, after asking a question, typically wait less than one second for students to respond before interrupting, prompting, giving the answer themselves, or calling on another student (Rowe, 1974, 1986). This pause between a question and a teacher interruption or interjection is called **wait-time** and represents the extent to which teachers provide students with an opportunity to think. José employed wait-time with nearly all of his questions. When students responded slowly or were unable to respond, he gave them ample time before he intervened.

The research on wait-time began with the classroom observations of Mary Budd Rowe, who was originally interested in the quality of discourse in science lessons. In observing classrooms at both the elementary and secondary levels, she saw a preponderance of drill-like questioning strategies that she likened to "inquisition-type" interrogation. In most of the classrooms observed, Rowe found that, in addition to typically waiting less than a second after a question, teachers also "cut off" students' responses rather than letting them present their answers as fully as possible. Unfortunately, both of these problems are more pronounced when students are perceived as low achievers.

Rowe further found that the pattern of short wait-times occurred at all school levels, from elementary to college classrooms, and in varied settings, from museum instructional programs (Marsh, 1978) to special education classes for both gifted and talented and people with mental disabilities (Korinek, 1985; Lee, 1985; Rowe, 1986). Cross-cultural studies also indicate that the phenomenon is not unique to American classrooms (Chewprecha, Gardner, and Sapianchai, 1980; Tobin, 1983). However, if you're aware of this tendency and make a conscious effort to give students more time to think, you can readily improve the use of this simple skill. Both you and your students will quickly become comfortable with the brief periods of silence that occur when you wait as they consider their answers.

An ideal pattern is illustrated in Figure 5.7.

A number of benefits are derived from lengthening wait-time. Rowe (1974, 1986) found that wait-times shorter than 3 seconds did not make a substantive difference in either teacher behaviors or student answers, but when the waiting period was extended beyond 3 seconds, teacher behavior and student performance were both improved. The benefits, which are very impressive, include the following:

1. Lessons are smoother and more focused (Rowe, 1986).
2. Teachers become more responsive to students by matching the wait-time to the difficulty of the question, improving equitable distribution, and increasing participation from minority students (Rowe, 1974, 1975).

**FIGURE 5.7** Effective Use of Wait-Time

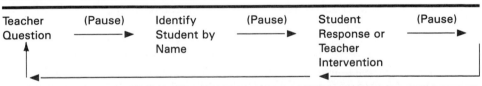

3. The length and quality of student responses increase, including more statements of inference with supporting evidence and more speculative thinking (Anderson, 1978; Rowe, 1986).

4. Failures to respond are reduced, and the variety of students participating voluntarily increases (Tobin, 1987). The number of disciplinary interruptions by the teacher decreases, and students are more actively involved in the lessons.

5. Finally, and perhaps most importantly, increased wait-times result in increased performance on subsequent tests in classrooms, ranging from kindergarten through college (Tobin, 1987; Tobin and Capie, 1982).

As with any skill or procedure, wait-time must be implemented with professional judgment. Our purpose in studying the research is to understand why some actions and behaviors are more desirable than others. With this understanding comes the ability to make considered decisions about the application of techniques and skills.

In the case of wait-time, the reasons for its effectiveness are simple. As the teacher waits longer, students are given more time to think and integrate their knowledge into a larger framework. In the cases of drill and practice, activities in which overlearning and automaticity are desired (such as multiplication facts), prompt and quick answers are desirable (Rosenshine and Stevens, 1986). In these activities, long wait-times would be undesirable.

Teachers sometimes argue that the use of wait-time puts shy students on the spot, but our experience doesn't support this concern. When a pattern of waiting is established so students see that the teacher waits for everyone, anxiety is eliminated quickly. As a climate of support is established in which all students are called on, and they all know that the teacher will help them provide an acceptable answer through prompting, lengthened wait-times serve to enhance the overall benefits to the students.

However, for teachers still uneasy about implementing the practice of longer wait-times in their classes, a practical solution to this potential problem is to introduce an "I pass" option to students. Researchers found that students who exercised this choice were 70 percent more likely later to reenter the discussion spontaneously than they were under regular classroom conditions (Rowe, 1986).

## Questioning: High- versus Low-Level Questions

We closed the last section with the suggestion that the kind of question affects the amount of time a teacher should wait for a response. This observation leads to a related issue: How does the level of teacher question affect achievement? In this section, we consider the benefits of low-level questions (e.g., "Who wrote *Hamlet*?) versus high-level questions ("Why is Shakespeare's *Hamlet* considered a tragedy, in the classical sense of the term?").

As we've already discussed, success is a major variable affecting student achievement. Effective teachers promote high levels of student success with their questions, assignments, and homework. We have also found that students need to be about 90 percent successful on homework and seatwork for them to gain the most benefit, and a success rate of over 80 percent is desirable in questioning episodes (Brophy and Good, 1986; McGreal, 1985). This high percentage for questions is important for active involvement as well as motivation; if questions are too hard to answer, most students will soon stop trying.

Question level interacts with success rate. Because low-level questions are easier to answer than high-level questions, should teachers ask more of them? Asking questions such as these is like asking, "Is a hammer better than a saw?" Better for what? Let's look at some research.

Some studies have found a positive and significant correlation between higher level questions and achievement (Redfield and Rousseau, 1981), while others found no relationship between the level of teacher questions and student achievement (Rosenshine and Furst, 1973; Winne, 1979), and still others have found a negative correlation between high-level questions and achievement (Dillon, 1981; Stallings, 1975). How might these contradictory findings be resolved?

The answer is actually quite simple, and it relates to the teacher's goal. Presumably, the goal is appropriate for the topic, the age of the students, and their backgrounds, so the goal will drive the level of questions. For instance, if the goal is fact-level achievement with young children, such as knowing multiplication facts, a high percentage of low-level questions is appropriate. On the other hand, for more complex goals, such as understanding the impact of Columbus's discovery of the new world, more high-level questions will be required. Students with limited backgrounds about a topic will—at least initially—be asked many low-level questions, and the number of high-level questions will increase as their background improves.

This is the only sensible approach to question level. In the complexities of teacher-student interaction, teachers don't consciously decide, "I will now ask a high-level question," or "It is now the time for a low-level question." This approach is both fragmenting for the lesson and energy consuming for the teacher. The solution is to have a clear and precise goal in mind prior to the lesson and to be alert, sensitive, and responsive to students as the lesson proceeds.

This was illustrated in José's work with his students. As we saw earlier in this chapter, his goal was very clear; he knew exactly what he wanted from the students. The responses of the students and his goal, rather than preconceived decisions about level, guided his questioning. For example, he began his lesson with low-level questions—simple descriptions and comparisons. However, knowing that he wanted to establish and confirm that the two systems were the same size, he asked a much higher level question when he asked Dan how he knew the amount of air was the same in each system. (Note also that José didn't reserve his higher level questions for his high achievers. All students were treated equally.) When he called on Dan, he was not thinking, "I will now ask a high-level question." Instead, he was working toward a goal, which we've already seen in effect when José prompted Dan. This goal-driven flexibility is the essence of expert teacher questioning.

As we saw in Chapter 3, Bloom's Taxonomy can be a useful planning tool, helping teachers to sequence objectives as well as lessons. It can also help teachers sequence their questions in a meaningful way, using each question as a foundation for later ones. This sequencing value comes from the hierarchical nature of the taxonomy (Bloom et al., 1956).

# Bloom's Taxonomy: A Sequential Questioning Strategy

Bloom's taxonomy is a hierarchical classification system based on the cognitive processing demands placed on students. Its development was pioneered by Benjamin Bloom (1956), thus the name. Though more than 30 years old, the taxonomy has been used in a variety of settings to analyze objectives, classroom questions, text problems, exercises, and test items. Its value in structuring classroom questions centers on its hierarchical structure.

*Hierarchical* means that the upper levels are dependent on and subsume the lower. This characteristic is important for questioning strategies because it requires that teachers build an informational base at the lower levels before proceeding to higher ones.

Let us illustrate these ideas by looking at the six levels in the taxonomy and considering how they function in a classroom setting.

*Knowledge.* The knowledge category, the lowest in Bloom's taxonomy, helps build an informational base for subsequent questions. Processes involved in the knowledge category include recognition and recall. Some examples of knowledge-level questions include the following:

Who wrote *Uncle Tom's Cabin*?
What is the chemical symbol for iron?
How many minutes in a basketball game?

*Comprehension.* Comprehension requires processing information so the meaning is clear. If the meaning of information being taught isn't clear, then the teacher needs to slow down or even back up to make sure that students understand. Comprehension is broken down into the subcategories of translation, interpretation, and extrapolation. Students show that they comprehend something when they can translate it into a different form (e.g., verbally describe numerical data presented in graph form), interpret it (e.g., explain why a phenomenon occurs), or extrapolate it (e.g., project a trend beyond the data given). Having students provide examples is another type of comprehension question. Comprehension questions attempt to determine if students understand information in a meaningful way. For example,

Can you tell us, in your own words, the major events in the story so far?
The book says rust occurs when iron is oxidized. What does that mean?
Who can find an example of an oxymoron in our poem?

*Application.* The third level of Bloom's taxonomy asks students to take some information they have learned and apply it to a new situation. Solving new or novel word problems in math would be an example. The process of application actually occurs in two phases. In the first, some abstraction, formula, equation, or algorithm is learned; in the second phase, students encounter a new situation or problem and are asked to apply the previously learned information. Teachers who try to get students to apply information at a later date verify that this second phase is a difficult one. Practice is essential here, and classroom questions provide an excellent opportunity for this practice. For example,

> Who can apply what we've learned about sonnets and finish this poem?
>
> Now, we're trying to find the length of this diagonal line. Any ideas? What formula should we use?
>
> So, we want the fish to be crisp on the outside but not overdone on the inside. How should we cook it?

Notice how in each of these examples students are being asked to use or apply information they've acquired previously.

*Analysis.* Analysis-level questions develop students' ability to take apart some complex phenomenon to show how it works. The medium involved in the analysis will vary with the content area involved. In English, it could involve the examination of a speech, a poem, or a book and some type of explanation of how the work holds together and how the different components add to the power of the work. In the area of art, the process of analysis could focus on a painting and show how various components such as color, line, and texture interact to produce an effect. Similar examples occur in every area of the curriculum in which student understanding of something is dependent on an understanding of how the interrelated components or parts work together.

> Let's write down the major historical events that have occurred in the Middle East. Then let's ask how these are interrelated and why we are where we are today.
>
> Let's look at this table and try to determine why it's so sturdy and why it has lasted so long.
>
> Who can take this paragraph and explain why it is such a powerful way to start this paper?

*Synthesis.* Synthesis questions are different from those in the other levels in several important ways. As opposed to the other levels, which focus more on analytical skills, the synthesis category focuses on creativity. In addition, the synthesis category is product oriented; there is typically a tangible product that is the result of the synthesis operation. Although most often associated with the fine arts areas of art and literature, synthesis questions also have applications in other areas. For example, creativity can be a central dimension in the design of a science experiment. In the area of home economics, synthesis-level skills can focus on clothes or food preparation. In other vocational areas, creativity can be a central component of woodworking and other vocational classes. Note how each of these questions asks students to be creative in producing some product or plan.

> Okay, we know that garbage is a major problem for big cities. What are some creative ways to solve this problem?

Remember, we're on a limited budget for this meal. What are some ways we can stretch our dollars and still produce an exciting menu?

You've viewed the first half of the game on videotape. What would you do differently in the second half to turn your team around? Be creative.

*Evaluation.* The highest level of Bloom's taxonomy is evaluation, which involves judging the merit or worth of some object or work. The process of evaluation occurs in two steps: The first is the establishment of some criteria, and the second is the application of these criteria to some object or idea. For example, in social studies, we can ask students to evaluate a proposed solution to world hunger. This process would involve first some description of the specifics of the problem — givens, resources, and limitations to work with — and then an analysis of the extent to which the proposed solution addresses these parameters. In literature, students can evaluate a written work, describing its strengths and weaknesses. In other areas, such as physical education and home economics, students can evaluate a game plan or a plan of operation such as a menu. Some examples of evaluation questions include the following.

How well did the North use its resources in the Civil War?

Was Hemingway a great American writer? When you answer that, you'll have to define greatness first.

We've read several theories about why the dinosaurs disappeared from the earth. Which makes the most sense? Why?

**The Taxonomy: A Classroom Example**    The following is an excerpt of a teacher using Bloom's taxonomy to structure a lesson on Shakespeare's *Romeo and Juliet*. Note how the teacher uses lower levels of the taxonomy to serve as a foundation for higher levels. To help you do this, we've labeled the level of the question in brackets.

Lynn Bell's junior English class had been reading Shakespeare's *Romeo and Juliet* for several weeks. Although they had known it was a tragedy, the class was disturbed at the gory ending. Lynn was trying to get them to pull it all together and to view the play in the larger context of a tragedy.

*Lynn:* Class, it's been a long weekend, so let's review some of the major characters in the play and try to remember some of the major events. [K] Someone? Jack?

*Jack:* Well, the most important characters were Romeo and Juliet. They fell in love, and that's how all the trouble started.

*Lynn:* Good, Jack. That's a good starting point. Let's follow up on that. What houses did they belong to? [K] Sandy?

*Sandy:* Juliet was a Capulet and Romeo was a Montague.

*Lynn:* Okay, now why is that information important to the play? [C] Anyone? Cassy?

*Cassy:* Because these two houses had been feuding for a long time.

*Lora:* And, in terms of Romeo and Juliet, they shouldn't have fallen in love.

*Lynn:* Good. Now let's return to an idea we discussed briefly earlier. What is a tragedy? **[K]** Shawn?

*Shawn:* It's a story that ends unhappily?

*Lynn:* Anything else? **[K]** Franco?

*Franco:* The people in it can't help what's happening.

*Lynn:* Why is that important? **[C]** Brad?

*Brad:* Because the people in the audience can see what's happening but the characters in the play can't. They're just kind of swept along by the events.

*Lynn:* Any other characteristics of a tragedy? **[K]** Pam?

*Pam:* In my notes, it says there is often "growth toward knowledge."

*Lynn:* Good note taking, Pam. What does that mean? **[C]**

*Pam:* Beats me. I just wrote it down.

*Lynn:* Who can help her out? Did growth toward knowledge occur in this play? **[C]** Ken?

*Ken:* Well, at the end the Montagues and Capulets got together and agreed to stop the feuding.

*Lynn:* Excellent, Ken. Now let's take this one step farther. Romeo and Juliet got married. Was it Act II, Scene 5? **[K]** Scene 6, okay. Now I want each of you to take a few minutes to devise another ending for the story that would still make it a tragedy. **[App]** When you're done with that, we'll share these with the rest of the class and they'll have to decide if your ending qualifies as a true tragedy. **[An]**

Let us take a few moments to comment on the lesson. First, note how the teacher began with knowledge-level questions, and, after establishing a factual base, proceeded to comprehension questions that checked for understanding. Then, after she felt confident that her students understood the concept of tragedy, she asked them to apply this information to develop a different ending. Finally, the lesson ended with an analysis question, asking students to examine one another's new endings to determine if these were truly tragedies.

Actual classroom lessons do not proceed this smoothly. They will progress in fits and starts, and the teacher will need to exercise that flexibility stressed earlier, adjusting questions to the background of students and the momentum of the lesson. The lesson recorded here was provided as a prototype so that you could see the progression of ideas.

Though somewhat unrealistic, the lesson did illustrate several important ideas. One is the value of the taxonomy as a guide to sequencing questions. A second related idea is the importance of using lower level questions to (1) involve a number of students, (2) establish an informational base, and (3) warm up the class at the beginning of the lesson. Also, note that at the end of the example as the teacher asked an application question requiring more thinking, she provided the class with the necessary wait-time (several minutes) to apply the information they had learned.

Finally, if the lesson had continued, how might the teacher have used the synthesis and evaluation categories to think about the play further? We offer these as possible alternatives but invite you to construct your own.

### Synthesis

Write a version of *Romeo and Juliet* in the twentieth century. Find a present-day story with the potential for being a tragedy. Flesh out the story in enough detail so that your thinking is evident.

### Evaluation

Some people call *Romeo and Juliet* a love story; others consider it to be a tragedy. Which do you believe is more correct and why?

Some critics call Shakespeare a master of settings, getting the most from his plays by having the scenes set in dramatic places. Do you agree with this assessment? Defend your answer with examples from *Romeo and Juliet.*

Bloom's taxonomy can provide a useful conceptual tool to ask higher level questions. It can help us sequence these questions, building on prior knowledge and using previous skills as the foundation for later ones. It can also help us understand why students have problems with questions requiring higher level answers. Finally, it can serve as a reminder of the breadth and variety of cognitive tasks available to us as we involve our students in the process of thinking. We'll return to the taxonomy in Chapter 9 when we discuss the topic of thinking skills, but for now we turn to student collaboration as a vehicle for promoting student involvement.

# PROMOTING INVOLVEMENT: STUDENT COLLABORATION THROUGH GROUPWORK

A kindergarten teacher is teaching her students basic shapes. After explaining and illustrating each with cardboard shapes, she divides the class into groups of two and asks each group to find examples of circles, squares, and triangles in the classroom. When the class comes back together, students share their examples.

A junior high math teacher is teaching how to solve word problems involving areas of different geometric shapes. She divides the class into teams of three students and asks each team to solve the next problems. The teams take turns at the board explaining how they solved the different problems.

A senior high English teacher is reviewing literary devices like simile, metaphor, personification, and alliteration. He assigns a scene from Shakespeare's *Julius Caesar* and asks students in groups of two to identify as many of these devices as they can. The whole class compares their findings after 15 minutes.

In the previous section of this chapter, we discussed ways expert teachers use questioning to involve their students in learning. Asking many questions, calling on all students equally, prompting, repetition, and wait-time were discussed as ways to induce and maintain this involvement.

These techniques are excellent, but they are very demanding, requiring both energetic and skilled teachers. In addition, because of the nature of questioning in crowded classrooms, it is all too easy for quiet or less confident students to become uninvolved. Unfortunately, in classrooms of 25 to 30 students, students soon learn that the odds of being called on are small, and the less attentive ones often drift off. To reduce some of this demand and elicit the participation of all students, other procedures can be employed without sacrificing student learning. This is most effectively accomplished with student **groupwork,** which involves "students working together in a group small enough so that everyone can participate on a task that has been clearly assigned" (Cohen, 1986, pp. 1–2). The purpose of groupwork is to provide opportunities for each student to become actively involved in the thinking task at hand.

In this section we focus on simple collaboration as a form of groupwork. We discuss cooperative learning as a more sophisticated form of groupwork in Chapter 10.

## Elements of Effective Groupwork

To begin our discussion of student collaboration, consider again the teaching episodes at the beginning of this section. In each the teacher presented a cognitive task to students that built on and reinforced lesson content. In each the teacher broke the class into manageable groups and required that each member become actively involved in the learning task at hand. Finally, the teacher provided feedback by discussing the products of the groups. The combination of these elements—focus on lesson content, active involvement, and feedback—combine to make groupwork effective.

José Alvarez also employed groupwork in his science lesson.

"Now . . . work with your partner, and make as many comparisons as you can of the two bottles. As always, write them down. Work quickly now. You have 3 minutes."

The students, all of whom were sitting next to their partners, turned to each other and immediately went to work.

José used the same strategy later in his lesson when he asked groups of students to compare the drawings of the molecules in the bottles. Let's examine more closely how these different teachers combined groupwork into an effective lesson.

## Organizing and Conducting Groupwork Activities

The goal of groupwork is to provide opportunities for all students to become involved in the learning task. The assignment of the task by the teacher provides cognitive focus; the fact that the task is done within small groups of students provides opportunities for student interactions, which can be both instructionally and motivationally beneficial. Effective use of groupwork requires careful planning and organization to make sure that the task and the interactions are beneficial. If the process isn't well organized, a great deal of instructional time can be lost in the transitions to and from the groupwork. Goals and directions to the students need to be very clear to prevent the activities from disintegrating into aimless "bull sessions."

Suggestions for planning and organizing effective groupwork activities include the following:

- Train students in groupwork with short, simple tasks, such as José used with his students. Have students practice moving into and out of the groups quickly.
- Seat group members together prior to the groupwork activity. José did this, and the transition from the whole-class activity to student groups and back again was accomplished with a minimum of disruption.
- Give students a clear and specific task to accomplish in the groups.
- Specify the amount of time students are allowed to accomplish the task (and keep it short). José gave his students 3 minutes in their first groupwork activity and 2 minutes in the second.
- Require that the students produce a product as a result of the groupwork (such as the papers with comparisons written on them that José's students produced).
- Monitor the groups while they're involved in the activity.

Effective use of student groups requires that all of the elements be employed. For instance, seating students together prevents loss of instructional time in transitions. Clear directions, a specific and short time allotment, a required written product, and monitoring all help keep students on-task and academically focused.

The process of repeatedly moving back and forth from groupwork to whole-class responses requires considerable logistical planning. One way to manage the process is to provide a signal such as turning off the lights, or a clacker that makes a noise loud enough for all to hear. Another is for you to raise your hand as a signal to reconvene, and students are taught to raise their own hands and stop talking when they see this signal. Students need to stop immediately when they see or hear the signal, or valuable instructional time will be lost in the repeated transitions from whole-class to groupwork and back again.

## Working in Pairs: Introducing Groupwork

The simplest form of groupwork involves organizing students in pairs and giving each pair a cognitive task to accomplish. This strategy, which Kagan (1989) called Think-Pair-Share, encourages students to think about content, compare their thoughts with their partner, and share their answer with the whole group. José used this strategy in his lesson, as did the elementary and high school teachers in the episodes at the beginning of this section.

Simple collaboration in pairs has several positive features.

- It is easy to learn. For example, students can learn to make comparisons in visual displays with little training.
- Working in pairs encourages each member of the pair to contribute, and the likelihood of one or more members of a group being left out is less than it would be in groups of three or more.
- For purposes of equitable distribution, the class is effectively cut in half. Involvement is high when the pairs are working, and teachers have to call on only half as many students as they would during a whole-class discussion, since each is speaking for a pair. This is much less demanding than trying to call on each student in a class individually, and the need for prompting is reduced, since the students are reporting results from their groupwork.

Another strategy to employ in working with groups is called "pairs check" (Kagan, 1989). In this arrangement, pairs of students are provided with handouts containing a number of problems (e.g., math, capitalization, or punctuation problems in English). Students on the teams take turns attempting to solve individual problems, while the other student is responsible for checking the solution. After every two questions or problems, each pair checks with another group to compare answers. The class can then discuss areas of disagreement or confusion after all the groups have had a chance to complete the assignment.

## Working with Larger Groups

Collaboration in pairs is the group arrangement that is easiest to manage, and it is a good place to begin when you are first introducing your students to groupwork. There are times, however, when you may want students to work in groups of three, four, or five. Groups larger than five are unwieldy, and they are generally not recommended (Cohen, 1986).

The primary advantage in having students work in groups of three or more is the opportunity to promote collaboration and social skills in addition to the cognitive goals of the lesson. For example, José could have organized his students into groups of four, with one designated as the group leader, two others responsible for making the comparisons, and the fourth serving as the facilitator/group leader. The cognitive task would be the same as illustrated in the case study, but the students would also be given practice in fulfilling different group roles. Resnick (1987b) noted that an important difference between learning in and out of school is that in-school learning is primarily individual, while out-of-school learning is usually collaborative. Giving students practice in collaborating while they work on cognitive tasks helps bridge this gap.

## Combining Pairs

Combining pairs is a group arrangement that retains the simplicity of a single pair yet promotes the social skill development of larger groups. It is effective for groupwork on comprehension and application-level activities in either a seatwork or class discussion setting. We look at its implementation in a seatwork arrangement first.

**Combining Pairs with Seatwork**   The process is organized and implemented in the following steps:

1. Student pairs are formed.
2. Pairs are combined into groups of four. The groups of four can be seated together, as illustrated in Figure 5.8. In this arrangement, the pairs are seated side by side facing the opposite pairs.
3. Students are given a series of exercises with convergent answers, such as solving math problems, identifying parts of speech in sentences, or applying a grammar or spelling rule.
4. Individuals respond to an exercise.
5. Partners compare their answers.
6. When the partners cannot agree on the correct answers, they confer with the other pair.

In classes not divisible by four, one or more groups of five can be arranged, and in those groups, a pair and a trio will work together. As with all forms of groupwork, this arrangement requires careful monitoring to prevent some individuals from deferring to their partners or "free-loading" by merely copying their partners' answers.

**Combining Pairs in Class Discussions**   Combining pairs in class discussions is a groupwork process that can be used effectively in question and answer sessions. It is similar to combining pairs with seatwork. The steps in organizing and implementing the process are as follows:

**FIGURE 5.8**   Seating Arrangement for Combined Pairs

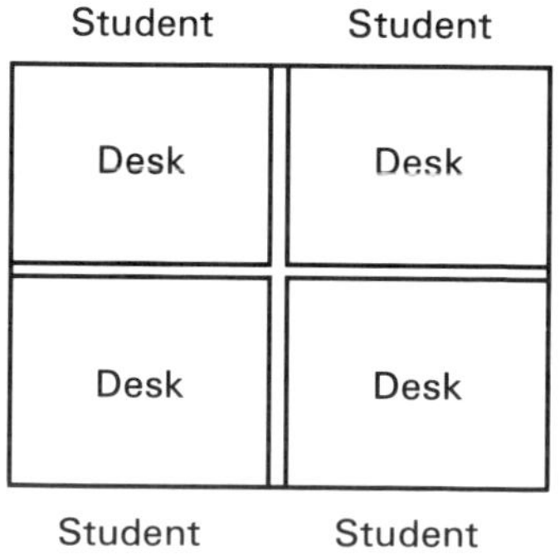

1. Groups of four are formed (with one or more groups of five).
2. The group members are assigned a number from one to four (or five).
3. The teacher asks the class a question with a convergent answer, such as the solution to a problem, the longitude of a designated city, or the correct punctuation of a sentence.
4. The group members are responsible for seeing that all members of their group know the answer and are able to explain *why* that answer is correct, so that any member of the group can explain it to the whole class.

The teacher can then call a number from one to four (or five), and the students in the groups with those numbers raise their hands. The teacher calls on an individual to answer and *explain* why that is the answer.

A simple incentive system can also be implemented with this process. If the individual answers correctly, every student in his or her group gets a point. If the student provides an adequate explanation, each member gets an additional point.

The incentive system can be made more complex and competitive among groups if the teacher chooses to do so. For example, one group could be called on to answer the question, and a second could be asked to provide the explanation, which would allow two different groups to earn a point. If a group member is unable to answer, or explain, a different group would have the opportunity to respond and earn the point.

This process is simple and promotes high levels of student involvement, even in large classes. For example, a class of 33 would have seven groups of four and one group of five. In a typical question and answer session, each group would have several opportunities to respond and earn points. Students of all ability levels are motivated, because the whole group is rewarded if the individual called on is able to respond correctly. High achievers will explain and even tutor others in their group with less understanding, and the lower achievers experience success and the rewards of contributing to their group.

## Groupwork with Higher Level Tasks

In José's lesson, the task was relatively simple; students had to make comparisons in the information that was displayed for them. As a result, contributions from individual members of the pairs were essentially equal. However, for higher level tasks, such as collaboration on problem solving, lower achievers or less aggressive members of the pairs may defer to the higher achievers or more aggressive partners, resulting in less involvement by less able students.

While there is no simple answer to this problem, you can take steps to encourage equal participation. First, require that students solve each problem individually before conferring with their partners, explaining the rationale for this action to students. Second, monitor the groups to be sure they are following your directions, encouraging equal participation as you circulate around the room. Third, strategically call on non-volunteers in groups, reminding the class that both members of the group need to understand how to solve the problems.

Groupwork provides an effective strategy for promoting and maintaining high levels of student involvement, by engaging students in tasks to be solved in a group. When combined with skilled questioning, it can also help students develop social skills, and it can be used to promote the development of higher order thinking skills, as we will see in Chapter 9.

## SUMMARY

In Chapter 4 we found that learners must be actively involved to learn most effectively. Expert teachers encourage involvement in two primary ways—skilled questioning and student groupwork. They often combine the two.

Effective teachers ask many questions, direct questions equally to all students in the class (whether or not they volunteer) and give individuals adequate time to think about their answers. They first ask the question, pause briefly, and then call on an individual student by name to answer. When students are unable to respond, or respond incorrectly, expert teachers provide cues or other questions that help students give acceptable answers rather than leaving them in favor of other students.

Call-outs pose an obstacle to equitable distribution by allowing the quicker or more vocal students to dominate a discussion. The exception here is with low socioeconomic status students, where call-outs can be used to encourage reticent students to respond.

Choral responding encourages active participation—if all students respond. This strategy is particularly effective for drill and practice of facts or skills when the teacher is able to ensure that all students answer at the same time.

Expert teachers often combine skilled questioning with student groupwork to promote involvement and reduce the energy required to maintain attention in whole-group activities.

Groupwork can be conducted with simple collaboration in pairs, or by combining pairs either for question and answer sessions or seatwork.

## ADDITIONAL READINGS FOR PROFESSIONAL GROWTH

Cazden, C. (1988). *Classroom discourse.* Portsmouth, NH: Heinemann. This text examines classroom interaction from a linguistic perspective. While not easy reading, it offers a number of fascinating insights into classroom interaction patterns.

Gall, M. (1984). Synthesis of research on teachers' questioning. *Educational Leadership*, *42*(3), 40–47. This article provides an excellent overview of the research on effective questioning.

Tobin, K. (1987). Role of wait time in higher cognitive level learning. *Review of Educational Research 57*(1), 69–95. Tobin does an excellent job of untangling the issues involved around the controversy of high- versus low-level questions.

# EXERCISES

Refer again to José Alvarez's lesson earlier in this chapter, and answer the following questions based on the episode.

1. Make a list of the students José called on. How does it relate to the concept of equitable distribution? What did he do for his lowest achievers?

2. Examine the following sequence taken from José's lesson.

   **a.** How does it illustrate José's responsiveness to his students?

   "How do we know it was heated? Ginny?"
   "I, er, I didn't hear the question," she answered sheepishly.
   "What did I do with this bottle, Ginny?" he asked, holding up the bottle with the red balloon.
   "You put it in the coffee pot."
   "Yes, I did, Ginny. . . ."

   **b.** How does this sequence relate to the concept of equitable distribution?

3. Consider the following sequence taken from José's lesson.

   "Yes, indeed. Very good conclusion, Nikki. What was one of the characteristics of air that we've discussed, Christy?"
   "It's all around us," Jason interjected.
   "That's right. Air is all around us. Well done, Jason."

   This sequence best illustrates which of the following?

   **a.** An open-ended question

   **b.** A choral response

   **c.** A prompting question

   **d.** A repetition question

   **e.** A call-out

4. How did José handle the situation in the segment illustrated in exercise 3? What are the probable outcomes in dealing with it as he did? Identify two other options he might have employed.

5. Identify an example of a choral response in the José Alvarez case study. Decide whether the choral response was appropriate and provide a rationale for your decision based on the discussion in the text.

6. Look at the following questioning segment.

   "Look at the two sentences on the board everyone," Mr. Walker directed. "How are the two alike? Helen?"
   "They are both very descriptive."
   "Good, Helen. Keith, . . . in what other way are they alike?"

   How is Mr. Walker's questioning of Keith in this short segment different from the typical way that José Alvarez questioned his students (other than the fact that the topic was different from José's)? What might occur if this were the dominant pattern? Why might Mr. Walker have chosen to act as he did?

7. Look at the following segment adapted from José's lesson.

"And what is in the bottles, Reginald?"
    ". . ."
    "Steve?"
    "Air," Steve responded.

What happened in this sequence? What are potential negative aftereffects of this? What would our discussion in this chapter suggest as a preferable procedure?

8. You are working with your students on the topic of adjectives and adverbs, and you are now in a question and answer session with them. You have displayed the following sentence on the chalkboard: "Alice and Joe walked quickly toward each other and embraced." You then ask, "What is the adverb in the sentence, Carl?" Carl sits without saying anything. List at least three different prompting questions that you could ask to elicit a response from Carl.

## DISCUSSION QUESTIONS

1. What kinds of things can a teacher do to encourage all students to form individual responses to their questions?

2. How might the following variables influence the number of questions asked in a class?

    a. Grade level

    b. Content area (e.g., math versus art)

    c. Subject-matter expertise of teacher

    d. Ability level of students

    e. Goals of the lesson

    f. Place of the lesson in a unit (e.g., beginning or end)

3. The text discusses the diagnostic, instructional, and motivational functions of questions. How would the variables in question 2 influence which of these functions would be emphasized in a given lesson?

4. Why should the success rates for questions be relatively high? Are there times when this should vary?

5. Are high-level questions better than low-level questions? When? Why?

6. Why is the practice of calling on volunteers to answer a question so prevalent? What are its advantages? What are its disadvantages?

7. Discuss the effects of the following questioning variables in terms of the concept of active involvement discussed in Chapter 4.

    a. High-level versus low-level

    b. Calling on volunteers versus calling on students randomly

**c.** Wait-time

**d.** Redirected questions

# APPLYING IT IN THE SCHOOLS

1. *Difficulty Level.* Tape a class in which questioning plays a significant role (this might be your class or someone else's). Listen to the tape and count the number of times

   **a.** The original question was answered correctly.

   **b.** The original question was answered partially correctly.

   **c.** Your original question was answered incorrectly.

   **d.** Your original question elicited no response.

   Add the number of questions in *a* through *d*. Divide the number in *a* by this total. This gives you the average success rate of your questions. Now respond to these questions:

   **e.** Was the difficulty level appropriate for this type of class?

   **f.** What do the numbers in *b*, *c*, and *d* tell you about your questions?

2. *Questioning Level.* Tape a lesson in which questions play a major role. Play the tape and jot down the questions in the order they were asked. Now, classify these questions in terms of whether they are low level (knowledge) or high level (comprehension and above). What is the ratio of high to low? Is there any pattern in terms of the sequence (e.g., LLLH or LHLH)?

3. *Choosing a Student to Respond: Volunteers.* Tape a questioning lesson in which volunteers are used to respond. Listen to the tape with a seating chart in front of you, and mark the number of times different students are called on. Respond to the following questions:

   **a.** Were the questions evenly distributed in terms of ability level?

   **b.** Were the questions evenly distributed in terms of student gender?

   **c.** How did student location in the classroom affect participation?

4. *Choosing a Student to Respond: Random Selection.* Teach and tape another lesson with a questioning format, and this time use a deck of cards with the students' names to respond. (Tell students beforehand what you are doing.) Analyze the tape and respond to these questions:

   **a.** Was this lesson harder or easier to teach than one in which you selected students in some other way?

   **b.** Did the pace of the lesson differ from the first? How?

   **c.** Comment on students' attentiveness. Was it higher or lower? How could you tell?

   **d.** What changes in your questioning style did you have to make to adapt to this modification?

5. *Questioning Strategies.* Plan a sequence of questions leading up to some point or conclusion. Tape record yourself as you implement this sequence in the classroom. Analyze the tape afterward, and compare the sequence that occurred with the one you planned. What caused you to change this sequence? How helpful is planning a sequence prior to a class?

6. *Wait-Time.* Tape yourself as you use questions in a lesson and then listen to yourself and try to determine how long you wait after asking a question before calling on a student, how long you wait for a student to answer before intervening, and how long you wait for the student to complete his or her answer. Also, identify the student selected to respond and whether he or she was a high or low achiever. Then respond to the following questions.

   **a.** What was your longest wait-time? What question did it follow?

   **b.** What was your shortest wait-time?

   **c.** What was your average wait-time?

   **d.** Did your wait-times differ for students of different abilities?

   Teach and tape another lesson and consciously try to respond to any difficulties uncovered in answering the parts of this question. Were you able to do this? What difficulties were encountered?

7. *Collaborative Groupwork.* Plan and teach a lesson incorporating collaborative groupwork. Teach and evaluate the lesson in terms of the following criteria:

   **a.** Did the groupwork reinforce lesson content?

   **b.** Was the task for students during the groupwork clear and unambiguous?

   **c.** Were the directions for students to break into groups simple and easily understood?

   **d.** Were students actively involved during groupwork?

   **e.** Were students able to perform the task required of them during groupwork?

# CHAPTER 6

# Adapting Instruction for Different Goals: Teaching Facts, Concepts, and Generalizations

## OVERVIEW

In Chapter 4 we discussed effective teachers' use of time and then outlined a general model of instruction. We found that teacher characteristics such as enthusiasm and high expectations, together with the ability to conduct effective reviews, provide focus and feedback, and reach meaningful closure, increase learning in students of all ages and for all content areas and topics. In Chapter 5 we described ways teachers can promote learning by actively involving students in learning activities.

We now want to build on the structure we began in the last two chapters and discuss how teaching can be adapted to help students reach specific instructional goals. In this chapter we examine what students actually learn—facts, concepts, and generalizations—and discuss strategies that promote this learning. In Chapter 7 we extend this discussion to the learning of organized bodies of knowledge, which interrelate facts, concepts, and generalizations. As with other topics, the research literature gives us information which, combined with teacher artistry and informed decision making, can help students reach these goals.

## MAIN IDEAS

### Facts, Concepts, and Generalizations: The Building Blocks of Learning

*Facts* are units of information that are either valuable in and of themselves or are used to form concepts and generalizations.

When events, objects, or ideas with similar features are grouped into categories, *concepts* are formed.

Relationships among concepts are described in *generalizations*, *principles*, and *academic rules*.

### Teaching Concepts Inductively and Deductively

Planning for teaching concepts involves *selecting the topic*, *identifying a precise goal*, and *selecting examples*.

Concepts are taught *inductively* when examples are presented and learners are guided to the definition.

When learners are presented with a definition followed by examples, a *deductive approach is used*.

### Teaching Generalizations Inductively and Deductively

Planning for teaching generalizations is basically the same as planning for teaching concepts.

With an *inductive* approach, examples are presented and learners are guided to the relationship described in the generalization. A *deductive* approach uses the opposite sequence.

Mike Lee is a fourth-grade teacher with 25 students in his class. He has his schedule arranged in the following way.

| | |
|---|---|
| 8:30–10:00 A.M. | Reading |
| 10:00–11:00 A.M. | Math |
| 11:00–11:30 A.M. | Science |
| 11:30–12:00 noon | Lunch |
| 12:00– 1:30 P.M. | Language Arts |
| | (Spelling, Grammar, Writing) |
| 1:30– 2:00 P.M. | Social Studies |
| 2:00– 3:00 P.M. | Resource |
| | (Art, Music, PE, Computer) |

At 10:59 A.M. Mike is walking among his students as they finish their math seatwork. He glances at the clock and says, "All right everyone, put your work in your folders. For those of you who haven't already completed your work, finish it tonight and put it in your folders as soon as you come in the room in the morning. Now get ready for science."

Several of the students get up, put their papers in their folders, and return to their desks.

At 11:01 A.M. Mike begins, "Okay, class, we've been talking about heat and energy. What is one way that heat is transferred, Keith?"

"Radiation?"

"Yes, good, Keith," Mike smiles at Keith. "Now give us an example. Bev?"

"Umm, when you hold your hand over a hot burner on a stove, your hand gets warm."

"Good, Bev! How about one more example? Jim?"

"When we stand out in the sun, it warms us up."

"And what do we know about radiation, Sally?"

"It travels through a vacuum. . . . Like from the sun to the earth."

"Outstanding, Sally! And what else? Gary?"

"It travels in waves."

"Yes, Gary. Very good. Now remember everyone, radiation is a form of heat energy that travels in waves, and it doesn't need any matter to travel through. We can't see the waves, but they move, such as going from the burner to our hand. We know the waves moved because our hand gets warm."

Mike continues, "Now we're going to leave radiation for a while and turn to a new type of heat transfer. As we go through this, I want you to try and figure out how this form is different from radiation. I know you're all good thinkers, so I'll bet you can figure this out. Everybody ready. . . . [He scans the room.] Good."

"Now look at this," Mike says, gesturing to a coffee maker that he set up in the front of his room.

"It's a coffee maker," Jane volunteers.

"My mom uses one every morning," Ron adds immediately.

"Elizabeth, put your finger near the bottom here," Mike directs. "Be careful. Put it close but don't touch the plate."

"It's hot!" Elizabeth says, as she quickly jerks her hand from near the hot plate of the coffee maker.

"Now take a look at this," Mike says, bringing out the coffee pot.

"You can see through it 'cause it's glass," Carmen says.

"Go ahead and feel it, Chet," Mike requests.

"It's cold," Chet says, as he touches the pot.

"Okay, let's just set this down," Mike says, and he puts the coffee pot on the hot plate of the coffee maker.

"I have a question, Mr. Lee," Elizabeth asks. "When I put my hand near the burner, I could feel some heat. Is that radiation?"

"Excellent thinking, Elizabeth. Yes, indeed it is. Did everyone hear Elizabeth's question?" [Mike has her repeat it and confirms why it is an example.] "This is the kind of thinking we're looking for. Elizabeth is relating what we're doing here to what we did yesterday. Excellent!"

Mike continues, "Now take a look at this. What do you see?" [He brings out a small pan that he puts on a stand with a lighted candle under it.]

"It's a candle, and it's lit," Debra offers.

"There is a little pan on the stand," Sue comments.

"What else, Steve?" Mike queries.

"The pan will be hot," Steve suggests.

"Go ahead and check it, but be careful," Mike directs.

"It is hot," Steve verifies as he gingerly puts his hand near the pan.

"Now look at this," Mike says, holding up a spoon. "Tell me about it, Cathy."

". . ."

"How does it feel, Cathy?" Mike asks, extending the spoon.

"Well, it's sort of smooth and made of metal," she answers.

"How is its temperature different from the pan's, Celeste?"

"It's cold and the pan is hot."

"Okay, good. Let's just put the spoon in the pan for a minute, and let's check back on the coffee pot. What did we say about the temperature of the coffee pot? Rachel?"

". . ."

"What did Chet say when he touched it?"

"It was cool," Rachel recalls.

"Yes, very good, and how did the coffee maker feel?"

"It was hot," Elizabeth blurts out.

"Now put your hand near the coffee pot. Be careful," Mike directs.

"It's hot, too," Linda volunteers as she holds her hand near the pot.

"And what did we say about it before?"

"It was cold!" Chet speaks up.

"Good, Chet. You were listening when we said that earlier. And what was the difference? Tommy?"

". . ."

"Where is it sitting?"

"It's on the coffee maker," Tommy answers.

"Yes, it is! We could say it's what? Toni?" Mike asks.

"It's . . . ," Toni hesitates.

"It's in contact or not in contact?" Mike continues.

"In contact!" Toni gushes.

"Yes, good!" Mike says, delighted.

"Now let's look at the spoon and the pan. Go ahead and touch the spoon handle, Chris," Mike says.

"It's warm," Chris returns.

"And what do we know about the spoon and the pan?"

"They're in contact!" Carmen and Jane say together.

"Yes, super! Now let's see how well you're all thinking. Let's try and pull all this together. This is tough. Do you think you can do it?" Mike smiles.

"You can't stump us, Mr. Lee!" Carmen shoots back.

"Good!" Mike says. "We have been talking about a particular form of heating. Now I want you to help me form a definition of it. Where do we start? Dorothy?"

"Well," Dorothy starts hesitantly, "it's a form of heat transfer."

"Yes, good," Mike nods as he starts to write what Dorothy has said on the board. "Go on."

"One object heats another object," Ron adds.

"How, Ron?" Mike continues.

"Well, the coffee maker heated the pot, and the pan heated the spoon."

"Good use of examples, Ron."

"And the two objects are in contact," Debra concludes.

"Yes, outstanding, everyone," Mike praises. "Can anyone give me the name of this type of heat transfer?" After waiting a few seconds, Mike says, "We call this *conduction*. So, remember, conduction is a form of transferring heat where the object being heated and the object doing the heating are in contact with each other. Now, how are radiation and conduction similar and different?" [Mike then has the class compare and contrast the two forms of heat transfer.]

Finally, Mike says, "For tomorrow I want you to go home and find at least three examples of conduction and two more examples of radiation that we haven't talked about in class so far."

At 11:28 Mike says, "OK everyone, go ahead and take out your language arts books."

Think about Mike Lee's lesson in the context of the general instructional model outlined in Chapter 4. We see that he first *reviewed* radiation and then provided for *introductory focus* by asking the students to think about the relationship between radiation and the new form of heat transfer. His coffee maker and pan provided excellent forms of *sensory focus*, and he developed the lesson with high levels of *student involvement*. He came to *closure* with a careful description of "conduction." Further, we see evidence of *enthusiasm* and *energy* in his manner, and his *expectations* for his students were demonstrated in his challenging statements. Finally, he used his *time* efficiently.

In examining Mike's lesson, however, we see that a more detailed analysis is necessary to understand fully what he did and how it relates to the content students learn in their classes. This chapter is devoted to a description of this analysis.

# FACTS, CONCEPTS, AND GENERALIZATIONS: THE BUILDING BLOCKS OF LEARNING

When students study an area of content, they are often required to learn different kinds of content. These different kinds of content require different study strategies for the learner and suggest different instructional strategies for the teacher. Let's see how these ideas operate in a social studies class on cities of the United States.

"Class, let's pick up where we left off by reviewing some of the major ideas we discussed yesterday," Leona Harris began as she surveyed her middle school class. "Who remembers some of the important ideas we talked about yesterday? Eddie?"

"The biggest cities in a state are often trade centers," Eddie responded.

"Good, Eddie. Can you give us some examples of trade centers?"

"Uh . . . San Francisco, New York, and Chicago."

"Good thinking, Eddie. And what do these three cities have in common that makes them trade centers? Mindy?"

"Umh, they're all on water so ships can get there."

"Good, Mindy. And who can remember some other reasons for the growth of cities in the United States? Carlos?"

"Well, sometimes they're state capitals."

"Like. . . ."

"Oh, like Atlanta and Indianapolis."

"Good examples, Carlos. Now, why might state capitals grow in size? Deena?"

"Because that's where the governor and the legislature meet, and there are lots of offices like the Department of Transportation."

"Excellent answer, Deena. And who can remember an effective way to remember some of these state capitals? Think about the capital of ARKansas. Deena?"

"You told us to make a picture in our minds like an ark sitting on a little rock—Little Rock, Arkansas!"

"Good, Deena. Class, we'll work more on this way of remembering capitals later in the week. For now I'd like to consider some cities that don't seem to follow the patterns we've talked about so far. . . ."

In this class the teacher wanted her students to learn a number of different content forms. One of these was facts. Examples here included the facts that Atlanta and Indianapolis were capitals and that they both weren't located on major waterways. Leona Harris also wanted her students to understand concepts like trade centers and state capitals. In addition, she wanted her students to understand generalizations linking the size of a city and reasons for the city's growth. Each of these was a different form of content.

These different forms of content have implications for the way that we teach them. We teach facts through a variety of methods ranging from repetition and review to visual mnemonics like visualizing an ark sitting on a rock. When we teach concepts and generalizations, we want students to understand the abstraction and be able to link them to examples that illustrate the idea. Again, we can see how different content forms are taught differently. In this chapter we discuss each of these content forms, beginning with facts.

# FACTS

**Facts** are isolated pieces of information. They are the building blocks of more advanced forms of knowledge, and enormous numbers of facts can be found in every area of the curriculum. The following are a few examples.

- Mercury is the planet closest to the sun.
- $7 \times 8 = 56$
- The first Crusade began in 1095.
- The Spanish equivalent of *love* is *amor*.
- The word *climb* is pronounced "clime," but the word *limb* is pronounced "lim."

A number of facts were identified in Mike's lesson as well. For example,

- The burner on the coffee pot was hot.
- The pot was cold when it was placed on the burner.
- After a period of time, the pot on the hot burner was also hot.

We see that all of these items are isolated bits of information, and taken alone they do little to help us understand the world. However, when related to each other in patterns, they become powerful tools for understanding. We examine these patterns as the content of this chapter is developed.

The emphasis placed on learning facts has varied over time in American education. In Colonial days—before textbooks were readily available—rote memorization of facts was the primary form of learning. Even in this century, proponents of "faculty psychology" advocated (incorrectly) the memorization of large bodies of information to develop memorizing power. More recently, a reemphasis on basic skills, new impetus for the development of thinking skills, and a better understanding of the ways learners process information have marked a decline in the importance of fact learning in classrooms.

These changes have not occurred without resistance. A study of high school students' knowledge of history and literature facts conducted in the late 1980s found that 32 percent didn't know that Columbus reached the new world before 1750, and one student in five did not know when, where, and by whom the first atomic bomb was dropped (Ravitch and Finn, 1987). These findings are disturbing to even the strongest opponent of fact learning.

Some knowledge of facts is valuable because subsequent learning depends on it. For example, knowing the order of the planets from the sun not only allows students to infer planet characteristics, such as surface temperature, but also provides background when they examine theories about the solar system's origin. Also, children must have basic addition and multiplication facts memorized for immediate recall, or their subsequent use in problem solving will be very inefficient. Some dates, persons, and events are important because they serve as the building blocks for more advanced forms of knowledge.

On the other hand, research indicates that fact learning is vastly overemphasized in schools. Goodlad (1984), in reporting his research on more than 1,000 classrooms in America, concluded as follows:

> Only rarely did we find evidence to suggest instruction (in reading and math) likely to go much beyond merely possession of information to a level of understanding its implications and either applying it or exploring its possible applications. Nor did we see activities likely to arouse students' curiosity or to involve them in seeking a solution to some problem not already laid bare by teacher or textbook.
>
> And it appears that this preoccupation with the lower intellectual processes pervades social studies and science as well. An analysis of topics studied and materials used gives not an impression of students studying human adaptations and exploration, but of facts to be learned. (p. 236)

There are two problems with this emphasis. First, research in cognitive psychology suggests that passive memorization is one of the most inefficient ways to learn (Glover et al., 1990; Mayer, 1987), and second, a fact-heavy curriculum deemphasizes more important learning, such as the development of thinking and problem-solving skills.

The decision about what facts are important enough to be emphasized is left to the teacher. Jarolimek (1990) offered the following criteria for assessing the value of facts.

- Will the information remain important over a long period of time?
- Is the information used frequently in everyday living?
- Is the information needed to explain or elaborate on more important ideas or generalizations?

Unless the answer to these questions is yes, including the fact in the curriculum is questionable. For example, the answer is obviously yes for number facts, while knowing that Elias Howe invented the sewing machine is little more than an interesting piece of trivia.

## Teaching Facts

Strategies for teaching facts can be described according to the extent to which they emphasize simple memory versus meaningful relationships. At one end of the continuum we have limited emphasis on meaning, with repetitious drill and recitation; at the other students are asked to integrate the facts with other content that they know. This continuum is illustrated in Figure 6.1.

**FIGURE 6.1** Strategies for Teaching Facts

| Limited Emphasis on Meaning | | Extensive Emphasis on Meaning |
|---|---|---|
| ◄─────────────────────── | | ──────────────────────► |
| | Strategies | |
| Drill, Recite, Copy, Underline | Outline, Diagram, Tabularize, Peer Teachback | Imagery, Mnemonics, Compare and Contrast, Infer, Predict |

*Source:* Adapted from Corno, 1987

From Figure 6.1, we see that simple drill and practice, or "brute force," is the strategy that least emphasizes meaning. It is also the oldest and crudest way of learning facts. Drill and practice is a form of stimulus-response learning where one part of the fact, $7 \times 8$ for example, is linked to the second part, 56. The stimulus-response bond is strengthened through practice and repetition, but it takes both time and effort and it isn't much fun. Sometimes, though, teachers will need to bite the bullet and do it.

Research identifies three important patterns about the effectiveness of drill and practice, or simple rehearsal (Dempster, 1988). First, the effectiveness of rehearsal increases with the number of repetitions; second, these repetitions should be spaced over time; and third, learners should be in an active role in the process. These patterns are summarized and illustrated in Table 6.1.

To maintain students' interest in the rehearsal process, teachers use a variety of motivational devices. One teacher we know gives students a series of facts on a dittoed sheet every day and times the students as they respond. If the children can improve from one day to the next, they receive bonus points on their final average. She also gives bonus points for all the children who get all of the facts right in the allotted time to maintain incentive for the high achievers. When all or nearly all the children are at mastery, she moves on. This strategy is a simple but effective way to enhance the drill and practice involved in fact learning.

Drill and practice works at the upper levels as well. One creative chemistry teacher decided that his students needed to know the chemical symbols for the 20

**TABLE 6.1** Increasing the Effectiveness of Rehearsal

| *Research Result* | *Example* |
|---|---|
| Memory for information increases with the number of repetitions. | The more students practice with flash cards, the better they will remember their multiplication facts. |
| Spaced practice is more effective than massed practice. | Ten minutes a day is better than 50 minutes once a week. |
| Active is more effective than passive practice. | Writing the answer is better than listening to a classmate state the answer. |

most common elements, so he began each of his classes for a week with a quiz-show format. The students thought he was a little "wacky," but they learned their chemical symbols. Contests, games, and flash cards to take home or use with classmates are all effective in providing the repetition necessary for teaching facts such as the multiplication tables. All involve the necessary practice needed to make the facts automatic.

While rehearsal is effective for information such as number facts or chemical symbols, for other material it often leads to memorized strings of words that have little or no meaning for students. A classroom incident that William James recalled near the turn of this century illustrates a problem that still exists today:

> A friend of mine, visiting a school, was asked to examine a young class in geography. She said, "Suppose you should dig a hole in the ground hundreds of feet deep, how should you find it at the bottom—warmer or colder than on the top?" None of the class replying, the teacher said, "I'm sure they know, but I think you don't ask the question quite rightly. Let me try." So taking the book she asked, "In what condition is the interior of the globe?" and received the immediate answer from half the class at once, "the interior of the globe is in a condition of igneous fusion." (James, 1914, p. 150)

Obviously, the condition of the earth below the surface had no meaning for these students, nor did "igneous fusion." This is a common problem in schools.

## Improving Fact Learning: Making Facts Meaningful

**Meaningfulness** is a term used to describe the number of connections or associations between one idea and other ideas in our memories (Eggen and Kauchak, 1992). This simple idea is one of the most powerful in learning. To learn and remember ideas, we must associate them with other ideas. Grouping on the basis of similarities, ordering on some dimension, such as chronology or size, and outlining in either tabular or diagram form all encourage students to relate specific items of information to each other. Presentations followed by peer teachbacks are also effective. For example, the class can be broken into groups of four or five and each member of the group is responsible for presenting some part of the important information.

Another effective alternative is to emphasize the meaningful patterns found in bodies of facts. For example, when we subtract nine from any number, the units place adds one, so $18 - 9$ is 9 (8 + 1) and $13 - 9$ is 4 (3 + 1). Similar patterns exist in other areas. For instance, we remember how to spell words such as *siege*, *ceiling*, and *receive* by following the rule "i before e except after c."

Probably the most powerful and widely applicable approach to teaching facts stresses their meaningful integration into a larger conceptual framework (Kuhara-Kojima and Hatana, 1991). This is done by asking students to identify relationships among the individual items of information. For example, a history teacher wanting students to remember dates of important Civil War events proceeded as follows:

*Teacher:*  What year did we say the Civil War began? Jane?

*Student:*  1859?

*Teacher:*  Let's back up a minute. What year did we say Lincoln was elected?

*Student:*  1860.

*Teacher:*  Good, and how were his election and the start of the Civil War connected?

*Student:*  The South felt that Lincoln as President would try to abolish slavery, so they felt they had no choice except to secede.

*Teacher:*  So, would the start of the Civil War be before or after the election of 1860?

*Student:*  Now I remember. It was 1861.

*Teacher:*  Good. Now let's focus on the end of the war. Did it happen before or after Lincoln's reelection? I'll give you a hint. Think about Lincoln's vice presidents and who succeeded him after he was assassinated.

Here, instead of treating the facts in isolation, the teacher attempted to make the beginning date of the Civil War more meaningful by associating it with Lincoln's political views and the date of his election. She then did the same thing with the ending date. These relationships help students remember the specific facts at some later time.

Facts can also be made more meaningful with **mnemonics**, which are simple strategies for forming associations in information. Some common examples are illustrated in Table 6.2.

In Table 6.2 we see that "Homes," for example, is more familiar and meaningful than is the name of each lake. By associating the two, the names of the lakes are easier to remember.

**TABLE 6.2**   Mnemonic Devices

| *Content Area* | *Example* |
| --- | --- |
| *Biology*<br>Kingdom, class, order, family, genus, species | Kennels can order fine German Shepherds. |
| *Astronomy*<br>Mercury, Venus, Earth, Mars, Jupiter, Saturn, Uranus, Neptune, Pluto | Men very easily make jugs serving useful nocturnal purposes. |
| *Music*<br>Musical scale, E, G, B, D, F | Every good boy does fine. |
| *Social Studies*<br>Names of the Great Lakes — Huron, Ontario, Michigan, Erie, Superior | Homes |

Other strategies can be used as well. For example, in the case of the Great Lakes, seeing a map can help students use **imagery** — being able to visualize the lakes makes their locations and names more meaningful.

The teaching of facts for long-term retention has important implications for instruction. First, whenever possible, students should be encouraged to relate new facts to information they already know, rather than merely memorize them. Accordingly, learning activities and materials should minimize drill and practice and instead should emphasize the meanings of the facts in a larger context. Finally, exercises and quizzes should require that students integrate new facts rather than merely state them in isolation. We discuss these ideas further when we talk about teaching organized bodies of information in Chapter 7.

# CONCEPTS

Concepts are one of the most important forms of learning, both in and out of classrooms. They guide our thinking and communication and help us understand our environment. When we read a newspaper columnist and conclude that he or she has a strong conservative bias, we are using the concepts *conservative* and *bias*. These concepts help us both understand the author and communicate our understanding to someone else. When we make a comment about conservatives, a receiver with a similar concept understands what we mean.

Concepts represent a major portion of the school curriculum, and much of teachers' efforts is directed at teaching them. The list of concepts taught in schools is virtually endless. A brief list is illustrated in Table 6.3. From the list, we see that some concepts, such as *square* or *noun*, are simple and can be taught to young children, while other more abstract ones, like *mercantilism*, require advanced and sophisticated learners.

Let us examine concepts further and see how they are learned. Consider the underlined words in each of the following sentences.

Suzy runs very fast.
I studied for this test for four hours.
You are reading the information in this section.
Jim drove the ball out of the park.
Kathy is a good math student.

**TABLE 6.3**  Concepts in Different Content Areas

| Language Arts | Social Studies | Science | Math |
| --- | --- | --- | --- |
| Gerund | Culture | Acid | Composite number |
| Noun | Republican | Conifer | Equivalent fraction |
| Plot | Conservative | Compound | Square |
| Simile | Mercantilism | Force | Multiplication |
| Direct object | Gross national product | Momentum | Ellipse |

In looking at the underlined words, we see that they are quite dissimilar—their spellings are different, some indicate an event in the past while others are in the present, one involves two underlined words, and some suggest more energy than do the others. However, despite their differences, they are all similar in that they *describe an action or a state of being.* Because of this common feature, we put them in a class or category into which all words that indicate action belong. We have formed the concept *verb.* This is the way concepts in general are formed. **Concepts** are categories, or classes of objects, events, or ideas, illustrated by examples and defined by common characteristics. Let us consider this definition in more detail.

## Characteristics

**Characteristics**, **features**, or **attributes** are the common elements that describe a concept. As we saw in our example, the characteristics of verbs are that they *describe an action or state of being.* These are the features that make individual words members of the class.

Many concepts have well-defined characteristics. For example, squares have four essential characteristics—closed, straight lines, equal sides, and equal angles. Other features, such as color or size, are not essential, so learners put both red and green and large and small squares into the category. These features don't alter the concept's "squareness." When the characteristics are clear and identified, concept learning is easier.

**Concept Prototypes: Examples and Nonexamples**   Not all concepts have well-defined characteristics, however. For example, *conservative* doesn't have cut-and-dried features, like squares, circles, and triangles, and instead has somewhat "fuzzy boundaries" (Schwartz and Reisberg, 1991). "Conservatives" vary widely in their political views, for example. As a way of confirming this idea, if you asked 10 people what a square is, you would get largely consistent answers, but if you asked the same people to describe a conservative, the answers would vary considerably, and some wouldn't be able to give any answer.

Some researchers believe that concepts, such as *conservative,* are best represented by a prototype, or a case that is a good example of the concept (Nosofsky, 1988; Schwartz and Reisberg, 1991), rather than specified characteristics. These prototypes, or examples, help students learn and remember complex concepts by providing a concrete reference point.

To illustrate the importance of examples, we turn now to some simple illustrations of concept learning as it occurs naturally. Let's take a very elementary concept—*dog*—and trace its development. This analysis provides us with insights into the nature of concepts, how they are learned, and how they can be taught.

We'll begin by asking a basic question: How do young children learn concepts? Or, from a psychological perspective, how does a child acquire the ability to discriminate dogs from other animals? For young children, the process begins with examples and nonexamples. We learn about dogs by encountering collies, terriers, poodles, chihuahuas, and many others. Our parents and other adults help us with statements such as, "Look, Mandy, there's a dog!" As with the *verb* illustration described earlier, the dogs are dissimilar in many ways. However, having been told that all the examples are dogs, we identify similarities among all the dissimilarity, and the concept begins to develop.

The development process is also aided by nonexamples such as cats and bears, and later more closely related cases such as coyotes, wolves, and jackals. In these instances, we are told, "No, Matt, that's not a dog. It's a kitty. Listen to him meow," or, "No. It looks very much like a dog and is related, but it's a wolf. It lives in the wild and not with people."

The examples tell us what the concept is by illustrating its essential characteristics, and the nonexamples help us discriminate between the important characteristics and those of closely related concepts. Consider the following examples:

Sammy, the running back, was a freight train moving down the field.

As a running back, Sammy was like a freight train moving down the field.

Obviously, the two statements are very closely related. However, they illustrate two different but closely related concepts. The first is a metaphor, which involves a nonliteral comparison. The second is a simile, which also makes a nonliteral comparison but includes the word *like* or *as*. The essential characteristics of metaphors are illustrated in the first example, and a key discriminating characteristic is shown in the nonexample. As students learn the concept *metaphor*, nonexamples such as *similes* are crucial to prevent them from overgeneralizing and including inappropriate examples in the category. The same thing occurs when we tell young children that foxes and wolves are not dogs.

Nonexamples are important because they clarify the boundaries of a concept. In the case of metaphors and similes, they are crucial because the concepts are so closely related. They are also valuable in helping learners understand where the edges of a fuzzy concept lie. For example, when a teacher says, "Class, this is not acceptable behavior, and we will not permit it in this classroom," she is trying to clarify an amorphous concept, *acceptable behavior.* Assuming that the teacher has already defined and illustrated acceptable behavior, such as "We do not talk while someone else has the floor," a strategically placed nonexample can help clarify the boundaries.

From this discussion we see that concept learning as it occurs naturally and concept learning in a formal school setting share several similarities. The learner either encounters examples or nonexamples accidentally—as the *dog* illustration indicates—or is presented examples and nonexamples—as demonstrated with *verbs*. In both cases the concept is learned by identifying its essential characteristics and discriminating them from closely related concepts. What differentiates the two is the teacher's conscious effort to provide students with adequate examples.

**Concepts: Ease of Learning**    The ease of learning a concept is directly related to the number of characteristics it has and how tangible and concrete they are (Tennyson and Cocciarella, 1986). *Square* is easy to learn, for example, because it has few characteristics and they're very concrete. *Conservative*, by contrast, is much harder.

As we noted earlier, most people would have difficulty precisely describing what makes a conservative a conservative.

These differences are reflected in the sequence in which concepts are taught in the school curriculum. Shapes, such as square and circle, are taught in kindergarten or before, while the concept of *conservative* doesn't appear until the middle school years or later.

## Making Concepts Meaningful: Superordinate, Coordinate, and Subordinate Concepts

In the previous section we discussed how to make facts meaningful by connecting them to other information. The same process can be applied with concept learning. Rather than learning concepts in isolation, we want them to be linked to other concepts (Glover et al., 1990). For example, we learn that *verb* is a *part of speech* and that other parts of speech also exist, such as *nouns*, *adjectives*, and *adverbs*. We go even further to find that there are special kinds of verbs called *helping verbs*.

We can summarize these links by describing *parts of speech*, *noun* (and adjective and adverb), and *helping verbs* as superordinate, coordinate, and subordinate concepts, respectively. **Superordinate** concepts are larger categories into which the concept fits (part of speech), **coordinate** concepts are "parallel" concepts that fit the same category (noun, adjective, and adverb), and **subordinate** concepts are subsets of the concept we're focusing on (helping verb).

We use superordinate concepts in several ways. One of the most important is to understand what a new concept is. What is a dog? A dog is a mammal. What is a republic? A republic is a form of government. If these superordinate concepts are understood, the new concept then has a cognitive hook on which to hang. This classification makes the concept more meaningful to the student by providing associations between it and related concepts (Gage and Berliner, 1992). We call this function of superordinate concepts "definitional," because definitions of concepts begin by placing the concept into a larger category. (You may want to verify this with a dictionary.)

A second function that superordinate concepts perform is inferential. Knowing that a concept belongs to a larger category allows us to infer characteristics from that category. For example, when students learn that kayaks and yawls are both boats, they can infer that both are vehicles designed for travel on water. They can also infer other characteristics like watertightness and a size large enough to carry people.

Studies on the organization of the mind suggest that the concepts we know are often organized hierarchically. Sometimes referred to as schemas (Rumelhart, 1980) or networks, these hierarchies allow us to relate and organize information for both storage and retrieval. For example, consider the network shown in Figure 6.2. (This hierarchy is incomplete for the sake of brevity.)

As a youngster's understanding of dogs gradually expands, it begins to fit into a larger and larger structure. Dogs fit into a larger (superordinate) category called canines, which in turn fits into mammals, and mammals belong to the category of warm-blooded vertebrates. This hierarchial structuring makes the concept vastly more meaningful to the learner than storing it in isolation.

**FIGURE 6.2**    Conceptual Hierarchy

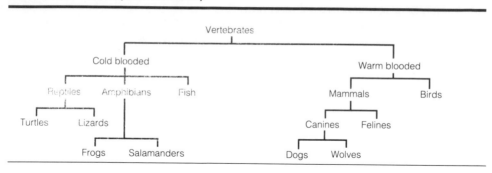

**Defining Concepts**    An efficient way of making concepts meaningful is to link them in a definition, which is a statement relating the concept, a superordinate concept, and characteristics. For instance, we could define *verb* as follows: "A verb is a part of speech that describes an action or state of being." *Verb* (the concept) is linked to *part of speech* (a superordinate concept), and *action or state of being* (characteristics). We can readily see that defining a concept such as *conservative* would be much harder, which is one reason it is less meaningful for people.

**Concept Name**    Table 6.3 shows a list of concepts. Technically, we provided a list of *labels* or *terms* we use to *name* concepts. In practice, no harm comes from simply calling the labels concepts as long as we remember that the labels are not the concepts themselves. The problem occurs when concepts are not illustrated with examples and students memorize definitions that are attached to labels. For instance, consider the following definition:

> An oxymoron is a statement that uses contradictory language or terms juxtaposed in the same sentence.

Students are fully capable of memorizing the definition and associating it with the name *oxymoron*, just as the students did when they memorized the string of words describing the inside of the earth. However, it is not likely to be meaningful in its present form, instead being reduced to the level of fact learning because it is memorized. If, in addition to this definition, we also provide examples like *cruel kindness* and *sweet pain*, we've given students concrete referents to make sense out of the words.

## Teaching Concepts

As the students entered Simone Torrez's English class, they saw the following sentences displayed on the overhead.

a. Running is an excellent form of exercise.
b. Look at the running girl.
c. See how fast she is running.

**a.** Talking without permission is against the rules.
**b.** We've all heard slang about "talking heads."
**c.** Karen was talking so fast that I couldn't understand her.

**a.** We all have trouble with thinking now and then.
**b.** Humans would like to believe that they are the thinking species on earth.
**c.** I've been thinking about this stuff all day.

Mrs. Torrez told the students to work in pairs [work in pairs was a part of her classroom routine and was arranged in advance], to focus on the words ending in "ing," and to see what the "a" sentences had in common, what the "b" sentences had in common, and the same for the "c" sentences. She also had them compare the three groups to each other.

After the groups had searched for similarities and differences, she brought them together and guided them into recognizing that all the "ing" words were verb forms, but they were used as nouns in the "a" sentences, as adjectives in the "b" sentences, and as verbs for the "c" sentences. She then labeled their use in the first two cases as *gerunds* and *participles*, respectively. Finally, she assigned the students to write a paragraph in which at least three gerunds and three participles had to be embedded.

Let's think about Mrs. Torrez's lesson, Mike Lee's lesson at the beginning of this chapter, and our illustration with verbs and ask ourselves what they have in common. First, they all involve concept learning; *conduction, gerund, participle,* and *verb* are all concepts. In this section of the chapter we will examine the other common features of these lessons, starting with the process of planning.

**Planning for Teaching Concepts**   The planning process for teaching concepts involves the three essential steps outlined in Figure 6.3.

*Identifying a Topic.* In Chapter 3 we found that teachers typically begin their planning with a topic or a learning activity. The topic typically comes from a textbook, curriculum guide, or the teacher's past experience. For the purposes of this section, we're dealing with topics that involve the teaching of concepts.

*Identifying a Precise Objective.* Once the topic has been identified, the teacher must decide, "Exactly what do I want my students to know about this topic?" In some cases—teaching small children *square, circle,* and *triangle,* for example—this is simple. We want the children to be able to name or identify the shapes. In others,

**FIGURE 6.3**   Planning for Teaching Concepts

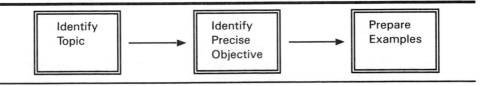

however, some decisions must be made, even in the cases of seemingly simple concepts, such as *mammal.* For example, if you are a kindergarten teacher, you might want the students to know the following attributes of mammal:

- Warm
- Furry
- Nurses young.

If you're a middle school teacher, however, the characteristics you focus on might be quite different, such as

- Placental
- Four-chambered heart
- Seven cervical vertebrae.

Both sets of characteristics are valid, but we see that they're very different. It is critical that teachers are clear about the characteristics they choose to focus on. We learn why in the next section.

***Preparing Examples.*** The purpose in having a clear objective in mind is to guide teachers in their selection of *examples* (we saw earlier in this chapter how important examples are in concept learning). When teachers determine exactly what they want their students to know, they then understand what they must illustrate. For instance, if a kindergarten teacher wants her students to know that mammals are warm, furry, and nurse their young, she must find examples that illustrate those characteristics. Likewise, the middle school teacher must figure out a way to illustrate placental, four-chambered heart, and seven cervical vertebrae.

As a teacher, an essential question to keep in mind as you prepare to teach concepts is, "*What can I show the students, or what can I have the students do that will illustrate the concept as clearly as possible?*"

*We cannot emphasize this step strongly enough!* Carefully selected examples are the key to your students' learning. Ineffective examples result in vague and uncertain learning. A clear illustration means that the characteristics of the concept are observable in the examples or the example is the best prototype available (Ranzijn, 1991).

When the concept can be confused easily with a closely related concept, both *positive* and *negative* examples are necessary (Tennyson and Cocciarella, 1986). Positive examples tell the learner what the concept is, while nonexamples (negative ones) illustrate what the concept is not. For example, if a teacher wants her students to understand the concept *adjective,* she would include sentences such as, "Suzy *quickly* ran to the store to get some milk," as nonexamples, so that students don't confuse adjectives and adverbs.

The selection of examples is a simple enough idea, but putting it into practice can be difficult. For instance, how might you illustrate concepts such as *atom* or *culture*? When teachers have difficulty finding or creating good examples, they often revert back to definitions alone, which students then memorize. The memorized definitions then exist in isolation, which makes them little more than forms of fact learning.

Table 6.4 describes some forms of examples that are useful in classrooms.

The ideal in illustrating any concept is obviously the real thing, and teachers should always use actual objects and demonstrations whenever possible. Sometimes this is impossible, however, and each of the other alternatives is appropriate depending on the concept being illustrated. For example, while heat and expansion are easy to illustrate by putting a balloon-covered soft drink bottle in a pot of hot water, this gives us no information about the movement of the molecules. A model drawn with the dots and arrows to represent the moving molecules is then an appropriate supplement, particularly when combined with the bottle and balloon—a concrete object. **Model**, as used with the dots and arrows, means a device *to help us visualize what we cannot observe directly*, and models are useful in science, particularly when dealing with topics such as atoms, molecules, and atomic structure.

Just as models are useful in science, simulations are commonly used in social studies to illustrate concepts impossible to illustrate in other ways. In the 1970s a teacher in California developed a simulation of Fascism with his students (without them knowing it was Fascism) that was so real to them that emotional upheaval and controversy resulted. Because of its notoriety, it was made into a motion picture called *The Wave*. The point is that this teacher was in essence doing nothing more than providing an example of a concept—an enormously clever and creative example, but an example nevertheless.

The use of case studies is another very powerful tool that can be used to illustrate difficult concepts. We frequently use case studies in this text—such as those at the beginning of each chapter—to illustrate essential teaching concepts that would be impossible to illustrate otherwise in writing. Case studies are the backbone of much of the instruction in some courses in law school curricula.

**TABLE 6.4**  Types of Examples and Illustrations

| Type | Illustration |
|---|---|
| Realia (the real thing) | Mike Lee's coffee maker<br>A school store to illustrate credit and debit, profit and loss<br>A frog dissection in biology<br>A basketball as an example of a thing for the concept *noun*<br>Actual compositions or passages in English<br>Actual art objects |
| Pictures | Pictures of the Rockies and Appalachians to illustrate young and mature mountains |
| Models | A plastic heart illustrating the heart's structure<br>A drawing of dots and arrows to illustrate the movement of heated and unheated air |
| Case Studies | A written conversation between two people illustrating opinion compared to fact |
| Simulations | A mock trial to illustrate the judicial system at work |

Case studies are also effective for illustrating many complex concepts taught in our schools today. As an example, consider the following:

Pedro is a boy living in a small Mexican village. Every day he rises early, for he must walk the 2 miles to his school. He has a breakfast of beans and bread made from ground corn, leaves the house, and begins his trek. He likes the walk because he can wave to his papa toiling daily in the cornfields that provide the food and income for the family.

When Pedro comes home from school, he often plays soccer with his friends in the village. After dinner, his mother usually plays songs on a guitar while Papa sings, but this evening she must go to a meeting of the town council, where they are trying to raise money for a new addition to the school. No decisions can be made without the approval of the council.

Chu is a young girl living in a city in Japan. Chu is up early and helps her mother with breakfast for her younger brothers and sisters. Chu loves the rice smothered in a creamy sauce made from raw fish that she often eats in the morning.

Chu skips out the door, bowing to her father as she goes. He is preparing tools to go to the docks, where he will meet his partner for their daily fishing expedition. He has been a fisherman for 30 years.

Chu comes home from school, finishes her work, and then goes down the street to play ping pong with the rest of the neighborhood boys and girls. She is the best one in the area. Before bed, Chu listens to stories of the old days told by her grandfather, who lives with them.

These case studies illustrate the concept *culture* and provide a form of semiconcrete experience for students that they would not get otherwise. As we teach a concept such as *culture*, we often describe it verbally as consisting of factors such as the food, work, recreation, and music of a people. Rarely, however, do we actually *illustrate* these characteristics, and as a result, the concept is less meaningful for students. Case studies can help build that meaning when other forms of examples are not available.

*Quality of Examples.*   When we select examples for the concepts we want to teach, we naturally want the best ones we can find. But what does that mean? In this case, quality of examples has a precise definition. An example is effective to the extent that *all the essential characteristics of the concept are observable (through any of the senses) in it*. This is the ideal we strive for, and this is the reason we use pictures, models, and case studies when the real thing is not available. This also guides us as we select our examples. Once we know the essential characteristics we want the students to identify in the concept, we then select or create the examples that best illustrate those characteristics. This will often call for different media. For instance, to illustrate *mammals* we need a combination of the real thing and pictures. A hamster would allow the children to feel its warmth and fur, and pictures or models would illustrate other characteristics, such as vertebrae and heart chambers.

**TABLE 6.5** Analysis of the Concept *Metaphor*

| Concept Name | Metaphor |
|---|---|
| Definition | A metaphor is a figure of speech that makes a nonliteral comparison between two ideas. |
| Characteristics | Comparison, nonliteral |
| Examples | His eyes were limpid pools of longing. Her mind is a steel trap. |
| Superordinate concept | Figure of speech |
| Subordinate concept | Mixed metaphor |
| Coordinate concept | Simile, hyperbole, personification |

## Concept Analysis: A Planning Tool

**Concept analysis** describes concepts in terms of their characteristics, related concepts, and representative examples. A concept analysis for the concept *metaphor* is illustrated in Table 6.5.

This type of analysis offers several benefits. First, writing a definition helps clarify the teacher's goal by specifying the characteristics he or she will focus on. Identifying coordinate concepts guides teachers in their choice of nonexamples; similes, hyperboles, and personifications used as nonexamples help students clarify their understanding of *metaphor.* Meaningfulness is increased by linking all the concepts under the superordinate *figures of speech.*

## Implementing Lessons for Teaching Concepts

We teach concepts in two ways. If we use an **inductive approach,** we present the students with examples (and nonexamples) and lead them to the concept based on the similarities they observe in the examples. We arrive at closure by having the students form a definition of the concept.

If instead we use a **deductive approach,** we present a definition and use the examples to illustrate it. The key to the success of either method is the quality of the examples teachers use to illustrate the concept. Effective teachers are skilled with both.

**Teaching Concepts Inductively**   Let's look again at Mike Lee's lesson at the beginning of this chapter. We see that he began with a review of the concept *radiation* and then displayed his coffee maker. He guided his students into observing the warm burner of the coffee maker, the cold pot, and the fact that the pot was later warmer. He then compared this example with the pan and spoon heated over the candle and finally led the students to a definition of conduction. He had the students apply what they had learned by finding examples of conduction in their everyday experience. The procedure Mike used is summarized in Figure 6.4.

**FIGURE 6.4** An Inductive Teaching Model

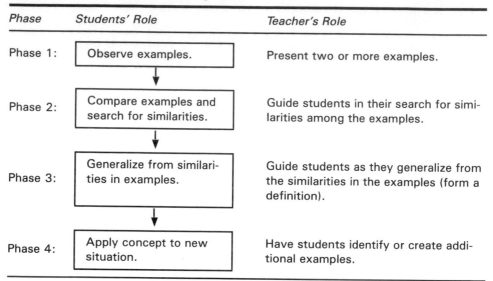

| Phase | Students' Role | Teacher's Role |
|---|---|---|
| Phase 1: | Observe examples. | Present two or more examples. |
| Phase 2: | Compare examples and search for similarities. | Guide students in their search for similarities among the examples. |
| Phase 3: | Generalize from similarities in examples. | Guide students as they generalize from the similarities in the examples (form a definition). |
| Phase 4: | Apply concept to new situation. | Have students identify or create additional examples. |

Now let's look at Simone Torrez's lesson on gerunds and participles, in the context of the teaching procedure and Mike Lee's lesson. We see that some differences exist:

- Mike used two examples to teach his concept, and Simone used three.
- Mike presented his first example, had the class discuss it, and then did the same with his second example. Simone presented all her examples at once.
- Mike conducted his lesson in a large group. Simone first had her students work in pairs and then came together as a large group.
- Simone taught two coordinate concepts—*gerund* and *participle*—simultaneously, with the examples of one serving as the nonexamples of the other. This is an effective way of teaching pairs of coordinate concepts (Tennyson and Cocciarella, 1986).

These differences are minor, however, and merely illustrate the flexibility in the procedure. Both teachers captured the essence of inductive teaching, and both were effective because they developed their lessons around examples.

**Teaching Concepts Deductively**  Now, let's look at a lesson where a concept is taught deductively.

Al Lombana had completed direct objects as part of his grammar unit and was now moving to indirect objects.

As the class bell rang, he began by saying, "We've been talking about direct objects. Let's see what we remember. Give me a sentence with a direct object in it. Ron?"

"Jack threw the ball to Shelly," Ron responded.

"Very good," Al smiled reassuringly, "And what is the direct object in the sentence?"

"The ball."

"Yes," Al smiled again. "And how do we know that 'ball' is the direct object? Tina?" [After hearing Tina's explanation, Al had the class produce and explain another example of direct objects.]

Al continued, "Now keep direct objects in mind, because we're going to begin studying a closely related idea. It's called an *indirect object*. I've written a definition of it on the board. Read that definition for me, Karen."

"When a direct object (answering the question 'What?' or 'Whom?') is used, an indirect object is sometimes used also, answering the question 'To whom?' or 'For whom?' "

"OK, good Karen. Now, let's look at Ron's sentence again. We said that 'ball' is the direct object. Now let's answer the question, 'To whom?' To whom was the ball thrown? Ken?"

"To Shelly."

"Yes! Excellent! Shelly is the indirect object."

Al continued, "Let's look at another example. See if you can identify the indirect object in this one [writing on the board]: 'Mom bought Jim the car.' What is the indirect object and why? Mario?"

"I think it's Jim, because it tells who Mom bought the car for."

"Excellent, Mario. Now let's try this one." Al wrote the following sentence on the board: 'He told the policeman the details of the accident.' "What is the indirect object, Sally?"

"Policeman," Sally responded, "because it describes who received the details."

"Good! That's exactly correct. You've identified precisely why the policeman is the indirect object. Now how about this one? 'The student gave the teacher her homework.' What do you think, Kim? Which is the indirect object?"

"Homework?"

"Look again, Kim. What did the student give?"

"The homework."

"Okay," Al smiled. "So what's that?"

"The direct object," Kim continued, hesitantly.

"OK! Good thinking! Now, who did she give it to?"

"The teacher."

"Good, Kim. So what is teacher?"

"An indirect object."

"Excellent. Well done, Kim!"

Al then gave the students the example, 'Santa Claus brought the kids presents,' had them analyze it, and asked individual students to present examples for analysis. After four different students had each given an example, he went on.

"Okay, everyone, you've done very well. Now once again. What did we learn today? Everyone."

"INDIRECT OBJECTS!" they all said in unison.

"Outstanding! And give me one more example. Doug."

After Doug gave an example, Al directed the students to write a short paragraph that had at least three direct and three indirect objects in it. To help them get started, he had a student offer a beginning sentence for a paragraph that contained both. He continued with the process, developing a short paragraph as a total group. He then had the students prepare their own paragraphs.

Let's analyze the steps involved in Al Lombana's lesson. He first reviewed direct objects and then began his lesson by displaying a definition of indirect objects. He continued by presenting the students with examples and having them identify and link the indirect objects to the definition. Finally, he had them apply their understanding by writing a paragraph that included additional examples of indirect objects. These steps are summarized in Figure 6.5.

**Inductive and Deductive Concept Teaching: A Comparison**   Let's compare the deductive teaching model as illustrated in Al Lombana's lesson to the inductive model lessons represented by Mike Lee and Simone Torrez. They were similar in several ways:

- Each teacher incorporated the elements of the general instructional model with appropriate lesson beginnings, lesson development, and closure. They were energetic, well organized, and used their time well.
- Planning for each lesson was essentially the same. All the teachers identified a precise goal and found or created examples to illustrate the concept.

**FIGURE 6.5**   A Deductive Teaching Model

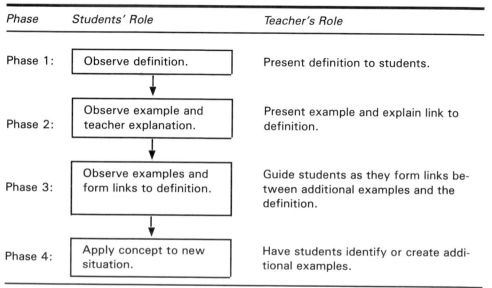

| Phase | Students' Role | Teacher's Role |
|---|---|---|
| Phase 1: | Observe definition. | Present definition to students. |
| Phase 2: | Observe example and teacher explanation. | Present example and explain link to definition. |
| Phase 3: | Observe examples and form links to definition. | Guide students as they form links between additional examples and the definition. |
| Phase 4: | Apply concept to new situation. | Have students identify or create additional examples. |

- In each case, the teacher helped students learn the concept with a combination of examples, nonexamples, and a definition.
- The last phase is the same for both models. Each teacher had the students reinforce the concepts by supplying additional examples. They were further applied with a homework assignment.
- The teachers were highly interactive in all cases.

Let's look at the differences in the two approaches. First, the sequence is reversed for the two. Mike and Simone began with examples and concluded with a definition; Al began with a definition followed by examples.

The teacher's and students' roles are different for the two. With an inductive sequence, the teacher's primary role is to guide the students' learning. Mike Lee, for example, guided the students as they made comparisons, found patterns, and finally arrived at a definition. The students were active throughout. In a deductive sequence, the teacher presents and explains in the first two phases — Al Lombana presented his definition and explained the first example's link to it — and then guides the students. The students are more passive in the first two phases of a deductive sequence than they are in the inductive procedure.

The students' thought processes are different for the two. With an inductive sequence, the students are looking for similarities and finally generalizing on the similarities they observe. With a deductive sequence, their thinking is focused on understanding and identifying the link between the examples and definition. These similarities and differences are summarized in Figure 6.6.

Each procedure has advantages. The inductive model capitalizes on a sense of the unknown in the students, and together with their active role and the safety of open-ended questions, it is effective for motivating learners — particularly low achievers. It is also effective for developing thinking skills in students, and it offers the opportunity for more incidental learning. (We examine the inductive approach again in Chapter Nine when we discuss the development of student thinking skills in detail.)

On the other hand, because a role of guiding the students' learning requires that the teacher's questions are based on student answers, the inductive model requires teachers who are confident in their understanding of subject matter and have the ability to "think on their feet." The inductive model requires highly skilled teachers.

Because lessons start with a definition to which all the examples are linked, lessons presented deductively are more focused, and they tend to be more time efficient and less demanding for teachers.

The essence for both models is the quality of the examples teachers use. Effective teachers are skilled with both procedures and use both regularly.

**Spontaneous Concept Teaching**    While most of the concepts we teach are preplanned, others periodically "pop up" during lessons, and their meaning often isn't clear. Sometimes students will tell us that they don't understand a term (concept); at other times we have to infer it from frowns or blank looks. Either can serve as the springboard for a 5-minute mini-lesson on the confusing concept. The following is an example:

**FIGURE 6.6** Inductive and Deductive Concept Learning

| | Similarities | Sequence | Teacher Role | Student Role |
|---|---|---|---|---|
| I N D U C T I V E | Both use examples<br><br><br>Concept is defined in terms of characteristics | Examples<br>↓<br><br>Definition | Present examples and help students analyze examples to extract essential characteristics | Analyze examples to define concept |
| D E D U C T I V E | Essential characteristics linked to example | Definition<br>↓<br>Example | Define concept and assist students to link definition with examples | Link definition to examples |

A fourth-grade language arts class was reading a story about the pioneers' adventures as they traveled west. As they were reading, they ran across the word *crik.*

"What's a *crik?*" asked Tom.

"It's a word the pioneers used for the word *creek,*" Mrs. Horton, their teacher responded. "Does anyone know what a creek is? . . . No one? Well, what does the story tell us? How is it used in the story?" Mrs. Horton asked.

" 'When we come to the next crik, we'll stop to let the horses drink,' " Tony answered after looking back at what they had read.

"So we know it has water in it. Well, a creek is kind of like a river but it's smaller, and the water in it moves. That's one thing that makes it different from a lake or pond."

Just then, Mrs. Horton remembered a picture in *National Geographic* that showed a creek meandering through a meadow. She got up, went to the table, got the magazine, and showed the picture to the class.

Mrs. Horton capitalized on the essence of effective concept teaching in her brief presentation. Foremost, because she happened to have the magazine with the picture in it, she was able to give the students a visual example of the concept. This is the ideal, and teachers should always try to supply an example if it is possible to do so. However, since examples may not be available, teachers need other options, and Mrs. Horton capitalized on them as well. These are outlined in Table 6.6.

**TABLE 6.6**   Strategies for Spontaneously Teaching Concepts

| Strategy | Example |
|---|---|
| Link to superordinate concept | It's a body of water. |
| Compare to coordinate concept | It's kind of like a river. |
| Identify characteristics | It has water in it.<br>It is smaller than a river.<br>The water in it moves. |
| Present nonexamples | It is different from a pond or lake. |
| Analyze context | How is it described in the story? |

This completes our discussion of concepts and how they're taught. We turn now to generalizations, even more powerful forms of content — powerful because they describe relationships among concepts and, as a result, have the ability to summarize large amounts of information.

# GENERALIZATIONS

Let's think again about Mike Lee's lesson at the beginning of this chapter. Mike's objective was for his students to understand the concept of *conduction*. He then presented examples and guided his students to a definition of the concept.

Assuming that students understand the concept, suppose that Mike now wants them to understand, "Dense materials conduct heat faster than do less dense materials." (Coffee cools off faster in a ceramic cup than it does in a styrofoam cup.) This goal is a **generalization**, which is a statement that describes a relationship between two or more concepts. In our example we said that the goal is to understand the relationship between *conduction* (one concept) and *density* (another concept), and this statement can be used to explain different rates of heat transfer in a wide variety of situations.

As with concepts, generalizations abound in the curriculum. The following are a few examples.

Herbivores have longer legs than do carnivores.

The earlier the musical piece, the fewer the instruments in the orchestra.

Objects at rest remain at rest, and moving objects remain moving in a straight line unless a force acts on them.

Complementary colors balance each other, with the brighter ones standing out and darker ones receding.

The farther from the equator, the longer the days in summer and the shorter the days in winter.

Pronouns must agree with their antecedent in number and gender.

Adjectives precede the noun in English but follow the noun in Spanish.

In our discussion of concept learning, we saw how learners identify similar characteristics in examples and, based on the similarities, form concepts. Forming generalizations involves a similar process. Learners identify patterns in a series of facts and employ concepts to help describe the pattern.

The relationships among facts, concepts, and generalizations are illustrated in Table 6.7.

We can see the dynamic relationship that exists among facts, concepts, and generalizations. None of the facts in isolation is especially meaningful; for example, knowing that Randall Kelly came to this country after the potato famine tells us very little. However, the summarized relationship between economics and immigration is very useful, because it provides the basis for explaining and predicting other events. For instance, we meet a new colleague from India, and we are likely to infer that he or she thought that more opportunity existed here than in his or her native country. If economic conditions continue to improve in Mexico, we would predict less of an influx of people across the Rio Grande; conversely, if they worsen, a greater migration rate would be expected. The explanation and prediction are both based on the generalization relating immigration and economics.

## Laws, Principles, and Academic Rules

As we think about the preceding section, we might say to ourselves, "Wait a minute. I know examples of immigrants who left their native country in spite of being very successful economically." This is undoubtedly true. People immigrate for political and religious reasons (and others), so the generalization relating immigration to economics doesn't apply in all cases. When we intuitively think of generalizations, we usually think of patterns for which there are obvious exceptions, and this is the case in our example with immigration.

However, some generalizations exist for which there are no known exceptions, or the exceptions exist only in extreme cases. We call these statements laws or principles. (While some scientists discriminate between the two terms, we use them synonymously.) A **law** or **principle** is a generalization that we accept as true for all cases. For example, when we say, "Objects at rest will remain at rest unless a force acts on them," we are stating a law. This is part of Newton's first law, or the law of inertia. As with any generalization, it describes a relationship among concepts (motion and

**TABLE 6.7** Relationship among Facts, Concepts, and Generalizations

| Type of Content | Example |
| --- | --- |
| Facts | Randall Kelly came to this country shortly after the Irish potato famine. Soo Ling was recruited to work on the transcontinental railroad. Pablo Martinez left Mexico because he could not support his family on his small farm. |
| Concepts | Immigration Economics |
| Generalization | People immigrated to this country for economic reasons. |

force), and we can use it to explain and predict other events. For example, we see a tennis ball sitting on a level floor, and we would predict that it will stay there forever if someone does not pick it up, kick it, or hit it with something.

Because we accept principles as "true," some learners are inclined to confuse them with facts. Notice, however, that the law of inertia does not describe a single event, but rather summarizes all cases involving objects, motion, and force. In isolation, seeing the tennis ball sitting on the floor is a fact, and it allows no prediction or explanation. The law summarizes this and other cases of resting objects into a relationship allowing both explanation and prediction. The single incidence is a fact; the summary statement is a principle or law.

Look again at the statement, "Adjectives precede the noun in English but follow the noun in Spanish." This statement is an **academic rule**, which is a generalization that has been arbitrarily developed by humans. For instance, deciding that the adjective precedes the noun in English is strictly arbitrary. When the language evolved, it would have been equally valid to have the adjective follow the noun, as in Spanish and French. This is the case with all our rules of grammar, spelling, and punctuation. Rules are important, of course, because they provide for consistency in communication.

While we most commonly think of rules in language arts, they exist in other areas as well. For example, we round off the number 64 to 60 and the number 65 to 70, because the rule says round "up" if the number is five or more. As with grammar, this is an arbitrary rule or convention that we follow to make the process uniform.

## Teaching Generalizations

How are generalizations and principles learned, and what implications does this have for the classroom? Like concepts, they are abstractions whose meaning depends on examples, and these examples can be presented inductively or deductively. The generalization "People immigrate for economic reasons" is meaningful only if learners can relate the abstract statement to real-world events. This is especially true for young children, whose capacity for abstract thought is hampered by limited vocabulary, verbal ability, and experience.

As with concepts, the abstraction-example sequence has important implications for the type of interaction that occurs in the classroom. In an inductive format, we first provide students with a number of facts and through our questions help them find patterns in the data. In a deductive format, the generalization is first stated, terms within it are defined, and it is then related to examples or instances. Let's see how these ideas work in an art class.

David Smith had his art class involved in a study of the Impressionist school of art. He began his third-period class by saying, "Let's take a look at some paintings today done by Impressionists. This one is by Vincent Van Gogh. It's called *Seascape on Saintes Maries.* Since there are boats and water that makes sense, doesn't it? The other is by Monet. What do you think it might be called? Sherry?"

"How about 'Harbor Scene'?" Sherry responded after gazing at the picture.

"That's a good idea. How about you, Tim?"

"Maybe . . . 'Sailboats'?"

"Actually you're both close. It's called *Bridge at Argenteuil*. Argenteuil must be the name of a harbor with a bridge that Monet painted. He has other paintings located here. Let's take a look at these paintings and talk about how the artist put them together. Let's focus on the Van Gogh first. What do we see in it? Harry."

"I see a bunch of boats on a choppy sea."

"OK, good," David smiled. "Anything else, Meg?"

"They look like small fishing boats because they only have one mast."

"Good observation, Meg. . . . How does the painting make you feel? Jan?"

"Kind of like I'm right on the water."

"Why do you think it does that?"

"Well, I'm not quite sure. . . . You can see, almost feel, the waves in the front of the painting. They sort of look almost alive, if that makes any sense."

"That's an excellent description, Meg!" David responded enthusiastically. "Keep what Meg said in mind, everyone. Now, look. Does everyone see these waves here? Why do they stand out? Gary."

"Got me," Gary shrugged.

"What color are they?" David prompted.

"Yellow."

"OK, and what color is the background?"

"Blue-green."

"OK. Does anything else in the painting stand out? Jeremy?"

"The sails on the boats. Hey, they're yellow too."

"Good," David smiled in response to Jeremy's revelation. "Now, notice the color of the sky surrounding these sails. What color would you call it? Michelle?"

"Mmm, purple, almost violet."

"Okay, let's keep those combinations in mind as we look at the next picture. This one is the Monet. And it's a water scene, too. But look at the water. How is it different from Van Gogh's *Seascape*? Stan?"

"It's really calm. There are only little waves and not much is moving."

"Fine, Stan. Now, let's look at this painting more closely. What do we tend to focus on when we see it? . . . What does Monet want us to look at here? Anyone? Sam?"

"I think it's the sailboat."

"Why do you think so?"

"Well, for one thing it's in the center of the picture."

"Good, the position of an object pulls the viewer toward it. Why else are we drawn to the sailboat? Look at its mast. What does the mast do for this painting? Sandra?"

"It really sticks out."

"Why do you think so?"

"Well, I don't know. It just does."

"Think about our observations of Van Gogh's *Seascape on Saintes Maries.* How does our Monet compare to that picture?"

"Well, they both have light colors next to dark," Sandra responded, looking back and forth from one picture to the other.

"Excellent, Sandra! Now, I'd like you to look at this painting that I put together just this morning. What does it look like? Fred."

"A bullseye."

"Good, and what colors do we have here? Sarah?"

"Red and green."

"Okay. What happens when we put these two colors together? What does it do to the painting? Sonya?"

"The red kind of jumps out at you and the green sort of fades."

"Good. Who remembers what we call color pairs like the ones we've been discussing? Let's write them up on the board." David then wrote

Yellow-Violet
Orange-Blue
Red-Green

"George, do you remember?"

"They're complementary colors."

"Excellent! Everyone, look at the color wheel. Note how the color pairs are at opposite sides of the color wheel. Now, let's look back at the three paintings we've been discussing to see if we can make a statement about what happens when we put complementary colors next to each other. Think for a minute. . . . Give it a try, Nancy."

"I think they do two things. One is that they really make each other stand out. It's a really sharp contrast. The other is that the dark colors look like they sink," Nancy said hesitantly.

"Good ideas, Nancy. Did everyone hear them? Let's write them down here so everyone can see. What did Nancy say? Janet?"

"Complementary colors next to each other make each other stand out," Janet repeated.

"Excellent, Janet! That's a precise statement of the relationship we found. Now, what else? Steve?"

"The brighter color in the pair stands out and the darker one recedes," Steve responded confidently after hearing Janet's description.

"Okay! Good work, all of you. Now, let's take a look at one more painting, and I want everyone to see if these statements make sense. This one is called *The Dance*, and it's by Henri Matisse. Which colors stand out and which recede? Tony."

"The oranges really jump out and the greens and blues recede."

David continued, "Excellent! And why is that the case? Ken?"

"The orange is lighter, so it stands out, and the greens and blues are darker, so they recede."

"Very good explanation, Ken, and good work everyone," David exclaimed. "Now let's see if we can apply these ideas to our own paintings. I've set up some still lifes over here for us to paint. Let's try to use some of the complementary colors that we discussed to emphasize objects in our paintings."

The students then went to work on their paintings and continued through the rest of the period.

Let's look at David's lesson and see how it illustrates the ideas we've been discussing.

**Teaching Generalizations: Planning**    In recalling the planning process for teaching concepts, we found that three essential steps were involved:

- Identifying the topic
- Determining a precise objective
- Preparing examples

The planning process involved in teaching generalization includes the same three steps.

David's topic was the effect of color on paintings. His precise goal was two generalizations; one related the concept *complementary colors* to *visual prominence*—"Complementary colors next to each other make each other stand out"—and the other related *lightness/darkness* to *prominence*—"The brighter color in the pair stands out and the darker one recedes."

Having determined his precise objective, David identified excellent examples. His lesson didn't focus on either complementary colors or visual prominence in isolation. Rather, he taught the *relationship* between the two, and his examples were good because each illustrated this relationship. This is the case whenever a generalization is illustrated effectively. Think back for a moment to José Alvarez's lesson in Chapter 5. He taught his students the generalizations, "Heat makes materials expand" and "Heat makes molecules move faster," and his examples concretely illustrated the *relationship* between heat and expansion as well as the relationship between heat and molecular movement.

**Implementing Lessons for Teaching Generalizations**    As with planning, implementing lessons in which generalizations are taught is very similar to implementing lessons for teaching concepts. David Smith used an inductive approach, and he followed a procedure nearly identical to the inductive model we presented in Figure 6.2. The only minor difference was that David guided his students to a *statement of the generalizations* he identified in his objective instead of guiding them to a *definition* as would be the case if a concept were taught. He then had his students explain the use of colors in another painting using the generalizations, which is analogous to having them identify additional examples of a concept. Using a deductive approach would be similar. Instead of presenting a definition and linking examples to it, as would be the case if a concept were taught, David would state (or write) the generalizations he wanted his students to understand, and he would then link the use of

**TABLE 6.8**  Inductive and Deductive Strategies for Teaching Generalizations

| Phase of Lesson | Inductive Sequence | Deductive Sequence |
|---|---|---|
| Introduction/ Beginning | Examples presented. Students make observations. | Teacher states generalization. Ensures all concepts in it are understood. |
| Development/ Main part | Teacher questions direct student observations to critical variables. Comparison-and-contrast questions encourage student inference. | Teacher questions link generalization to examples. |
| End/Closure | Teacher tests student understanding through application of generalization. | Teacher tests student understanding through application of generalization. |

colors in his pictures to the generalizations. The application phase would be the same as the application phase in David's lesson. These similarities and differences are summarized in Table 6.8.

When teaching generalizations, we want students to understand the relationship between the abstraction and the data being summarized. We do this by linking the generalization to examples. In an inductive sequence, the examples are presented and the teacher uses questions to help students find patterns; in a deductive sequence, the generalization is first explained and then illustrated with examples.

This concludes our discussion of teaching strategies designed to teach facts, concepts, and generalizations. In the next chapter, we consider ways of linking these forms of content into organized bodies of information. But before you turn to that chapter, please read the chapter summary and complete the exercises that follow.

## SUMMARY

Facts comprise one important, if overemphasized, part of the school curriculum. Screens to use in assessing the value of facts in the curriculum include their future utility and whether they will remain important over time.

Strategies for teaching facts range from memorization through repetitious drill and practice to more meaningful processing. These latter strategies provide not only better immediate results but also greater long-term retention through the integration of facts with other meaningful material.

Concepts are abstract categories that we use to classify objects, events, and ideas. We learn new concepts by encountering examples and nonexamples and identifying the similarities in the positive examples (the psychological process of generalizing) and how they are different from the negative ones (the process of discrimination). As we encounter examples, we learn abstract characteristics that differentiate positive and negative examples and help define the boundaries of the concept. Words allow us to put labels on the essential characteristics of concepts and to use these characteristics to differentiate between additional positive and negative examples of the concept.

Superordinate concepts are larger categories into which the concept fits. Coordinate concepts are additional subsets of the superordinate concept. This organization has implications for instruction. Studies from diverse areas such as comprehension of reading passages, lecturing, and questioning all indicate that content organization helps not only initial learning but also long-term retention. The more we can help our students see the logical relationship between concepts, the better they can learn and retain these ideas.

When we teach concepts, we want students to understand (1) the concept's essential characteristics, (2) how these relate to positive and negative examples, and (3) the relationship of the concept to other ideas. This last function is accomplished by linking the concept to superordinate and coordinate concepts.

Concepts are taught in two major ways. In deductive teaching, a definition is presented and linked to positive and negative examples. An inductive sequence presents students with examples and then asks students to analyze the examples to identify essential characteristics. Both types of concept lessons are interactive to encourage student involvement and to allow the teacher to gauge whether students are understanding the concept.

Spontaneous concept teaching occurs when ambiguous concepts are encountered in the course of a lesson. The same essential components of effective concept teaching apply here: (1) positive and negative examples, (2) characteristics, (3) superordinate concept, and (4) coordinate concepts.

Generalizations, a second major form of abstraction taught in classrooms, summarize large amounts of information in statements linking important concepts. Their value in the curriculum lies in their ability to relate a large number of facts as well as their use in prediction and explanations.

When teaching generalizations, we want students to understand the relationship between the abstraction and the data being summarized. We do this by linking the generalization to examples. In a deductive sequence, the generalization is first explained and then illustrated with examples; in an inductive sequence, the examples are presented and the teacher uses questions to help students find patterns.

# ADDITIONAL READINGS FOR PROFESSIONAL GROWTH

Eggen, P., & Kauchak, D. (1992). *Educational psychology: Classroom connections.* Columbus, OH: Merrill. This book places the learning of facts, concepts, and generalizations within a cognitive learning perspective.

Hyde, H., & Bizar, M. (1989). *Thinking in content: Teaching cognitive processes across the elementary school curriculum.* New York: Longman. Though focusing on elementary instruction, this book provides insights into teaching concepts at all levels.

Tennyson, R., & Cocciarella, M. (1986). An empirically based instructional theory for teaching concepts. *Review of Educational Research, 50,* 55–70. An excellent overview of the issues involved in teaching concepts.

## EXERCISES

**1.** Read this passage and answer the questions that follow.

Elephants are interesting animals. Like all mammals, they are warm blooded, bear their young live, and nurse their young. They also have hair, but unlike other mammals like tigers and horses, this usually doesn't cover the entire body. There are two kinds of elephants, Asian and African. The African elephant is larger and has bigger ears. As in most animals, the length of the gestation period is related to the size of the animal (and the size of the baby). We can see why it might take a female elephant up to 22 months to have a baby if we consider that at birth the baby may weigh 200 pounds. Elephants have been used by humans over the years. Hannibal used elephants as living tanks to carry his troops. Elephants also have been used as beasts of burden in warm countries.

**a.** From the passage, identify a superordinate concept and two coordinate concepts to the concept *elephant*.

**b.** List two facts in the passage.

**c.** Identify a generalization in the passage.

**2.** In the following passages, indicate whether the lesson was inductive or deductive and explain why.

**a.** Miss Kennedy was teaching a lesson on different kinds of plants. She began the lesson by showing the class a jade plant and saying, "This is a succulent. It's a perennial that can exist on very little water. Notice the leaves. They're waxy on the outside to retain moisture and they are thick to store water within them. Here's another succulent. What do you notice about it?" With that, she held up a cactus.

"Ooh, it has sharp spines," observed Jim.

"Yes, those are modified leaves. They not only help protect the plant but also help by minimizing transpiration." Miss Kennedy then brought out a philodendron and had the class classify it.

**b.** Mr. Eyring was trying to teach his junior high social studies class about the laws of supply and demand. He began by sharing the information in Table 6.9.

**TABLE 6.9**  Price of Tomatoes

| *Month* | *$/lb.* |
|---------|---------|
| June    | $ .79   |
| July    | $ .59   |
| August  | $ .39   |

After they discussed this information, he shared the following information with them:

> Price of salmon in Seattle (9/1/92) — $2.79/lb.
> Price of salmon in Denver (9/1/92) — $3.29/lb.

Mr. Eyring encouraged the class to compare the two bits of information. Then, he showed them the following headline:

> FROST DAMAGES CITRUS CROP
> ORANGE JUICE PRICE SKYROCKETS

After some discussion, the class concluded that price is inversely related to the supply of something. Mr. Eyring went on to tackle the topic of demand.

3. Read this passage and answer the questions that follow.

> Miss Handy wanted to teach her fourth-grade health class about sources of protein. She began her lesson by showing the class a picture of a piece of cheese and saying, "This is a source of protein. It is an animal product that we eat that our body needs." She then showed them a picture of a steak and said, "This is also a source of protein." Then she showed them a picture of a roast turkey and asked them, "Is this a source of protein?" Johnny eagerly answered, "Yes, because it's an animal product that our body can use." "Good," replied Miss Handy, "now look at all these pictures and tell me something about protein." Mary raised her hand and stated, "They're all farm products." "Excellent," said Miss Handy. "It is important to know where protein comes from because it is an essential part of our diet. We should eat protein every day."

a. Was the procedure inductive or deductive? Explain.

b. Assess the quality of the lesson, and provide a rationale for your assessment.

# DISCUSSION QUESTIONS

1. How does the optimal mix of facts, concepts, and generalizations vary in terms of
   a. Grade level (e.g., Would you recommend relatively more fact learning in the first few grades than in high school?)
   b. Ability level (e.g., Do lower ability students need more or less emphasis on concepts?)

c. Subject matter (How does the specific focus of a content area, like social studies or art, influence content goals?)

2. In 1987, the book *Cultural Literacy: What Every American Needs to Know* (Hirsch, 1987) was on the *New York Times* Best Seller List for months. The basic idea behind this book is that our cultural heritage can be defined by a list of terms that every literate citizen should know. Examine the following items from Hirsch's list and answer the questions that follow:

| | |
|---|---|
| Truman–MacArthur controversy | trust busting |
| trump card | Truth is stranger than fiction. |
| trumpet | Truth will win out. |
| Tucson, Arizona | Tutankhamen |
| Tudor monarchy | Twain, Mark |
| Tulsa, Oklahoma | Tweed, Boss |
| tundra | Tweedledum and Tweedledee |
| Tunis | Twenty-third Psalm (text) |
| Tunisia | Twinkle, Twinkle Little Star |
| turbine | Two China Policy |
| Turk, Young | Two heads are better than one. |
| turkey | Two's company, three's a crowd. |
| Turkey in the Straw (tune) | two shakes of a lamb's tail |
| Turn about is fair play. | Two wrongs don't make a right. |
| Turner, Nat | tycoon |
| turn over a new leaf | typhoid fever |
| turn the other cheek | Typhoid Mary |

(1987, pp. 210–211)

a. What kinds of content are contained in this list?

b. Who should be responsible for teaching this type of content?

c. How does the list fare in terms of the criteria listed in this chapter for including facts in the curriculum?

3. Some workers in the area of concept learning have suggested that the optimal number of positive/negative examples to be used in teaching a concept is three. What factors might influence this optimal number?

4. What advantages are there in asking students to generate their own examples and nonexamples of concepts and generalizations? Are there any disadvantages?

5. What are the advantages and disadvantages of inductive and deductive learning? How does your particular grade-level focus (elementary or secondary) influence the value of either?

6. In Chapter 4, we talked about the idea of modeling. How do the examples in concept learning relate to this idea? How are they different?

7. In Chapter 4, we discussed the following general characteristics of effective teaching. How do these apply to inductive and deductive concept teaching?

   a. Focus

   b. Organization

   c. Pacing

   d. Practicing and feedback

   e. Review and closure

8. At the beginning of this chapter, we asserted that what you teach should influence how you teach. Relate this idea to the following:

   a. Facts

   b. Concepts

   c. Generalizations

9. What are the implications of this chapter in terms of planning for the following?:

   a. Fact teaching

   b. Concept teaching

   c. Teaching for generalizations

10. What are the implications of this chapter in terms of testing for the following?:

    a. Facts

    b. Concepts

    c. Generalizations

## APPLYING IT IN THE SCHOOLS

1. *Cognitive Goals.* Examine a school district's curriculum guide for a specific area of the curriculum (e.g., fourth-grade social studies or high school biology). What percentage of the goals correspond to each of these areas of the cognitive domain? (In your answer, include a concrete example for each category.)

   a. Facts

   b. Concepts

   c. Generalizations

2. *Textbook Content Goals.* Analyze a chapter from a content-area text book in your area (e.g., second-grade science or eighth-grade English). How much emphasis (pages or sections) is given to the following?:

   a. Facts

   b. Concepts

   c. Generalizations

Critique this distribution in terms of your views of the purpose of that course.

3. *Facts.* Select one of the facts identified in question 2. Using the screening criteria suggested in this chapter, evaluate whether it should be included in the curriculum.

4. *Interactive Teaching.* Observe and audiotape a classroom lesson. Analyze the content of the lesson in terms of the ideas in this chapter (i.e., which content was facts, concepts, and generalizations?). Diagram the structure of the content with some type of schematic diagram. Answer the following questions:

   **a.** Was the organization of the content apparent?

   **b.** Was there an appropriate mix of the different forms of content?

   **c.** Were the concepts and generalizations illustrated with examples?

5. *Concept Teaching in Textbooks.* Identify a concept being taught in a school text. Analyze the quality of the concept teaching in terms of the following criteria:

   **a.** Characteristics (clearly defined?)

   **b.** Examples and nonexamples (linked to characteristics?)

   **c.** Superordinate concept (familiar to students?)

   **d.** Coordinate concept (clearly differentiated from the target concept?)

6. *Interactive Concept Teaching.* Observe a teacher teaching a concept (or teach one yourself) and critique the lesson in terms of the criteria in numbers.

7. *Interactive Teaching of Generalizations.* Observe (or tape) a lesson in which a generalizaiton is being taught.

   **a.** Identify the generalization.

   **b.** What examples were used to illlustrate the generalization?

   **c.** Was the sequence inductive or deductive? Explain.

   **d.** Were students asked to apply the generalization? How?

# CHAPTER 7

# Organized Bodies of Knowledge: Integrating Facts, Concepts, and Generalizations

## OVERVIEW

Our analysis of instructional strategies designed to teach specific forms of content continues in this chapter. In Chapter Six we examined facts, concepts, and generalizations—the building blocks of learning. These forms of content often can be isolated and taught individually using specific instructional strategies. Often, however, facts, concepts, and generalizations are all embedded in larger contexts where the focus is on the interrelationships among them. We call these relationships *organized bodies of knowledge*, and we now turn to a study of them. Lectures, lecture/recitation, and inductive approaches to teaching organized bodies of knowledge provide us with instructional alternatives. This chapter is devoted to a discussion of these alternatives.

## MAIN IDEAS

### Organized Bodies of Knowledge

*Organized bodies of knowledge* subsume facts, concepts, and generalizations.
Organized bodies of knowledge focus on complex *relationships* among facts, concepts, and generalizations.

### Visual Ways of Organizing Bodies of Knowledge

*Matrices* allow specific information to be placed in cells for analysis.
Complex relations are visually illustrated in *networks*. *Schematics* represent both content and sequencing of data.

### Teaching Organized Bodies of Knowledge Deductively

*Lectures* are commonly used to present large quantities of information.
Information presentation and student interaction are combined in the *lecture-recitation* cycle.
The lecture-recitation cycle includes *information presentation*, *monitoring comprehension*, and *integration*.

### Teaching Organized Bodies of Knowledge Inductively

When using inductive approaches, the process begins by establishing a *data base*.
Finding relationships is accomplished through *description and comparison* of elements in the data base.
Relationships are explored by identifying *cause and effect*.
*Application* and *hypothesizing* extend understanding and thinking skills.

Henry Myer watched as the last of his students turned in their quizzes on the circulatory system. Glancing at the clock to see how much time was left in the period, he moved to the front of the classroom, waited briefly until all the students were looking at him, and said, "Within the next hour you are going to witness a scientific miracle, and it's going to start in our school cafeteria."

"Do you mean students will eat there and not die?" Larry commented, pleased with his wit.

"Close, Larry," Henry responded, smiling as he waited for the class to stop laughing. "Think about it. You'll see people putting the most dissimilar stuff in their mouths—carrots, milk, hamburgers, chips, candy and all kinds of garbage. Their bodies take it all in and 28 feet and 36 hours later have efficiently turned it into fuel and gotten rid of the rest. That's what we're going to learn about today. We're beginning our study of the digestive system."

Henry then displayed the information shown in Figure 7.1 on the overhead.

"As you can see on the overhead," Henry continued, "there are six major parts of the digestive system. We are going to examine each of these sequentially, analyzing both the organs in each and the functions they perform. If you'll recall, we did this with the circulatory system, emphasizing form and function. When we're done, we'll have a chart that will look something like this." Henry displayed the chart shown in Figure 7.2. "When we complete this unit, you should be able to trace a bite of food through the whole system, describe what happens to it and explain why."

Henry continued, "The digestive system is like an ore-refining factory. Big chunks of ore-bearing rocks are brought into the factory. These need to be broken down and the valuable ore separated from the dirt and the other stuff. Then the valuable ore needs to be collected in a usable form and the rest discarded.

"The same thing happens in our digestive system. We first need to break down the big clumps of food so they can be processed. Then we need to separate out the parts the body can use. Finally, the nonusable parts are discarded.

**FIGURE 7.1** Schematic Diagram of Digestive System (Adapted from Vaughan, 1984)

| Organs | Mouth | Function |
|---|---|---|
| | Swallowing tubes | |
| | Stomach | |
| | Small intestine | |
| | Large intestine | |
| | Colon and rectum | |

**FIGURE 7.2**  Matrix Summarizing Digestive System

|  | Major Structures | Functions | Products | Length/Time |
|---|---|---|---|---|
| Mouth |  |  |  |  |
| Swallowing Tubes |  |  |  |  |

This all starts with the mouth." With that, Henry drew on the board the chart shown in Figure 7.3.

Henry continued, "When we talk about the different parts of the digestive system, we'll analyze them in terms of the reciprocal processes of breaking down and absorption. Breaking down food, or digestion, makes food into smaller pieces so it can be processed and so the nutrients are transportable. Absorption refers to soaking up the nutrients in the food so other parts of the body can use them. Let's stop for a second and make sure these ideas are making sense.

"How does the mouth help break down foods? Jeremy."

"The teeth."

"Go on."

"Well, the teeth help us grind up food into smaller pieces so we can swallow."

"Good, and what else is in our mouths that aids digestion?"

". . ."

"No one? Try this. It's getting toward lunch time. Think about food you really like, like a juicy hamburger or hot, steaming pizza. What's happening in your mouth? That's right, your mouth is watering. That's saliva, and saliva contains an enzyme called ptyalin that converts starch to sugar. Why is that important? Kerry?"

"The blood."

**FIGURE 7.3**  Reciprocal Processes of Digestion

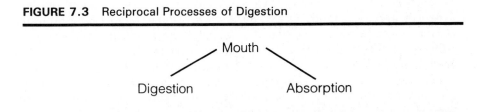

"Say more."

"We just studied about the blood, and one of the things it does is carry sugar to the rest of the body for energy."

"Good, Kerry. The digestive system is linked to the circulatory system, so the blood can carry food to the rest of the body. The circulatory system does this by absorbing sugars through the walls of the digestive system. Look up on the board at the two functions, digestion and absorption. The mouth starts these by chewing up the food and by secreting an enzyme that helps our bodies absorb starches later on. What would happen if the starch weren't converted to sugar? Zach?"

"It would have to happen somewhere else."

"Good, Zach, and why might that be a problem? Kim?"

"Because it would take longer for the body to get energy then."

"Excellent, Kim! Let's talk a little more about how the mouth does this."

The discussion of the mouth continued, proceeded to a consideration of the esophagus and pharynx, and then Henry noticed the clock.

"I see we're running out of time, so before we stop, let's give ourselves a few minutes to wrap up what we've done. Who remembers some of the important ideas we talked about so far? Shannon."

"Digestion means breaking food down, and absorption helps move it into the blood."

"Good, and where does this all start? Matt."

"The mouth. It chews food into small parts and something called. . . ."

"Look on the board."

"Oh yeah, ptyalin converts starch to sugar."

"Fine, Matt. So then, where does it go from there? Pat."

"Through the pharynx and down the esophagus."

"Okay, class, that's enough for now. Tomorrow we'll pick up here [pointing to Figure 7.1 on the overhead] and continue our journey through the digestive system. Please note your reading assignment on the board for tomorrow. As you're reading, remember the two concepts—digestion, or breaking down, and absorption. They're the keys to understanding the digestive system. Think about them while you're eating your lunch. Okay, you can go now."

As we began Chapter 6, we asked you to think about Mike Lee's lesson on conduction in the context of the general instructional model. We saw that he incorporated most of the elements of the model in his teaching, and he adapted it where necessary to meet his specific goal—teaching a concept.

Let's do the same with Henry Myer's teaching. To what extent did he use the general instructional model as a guide, and where did he adapt? He established *introductory focus* by suggesting that the students were going to witness a miracle and relating it to the variety of foods the students were eating. We also saw in Chapter 4 that *advance organizers* can be used as a form of introductory focus, and Henry capitalized on their use by comparing digestion to the refining of ore. While he didn't conduct a formal *review*, the students had just finished a quiz on the circulatory system, and he related digestion to the circulatory system as the lesson progressed.

His schematic, matrix, and hierarchy provided forms of *sensory focus*, and he maintained high levels of *student involvement* with his questioning. When he saw that he wouldn't be able to finish the lesson, he conducted a lesson-ending review that served as a form of *closure* for the day. He also conducted the lesson with *enthusiasm* and *energy*. Like Mike Lee in Chapter 6, Henry effectively applied the elements of the general instructional model as he introduced, developed, and completed his lesson.

As with Mike's teaching, we need to examine Henry's work in more detail to understand fully how he adapted the general instructional model to meet his goals. We do so in the sections that follow.

# ORGANIZED BODIES OF KNOWLEDGE: INTEGRATING FACTS, CONCEPTS, AND GENERALIZATIONS

To examine Henry's lesson more specifically, let's analyze his lesson's content. It focused on the general topic of *digestion*. Within this broad area were facts, such as the specific foods the students were eating in the cafeteria, parts of the digestive system (each of which are concepts), and generalizations like "Digestion begins in the mouth." However, unlike Mike Lee's lesson in Chapter 6, which focused specifically on the concept of conduction, Henry's wasn't directed at any of these elements specifically; rather it was aimed at the relationships among all these parts. It included information such as the role the teeth play, the connection between absorption and digestion, and how waste is discarded. Henry was teaching an **organized body of knowledge**, which is a combination of facts, concepts, and generalizations integrated with each other.

As another example, suppose you're comparing novels by twentieth-century American writers. Your study would deal with the relationships among a number of facts; concepts like *plot*, *setting*, and *character*; and generalizations, such as "Writers' life experiences are reflected in their writing." It wouldn't focus on any of the elements separately.

As with concepts and generalizations, organized bodies of knowledge are an important part of the school curriculum. For example, geography students study the topography, climate, culture, and politics of one country and compare them to the same elements in other countries. In a study of immigration in the late nineteenth and early twentieth centuries, American history students examine reasons immigrants came to the United States, the difficulties they encountered, and the ways they were assimilated into our culture. Chemistry students study the characteristics of the elements in the periodic table and the relationships among them. These are all organized bodies of knowledge.

One specialized subset of organized bodies of knowledge are **theories**, which have precisely described relationships among the concepts and generalizations that comprise them. In science, for example, we have the theory of evolution, the molecular theory, and theories about the origins of the universe. In the social sciences, we have learning theories such as behaviorism and information processing; sociological theories such as Durkheim's theory of suicide; and economic theories such as supply economics.

Other writers use different labels to describe organized bodies of knowledge. Calfee (1986) used the term *explicit explanation* and stressed the importance of precise descriptions of the connections between ideas. Other labels include *declarative knowledge*, *factual knowledge*, *explaining*, or simply the learning of *content* (Rosenshine, 1986). Rosenshine differentiated this type of content from skills: "It is not the 'how to' of skills; rather, it is the who, what, where, when, why, and how of content knowledge—what happened, how did it happen, and why did it happen?" (p. 7). When the answers to the who, what, and why questions are tied together in a meaningful way, we have an organized body of knowledge.

# TEACHING ORGANIZED BODIES OF KNOWLEDGE: PLANNING

How large are organized bodies of information, and how does this size affect learning? Ideally, we want all of the information that students learn to be integrated in a meaningful way. More practically, we can think of these bodies as occurring at three levels: the course, the unit, and the lesson. We try to organize our courses coherently, providing an overview at the beginning and tying it up at the end, hoping that students exit with a body of interrelated ideas. Similarly, the units we construct are bounded structures with beginning and end points. Finally, a lesson focusing on an organized body of information ought to have internal coherence and organization characterized by a structured introduction, a logical development, and a comprehensive summary. When this coherence is present, students have something meaningful to remember.

When we discussed planning for teaching either concepts or generalizations, we identified three essential steps:

- Identifying the topic
- Determining a precise objective
- Preparing examples.

In planning to teach an organized body of knowledge, you must also identify a topic, and you must have a clear idea of what you want your students to know or understand; so the first two steps are similar to those when you plan to teach a concept or generalization.

The third step is different, however, and is more complex. While finding good illustrations of concepts or generalizations can be difficult, at least the task is well defined. For example, in the previous chapter Mike Lee knew that he needed clear examples of *conduction*, and David Smith knew he needed paintings that illustrate prominent and receding complementary colors. When teaching an organized body of knowledge, teachers have to make more decisions about what will be taught, how the parts will be organized, and how the information will be represented for the students.

This part of the planning process requires careful decision making. The following questions can be helpful:

- How does this topic relate to previous ones?
- Which prerequisite ideas do students need to know?
- How can I organize the information so important ideas are interrelated?
- How should I present the organized information to the students?

Assuming now that you've answered the first two questions, the key is careful organization of the content you plan to teach. The following sections describe some different forms of organization.

## Organization through Spatial Representations

The term *organized* implies that the individual ideas making up the body of knowledge are related and connected, and the form the information is presented in must then imply these connections.

Bodies of knowledge can be organized and represented in several different ways. Each provides sensory focus for the students and illustrates the relationships among the different parts. Spatial techniques such as matrices, networks, hierarchies, and schematic diagrams are all effective (Holley and Dansereau, 1984; Novak and Gowin, 1984).

**Matrices**   Matrices are two-dimensional tables that are useful for comparing and contrasting major concepts. The ideas being compared are placed on the left margin, and the key dimensions or characteristics being considered are displayed along the top. These can be simple tables for elementary students, such as the matrix in Figure 7.4, or they can be more elaborate, like the one Henry Myer used in his lesson (Figure 7.2).

**Networks**   Networks are simple diagrams that link related ideas, and they have been demonstrated as effective in helping students learn from textbooks (Holley and Dansereau, 1984). These same networks, when shared on an overhead or blackboard, can help students understand the interrelationship of ideas when a body of knowledge is being taught. A network from the area of physical education is illustrated Figure 7.5.

**Conceptual Hierarchies**   A special type of network, conceptual hierarchies connect superordinate and subordinate ideas to each other. For instance, in Figure 7.6 we see that nouns and pronouns are subsets of naming words, and adjectives and adverbs are subsets of modifying words. Hierarchies spatially illustrate these superordinate–subordinate relationships.

**Schematic Diagrams**   Another variation of the network concept is the schematic diagram, which physically represents complex phenomena in simplified form. Henry Myer used a schematic in his presentation of digestion (shown in Figure 7.1). Henry's

**FIGURE 7.4**  Elementary Matrix Comparing Two Concepts

| | Examples | How They Grow |
|---|---|---|
| Fruit | | |
| Vegetables | | |

diagram is a shorthand representation of the more complex real system. It is simplified so that the major parts or components can be seen without confusing detail. As the lesson progresses, the schematic diagram provides an outline for the lesson as well as conceptual hooks onto which students hang new ideas.

Spatially representing the body of knowledge helps both the teacher and stu-

**FIGURE 7.5**  Network in Physical Education (Adapted from Novak and Gowin, 1984)

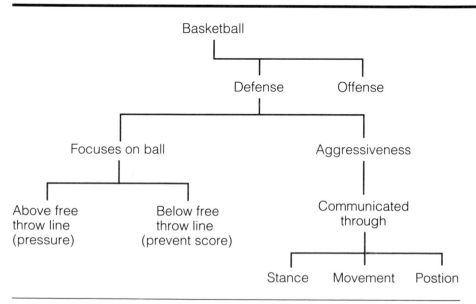

**FIGURE 7.6**   Partial Hierarchy for Parts of Speech

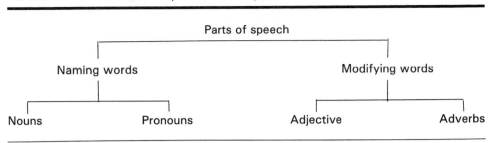

dents. During the planning process, it helps the teacher break large amounts of content into manageable parts. As the lesson is implemented, it provides both sensory focus and a form of conceptual organization for the students. In practice, teachers often use two or more of the organizational forms together, as we see in the next section.

Your overriding goal in the planning process is to define the boundaries of the body of knowledge you plan to teach, to link important ideas, and to organize the information so these links can be identified. Once this is accomplished, you're ready to implement the lesson.

# TEACHING ORGANIZED BODIES
# OF KNOWLEDGE: IMPLEMENTATION

In teaching organized bodies of information, teachers have two closely related goals—to understand the separate items of information in the body of knowledge, and to understand the relationships among them. In this section of the chapter we analyze different ways of reaching these goals.

## Lectures

> *Lectures were once useful; but now when all can read, and books are so numerous, lectures are unnecessary. If your attention fails, and you miss a part of a lecture, it is lost; you cannot go back as you do upon a book.*
>
> —Samuel Johnson, 1799

Samuel Johnson, usually a very astute observer of the world around him, was mistaken. Lectures have continued as the primary form of instruction in colleges and universities ever since Johnson made this observation, and they are still firmly if unfortunately entrenched in many junior high and high school classrooms (Cuban, 1984).

There are several reasons why lecture remains so entrenched:

- They're easier for the teacher. Simply "telling" students helps teachers maintain control, and they don't have to do the "thinking on their feet" that guiding students through questioning requires. As we discussed in Chapter Three, teachers have a strong need to simplify their instruction. Lectures are simple and safe.
- They are efficient; planning time is devoted to organizing the content. Little attention needs to be devoted to teaching strategy.
- They are flexible and can be adapted to a wide range of subjects.
- Most people can learn to lecture well enough to survive in a classroom of existing instructional strategies. Lecturing is easier to learn than most teaching techniques.

Lectures have two serious flaws, however. First, they put the learner in a passive mode and, as a result, student engagement is often very low. Research on how students learn most efficiently indicates that they must be actively involved if information is to be comprehended and linked (Eggen and Kauchak, 1992) . Lectures permit—even encourage—passive learning. Lectures are basically monologues in which the teacher talks and students listen. The teacher presents and explains the content, sometimes supplementing the information with charts, graphs, or words and diagrams on the chalkboard. The students' job is to understand what the teacher is trying to explain. Some take notes, and sometimes these help.

This arrangement works for most college and some high school students—the motivated ones. College students pay for their education, and the decision to attend class is theirs. Successful high school students also are motivated; they get the reinforcement of good grades, and they have developed skills to learn from lectures. They understand the need to monitor their own attention; when they catch themselves drifting off, they pull themselves back. They take notes and use them later as a resource.

Poorly motivated high school students, typical junior high students, and virtually all elementary students don't have these skills. If you talk longer than 5 minutes to first and second graders, they start fidgetting and looking out the window. They are bored; there is nothing to do. Lectures do not provide for active learning.

A second flaw of lectures is that they don't provide a means for gauging student understanding. An interesting contrast exists between elementary students and high school students in terms of induced boredom. Elementary students will openly yawn and fidget, while high school students are usually more subtle; they often try to hide their yawns, and their glances at the clock are often veiled. But, because of this politeness, the teacher often doesn't know when he or she has lost students. Because one-way lectures do not afford opportunities to assess comprehension, students can become confused or disinterested, and the teacher may not know until much later. It is *literally impossible* to determine whether or not students understand your examples and descriptions without interacting with them. This means you must *call on them* or in some other way have them describe what they are learning on a regular basis, or your teaching is not as effective as it could be.

Lecture is one of the great ironies of teaching. It is one of the most ineffective yet remains the most popular mode of instruction today.

## The Lecture Recitation: Involving Students in Learning

**Lecture recitation** is a teaching strategy that combines short periods of teacher presentation with extensive teacher–student interaction. This strategy combines the positive aspects of lecture flexibility and economy of effort with the beneficial aspects of interactive teaching. It is an instructional hybrid effectively suited to teaching integrated bodies of information.

Effective lecture recitations use the lecture-recitation cycle as the building block of the lesson. The **lecture recitation cycle** is a recurrent sequence of *information presentation*, *comprehension monitoring*, and *integration*. The basic structure of this cycle is summarized in Table 7.1. Lasting approximately 5 minutes (shorter or longer depending on the topic and the age of the students), it is the basic building block of lecture-recitation lessons. By stringing together several of these cycles, the teacher can tie together the ideas in an organized body of knowledge. Let's see how this works in a high school social studies lesson.

Velda Houston is a ninth-grade American government teacher continuing a unit on the Constitution and including topics such as the electoral college, the branches of government, and the role and function of each branch.

As Velda planned the lesson, she sat and outlined her information. In her notebook she sketched the information shown in Figure 7.7.

She put the information on a transparency and headed for her first-period class.

The students sat down as the bell rang, and Velda began, "Listen everyone. . . . To begin our lesson on the Constitution, I'd like to pose a problem to you. Mrs. Brown [another teacher in the school] has a special project she wants done, and she wants the smartest kid she can find to do it. Tim wants the job and thinks he is qualified. He's a good writer and gets good grades on his essays. However, Jo also wants the job, and she thinks she is better qualified than Tim. She's a whiz in math. What is Mrs. Brown going to do?"

**TABLE 7.1**  The Lecture-Recitation Cycle

| Phase | Function(s) | Teacher Action | Student Outcome |
|---|---|---|---|
| Present information | Establish information base | Teacher lecture | Information intake |
| Check comprehension | Involve students, check comprehension, encourage meaningful encoding | Teacher questions: a) Summarize b) Paraphrase c) Explain d) Examples | Understand material |
| Integration | Explore relationships in content | Teacher questions: a) Comparisons b) Causes and effects c) Similarities and differences | Relate new material to other ideas |

**FIGURE 7.7**  Organizational Scheme for Lesson on Constitutional Compromise

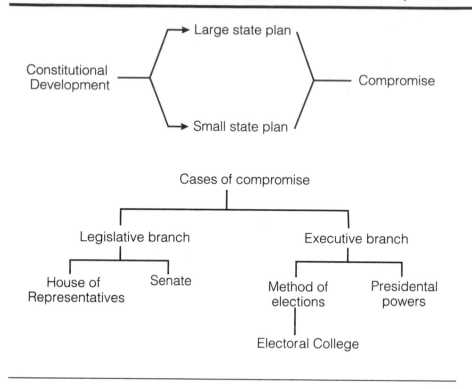

"What are they supposed to do in the project?" Katy wondered.

"Well, a variety of things," Velda responded. "Mrs. Brown will have them doing different things at different times."

"Boy, it's hard to tell," Ken added. "How would you know?"

"Maybe take them both," Sue suggested. "Could she do that?"

"That's an excellent idea, Sue. Think about that, everyone." Velda paused a moment and then went on, "The situation we're going to discuss today is sort of an analogy to Mrs. Brown's problem. The makers of our country's Constitution were in a dilemma when it came to making a decision about how to elect our leaders. The compromises that had to be made are what we're going to discuss today."

Velda then strode across the front of the room, gesturing animatedly with her hands, emphasizing key points, saying, "I know I've said it before, but it's so important I'll have to repeat it again. The Constitution was a series of compromises between people like you and me. Just as Mrs. Brown could compromise and perhaps take both Tim and Jo, the people who developed the Constitution had very different views of where this new country was heading. To arrive at a product they could all agree on, they had to compromise."

"The forms of the compromise are diagrammed on the transparency you see," Velda said, displaying the information she had outlined on the overhead.

She continued, "The nature of this compromise process came out very clearly in the part of the Constitution having to do with the way we elect the members of Congress. Originally, when our forefathers were writing the Constitution, there was a lot of disagreement about how votes in the legislature should be allocated. States like Rhode Island wanted each state to have the same number of votes. Delaware felt the same way. On the other hand, New York and Pennsylvania wanted the votes to be determined by the number of people in the state. . . . Each idea seemed the most fair to the states who proposed them. The small states wanted them allocated by state; the large states wanted the votes to be distributed on the basis of population. Both of the ideas seemed fair, and neither side wanted to give in."

"So, as a compromise, they created a legislature with two bodies. The House of Representatives was based on population (today we have 435 representatives), and the most populous states have many more representatives than smaller ones. On the other hand, the Senate has two members from every state. So, now we have 50 states times two equals 100 senators."

"Now, let's analyze this process of compromise. How were the states supporting the two proposals different? Miguel?"

"New York was a large state, and Rhode Island was a very small state."

"Yes, good, Miguel," Velda smiled. "And what does that mean? Jamie?"

"Well, it was bigger," Jamie responded hesitantly.

"Bigger land area or bigger population or what?" Velda continued.

"Both, I think," Jamie continued, "But probably the bigger population was the most significant."

"Yes, good, Jamie. Now why would the large states feel the way they did, and also why would the small states feel the way they did? What do you think? Dick?"

"It would relate to power," Dick answered. "If the representation was made on the basis of population, the large states would be much more powerful than the small states."

"On the other hand, what would happen if representation were completely equal among the states?" Velda continued. "Toni?"

"It would sort of throw the balance in the favor of the smaller states. It would mean a state like Wyoming with very little population could maybe stop a proposal from a very populated state like California."

"So as part of the process of compromise what part of the legislature is based on population? Camille?"

"Hmmm? The House of Representatives?"

"Excellent, Camille. The total number of representatives is 435. The number of representatives from each state is determined by population. That would make populous states happy. And what part of the compromise made the smaller states happy? Kareem?"

"The Senate?"

"Why, Kareem?"

"Because every state gets two, no matter how big or small they are."

"Excellent thinking, everyone!" Velda enthused.

Let's interrupt the lesson at this point and take a look at it. First we see that Velda used both a schematic and a hierarchy in organizing the total lesson. Then she proceeded by beginning the first of several lecture-recitation cycles. In the first phase of the cycle, Velda **presented information** about the conflict between large and small states, setting the stage for the importance of compromise. The purpose of this short presentation was to establish an information base for the discussion that followed. But before she asked students to analyze and integrate the information, Velda first determined that students understood the basic ideas in her presentation. This is the **comprehension-monitoring** phase of the cycle. She did this by asking questions such as the following:

How were the states supporting the two proposals different?
Bigger land area or bigger population?

These comprehension checks were important because ideas can't be related unless they are first understood. The comprehension-monitoring phase of the cycle serves several important functions. First, it makes the lesson interactive and draws students into the process. When students expect to be called on about material that was just covered, it gives them an added incentive for listening and reinforces them for doing so. This is related to two elements of the general instructional model — positive expectations and accountability. If teachers expect all students to listen and participate and hold them accountable by asking questions addressed to the whole class, students are more likely to enter into the lesson. Conversely, if teachers talk for extended periods without engaging students, or ask questions that are answered by only a few, the rest of the class will tune out the lesson. The teacher needs to communicate by his or her actions that this is important material that all should learn.

Getting feedback is a second important function that comprehension-monitoring questions perform. The quality of student response helps teachers gauge whether or not they understand the material, and teachers can pace the presentation accordingly. If students are not understanding, there is no point in proceeding; teachers need to slow down and reteach the misunderstood or confusing material. In Velda's lesson, if students didn't understand that population differences were central to the idea of compromise, the rest of the lesson wouldn't make sense.

The questions also give the students feedback. Their ability to answer helps them monitor the extent to which they understand the material. The questions also require students to process the information in a deeper, more meaningful fashion. Questions encourage them to try to understand the information and not just memorize it.

In the third phase of the cycle — **integration** — the students are asked to identify and explore relationships among the different items of information as well as consolidate new information with content they already know.

The integration phase is the natural extension of comprehension monitoring, and the line between the two is often blurred. It is also accomplished with teacher questioning. The difference is in the type of questions teachers ask. In the integration phase, students are asked to identify similarities and differences, explain information, establish cause-and-effect relationships, make predictions, and hypothesize.

The exact kind of question depends on the content being taught; the essential characteristic is that the questions cause students to search for links with other important ideas in the lesson. Velda Houston did this, for example, when she asked her students why the big state/small state positions were important. Understanding these different perspectives was essential to understanding the need for compromise, the central focus of this cycle. Let's return to this lesson and see how lecture-recitation cycles are linked together.

"Now that we understand how compromise produced the present form of our Congress, let's turn to the electoral college and see how the process of compromise shaped the way we elect our President. Note that on the overhead we just talked about legislative branch," Velda continued, pointing at the left side of the hierarchy on the overhead. "Now we're turning to the presidential or executive branch. This is Article 2 of the Constitution. Let's see how our President is elected. Every four years, sometime in December, 535 people in the electoral college get together and cast their votes for the next President of the United States. When people vote for the President in the November elections, they are actually voting for the members of the Electoral College and not directly for the President. Let's think about this one for a while. Why are there 535 members? Where did it come from? Where have we seen that number before? Sherry?"

"Well, we just learned that there are 435 members of the House and 100 members of the Senate. Is it the two combined?"

"Good, Sherry. And how are the members of the Senate distributed between the states? Leroy?"

"Two each."

"Okay, two per state times 50 states is 100. And what about the House? Who remembers? Terry?"

"They're divided between the states on the basis of population. The states with the most population, like California and New York, have the most, while those with the least, like North Dakota and South Dakota, have only two or three."

"Good complete answer," Velda smiled at Terry. "So, we see that there are 535 members, which are the combined numbers of the house and senate. Using this information now, how is this another example of compromise? Kate?"

"Again, there were two views as to how the President should be elected. The small states wanted each state to have equal representation, while the big states wanted it done on the basis of population. Using both was a form of compromise."

"Now, let's ask a big question that pulls this information together. Why was compromise necessary in designing the electoral college? What difference does it make? Kate?"

"The President is a very powerful person who can influence the country. If we had a President who favored the populous states, the smaller states would be unhappy. And the opposite is true, too. If they elected a person who only helped the less populated states, then the other states would get mad. So they had to develop a system that all could live with."

"Good description, Kate. That's an excellent analysis. Now, let's examine a third compromise dealing with why the President isn't elected directly, instead being chosen by an electoral college. To do that, we need to know about a fellow by the name of Rousseau and his idea of an enlightened aristocracy."

Let's pause again and analyze how this second cycle was structured and how Velda skillfully integrated the two. In the presentation phase of the second cycle, she referred her students to the outline and talked about the electoral college. Her outline together with her statement, "Note that on the overhead we just talked about legislative branch. . . . Now we're turning to the presidential or executive branch . . ." provided a link between the first cycle and the second. Remember from Chapter Four that transition signals are important communication skills in effective teachers, and Velda demonstrated this skill in her teaching.

In the comprehension-monitoring phase of the second cycle, Velda checked to see if students remembered and understood the information about the structure of the legislature. She did this by asking questions such as the following:

Where have we seen that number before?
Where did it come from?

Having determined that students understood the link between the number in the electoral college and the legislature, she then began to explore the implications of this connection.

Velda did an effective job of exploring relationships by asking questions such as, "Why is that number significant?", "How is this another example of compromise?", and "Why was compromise necessary in designing the electoral college? What difference does it make?" Her questions linked the electoral college, which was discussed in the second cycle, both to the number of Representatives and Senators — discussed in the first cycle — and to the concept of compromise, which was the theme of the lesson. Once these links were made, the next cycle was ready to begin with the presentation of new material. As teachers guide students with questions such as these, students eventually develop the inclination to look for these relationships without being prompted by the teacher.

## Research and the Lecture-Recitation Cycle

Evidence supports the effectiveness of the lecture-recitation cycle. Research on lecturing shows that the amount learned from a verbal presentation decreases as the length of the presentation increases (Gage and Berliner, 1992). These results were obtained with college students, so we can safely predict the effects to be even greater with younger learners. Active listening is hard work, and fatigue quickly sets in.

How long is too long when it comes to teacher talk? As with so many instructional questions, the answer to this one is contextual, but a ballpark figure is 5 minutes. Shorter periods are necessary with younger, slower, or poorly motivated students. Similarly, complex or abstract material requires shorter presentations and more frequent questions. The best answer to this question comes from actual classroom experience. Nonverbal behavior during the presentation phase gives clues to inattention, and student performance during the comprehension-monitoring phase provides additional data.

Further empirical support for the lecture-recitation cycle comes from research on reading. We've all caught ourselves "drifting off" while reading. Research indicates that questions interspersed in text material increase comprehension (Anderson and Armbruster, 1984) and that greater comprehension is due in large part to increased reader attention (Reynolds and Shirey, 1988). Questions attract attention and direct the reader to focus on important material. The process is similar with classroom processes.

Additional support for the interactive lecture-recitation cycle comes from research examining the link between teacher actions and student attention in secondary science classrooms. As researchers observed naturally occurring lecture-recitation cycles, they found that attention increased when a question was asked and decreased when a student was called on (Lemke, 1982). (Remember what we said in Chapter Five about asking a question first and then calling on a student?) Student attention was also high at the beginning of a teacher monologue but dropped significantly during it. Students attention improved during demonstrations, debates, and student-initiated questions, providing strong support for the idea of active student involvement.

This cycle is effective from a learning perspective because it breaks content into smaller parts and allows the teacher opportunities to teach, not just talk about these parts. Students are presented information in small, learnable chunks and are helped to understand and connect these subunits through teacher questions.

The lecture-recitation cycle works for teachers as well as students. It allows teachers to break instruction down into manageable parts, not only during instruction itself but also in the planning process. This chunking allows teachers to divide up a potentially overwhelming body of content into subparts that are teachable and learnable.

But just as a house is more than a pile of bricks, a good lecture-recitation lesson is more than just an accumulation of segments. There must be structure and continuity for the total lesson to hang together.

**Lecture Recitation: The Total Lesson**    In this section, we look at the problem of teaching organized bodies of information from a total lesson perspective. As with the length of an individual cycle, the length of the total lesson is influenced by developmental considerations, with those at the lower elementary level shortened to 15- or 20-minute segments, and those at the secondary level lasting a whole period.

A lecture-recitation lesson has three phases: introduction, development, and summary. The introduction frames the lesson in a larger context, provides an overview of the content to be covered, and introduces the structure or organization of the lesson. In the development part of the lesson, the lecture-recitation cycle described earlier is used to introduce, integrate, and consolidate new information. New ideas are introduced systematically, and links with previous ideas are explored. In the final, or review-and-closure phase of the lesson, major points are restated and linked to the organizational structure. As we discuss these phases, see if you can identify each of these phases in the lesson on digestion at the beginning of this chapter.

*Introducing a Lecture Recitation: Introductory Overview.* A well-thought-out introductory overview is essential to the success of a lecture-recitation lesson. If done well, the organized body of knowledge is presented as a coherent, learnable piece of information with a logical beginning and end, an internal organization, and linkages to what students already know. When done ineffectively, the lesson becomes a garbled set of mini-lessons with no connecting theme.

An effective introduction not only provides an overview of the new content to be covered but also links new content to old. The overview provides students with a cognitive map of the new material to be learned. An effective introduction also creates linkages with previously learned materials. For new bodies of information to be integrated with previously learned material, explicit connections need to be made. One way of doing this is through a structured summary that briefly condenses major ideas and links them to old ones. Often this is as simple as, "Yesterday we talked about A. Today we're going to discuss B, an idea related to A in this way."

*Advance Organizers.* An alternate way to integrate the new content is through an advance organizer (Ausubel, 1963, 1968, 1978). An advance organizer is an initial statement about the topic to be learned that provides a structure for the new information and relates it to information students already possess.

One way of doing this is to use concepts or generalizations that students already understand to frame the new material. Henry Myer did this when he described the digestive system in terms of form and function, an organizational scheme used with the circulatory system. Student familiarity with the ideas of form and function would then help them to understand the digestive system. Velda Houston did this when she discussed the electoral college in terms of the concept of compromise. Since students already understood this concept from the previous lecture-recitation cycle, Velda was able to hook new information about the electoral college to this conceptual anchor.

An alternative kind of advance organizer, called comparative, uses an extended analogy to link new, unfamiliar information with something that is already learned and understood. Henry Myer used a comparative advance organizer to compare the workings of the digestive system to an ore-mining factory. Students' understanding of the mechanics of an ore-mining factory were then used to help them understand the new material on the functioning of the digestive system. The following are some additional examples of comparative advance organizers:

1. A tree can be thought of as a city of cells in which each type of cell has a job to do and depends on the jobs of other cells.
2. A schema is like a computer program; the content and the relations between the content are dependent upon the learner (programmer).
3. Birds are reptiles with feathers; except for flight, their bodies work primarily the same way.

4. Outer space is the last frontier. The same dangers and hardships faced by the pioneers are encountered by the astronauts.
5. A novel is like a movie, in that it has a plot which usually tells a story.
6. Red blood cells are our bodies' oxygen railroad. (Eggen and Kauchak, 1988)

In each of these examples, a familiar frame of reference is used to present new and unfamiliar content. Through the process of analogy, hooks are provided on which to hang the new material. The more familiar the old material and the closer the fit of the analogy, the more learning is facilitated.

*Development.* Once the content is organized and represented diagrammatically, the main part of a lecture-recitation lesson consists of the gradual development of the ideas. The lecture-recitation cycle is the basic building block; the organizational schemes provide the superstructure. A major teacher task during the development is to link continually the content within each lecture-recitation cycle to the larger organizational structure of the lesson. Organizational and transitional links that bind together ideas are essential here. Table 7.2 is an example of what these links would look like in the lesson on the digestive system.

The purpose of these links is to point out connections in the content being discussed, helping to integrate this content into an understandable whole. They are, in a sense, the conceptual glue or mortar that holds the lesson together. In their absence, the lesson consists of a string of unconnected ideas. Research on these connective links supports their use, both in lesson clarity and student achievement (Cruikshank, 1985). This makes intuitive sense. When a lesson is clear, students understand it better, and better learning results. By providing not only structure but also connections between content, links help ensure that the new content is being learned as a coherent and interconnected body.

**TABLE 7.2**  Integrative Links

| Content | Example | Type of Link |
| --- | --- | --- |
| Mouth and esophagus | From the mouth, the food then travels to the esophagus. | Sequential |
| Stomach | The esophagus is primarily a tube. In comparison, the stomach is a holding tank. | Comparison: similarity/difference |
| Small intestine | The food that has been broken down by the stomach then goes to the small intestine for absorption. | Functional |
| Large intestine | The large intestine is also concerned with absorption, but this absorption is more with water and salts. | Comparison: similarity/difference |
| Colon and rectum | Finally, the wastes that have been accumulating from the processes of the rest of the digestive system end up in the colon. | Concluding/summarizing |

*Review and Closure.* One characteristic of all good teaching is some attempt to pull the lesson together at the end. We discussed this idea in Chapter Four when we talked about general dimensions of effective teaching. This is especially true in teaching organized bodies of knowledge because of their scope and complexity. Because of the amount of information presented, it is easier for students to lose track of the lesson's direction and the overall structure of the content. One way to prevent this is to tie the content of the lesson together in a strong summary.

A powerful way to conclude is to refer students back to the organizational scheme that was introduced at the beginning of the lesson. The spatial organizational devices that have proved so useful so far have one final function. They provide a visual means of pulling the lesson together at the end. Henry Myer did this when he called attention to the diagram on the board at the end of his presentation. Velda Houston, in her lesson on the Constitution, could do this by referring students back to the overhead that began the lesson. Because they are visual, these organizational devices provide an economical and alternate (visual) way of remembering the lesson's content. Research on imagery (Paivio, 1971) as well as on learning styles (Dunn and Dunn, 1978) supports the idea of visual summarizing devices.

## Teaching Organized Bodies of Knowledge Inductively

Teaching integrated bodies of knowledge through lecture recitation works. It is a time-tested, efficient, and effective way of teaching content. But alternatives, which emphasize alternative thinking processes, exist.

The lecture-recitation model is a deductive strategy that emphasizes expository teaching and meaningful verbal learning. It is "top-down" in two respects. First, the teacher presents the information and students assimilate it, and second, the flow of ideas is from the larger, more general ideas to those more specific.

When teachers use an inductive approach to teaching integrated bodies of knowledge, they present specific information to students and, through questioning, guide them into identifying the relationships and links among the specific items. This type of strategy can be more time consuming that the lecture-recitation model, and it requires sophisticated questioning skills in the teacher. On the other hand, it is effective for promoting student involvement, encourages incidental learning, and helps develop students' thinking. As with teaching concepts and generalizations, effective teachers are skilled with both approaches.

The planning process is the same whether the approach is inductive or deductive. A topic is selected, teachers must have a clear objective in mind, and they must organize the information to be presented to the students.

**Phases in the Inductive Approach**   There are four sequential steps or phases in implementing this teaching strategy. In the first stage, *forming a data base*, students are presented with data relevant to the topic. Through questioning or student collaboration, teachers assist students in the second phase to *identify similarities and differences*. In the third phase, the class further analyzes the data, attempting to *identify cause-and-effect relationships.* In the fourth and final stage, students *apply the information* and use it to hypothesize. These steps are summarized in Table 7.3.

Let's look now at a teacher who is implementing these phases in a social studies lesson.

Leon Wilson is a secondary American history teacher and is discussing the events prior to the American Revolutionary War. We join him as he begins his class.

"We just made a bare beginning yesterday. Let's take a quick look at what we discussed," he began, after the bell had signaled the beginning of class. "Where did we leave off? Juan?"

"We started discussing French and British expansion into what is now Canada and the American Midwest."

"Yes, good, Juan," Leon smiled. "And what did we find out? John?"

"Champlain came down the St. Lawrence River and formed what is now Quebec City. We located it on the map."

"Good. What time period are we talking about? Mike?"

"This was in the seventeenth century, wasn't it?"

"Yes, good, Mike. What year did Champlain actually establish Quebec City? Roger?"

"1608, I believe," Roger replied.

"Yes it was," Leon smiled back. "And what else did we mention? Judy?"

"This was a year after the British established their foothold at Jamestown," she responded.

"Okay. David?"

"The whole thing actually started with the Vikings, who landed in Canada over a thousand years ago."

"Yes, fine, David, and good, everyone. Now let's look forward. From our readings, let's examine some of the facts about the French that occurred during this period. Go ahead, Jim."

"The French fur traders were the first ones into the new continent."

"Ted?"

"At least 35 of the 50 states were discovered or mapped by the French."

**TABLE 7.3** Phases in an Inductive Sequence for Teaching Integrated Bodies of Knowledge

| Phase | Description |
| --- | --- |
| **1.** Establish data base | Topic-relevant data are presented which form the focal point for the rest of the lesson. |
| **2.** Find relationships | Teacher questions help students identify important concepts and generalizations. |
| **3.** Identify cause-and-effect relationships | Further analysis of the data attempts to establish causal connections in the data. |
| **4.** Application and hypothesizing | Students use the data in the hypothetical thinking to apply information learned. |

"And prominent place names such as Detroit, St. Louis, New Orleans, and Des Moines are of French origin," Ann volunteered.

"They established an empire stretching from Hudson Bay to the Gulf of Mexico," Mindy noted.

"During the late seventeenth and beginning eighteenth centuries, the French established a string of forts that lined the Ohio-Mississippi Valley," Mary added.

"Very good, everyone. Now how about the British? Donna?"

"After Jamestown, they began to firm up their hold on what is now the eastern United States."

"Yes, Donna. Go on, Marianne."

"They started moving west and eventually went over the Appalachians."

"Well done, everyone. Now look at the list and see what else we should add," Leon said, referring the class to a list of items he had written on the board in response to their answers. "Cheryl?"

". . ."

"How was the original French settling of the New World managed?"

"I think they called it a seigniorial system, where the settlers were given land by the French government if they served in the military."

"Bravo, Cheryl. Now what else? Leroy?"

"The French were more friendly with the Indians than the British were."

"The Iroquois nation was the most powerful force in the area. More than either the French or British," Jan added.

Nikki continued, "The British and French started fighting seriously in 1689."

"And what was that called?" Leon continued.

"That was King William's War," Don answered.

"There were a series of wars after that, culminating in what is called the French and Indian in the mid-1700s," Kathy went on.

The class continued presenting information, with Leon recording the key items on the board until they had a list that appeared as follows:

| French | British | Conflicts |
|---|---|---|
| Quebec 1608 | Jamestown 1607 | King William's War (1689–1697) |
| Fur traders | Expanded west | Iroquois Nation dominant |
| Hudson Bay to Gulf of Mexico | New York—center of trade and commerce | Seven Years' War (1756–1763) |
| Forts on Ohio-Mississippi Valley | Wars incredibly costly | Washington taken prisoner 1754 |
| Influence waned after 1763 | Colonialists taxed | British naval blockades |
| 80,000 population | Administrative difficulty in colonies | Quebec falls—1759 |
| | 1,500,000 population | Treaty of Paris—1763 |

After recording the information, Leon went on, "Now, everyone, let's take a look at the information we have here. We want to see what kinds of relationships we can find between some of the events. Anyone see any similarities or differences in the information up here? Andrew?"

"The British landed on what is the present-day United States, while the French settlements got started in Canada," Andrew volunteered.

"Okay," Leon responded. "What else? I haven't heard from you, Sue," he smiled at her.

"The French initially expanded down the Ohio and Mississippi valleys, while the British stayed on the eastern seaboard," Sue answered.

"Fine, Sue. What else, Jason?"

"The French got along better with the Indians than the British did."

"Good point, Jason. Christy?"

"Their relationship with the Indians helped them to be more successful initially when they started fighting with the British."

"Good thinking, Christy. And why do you suppose the British and the French initially began to fight in these areas? Tom?"

". . ."

"Look at the list you see under the British and under the French, Tom," Leon encouraged.

"The British were expanding to the west," Tom went on hesitantly.

"Yes! And what about the French?"

"They had them blocked with their forts!" Tom blurted out with a flash of insight.

"Good! That's the idea! Now let's continue," Leon enthused. "Someone else?"

After waiting a few seconds, Leon continued, "How did the points of original settlement influence the events during this period? Sarah?"

"The British initially were fenced in by the Appalachian Mountains, which gave the French free access to all the western territory. Once the British began to move west, the trouble started."

"Good thinking, Sarah! Why do you suppose the French originally were more successful than the British in the Seven Years' War? What do you think? Dan?"

"Maybe it had something to do with their original system. They had that military seigniorial system, which meant they had a stronger military orientation from the beginning."

"Good thinking, Dan. Any other thoughts? Bette?"

"We already said that the French had a better relationship with the Indians, and the Iroquois nation was dominant at this time, so they got a lot of help from the Indians."

"Also good thinking, Bette," Leon praised.

"Maybe their military leaders were smarter," Gordon offered. "We read that Montcalm was brilliant in the sort of unorthodox, semiguerrilla war that was going on in the American wilderness."

"Excellent, but what advantages did the British have? Stan?"

"Well, there were more British than French. We see that there were approximately 1,500,000 British settlers but only 80,000 French. Also, the British came here with their families seeking religious freedom. So they had a reason to fight for land. Many of the French were trappers and traders, and land wasn't as important for them. If trouble came, they could just get in their canoes and paddle away."

"Good points, Stan. So then what happened to turn the tide against the French?"

"They were hurt economically," Eric volunteered. "You wrote on the board that the British had blockaded the French in both the New and Old World, meaning that they had superior naval forces. This would hurt the French in the long run."

"Also, the role of the Indians was declining," Ryan continued. "They had been decimated by small pox, and the superior British weaponry was also hurting them."

"Outstanding thinking, everyone!" Leon enthused. The lesson continued, with Leon guiding the students' analyses of the information they had listed as well as other information they recalled. They considered the impact of the original British and French landing positions on the American continent, the role the Appalachian Mountains played in preventing earlier British expansion, the fall of Quebec, and the cost of the war to the British. Leon then went on.

"Suppose the outcome of the war had been different," Leon suggested. "Imagine what would have happened if the French had won the war. What might have been the outcome? Someone?"

"I think the whole world would have been different," Karen suggested after a moment's hesitation.

"Go on, Karen."

"The wars ultimately determined who would dominate the New World. If the French had won, we could very well be French speaking, and our culture would be dominated by French rather than English traditions."

"I don't agree," Scott countered. "The French weren't a migrating people, and I think they would have strengthened their hold on what they had, but otherwise the world might be about the way it is today, particularly on other continents. Most other colonial empires have collapsed anyway."

"Those are both good views," Leon noted. "We, of course, will never know for sure."

He continued posing hypothetical questions for a few minutes and then, seeing that the period was nearly over, began to close the lesson.

"Now for tomorrow, I want you to consider a different question," he said. "We know what happened in the French and Indian Wars, and we also know that the American Revolution followed in a matter of a few years. I want you to write a paper of no more than one page discussing the relationship between the two. Be sure that you support your statements with information that we've read or discussed."

Now let's consider the procedures Leon used in his lesson. For the sake of clarity and organization, we described the process in four sequential phases. As we identify each step in the lesson, remember that with some topics the lesson might still be effective even though a step is skipped or eliminated. The procedure is flexible and highly adaptable.

***Phase One: Forming a Data Base.*** As we began our discussion of organized bodies of knowledge, we said that they are combinations of facts, concepts, and generalizations integrated with each other. In the first phase of the process, these facts, concepts, and generalizations are identified and organized.

In preparing a data base, teachers have two options. They can develop it in a class discussion, as Leon did when he had his students recall facts from their reading and a review of the previous day's work. He simply asked them what they remembered, and he listed and organized the information the students supplied. The following information made up part of the list:

> Quebec established in 1608
> The Seven Years' War (1756–1763)
> String of French forts in the Ohio-Mississippi valley
> British blockade of French coast
> Fall of Quebec—1759
> Heavy tax on American colonies after 1763.

The information then provides the background on which the students' understanding will be developed.

The other option is to prepare the data base in advance and bring it to class ready-made. This option has several advantages:

- It simplifies the lesson for the teacher. For example, Leon had to monitor the process to be sure the students supplied the material essential to the topic, and he had to arrange the items on the board as they were presented.
- It gives teachers time to reflect and think about the best way to organize the information to make it most meaningful for the students.
- Once the data base is prepared, it can be used again with little or no additional preparation.
- It allows teachers to teach state- or district-mandated topics that aren't covered in the text.
- It helps students who are unable to comprehend the information in the text.

Establishing a data base is critical to the process, whether or not it is prepared in advance and regardless of topic. For example, Leon Wilson's students needed to know that the string of French forts existed to understand why conflicts occurred as the British expanded westward, and they couldn't understand the impact of the French and Indian Wars on the American Revolution if they did not know the chronology of each.

The same interdependence of ideas would be true in other areas. For instance, to understand the impact of twentieth-century American writers, such as F. Scott Fitzgerald or Ernest Hemingway, students would need information about the context in which they wrote, such as the times their novels were written, facts about the society at that time, and some information about their personal lives. Similarly, as students study immigration, they need to look at some representative immigrant groups, when they came, where they landed, the conditions in their home country, and their experiences when they arrived. The integration of all this information provides background that makes the process of immigration understandable. All this information would be displayed in the data base.

With some topics, ready-made data bases already exist. For instance, the periodic table could be used as a data base in a chemistry class; it is rich with the opportunities for analysis. Tables and graphs are also excellent sources of already-existing information. Further, a number of data bases now exist on computer software, so the process of creating one is eliminated.

Having the information displayed on the chalkboard or overhead is important for two reasons. First, it provides a form of sensory focus for the students; and second, it helps reduce the variation in individual students' backgrounds. Since the same information is displayed for all the students, someone who didn't remember a certain fact — or perhaps didn't read the assignment — isn't at as much a disadvantage as he or she would be if the lesson were mostly verbal. This is particularly important for poorly motivated or at-risk students. If the data base doesn't already exist, it should be displayed as it is developed, as Leon did in his lesson.

We are now on firm footing. Our students have access to the data base, and a common ground for discussion has been established. This unconnected background isn't enough by itself, however. The relationships among the data are the critical elements of the lesson.

***Phase Two: Identifying Similarities and Differences.*** The process of finding relationships begins with identifying similarities and differences in different items of information. Leon did this at several points in his lesson. He initiated the process by simply saying, "Anyone see any similarities or differences in the information up here?" and the students responded with the following statements:

> "The British landed on what is the present-day United States, while the French settlements got started in Canada."
>
> "The French initially expanded down the Ohio and Mississippi valleys, while the British stayed on the eastern seaboard."
>
> "The French got along better with the Indians than the British did."

Leon's students responded quickly when asked to make these comparisons. Learners are not always that responsive, however, and sometimes a more explicit question may be necessary, such as, "How did the French and British relationships with the Indians compare?" or "How did the French expansion compare to that of the British?" These prompts communicate intent while providing more assistance to students.

The same process of using questions to encourage comparisons would apply in other lessons. For example, we would want to ask questions such as "How would you compare Fitzgerald's childhood background to Hemingway's?" in our literature example, or "How many unpaired electrons do the elements in the first column have? How about those in the second column?" in a chemistry lesson using the periodic table.

The comparisons that we ask students to make are determined by the lesson's focus. For example, the respective points of initial settlement for the French and English were important because they set the stage for many of the events that followed. A comparison of unpaired electrons in the chemistry class signals to students that this information is important and will be used later. In a similar way, Fitzgerald's and Hemingway's backgrounds are important because they influenced later writing themes.

When the data base has been established firmly and important comparisons have been made, students are ready for the next step.

**Phase Three: Identifying Cause-and-Effect Relationships.** One of the most important elements in understanding an organized body of knowledge is the identification of cause-and-effect relationships that exist within it. Once Leon's students had established a data base and made the explicit comparisons necessary to form a foundation for their understanding, they began this process. Sometimes it occurs spontaneously, as was the case when Kristy said, "Their relationship with the Indians helped them to be more successful initially when they started fighting with the British." In other instances, Leon initiated the analysis with these questions:

"And why do you suppose the British and the French initially began to fight in these areas?"

"Why do you suppose the French originally were more successful than the British in the Seven Years' War?"

"What happened to turn the tide against the French?"

In discussing American authors, the teacher might ask questions such as the following:

Why were Fitzgerald's best novel, *The Great Gatsby*, and one of Hemingway's best, *A Farewell to Arms*, written about such divergent topics?

Why was Hemingway so attracted to the outdoors while Fitzgerald loved society's "bright lights"?

How did Hemingway and Fitzgerald both come to be expatriates?

These questions would be based on analysis of the data base and comparisons in the same way Leon guided his students. The function of these questions is to encourage students to establish links in the content they're analyzing.

**Phase Four: Application and Hypothesizing.** In the final phase of the process, the teacher encourages students to apply the information to new situations and to think hypothetically. For example, Leon asked the following question that encouraged hypothesizing in his students:

> "Suppose the outcome of the war had been different. . . . Imagine what would have happened if the French had won the war. What might have been the outcome?"

As we saw in the case study, the question generated some interesting thoughts and even some disagreement in the students.

This process serves three important functions. First, it allows the teacher to further assess students' understanding of the material. For instance, suppose Leon asked the question, "What if the British and the French had both initially settled in the present-day United States. How might that have affected the history of this period?" In response, he would expect students to consider possibilities, such as conflict occurring earlier than it did, or present-day Quebec being different from the way it is. As students hypothesize, the teacher can listen to the information brought to bear on their analysis and use this information to diagnose their understanding.

In a similar way, the teacher comparing the works of Hemingway and Fitzgerald might have asked,

> How might the novels of Fitzgerald and Hemingway have been different in their early lives had been switched?

Expected responses might include,

> Hemingway's novels wouldn't have been set in the outdoors or in wars.
> Fitzgerald's novels might have taken a different focus.
> The themes would have been different.

If the class fails to see these interrelationships or if the question elicits nothing but quizzical looks, the teacher knows that the point has been missed.

A second function of hypothetical questions is motivational. As opposed to the rigidity of learning facts, concepts, and generalizations, with their precise definitions and characteristics, hypothesizing allows students to operate in the arena of conjecture and possibility. This is stimulating. With experience, students begin to feel that they have some control over the topics they're learning rather than being constrained by learning content in a carefully prescribed way.

Finally, hypothesizing is an important thinking skill. We consider it again when we take up the issue of teaching thinking skills in the classroom in Chapter 9.

This concludes our discussion of inductive strategies to teach organized bodies of knowledge. We encourage you to read the summary before proceeding to the exercises that follow.

## SUMMARY

Organized bodies of knowledge are areas of content that have boundaries, are interconnected, and contain within them facts, concepts, and generalizations. The boundaries and organization give them form; the facts, concepts, and generalizations give them substance. When instructors teach organized bodies of information, they want students to understand the logical relationship of the ideas within them. One effective way of doing this at the lesson level is through the lecture-recitation.

The lecture-recitation, combining the positive aspects of lecture flexibility and economy of effort with the beneficial aspects of interactive teaching, is an instructional hybrid effectively suited to teaching organized bodies of information. Effective lecture recitations use the lecture-recitation cycle as the building block of the lesson.

The lecture-recitation cycle offers an effective way to break a large body of integrated knowledge into teachable and learnable segments. Each cycle consists of three phases, beginning with teacher presentation followed by questions to assess comprehension. In the third phase, questions help students link the new content with the larger body of knowledge.

Organizational aids serve several functions in the development of the lesson. They summarize main points and display this information in an economical way. They also provide the teacher with a blueprint for the lesson's direction. From the student's perspective, they provide effective vehicles to encode, store, and retrieve information. At the end of the lesson, they also provide an effective way to summarize the main points and pull the lesson together.

Induction provides an alternate format for teaching organized bodies of information. This process begins with establishing an information base, which can occur through questioning or a prepared matrix. In the second stage, comparison questions are used to find relationships in the data. Once these are established, causal relationships are explored, and, finally, students are encouraged to apply the information they have learned through hypothetical questions.

## ADDITIONAL READINGS FOR PROFESSIONAL GROWTH

Cuban, L. (1984). *How teachers taught: Constancy and change in American classrooms*. New York: Longman. Cuban provides an interesting historical look at the perseverance of the lecture method over time.

Mayer, R. (1987). *Educational psychology: A cognitive approach*. Boston: Little Brown. This is one of the best cognitively oriented texts on the topic of learning.

Novak, D. J., & Gowin, D. (1984). *Learning how to learn*. New York: Cambridge University Press. The theory and research behind concept maps is described and illustrated.

## EXERCISES

**1.** Read the following description of a lesson focusing on an organized body of knowledge and answer the questions that follow.

Shirley Hathaway, a physical education teacher at North Ridge High, was beginning her unit on exercise physiology and wanted to give her students an overview of the topic. After assembling the class and taking roll, she began by showing the class pictures of two women, one a weight lifter with sharply defined muscles and the other a lean, lightly muscled jogger.

She started the lesson by asking, "Which of these is more physically fit?" The discussion that followed revealed differences of opinions, including different definitions of physical fitness.

She continued. "Okay, we've heard a number of different opinions about which person is more physically fit and each of you is partially right, depending on how we define fitness. Physical fitness actually has several dimensions. Our first person is a champion weight lifter and holds several U.S. records. This other woman won the last state triathlon, which includes running, bicycling, and swimming. Each is superb at what she does and each physical fitness program matches the individual's goals.

With that, she put the diagram in Figure 7.8 on the overhead. She continued, "Remember when we talked about nutrition? We discussed the idea of matching your diet to your goals; even though all diets have some basic components, the specifics of the diet can help you gain or lose weight. Exercise is the same way; you can use different kinds of exercise to do different things."

After a short overview of the five dimensions of exercise, she focused her lesson on strength, discussing the differences between isometric and isotonic exercise. After this discussion, she put the matrix in Figure 7.9 on the overhead and began. "Let's review some of the ideas we just talked about. Who can give me a definition of isometric exercise? Jill?"

"It's where the muscle stays the same length," Jill responded hesitantly.

"Good, for example? Adam?"

"Like, if one hand pushes against the other," Adam answered, demonstrating with his hands.

"Good example," Shirley waved. "Now, someone give us another example of an isometric exercise? Toni?"

"Well, you could use a leather belt and buckle it and put one end of the loop under your foot and hold the other."

**FIGURE 7.8**  Introductory Overhead

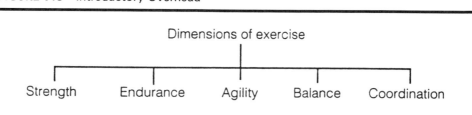

**FIGURE 7.9**  Exercise Matrix

|  | Examples | Advantages | Disadvantages |
|---|---|---|---|
| Isometric |  |  |  |
| Isotonic |  |  |  |

"Excellent," Shirley nodded, smiling. "Others? Shannon?"

"You could also stand in a doorway and push against the sides."

"That's another good example. . . . Now, let's write our definition in this box and put in these examples."

Shirley then continued, "And what about isotonic exercises? How are they different from isometric? Tanya?"

"I think with them you move your muscles but the weight stays the same."

"Good, Tanya," Shirley responded, gesturing for emphasis, "and what could be included under these weights? Steve?"

"Oh, it could be barbells or big cans of food or it might even be your own body like in push-ups or pull-ups."

"Excellent examples, Steve! Now, as we consider advantages and disadvantages of these two forms of exercise, I'd like you to think back to the overhead I put up at the beginning of class, listing the different dimensions or goals of physical fitness."

She waited a moment, surveyed the class, and continued, "How might these two forms of exercise meet other goals? Karen?"

"If you did isometrics over and over again for a long period of time, you might build up endurance."

"Okay, let's list that under 'advantages,' " Shirley nodded. "Any others, Wendy?"

"If you planned them right, isotonics might also build up coordination. Like if you had a dance routine with light barbells."

The lesson continued with a consideration of endurance, agility, balance, and coordination. As the period was drawing to a close, Shirley said, "As we summarize the important points that we discussed today, let's go back to our two pictures and ask the question again, Which one is more physically fit? As we answer our question, I'd like you to use this overhead." She then put Figure 7.8 back on the overhead.

**a.** We identified organized bodies of knowledge as combinations of facts, concepts, and generalizations integrated with each other. Identify two facts, two concepts, and two generalizations in the passage. Explain why we would describe Shirley's lesson as teaching an organized body of knowledge.

**b.** Shirley's pictures and initial question about which woman was more fit illustrates what concept from the general instructional model discussed in Chapter 4?

**c.** What did Shirley do to organize the lesson content?

**d.** There was a partial lecture-recitation cycle contained in the lesson. Describe approximately where *teacher presentation* and *comprehension monitoring* occurred in the lesson.

**e.** Comment on the quality of the teacher's lesson summary in terms of the criteria listed in this chapter.

2. Return to Henry Myer's lesson on the digestive system. In the lecture-recitation cycle on the mouth, identify where the following phases occurred:

**a.** Information presentation

**b.** Comprehension monitoring

**c.** Integration

3. In the text we partially described a lesson comparing Hemingway and Fitzgerald. The focus of the lesson was to show how a writer's life influences his or her writing. Draw a matrix that could be used to establish a data base to teach this content inductively.

## DISCUSSION QUESTIONS

1. Are organized bodies of information more important at some grade levels or in some content areas than others? Which and why?

2. How is the importance of organized bodies of information influenced by timing; that is, is this type of content more important at the beginning or end of a course or unit?

3. How should students' understanding of organized bodies of information be evaluated? Comment on the appropriateness of the following item types:

**a.** True–false

**b.** Multiple choice

**c.** Completion

**d.** Essay

4. How does the lecture-recitation cycle address the basic problems inherent in lectures?

5. How do the following factors influence the optimal length of one lecture-recitation cycle?

    **a.** Age of students

    **b.** Difficulty or complexity of material

    **c.** Background knowledge of students

    **d.** Student motivation

    **e.** Teacher's presentation skills

  **6.** Advance organizers have been called cognitive roadmaps. Why is this an appropriate analogy?

  **7.** How is the process of organizing information to be presented with the lecture-recitation model similar and different from forming a data base with the inductive approach to teaching organized bodies of knowledge?

  **8.** How do the following lesson components contribute to cohesiveness within organized bodies of information?

    **a.** Introduction

    **b.** Spatial representations

    **c.** Transitional links

    **d.** Summary

  **9.** What are the advantages and disadvantages of deductive versus inductive strategies for teaching organized bodies of information?

**10.** Compare and contrast each of the steps in the lecture-recitation model to those in the inductive approach.

## APPLYING IT IN THE SCHOOLS

  **1.** *Organized Bodies of Knowledge: Textbooks.* Examine a chapter in a textbook used in your teaching area that deals with an organized body of information. Analyze it in terms of the following variables (providing specific examples, if possible):

    **a.** Introduction/overview—Is there an introduction at the beginning that provides an overview of the content to follow?

    **b.** Organizational structure—Are there any aids (e.g., diagrams, outlines) that describe the organization of the content?

    **c.** Comprehension checks—Are there questions inserted in the text to check comprehension?

    **d.** Integrative links—Do questions or exercises encourage students to link ideas from one section to another?

    **e.** Summary

  **2.** *Organized Bodies of Knowledge: Organizational Aids.* Take the content in exercise 1 and organize it using one (or more) of the following organizational aids:

    **a.** Outline

    **b.** Matrix

    **c.** Network

    **d.** Schematic diagram

    **e.** Conceptual hierarchy

**3.** *Interactive Teaching: Organization.* Observe (and audiotape, if possible) a lecture or lecture recitation. Take notes from the presentation. Organize the content in terms of one (or more) of the organizational aids listed in exercise 2.

**4.** *Lecture Recitation: Patterns of Interaction.* Observe a teacher (or professor) using a lecture-recitation format (determine beforehand that the lesson will not be entirely lecture). Analyze the lesson in terms of the following:

    **a.** The length of each lecture-recitation cycle (i.e., how long does the teacher talk before asking a question?)

    **b.** What kinds of questions does the teacher ask? (Jot these questions down in order with times attached to them. Later determine whether these were comprehensive or integrative.)

**5.** *Lecture Recitation: Applying It in Your Classroom.* Plan, teach, and tape a lesson using the lecture-recitation format. Analyze the taped lesson in terms of the following variables:

    **a.** Introduction/overview

    **b.** Organizational aids

    **c.** Average length of one lecture-recitation cycle

    **d.** Comprehension checks in each cycle

    **e.** Integrative links in each cycle

    **f.** Summary

**6.** *Advance Organizer.* Construct two advance organizers for an organized body of information; one of these should be a comparative advance organizer. Analyze these in terms of how well they do the following:

    **a.** Take into account students' background knowledge

    **b.** Provide a roadmap of information to come

# CHAPTER 8
# Skills Instruction

## OVERVIEW

We continue our study of teaching strategies and their effect on student learning. We have examined facts, concepts, and generalizations and how these forms of content are woven together in organized bodies of knowledge. However, much of this learning would be impossible without the skills students need to analyze and develop the more advanced forms of knowledge. In this chapter, we discuss skills that range from operations in arithmetic, through rules for grammar and punctuation, to such far-ranging abilities as word processing and map reading. In addition, we examine the research on how to teach skills in the classroom to ensure their long-term retention and transfer to other settings.

## MAIN IDEAS

### Skills in the School Curriculum

*Procedural skills* are cognitive abilities that allow useful processing of information according to established rules.

Common procedural skills exist in the form of *academic rules*.

One goal of skill learning is *automaticity*, which occurs when skills are overlearned to the point that they can be performed quickly and effortlessly.

*Transfer* of skills occurs when skills can be used in new learning situations.

### Planning for Skills Instruction

*Task analysis* helps the teacher break down skills into learnable parts.

### Teaching Skills

Skill learning occurs when students move from *dependence* on the teacher to performing the skill *autonomously*.

Teachers initially introduce a skill by explaining how and why it is used.

*Modeling* by the teacher allows students to see the skill in action.

*Teacher-directed practice* allows students to practice the skill under the supportive supervision of the teacher.

*Independent practice* provides opportunities for students to practice the skill on their own.

*Extended practice* is used to develop long-term retention and transfer.

Jenny Reeder opened the teacher's edition of her second-grade math text to refresh her memory about the next topic for study. She saw problems like the following:

$$\begin{array}{ccccc} 43 & 92 & 18 & 23 & 34 \\ -24 & -74 & -\ 9 & -15 & -17 \end{array}$$

"Oh no, subtraction with borrowing. Are we ready for this?" she thought. She remembered last year when she introduced this topic. Some of her students got it right away, some of her students struggled first and then picked it up, while still others had problems with it throughout the year. She had to do a better job this year.

# SKILLS IN THE SCHOOL CURRICULUM

Subtraction with regrouping or borrowing is a skill, as are the enormous number of mathematical operations that children are required to learn. The four basic algorithmic operations—adding, subtracting, multiplying, and dividing—are all skills. Simplifying expressions such as $9 + 3 \times 8 - 10/5$ or solving equations like $3(2x + 6) = 24$ in algebra are also skills. Such skills obviously require a more developed and sophisticated learner than a simple subtraction problem does, but they are skills nevertheless.

Skills are not limited to arithmetic and algebra, however. They include the academic rules we follow as well. For instance, consider the following examples:

get   getting
jump   jumping
play   playing.

The rule we follow for adding -*ing* endings to words is "Double the ending consonant if it is preceded by a short vowel sound, but do not if it is preceded by another consonant or a long vowel sound." This is a skill, as are the rules for capitalization, punctuation, subject–verb agreement, and many others in the language arts curriculum. Skills can be very basic, as in the subtraction problem at the beginning of this section, or very sophisticated, such as verifying identities in trigonometry.

Skills instruction permeates the K through 12 curriculum. In fact, the emphasis on skills begins in preschool, where teachers help toddlers work on skills like dressing themselves, fastening buttons, zipping zippers, and tying shoes. Preschools and kindergartens also focus on more academically oriented skills, called readiness skills, which prepare students for their introduction to reading, writing, and arithmetic. These include skills like coloring, pasting, and cutting with scissors, which not only develop eye–hand and small muscle coordination but also introduce concepts like left–right and top–bottom, which are important later on.

Skills instruction also makes up the major portion of the content in elementary schools, with its emphasis on reading, language arts, and arithmetic. This is where we get the term *basic skills*. These skills are called basic because they form the foundation for later learning; if a student can't read, write, and do fundamental arithmetic operations, he or she will have problems later on in other subjects. Skills instruction goes beyond these basics, however, to include activities like map reading in social studies, designing and executing experiments in science, and developing aesthetic skills in art and music.

Secondary teachers also make skills an integral part of their curricula. English teachers continue to stress writing and study skills such as summarizing and outlining. Social studies teachers attack thinking skills like recognizing propaganda and analyzing arguments. Science teachers stress processes like observation, controlling variables, and analyzing data, and the secondary math curriculum is literally packed with cognitive skills.

Schools have always taught skills, but the recognition of their importance in the curriculum and the way in which they are taught has changed dramatically. Within the last decade, skills—both basic, or procedural, and higher level thinking skills—have been targeted as crucial dimensions of the curriculum. Interestingly, this emphasis on skills occurred at the same time that computers were becoming a central component of American life and work. The need for people who can think and who can use computers and modern technology in an intelligent manner has replaced the need for people who can remember large amounts of information.

## How Skills Are Taught

In addition to a renewed emphasis on skills, there has also been a change in the way skills are taught. In the past, skills instruction consisted of the exposure method; the implicit belief was that the more times students were "exposed" to a skill, the better they would get at it. This method of skill instruction was a byproduct of behaviorism, which stressed the need for large numbers of repetitions to strengthen stimulus–response bonds.

The exposure method consisted of a three-step sequence, beginning with mentioning the skill, followed by practice, and concluding with assessment. The teacher's role in the process was more managerial than instructional; there often was not much real teaching going on. In a similar way, the students' role was passive; they were expected to look and listen, but their role was unclear beyond that. All that has changed.

Present-day conceptions of skills teaching and learning emphasize the central role of the teacher in clarifying the structure and function of the skill being taught. The teacher does this by explaining (1) what the skill is, (2) how it can be applied, (3) why it is useful, and (4) when it should be used (Pearson and Dole, 1985). These dimensions of skills learning attempt to teach the skill so that it will be understood and usable in later contexts. The name given to this type of teaching is direct or explicit skill instruction (Rosenshine and Stevens, 1986), which underscores the teacher's central role in explaining the skill and how it can be applied.

In this chapter, we examine the research on skill instruction and describe a skill model appropriate for teaching basic skills. In the next chapter we examine the topic of thinking skills, contrasting them with basic or procedural skills, and analyze ways to teach these in the classroom. But before we proceed further, let's make sure that we understand the nature of the beast we'll be wrestling with later.

## Skills: A Definition

**Skills** are cognitive strategies that allow us to process information in some useful fashion. These strategies are free of context and content; they can be generalized across a broad span of situations. In addition, skills are functional; they provide the means to complete some kind of task. For example, the skill of addition allows us to combine apples as well as dollars and cents. What we are adding does not matter; addition is a skill that is content and context free. In a similar way, the ability to punctuate a sentence properly allows us to communicate in term papers as well as in love letters. In both of these instances, the functional nature of skills can also be seen—they enable us to do something, whether that something is counting our money or wooing our loved one. Rosenshine (1983) called this the "how to" of learning versus the what, how, or when. When students have learned a skill, they know how to do something, hopefully something that will be useful in later learning.

## Procedural Skills

An important area of the elementary school curriculum involves the learning and overlearning of procedural or routine skills. These skills require students to apply a standardized algorithm or formula to generate answers. Common examples are found in mathematics, where students learn to perform operations such as multiplying three-digit by two-digit numbers, subtracting with borrowing, and adding fractions with unlike denominators. Other examples involve the application of grammar rules, rules for forming plurals, and phonetic decoding in reading. Much of the early elementary curriculum's emphasis on basic skills is in this category.

    **Procedural skills** are a subset of skills characterized by a relatively tight sequence of standard operations and convergent products. Both of these characteristics—a sequence of actions and convergent products—have implications for instruction. For example, when performing this addition problem,

$$487$$
$$+348$$

you first add the 8 and the 7, carry the 1 to the tens column, and then add the numbers in the tens column. This sequence of operations influences how we present this complex skill to students as well as the kind of practice we provide. We discuss this idea further when we describe how to plan for skills instruction.

    The second characteristic of procedural skills, that they result in convergent or correct answers, also has implications for instruction. As we saw in Chapter 4, opportunities to practice with feedback are important for all learning and are essential with procedural skills. To master a skill, students must have ample opportunities to practice the skill over time and under a variety of circumstances until the skill becomes grooved or automatic.

The process of learning procedural skills is similar regardless of the level of sophistication. For example, in high school algebra, students encounter the following problem:

Solve the following equations for $x$ and $y$.

$$4x + 2y = 14$$
$$6x - y = 9.$$

The numerals and the $x$ and $y$ are all symbols, and we have sequential procedures we follow for solving simultaneous equations. Again, we get precise results: $x = 2$, and $y = 3$. In learning to do this we have acquired another procedural skill.

The same thing applies in other areas. When we say, "We are studying this material," rather than "We is studying this material," we are using language symbols according to a set of grammar and pronunciation rules. When we locate the longitude and latitude of Chicago, we also follow a procedure prescribed for us. From these examples, we can see how the label *procedural skill* is derived.

As with all skills, procedural skills are important because they provide us with cognitive tools. Once we know how to add and subtract, these tools remain valuable to us for a lifetime, and once we know the rules for subject–verb agreement, we have the beginning capacity to write clear, literate prose. From these examples, we can see how facility with procedural skills is critical to the development of our cognitive structures and crucial to subsequent learning.

## Automaticity and Transfer: Two Goals of Skills Instruction

When we teach skills in the classroom, we want students to overlearn them to the point that they can perform them effortlessly, even unconsciously. We call this the point of automaticity. In addition, when we teach skills, we want them to carry over or transfer to other subjects and to be used in real-life situations. Let's examine these concepts.

**Automaticity** occurs when skills are overlearned and can then be used with little or no mental effort. Learning to drive a car is an example. Initially, we clutch both hands to the wheel, devoting all of our attention to the cars and posts that are trying to hit us. As automaticity develops, we can drive almost unconsciously while performing other operations like talking and listening. Skills that are automatized are (1) fast, (2) effortless, (3) consistent, and (4) free of the need for conscious control (Logan, 1988). These characteristics allow us to "plug in" automatic skills while we perform other cognitive operations.

This last point is a strong argument for overlearning. When we overlearn skills, this frees us to insert these skills into larger, more complex operations. For example, we have a paper to write. If we have learned word processing skills to the point of automaticity, we can plug these skills into the total operation, performing these effortlessly and concentrating on other things like organization, transitions, and clarity. The same applies for grammar and punctuation skills; overlearning frees us to concentrate on other aspects of the writing process. In a similar way, if students have overlearned basic math operations, they can plug into these when needed to solve word problems and not expend all of their efforts counting on fingers and toes.

When we teach skills, we also want to teach for transfer. **Transfer** occurs when something learned at one time is applied in another setting. Transfer occurs in the school curriculum when writing skills learned in English class are applied in writing assignments in science and social studies. Transfer also occurs when a student learns map-reading skills in a social studies classroom and uses that skill to help plan a family trip. As we can see, our ultimate goal in teaching skills is to have them transfer not only across subject-matter areas but also into real life.

To accomplish both of these tools — automaticity and transfer — teachers must consciously plan for these to occur, which is the topic of the next section.

## PLANNING FOR SKILLS INSTRUCTION

In planning for skills instruction, the teacher's major task is to break the skill into teachable and learnable parts. In doing this, the process of task analysis, introduced in Chapter Three, can be valuable. In that chapter we described the process in four steps:

- Specify terminal behavior.
- Identify prerequisite skills.
- Sequence subskills.
- Diagnose students.

The purpose of task analysis in skills teaching is to break large complex skills into simpler, more learnable ones. Brown (1982) called this process "headfitting," which is the modification of the material to be learned so that it matches students' existing capabilities.

In addition to task analysis, planning for skill teaching requires that the teacher provide multiple opportunities for student practice and feedback. In Chapter 4, we identified practice and feedback as characteristic of good teaching in general. Opportunities for active involvement in which students practice a skill under the watchful eye of a teacher are essential for skills instruction. Let's return to Jenny Reeder to see how these ideas apply to her teaching situation.

As Jenny sat at her desk and pored over her notes from last year, she found these comments:

Kids don't know place value.
Some having trouble with subtraction facts.
Students are subtracting smaller from larger numbers.

As she pondered these, she asked herself where to begin. She started by writing down this problem and saying to herself, "Here's what I want them to be able to do.

$$\begin{array}{r} 43 \\ -24 \\ \hline \end{array}$$

Subtract a two-digit number from another two-digit number with borrowing. Hmm, what do they have to know to do this?" She then wrote the following on her planning sheet:

Understand place value

Understand subtraction

Know subtraction facts

Understand how to borrow

Understand two-digit subtraction without borrowing

Know how to subtract a one-digit number from a two-digit number with borrowing.

"Well, they already understand subtraction. We've been doing that for weeks. And most know their subtraction facts. But some of them are having problems with place value. I'd better review that and also review two-digit subtraction without borrowing. If they can do that, then we can move on to borrowing. Before I do anything else, I'd better find out who knows how to do what."

She then proceeded to construct a short diagnostic quiz that contained the following subparts:

Subtraction facts
Place value
Two-digit subtraction without borrowing
One-digit subtraction from two digits with borrowing.

As she administered this quiz to students the next day, she used the time to comb through her files and other teacher editions for examples and worksheets she could give her students for practice.

Like so much of good teaching, skills instruction requires careful and thorough planning. You need to identify the skill you're going to teach and the prerequisite skills that lead up to it. In addition, you should know which students will be able to perform these prerequisites. Finally, you need to prepare a number of sample problems or examples to use in your teaching and for students to practice with.

# TEACHING SKILLS

Procedural skills typically are taught by having the teacher first explain and model the skill, then guide the students through initial practice, and finally provide for independent practice (Rosenshine and Stevens, 1986). This transition from teacher control to student autonomy is termed the gradual release of responsibility in skill learning (Pearson and Dole, 1985). Initially, the teacher is responsible for identifying the skill, explaining its functions, and modeling its uses. During the course of instruction, students become more knowledgeable about and confident with the skill and more autonomous in their learning. Finally, if instruction is successful, the students no longer need the teacher; students can perform the skill on their own on playgrounds, in stores, or at home. This transition of responsibility is a central characteristic of skill instruction. Let us examine this process from a psychological perspective.

## Vygotsky: The Teacher as Scaffold

Vygotsky (1978) was a Russian psychologist who wrote about learning in the 1930s. Unfortunately, he died before his major works could be published, and they were not translated into English until the 1960s and 1970s. In his writings, Vygotsky focused on the process of language acquisition and the role of adults in helping children develop their linguistic skills. His observations of parents working with their children led him to develop the concept of the zone of proximal development.

The **zone of proximal development** is the distance between what the child can do under the guidance of a teacher and what the child can do independently. As such, it represents the arena in which successful skills learning can take place. At one end of this zone, the teacher helps the child through a structured environment to perform the skill. This may be accomplished through teacher talk, modeling, or props. At the other end of the zone, the student is able to perform the skill with no assistance from the teacher. The task for the teacher is to move the student from one end of the zone to the other with as few psychological bruises (failures) as possible. The teacher does this through instructional scaffolding (Brown and Palincsar, 1985). Instructional scaffolding closes the gap between task requirements and the skill level of the learner. In doing this, the teacher metaphorically becomes a scaffold for the learner.

Let us illustrate these ideas with an example from everyday life. How do we teach youngsters to ride a two-wheeler? We begin (though probably quite unconsciously) by having them practice on a tricycle. The learning situation is safe, and there is no penalty for sitting in the seat, thinking about the world, and not pedaling (a situation that would be disastrous on a two-wheeler). Then we move to a two-wheeler with training wheels. Again, there is a structured, safe environment with minimal penalty for failures. Finally, the big day arrives. Mom or Dad holds onto the bike as the youngster works up speed. When to let go? A delicate dance occurs. The parent subtly lets go for a moment and then grabs on again. Later, the parent lets go again, this time for a longer time. Finally, the chase is over and the parent stops running. Through scaffolding, the bike learner has reached the other end of the zone of proximal development with as few bruises and scrapes as possible.

Consider this scaffolding metaphor in more detail. A construction scaffold provides support to the worker; in a similar way, instructional scaffolding provides support to the learner. In the bike example, training wheels and parental propping provided both literal and figurative support to the learner. In the classroom the teacher does this by breaking the skill into small steps, by modeling the skill, by providing practice with prompts, and finally by letting go when the learner is ready. The scaffold also functions as a tool for both the worker and student, helping the one perform his or her job and the other learn a new skill. The scaffold does this by extending the range of the worker (learner), allowing him or her to accomplish tasks not otherwise possible. If a child were faced with a two-wheeler with no intermediate props, he or she might never learn to ride it. In a similar way, some skills-learning tasks are so formidable that they cannot be accomplished without continual teacher support along the way. This is where a skilled teacher is essential. A final characteristic of scaffolds is that they are used selectively and only when needed. A painter does not need scaffolding to paint at ground level; to use one would be counterproductive. Similarly, as students gain confidence in their skills learning, aid from the teacher becomes unnecessary, if not counterproductive. The learner is ready to move out on his or her own.

The implications for skills instruction are clear. The teacher must provide a learning environment that is safe but not too safe. Here the concept of success rate, introduced in Chapter 4, is important. The success rates that students encounter as they learn a skill provide tangible evidence of successful scaffolding. When success rates are too low, the scaffolding is insufficient; as they approach 80 to 90 percent, the instruction is both challenging and supportive. As they move higher, the need for scaffolding disappears. The teacher can move on, ensuring that the skill is automatic and can transfer or be applied in diverse situations.

How this all can occur in a classroom is the topic of the next section.

## A Skills Model

The skills model described in this section has five phases, arranged along a continuum of decreasing teacher control. In the first phase, the teacher assumes complete responsibility for learning by initially structuring the skill and explaining its purpose in the total school curriculum. This phase is followed by teacher explanation and modeling.

The transition to student responsibility occurs in the third phase, when group practice allows students to try out the skill and receive feedback from the teacher. Students are now ready to practice the skill on their own, and independent practice, both at their desks and at home, provides opportunities for this function. Finally,

**TABLE 8.1**  Components of the Skill Model

| Phase | Primary Focus | Teacher Actions |
|---|---|---|
| Introduction | Students learn about the skill, why it is important, when used and how applied. | Teacher verbally introduces the skill. |
| Explanation | The mechanics and subcomponents of the skill are explained. | Teacher models skill and explains how it works. |
| Teacher-directed practice | Students try the skill out under teacher supervision. | Teacher leads guided practice to further explain skill and ensure high success rates. |
| Independent practice | Students practice the skill on their own. | Teacher monitors practice to identify problem areas. |
| Extended practice | Automaticity, long-term retention and transfer | Teacher assigns homework and conducts long-term reviews. |

during extended practice, maintenance and broad integration of the skill into the learner's cognitive structure occur. These phases are summarized in Table 8.1 and are discussed next.

**Phase 1: Introduction**  Let's return to Jenny Reeder to see how she introduces her students to this subtraction skill.

"Class, I'd like everyone to look up here at the board. We've got an important new idea to learn today, and I need everyone's attention. Good.

"Now, we've been working on our subtraction, and we're getting pretty good at taking away. Today I'd like to introduce a new kind of subtraction problem that's kind of like the old ones but just a little different.

"Suppose we went to our school bookstore with 27 cents and bought an eraser for 9 cents. How much would we have left? This is a subtraction problem. We've done these kinds of problems before, so let's write it down like this:

$$\begin{array}{r} 27 \\ -\ \ 9 \\ \hline \end{array}$$

"So, let's see, seven take away nine. Wait a minute. Nine is more than seven. What are we going to do? Sometimes we'll run into subtraction problems like this, and we'll need to borrow. Borrowing allows us to subtract numbers like this. That's what we're going to learn about today.

"This is an important skill that all of you need to learn and *can* learn. We're going to work hard at this skill until everyone understands it. To do that, let's take out our play money chips and see if we can figure out this problem."

In the first phase of the model, characterized by large amounts of teacher talk, the teacher introduces the skill and explains its relationship to the total curriculum.

An important function here is to focus students' attention on (1) what will be learned, (2) why it is important, (3) when it will be useful, and (4) how it should be applied. This part of the lesson corresponds to lesson focus, described in Chapter 4. The purpose of this introduction is to provide students with an overview of the lesson and of how the lesson content will be useful to them. The teacher will return to these *how*, *what*, *why*, and *when* questions in the explanation phase to reinforce this information; here, the purpose is to develop an initial framework.

Madeline Hunter (1984), in her popular approach to skills instruction, called these preparatory devices anticipatory set and objective and purpose. The anticipatory set focuses students' attention on the lesson; objectives and purposes describe what will be learned and why. This introductory structuring may appear to be an obvious component of all skills instruction, but Brophy (1982a) found that 20 percent of all skills lessons begin with little or no formal introduction.

Jenny Reeder introduced the skill of borrowing by relating it to the students' real world. Through a real-life but simple problem, she was able to introduce the topic to be learned (subtraction with borrowing), why it was important ("Sometimes we'll run into problems like this"), and when it should be used and applied (in real-life situations where the top number is less than the bottom). Because of this initial structuring, the new skill became not only real but also attached to what students already knew (subtraction without borrowing).

***Structuring the Lesson.*** The exact content of the structuring segment of the lesson will vary with content, but some components cross content lines: objective, content, and procedures (Murphy et al., 1986). The objective tells students what they will be able to do after the lesson, the content describes the essential parts of the skill, and the procedures outline the activities and procedures for the lesson.

To these three, we would add a contextualizing component, which describes the relationship of the new material to material already learned. Our second-grade teacher did this when she explained the new skill as just another kind of subtraction. A junior high science teacher introducing controlling variables might do this by describing the skill in this way:

> We talked yesterday about experiments and how experiments help us learn about cause-and-effect relationships. We talked about manipulating or changing something, like in our gerbil food experiment. Today, we're going to talk about how to control variables to make our experiment more precise. Let's talk about the experiment yesterday.

Similarly, an art teacher who has been working on two-point perspective and who is making the transition to three-point would point out similarities and differences between drawing the two types of pictures.

In each of these examples, the teacher links new material to old, thus ensuring that the new skill is integrated with familiar ones. Meaningful integration, an important idea in the previous chapter, is a central concern in skills instruction.

A final element in the introductory phase of the model addresses motivation. Research is clear that positive teacher expectations and student accountability for learning contribute to student achievement (Good and Brophy, 1991). The teacher can address both of these variables by communicating to students that (1) the skill is important, (2) it is one that all can learn, and (3) individual effort and perseverance will result in positive achievement. The teacher does this both verbally and nonverbally, as we saw in Chapter 4. Enthusiasm, animation, and gestures are probably as important as any spoken words.

Having set the stage both cognitively and affectively, the teacher is ready to move to the next stage.

**Phase 2: Explanation**    In the explanation phase of the model, the teacher further describes the skill, defines its place in the curriculum, and demonstrates how it is performed. Also called the development phase (Murphy et al., 1986), the presentation phase (Rosenshine, 1983), or input and modeling (Hunter, 1984), this part of the lesson is not only the most crucial to skill instruction but also the most difficult to implement (Duffy, Roehler, Meloth, et al., 1985; Duffy, Roehler, and Rackliffe, 1985).

Why is this so? One explanation considers socialization and suggests that teachers are used to the exposure method of teaching skills, with its emphasis on practice, and their lack of experience makes the transition to a more active teacher role difficult. Teachers talk about this difficulty:

> "I've never thought through (how to teach a cognitive skill). The most difficult thing is to think it through." (Duffy and Roehler, 1985, p. 6)

> "Figuring out how to model [the skill] is a hard thing for me. . . . I have to really sit down and write it out. I mean, I am still doing that pretty much, like every day with that group." (Duffy and Roehler, 1985, p. 6)

The process of task analysis discussed earlier can be helpful in breaking a complex skill into teachable parts. A second explanation suggests that teachers have difficulty in verbalizing a skill that is for them already internalized. For example, how would you teach someone to tie a shoe? We all do this so automatically that we have trouble putting words to our actions. This is the case with many of the skills teachers try to explain to their students.

Teachers have two goals in explaining a skill. First, we want students to understand the skill and how it works; second, we want them to understand its usefulness and importance. Consider how a teacher does this in a lesson on semicolons.

> *Teacher:* Class, today we're going to continue our discussion of different kinds of punctuation. Who remembers the different kinds of punctuation we've learned about so far? Shelly?
>
> *Student:* Commas and periods.
>
> *Teacher:* Good, and who can tell us why we use punctuation in our writing? Jon?
>
> *Student:* To help the reader understand what we're trying to say.

*Teacher:* Fine. Now we are moving on to semicolons. After today's lesson you'll be able to use semicolons to punctuate your sentences. Semicolons are a hybrid or mix between commas and periods. They tell the reader, "There is a pause here—pause a little longer than a comma but not as long as a period." Because they're a hybrid, they look like this ";". One use of a semicolon is between two independent clauses that are not joined by *and*, *but*, or *or*. For example, look at this sentence: "The teacher was concerned about the quiz scores; he planned a special review session." What are the two independent clauses here? Sarah?

*Student:* "The teacher was concerned about the test scores" and "he planned a special review session."

*Teacher:* Good. Notice how the ideas in the two clauses are related. That's why we don't use a period. Note, too, that the sentence could also be written this way,

> The teacher was concerned about the quiz scores, so he planned a special review session.

In this case, we wouldn't need a semicolon. Let's take another sentence and see how a semicolon would work here:

> We had to wait in line for hours but the rock concert was well worth the wait.

Let's see, the two independent clauses are "We had to wait in line for hours," and "the rock concert was well worth the wait," so I would write the sentence like this:

> We had to wait in line for hours; the rock concert was worth the wait.

Note how in explaining the skill the teacher described (1) what the skill was, (2) how it was applied, (3) why it was useful, and (4) when it should be used. In addition, in modeling the skill, the teacher used actual examples to illustrate the skill. These are all essential components of effective skills instruction.

***Explaining with Examples.*** The importance of examples in skills learning cannot be overemphasized. As we saw in Chapter Seven, examples help students link concepts and generalizations to the real world. For skills, examples provide a concrete arena in which the skill is performed. Modeling and think-alouds, in which the teacher talks through his or her thinking while working with examples, help students understand how the skill works. To illustrate this idea, let us return to our teacher who was introducing the skill of subtracting with borrowing:

"Okay, now everyone go into your money box and take out two dimes and seven pennies. How much is that? Susan?"
    "Twenty-seven cents!"

"Good. Now let's look at our problem on the board again. It says subtract nine cents from the seven. . . . But, wait a minute! We don't have enough pennies. We can't take nine from seven because seven is already less than nine. Hmmm? So we have to borrow from a dime. Let's do that. Let's go into our money boxes and trade a dime for ten pennies. So, we put a dime away and trade it for ten pennies [illustrating this with pennies and a dime on a felt board]. Now we put the ten pennies with the other seven and we have seventeen. That's called borrowing. Now we can take away the nine pennies like the problem says. Let's do that."

This is a hard idea for second graders. The teacher helped them by using a concrete example and thinking aloud or modeling as she worked through the problem. Effective teaching!

**Phase 3: Teacher-Directed Practice**  Once the teacher feels that the class has a basic understanding of the skill, the class is ready for teacher-directed practice. In this phase of the model, the teacher guides the class through the skill with scaffoldlike instruction that helps students bridge the gap from novice to expert. Using a recitation format, the teacher provides a number of examples of the skill and walks students through the procedures of the skill with as much, or as little, help as is needed. In addition to modeling and explanation, the teacher adds practice and feedback, variables we have seen that contribute to learning. Other names for this stage of skills instruction include monitored practice (McGreal, 1985), checking for understanding, and guided practice (Hunter, 1984). Implicit in all of these terms are the ideas of scaffolding and the gradual release of responsibility discussed earlier.

In this phase of the model, several important transitions occur. There is less teacher talk and more student talk, and, perhaps more importantly, the teacher talk is focused more on questioning, ascertaining what aspects of the skill students do and do not understand. There is a concomitant change in the students' role. In previous phases, their role was to understand the skill and how it could be used. Now they are being asked to try out the skill under the direction of the teacher. In this phase of the model, the gradual release of responsibility occurs most dramatically. If instruction is successful, students will exit this phase as competent bike riders; if unsuccessful, they can become discouraged learners. Let us see how this works in the math lesson we have been following:

"Now, let's try another one. Everyone look up at the board and try this one on your chalkboards. [Each student had a chalkboard slightly larger than a piece of notebook paper on which to work the problem.]

$$\begin{array}{r} 33 \\ -\phantom{0}7 \\ \hline \end{array}$$

"Hmm . . . three minus seven. Can we do that? Why not? Jane."
"Because seven is more than three."
"Good, so what do we have to do? Alice."

"Borrow."

"Excellent. Now look at this problem. It's a little different from our first one because we have a three in the tens place. What does that mean? Jason."

"Thirty."

"Good, because the three is in the tens place it means three tens or 30, so we have 33. Now, we need to borrow 10 from the 30. Let's do that with our coins."

Student answers and success rates are essential barometers here. As students begin this stage, their success rates may approximate chance; when they leave, they should be at the 80 to 90 percent level. The teacher's ability to choose appropriate examples, to sequence these from simple to complex, to provide or elicit clear explanations as the students practice the skill, and to provide appropriate feedback to incorrect or partially correct answers all influence whether success rates improve. In no other stage of the model will so many crucial interactive teaching skills come together at one time. Teacher judgment in applying these skills is essential.

*The Transfer of Responsibility.*  In the first part of this stage, the teacher presents a problem that elicits the skill. This is typically done on the board or an overhead so that all can see and so the teacher can observe the faces of the students as they work with the problem; nonverbal cues on student faces provide invaluable information. Initially, the teacher works the class through the skill, explaining his or her actions as the lesson goes along. If the teacher thinks that the class understands the skill, he or she might call for volunteers to do the next problem at the board. This performs several functions. First, it further models the skill being performed correctly. Second, it provides an opportunity for the teacher to ask students to explain their answers and procedures, thus furnishing an alternate description of the skill. Finally, it provides access to student errors, thus providing an opportunity to correct or "debug" common errors (Nickerson, 1985; Young and O'Shea, 1981) . Let's see how this works.

Jenny Reeder continued with her lesson by saying, "Let's try one more. Kim, Mario, Kevin, and Susan come up to the board and try this one. The rest of you work it at your seats and see if they get the right answer." With that, she wrote the following on the board:

$$\begin{array}{r} 46 \\ -\phantom{0}8 \\ \hline \end{array}$$

As she observed the students at the board, she noticed that all had done the problem correctly except Kevin, who was staring at the board. She walked over to Kevin, put her hand on his shoulder, and said, "Kim, can you give Kevin a hand?"

. . . (No answer).

"What did you do first, Kim?"

"I tried to subtract eight from six."

"And what happened?"

"I couldn't."

"Why not, Kim?"

"Because eight is larger than six."

"So then what did you do, Kim?"

"I borrowed."

"Did everyone hear that? Kim tried to subtract eight from six but she couldn't. So she had to borrow. Show us how you did that, Kim."

"Well, I went to the four and crossed it out and made it a three."

"Why did you do that, Kim?"

. . . (Silence).

"What does the four in the tens column represent?"

"Oh, 40."

"So when you crossed out the four and made it a three, what were you doing?"

"Borrowing! Uh . . . I was borrowing 10 from the 40 and making it 30."

"Excellent, Kim. And where did that 10 go? Kevin, do you know?"

"Did we add it to the six?"

"Good thinking, Kevin. Now can you subtract the 8 from 16?"

"Eight?"

"Good, write it down. And how much is left in the tens column?"

"Three—I mean 30."

"Write that down, too. So what is the correct answer, Kevin?"

"Thirty-eight."

"Good work, Kevin. Now let's try another one to be sure."

As students become more proficient at the skill, the teacher can place more and more of the responsibility for explaining answers on students. Concomitantly, teacher talk changes from explaining to questioning. Even the nature of questions change; initially, the question stem is long and the student response is short; later the question is short with a concomitant increase in the length of student replies. Students are understanding and becoming competent in verbalizing the skill.

*Checking for Understanding.* Student responses are essential for gauging student progress. Workers in this area emphasize several principles of effective interaction during this stage of the model (Rosenshine and Stevens, 1986). First, be sure to call on nonvolunteers as well as volunteers. Make a special effort to call on all students, including those whose hands are not raised. This provides a more accurate overall measure of the rate of skills acquisition in the classroom. An alternate procedure would be to have students work several problems and then check the work by switching papers among students. A subsequent quick show of hands can provide valuable feedback concerning the number each got correct. Finally, avoid questions like "Are there any questions?" If there are, the students who have them will not have the courage to admit it. (Think back on your own experience in classrooms; no one wants to admit that they don't understand something—everyone assumes he or she is the only one who does not understand something.)

In listening to student answers during this phase of the model, the *how* is as important as the *what* (Rosenshine, 1983). Correct, quick, and firm answers indicate that students understand the skill, and the teacher can maintain a brisk lesson pace through additional examples or problems. Correct but hesitant answers suggest that students are not confident about the new skill, and the teacher can respond with appropriate supports such as interspersed explanations and encouraging feedback (e.g., "Good answer" or "It looks like we're getting this").

Incorrect but careless answers also need to be differentiated from more serious problems. If the teacher thinks the student understands the process but got the answer wrong because of a rushed answer (e.g., a computational error), the teacher should correct the error and move on. If, however, the mistake appears to be grounded in a fundamental misunderstanding of the skills, the teacher probably needs to reexplain the skill, walking students through the process and using questions to find out where the problem lies. High error rates (or, conversely, low success rates) distributed over the classroom are one clear indicator of the need to reteach material.

The cycle of problem presentation, solution, and explanation continues until the class is ready to make the transition to independent practice in seatwork. Teacher judgment is essential in this transition. If it occurs too soon, students will practice mistakes and experience frustration; if too late, students will become bored and lesson momentum will suffer. A show of hands (or nonobtrusive thumbs up or down on the chest) from the whole class to signal correct or incorrect answers is useful in gauging competence here. Again, the general ballpark figure of 80 to 90 percent can be used as a gauge.

**Phase 4: Independent Practice: Developing Automaticity**    During independent practice, students individually practice the skill to develop automaticity. This practice occurs in two sequential stages. In the first, called supervised study, students practice the skill under teacher supervision, raising their hands if they encounter problems as the teacher circulates around the room, not only responding to raised hands but also spot-checking student progress. In the second phase of the independent practice stage, students practice the skill at home (Murphy et al., 1986).

As with previous stages, several transitions occur here. One is in the nature of student interactions. In previous stages, student interactions were with the teacher; in this stage, student interactions are primarily with materials. These interaction changes reflect shifts in emphasis from skill acquisition to practice.

A related transition occurs in the purposes of instruction. Initially, the focus was on understanding the skill and how it should be performed. Later, in the practice stages of the model, emphasis is placed on skill mastery. Mastery is characterized by skill automaticity, in which students can perform the skill without consciously thinking about it. This automaticity grooves the skill and allows students to use the skill without a great deal of conscious effort. This frees students to concentrate on other more complex problems at hand. When automaticity fails to develop, students are required to focus their energies on both the skill and the problem to be solved. Research has shown that one of the reasons poor math students have particular problems with word problems is that they are required to concentrate not only on the immediate problem to be solved but also on the computational skills needed to solve the problem (Leinhardt, 1987). It is a tough juggling act to perform.

*Effective Independent Practice.* Research has identified some general guidelines to follow during independent practice:

**1.** Precede individual seatwork by substantive interactive practice; this ensures that students understand a skill before being asked to practice it alone.

**2.** The examples or exercises assigned for independent practice should be directly related to the content covered in the earlier phases of the model. This seems self-evident, but, surprisingly, assigned homework often is not related to the class content (McGreal, 1985). A guiding principle for seatwork and homework could be: Seatwork and homework do not teach—they reinforce!

**3.** Circulate around the room while students are working at their desks. This not only allows you to monitor student progress but also increases engagement rates. In one study, teachers who circulated during seatwork had engagement rates that were 10 percent higher than those of teachers who sat at their desks (Fisher et al., 1980).

**4.** Use "response-to-need" questions as one measure of effectiveness for the independent practice (McGreal, 1985). Response to need means that the students are raising their hands because they need help and they are "responding to the need." Some students will naturally need some help, and it is totally appropriate to help them. However, if too many students are raising their hands, or if the required explanations take too long (about 30 seconds or more), independent practice is not accomplishing its goal. If this is the case, the teacher should move back to phase 3 or even phase 2 before continuing. No quantitative measure exists to tell the teacher exactly how many response-to-need questions are too many, so judgment will again be required.

We have observed classes in which the teacher was involved in a skills lesson, and the students paid little attention in phases 1 and 2. Phase 3 was omitted entirely, and the teacher proceeded directly to phase 4. Students obviously had little idea of what they were supposed to do, so hands were up all over the room, and the teacher was "running herself to death" trying to keep up with them. Unconsciously, the teacher had individualized instruction; each student had the skill explained to him or her as individuals. This is inefficient and enormously demanding teaching; predictably, classroom management problems also develop because students are unable to do the seatwork exercises.

**5.** Use success as a second measure of the effectiveness of independent practice. Students should be about 90 percent successful in their seatwork if it is to be optimally effective (McGreal, 1985). If students are struggling to complete exercises successfully, a return to phase 2 and/or 3 is necessary.

**Phase 5: Extended Practice: Teaching for Retention and Transfer**   In this phase of the model, the instructional emphasis changes in several ways. In earlier stages, the emphasis was on learning; here, the focus changes to retention, or the long-term strengthening of the skill. In addition, in earlier phases, the skill was simplified and taught in isolation so that students could focus their energies on the task at hand. In this phase, the integration of the skill into the learner's total skill repertoire is stressed through transfer, which occurs through the reciprocal processes of generalization and discrimination.

**Generalization** occurs when students are able to transfer the skill broadly to new situations. For example, capitalization skills are generalized when students spontaneously use the skill in writing social studies or science reports even though these areas were not covered in the original instruction. **Discrimination** occurs when students are able to differentiate appropriate from inappropriate times to apply a skill. Students are discriminating when they are able to solve a series of problems, some of which call for addition; others for subtraction, multiplication, or division; and still others for various combinations of the operations.

What can the teacher do to foster retention and transfer? In a word, the answer is practice, but the practice must be spaced and focused strategically. It must occur periodically at spaced intervals after the initial instruction and must include opportunities for students to practice the skill in complex, real-life situations. It is one thing to use semicolons in an exercise within the context of a lesson on semicolons, and something else for students to use semicolons spontaneously in their own writing. This type of transfer is the ultimate goal of skills instruction, and the extended practice phase of the model is designed to address that concern. The two most powerful ways of accomplishing this goal are homework and systematic review.

*Homework.* One efficient means of providing for long-term transfer is through the use of homework. Homework is an alterable variable (i.e., one that teachers can influence) that can be used to increase the amount of time students spend on a subject. Research on the cognitive effects of homework is mixed but generally positive (Harvard University Press, 1985; Walberg, Paschal, and Weinstein, 1985); the former finding is probably due more to variability in the quality of homework than the practice itself. An analysis of 15 studies comparing differing amounts of homework found an average effect of .36 standard deviations (Walberg et al., 1985) This effect was large enough to move a student from the fiftieth percentile in achievement to the sixty-fifth percentile. Researchers also found that, in addition to amount, the frequency of homework was also important (e.g., 10 problems every night vs. 50 once a week).

For homework to be effective, it must be a logical extension of classroom work (Gage and Berliner, 1992). In addition, the teacher should ensure that the skill has been learned well enough that students will experience high rates of success on the assignments. Estimates here are around 90 percent, and experts in this area suggest that success rates during homework should be higher than either classwork or seatwork (Berliner, 1984). The reason is that, because homework is done at home, no one is available to help if the student encounters problems. Homework is also made more effective if assignments are written on the board rather than given orally, and if the assignment of homework is a daily part of the class routine. Finally, homework needs to be collected routinely and graded. This provides both students and teachers with feedback about skills acquisition. Alternatives for grading homework are discussed in Chapter 12 on classroom assessment.

In terms of skills, there are two different types of homework assignments. The first is targeted at the lesson level and focuses on one particular skill. The purpose is to reinforce that particular skill to the point of automaticity. The second type of homework is more integrative and attempts to pull together and connect several related skills. Examples include a language arts assignment combining the different rules of capitalization or a math assignment focusing on different subsets of percentage word problems. This type of assignment would come at the end of a unit and should be preceded by review of the major ideas and skills involved.

Homework assignments should be kept relatively short. McGreal (1985) suggested that no assignment should take an elementary student longer than 20 minutes to complete. You may disagree with this figure, but, unquestionably, many teachers' homework assignments are excessive. If phases 2 and 3 are properly executed, students should be able to complete their assignments quickly and effectively. Performance improves and motivation increases.

*Review.* Homework used for extended practice is most effective when it is combined with systematic review. In their research with both elementary and secondary math teachers, researchers concluded that the most effective math teachers included provisions for regular and systematic review in their planning (Good et al., 1983). This began at the lesson level, where teachers reviewed information in context every day for 5 minutes at the beginning of a lesson. This provided both continuity and reinforcement. They also spent one half of every math period on Monday reviewing material from the previous week. Special emphasis was given to any problems with concepts or processes that had shown up the week before in classwork or homework. Finally, once a month, a whole class period was devoted to review and practice of major skills covered in the last 4 weeks. To break up the potential for monotony or boredom, the researchers recommended the use of games, contests, or quiz-show formats. The teachers' systematic efforts make this approach to retention and transfer effective.

While systematic review and practice is important, opportunities for reinforcement and practice periodically will occur spontaneously, and alert teachers can capitalize on the strategic moment. This happened when a teacher had been working on differentiating between fact and opinions in literature. Several days later, during a class discussion, two students were disagreeing about the movie *Raiders of the Lost Ark*. One asserted that it was boring, and the other disagreed. The teacher intervened as follows:

*Teacher:* Remember what we talked about last time? Fact and opinion?

*Student:* Yes, and that was my opinion.

*Teacher:* That was your opinion, but it sounded like you were saying that she was wrong.

*Student:* No, but I don't think it was boring.

*Teacher:* Okay, different people have different opinions. Is there any fact to any of those?

*Student:* I know one fact. They both have opinions. (Roehler and Duffy, 1984, p. 275)

Teachers cannot plan for opportunities like these, but when seized, they provide valuable opportunities to help students see the relationship of classroom instruction to the real world. This connection to reality often makes spontaneous instruction and review the most valuable form. Being able to recognize opportunities such as these is effective teaching at its best.

# SUMMARY

To summarize our discussion of the skills model, let us analyze it in terms of five characteristics of effective instruction identified earlier: (1) focus, (2) organization, (3) pacing, (4) practice and feedback, and (5) review and closure.

*Focus.* The skills model provides focus during the introductory phase of the model in a number of ways. The teacher states the objective for the lesson, provides an overview of the content, explains how the new skill relates to previous information, and outlines the procedures for the lesson. These lesson components spell out the direction for the lesson.

*Organization.* The entire lesson is built around the idea of the gradual release of responsibility. Through instructional scaffolding, the teacher gradually but systematically gives more and more of the responsibility for performing the skills to students. Concomitantly, as student expertise and confidence increase, the teacher releases control until students are finally competent with the skill. Initially, during teacher-directed practice, the teacher assumes a very supportive role, explaining and modeling procedures and clarifying problem areas. During independent practice, more responsibility is placed on students to demonstrate the skill. Finally, during extended practice, students use the skill on their own in a variety of contexts.

*Pacing.* Pacing is crucial to the skills model and depends heavily on student responses, both verbal and written. The transitions from the explanation phase to teacher-directed practice to independent practice and finally to extended practice are determined by student success rates. When they are high enough during one phase, the teacher can proceed to the next.

*Practice and Feedback.* Practice and feedback are also essential. The model provides a number of opportunities for students to practice the skill and receive feedback. Correspondingly, this feedback is geared to the needs of the students. If they understand the skill, positive feedback may be all that is necessary; if students are experiencing problems, corrective feedback may be necessary.

*Review and Closure.* Finally, review and closure occur in the skills model at several places. At the lesson level, they occur when students are provided with seatwork and homework exercises. These reinforce the skill and provide additional opportunities for practice. Review and closure also occur during the extended practice phase of the model through planned maintenance and review. Here, the class returns periodically to important skills, which are integrated into the students' overall repertoire.

# ADDITIONAL READINGS FOR PROFESSIONAL GROWTH

Brophy, J., & Good, T. (1986). Teacher behavior and student achievement. In M. Wittrock (Ed.), *Handbook of research on teaching* (3rd ed., pp. 328–375). New York: Macmillan. This chapter embeds the research on skills instruction in the larger context of effective teaching.

Good, T., Grouws, D., & Ebmeier, H. (1983). *Active mathematics teaching.* New York: Longman. Though this book focuses on research on mathematics instruction, it makes valuable reading for anyone interested in skills instruction.

Hunter, M. (1982). *Mastery teaching.* El Segunda, CA: TIP Publication. This short, readable book describes Hunter's approach to teaching skills.

Rosenshine, B., & Stevens, R. (1986). Teaching functions. In M. Wittrock (Ed.), *Handbook of research on teaching* (3rd ed., pp. 376–391). This is an excellent overview of the research on effective teaching.

# EXERCISES

1. In the following lesson, identify where each of the following five steps in the skills model occurred:

   a. Introduction

   b. Explanation

   c. Teacher-directed practice

   d. Independent practice

   e. Extended practice

   Mr. North, a sixth-grade teacher, began his lesson on writing by saying, "We've been working on writing paragraphs. Today we are going to learn some steps that you can use when you have to write a composition. A composition is nothing more than a bunch of paragraphs put together logically. We'll use compositions when we write our book reports, and each of you will get to write a composition about your experiments in science. This is a valuable skill to know and one you'll use in every grade level. Besides, I think writing is kind of fun. The trick to a good composition is to follow the steps we're going to learn about. These steps will help you to be clear about your ideas so that when other people read them they will know what you mean. Kareem, you had a question?"

   "Sometimes I can't think of enough stuff to say on my compositions."

   "I think the steps we are going to discuss will help you organize and arrange your ideas so that you can explain them clearly. Let's run through these steps so you can see how they go together. Everyone look up here at this overhead for a minute:

1. Brainstorm
2. Organize
3. Take notes
4. Write
5. Revise

"When you're writing a composition, the first thing you do is write down any ideas you can think about your topic. That's brainstorming. Then, you organize your ideas into an outline. Then, you make notes on your outline to help you remember things you want to say. Then, you're ready to write your ideas down. When you're all done, then you go back and check to see if it all makes sense. That's called revision."

Mr. North then proceeded to show his class how these steps worked with a composition he wrote in front of them entitled "Mr. North Gets Ready for Work in the Morning." When he was done, he asked the class to try one.

"Your topic for today is 'This School Year at Brookwood.' Get a piece of paper and write down as many ideas as you can think of about this year. Let's do this together. Who wants to share theirs with us, Mandy?"

"I can think of six things that happened so far this year: the first day of school, the PTA fair, our field trip to the museum, the class spelling bee, our Halloween party, and the guest speaker from the zoo."

"Good. Now that's our first step. When you brainstorm, don't worry if all the ideas fit. Get as many down as possible. Does everyone have his or her own list? It'll probably be different from this one because everyone thinks differently. Now we're ready for the next step. That's organizing. That means which things go together. Mandy, look at the list and tell us which ones go together and why."

"Hmm. How about field trip and guest speaker? They go together because they're both things we learn from outside the classroom."

"Okay. Any others?"

"We could put the spelling bee and Halloween party together."

"Why, Mandy?"

"Because they're both fun things that we did."

"And what about the first day?"

"It was just different—different from any other day because it was so new."

"And if you were going to tell someone about these different things, which would go first and which last?"

"Well, the first day would come first and our field trip last because we just did that last week."

"So, now we have an outline for our composition that looks like this."

The lesson continued as Mr. North walked his students through the remaining steps.

When Mr. North thought that students were comfortable with these steps, he assigned the following topic for an in-class writing project: "Eating in the Cafeteria." As they began their assignment, Mr. North circulated around the room fielding questions.

Later on in the week, Mr. North asked the students to write a composition for homework on a topic of their choice.

2. Imagine that you are a fourth-grade teacher teaching the procedural skill (rule), "When forming contractions for two words, you combine the words, drop the vowel, and add an apostrophe to indicate that the vowel is missing (e.g., did not = didn't)."

   **a.** Design a lesson including the five steps of the skills model.

   **b.** What kinds of examples will you use to illustrate this procedural skill?

## DISCUSSION QUESTIONS

1. How do the following factors influence the importance of skills in the curriculum?

   **a.** Grade level

   **b.** Subject matter

   **c.** Aptitude of students (e.g., high versus low ability)

2. As you read about skills instruction in this chapter, you may have seen some parallels with concept teaching. Discuss similarities and differences in terms of the following:

   | Concept Teaching | Skill Teaching |
   |---|---|
   | Superordinate concept | Contextualizing |
   | Definition | Explanation |
   | Positive examples | Modeling |
   | Student differentiation of positive and negative examples | Practice and feedback |

3. Why is automaticity important to the following skills?

   **a.** Learning to print in first grade

   **b.** Learning to play a musical instrument

   **c.** Learning a foreign language

4. Teachers often have to make professional compromises: You've just begun a skills lesson and find out that, because of a changed school schedule, you only have half as much time as you had planned. How will you adjust your teaching in terms of the five phases of the skill model? Why?

   **a.** Introduction

   **b.** Explanation

   **c.** Teacher-directed practice

   **d.** Independent practice

   **e.** Extended practice

5. In this chapter, we described the process of "headfitting" as modifying content to students' backgrounds and capabilities. Explain how this process would apply to the following teaching situations.

   **a.** Teaching about farm animals to inner-city urban first graders

   **b.** Helping 8-year-old physical education students learn to shoot baskets when they can't throw the ball high enough to hit the rim

   **c.** Teaching high school students about a religion (e.g., Buddhism or Hinduism) in a country you're studying

6. How appropriate would the five-phase skills model described in this chapter be for psychomotor skills such as those found in physical education? What modifications would have to be made?

7. Why is modeling important in skill learning? How can teachers increase the effectiveness of their modeling?

8. How would you teach for transfer in the following lesson?

   **a.** Teaching map-reading skills to junior high students

   **b.** Teaching punctuation skills to fifth graders

   **c.** Teaching percentage word problems to high school basic math students

9. What implications does the skills model have for testing and measuring skill acquisition?

10. How much homework should a student have each night? How does your answer to this question vary with the following?

   **a.** Age level

   **b.** Ability level (e.g., slower vs. higher ability students)

   **c.** Motivation

   **d.** Subject matter

## APPLYING IT IN THE SCHOOLS

1. *Skills and State and District Curriculum Guides.* Inspect an appropriate curriculum guide in your area or level and answer the following questions:

   **a.** What skills are identified?

   **b.** What suggestions or recommendations are given about how they should be taught?

   **c.** How are the skills sequenced?

   **d.** How is skill acquisition measured?

2. *Textbooks and Skills*. Examine a text in your area and answer the following questions:

   **a.** How much of the text is devoted to skills?

   **b.** How are the skills sequenced?

   **c.** What provision is there for practice and feedback?

   **d.** How does the text deal with long-term retention and transfer?

3. *Homework*. Interview a teacher or student and ask the following questions:

   **a.** How often is homework given?

   **b.** Is there any pattern to homework assignments (e.g., end-of-week or end-of-unit reviews)?

   **c.** Is homework graded and returned?

   **d.** How does it count toward the final grade in the course?

4. *Interactive Skills Teaching*. Observe and audiotape a skill-oriented lesson. Analyze it in terms of

   **a.** Introduction

   **b.** Explanation

   **c.** Teacher-directed practice

   **d.** Independent practice

   **e.** Extended practice

5. *Interactive Skills Teaching: Trying It Out*. Plan for, teach, and tape a skills lesson using the basic skills model. In your plan, make sure you address these phases:

   > Introduction
   > Explanation
   > Teacher-directed practice
   > Independent practice
   > Extended practice

   Listen to your tape and address the following questions:

   **a.** Was your introduction clear? Did it include the following?:

      **(1)** What the skill was

      **(2)** How it can be applied

      **(3)** Why it is useful

      **(4)** When it should be used

   **b.** Did you state an objective for the lesson?

   **c.** Did you relate the skill to material previously covered?

   **d.** Did you think aloud while modeling the skill?

   **e.** What did student success rates during the following suggest about your pace?

      **(1)** Teacher-directed practice

      **(2)** Independent practice

      **(3)** Extended practice

**f.** How did the amount of teacher talk vary throughout the lesson?

**g.** What percentage of the class can perform the skill at an acceptable level? Define what this level is and why.

# CHAPTER 9
# Teaching Thinking Skills

## OVERVIEW

To this point, we have focused on teaching students specific forms of content and skills, such as facts, concepts, and generalizations (Chapter 6), organized bodies of knowledge (Chapter 7), and procedural skills (Chapter 8).

We now change our orientation to focus on the intellectual abilities—commonly described as thinking skills—students use to make learning concepts and the other forms of content more thorough and efficient. As students' thinking improves, their ability to learn the content and skills found in the curriculum also improves, as does their ability to assess the validity of others' assertions and their ability to make decisions based on information rather than emotion or whim.

In this chapter we examine the different aspects of thinking and describe specific strategies teachers can use to promote thinking in their students.

## MAIN IDEAS

### Models of the Thinking Process

*Domain-specific knowledge*, *basic processes*, *metacognition*, and *attitudes and dispositions* are dimensions of the thinking process.

*Domain-specific knowledge* refers to knowledge in a specific content area.

*Basic processes* are the intellectual skills involved in thinking.

Awareness and regulation of our own thinking is described as *metacognition*.

Our *attitudes* and *dispositions* influence our inclinations to use thinking as a way of acquiring and confirming understanding.

### Principles for Teaching Thinking

Teachers should target a small number of thinking skills and teach these intensively.

*Explanation, modeling*, and *practice with feedback* help students understand and use thinking skills.

Teachers influence students' *motivation* toward thinking skills through the instructional strategies they employ.

### Teaching Thinking

Planning for teaching thinking involves *identifying a content topic*, *considering content and thinking-skills goals*, and *preparing examples or data displays*.

*Explicit* thinking-skills instruction defines a specific skill, models it, and reinforces it through teacher-directed practice.

*Complementary* skills instruction incorporates thinking skills into content-oriented lessons.

Inquiry strategies provide students with opportunities to use and practice thinking skills through the processes of hypotheses generation, data gathering, and data analysis.

Carmen Padilla is beginning the study of singular and plural possessives in her junior high English class. She has taught the rule for forming plurals of nouns ending in *y*, and students have practiced writing paragraphs that include both singular and plural nouns that end in *y*. We join her class now as she begins a review of the earlier work.

Carmen's students have their language arts books on their desks and are waiting. Carmen says, "Now look at the overhead, everyone. We want to briefly review the ideas we covered yesterday."

She then displays the following information.

| | | |
|---|---|---|
| **1.** | There is a fly in my soup. | Three flies are buzzing around my head. |
| **2.** | Put a cherry on your ice cream. | I love a bowl full of fresh cherries for dessert. |
| **3.** | Look at the beautiful baby. | A bunch of babies are in the nursery. |
| **4.** | Gee! He's a good-looking boy. | All the boys in this class are good looking. |
| **5.** | Don't spill the stuff on your tray. | Look! There are trays of food everywhere. |
| **6.** | We had turkey for Thanksgiving. | Hey, you turkeys! Don't any of you ever listen? |

"OK. Look carefully at the sentences, everyone."

Carmen pauses and surveys the class as they study the sentences quietly. After several seconds, she asks, "How do these sentences illustrate the rule we have been studying? . . . Dwain?"

"All the sentences over here [pointing to those on the left] talk about only one, and those [pointing to the ones on the right] talk about more than one."

"Excellent, Dwain. Now, look a little more carefully, everyone. What do you notice about the spellings? . . . Kristen?"

"We dropped off the *y* and added *ies* in those [pointing to the first three pairs], but we just added an *s* in those."

"And why did we do that? Ellen?"

"The ones at the top had a consonant before the *y*, and the ones at the bottom had a vowel in front of the *y*."

"Excellent description, Ellen. Very thorough. Now, let's say the whole rule again. . . . David?"

"If the word ending in *y* has a consonant in front of the *y*, we drop the *y* and add *ies*, but if there's a vowel in front of the *y*, we only add *s*."

"And what kinds of words are we talking about? Ann?"

"Nouns."

"Outstanding, everyone. You've done very well. Now," Carmen continues, raising her voice as if offering a challenge. "We'll really need to be good observers and good thinkers today, and we need to keep the rule we just reviewed in mind. . . . Look at these sentences on the overhead." She displays the following:

1. Yuk! He's pulling off the wings that belong to that fly.

2. Yuk! He's pulling off that fly's wings.

3. Look! He pulled the wings that belong to all three flies off.

4. Look! He pulled all three flies' wings off.

After giving the students a few seconds to look at the sentences, Carmen smiles and says, "OK, here we go. Look at sentences one and three. What do they have in common? Terry?"

"They're both talking about pulling wings off flies."

"What other word do you see in both sentences? Robert?"

"*Belong*?" Robert says uncertainly after looking back and forth at the two sentences.

"Good, so what are the sentences talking about? Ginger?"

"Pulling off wings that belong to flies."

"Yes, excellent, Ginger. Now, look at sentences two and four, and compare them. . . . Steve?" she continues, after giving the students a few seconds to study the sentences.

"They both have apostrophes in them," Steve responds.

"Good, Steve, so what must the apostrophes mean? Stephanie?"

No answer.

"Look back at sentences one and three. What did we say they were talking about?"

"Pulling wings off flies?" Stephanie responds uneasily.

"Yes," Carmen smiles. "And what else?"

"Belonging?"

"Right! Very good. So, what must the apostrophes mean?"

"They must show that something belongs to something else."

"Excellent thinking, Stephanie. And how do we know that? Debbie?"

". . ."

"Look at the meaning of sentences one and two. Do they mean the same thing or do they mean something different?"

"I would say same."

"Yes, excellent. So, can you say that in a statement?"

"The sentences mean the same thing."

"And the second one has what in it?"

"Oh, I get it," Debbie replies. "They mean the same thing, and the second one has an apostrophe, so the apostrophe shows belonging."

"All right!" Carmen responds with enthusiasm, pleased with what she has been able to draw from the students.

"Wait," Kevin interjects, "there's another apostrophe in the second sentence, and it doesn't look like it shows belonging [pointing to the *He's* in the second sentence]."

"Terrific, Kevin," Carmen comments enthusiastically. "So, now what do we know? Ellie?"

"An apostrophe doesn't always show belonging, I guess."

"Exactly, and how can we tell when it shows belonging? Anyone?"

The class studies the sentences intently, and finally Josh offers, "I think you have to look at the sentence. You can sort of tell by looking at it."

"Yes! Outstanding, Josh. We use the term *context* for what you've just said. We can tell by looking at the apostrophe in the *context* of the sentence. Now, let's keep that in mind while we look at the rest of the sentences."

She then uncovers the rest of the overhead, displaying all 10 sentences.

1. Yuk! He's pulling off the wings that belong to that fly.

2. Yuk! He's pulling off that fly's wings.

3. Look! He pulled the wings that belong to all three flies off.

4. Look! He pulled all three flies' wings off.

5. The baby's crib is full of toys.

6. Both babies' bottles are on the floor.

7. The boy's hair was messy when he got up from his nap.

8. The two boys' faces were red when they came in from the hot sun.

9. The turkey's beak was sharp and pointed.

10. All four of the turkeys' feathers are smooth and sleek.

Carmen continues, "Now, work with your partners, and let's see what kind of thinkers you can be. Look at all the sentences, and see what conclusions you can make about them. And when you do that, what process will we be practicing?"

"I think we will be finding patterns," Jeneria volunteers.

"Good, Jeneria," Carmen smiles. "Can you explain why?"

"We're supposed to look at all the sentences and see what they have in common."

"Excellent. And what other skills will we practice?"

"We'll also find differences," Thomas adds.

"And you'll ask us how we know that," Jerry adds with a mock grimace. "You *always* ask us how we know."

"That's really hard, isn't it?" Carmen responds, "But look at what good thinkers you're getting to be. OK, let's get started. You have 3 minutes."

The students quickly go to work, and a buzz of activity can be heard in the room as Carmen walks up and down the aisles, monitoring their work.

At the end of the 3 minutes, Carmen flicks off the lights, and the students look up and stop what they are doing. She then calls on different pairs to share their conclusions. Several pairs respond with statements such as,

"All of the sentences have apostrophes in them."
"The numbering of the sentences looks funny."
"They're all complete sentences."
"They're all telling [declarative] sentences."

When Jeff and Loretta's turn comes, Loretta adds, "We decided that they all show belonging," speaking for herself and Jeff.

"Outstanding," Carmen responds, pleased with their answer. "And how do you know that?"

Jeff continues, "They all have apostrophes in them, and we found out that apostrophes mean belonging."

"Where did we find that out? Teresa?" Carmen asks, turning the question to another pair.

"Up in those," Teresa answers, pointing to the first four sentences.

"Super! What else did you find? Beth and Jared?"

Beth looks down at their paper and then answers, "We don't get this. Some of the apostrophes came before the *s* in the words and others came after the *s.*"

"Excellent observation, Beth," Carmen praises. "Let's see if we can figure out why that is the case."

"The ones on that side are all more than one," Stewart interjects, pointing to the sentences on the right of the overhead.

"Good thinking, Stewart, and how do we know that? Anyone?" Carmen continues, deciding not to admonish Stewart for his call-out.

"Go ahead, Kelly," Carmen points, responding to Kelly's raised hand.

"It's the way they're spelled. Those are spelled *flies* and *babies.*"

"So, what have we decided about the sentences on the right? Cheryl?"

"They all show more than one."

"And those on the left?"

"Only one."

"Now, let's look again at the apostrophes. Where did we say they were located? Todd?"

"Some were before the *s* and some were after the *s.*"

"Which ones were before the *s*? Josh?"

"Those," Josh answers, pointing to the sentences on the left side of the overhead.

"And which ones are those? Cheryl?"

". . ."

"Those showing just one, or those showing more than one? Ray?"

"Showing just one."

"So, what do we know about the apostrophe if the statement shows only one? Shawn?"

"The apostrophe comes before the *s,*" Shawn answers after thinking for several seconds.

"Outstanding thinking, Shawn, and everyone else too."

Carmen then goes on to examine the location of the apostrophe with plural possessives. She has the students restate the rule, and again they review the skills they have been practicing.

She then continues by writing the following sentence on the board.

The dresses belonging to the two girls are red.

"Now, let's rewrite the sentence using an apostrophe to show that the dress belongs to the two girls," she directs. "Everyone write a sentence. You have 1 minute."

She watches as the children write their sentences, and then she calls on a volunteer to read a sentence. "I think it is *The two girls' dresses are red*," Helen volunteers.

"Excellent," Carmen smiles. "Now, let's think about the location of the apostrophe. Where should it be? Jan?"

"After the *s* on *girls*, I think," Jan responds after thinking for a few seconds.

"And, why do you think that?"

"The *s* is already there."

"That makes sense alright," Carmen nods, "but let's think about it a little farther. Do we have one girl, or do we have more than one?"

"Two."

"Good! And, what is the rule if something belongs to more than one thing?"

"*S* apostrophe."

"Excellent thinking, Jan. Yes, it makes sense, and that's what this is all about."

Carmen then examines some additional examples and moves to guided practice, where she asks each student to write two sentences, one using a singular possessive and the other using a plural possessive.

She closes the lesson by assigning a paragraph in which at least two examples of each form of possessive are embedded.

# DEVELOPING THINKING SKILLS: A GOAL FOR ALL LEARNERS

Since *A Nation At Risk*—a powerful publication warning that American children were receiving a poor-quality education—was published in 1983, increased attention has been given to the task of "teaching our kids to think" (Carnegie Task Force on Teaching as a Profession, 1986). This doesn't mean that teachers, schools, or our nation cared little about "thinking" before then, but rather that the explicit emphasis on student thinking skills has greatly increased since that time.

Several factors have contributed to this movement. One is that American students' standardized test scores were low compared to the scores of students from other industrialized countries. As one expert on thinking skills observed, "The increasing interest in the teaching of thinking skills and in particular in the desirability of teaching them explicitly, stems in large part from concerns about such documented failings of the current system" (Nickerson, 1984, p. 29). Developing students' thinking skills was seen as one way to improve student performance on standardized tests.

In addition, our country's leaders saw America's status as the economic leader of the world slipping. A connection was made between thinking skills and economic growth and development. This point was illustrated by a Japanese industrialist's highly controversial comments in January of 1992. He described American workers as undereducated and ill equipped to help America compete in the modern world marketplace. While the causes of these national trends are hotly debated, many look to the emphasis on thinking as one way of improving our schools.

All teachers teach thinking skills, but not all teachers do it well. Some do it consciously in an organized, systematic fashion, and others do it unconsciously in a disorganized, chaotic fashion. A major goal of this chapter is to help teachers understand the process of thinking-skills instruction and apply this information in their classrooms.

Having said that all teachers teach thinking skills, we need to qualify this with "to varying degrees." Research suggests that most classroom instruction is geared to "mere possession of information" and "facts to be learned" to the exclusion of the development of thinking skills (Goodlad, 1984). A historical look at classroom teaching confirms that this tendency toward memorization is not new, extending back into the nineteenth century (Cuban, 1984). An examination of classroom testing procedures corroborates this conclusion. One analysis of teachermade tests found that both elementary and high school teachers wrote 69 percent of their test items at the knowledge level, and junior high school teachers were even worse, writing nearly 94 percent of their questions at the lowest intellectual level (Fleming and Chambers, 1983). If teachers' tests match what they are teaching, we have a serious problem because students are being taught what, not how, to think.

Students need to learn to think, because the ability to think through ideas is as important as the ideas themselves, and classrooms should play a major role in this area of development. As with other areas of the curriculum, effective teachers can have a considerable impact on students, helping them develop and refine their thinking abilities. To do this, teachers must understand what thinking skills are, how they are learned, and what they can do to develop them. These are the topics of the next sections of this chapter.

## THINKING SKILLS: WHAT ARE THEY?

We are not the first to admit that thinking skills are elusive creatures to define (Beyer, 1984) . Let us start the process with the tried and tested approach advocated earlier in Chapter 6—examples. Various workers in the area of thinking skills have offered the following:

| | |
|---|---|
| Comparing | Classifying |
| Contrasting | Summarizing |
| Inferring | Identifying irrelevant information |
| Generalizing | Planning |
| Controlling variables | Hypothesizing |
| Making conclusions | Predicting |

To these skills, we would add the top five levels of Bloom's taxonomy (1956) discussed earlier: comprehending, applying, analyzing, synthesizing, and evaluating.

But even with these additions, the list is not complete. Each of you, in various content areas and at different levels, can add to these.

Let us try another tack—a definition. **Thinking skills** are context-free, open-ended, sequential cognitive processes that allow students to transform information in a strategic manner. Thinking skills are similar to the procedural skills we studied in Chapter 8 in that they are context free; like procedural skills, this is what makes thinking skills so valuable. When we learn to plan, infer, or generalize, we can use these skills in a variety of situations.

Thinking skills differ from procedural skills in that they are more open ended. While procedural skills typically have one right answer, thinking skills can have a range of acceptable answers. Let us illustrate this difference with two examples, predicting and summarizing. When we ask students to summarize a passage or predict based on a body of information, we have general criteria in mind, but the final product will differ in terms of the particular approach that the student took and the information used.

In addition to being open ended, thinking skills are also typically sequential, a characteristic that has implications for instruction. For example, the process of classifying typically begins with observing, proceeds to identifying similarities and differences and grouping on the basis of similarities, and concludes with the labeling of groups. When we teach this skill, we break it down into subskills, present it in a sequential manner, and provide practice at each of the stages.

Now let us return to the last characteristic in our definition—thinking skills allow students to transform information in a strategic manner. Thinking skills are useful because they allow us to process ideas and information to accomplish certain goals. If information is too large or cumbersome, we summarize; if we need to determine the effects of different variables, we control them in an experiment. The specific skill is selected to match the goal being achieved.

One final characteristic that has important consequences for instruction needs to be mentioned. Thinking skills, once acquired, tend to become automatic, and because of this automaticity are often hard to describe. Let us illustrate this idea with an example. Classify the following items in groups:

|  |  |
|---|---|
| Shoe | Vine |
| Apple | Banana |
| Tree | Bush |
| Watermelon | Coat |
| Shirt | |

How did you do this? Which did you do first? Then what? How would you teach a third grader how to do this? As with other skills, thinking skills often become so automatic that they are unconscious and difficult to teach other people. This is unfortunate because workers in the area of thinking skills stress the importance of explaining the skills through the process of thinking out loud (Palincsar, 1991; Pressley et al., 1990). Through this process, experts are able to share their understanding of the skill with novices. We return to this idea in a moment when we describe different approaches to teaching thinking skills.

# THE DIMENSIONS OF THINKING: COMPONENTS THAT INFLUENCE PERFORMANCE

While approaches vary (Nickerson, Perkins, and Smith, 1985), four dimensions of thinking are commonly identified (Nickerson 1988; Pressley et al., 1990) . The first, and perhaps most central, component consists of basic processes which students use when they think. These include processes like observing, comparing and contrasting, inferring and predicting. During the process of thinking, these basic processes are applied to some content area or domain. This domain-specific knowledge provides a content arena in which basic processes can be applied. To think effectively, students must also know when different processes are appropriate. For example, when we want to condense information we summarize; when we want to group items we classify. This knowledge about thinking is called metacognitive knowledge. Finally, effective thinking requires a willingness on the part of students to use basic processes in different content areas and in their everyday lives. Without positive attitudes, thinking skills remain unused in students' minds. These four dimensions are illustrated in Figure 9.1.

Using Carmen Padilla's lesson as a focus, these dimensions help us understand why the lesson was successful and how the teacher planned and taught for promoting thinking in her students. Let's examine each of these dimensions more clearly.

## Basic Processes

**Basic processes** are the fundamental constituents or building blocks of thinking. They are our thinking tools that we use to transform and evaluate information. While experts label these basic processes in different ways, using terms such as *information processing skills* (Beyer, 1988), *core thinking skills* (Marzano et al., 1989), or *essential cognitive processes* (Presseisen, 1986), most include the processes summarized in Table 9.1 (Eggen and Kauchak, 1992, p. 392).

**FIGURE 9.1**   Dimensions of Thinking

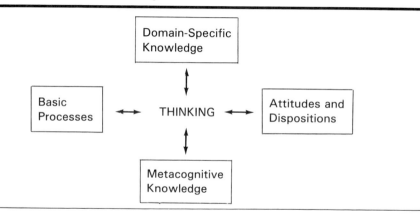

**TABLE 9.1**   Basic Processes in Thinking

| *Process* | *Subprocesses* |
|---|---|
| Observing | Recalling<br>Recognizing |
| Finding patterns and generalizing | Comparing and contrasting<br>Classifying<br>Identifying relevant and irrelevant information |
| Forming conclusions based on patterns | Inferring<br>Predicting<br>Hypothesizing<br>Applying |
| Assessing conclusions based on observation<br>Thinking critically | Checking consistency<br>Identifying bias, stereotypes, clichés, and propaganda<br>Identifying unstated assumptions<br>Recognizing over- or undergeneralizations<br>Confirming conclusions with facts |

Rationales for these processes come from several sources.

- These basic processes allow us to make sense of the world, pulling together discrete bits of information into understandable and coherent patterns (Bruner, 1966; Carnine, 1990).
- Each of the processes is based on the theme of *forming conclusions based on evidence*, which is the dominant view of the way knowledge should be acquired and validated in our culture. For example, patterns are based on relevant information; the patterns form the basis for inferring, predicting, and hypothesizing; and the description of critical thinking as "assessing conclusions based on observation" is consistent with most experts' definitions (Beyer, 1987; Paul, Binker, and Charbonneau, 1987; Presseisen, 1986).
- The ability to reason inductively—to generalize—and the ability to reason deductively—to infer, predict, and hypothesize—are described as characteristics of intelligence itself (Nickerson et al., 1985; Sternberg, 1986).

When we teach thinking skills, we provide students with opportunities to use and practice these basic processes. The most effective way to do this is to encourage students to apply these processes to the content they're learning.

## Domain-Specific Knowledge

There are two general philosophical stances regarding teaching thinking skills. One is to develop separate curricula, such as a course students would take that is devoted to the study and development of thinking. A number of these programs now exist, developed by prominent leaders such as Robert Sternberg (1987), Mathew Lipman (1987), and Edward deBono (1983), among others.

An alternate approach is to infuse thinking as an explicit goal into the regular curriculum. This is the position we take, for two reasons. First, while the separate curricula have many positive features and are well conceived, little evidence exists supporting the effectiveness of these programs. As Nickerson (1984) concluded, "Evidence regarding the effectiveness of specific programs for teaching thinking is sparse" (p. 36).

The second reason that we recommend a content-based approach to thinking skills is a growing body of research that highlights the importance of content background for effective thinking (Glover et al., 1991; Mayer, 1987). In short, students can't think effectively about a topic if they don't know anything about it. Nickerson observed, "The importance of domain-specific knowledge is not really debatable. To think effectively in any domain one must know something about the domain, and, in general, the more one knows the better" (1988, p. 13). Resnick and Klopfer reinforced this position: "Recent cognitive research teaches us to respect knowledge and expertise. Study after study shows that experts on a topic reason more powerfully about that topic and learn new things related to it more easily than they do on other topics" (1989, p. 4).

**Domain-specific knowledge** refers to knowledge in a particular content area—language arts, in Carmen's case. Carmen's students could not have formed conclusions about possessives if they didn't understand basic grammar and spelling rules, and more particularly, they couldn't have formed the rule for forming plural possessives without understanding the prerequisite rule for forming plural nouns. Teachers accommodate domain-specific knowledge when they teach *both* content and thinking skills during their lessons.

## Metacognitive Knowledge

Effectively developing students' thinking also requires metacognitive knowledge. **Metacognition** is individuals' awareness of their own thinking. "Metacognition has also come to connote the management of one's own cognitive resources and the monitoring and evaluation of one's intellectual performance" (Nickerson, 1988, p. 19). Presseisen (1987) suggested that the emphasis on metacognition is what sets the present thinking-skills movement apart from previous efforts.

The focus on metacognition suggests that students should be aware of the processes and strategies they're using. This means that students should know when they're using basic processes, what processes they're using, how they relate to the content they're learning, and why they're being used. They should not only find patterns and form conclusions based on them, for example; they should also be keenly aware of what they're doing.

McTighe (1987), in asking how we might develop students' thinking abilities, described three complementary approaches. Teaching *for* thinking amounts to involving students in thinking as they learn content, teaching *of* thinking "utilizes a direct teaching strategy whereby a specific thinking skill, such as comparing, becomes the content of the lesson" (p. 25), and teaching *about* thinking helps make students become more aware of their own learning and thinking. As students learn about thinking they develop "inner speech," which is the use of language to describe steps in reaching a goal. (This is similar to the teacher think-alouds that we mentioned earlier.) Capable learners develop inner speech, and the use of inner speech increases as tasks become more complex, helping learners talk themselves through difficult cognitive tasks (Palincsar and Brown, 1989). Talking and teaching about thinking can help students become more efficient and better self-directed learners.

Carmen's efforts to promote metacognitive knowledge in her students is illustrated by the following segment taken from the introductory case study.

> "And when you do that, what process will we be practicing?"
>
> "I think we will be finding patterns," Jeneria volunteers.
>
> "Good, Jeneria," Carmen smiles. "Can you explain why?"
>
> "We're supposed to look at all the sentences and see what they have in common."
>
> "Excellent. And what other skills will we practice?"
>
> "We'll also find differences," Thomas adds.
>
> "And you'll ask us how we know that," Jerry adds with a mock grimace. "You *always* ask us how we know."

By actively talking about these processes as they appear in lessons, teachers help students become aware of their uses in their own thinking.

Research in the areas of metacognition indicates that these abilities can be taught (Gavelek and Raphael, 1985; Miller, 1985). A supportive classroom structure, together with class discussions and teacher modeling, have been demonstrated as effective teaching strategies. The results of this research suggest that explicit focus on metacognition is productive and worthwhile.

## Attitudes and Dispositions

To be valuable, thinking skills must not only be learned but also used. Hopefully, learners' awareness and understanding of the processes and strategies they're using will lead to the disposition, or inclination, to use them spontaneously. For example, when students encounter the advertising claims of one miracle diet over another, they will be inclined to ask "Which diet *is* better?" and "What data exists to support these different claims?"

To illustrate this process, consider an elementary science classroom. A soft drink bottle is covered with a balloon, and the system (bottle, balloon, and the air inside) is placed in a pot of hot water. On the basis of their observations, learners are helped to conclude that the pressure in the system has *increased*. At a later point, they find that the pressure inside a heated duplicating fluid can has *decreased* when it is heated. A hoped-for inclination in learners is that they spontaneously ask themselves if the second experience is related to the first, and if it is, how? (With a little guidance, they recognize that the first system is closed, which prevents the air from escaping, while the second is open; the cap is off the can.)

These dispositions were briefly illustrated in Carmen's lesson by Beth's comment, "We don't get this. Some of the apostrophes came before the *s* in the words and others came after the *s*." Carmen's positive response to Beth then affirmed that this kind of inquiry was important and valued in her class. Other examples of attitudes and dispositions include, "fair-mindedness and openness to evidence on any issue; respect for opinions that differ from one's own; inquisitiveness and a desire to be informed; a tendency to reflect before acting; and numerous others" (Nickerson, 1988, p. 21).

Experts are becoming increasingly aware of the role attitude plays in the development and use of thinking skills (Ennis, 1987; Resnick, 1987a; Swartz, 1987). Unfortunately, students don't necessarily acquire these dispositions as part of the normal developmental process. "Open-mindedness may be the proper, but is not the 'natural' disposition of the human mind" (Paul, 1984, p. 7) . We have all been frustrated with students who, rather than reasoning for themselves, would rather be simply told. The old joke, "Don't confuse me with the facts. My mind is made up," often applies.

This suggests that inclinations should be taught, but can they be? Research suggests that students can be taught to value the power of thinking skills, and this valuing results in increased use (Pressley et al., 1990). In addition, our own work in classrooms gives us reason to be optimistic. For example, in training teachers to follow students' answers with requests for reasons, explanations, or supporting evidence, we have found that even young learners quickly warm to the task and begin supplying their explanations and supporting evidence along with their answers, documenting their answers spontaneously.

Attitudes and inclinations develop over time and as a result of the positive experiences students encounter with thinking in the school curriculum. Ideally, as these experiences accumulate over the school year, students develop the inclination to compare examples and look for differences without being prompted or coached each time they occur. When these inclinations eventually become automatic, students acquire powerful aids that help them become self-directed learners both in and outside of classrooms.

# PRINCIPLES FOR TEACHING THINKING

As we move from the dimensions of thinking themselves to specific procedures for teaching thinking, several principles help us form the bridge between the two (Pressley et al., 1990):

- Target specific thinking skills and teach these intensively. Avoid the temptation to teach a smorgasbord of skills; instead focus on a few in a concerted effort.
- Model and talk about thinking skills. Thinking skills can be abstract and elusive entities. Help students understand them by using concrete examples to teach thinking skills and talking about them often.
- Explain where and when to use different thinking skills. This should be done when thinking skills are first introduced and also when they reappear later on.
- Reinforce thinking skills. Use thinking skills across the curriculum, helping students see their application in various subject-matter areas.

- Develop student motivation to use thinking skills. Emphasize their utility in thinking about the world and learning new content. Encourage their use in students' daily lives.

These principles are general ones which apply to whatever particular teaching strategy you use to teach thinking skills. In the next section, we consider specific strategies to use when teaching thinking skills.

# TEACHING THINKING: INSTRUCTIONAL STRATEGIES

In the first sections of this chapter, we identified different dimensions of thinking and implications for teaching thinking. At this point, you might wonder, "How can I apply this information in my classroom?"

The goal of this discussion is to present generalizable strategies that will allow you as a teacher to integrate the teaching of content and thinking. *Generalizable* means that the strategies are both practical and usable regardless of grade level, content area, or topic. However, these strategies are not presented as rigid sets of rules to be followed without question or modification. Instead, they are intended to illustrate the general processes involved in teaching thinking. From these guidelines you must use your professional judgment about appropriate adjustments and modifications.

We describe the strategies for teaching thinking skills in the following sections. First, we examine the planning needed for teaching thinking, and then we discuss strategies for actual classroom implementation.

## Planning for Teaching Thinking

Planning for teaching thinking requires three essential steps.

- Identify a topic.
- Specify content and thinking skills objectives.
- Prepare examples of data.

As we look at these steps, we see that they are similar to those we originally presented in Chapter 6 when we discussed planning for teaching concepts. In fact, the first step is identical to the first step in Figure 6.3. — identify a topic.

**Identify a Topic**   Imagine you're at your desk and are planning for your next week's instruction. Where does your planning begin? If you're a typical teacher, it might start with a topic or a learning activity (Clark and Peterson, 1986) . The topic could come from a textbook, curriculum guide, or your past experience. The topic could be flowering plants, longitude and latitude, equivalent fractions, or singular and plural possessives, as was the case in Carmen's lesson. Identifying a topic is where instruction typically begins, and it is a productive beginning point for planning for teaching thinking as well.

**Consider Content and Thinking-Skills Objectives**   At this point, content-oriented instruction and teaching thinking begin to differ. Typically, once a topic has been identified, you specify a content objective: "What do I want my students to know, understand, or be able to do with respect to my topic?" For instance, in Carmen's case, the content objectives might be as follows:

- Understand the rule for forming singular and plural possessives.
- Be able to apply the rule for forming singular and plural possessives in writing.

When we teach for thinking, however, not only are the content objectives themselves important, but the *way we reach them is of equal importance*. Having students practice basic thinking processes and having them know that they're involved in these processes are as important as the content objectives themselves. In other words, *active involvement in the thinking process is an objective in and of itself*.

This means that each thinking-oriented lesson has two simultaneous sets of objectives. One is the set of traditional content objectives, and this is where the planning process begins. The other is the set of objectives for involving students in the thinking process. In a thinking-skills lesson the two are inseparable, and one is no more important than the other. In Carmen's case, not only did she want her students to understand the possessive rule, but she also wanted them to practice identifying similarities and differences, finding patterns, and forming inferences and hypotheses.

The acceptance of the value of simultaneous sets of objectives is important. Teachers making the effort to increase their emphasis on student thinking are commonly concerned about the extra time they believe the process will take. When they accept the idea that involvement in the thinking process is a objective in itself, using extra time is justified.

**Preparing Data**   Having identified a content area and objectives, the next step is to determine how you will teach the topic so that students can reach the content objectives using basic thinking-skills processes. The question you're asking yourself at this point is, What can I provide the students, or what can I have them do that will allow them to practice their thinking skills while reaching the objective?

We emphasized this step in Chapter 6, and we reemphasize it here. Its importance is difficult to overstate. The overall effectiveness of your teaching for thinking will depend significantly on the information you provide to illustrate your topic. The ideal you're striving for is as follows: *All the information students need to reach the content objective is observable in the information displayed or can be directly inferred from the display.* The form of the display depends on the topic. In Carmen's case, all the information about singulars and plurals, possession, and apostrophes was observable in the sentences that illustrated the rule. Carmen didn't have to "tell" the students anything.

Carmen's topic was a punctuation rule. On the other hand, if the topic was a generalization (or series of generalizations), such as José Alvarez's lesson on heat, expansion, and the motion of molecules in Chapter 5, the information was in the form of a demonstration and model that illustrated the generalizations. If it is a concept, such as Mike Lee's lesson on conduction in Chapter 6, the information would be examples of the concept. If the topic is a body of knowledge, such as Leon Wilson's lesson on the events leading up to the Revolutionary War in Chapter 7, the information could be presented in the form of a matrix. In each case, all the information the students needed to use and practice their processing was displayed for them.

We are all familiar with the emphasis that is placed on concrete and hands-on experiences for learners, and now from a thinking perspective we see why they're important. These experiences are the most likely to provide learners with the information needed to understand the topic being presented, and through the processing of information they also allow learners to be actively involved in learning.

Providing illustrations that contain all the information needed to reach the objective serves another vital function. As we know from Chapter 2, our students come to us with widely varying experiences. Some have elaborate backgrounds—sometimes called "cultural capital" (Ballantine, 1989)—while others' backgrounds are not as rich or varied. By providing all the essential information in the examples, we minimize those background differences. In a sense, the examples become the experience, helping all students learn content and develop their thinking skills.

# EXPLICIT AND COMPLEMENTARY SKILLS TEACHING

The pressures against better skills instruction alluded to earlier in this chapter are real. There are a limited number of hours in the day, textbooks and curriculum guides are oriented more toward content, and parents as well as administrators often value content acquisition more than the development of thinking skills. A common comment teachers make is, "I am expected to teach so many things already. How can I be expected to focus on thinking as well?"

This concern is real, because classrooms *are* busy places. So, teachers who value the development of thinking skills must do two things. First, when they explicitly teach a thinking skill, they must do this as effectively as possible. Second, to reinforce these thinking skills and ensure their generalization to all areas of the curriculum, they must be able to integrate thinking skills into their ongoing lessons. We call these two approaches explicit and supplementary strategies for thinking-skills instruction. As we describe these two approaches, think of them as points on a continuum rather than discrete categories.

In **explicit thinking-skills instruction**, the teacher identifies skill acquisition as a primary goal and teaches toward that goal in a direct manner. Content becomes a vehicle to teach the thinking skill. The instructional steps in the skills model described in Chapter 8 are relevant here. Teachers explain the skill, model it, and provide students with relevant practice. We look at an example of this strategy in a moment.

In **complementary skills instruction**, the tension between content and thinking-skills development is more apparent. Content goals become more important, and the need to develop lesson momentum, organization, and continuity are real. Thinking skills are still taught, but these are complementary to the content vector of the lesson. Sometimes the teacher will not take time to explain the skill explicitly, instead mentioning its existence in the course of a content lesson. Similarly, the modeling and practice are provided as an integral part of the content lesson. A difficult juggling act, yes, but a teacher can have the proverbial best of both worlds. Let us see what each of these would look like in the classroom.

## Explicit Thinking-Skills Instruction

Tanya Winkowsky's third-grade class was discussing their field trip to the zoo. Her content goal for the lesson was for students to understand similarities and differences between the major subgroups of animals like mammals, reptiles, and birds. To do this, she first had students list all the things they saw at the zoo. The board looked like this:

| | | |
|---|---|---|
| elephants | lions | crocodile |
| seals | wolves | otters |
| giraffes | cheetah | zookeeper |
| eagles | monkey | rhinos |
| antelopes | baboons | bears |
| hippos | deer | ostrich |
| iguana | cobra | |

She then proceeded, "Class, that's a real good start. You were really observant. Now let's take the list and classify the animals into groups so we can talk about them. Who wants to start?"

Silence.

Tanya's experience is not unusual. As teachers, we'll often ask our students to use thinking skills that they are unfamiliar with or unable to use. When this occurs in a lesson, we'll need to place the content goal on hold for a while and concentrate on the thinking skill. This is called an explicit approach to teaching thinking skills because the lesson focus is on the direct development of a specific student thinking skill.

In an explicit approach to teaching thinking skills, the teacher wants students to understand the skill and how and when it is used, as well as be able to use it in the classroom and other settings. The same principles of decreasing teacher control and gradual release of responsibility that we discussed in Chapter 8 apply here. Let's return to Tanya's lesson and see how she might teach the classification skill using a direct instructional model.

"Well, I thought everyone knew how to classify, but I can see we don't. So, we better learn how to do it. *Classify* means to put things into groups and label the groups. Let's write that on the board."

Classify—Put similar things into groups and label the groups

"This is an important skill that we'll be using all year long, not only in science but in other areas as well. If you know how to classify, you'll be able to group things that are similar. First, I'm going to show you how I classify. Then I'm going to ask one of you to try it in front of the rest of the class. Then, I'm going to ask each of you to do it on your own.

"When we classify, here are the steps to follow." She then wrote the following on the board:

### Steps in Classifying

1. Skim (look) over all objects.
2. Choose two that are alike.
3. Label that group.
4. See if any others belong in that group.
5. Find two more that belong together.
6. Label that group.
7. See if any others belong in that group.
8. Do steps 5, 6, and 7 until all items are in a group.

"Now I'm going to show you how to classify using these steps. Listen very carefully because I'm going to ask you to do it next. When we're all done, each of you will be able to classify on your own.

"First, what can we classify? We can classify anything because classification is a skill that works with all kinds of things. Let's see, since it's getting close to lunch, let's classify the things in my lunch bag. Everyone watch while I put these on the table."

She then placed the following items on the table for the class to see:

| | |
|---|---|
| Sandwich | Apple |
| Fork | Milk |
| Salad | Straw |

"Hmm, now let's go back to the steps that I wrote on the board. First we skim over everything we're going to classify. *Skim* means look. Okay . . . sandwich, fork, salad, apple, milk and straw. Now, step 2. Which two of these go together? Hmm? How about sandwich and salad. They go together because they're things to eat. That's the label for the group. To help us remember that, let's put E's in front of them and put 'E = Things to eat' on the board.

"Now we're ready for step 4. Are there any other things that belong in that group? Hmm, things to eat. Fork, no. Apple, what do you think? Yes, apple is something to eat, so let's put an E by it."

The lesson continued until all the items were classified.

Tanya was explicitly teaching a thinking skill through the use of the skills model introduced in Chapter 8. Note how in the introduction phase of the model the teacher described (1) the objective of the lesson, (2) the content of the lesson, and (3) the procedures to be followed in the lesson. This was followed by the explanation phase, in which the teacher thought out loud as she went through the classification steps. This allowed her students to observe her thinking as she modeled the skill. Now the students are ready to try the skill themselves. Let's return to Tanya's classroom and see how the teacher handles teacher-directed practice.

"Now that you've seen me classify, let's see if you can do it yourselves. I'm going to put some things up on the board, and I want each of you to see if you can classify them using the first four steps on the board. Look up here on the board, and everyone try to classify these. Then I'll call on someone to explain how they did it."

> Car      Boat
> Plane    Jet
> Bus

After a short pause to give the class time to think, Tanya continued, "Who would like to come up here and show us how they classified these? Jeremy?"

"Well, first I put *car* and *bus* together and put an *L* by them for *land*. Then I put *plane* and *jet* together and put an *A* by them for *air*. Then I didn't know where to put *boat*, so I made a new group called *water*."

"Excellent, Jeremy, you did a fine job of classifying all the items. How many people classified it like Jeremy? Thirteen, fourteen, fifteen. Good. How about the rest of you? Phil?"

"I put *car*, *plane*, *bus*, and *jet* together because they all have wheels. Then I put *boat* in its own group like Jeremy and called it *water*."

"Did anyone else do that? Martha, you did. Sam, okay. That's something I forgot to mention before. It's okay to classify things in different ways—just so your system makes sense. Now let's try another group of items."

During teacher-directed practice, the teacher provides students opportunities to practice the skill under close teacher supervision. This ensures that students understand the skill before being asked to perform it on their own. As students practiced the skill, note how Tanya encouraged Jeremy and Phil to think out loud. This provides additional modeling of the skill as well as allowing students access to other students' explanations of the skill. Often students can explain things better than the teacher.

Note, too, how Tanya used student responses to gauge whether to go on or to repeat her explanation. Had the success rate been lower, she would have gone back and retaught the skill rather than proceeding on to independent and extended practice. Once Tanya felt confident about her students' grasp of the classification skill, she returned to the zoo lesson, using this content to extend and reinforce the thinking skill of classification.

In an explicit approach to thinking-skills instruction, the lesson focuses primarily on the thinking skill and the teacher uses explanation, modeling, and directed practice with feedback to help students understand and practice the skill. This approach to skills instruction is recommended when a new thinking skill is being introduced because it allows students to focus their attention on the specific thinking skill at hand and not concern themselves with new content. Note how Tanya employed familiar objects, like her lunch and transportation vehicles, to teach this skill. This minimized the number of cognitive balls students had to juggle.

An explicit approach works when teachers want to introduce a thinking skill and specifically provide explanation, modeling, and opportunities for practice. At other times teachers will prefer to integrate thinking-skills instruction with a content lesson. Carmen Padilla did this with her lesson on possessives. Let's examine the structure of this lesson more closely.

## A Complementary Strategy for Teaching Thinking Skills

Having identified both content and thinking-skills objectives, and having prepared information for students' use as they employ their thinking skills, you are now ready to begin the lesson. To reach both content and thinking-skills objectives, a complementary strategy has a content focus while providing for student practice in thinking. The following strategy, outlined in Figure 9.2, is classroom tested and allows teachers to pursue both goals.

The phases in this strategy typically occur in sequence, but it isn't necessary that they do. They are not a rigid set of steps that must be followed in order. For instance, students might make several inferences before they generalize, and identifying the thinking skills they're using certainly doesn't have to occur only at the end.

**FIGURE 9.2**   Teaching Thinking: A Complementary Instructional Model

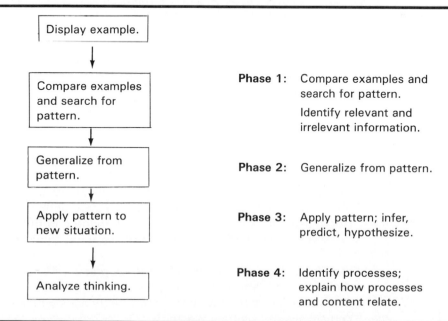

**Beginning the Lesson**   When using this instructional strategy, rather than sharing a content objective at the beginning, teachers introduce their lessons by telling students that they are going to present some data or have students do some activity, and the students' task is to carefully observe and analyze the data. Teachers can be as general or as specific as they choose to be; the specificity can depend on the students and the preferences of the teacher.

Carmen began her lesson by reviewing the spelling for singular and plural nouns, displaying her first four sentences and saying simply, "We'll really need to be good observers and good thinkers today," and then "OK, here we go. Look at sentences one and three. What do they have in common?" This simple introduction actively involved students by posing a problem for all to consider.

**Developing the Lesson**   Once the lesson was introduced, Carmen used the procedure outlined in the model as a framework. She had students compare singular and plural possessives, searching for patterns. When they were able to identify the rule linking singular and plural possessives, she asked them to apply the pattern to new examples. However, in using this basic pattern she didn't follow it rigidly. For example, when Kevin said, "Wait, . . . There's another apostrophe in the second sentence, and it doesn't look like it shows belonging," Carmen seized on the opportunity to help students understand the use of context to determine meaning. A teacher with less expertise might have missed the opportunity or brushed over it.

**Analyzing Thinking**   In addition to a content emphasis, Carmen focused specifically on the basic processes during the course of her lesson, and this focus and emphasis is what separates a thinking-skills lesson from a lesson with a pure content focus. As Carmen taught her students about forming possessives with apostrophes, she also emphasized thinking skills in two ways.

- She provided systematic opportunities for students to practice the processes while the lesson moved toward the content goal; the development of thinking skills was a goal in and of itself.
- In addition to having the students practice the thinking skills, Carmen had them explicitly identify and discuss the basic processes they were using during the course of the lesson.

The following segment taken from the lesson illustrates how she did this.

"And when you do that, what process will we be practicing?"
"I think we will be finding patterns," Jeneria volunteers.
"Good, Jeneria," Carmen smiles. "And why do you think that?"
"We will look at all the sentences and see what they have in common."
"Excellent. And what other skills will we practice?"
"We'll also find differences," Thomas adds.
"And you'll ask us how we know that," Jerry adds with a mock grimace. "You *always* ask us how we know."

Explicitly using and talking about thinking skills helps students become knowledge-able about these processes.

**Motivating Students: Teaching Positive Attitudes toward Thinking Skills**  Ear-lier in this chapter, we suggested that positive attitudes toward thinking skills can be developed, but we didn't explain how. At this point we readdress this topic.

Positive attitudes can be taught in two complementary ways. The first is by teacher modeling in think-alouds. For example, when beginning a new topic a teacher might say aloud, "Hmmm. I wonder how this relates to what we've already done," or "Hmmm, we don't know the meaning of this word. What thinking skill might be useful here?" This process encourages students to look for opportunities to use their newly acquired skills and fosters a climate in which students realize that questions, conjecture, and original thought are valued. The fact that Kevin was quick to question the inconsistency in the use of apostrophes suggests that Carmen had developed a climate in which questioning and critical examination were valued.

Teacher think-alouds and modeling can then be followed with specific focus on encouraging the transfer of thinking skills, as illustrated in the following example:

*Teacher:* Whenever we see examples of something, like our sentences, what do we want to ask ourselves?

*Student:* How are they similar or different?

*Teacher:* What else do we want to know?

*Student:* Why things happen.

*Teacher:* Such as?

*Student:* Why the apostrophe came before the *s* in some cases but after the *s* in other cases.

Admittedly, Carmen didn't practice this process with her students, but the seg-ment illustrates how readily it could be done. A teacher won't focus on all the dimen-sions of teaching in every lesson. If teaching for thinking becomes a pattern, each of the dimensions will be emphasized when it is the easiest to do so.

**Reaching Closure**  As the lesson moves toward closure, the abstraction (or rule, in Carmen's case) that served as the content focus can be used to explain other exam-ples, such as the example with the girls' dresses which occurred at the end of Car-men's lesson. This example was an application of the rule, which required inferences from the students to apply the rule. This step reinforces the rule and promotes trans-fer while at the same time giving students practice with the basic processes. The thinking processes can again be made explicit at this point if the teacher chooses to do so.

We see all the phases of the model in the illustration at the beginning of the chapter, and we also see that they don't have to occur in order. A creative teacher capitalizes on the opportunities to have the students practice thinking whenever they occur. This practice is woven into the fabric of the lesson as students move toward the content objective.

The lesson comes to closure when the content objective is reached and is reinforced with application. The thinking-skills objectives are not "reached" in the same sense. Rather they are woven into every lesson, providing students with abundant, ongoing, and continuous practice.

**Adapting the Complementary Strategy: Additional Examples**   The model can be readily adapted to a wide variety of topics. For instance, let's briefly look back at José Alvarez's science lesson in Chapter 5. In comparing the heated and unheated bottles, he could have easily increased the emphasis on thinking with a questioning sequence, such as the following:

*Teacher:*  How do the masses of the air in the two systems compare?

*Student:*  They're the same.

*Teacher:*  How do you know?

*Student:*  No air was allowed in or out of either system.

*Teacher:*  How about the densities?

*Student:*  The density in the heated system has decreased.

*Teacher:*  How do you know?

*Student:*  The masses are the same, but the volume of the heated system has increased, so its density has decreased.

This sequence illustrates the intimate relationship between thinking and domain-specific knowledge. For example, students are making an inference when they conclude that the density in the heated system has decreased, and they are asked to document it when the teacher asks, "How do you know?" Through the use of questions designed to teach thinking skills, teachers are also able to teach content in a more meaningful fashion.

# TEACHING THINKING SKILLS THROUGH INQUIRY

An English class is discussing the novel *To Kill a Mockingbird*, which they have just read. Though all the students enjoyed reading the novel, members of the class differed on why. The teacher uses this difference of opinion to spark a discussion of factors that influence the popularity of novels. To do this he poses the question, "What makes a novel popular and well liked?" As students offer a number of different ideas, the teacher writes these on the board. Then he asks students to list several novels that they have read and to rank order these in terms of preference and explain in a few sentences why they liked each. He collects this information and presents it to the class to analyze the next day.

A social studies class is looking at the United States' economy and is investigating factors that influence it. One of these is advertising. As the class discusses this topic, the powerful impact of television advertising surfaces. Through the teacher's encouragement, the class decides to investigate factors that influence the shape and content of TV commercials. To do this, the class divides into groups and each group strategically watches different channels on different days and times, looking for both content, approach, and length. Later the whole class compares results.

In previous sections, we discussed two different strategies to teach thinking skills. Though both were structured differently and placed different amounts of emphasis on content versus thinking-skill development, both used content as a vehicle to teach thinking skills. They did this by identifying a content area as an arena in which students could develop and practice their thinking skills. Inquiry lessons provide additional opportunities to develop students' thinking skills through student investigations.

**Inquiry** is a process for answering questions and solving problems based on facts and observations. Inquiry lessons involve students in this process by posing a question or problem to be solved and involving them in the collection and analysis of data. Through these processes, students not only learn content but also develop thinking skills through their use in the lesson. Let's see how this occurs.

## Implementing Inquiry Lessons

Inquiry lessons occur in four sequential steps (Eggen and Kauchak, 1988). In the first of these, a question or problem is identified. During the second phase, hypotheses are offered in an effort to explain or frame the problem or question. These hypotheses then guide data-gathering procedures, which occur in phase three. In the final phase, data is analyzed and hypotheses are evaluated. These phases are summarized in Table 9.2 and discussed next.

Inquiry lessons begin with a question or problem that frames the class's investigation. In the English class, the teacher used the question, "What makes a novel popular and well liked?" In attempting to answer this question, students generate a number of alternate hypotheses. These might include

- The setting
- Characters

**TABLE 9.2** Phases in Inquiry Lessons

| Phase | Description |
| --- | --- |
| 1. Question or problem identification | A question or problem is raised that serves as the focus for the lesson. |
| 2. Hypothesis generation | Students conjecture about different explanations for the question or problem. |
| 3. Data gathering | Data is gathered in an attempt to test alternative hypotheses. |
| 4. Data analysis | Students analyze data and form conclusions. |

- The plot
- The reader.

As students wrestle with the question or problem, opportunities to use and practice thinking skills occur in the generation of hypotheses.

The hypotheses generated then help to guide data-gathering procedures. The scope and variety of these data-gathering procedures vary with the content being considered, the age of students, and resources available. Some options in different content areas are listed in Table 9.3. Through these data-gathering activities, students are actively involved in learning about the topic and are provided opportunities to discover connections between the ways questions are asked and knowledge is generated.

After the data is gathered, students are encouraged to analyze this data in terms of the hypotheses generated. The process of data analysis provides valuable practice in basic processes like observing, comparing and contrasting, classifying, inferring, and confirming conclusions with facts. At a broader level, inquiry activities provide opportunities for students to see connections between conclusions and the evidence on which they are based.

As with the complementary strategy, inquiry offers opportunities to teach thinking skills within the context of content-oriented lessons. Through the processes of hypothesis generation, data gathering, and analysis, students are provided with opportunities to use and practice thinking skills in the generation of knowledge.

## SUMMARY

Emphasis on the development of student thinking skills has increased since the early 1980s, when our nation's leaders realized that America's students weren't acquiring the skills needed to keep our country competitive in an information-oriented, technology-driven, global marketplace.

Thinking skills are a combination of four dimensions: knowledge in a particular content area—called domain-specific knowledge, basic thinking processes, metacognitive knowledge, and attitudes and dispositions. None of the four exists in isolation, and thinking is a combination of all four.

**TABLE 9.3** Alternative Data-Gathering Procedures

| *Content Area and Problem* | *Possible Data Sources* |
| --- | --- |
| 1. History—growth patterns in cities | 1. Census data and history books |
| 2. Home economics—factors influencing the baking of bread | 2. Experiments varying variables like oven temperature, kneading, and amount of yeast |
| 3. Science—sunlight and plant growth | 3. Bean plants are grown under different amounts of sunlight. |
| 4. Social studies—voter preference on issues | 4. Questionnaires and interviews |

*Source:* Adapted from Eggen and Kauchak, 1988

Thinking is most effectively taught when specific skills are targeted and intensively taught through explanation, modeling, and practice and feedback.

Planning for teaching thinking includes identifying a topic, considering content and thinking-skills objectives, and preparing examples or other forms of data.

Explicit thinking-skills instruction targets a specific thinking skill and uses the direct instructional model to explain the skill and provide practice and feedback.

Complementary teaching for thinking follows an inductive procedure which allows learners to practice basic processes, such as comparing, inferring, predicting, and hypothesizing, while learning content.

Inquiry strategies teach thinking skills by involving students in hypotheses generation, data gathering, and data analysis.

Teachers help students acquire positive attitudes toward thinking skills by modeling and focusing specifically on the dispositions and by helping students understand how thinking skills can be useful in other areas.

## ADDITIONAL READINGS FOR PROFESSIONAL GROWTH

Beyer, B. (1987). *Practical strategies for the teaching of thinking.* Boston: Allyn & Bacon. This book provides an eclectic overview of the issues involved in teaching thinking skills.

Costa, A. (Ed.). (1985). *Developing minds.* Alexandria, VA: Association for Supervision & Curriculum Development. This edited work contains a valuable assortment of articles covering different perspectives on thinking-skills instruction.

Eggen, P., & Kauchak, D. (1988). *Strategies for teachers: Teaching content and thinking skills.* Englewood Cliffs, NJ: Prentice Hall. This book relates thinking skills to information processing theory and presents several teaching models that combine the two.

Resnick, L. (1987). *Education and learning to think.* Washington, DC: National Academy Press. Resnick provides an excellent overview of the conceptual issues surrounding our attempts to teach students to think.

## EXERCISES

1. In this chapter the skills model was suggested as one effective strategy to explicitly teach thinking skills. Reread the case study describing Tanya Winkowsky's lesson on classification and identify where the following phases occur. Use specific information from the lesson, if possible, and also specify if any phases were missing.

   **a.** Introduction _____

   _____

    **b.** Explanation _____

_____

    **c.** Teacher-directed practice _____

_____

    **d.** Independent practice _____

_____

    **e.** Extended practice _____

_____

2. Analyze the lesson that Carmen Padilla taught using the phases of the complementary skills strategy described in this chapter. Identify where in the lesson each of the phases occurred and tell if any were missing.

    **a.** Display examples, compare examples, and search for patterns _____

_____

    **b.** Generalize for pattern _____

_____

    **c.** Apply pattern to new situation _____

_____

    **d.** Analyze thinking _____

_____

3. Read the following episode and answer the questions that follow.

    David Burnett was beginning a unit on quadrilaterals in math, and he began his first lesson by placing the following geometric shapes on the overhead.

        square            trapezoid
        parallelogram   rhombus
        rectangle

    He continued by asking, "Now, what do you notice about these shapes? Sandra?"

    "We can see that they all have four sides," Sandra responded after thinking for a few seconds.

    "Good, Sandra. Anything else, class? Mindy?"

    "They all have four interior angles."

    "Excellent, Mindy. Anything else, Toby?"

    "The interior angles equal 360°," Toby replied after a moment's hesitation.

"Hey, wait, how do we know that? We didn't measure them!" interjected Deena.

"Good question, Deena. Class, how do we know that, or do we?" After a pause, David returned to Toby.

"We don't have to measure, we can infer it. Remember what we learned about plane closed figures. . . ."

    **a.** How does the episode illustrate the need for domain-specific knowledge in the process of developing thinking skills?

    **b.** How does the episode illustrate metacognition on the part of the students? Cite specific information from the episode to support your answer.

    **c.** How does the episode illustrate student dispositions? Cite specific information from the episode to support your answer.

**4.** McTighe (1987) discussed teaching *for*, *of*, and *about* thinking. Think again about Carmen Padilla's lesson that introduced the chapter. Which of McTighe's three approaches did Carmen *least* emphasize? Explain.

**5.** Return to the social studies episode involving TV advertisements at the beginning of the section, "Teaching Thinking Skills through Inquiry." Describe how a teacher might structure a possible inquiry lesson that would include the following components:

    **a.** Question or problem _____

    _____

    **b.** Hypotheses _____

    _____

    **c.** Data gathering _____

    _____

    **d.** Data Analysis _____

    _____

## DISCUSSION QUESTIONS

**1.** How are procedural and thinking skills similar? different?

**2.** Are there some content areas where it is easier to include thinking skills in the curriculum? Which and why?

**3.** Some critics see the current emphasis on thinking skills as a fad. Others view the development of thinking skills as antagonistic to content acquisition (e.g., the idea of cultural literacy mentioned earlier). How would you respond to these critics?

4. How is the complementary strategy of promoting thinking skills, as presented in this chapter, different from the inductive approaches to teaching content that were presented in Chapters 6, 7, and 8? How could the teachers in those chapters have made their teaching more thinking-skills oriented?

5. Could procedural skills, as presented in Chapter 8, be taught with a thinking-skills orientation? If so, describe an example that illustrates how it might be done.

6. Most teachers agree that teaching thinking skills is important. Since this is the case, why is teaching thinking so rarely done? List several reasons. What might be done to overcome these obstacles?

7. Consider content goals that are concepts, principles, rules, or organized bodies of knowledge. How is teaching thinking skills with each of these forms of content similar and different? Which of the four is least like the other three? For which is teaching thinking the easiest? the hardest? Why do you think so?

8. Look again at Carmen Padilla's lesson at the beginning of this chapter. Critically assess her teaching using the information from Chapters 2, 4, 5, and 6 as a basis for your assessment.

## APPLYING IT IN THE SCHOOLS

1. Interview a teacher. Ask how much emphasis is placed on teaching thinking in class. In the process, ask what is meant by *thinking skills*. Ask for a specific example of how approaches to thinking are taught to students.

2. Observe a class in which the teacher is focusing on some type of thinking skill. Use the following simple classification system for the questions the teacher asks:

   a. Factual/recall question

   b. Question that calls for a comparison, such as "How are these similar (alike, the same, different, etc.)?"

   c. Question that calls for an explanation, such as "Why?"

   d. Question that calls for documentation, such as "How do you know?"

   e. Question that calls for a hypothesis, such as "What would happen if?"

   Tally the number of questions that the teacher asks in each of the categories. Add additional categories if needed.

   a. How often are these questions asked?

   b. How do students respond to these questions?

   c. What could the teacher have done to promote the development of thinking skills during the lesson?

3. Observe another class. Look for any evidence of the teacher trying to teach meta-cognition or attitudes and dispositions. Describe specifically what the teacher did in any cases that you observe.

4. Plan and teach a thinking-skills-oriented lesson using one of the strategies described in this chapter.

    a. How did your planning differ from other lessons?

    b. What information did you provide students to think about?

    c. How did students respond to your questions asking them to use thinking skills?

    d. What evidence do you have that students actually developed their thinking skills?

# CHAPTER 10
# Alternatives to Direct Instruction

## OVERVIEW

The instructional strategies that we have discussed so far have been teacher centered and have focused on the cognitive domain. Alternatives to this whole-class format exist and can be used to reach other instructional goals. In this chapter, we examine topics such as peer tutoring, cooperative learning, and small- and large-group discussions. These strategies, combined with a look at advances in available technology, provide teachers with effective alternatives to teacher-centered, whole-group instruction.

## MAIN IDEAS

### Students as Resources

Older or more able students can be used as *peer tutors* to help younger or less able students.

*Cooperative learning* involves student teams of mixed ability who are rewarded for group effort in addition to individual effort.

*Group investigations* focus on collaborative efforts in solving problems.

Individuals are responsible for developing and teaching specific portions of organized bodies of knowledge when *jigsaw techniques* are used.

### Discussion Strategies

*Discussions* promote student thinking at high cognitive levels when focusing on organized bodies of knowledge.

*Discussions* in the *affective domain* often focus on values and moral issues.

*Discussions* require extensive *student background* and skilled teacher facilitators.

*Small-group discussions* develop social skills, such as compromise, communication, leadership, and open-mindedness.

### Technology and Teaching

*Computer literacy* involves knowledge and skills all people need to function in a computerized world.

Computer applications include *computer-assisted instruction*, *tutorials*, *simulations*, and *games*.

*Computer-managed instruction* uses the computer for record keeping, grading, and organization.

The previous four chapters on instruction have focused teacher-centered, whole-group instruction aimed primarily at cognitive goals. This approach is called *direct instruction*, and research supports its effectiveness when teachers want students to learn concepts, principles, skills, and organized bodies of information—the major goals of today's classrooms (Brophy and Good, 1986; Doyle, 1986; Slavin, 1988).

Teachers have goals, however, that can't be reached with a direct instruction approach. How many times have we heard or even said, "I don't know what I'm going to do with that class. They won't listen to each other, they're rude, and they think they're right about everything," or "They're so narrow-minded. They won't even consider anyone else's point of view." These expressions reflect concerns about students' attitudes, values, and interpersonal skills. We want, for example, to develop our students' ability to listen, to work with their classmates on group projects, or to cooperate in solving problems. For these goals, alternatives to whole-group, teacher-centered instruction are needed. This chapter is devoted to instructional alternatives designed to reach these goals.

The role of technology—another instructional alternative—in teaching and learning is expanding rapidly. To work successfully in the technology-driven information age in which we now live, we need a computer literate society, and the first goal of technology education is to develop this literacy. Computers can also be used to provide practice and feedback, to promote problem-solving and thinking skills, and to manage instruction.

We also address computers and their use in this chapter.

# INSTRUCTIONAL ALTERNATIVES: STUDENTS AS RESOURCES

Effective teachers use all available resources to promote learning, one of which is the students themselves. In this section, we discuss instructional alternatives that allow the teacher to use students to help each other learn content while at the same time developing skills outside the cognitive domain. These alternatives provide variety, flexibility, and some degree of individualization. We begin this section with a discussion of peer tutoring, an instructional strategy that uses students to teach each other.

## Peer Tutoring

Jim Corbin, an exceptional education resource teacher, and Maria Sandoval, a first-grade teacher, were talking in the teachers' lounge over lunch. Both were having problems with their students' reading.

"I just don't have enough time to spend with my slower students," Maria commented. "I know what they need—time in small groups where I can give them individual help and encouragement, but I've got 27 students in that class, and when I spend extra time with them, I feel guilty about slighting the others."

"I know how you feel," Jim replied. After hesitating briefly, he continued,

"Numbers aren't my problem; it's motivation. I'm working with fourth and fifth graders who are really discouraged. They just don't think they can do it."

As Jim and Maria talked, they wondered if there was any way that they could help each other. They'd both heard of peer tutoring but had never heard of special education students acting as tutors for regular students. They both had their doubts, but they agreed to give it a try.

For the next week, Jim prepared his students, teaching them to model and demonstrate the reading skill they were teaching, and showing them how to provide helpful praise and feedback. Maria helped by pulling together concrete reading materials for the tutoring sessions.

The next Monday, Jim brought his nine resource students down to pick up the first graders. When they returned to the resource room and began working, Jim watched each pair's progress carefully. As he had anticipated, some tutors did better than others, but all groups seemed to work reasonably well. He could tell it was working for his students by the way they came into his classroom and got ready for the tutoring sessions. Before, they dragged themselves in, and it was like pulling teeth to get them to work. Now, they arrived on time and appeared eager. He wondered how it was working for Maria's students. (Adapted from Top and Osguthorpe, 1987)

Peer tutoring, as the term implies, involves students teaching students. Peer tutoring offers two specific benefits. First, because the sessions are one to one, the teaching is individualized, which is effective for all teaching situations and especially for skill learning. Second, peer tutoring can be motivational, both for the tutor and the one being helped. Helping someone learn is intrinsically motivating for the tutors (Slavin, 1991), and the satisfaction that comes with increased understanding motivates those being helped.

The idea of students helping students is not new. The ancient Greeks and Romans used tutors, and in nineteenth-century Lancastrian England, where pupil-teacher ratios of 400 or 500 to one existed, teachers coped by first teaching older monitors, who then worked with younger students. Teachers in America's one-room schoolhouses dealt with the differences in grades one through eight by having older or more capable students help others.

Two primary peer tutoring arrangements exist. Cross-age tutoring, like the Lancastrian system, uses older students to help younger ones. It benefits from the more mature tutor's knowledge and skills but is hard to manage logistically. It is difficult, for example, to pull fifth graders out of class to help second graders. Same-age peer tutoring addresses this problem and can be used in any class where students are at different levels of learning.

As we saw in the introductory episode, peer tutoring has also been used successfully with special education students. In one study, upper elementary special education students were trained to act as reading tutors for first graders (Top and Osguthorpe, 1987). After 12 weeks of tutoring, researchers found that both the tutors and first graders outperformed comparable control students on reading achievement tests. In addition, the special education tutors showed significant increases in perceptions of their general academic ability as well as their ability in reading and spelling.

## A Basic Peer Tutoring Model

Peer tutoring is most commonly used to supplement typical teacher-led instruction. We call this the *basic tutoring model* and examine it in this section.

The model has two phases: planning and implementation, each having four steps. These steps are summarized in Table 10.1.

### Planning for Peer Tutoring

*Identify a Topic.* One-to-one peer tutoring can be used in any subject where the topic includes convergent information with clear right and wrong answers. For example, the algorithm for two-digit by one-digit multiplication, concepts such as adjectives or proper noun, finding the longitude and latitude of various locations, and a variety of grammar and spelling rules are all appropriate topics for peer tutoring. Organized bodies of knowledge and thinking skills, with their complexity and divergence, are less applicable to peer tutoring activities.

*Prepare Instructional Materials.* Convergent topics allow the teacher to construct specific practice and feedback exercises that provide structure for the tutoring sessions. Tutors then focus on the problems and exercises in the materials. Student tutors are largely incapable of providing initial or even supplementary instruction, so these materials are critical.

*Assign Students to Pairs.* One arrangement is to pair a high with a low achiever and let the more advanced student do the tutoring. A different option, called reciprocal tutoring, pairs students of comparable ability, and they take turns being the tutor. In this arrangement, students usually slide into a pattern in which they simply work together instead of one acting as tutor for a period of time and then switching.

*Train Students to be Effective Tutors.* Like teachers, effective tutors are made, not born. The preparation both the tutors and the students being tutored receive is im-

**TABLE 10.1**   Steps in Planning and Implementing Peer Tutoring

*Planning*
1. Identify a topic.
2. Prepare instructional materials.
3. Assign students to pairs.
4. Train students to be effective tutors.

*Implementing*
1. Conduct group presentation.
2. Break into peer tutoring groups.
3. Monitor progress.
4. Evaluate tutoring pairs.

portant in the effectiveness of the process (Slavin, 1991). Untrained tutors often imitate the worst from their teachers, including punitiveness and a lack of helpful feedback. A list of effective training components includes the following:

- *Explaining objectives.* At the beginning of a session, the tutor should provide focus by identifying the skill or concept to be learned. The teacher can help by writing the objective at the top of the worksheet.
- *Staying on-task.* When an extraneous subject comes up, have the tutors remind their partners of the objective and call their attention to the number of examples, pages, or steps left to do.
- *Emotional support.* Encourage tutors to make supportive comments for incorrect answers, such as, "Not quite. Let's look at it again. What is the first thing you did?"
- *Praise and other positive feedback.* Discuss the importance of positive feedback and provide examples of different forms of praise (e.g., "Good answer!" "Great, you're really getting this."). If possible, have the tutor link the praise to specific behaviors ("Good, you remembered to carry the three to the hundreds column."). At the end of the lesson, have the tutor state what was learned and relate this to the session objective.
- *Encouraging verbalization.* Instruct the tutor to encourage thinking out loud, both for himself or herself and his or her partner. This makes the cognitive operations observable, providing a model for the partner and feedback for the tutor.

## Implementing Peer Tutoring Activities

*Group Presentation.* Teach the content in the same way that you normally would. You could use one or more of the strategies we presented in Chapters 6 and 8, remembering that organized bodies of knowledge, discussed in Chapter 7, are less appropriate for peer tutoring activities.

*Break into Peer Tutoring Groups.* Give the students the worksheets designed to reinforce the content you've just presented. Specify the amount of time they have for the tutoring session, and clearly state your expectations.

*Monitor Progress.* Circulate around the room to answer questions and ensure that the tutoring is proceeding smoothly. To the extent possible, answer only procedural questions. Answer content questions only when the tutor is unable to do so. Check the exercise sheets at the end of the session for any error patterns that might indicate areas for reteaching.

*Evaluate Tutoring Pairs.* If a tutoring pair is not functioning, rearrange the students. One of the advantages of peer tutoring is that students are exposed to different teaching styles and personalities. To take advantage of this, reconstitute the tutoring pairs periodically.

Peer tutoring works because it places students in an active learning role, individualizes instruction, and it can be easily combined with large-group direct instruction. Other, more comprehensive, student-centered instructional approaches place students on learning teams and reward group efforts. These are discussed in the next section.

## Cooperative Learning

Maria Sanchez began her Friday's sixth-grade language arts class by passing back the vocabulary and spelling quizzes from the previous day. As she circulated around the room, she overheard the following comments:

"Uh oh, Another D."
"I can't do this."
"I hate spelling."

Some didn't say anything, and instead looked at their papers, crumpled them up, and threw them in their desks. She couldn't really blame them; over one third *had* failed the quiz—the same one third that had problems every week.

Maria decided that something had to be done, and she went to work on it over the weekend. Though it was a grueling effort, she was ready Monday.

She began Monday's class with new enthusiasm, saying, "I know we've been having problems with our spelling and vocabulary quizzes, and I've decided it's time to try something different. I know you all can learn this information, so I've designed a different kind of activity to help you. We're going to help each other learn this information, and I'll show you how."

With that she broke the class into groups of four and explained how each group was a team, and they were to work as a team and help each other. She then had the teams move their desks together, told them that this is the way they would be sitting until further notice, and gave each team 5 minutes to decide on a team name.

She then went on to explain another new feature. "We're going to have some competition in here, and it's the best kind of competition there is. You all are going to be competing with yourselves. If your quiz score this week is above your average, you are going to get some 'improvement points' that contribute to your team. If your whole team improves, you will be eligible for some rewards. You'll all see how it works when we get started."

She then went over the spelling and vocabulary words as she normally did on Monday, explaining their definitions and helping students understand the structure of each word. Then she asked each student to take out a sheet of paper for a pretest, similar to the one they'd receive on Thursday. She explained that the pretest wasn't for a grade but was only designed to help each student find out which words they knew and which they didn't.

After they took the quiz, students exchanged their papers and graded each other's. Then Maria passed out an envelope and four sets of different-colored flash cards to each group. She explained how each set was for a different student in the group and that each student was to write the definition and correct spelling of each word that he or she had missed to study in class on Tuesday.

She began Tuesday's class by reminding the students of where they were sitting. Each student then chose a partner for that day and the next. As Maria circulated around the room, students took turns helping each other either spell the word or provide the definition. Maria reminded them that they were finished only when all the members of their teams knew the spellings and definitions perfectly. Some pairs did this very effectively, while others needed extra guidance from Maria.

On Thursday they took the quiz as usual. Maria was struck by their comments as they left the class.

"Easy, Miss Sanchez. Piece of cake."

"Miss Sanchez, I think I got all of them right."

Even Randy, who pretended to dislike anything academic, admitted, "It was okay. I think I did all right."

At lunch time, rather than joining the other teachers, she decided to score the papers to see how they did.

"A miracle?" she thought as she recorded the last score in her grade book. "No, not quite. Some of the students are still struggling, but over 90 percent of the class got a B or better, and only two students had failed."

**Cooperative Learning: Essential Components**   Cooperative learning is the name of a collection of teaching strategies that use students to help each other learn. In that respect, these techniques are similar to peer tutoring. But they take this assistance a step further by organizing students in groups or teams for mutual support and learning. There is a variety of cooperative learning strategies, but research indicates that those most effective share the following characteristics (Slavin, 1990):

- Group goals
- Individual accountability
- Equal opportunity for success.

Think about a team sport, such as soccer or basketball. The team members are of unequal ability, but they all contribute to the team effort, and a game won rewards the entire team. Cooperative learning is analogous to this concept. **Group goals** reward students of unequal ability for working together and helping each other.

Too often, classroom activities and grading systems do just the opposite—place students in a position where they compete for the teacher's recognition and high grades. Less capable students soon learn that they cannot compete, and they stop trying. Group goals, in contrast, motivate students to help each other and give them a stake in one another's success.

Maria Sanchez implemented group goals when she divided students into teams of four and structured the activity so that each team member's score would contribute to the total team score.

**Individual accountability** means that each team member is responsible for learning essential content, and each student takes the quizzes individually. This is an essential idea. The teacher needs to communicate clearly that all students are expected to learn and that cooperative learning will culminate in an activity—usually a quiz—in which all students demonstrate that they've mastered the content. Maria Sanchez's regular Thursday quizzes demonstrated this characteristic.

**Equal opportunity for success** means that if all students try, they can expect to be rewarded for their effort. This is accomplished by implementing a system of *improvement points*, which are bonus points earned for quiz scores that exceed a student's average. This means that students only compete with their past performance and not with each other. Increased effort will result in individual improvement, which in turn results in improvement points that contribute to the team score. A low achiever who improves more than a high achiever will earn more improvement points and thereby contribute more to the team than does the high achiever. In this way, equal opportunity for success is accomplished.

**Why Use Cooperative Learning?**   The simplest answer to this question is that it works. Cooperative learning is one of the better researched instructional strategies, and the results of this research indicate that cooperative learning produces cognitive, affective, and interpersonal benefits (Johnson and Johnson, 1991; Slavin, 1990).

Let's briefly summarize these results. Compared to traditional instruction, cooperative learning strategies improve students' achievement, both on teachermade and standardized tests (Slavin, 1990). Slavin attributed these improvements to increased student motivation, greater time on-task, and active student involvement.

Slavin (1990) also found that students' self-esteem increased, they felt more in control of their academic success, and they began to link their success to their effort, an important factor in motivation. Low achievers tend to attribute their success or failure to luck or other forces outside their control, and cooperative learning helps change this pattern.

Cooperative learning also can produce impressive improvements in interpersonal relations. When groups were mixed by race, gender, and ability, the strategy resulted in improved attitudes toward different ethnic groups and increased interethnic friendships.

The same benefits can occur in helping exceptional students integrate into the regular classroom, in contrast with simply placing them in contact with other students, which does little to promote acceptance or help form friendships (Hardman et al., 1990). One teacher reported this success.

A special education student in the sixth grade was transferred to our classroom, a fifth/sixth grade. The classroom she was in has several special education students. The first—I'll call her Sara—was having behavior difficulties in her first classroom and was about to be expelled because of her unacceptable behavior with her peers. We offered her the opportunity to try our room with no special education students and with cooperative learning techniques being applied in various subjects along with TAI (cooperative learning) math. Sara was welcomed by her new classmates. We added her to one of the TAI math learning teams, and the students taught her the program's routine. Sara worked very steadily and methodically trying to catch up academically and to fit in socially. She began to take more pride in her dress and grooming habits. I have been working with Sara on her basic facts in preparation for the weekly facts quizzes. Her attitude toward her schoolwork and her self-concept have blossomed within the length of time she has been in our classroom. (Nancy Chrest, fifth/sixth-grade teacher, George C. Weimer Elementary School, St. Albans, WV, cited in Slavin, 1990, p. 42)

These are impressive results, especially when you consider that they were achieved with little additional teacher effort and without outside help. They are a testimony to the power of students helping students in general, and cooperative learning in particular.

**Types of Cooperative Learning**   Cooperative learning can be adapted to a variety of instructional goals ranging from basic facts and concepts to higher level thinking skills. In addition, through strategically selected learning activities, teachers can help students to analyze, synthesize, problem solve, and even learn to learn. Let's see how the different strategies accomplish these goals.

*STAD: Student Teams–Achievement Division.*   Probably the most popular type of cooperative teaching strategy, Student Teams–Achievement Divisions (STAD) uses four or five member teams to master basic content. Maria Sanchez used STAD to teach spelling and vocabulary. Other teachers have used STAD to teach a wide range of content goals. Some examples are presented in Table 10.2.

In STAD, the teacher presents the content or skill in a large-group activity in the regular manner, such as direct instruction and modeling. Then, as opposed to individual study, students are provided with learning materials that they use in groups to master the content. As students study the materials in groups, the teacher circulates around the room to monitor group progress and interaction. When students are ready, an individual quiz or test is administered and scored by the teacher, who then uses this information to compute improvement points (which we discuss shortly). These are added up for each team, and teams earning a specified number of

**TABLE 10.2**   Applications of STAD in Different Curricular Areas

| Subject Area | Possible Topics |
|---|---|
| • Language arts concepts and rules | Capitalization rules or rules for forming possessives |
| • Math concepts and skills | Addition, subtraction, fractions |
| • Science facts and terminology | Facts about the solar system, chemical symbols for elements |
| • Social studies names and dates | State capitals or major exports of countries |
| • Health concepts and terms | Parts of the circulatory system, different drug families |

improvement points are recognized (e.g., award, free time, or certificate of achievement). The teacher's actions in implementing STAD are summarized in Table 10.3.

In planning for STAD, the teacher's first task is to identify an area of the curriculum that is compatible with STAD goals. As with peer tutoring, STAD is most effective when used with facts, concepts, and skills that have convergent answers. The content can be introduced or taught as you normally would in a large-group format. When students break into their groups, they need to be supplied with learning materials that they can use to help each other learn the material. Exercises, worksheets, or quizzes with the correct answers available for reference can all be used. It is essential that these materials cover the same content that was presented by the teacher and that will be tested at the end of the activity.

In composing groups for cooperative learning, the teacher has two goals—balance and heterogeneity. In terms of balance, the teacher should attempt to place equal numbers of high-, medium-, and low-ability students in each group. One way to do this is to use pretest performance, students' averages from the last grading period, or their present average (if you begin cooperative learning sometime after the beginning of the grading period). Then place students in groups of four (or five) with a high, low, and two medium achievers in each group. Strategically pairing high- with low-achieving students provides not only academic balance but also effective tutors and models for lower achieving students.

A second goal is heterogeneity. As we saw earlier, one of the prime benefits of these strategies is that they allow students from different ethnic, socioeconomic, and ability groups to interact and work together. As you form the four-person teams for STAD (and other strategies), make a special effort to balance the groups by race and gender.

***Improvement Scoring.*** An essential component of STAD is the use of an improvement scoring system, which helps provide equal opportunity for success for all stu-

---

**TABLE 10.3**   Steps in Implementing STAD

*Planning*
1. Identify content or skills to be mastered.
2. Plan large-group presentation on topic.
3. Design interactive learning materials (e.g., flash cards, worksheets, sample quizzes) that students can use to reinforce their understanding.
4. Assign students to groups.

*Implementation*
1. Teach content as you normally would.
2. Divide students into groups and distribute interactive learning materials.
3. Circulate around the room to monitor group interaction and effectiveness.
4. Provide answer sheets when students are ready so they can check their work.

*Evaluation*
1. Administer quiz or test to evaluate individual learning progress.
2. Score quiz and calculate improvement points.
3. Add team scores and recognize team achievements.

dents. In computing improvement scores, the teacher first needs to compute base scores on the basis of past quizzes and tests. If these scores are in percentages, no additional changes need to be made; if they are in the form of grades, the figures in Table 10.4 can be used to convert to percentages.

The next step is to administer and score the test or quiz as you normally would. Then use the data shown in Table 10.5 to convert raw scores into improvement points.

The two systems for converting raw scores to improvement points — more and less difficult — provide you with options to use with a particular group of students. If students are poorly motivated with a past history of failures, the less difficult system can be used to encourage increased effort. Conversely, if you're working with highly motivated and competitive students, the more difficult system may provide more challenge.

As students progress through STAD, the tendency is for students to improve their scores over time. This is a desired sign of increased learning and motivation but also makes attaining improvement scores less challenging. One solution is to use a more challenging conversion system, like the one shown in Table 10.3, from the beginning or convert to it later. Another option is to recompute the base score to reflect students' new level of competence (Kagan, 1989). A formula to do this is as follows:

$$\text{Old Base} + \text{Last Quiz} + \text{Next-to-Last Quiz} \div 3 - \text{New Base Score.}$$

**TABLE 10.4**  Determining Initial Base Scores

| A | 90 |
|---|---|
| A – /B + | 85 |
| B | 80 |
| B – /C + | 75 |
| C | 70 |
| C – /D + | 65 |
| F | 60 |

*Source:* Kagan, 1989; Slavin, 1990

**TABLE 10.5**  Options for Awarding Improvement Points

| Improvement Points | Less Difficult | More Difficult |
|---|---|---|
| 0 | 5 or more below base | 0 and below base |
| 1 | 4 below to 4 above | 1–9 above base |
| 2 | 5–9 above base | 10–14 above base |
| 3 | 10 or more above base score or perfect score | 15 or more above base score or perfect score |

*Source:* Adapted from Kagan, 1989; Slavin, 1990

With either of these options, it is important to explain to students what you're doing, linking the change to increased effort and performance on their part. When done in this way, students will respond positively to the increased challenge.

*Jigsaw II.* In addition to learning basic facts, skills, and concepts, cooperative learning strategies can also be used to help students learn organized bodies of knowledge. Jigsaw II, developed by Robert Slavin (1990), assigns students to groups and asks each student to become an expert on one aspect or part of an organized body of knowledge. These experts then are responsible for teaching other team members, all of whom are then held accountable for all the information covered by each member. Let's see how this works in a junior high social studies class.

Tom Harris was passing back papers from a unit on Early Americans on the North American Continent. As he finished, he noticed that there were still 5 minutes of class time, so he called the class together. "Excellent job on this test! You all worked hard, and I could tell. It showed up on your last test scores. Class, we only have a few minutes, but I'd like to say a few words about our next unit of study. The topic is early explorers, and we'll be looking at the explorers from Europe who helped discover and explore not only our country, but other countries in North and South America. Who remembers one of these early explorers? Anyone? Think now, you've studied these before. Sal?"

"Mr. Harris, how about Christopher Columbus?"

"Good, Sal. Any others, class? Sal, did you have something else you wanted to say?"

"Yeah, Mr. Harris. Do we have to study this stuff again? We've done it so many times and it's boring."

"Sal, I know you've studied this before. . . ."

Just then the bell rang, and Tom concluded by saying, "Let's continue this on Monday. Everybody have a good weekend. No homework. See you then!"

As Tom thought about this class during his planning period, he shook his head. "Sal's right. This chapter can be a little dry. But still, they need to know this information. It's essential for their understanding of early settlements and why the New World took the shape it did. But how to get them involved and excited? Hmmm?"

The next Monday, Tom Harris began his American History class by saying, "Class, I thought a lot about our new unit over the weekend. Sal, you'll be interested to know that I listened to you on Friday. You probably *have* studied this information before, but I'm sure you haven't learned it in a systematic, organized way. That's important because we're going to use this information later on when we study related topics.

"To learn this material, we're going to try something different. We're going to form into teams of four, and each team member is going to become an expert on one group of explorers. Then that student will teach the other team members to get them ready for the quiz. To help us organize the information, I've constructed the following sheets."

With that, Tom passed out the following chart.

| Names | Places | Dates | Reasons for Exploring | Accomplishments |
|---|---|---|---|---|
| Spanish | | | | |
| Portuguese | | | | |
| English | | | | |
| French | | | | |

"I've divided the class into different teams of four," he continued, "and each of you will be responsible for one of these groups of explorers. To help you gather the information, I've gathered some other books that you can use. On Thursday the experts from each group will get together to check their information. That means all of the people studying the Spanish explorers will get together to review their findings. The same for the other groups. On Friday and Monday we'll go back to our groups, and each of you will share your information with other team members. Then we'll take our quiz on Tuesday. Questions? Maria?"

"Who gets which topic in the group?"

"Good question. That's the first thing you need to decide when you get into groups. Now I'd like group 1 to come up here and pull your seats together. That will be Xavier, Melissa, Brad, and Tanya. Group 2. . . ."

Jigsaw II is a cooperative learning strategy that uses task specialization to make individual students "experts" on a particular area or topic. It is similar to STAD in several respects. First, students learn cooperatively in groups and are held accountable for important information by a quiz at the end of the unit of study. These quizzes are graded like STAD, using improvement points to provide equal opportunity for success. In addition, the groups are heterogeneously constructed to ensure that all teams are equal and to provide opportunities for different types of students to work together.

Jigsaw II differs from STAD in several important respects, however. First, the goals of instruction are not specific facts, concepts, or skills, but rather students' understanding of interconnected bodies of knowledge. Though Tom Harris had students learn names and dates associated with the early explorers, his overall goal was to have students understand the significance of these to the larger picture.

The primary source of information also is different. In STAD, the teacher presents new information to be learned, while in Jigsaw II students rely on texts and other books.

A final difference relates to the idea of task specialization, from which the strategy gets its name. Each member of a Jigsaw learning group becomes an expert on a particular topic and uses this expertise to teach other members. When groups work together, the different parts of the jigsaw puzzle fit together to make a coherent picture. This task specialization is important because it promotes interdependence; each student must depend on his or her partners to learn their information. For teams to do well on the quiz, individual students must work and pull together as a group. When this occurs, students can see tangible evidence of their cooperative efforts.

The steps involved in using Jigsaw II in the classroom are summarized in Table 10.6.

An essential key to the effectiveness of Jigsaw II is the expert worksheets or charts that are given to students. Students will not, on their own, be able to identify key points of information. It is essential that the teacher organize and structure the content to guide the students' study and work with their peers. If the expert study guides are disorganized and disjointed, the students' understanding will be similar.

### Group Investigation.

Karen Selway was enjoying a good year with her third graders. Virtually all had made major progress on their basic skills, and she felt good about the foundation she had laid in reading and math. She still wanted them to work on their writing and library skills and still wanted to give them some experience in handling a large-group project.

After their return from lunch on Monday afternoon, Karen began by saying, "Class, today we're going to begin a new unit of study. And this time rather than all learning the same thing, each of you will have a chance to read and learn about something that you're specifically interested in. When I tried to think of a topic that we all could study, I asked myself, What's something that every third grader in my class likes? Guess what I decided? Think for a minute while I put this word on the board."

PETS

**TABLE 10.6** Steps in Implementing Jigsaw II

*Planning*
1. Identify an area of study requiring students to understand interconnected or organized bodies of information that easily break down into subtopics.
2. Divide area into three or four roughly equal subtopics that will allow students to specialize in their study.
3. Locate resources (e.g., textbooks, reference books, encyclopedias) that students can use to study the topic.
4. Develop expert worksheets or charts that ensure that students will learn essential information.
5. Divide students into heterogeneous groups.

*Implementation*
1. Introduce method and divide students into groups.
2. Hand out worksheets or charts and explain how they are to be used to guide individual study and group teaching.
3. Monitor study in the different groups.
4. Convene expert groups (use groups of six or smaller) to discuss and compare information.
5. Monitor students as they teach their topic to other members of the group.

*Evaluation*
1. Administer quiz or test as you normally would. Make sure quiz covers all topics and encourages students to interrelate information across topics.
2. Score, using improvement points.
3. Recognize team achievements and provide feedback about group performance.

She could tell from the wiggles and excited talking that she had guessed correctly. She then proceeded to brainstorm with the group about different pet topics. After considerable discussion, the class agreed to pursue the following topics:

| | |
|---|---|
| Dogs | Bunnies and hamsters |
| Cats | Fish |
| Birds | Other pets (turtles, hermit crabs, snakes) |

Students decided which topic they wanted to investigate, and Karen took down the names to group together into topic groups that night.

When the students came to class the next day, Karen had stacks of pet books from the public library on tables at the back of the room. She also had the names of different students divided into groups on the basis of interest. There were two groups of four each for both dogs and cats because of the high interest in these topics; other groups had between three and five members. After a general overview of each group's responsibilities and procedures, Karen broke the class into groups and had them begin.

As she circulated around the room, a number of questions surfaced:

"What do we do first?"
"Where do we find out about the pets?"
"Who is supposed to do what?"

She had anticipated some of these questions, and when they seemed common to all the groups, she called the class together and discussed them. Other questions, like "Do we want to report on all the different kinds of dogs?", were peculiar to an individual group, and when Karen encountered these she sat down with each group to help them work through it.

For the next 2 weeks, her students spent their time reading books, visiting the school library, visiting pet stores, interviewing people who owned these pets, and compiling a report on the classroom's computers, complete with pictures and posters. On Pet Day they invited parents and the principal to come in and visit the different groups, who were set up in different places around the room. Each member of the team was assigned the responsibility to talk about one aspect of the report. On the next day, Karen helped the class pull together all the information by using the following chart:

| Pet | Cost | Care and Feeding | Advantages | Disadvantages |
|---|---|---|---|---|
| Dogs | | | | |
| Cats | | | | |
| Birds | | | | |
| Bunnies | | | | |
| Fish | | | | |
| Other Pets | | | | |

*Analyzing Group Investigation.* This was an example of group investigation, a third type of cooperative learning strategy used in the schools today. Like the other two, it places students into cooperative groups to learn about some topic. Unlike the other two, content goals are relatively less important than the development of inquiry skills and group planning skills.

Group investigation is less structured than the other strategies you've been studying, and this lack of structure has advantages and disadvantages.

Group investigations provide opportunities for students to wrestle with ill-structured domains and tasks. These are the kinds of tasks we face in life. Seldom are we presented with situations where we are told what to learn and how to learn it. Instead we're required to clarify and then structure the problem before we solve it. So an advantage of this strategy is that it provides students with opportunities to wrestle with meaningful real-life learning tasks under the supervision of a teacher.

This is also a disadvantage. Some students are lost when first encountering this lack of structure. Karen dealt with this both individually and in whole-class discussions. Teachers using group investigation for the first time should anticipate these fits and starts.

One way to deal with these learning problems is to use some of the strategies that are so effective with skills learning. Modeling, think-alouds, and the liberal use of examples can help students learn these skills in an effective way. Some examples of these strategies applied to Karen's class can be found in Table 10.7.

*Implementing Group Investigation.* In implementing group investigation, the teacher's role changes from information disseminator to facilitator and resource person. As a facilitator, the teacher circulates around the room helping students in different groups work together cooperatively. As a resource person, the teacher helps students understand and structure the learning task and helps them access resources available to them. The specific steps involved in planning and implementing group investigations can be found in Table 10.8.

**TABLE 10.7** Strategies for Teaching Learning Strategies in Group Investigation

| Teaching Strategy | Example |
| --- | --- |
| *Modeling* | "Class, I've had several students ask about how to outline your reports. Let's look up on the board and I'll show you how you might do it with the topic of horses." |
| *Think-alouds* | "We're encountering some problems in finding our topics in the encyclopedia. Let's go over to the encyclopedia and brainstorm some words that might help us find our topics." |
| *Examples* | "There have been some questions about what kinds of pictures to put on your bulletin boards. Let me show you some examples of ones done last year. Remember, you don't have to do it just like these. They're just designed to give you some ideas." |

**TABLE 10.8**   Steps in Implementing Group Investigations

*Planning*
1. Identify a common topic that will serve as a focal point for the class as a whole.
2. Catalog or gather resources that students can use as they investigate the topic.

*Implementation*
1. Introduce the general topic to the class and have students identify specific subtopics that individual groups will investigate.
2. Divide students into study groups on the basis of student interest and heterogeneity.
3. Assist students in cooperative planning regarding goals, procedures, and products.
4. Monitor student progress, assisting students to work effectively in groups.

*Evaluation*
1. Use group presentations to share information gained.
2. Provide individual and group feedback about projects, presentations, and group effectiveness.

## Cooperative Learning: Getting Started

"I don't get it. What are we supposed to do?"
   "I can't hear, it's too noisy. "
   "Teacher, Ken won't share the materials."

Successful cooperative learning sessions don't just happen. Instead, they are the result of thoughtful teacher planning and preparation. Because they are instructional strategies with which students have little experience, the teacher needs to make a special effort in introducing cooperative learning to students.

Experts who have helped teachers implement cooperative learning strategies in their classes identify the following potential problem areas:

1. Noise
2. Failure to get along
3. Misbehavior
4. Ineffective use of group time (Kagan, 1989; Slavin, 1990).

Let's see how the teacher can address each of these potential problem areas.

*Noise.* Noise is often a healthy byproduct of productive student interaction. We should expect our classrooms to be slightly noisier because students are working and talking in small groups. Excessive noise, however, can interfere with group functioning, frazzle the teacher, and bother other classrooms.

The most common cause of noise in cooperative learning activities is student energy and enthusiasm. More often than not, students become so involved in their interactions with other team members that they don't realize that noise is becoming a problem.

Some teachers deal with the problem by discussing and modeling the social skill "Using quiet voices," which encourages the students to work together yet keep the noise level to a minimum. A system of rewards for using "quiet voices" then reinforces the skill. Other teachers use signals, such as flicking the light switch, as cues to remind students to lower the noise level. As the students' skills develop, noise becomes less and less a problem.

*Failure to Get Along.* Working together effectively is learned behavior; it doesn't happen automatically. Remember that in most of their learning activities students sit quietly, isolated from each other. Cooperative learning requires them to talk, listen, and help each other learn. The problem is compounded by the heterogeneous nature of the group.

Cooperative skill-building exercises include the following (Slavin, 1990):

1. *Name learning*—Allocate some time at the beginning of group formation for students to learn each other's names. Make this a game, and give an oral "quiz" in which other team members have to name each of their partners.
2. *Interview*—Extend the name-learning exercise to one in which students interview each other about interests, hobbies, and something that no one else knows about them. Have students present these in a short introduction to the rest of the class.
3. *Team name or logo*—Encourage students to develop a name for their group. In doing this, stress broad participation, consensus building, and respect for individual rights.

*Misbehavior.* Cooperative learning strategies are designed to be interactive, and often this freedom and lack of structure results in increased student management problems. Two solutions to this potential problem are task demands and agenda setting, and vigorous student monitoring.

As we see in the next chapter, many management problems occur because of unclear student roles and expectations (e.g., "What are we supposed to do? I don't know. Do you?"). Before you break students into groups, make sure that all students know what they are expected to do. Don't just describe student tasks; directly model them with the same learning materials students will be using.

Once students are in groups, productively monitor the groups by circulating around the room and helping individual groups. Public praise is a powerful tool to help other students understand effective and appropriate group behaviors (e.g., "Class, the Eagles group has gotten right down to work and is almost done with the first part.")

*Ineffective Use of Group Time.* Teacher monitoring, which we described as an effective tool against misbehavior, can also help combat wasted time. Stand back from time to time and observe the whole classroom. Which groups are working well? Which students are busy and which ones are dawdling or playing? Spend extra time with those groups that need extra help. Make sure that groups that do work effectively are rewarded with group recognition, and make a special effort to call the whole class's attention to the link between group work and group performance. This works on the individual level and should work at the group level.

# DISCUSSIONS

Shannon Wilson's sixth-grade language arts class had been reading *Sounder*, the story of a poor, black sharecropper family in the South during the Depression. The father, concerned about his family's diet and health, had taken to raiding rich people's smokehouses at night to put some meat on his family's table. Shannon's class was discussing the moral implications of his stealing.

"So where do you think the father goes at night when his wife can't find him?"

"He's going out to get food for his family," Tammy replied.

"And where is he getting this food? Ray?"

"From other people's smokehouses."

"Which other people? Tanya?"

"From the rich, white folks who have big farms."

"Okay, we've got the facts of the story down. Now let's focus on the stealing itself. Was the father wrong to steal? Ben?" Shannon continued.

"Well, I think he was, because he'll get caught and thrown into jail or something."

"Frank, do you have something to add?" Shannon continued.

"I agree with Ben. He shouldn't have done it because it's against the law."

"Sarah, did you have something to add?" Shannon nodded to Sarah.

"I just wanted to ask, what was he supposed to do, let his family starve?"

"Sarah asks a real good question, class. Anybody want to respond? Kerry?"

"I kind of agree with Sarah. Even though it's wrong to steal, he still couldn't let his children go hungry. It said right in the book that they weren't getting enough to eat."

"Frank?" Shannon added, nodding to Frank.

"But the law is the law. You can't just break it because you're hungry. The law is for everybody," Frank continued.

"Class, let's think about what Frank and Sarah are saying. . . ."

The lesson continued as the class wrestled with the moral dilemma raised by the book they were reading.

## Using Discussions to Promote Student Growth

**Discussions** are instructional strategies in which student-to-student communication is the primary vehicle for learning. They are characterized by decreased focus on the teacher, student-to-student interaction patterns, and high levels of student involvement. When effectively used, discussions can stimulate thinking, challenge attitudes and beliefs, and develop interpersonal skills (Oser, 1986; Slavin, 1991). However, if not organized and managed properly, they can be boring for students, frustrating for the teacher, and a general waste of time.

In contrast with the strategies we've discussed earlier in this book—which focus primarily on cognitive goals—discussions are effective for dealing with both cognitive and affective topics. We briefly discuss these goals in the following sections.

**Cognitive Goals** Discussions are an effective way to help students reach higher cognitive objectives. They are especially useful when we want students to investigate questions that don't have simple answers or to evaluate ideas with complex interconnections.

Gall (1987) explained the effectiveness of discussion in the following ways. First, because discussions focus on areas where there isn't a single best answer, students feel comfortable contributing, knowing that they won't be "right or wrong," and high levels of student involvement are likely. Second, students listen and contribute to other students, adding to each other's information base. Finally, discussions help students examine complex issues from different points of view.

**Affective Goals** As we saw in our introductory episode, discussions can also be used to help students examine their attitudes and values. By focusing on specific issues, discussions can provide the intellectual grist that allows students to examine their own beliefs and value structures. Through Socratic questioning by the teacher and by listening to the different opinions of a heterogeneous group, students are able to evaluate the adequacy of their own beliefs while comparing them to the beliefs of others. Research on discussions reveals that they can be an effective vehicle to clarify values and promote moral growth (Gall, 1987; Oser, 1986).

**Communication Skills** Because discussions provide extended opportunities for students to talk and listen to each other, they are a powerful tool in developing students' communication skills, and developing communication skills should be a concomitant goal for discussions that focus on either cognitive or affective topics. These social skills include the following:

- Expressing ideas and opinions clearly
- Justifying assertions
- Acknowledging and paraphrasing others' ideas
- Asking for clarification and elaboration when others' ideas aren't clear
- Avoiding monopolizing discussions
- Inviting silent group members to participate.

How can teachers use discussions to accomplish these diverse goals? We begin to answer this question by discussing the planning and implementation of cognitive-oriented discussions in the next section.

## Planning for Discussions

Planning for discussions is similar to planning for the use of any strategy. The teacher must identify the *topic* and specify a clear *goal*. In addition, however, *student background* and the *physical arrangement of the room* are even more critical when discussions are used than they are with other strategies. We examine each of these in this section.

**Identify Topic** As we noted earlier, discussions are effective strategies when the topics don't have cut-and-dried answers. For example, topics such as solving word problems in math, identifying parts of speech in language arts, or describing work and force in science would not be appropriate discussion topics. With them, there is little to discuss. Gage and Berliner (1992) recommended using discussions in low-consensus fields like social studies and the humanities, where questions are likely to have multiple answers.

**Specify Goals**   Merely identifying a topic isn't enough, however, as we see in this section. Let's look at the following two episodes.

Paula Marsh had assigned the chapter on the beginnings of the Revolutionary War to be read as homework, and she began her American history class by saying, "Today we begin our discussion of the Revolutionary War. We've been talking about all of the events that led up to the war. What were some of these? Jill?"

"The Stamp Act."

"Good. Brad?"

"The Tea Act and the Boston Tea Party."

"Fine, Brad. Any others? Mike?"

"The First Continental Congress."

"And when was that held? Does anyone remember? Go ahead, Mike."

"In 1774 in Philadelphia."

"And what was the major outcome from this meeting?"

We leave this room and walk across the hall, where Jean Levitt's American history class is studying the same topic.

Jean began, "We've been studying the Revolutionary War, and you all know a lot about it. But," she continued, "some historians, reviewing all the facts about the War, suggest that, on paper, the British 'should' have won. When they say this, they're not saying 'should' like 'ought' but rather that the British had important advantages but wasted them. I'd like for us to think about that notion today, and see if our conclusions agree with those of the historians. . . . What do you think? Take a little time to consider it while I put this statement on the board."

She then wrote, "The British advantages during the Revolutionary War should have ensured victory," on the chalkboard.

"Okay," she went on, "now that you've had time to think, does anyone want to take a stab at this? Shirley?"

"I basically agree with the statement," replied Shirley. "They had more soldiers, more guns, and better equipment, and should have won."

"I think Shirley's right," Martha added. "They not only had more soldiers, but the soldiers they did have were better trained. Also. . . ."

"If the British had treated the Colonists decent, there wouldn't have been a war in the first place," Ed interjected.

"That's an interesting point, Ed," Jean smiled. "But, given that there was a war, we're considering whether or not the British should have won. . . . Anything else, Martha?"

"No, not really, I was just going to say that they had a physical advantage."

"Okay, Martha," she nodded. "Hank; you look like you were going to say something."

"Oh, I was just going to say that the British soldiers often weren't in the right place."

"I don't know what you mean, Hank," Jeff put in.

"Well, even though they had a numerical advantage, this wasn't always important. Like at Saratoga. One big part of Burgoyne's army captured Philadelphia instead of going to Albany like they should have. So those troops were wasted. It would be interesting to wonder how history might have been changed if Burgoyne had gone to Albany. Maybe we'd still be British."

"That's a very interesting thought, Hank. Jeremy, do you have something to add?"

"Just that some of the troops the British had were mercenaries. They were just being paid to fight, so they didn't fight very hard."

"So numbers might not be the only thing to think about when we talk about advantages and disadvantages. Is that what you're saying?"

"I believe so."

"Okay! Very good, everyone. Now, let's return to our question on the board. What other advantages or disadvantages did the British have that influenced the outcome of the war?"

Now let's compare the two episodes. While the *topic was the same* for both lessons, and the teachers both focused the students on the content through their questioning, their *goals were very different*. Paula Marsh was reviewing facts about events leading up to the Revolutionary War, while Jean Levitt was trying to get students to identify relationships and make applications. To meet these goals, questions from the upper levels of Bloom's taxonomy served as a conceptual framework and guide. For example, the following questions might serve as guides in Jean's lesson.

*Analysis:* What were the relative strengths and weaknesses of the American and British forces? How did the French influence the outcome of the war?

*Synthesis:* Design a strategy or plan that would have used Britain's seapower to greater advantage.

*Evaluation:* Was the American victory the result of a lucky chain of events or superior strategy? Take a position and defend it.

Jean's goals did not stop there, however. If they had, we might argue that the processes are little different from those we discussed in Chapters 6, 7, 8, and 9. In addition to understanding organized bodies of knowledge, focusing on the Revolutionary War, and developing their thinking, Jean wanted students to develop other important skills, such as willingness to listen to another's point of view, cooperation, and the ability to take and defend a position. These are important goals for discussions. Because of these supplementary goals, the lesson is much less driven by the content per se, instead providing opportunities for students to use this content as they develop their discussion skills.

**Student Background**   When a teacher is considering using discussion as a strategy, student background knowledge is an essential factor in the decision. Unlike other strategies, where the content is taught as an integral part of the lesson, discussions require that students be thoroughly conversant with the information related to the topic *prior* to the lesson. This was clearly demonstrated in Jean Levitt's lesson. For instance, Shirley demonstrated her background knowledge by observing that the British had more soldiers, guns, and equipment. Martha's comment about the soldiers' training in response to Shirley reflected similar background knowledge. Hank's comment about the battle of Saratoga is perhaps more significant, because he demonstrated understanding of a cause-and-effect relationship in addition to a knowledge of facts. The quality of the discussion would have been impossible if students' background had been inadequate. Students must have something to discuss if a discussion is going to work, and the teacher must be sure that their background is extensive before using discussion as a strategy.

**Arranging the Room for Discussions**   A final planning task is to arrange the room to promote communication and involvement among participants. Research indicates that students are more likely to interact with other members of the class if they are face to face (Gall, 1987).

To accomplish this, you might consider either circles or half circles (Arends, 1991). Circles allow everyone in the class to see each other, and they position the teacher within the group. This communicates that the teacher is an equal among other participants and encourages students to take a more active role in structuring the lesson.

A half circle or horseshoe also allows students to see each other but places the teacher in a focal point at the open end. This allows the teacher to move easily from the circle to write points on the board or clarify ideas on an overhead.

## Implementing Discussions

In implementing discussion activities, we need to draw students into the lesson and help them understand the lesson's goal, refocusing them when necessary during the course of the lesson, and summarizing the discussion at the end. This is accomplished with the following three steps.

- Agenda setting
- Refocusing students during lesson
- Summarization.

**Agenda Setting**   Jean began her lesson by saying, "Some historians, reviewing all the facts about the War, suggest that, on paper, the British 'should' have won. . . . I'd like for us to think about that notion today, and see if our conclusions agree with those of the historians. . . . What do you think?" By introducing the topic in this way, she both clarified the goal and presented a question that attracted the students' interest. She then wrote the question on the board as a way of maintaining academic focus.

**Refocusing Students during Lesson**   It's easy in a discussion to "drift off the subject" and begin dealing with issues that aren't relevant to the goal of the discussion. For instance, Ed's comment, "If the British had treated the Colonists decent, there wouldn't have been a war in the first place," while appropriate as a discussion issue in itself, was irrelevant to the issue of whether or not the British should have won the war. A less alert teacher might have allowed the discussion to drift in that direction, but Jean refocused the class by saying, "That's an interesting point, Ed, . . . But, given that there was a war, we're considering whether or not the British should have won." The ability to recognize irrelevant information is an important thinking skill, and Jean's comment helped the class recognize Ed's comment as irrelevant. At the same time, her own social skills and positive manner refocused the class without "cutting Ed off" or admonishing him in any way. We examine this further in the next section.

### The Teacher's Role

Vance Wilson, a high school teacher in Atlanta, is discussing Joseph Conrad's *Heart of Darkness* in his English class. In the book, the ivory trader Kurtz dies in the Congo uttering the phrase, "The horror! The horror!" All through the novel the narrator, Marlow, has said he despises lies. Yet when he returns to Europe and encounters Kurtz's intended, he tells her that with his last breath her fiancé spoke her name.

Let's see how Vance Wilson handled this seeming contradiction in class.

"Why does Marlow lie to her?" I asked.

As usual I felt a physical urge to answer my own question quickly, to point them to the passage early in the book where Marlow reminds his listeners that London, the capital of civilization, was once itself a dark and horrific place. I could hear my own sweet voice within my head. "Don't you understand? We build our culture on blindly held illusions."

But instead I did the Curmudgeon count: one thousand one, one thousand two, one thousand three. . . . In the middle of my counting I recalled Milton's famous line, the one the *Norton Anthology* used to illustrate a snail's crawl of poetic rhythm: "Rocks, caves, lakes, fens, bogs, dens, and shades of death." The wait seemed endless.

Just before I gave in to answer my own question, Tommy shifted in his seat. "It wouldn't do any good to tell her the truth," he said.

Oh my God, I thought, he used "good" and "truth" in the same answer. My mind spun. I could allude to Keats's truth and beauty and tell them about his bitter-sweet love for Fanny Brawne—surely there was a connection there. But then I stopped myself.

"Why not?" I said. And I counted again. One thousand one, one thousand two, one thousand three, one thousand four. . . .

"Sometimes it's better to lie about things," John said.

"No, you should always tell the truth." It was Elizabeth, who had invited me to her church three or four times.

"And just because she's a woman doesn't mean she can't face the truth." This time, Millie. "We said the natives of the Congo had a different culture, didn't we? No better, no worse than the European one. She lives in a different culture from Marlow, that's all. It doesn't mean you have to go to the Congo to explore. And the truth of Kurtz' death might have opened her eyes."

"But are you going to tell the truth if it shatters someone else's carefully created illusion?" I said. And then, without thinking, I said, "It might lead to despair."

A terrible mistake. I knew it right away. I had offered an answer, and silence followed. No one knew how to respond to a teacher's statement.

But Parker, the most unlikely candidate, asked his own question: "Do you think we have illusions?"

"No, not really," Mike said.

"This school is built on more than one," offered a previously quiet voice.

"That's for damn sure."

Now I had to say, "Your language, please, John."

"I'm sorry, sir, but it's true about the school, about society. You're supposed to act a certain way, the civilized way, I guess. Rules and more rules. But lots of them are false. The whole thing is false. Something inside of you, you know."

"Is that bad?" Elizabeth asked. "I mean, that we're taught to act differently from our instincts."

"Of course it is. We ought to be who we are."

"But then we'd all be savages."

The bell rang. No one moved.

"It's a sham, man. A lie."

"It's the same illusion Marlow gave to that woman, and he said he never wanted to lie."

"He had to lie, he had to." Arthur pounded his desk. "The truth would have killed her."

"But somewhere in the story he says lies the smell of death," Millie said.

Suddenly we looked up at one another. I was speechless. And in a second they were gone.

John, hurrying out the door, looked at me. His face beamed. "That wasn't bad was it, Mr. Wilson?"

"Just great."

"We ought to do that more often. It's nice to see people in this room care about ideas." (Rock Kane, 1991, pp. 47–48)

In most classrooms, teacher talk is the dominant element, and the teacher uses this talk to steer a lesson in a clear direction (Cazden, 1986). This pattern of teacher control is effective when the goal is to learn some fact, concept, generalization, or skill, such as Paula Marsh's lesson on facts about the Revolutionary War. However, this type of interaction is less effective when the goals are for students to learn discussion skills and productive ways of interacting with each other. In contrast with Paula's class, both Jean Levitt's and Vance Wilson's lessons involved more student-to-student talk, and their roles changed from lecturer or knowledge source to facilitator of the discussion process.

Because the teacher's role in a discussion is less direct and perhaps less apparent, it appears to be easier. In fact, it is just the opposite. During discussions a teacher must listen carefully to each student's response, avoid commenting when students are interacting appropriately, interject questions when ideas need to be stimulated, and refocus the discussion when the students drift off, as Ed did in Jean Levitt's lesson. Effectively guiding a discussion requires more sophisticated skills than teacher-led lessons, because the teacher is not in direct control of the activity and a great deal of judgment is required. A skilled discussion leader must do all of the following:

- *Focus the discussion.* A primary role for the teacher is to keep the class on track, without taking ownership of the discussion away from the students, as Jean Levitt managed to do so skillfully. Periods of silence characterized by student thought are typical (and potentially unnerving), as Vance Wilson discovered.
- *Encourage thoughtfulness.* In conducting content-oriented discussions, the teacher must be skilled in using questions that solicit points of view, relationships, and hypothetical analysis rather than convergent, focused answers.
- *Maintain momentum.* The activity must be monitored constantly to ensure that its momentum is maintained, and the teacher must intervene when necessary. This requires careful judgment. If teachers intervene too often, the discussion reverts back to a teacher-directed activity, but if they don't intervene when necessary, the discussion can disintegrate into an irrelevant bull session. The teacher should intervene under the following conditions: (a) lesson digressions, (b) errors of fact, (c) logical fallacies, (d) a small number of students dominating the discussion, and (e) when the lesson should be summarized and brought to closure. As a rule of thumb, cut off a discussion too soon instead of letting it go too long.

To prevent teacher domination, some have advocated teachers not questioning at all (Dillon, 1981). This isn't realistic, however, and in doing so, teachers abdicate their important role. Teacher guidance is critical in effective discussions, as we saw in both Jean Levitt's and Vance Wilson's lessons. As teachers acquire expertise, they develop a feel for when intervention is and is not appropriate.

## Affective Discussions

As we said earlier, discussions can be used to reach both cognitive and affective goals. We have discussed the first. In the second, the purpose is for students to examine their attitudes and beliefs, compare them with others, and perhaps change them if they think a change is necessary. Let's look now at the use of discussions for reaching affective goals.

The place of attitudes and values in the school curriculum is controversial, with educators taking positions ranging from ignoring values completely to focusing explicitly on them. Advocates of a value-explicit curriculum argue that the schools have a responsibility for teaching students fundamental values such as honesty, hard work, and patriotism. With youth being bombarded by mixed messages about drugs, sex, and other sensitive issues from the media and society, the schools should play a vital role in helping students develop healthy and desirable values.

But which values should we teach? No consensus exists. Proponents of a value-free curriculum claim that there is so much disagreement that compromise is impossible. Differing positions on sex education are a case in point. Should we advocate abstinence or intelligent sexual behavior? What about contraception, and what should be the role of the schools in AIDS education? Answers to these questions differ sharply across the country. Because of the absence of consensus on topics such as these, some educators believe they should be avoided. Opponents of values education further argue that the schools' primary goal is to develop students intellectually, and watering down the curriculum with values education distorts this mission.

Proponents of *values clarification* attempt to take a middle position in this controversy (Hersh, Miller, and Fielding, 1980; Jarolimek, 1990). They contend that values do have a place in the curriculum, but teachers should not impose personal values on students. Instead, schools should help students understand their own values and what implication those values may have for life both now and later. Advocates hope that a better understanding of values will result in greater consistency between values and behavior. But integrating affective content into the curriculum without proselytizing or appearing heavyhanded is a delicate balancing act.

This problem is important for all teachers, as value-related discussions are impossible to avoid. Sometimes affective concerns are explicit, such as when freedom of speech and individual rights are discussed in social studies classes. Health classes deal with sex education, and evolution versus creationism continues to be debated in science classes in different parts of the country.

Other instances of affective issues are more subtle, however, and teachers often address affective issues without realizing it. For example, teachers who say, "Class, the Civil Rights Movement was perhaps the most important event in twentieth-century America," or "The effect of pollutants on our planet is the biggest problem facing modern humanity," or "Julius Caesar wasn't just a play about ancient Rome. It was a play about politics and democracy and the potential for demagoguery" are making value-laden statements that can lead to lively discussions.

Opportunities to examine values often occur as natural byproducts of other lessons. For example, a discussion in biology might consider benefits of pesticides, such as increased productivity, with negative side effects, such as the impact on wildlife. A lesson on ethnic groups could focus on the internment of Japanese Americans during the Second World War, resulting in a discussion of the importance of individual rights versus perceived risks to national security. A literature class reading *Lord of the Flies* might consider individual responsibility versus peer pressure. A class focusing on career choices might list different occupations and use this as a spring-board for a discussion of the values underlying different occupational choices. A conflict of values exists in each of these topics as well as a potential springboard for subsequent discussion.

**Clarifying Values through Moral Dilemmas**   Value-oriented discussions can also be started through moral dilemmas (Kohlberg, 1976; Oser, 1986). A **moral dilemma** presents students with an everyday problem, the solution to which involves the reso-lution of a value conflict. Shannon Wilson, in the teaching episode earlier in this chapter, used a moral dilemma as the focus for her lesson. Was it right for the father to steal to feed his children? This dilemma was embedded in the book the class was reading, which provided both background knowledge and motivation for her students. Vince Wilson used a similar strategy, focusing on the problem of being honest.

Teachers can also construct their own moral dilemmas to stimulate moral thought. Consider the following:

> John was working as a teacher's aid and ran across a copy of the final exam sitting on the teacher's desk. The exam was for a course that his best friend, Gary, was repeating for graduation. At lunch, Gary expressed concern that he wouldn't pass the course because his boss had made him work every night for the last 2 weeks, and the heavy schedule had pre-vented him from studying. Gary asked John to get him a copy of the test. If John didn't, Gary might not be able to graduate. John's refusal would almost certainly end their friendship. What should John do?

The conflicts here are honesty versus friendship. Some questions to encourage think-ing about this conflict could include the following:

> Which is more important?
> What would happen if John steals a copy of the exam?
> What if he doesn't?
> What circumstances in the problem make a difference?
> What other alternatives are there?

In leading a discussion involving a conflict of values, there are several guide-lines to follow (Oser, 1986). Students should be encouraged to take a personal posi-tion in terms of the dilemma (e.g., What would you do?). This encourages involvement and causes students to reflect on their own values. In doing this, an atmosphere of acceptance for various value positions should be established. Students should be encouraged to listen and respond to the views of others. One of the major advantages of discussing different value positions is each student's consideration of alternative views.

In dealing with any of these value-laden topics, the teacher's role is to help students understand the issues involved through strategic questions. These should establish what the problem is, what value positions are involved, and what alterna-tives exist. In addition, students should be encouraged to clarify and voice their own thoughts on the issues involved. The teacher should refrain from imposing his or her views on the students, and students should not feel pressured to respond.

## Small-Group Discussions

So far, we have been considering large-group, teacher-led discussions. There are some advantages to this format, primarily management and control. It is easier to maintain academic focus when the teacher is leading the discussion. But this control comes at a price. In a class of 25 to 30 students, opportunities for active involvement and direct student-to-student interaction are reduced. Students simply do not have enough opportunities to practice active listening, evaluation of ideas for relevance, idea building, and turn taking. These communication skills are important outcomes of discussions, and small-group work can help meet these goals.

In this format, the teacher arranges groups of varying size depending on the age of the students and the teacher's goal. Research suggests that groups of five to eight work best, with too few students reducing the diversity of opinions and interaction; above that number, certain members tend not to participate (Dillon, 1987). The benefits of small group size are supported by research, with smaller groups having greater participation rates, higher satisfaction, and greater academic achievement (Gall, 1987).

Many of the process goals designed for small-group activities are long range. These include the development of communication skills, leadership ability, open-mindedness, compromise, and persuasive arguing, among others. These skills and abilities are acquired slowly, and it may take a full school year before observable change can be detected. For student growth to occur, these goals must be valued, and patience is required. This is important, because teachers' goals aimed primarily at content acquisition can be reached much more efficiently with alternate strategies, such as those discussed in Chapters 6, 7, 8, and 9.

**Organizing Small-Group Discussions**   One of the primary problems with small-group activities is the potential loss of engaged time. Students can drift off-task very quickly, and the activity often disintegrates into a waste of time. These problems can be reduced, however, with careful organization. The following suggestions can help relieve this problem.

**1.** Give students precise directions for the activity. This begins with a focusing event or question that pulls students into the activity. For example, a ninth-grade government teacher wants to use small-group discussion to consider partisan politics in approval of Supreme Court justices. She might direct the group to take and defend a position regarding the following case study:

The United States has a Republican president, but a Democratic majority in the House and Senate. The president nominates a very conservative judge for the Supreme Court. The judge has a very good record, but his view contrasts sharply with Democratic party philosophy. The Senate rejects him, primarily on the basis of his views rather than his record. Should they have this right?

Here the teacher has asked a specific question, and students are directed to answer and provide a rationale for their answer. Directions that merely call for a "discussion" by the students quickly drift into a waste of time.

**2.** Develop background knowledge. As with large-group discussions, be sure that the students have enough background knowledge to bring information, as opposed to only their feelings, to the activity. This means that discussions should follow a lesson focusing on content, building on topics previously developed. One of the strongest criticisms directed at small-group discussions is the tendency to have students get together and "pool their ignorance." If dissemination of knowledge is the goal, small-group discussion is a poor vehicle for delivery.

**3.** Keep the time for the discussion relatively short. Plan for no more than 15 minutes (shorter for younger students). If you see that the students are interested and involved, you can always allow the process to continue. A time limit specified in advance encourages students to remain on-task.

**4.** Require that the discussion results in a product. In the example with Senate approval rights, the product would be a written statement with the group's answer to the question and a rationale. A product provides additional focus for the students and helps them reach consensus, because the statement must reflect the group's view rather than an individual's. It is also an additional incentive to remain on-task.

In a small-group discussion format, the reports from the different groups need to be shared with the other groups. This can be done through small-group reports or by having each group submit a written report to the teacher, which is edited, duplicated, and distributed to the whole class at the next meeting. Whatever form this takes, it is important to acknowledge the efforts of each discussion group through some type of consideration of their products.

**5.** Carefully monitor the activity. Because the teacher's direct control has been removed, monitoring is more subtle and informal, but it is no less important than it would be for any other activity.

This concludes our discussion of discussion strategies. In the next section we look at how computers can be used as an alternate instructional strategy.

## TECHNOLOGY AND TEACHING

There won't be schools in the future. . . . I think the computer will blow up the school. That is, the school defined as something where there are classes, teachers running exams, people structured in groups by age, following a curriculum—all of that. The whole system is based on a set of structural concepts that are incompatible with the presence of the computer. (Papert, in Cuban, 1986, p. 72)

Microcomputers are proliferating in our schools and unless a lot of people are wrong they're here to stay. But the $64 question is whether these computers will make any difference in the education of our children. When my daughter graduates from high school in the year 2000, will she have received a better education with the help of computers than I did without them? (Dale Peterson, in Cuban, 1986, p. 72)

Unquestionably, we live in an information age, and technology has certainly affected our world. A list of examples would be virtually endless. The way we check out groceries at a supermarket, our banking systems with automated teller machines, the quality of the music we listen to, the way our cars are built and run, the way we have stored the information to write this text, and many other activities have been dramatically affected by technology within the last 10 years. The examples could go on and on.

Technology has also affected the way schools are managed. Most school systems now have all their student records on computer, and scheduling is also computerized. Aids such as LUIS (Library User Information Service) are common. School systems commonly teach computer courses, so their students will be better equipped to cope with the technology in the future, and computer literacy is often a requirement in state curriculum frameworks.

The direct impact of technology on the classroom teacher is less certain, however. Advocates argue that education will be revolutionized, and our schools in the twenty-first century will bear little resemblance to today's schools. Critics snort skeptically and wonder if technology will have any significant effect on the day-to-day life of the classroom teacher. We examine some of these issues next.

## Computers in the Classroom

Computers are another alternative to teacher-centered group instruction and have received considerable attention as a way to improve classroom learning. Most schools have computers, and the number of computers in classrooms increases every day. Between 1983 and 1985, the number of computers in U.S. schools quadrupled from approximately 250,000 to over 1 million. This number more than doubled again by 1989 to reach 2,355,000 computers. In 1985, 86 percent of the nation's schools had access to computers, with 24 percent having 15 or more computers. By 1989, the number of schools with computers had climbed to 96 percent; 57 percent of these schools had 15 or more computers (Harvey, Kell, and Gadzuk–Drexler, 1990, p. 1). In response to this growth, a number of states have included knowledge of computers as an essential component of teacher education programs, which have responded in turn with courses in the area. The purpose of this discussion is to describe current uses of computers in education and to analyze the strengths and weaknesses of this new technology in terms of the realities of classroom practice.

## Computer Literacy

Probably the most widespread use of computers to date has been toward the development of computer literacy in students. The impetus for this direction is that computers have become such a major influence in our technological society that a basic understanding of computers is a necessity for all citizens.

Computer literacy can be approached from a general perspective (i.e., What kinds of knowledge and skills with computers should all people possess?) as well as a user-specific perspective (i.e., What do doctors or engineers need to know about computers?). One general definition of computer literacy calls for an appreciation of the general principles that underlie computer hardware, software, and the application of computer technology to various science, business, education, government, and entertainment objectives (Jones, Jones, Bowyer, and Ray, 1983, p. 4). Another definition of computer literacy views it as a three-step process, beginning with machine mastery, proceeding to mastery in a specific domain like word processing, and ending in the ability to use computers across a wide range of applications, including graphics and information storage and retrieval (Neudecker, 1989).

The concept of computer literacy applied to the field of teaching asks the question, "What knowledge and skills do teachers need to utilize computers in their classrooms effectively?" The following goals could serve as starters:

1. The ability to understand the impact of computers in education as well as society as a whole
2. The ability to understand and use computer terminology (e.g., computer literacy, hardware)
3. The ability to read and write simple computer programs
4. The ability to understand educational applications of computers in the classroom
5. The ability for continued growth and development in the area (Anderson, 1983).

Computer literacy can also be viewed as a continuum of knowledge and expertise (Rogers, Moursund, and Engel, 1986). At the lowest level, the continuum addresses the question, "What kinds of knowledge about computers should all teachers possess?" Teachers specifically assigned to teach word processing, computer literacy, and programming are at the other end of the continuum, and their knowledge and skills would be increased concomitantly.

## Instructional Application of Computers

Computers can be used to present information, provide practice, assess understanding, and provide additional information if needed. In addition to the general goal of computer literacy, computers have several specific applications in classrooms. These range from computer-assisted drill and practice to adaptive programs that provide feedback to student answers to simulations that teach problem-solving and thinking skills. Let's look at these different applications.

**Computer-Assisted Instruction**   Computer-assisted instruction (CAI) can provide an effective supplement to the teacher (Slavin, 1991). The most common form that CAI takes at present is drill and practice (49 percent of the software evaluated in one recent study focused on this dimension). Unfortunately, the use of computers to review previously learned material is one of the least efficient uses of the medium; workbooks or worksheets can perform this same function as efficiently and more inexpensively.

**Tutorials**   Tutorials that present information and then provide practice based on the responses and needs of students are another, more effective, instructional use of computers. We discussed peer tutoring in an earlier section. In a sense, the computer acts as the tutor instead of another student.

> A tutorial on high school accounting, for example, might first explain the formula "annual depreciation = cost/expected life" and then ask, "If an electric pasta machine costs $400 and is expected to last four years, what is the annual depreciation?" In response to the answer "$100," the computer would say, "Good," and go on to the next problem or concept. A student who typed $400 might be told, "Sorry, but you're probably not ready to work for H&R Block. $400 is the cost. To find annual depreciation, divide this figure by the expected life (four years). Please type the correct answer." (Hassett, 1986, p. 20)

The advantage of this adaptive approach to instruction is that it delivers all of the instruction in a responsive manner. So, for example, if the student already understood depreciation and did not need to be reminded, the computer would move him or her on to the next concept.

**Developing Automaticity**   Another computer program, called Fast Facts, helps students develop automaticity with math facts by adapting instruction to meet student needs. It begins by pretesting to determine entry skill levels. Building on existing skills, it then introduces new math facts at a pace that ensures high success rates. When students fail to answer or answer incorrectly, the program provides the answer and then retests that fact. To develop automaticity (and discourage finger counting), presentation rates are timed, and students' response times are shortened as they become more proficient. Research on the program showed both immediate and long-term gains on math skills (Hasselbring, Goin, and Bransford, 1988).

**Computers as Writing Tools**   Another promising instructional use of computers is to improve students' writing skills. Most readers of this text have already used computers in composition and will attest to their ability to make the process of writing and editing more manageable and efficient. Research indicates that computers can be an effective instructional tool to teach both keyboarding and mechanical editing skills (Barrett and Paradis, 1988; Ellis and Sabornie, 1986).

Computers have also been used to teach higher level editing skills. In one study, the computer was programmed to remind students during the writing process to think about their audience (e.g., "Is the reader a novice? Remember that he or she may need some facts about the topic."), about transitions in the manuscript (e.g., "How does this new idea relate to the last one?"), and about ways to edit effectively (e.g., "Is your argument supported by data that will convince your reader?") Results indicated that students receiving these prompts not only wrote better essays but also transferred the skill to writing where no prompts were used (Zellermayer, Salomon, Glaberson, and Givon, 1991).

**Using Computers to Teach Problem-Solving and Thinking Skills**   Computers can also be used to teach problem-solving and thinking skills. In one popular simulation, called Oregon Trail, students join a family of five who are attempting to make the 2,000-mile trek from Missouri to Oregon in 1847. Students are allocated $700 and a wagon and must decide how much to spend on items like food, clothing, and ammunition. As they make decisions, the simulation provides them with feedback about the impact of their decision on the journey's progress.

Other popular programs, such as "Where in the U.S. Is Carmen San Diego?" and "Where in the World is Carmen San Diego?" teach problem-solving skills along with geography facts. Faced with the task of capturing a criminal, students take notes and organize information as the program takes them to different geographic locations. The popularity of these programs is evidenced by their development into a program for public television.

A third way to use computers to teach thinking skills is as a networking tool to connect student researchers in different parts of the country. One project, called the National Geographic Kids Network, electronically joined thousands of fourth, fifth, and sixth graders in a research project on pets (Julyan, 1989). As students collected and analyzed data about pets across the country, they asked questions like these:

How do you define a pet?
Is an ant farm a pet?
Would you consider a pig a pet if it later became Sunday dinner?

As students attempted to answer questions like these, they shared information across the network and tried to find patterns in the data and explain anomalies. For example, one student found that the number of cats (7,713) and dogs (7,522) in the sample was quite similar, but the number of cat owners (3,777) and dog owners (5,107) was quite different. He concluded that the difference was due to the larger number of cats owned by individual cat owners. In a similar way, students in Maine and New Orleans attempted to explain why the Maine school had over 120 pets while the New Orleans school had only 25. As they pursued the question, they corresponded with each other to see if the numbers could be traced to rural/urban differences and whether the urban school was in a housing project where pets were not allowed. This ability to place students in real and simulated problem-solving situations is probably one of the more promising applications of computers in the classroom.

**Developing Reading Skills with Computers**   Computers have also proven effective in teaching reading skills. In one program, computers were used to help middle school students make inferences from text (Golden, Gersten, and Woodward, 1990). After group-based instruction, students were provided with individual practice identifying relevant from irrelevant inferences. For example, students were told the following:

The Fuentes family wants to take the shortest possible route to Fresno. They were then presented with passages that contained both relevant and irrelevant information, such as, "If you take Highway 99, you'll pass a lot of beautiful scenery," or "If you take Miller's Road, you'll pass a lot of gas stations. That's good if you have car problems."

Students trained on this program made both short- and long-term gains on this skill and had positive attitudes toward the immediate feedback provided.

**Computers as Instructional Management Tools**    Another effective use of computers is to help teachers track the learning progress of different students (Siegel and Davis, 1986). In computer-managed instruction (CMI), computers can be used to administer pretests and to suggest subsequent tracks for instruction, monitor time within lessons, administer posttests, and generally keep records of student progress. In addition, computers can assist in other evaluation functions, such as serving as test banks, scoring tests, identifying error patterns, and refining tests by computing test means, difficulty levels, and an index of discrimination for individual items (Gronlund, 1985a). CMI provides teachers with a powerful time-saving tool, allowing them to make more effective professional decisions.

When you first go into classrooms, the most common application of computers that you will probably encounter is their use in record keeping. Most computer companies now offer simple programs that allow teachers to enter student scores, and the program automatically computes and weights different assignments according to the teacher's wishes, creates averages, and keeps an ongoing record for the students. These programs can also be used to prepare and present interim progress reports and to compute final grades. The uses of computers for these purposes will almost certainly expand in the future.

The second most common application of computers that you are likely to encounter is their use in generating tests. Many commercially available banks of test items now exist, typically costing less than $100 (Bluhm, 1987). In addition, more and more classroom text series are being produced with accompanying computerized test banks. Teachers can access the bank, select the items they want to use, and quickly prepare their own custom-made tests using items field-tested for their validity. This is a promising prospect. Teachers often do not write their own test items, and when they do, the items are usually written at a low level. The demands placed on teachers often prevent them from having the time to create effective tests, and the use of commercial item banks that allow teachers to create their own tests quickly is a major technological breakthrough.

This concludes our discussion of alternatives to teacher-directed, large-group instruction. After reading the summary, please respond to the exercises that follow.

# SUMMARY

Students can serve as valuable resources within the classroom, and the way that they are used depends on the teacher's goals. The basic tutoring model uses peer tutors as supplements to direct instruction when information with cut-and-dried answers is taught. Research indicates that there are as many benefits for students doing the tutoring as for those being tutored.

Cooperative learning strategies place students on learning teams and reward group performance. Cooperative learning strategies can be used to teach both basic skills and other higher level skills. To be effective, cooperative learning strategies must stress group goals, individual accountability, and provide equal opportunity for success.

Student Teams–Achievement Divisions (STAD) are a proven effective way to teach facts, concepts, and skills. Group investigation places students in teams to attack a common problem from different perspectives. Jigsaw techniques assign different students on a team to investigate different aspects of a larger body. Subsequent sharing and quizzes or group projects make all students accountable for the information gained by the group. In all of these strategies, process skills are as important as content acquisition.

Discussions are interactive instructional strategies that can be used to teach higher level thinking skills, affective goals, and interpersonal communication skills. Content-oriented discussions use questions from the higher levels of Bloom's taxonomy to invite students to integrate previously learned information. Student content background is essential here. The teacher's role is less directive and obtrusive, first setting the discussion with a question or problem and then monitoring its progress through questions and clarifying statements.

Affective discussions are designed to help students clarify their own views through the dual processes of articulating their own and listening to those of others. As with content-oriented discussions, the teacher acts as facilitator and clarifier rather than position taker.

Small-group discussions, because they provide more opportunities for student-to-student interaction, provide greater opportunities for the development of discussion skills. To ensure that these discussions are productive, teachers need to structure them carefully in terms of goals and agenda.

Computers provide the teacher with other alternatives to direct instruction. Computer literacy and computer-assisted instruction are the most common uses to date, but tutorials and simulations which use computers to individualize and teach problem-solving skills hold the most future promise. Computer-managed instruction, with its potential for time-saving record keeping, is already being used in many classrooms.

# ADDITIONAL READINGS FOR PROFESSIONAL GROWTH

Collins, A. (1991). The role of computer technology in restructuring schools. *Phi Delta Kappan 73*(1), pp. 28–36. Collins looks at computers from an instructional perspective and asks how they can be used to improve instruction.

Cuban, L. (1986). *Teachers and machines.* New York: Teachers College Press. This book places computers in the larger, historical context of mediated instruction.

Johnson, D., & Johnson, R. (1991). *Learning together and alone* (3rd ed.). Englewood Cliffs, NJ: Prentice Hall. This book provides an excellent introduction to the theory and research behind cooperative learning.

Slavin, R. (1990). *Cooperative learning: Theory research and practice.* Englewood Cliffs, NJ: Prentice Hall. Slavin does an excellent job of describing and illustrating cooperative learning strategies and the research behind them.

## EXERCISES

1. Examine the following descriptions of teachers using different cooperative learning strategies and determine whether they are using group investigation, Jigsaw II, or STAD.

   a. Jim Prescott's middle school social studies class was studying different occupations and careers. He allowed students to select a career and break up into groups on the basis of that career. Students in each group then read about that career, interviewed someone in that career, and reported their findings to the whole group.

   b. Marsha Anderson wanted her high school English students to know about the major American authors of the twentieth century. She divided students into groups and allowed each student to focus on a particular author like Steinbeck, Hemingway, or Fitzgerald. These students were then responsible for teaching the other students in the group about this author. All students in all of the groups took a common test at the end of the unit.

   c. Ken Halloway was trying to teach his third graders the rules of capitalization. He presented the rules on Monday, explaining each and illustrating them with examples on the board. On Tuesday, Wednesday, and Thursday students practiced these in individual groups and took a quiz on them on Friday. Improvement points were used to determine team scores.

2. Examine the following list of goals and determine which ones are appropriate for discussion strategies.

   a. To remember the symbols for the chemical elements

   b. To understand the relationship between nutrition and health

   c. To analyze the causes of the Vietnam War

   d. To understand the difference between adjectives and adverbs

   e. To analyze the motives of characters in *The Great Gatsby*

   f. To examine the different value positions in different forms of socialism

3. Read the following case study and answer the questions that follow.

   Ralph Reynolds was beginning a unit on the Civil Rights Movement in the United States. He began the first class of the unit by saying,

   "Today we're going to begin Chapter 19, which describes the impact of the Civil Rights Movement on modern America. To begin this unit, I'd like us to break up into groups of four or five and discuss the major events of this movement. You can use your text if you need to. We'll do this for about half an hour and then compare results. Go ahead and break into your own groups."

After the class had settled into groups, Ralph ran down to the ditto room to run off the unit questions for the students. On the way, he was way-laid by the assistant principal and didn't return to his class until 11:05, five minutes before the class was to end. The noise from his room could be heard down the hall. As he entered the room, he shouted,

"Class! Hold it down. I can hear you halfway down the hall. Let's get back into our rows. Sorry I took so long, but Mrs. Peterson needed to talk to me about the field trip next week. Let's summarize some of the main points we discussed so far. Who can name an important figure or event during Civil Rights Movement?"

The class continued on like this until the bell rang.

*Question:* Ralph made several mistakes in his application of discussion strategies in his classroom. Identify at least four of these and suggest alternative courses of action.

## DISCUSSION QUESTIONS

1. How would you respond to parents who raise concerns about their son or daughter being involved in peer tutoring, either as a tutor or student?

2. In the text, we said there were advantages and disadvantages for both high- and low-ability tutoring pairs and matched-ability reciprocal tutoring pairs. What might these be?

3. Which of the three cooperative learning strategies—STAD, Jigsaw II, and group investigation—are most appropriate for the lower grades? upper grades? Why?

4. Are the three cooperative learning strategies more appropriate in some content areas than in others? Which and why?

5. Which of the three cooperative learning strategies would be most effective for fostering improved inter-group relations? Why?

6. What is the place of values in the curriculum? How would you respond to objections from people at the other end of the values continuum? What advantages and disadvantages does the values clarification approach have?

7. Which values should the schools try to develop? Examine the following values and rank order the five more important values from an educational perspective. Compare lists with other students in your class.

| | |
|---|---|
| Broad-minded | Logical |
| Forgiving | Loving |
| Honest | Obedient |
| Imaginative | Polite |
| Independent | Responsible |
| Intellectual | Self-controlled |

(Adapted from Rokeach, 1973)

8. To what extent should teachers consciously plan for affective goals? Or, should these goals be implicit in the classroom?

9. Are discussions more valuable in some areas of the curriculum than others? Which and why? How does the value of discussion vary with grade level? What is the lowest grade level that can still benefit from discussion?

10. What advantages do small-group discussions have over large groups? what disadvantages? Developmentally, which should you probably try first?

11. List three reasons why teachers need to be computer literate. How does the definition of computer literacy change with grade level? subject matter?

## APPLYING IT IN THE SCHOOLS

1. *Peer Tutoring.* Identify a classroom that is using peer tutoring. Observe a peer tutoring session and analyze it in terms of the following dimensions:

   a. Goals

   b. Instructional materials

   c. Type of peer tutoring (e.g., cross-age or reciprocal)

   d. Training (You will have to interview the teacher for this.)

   e. Teacher monitoring

   f. Teacher's evaluation of the process (Again, a short interview will be needed.)

2. *Cooperative Learning.* Identify a classroom that is using cooperative learning. Observe the classroom and answer the following:

   a. What kind of cooperative learning strategy was being used?

   b. What kinds of content goals were targeted?

   c. How were the groups composed (teacher interview)?

   d. How did the teacher promote (1) group goals, (2) individual accountability, and (3) equal opportunity for success?

   e. What special management strategies did the teacher use?

3. *Affective Goals.* Examine a blank report card. What do the categories in the report card say about the affective goals in that school?

4. *Discussions: Interaction Patterns.* The purpose of this exercise is to analyze the

interaction patterns in a discussion. To do this, sketch out a seating chart of the participants. Mark the first person who talks with a 1, the second with a 2, and so on. After the session, analyze your data in terms of the following questions:

**a.** How did the discussion begin?

**b.** Was the prevalent interaction pattern T-S-T or S-S?

**c.** What percentage of the students participated? What did the teacher do to influence this?

**d.** What role did the teacher play?

**e.** How did the teacher's questions guide the discussion?

**f.** How did the discussion end?

5. *Discussions.* Identify an instructor at either the elementary, secondary, or college level who is good at leading discussions and ask to sit in on one of his or her discussions.

**a.** What instructional activities (e.g., readings or lecture) preceded the discussion?

**b.** What kinds of interaction patterns developed?

**c.** What kinds of questions seemed most effective in provoking thoughtful interaction?

**d.** How was silence used?

**e.** How appropriate would this discussion style be in your content area or level?

6. *Computers.* The purpose of this assignment is to acquaint you with computer uses in your school.

**a.** How are computers being used in your school?

**b.** How many computers are there, and where are they located?

**c.** Who uses them, and for what purposes?

**d.** How do teachers use computers apart from instructional uses?

# CHAPTER 11

# Classroom Management

## OVERVIEW

If you anticipate getting in front of a group of students for the first time with some trepidation, you have a bit of company. This uneasiness is very common among student interns, first-year teachers, and occasionally even veterans. Often the concern stems from uncertainty about their ability to handle students, prevent disruption, and maintain an orderly learning environment successfully. In this chapter, we examine these factors and other concepts related to the topic of classroom management. You will learn about the impact of the physical environment, the students themselves, organizational factors such as rules and procedures, and instructional variables like momentum and smoothness on the overall management process.

## MAIN IDEAS

### Effective Management

Effective managers establish a *positive learning climate* with *high expectations*.

Classroom *organization* and effective *instructional skills* are critical to effective management.

### History

The *clinical view of management* tried to address the source of discipline problems.

Another perspective saw effective managers as *disciplinarians*.

*Managers of the total environment* is the prevailing view of discipline and management.

### Planning for Management

*Student characteristics* and *developmental levels* have an impact on management: Low achievers and junior high students often are harder to manage than other groups.

The *physical environment* should be arranged to allow traffic flow and easy access to materials and aids.

*Rules* should be few in number, behavioral, and have explicit consequences.

*Procedures* should be routine and should structure activities during the day.

### Implementing Management Plans

The patterns for the year are established the *first 10 days* of school.

*Orchestration* organizes and maintains routines and instructional activities throughout the year.

High-interest activities and student involvement help maintain lesson *momentum*.

Lesson *smoothness* is lost when irrelevant topics and events or disruptions detract from the thrust of the lesson.

Teachers demonstrate *"withitness"* when they are aware of everything in the classroom and *"overlapping"* when they can do two things at once.

## Situational Variables

*Laboratory* experiences, *seatwork*, and *small-group* activities pose special management problems.

Management *interventions* range from a simple squelch to removal from class. Clear communication helps deal with *individual problems*.

. . . . . . . . . . . . . . . . . . . . . . . . . . . . . . . . . . .

> *"If teachers met students individually, privately and voluntarily, there would be little need to talk about classroom management."*
>
> (Doyle, 1986, p. 394)

If . . . , but they do not. The typical teacher has a class of 25 to 35 or more students, several of whom would prefer to be somewhere else. In this situation, the teacher is supposed to create an environment that promotes both learning and healthy emotional development. Obviously, this is no easy task. The ability to handle students and keep them orderly is often the primary concern of student interns and first-year teachers (Veenman, 1984). Disorderly and disruptive students are an important cause of teacher stress and burnout, and some teachers even leave the profession because of problems in disciplining students. A common teacher complaint about their principals and other administrators is that they do not give the teachers adequate support in handling disruptive students. Historically, classroom management has been a major concern of school policy makers, parents, and the public at large (Elam, Rose, and Gallup, 1991).

A teacher's ability to manage a classroom is also linked to achievement. Good concluded, "Teachers' managerial abilities have been found to relate positively to student achievement in every process–product study conducted to date" (1979, p. 54). Students learn more in an environment that is orderly, clean, and physically and psychologically safe (Rutter, Maughan, Mortimore, Ouston, and Smith, 1979), and Purkey and Smith (1983) identified classroom management as one of the four key variables in an effective school. The importance of management is inarguable.

A teacher must be able to manage students to be effective; but the relationship of effective classroom management to other effective teaching behaviors is a close one. *It is virtually impossible to manage a classroom without simultaneous effective instruction.* What does this mean?

First, an effective manager establishes a climate with high expectations for all students; the teacher models appropriate behavior and is warm, enthusiastic, and dynamic within the boundaries of his or her natural personality, consistently communicating these factors both verbally and nonverbally.

Second, effective managers are well organized. They come to class prepared and on time; they have materials, demonstrations, and activities planned in advance and ready to go. Their daily routines maximize instructional time. They interact effectively with their students both on a personal level and through skilled questioning. They communicate clearly, and their assignments are consistent with their classwork.

Some researchers have gone so far as to define effective classroom management in terms of instruction (Emmer and Evertson, 1981). Effective teachers plan and implement classroom activities that result in high levels of student involvement. These activities are successful because they result in minimal amounts of student behaviors that interfere with the teacher's or other students' time. In sum, effective managers demonstrate the behaviors discussed in Chapters 3, 4, and 5.

Teachers with management problems often search for a simple and magic solution to their dilemmas. Unfortunately, none exists. In working with these people, we first ask to observe their teaching, and then we help them develop their teaching effectiveness. As it improves, many management problems disappear. Interestingly, an important additional factor, which often goes unrecognized until we identify it for them, is an increased level of confidence in their own ability. Students perceive the increased confidence and, as a result, behave better.

For those of you who are beginning teachers facing the uncertainty of a new situation, our first advice is to be certain that you are very well planned and prepared. In fact, be so well prepared that you do not have to depend on a lesson plan or other props when you face students. You will be surprised at how much good planning will help with management.

Unfortunately, effective instruction is a necessary but not completely sufficient condition for effective management. Research suggests that effective teachers complement their instruction with management strategies that enhance learning. This chapter is designed to help you to understand the results of this research and then to apply these findings in your own classroom. It is divided into three main sections. In the first, we define the concept of classroom management and examine its historical origins. In the second, we look at ways of organizing the classroom for learning. This preactive or planning stage is essential for classroom management because it provides an opportunity for the teacher to frame classroom activities in an integrated and purposeful way. Finally, we discuss the actions of teachers as they implement their management plans. But, first, a closer look at the concept of classroom management itself.

# CLASSROOM MANAGEMENT: A DEFINITION

Classroom management consists of all the teacher actions that create an orderly environment that promotes learning. As examples, consider each of the following:

> Mrs. Sweat has her first graders practice the routines of finishing seatwork and putting it in folders in front of the room. She has them finish a short assignment and then "walks them through" the process of taking the paper, filing it efficiently, and returning to their desks. She then has them repeat the routine with another short assignment.

Mr. Evans has a list of five rules written on a piece of poster paper in the front of the room. Each morning, he gives his fourth graders an open envelope with three slips of paper in it. When a rule is broken, he goes to the student's desk and takes one of the slips of paper. If a student loses all three of the slips in a day, he or she writes a note home explaining why he or she must stay after school. Any students who lose no more than two slips during the week are given a free hour Friday afternoon when they can bring treats and play games.

Mrs. Houson always carefully prepares each morning for her advanced placement American history class. "These kids are sharp, and their discussions get animated," she commented to a colleague in the faculty workroom. "If I'm not prepared, they know it, and their arguments get a little out of hand. They're good kids though, so all I have to do is tell them to tone it down a little, and they're fine."

Each of these situations is quite different from the others, but they all are part of the management process. Mrs. Sweat teaches small children who need to learn classroom routines, Mr. Evans developed a plan for systematically enforcing rules, and Mrs. Houston spent much of her effort in planning and preparation. Planning and organization, routines and procedures, and systems for handling disruption are all part of management, and we examine each in this chapter.

Before we proceed further, let us first place the concept of classroom management in historical perspective and see how early research in this area has affected the views we have today.

# MANAGEMENT: A HISTORICAL PERSPECTIVE

The area of classroom management has not always focused on the teacher as effective organizer and efficient manager. Early work in the area viewed the teacher as either clinical practitioner or exemplary disciplinarian (Doyle, 1986).

The clinical view of management stressed the teacher's role as counselor/therapist; if the teacher understood the sources behind student management problems, these could be solved. This approach proved inadequate for two reasons. Conceptually, it considered the teacher's role as diagnostic ear or therapist. While every teacher performs these functions at some time during the school year, this role is not a primary one in today's schools. Instead, teachers are expected to promote the cognitive growth of their students. The second reason for the demise of the clinical approach to management was logistical. It proved impossible for elementary teachers with 25 to 30 in a class—much less secondary teachers with five classes times 30 students—to spend the time needed to work on each student's individual problems. That is what school counselors and psychologists are hired to do. This is not to say that teachers do not deal with some management problems on a one-to-one basis. But this approach is so time consuming that it can drain the energies of the teacher and divert him or her from the central task of classroom learning. We discuss dealing with individual management problems later in this chapter.

A second perspective viewed the best classroom managers as successful disciplinarians. An effective manager, for example, would be one who could quickly quiet a class down when they had gotten too noisy, or get kids back in their seats after a classroom uproar. The research, however, simply failed to confirm the hypothesis that the best managers were the ones who could put out fires once they had started. The story behind this research is interesting.

Jacob Kounin (1970) is primarily responsible for turning our attention away from discipline strategies to more management-oriented concerns. But he did not do so without some fitful starts. He began his inquiry with the hypothesis that effective classroom managers use "desist" strategies that not only stop the immediate misbehavior but also have a "ripple effect" on other students. In studying these strategies, he focused on teacher variables such as language clarity and intensity. For example, "Johnny, please stop talking" is clearer than a statement such as "Class, pay attention," and "Get to work, *now*," is firmer than "I think we better get working." Tone of voice and the length of the reprimand were also included with intensity. He then measured student behavior, examining the amount of time they were attentive and on-task as well as the amount of student disruption. However, when the researchers went into classrooms, they found *no* relationship between the desist strategies of less and more effective classroom managers.

Reanalysis of the data provided some interesting information, however. In a study of 49 first- and second-grade classrooms from both middle-class and inner-city classrooms (Why is the selection of classrooms from both areas important?), he identified a variable he called "*withitness.*" A teacher exhibits withitness if he or she can work with a student individually without losing track of the rest of the class. Kounin described this skill as having "eyes in the back of the head." Actually, the awareness dimension is only part of it; the other part involves communicating this ability to students. The teacher does this by being continually watchful for misbehavior in the classroom, and nipping problems in the bud before they interfere with the class as a whole. "Withit" teachers are constantly scanning the room and monitoring students' behavior.

What is opposite of a "withit" teacher? We have all seen teachers who talk to an individual student with their backs to the rest of the class, or lecture to the ceiling or to a point above the students' heads while several individuals are daydreaming or even talking to each other, or sit with paperwork at their desk while students who are supposed to be doing seatwork are going wild. Other problems include reprimanding the wrong student for misbehavior or correcting a less serious infraction while overlooking a more serious one. Many of us have probably been victims of getting caught "hitting the student back" right after we have been hit. Each of these examples indicates that the teacher is not aware of what is going on in the classroom and is not "withit."

Beyond the immediate variables it identified, Kounin's work had a profound influence on classroom management studies that followed. Previous research had framed questions in terms of simple cause-and-effect relationships; that is, if the teacher says this, then the students will do that. Subsequent research viewed classrooms as extremely complex systems in which teacher actions determined only part of the flow. Philip Jackson's book *Life in Classrooms* (1968) also was influential in helping researchers understand the complex task that teachers faced. In addition, researchers switched to more observational studies that attempted to answer the question, "How do effective managers perform their juggling act in the buzzing, whirling world of real-world classrooms?"

One of the problems researchers encountered was the near invisibility of teachers' actions in smoothly running classrooms. Effective teachers managed their classrooms so well that it was difficult to pinpoint any one dramatic action that made a difference. In hindsight, we can see that this was one of the most important findings of this literature. Effective classroom management does not boil down to a simple formula. Instead, it is the complex interaction of a number of factors, many of which—like instructional and management planning—have been thought out in advance. This leads us to a consideration of plans for managing classrooms efficiently.

# PLANNING FOR CLASSROOM MANAGEMENT

Few teachers would think of getting up in front of a group of students without considering in advance what they were trying to accomplish. In other words, teachers plan before they teach. As they become more experienced, they often skip writing the plans down on paper, but they are clear nevertheless on what they want to accomplish and how they will accomplish it.

The need to plan for classroom management is no less important than it is for instruction, but, interestingly, beginning teachers often fail to consider plans for management. This oversight is a major mistake. Carefully plan and consider your strategies for management with as much effort as you would make for your lessons. It will make your job not only much easier but also more enjoyable.

In planning for management, our long-term goal should be the development of self-controlled students who assume responsibility for their own behavior. Research from the related areas of learning (Wittrock, 1986) and motivation (Ames, 1990) highlights the importance of students' beliefs in themselves as self-regulated and capable students. Let's see how teachers at different levels attempt to teach this.

Felicia Perez works with inner-city first graders. She describes her goals in this way: "I try to teach each student a sense of individual responsibility. We have choice time in the afternoon, when students get to select an activity or game and pursue it. They're on their own and I'm trying to get them to take responsibility for their own behavior."

Jeff Thompson teaches middle school science. His management goals are "to develop in them the ability to manage their own learning. I purposefully give them free time to work on individual projects. I want them to experience freedom *and* responsibility. Labs are especially difficult for them because there is all that equipment to mess around with. But we talk about it beforehand and we work with it. I'll even leave the room for a minute or two and stand outside in the hall and listen. I want to give them the feeling that *they're* in charge. Does it always work? No, but we're working on it."

Individual responsibility and self-control don't just happen. They develop over time through the efforts of conscientious teachers who plan for these goals through their management efforts.

Your plans for management should encompass three elements of your overall environment: the characteristics of your students, the physical environment in your room, and classroom rules and procedures. Your physical arrangement, rules, and procedures will depend on the characteristics of your students, so we consider this issue first.

## Student Characteristics

As we've stressed earlier, who you teach determines how you teach; this is also true in the area of management. The characteristics of your students are a major factor to consider as you plan for effective classroom management. As we saw in Chapter 2, some students pose greater management challenges than do others, and developmental differences influence the way rules and procedures are understood and interpreted. In studies of lower elementary classrooms, researchers found high-achieving students to be actively engaged almost twice as often as low-achieving students (Levin, Libman, and Amiad, 1980; Shimron, 1976). In addition, the low achievers were idle or engaged in inappropriate activities almost three times as often as high achievers. Part of these differences may result from learned self-monitoring behaviors in the students themselves, and part may be due to the quality of the instruction and its match with student needs and abilities. Whatever the reason, different types of students pose different management problems, and rules and procedures must be adapted to the students' backgrounds and needs.

The developmental age of the learner also influences the management plans a teacher makes (Brophy and Evertson, 1978). Children at different stages understand and interpret rules and procedures in different ways:

*Stage 1:* Students in the lower primary grades are generally compliant and oriented toward pleasing their teacher; their attention spans are short, and they tend to break rules more from simply forgetting or not fully comprehending them than for other reasons. Rules need to be carefully and explicitly taught, modeled, practiced, and frequently reviewed with students at this age. Role-playing and positive reinforcement for compliance can help solidify the rules in students' minds.

*Stage 2:* Grades two through six are characterized by children who have learned the game of schooling and generally are still interested in pleasing the teacher. Many elementary teachers believe this age group is the easiest to teach because of these characteristics. Rules are easier to (re)teach at this level, and the teacher's central management task becomes one of maintenance and monitoring.

*Stage 3:* This stage spans grades seven through ten and includes the tempestuous period of adolescence. As students become more oriented toward their peers, authority is questioned more often, and more disruptions result from attention seeking, humorous remarks, horseplay, and testing of limits. Classroom management can be demanding at this stage. Motivating students and maintaining compliance with the rules are the teacher's major tasks.

*Stage 4:* In the later high school years, students mature, becoming more personally adjusted and more oriented toward academic learning. Management becomes easier, and more time and energy can be devoted to instructional tasks.

Although these differences between developmental stages and ability groups suggest different emphases and approaches, the same basic principles that work with one type of student work with others. All students—whether they are high or low achievers; Hispanic, Asian, black, or white American; high or low socioeconomic status—require an understandable, coherent set of rules and procedures that are uniformly enforced (Brophy, 1980). Research with special education students who are mainstreamed in regular classrooms suggests they respond to the same structured approach (Hardman et al., 1990). In addition, all groups of students require a management system that is systematic and comprehensive in scope and that begins on the first day of class and is carried through the rest of the school year.

## The Physical Environment

"I can't see the board."
"I didn't get a worksheet. Kevin didn't pass them back."
"What did she say? I couldn't hear her!"

A second planning consideration is arranging the physical environment of the room so that the job of teaching and the task of learning are accomplished as efficiently as possible. Environmental concerns include locating the teacher's and students' desks, storage areas, overhead projector, screen, maps, and other instructional materials so they complement rather than detract from learning.

First, the environment must be arranged so all the students can see the board, overhead projector screen, and other instructional aids all the time. If they cannot, both management and achievement suffer. Surprisingly, some teachers fail to consider this factor. They display information on an overhead, but the projector itself obstructs the view of several students. As a result, students crane their heads to see, bumping other students in the process (who then protest out loud), or they holler from the back of the room that they cannot see.

In addition, the room should be arranged so the teacher can move from one aid to another, such as from the overhead to a map, without the students' having to slide their desks around or even to turn in the desks themselves. A simple process such as rotating 90 degrees in a desk can disrupt the flow of an activity for a rambunctious middle schooler.

Also, consider the location of other materials, such as paper and scissors, that should be accessed with a minimal amount of disruption. Moreover, procedures for using the drinking fountain, sink, and pencil sharpener need to be formalized. A simple rule for the teacher's desk and storage areas would be that they are off limits to students without the expressed permission of the teacher.

The question of desk arrangement has been studied, and researchers have found that the best arrangement depends on the situation. One study in fourth- and fifth-grade classrooms found that the quantity of work increased when students sat in rows, and teachers reported a concomitant improvement in classroom behavior (Bennett and Blundell, 1983). However, an experimental study in fifth- and sixth-grade classrooms found that during discussions rows were the most disruptive organizational pattern, clusters of four or five desks were intermediate, and a circle pattern was least disruptive (Rosenfield, Lambert, and Black, 1985). These researchers concluded that desk arrangement patterns influenced not only participation but also student thinking and the number of task-specific comments. The circular organization enhanced student-to-student communication while allowing the teacher to monitor all students for participation.

Sometimes room arrangement is a trial-and-error process. Consider the following situation encountered by a seventh-grade teacher.

> Ms. Holmquist had 33 seventh graders in a room designed for a maximum of 27 students. As a result, the students were very close together. She experimentally arranged the desks in her room in a two-ring semicircle with the outer row behind the inner.
>
> She soon moved the desks back to their original positions. Her explanation was that her low achievers could not handle the arrangement. "They weren't trying to be disruptive," she told us. "But as they faced each other across the front of the room, they would inaudibly mouth questions like 'What are you doing tonight?' or they would be pinching each other on the rear ends. They couldn't handle it, so I went back to a standard arrangement of rows. Interestingly, my advanced kids were okay. Once I told them, it was enough."

This example illustrates the need to consider both the physical arrangement of the room *and* the nature of the students involved as we plan for management. Our suggestion is to have flexible organizational structures and experiment with them just as Ms. Holmquist did. Initially, you may choose to start with rows because of the convenience involved with traffic patterns and easier initial management.

A question related to the arrangement of desks is where individual students should sit. Three factors affect this question. First, for students in the fourth or fifth through the eighth or ninth grades, the social aspects of schooling increase, and details of who sits next to whom become very important. Second, research has established an "action zone" in the classroom; students seated in the center and front of the classroom tend to interact most frequently with the teacher (Adams, 1969; Adams and Biddle, 1970). Finally, our experience indicates that the number of behavioral problems increases as students sit farther from the teacher. Students in the back and corners of the room are more likely to be off-task than those close to the front or the teacher's desk.

In response to these factors, some teachers change their room arrangement and the student seating charts on a regular schedule, both for the sake of variety and to put different students at the front of the room. They strategically use seat assignments as a tool to help students become involved and to maintain that involvement during the day. Many effective teachers begin the school year with arbitrary seat assignments, planning to modify those assignments after they have had several weeks to observe the patterns of behavior that evolve.

Should students be allowed to sit where they want? If you are a new teacher, a bit anxious about management, or have had management problems in the past, this is not a good option for the beginning of the year. Later, it can be used as a reward for good classroom behavior *and* on the condition that continuation of that arrangement is contingent on a smoothly functioning classroom. In short, student choice is a privilege rather than a right, and it may not be possible in the lower elementary grades where individual self-control has not developed.

## Classroom Rules

**Classroom rules** establish general guidelines for acceptable student behavior. They help eliminate student uncertainty by communicating what is expected, and they make the climate of the classroom predictable. They also help students understand the name of the classroom game.

The value of rules is well documented. When they are clear, specific, and enforced, desired student behavior is the result (Emmer, Evertson, and Anderson, 1980; Sanford and Evertson, 1981). As Kounin discovered, the most effective managers are teachers who are successful in preventing management problems rather than those with special skills in dealing with problems once they occur. Rules help in this process by establishing a safe and orderly environment that is conducive to learning.

The value of rules is clear, but are some ways of designing rules better than others? The answer is yes. The following guidelines were offered to us by experienced teachers:

**1.** *Consistent rules.* Rules must be consistent with the policies of the school and district. This statement may be obvious, but we include it as a reminder to check your school and district's policies before you prepare your own classroom rules.

**2.** *Reasonable number.* Rules should be few in number. No specific number exists, but a rule of thumb would be "The fewer the better." A reasonable number to consider would be five; if you go over six or seven, you have too many. Interestingly, our experience has been that the most common reason students break rules is simply because they forget. This tendency is particularly true with young children, but it is often the case with older kids as well. For example, junior high and high school students are often given legal-size sheets of paper with long lists of single-spaced rules typed on them, and rules are discussed the first day of class and not referred to again until they are broken. Under these conditions, we all would forget. The solution is to keep the number down to a few important rules that you intend to enforce unfailingly and consistently. Some examples follow:

**a.** Bring your book, notebook paper, and pencil to every class.
**b.** Talk only when called on by the teacher.
**c.** Remain in your seat until given permission to leave.
**d.** Do not touch another person or another person's belongings.

These sample rules are pertinent to many classroom problems. Teachers commonly complain that students come to class without their books, without pencils, and without notebook paper. Talking inappropriately and students' being out of their seats without permission are two of the most common management problems that teachers face. Researchers found that 80 percent of classroom management problems are related to students' talking inappropriately, and most of the remaining 20 percent are related to students' being out of their seats without permission (Jones and Jones, 1990).

Finally, teachers also complain about students' tendencies to hit, poke, shove, grab, and "fiddle around" with each other and each other's belongings. If the four rules we identified here were consistently enforced, most management problems would cease to exist.

**3.** *Be explicit.* State rules behaviorally. For example, compare the following rules:

**a.** Always come to school prepared.
**b.** Bring your book, notebook paper, and pencil to every class.

Rule *b* is clear and precise and explicitly describes the desired behavior; there is no mistaking its meaning. In contrast, rule *a* requires additional interpretation; interpretation adds to uncertainty, and, in extreme cases, it can even lead to controversy.

**4.** *Explain rules.* In presenting rules to students, carefully explain the reason for the rule. This might be as simple as explaining why one person talking at a time is necessary for learning or could involve a lengthier discussion about the need to respect the rights of others. Explaining classroom rules not only helps students understand the reasons for the rule but also places classroom management in the larger arena of promoting student growth and development.

**5.** *Display rules.* Write the rules down and have them displayed prominently in the classroom from the first day of class. This detail ensures that the rules are clear and available to students as the school year progresses. We consider this issue further when we discuss implementation.

**6.** *Plan consequences.* Plan consequences for breaking rules. This simply means decide what you are going to do when a student breaks a rule. Many teachers have difficulty with management because they have only a vague and uncertain idea as to what they will do next. Making these decisions is difficult because of the many and varied contingencies involved; making these decisions is especially difficult in front of 30 students. Consequently, we strongly urge you to consider carefully what you will do when students inevitably break rules *before this actually happens.*

In considering consequences, student characteristics are important. With advanced high school students who have been socialized to classroom rules, you may not need rules, much less consequences, and your planning can focus primarily on classroom procedures. On the other hand, if students are younger or less socialized into the rules and procedures of classroom life or if you anticipate a difficult class, you need to have very precise and explicit consequences in mind.

There are several options available in planning consequences. One is simply to tell the student to stop the rule-breaking behavior. This is a simple "desist" as Kounin (1970) described it. Another strategy is to stop the activity briefly, ask the student what the rule is, have him or her explain why the rule is important, and remind the student that all students must obey the rule. Our experience has been that this approach is effective if momentary memory lapses are the cause and if the rules are carefully taught in advance. At the other end of the spectrum, Canter and Canter (1976) advocated taking a very assertive stance. In their enormously popular but somewhat controversial approach, *assertive discipline*, they advocate a process of writing the student's name on the board for a first infraction, adding a checkmark for a second infraction, and so on until a specified number of checks are reached. At this point, the student is sent to the principal's office, given a detention, or some other agreed-on punishment.

The popularity of assertive discipline is probably due to two major factors. First, it stresses the idea that teachers have a *right* to teach in an orderly environment. This assertion strikes an appreciative note in beginning teachers and teachers who are unsure of their management rights. Teachers *do* have a right to expect students to comply with classroom rules and should expect parents and principals to help in this task. Assertive discipline emphasizes this right.

The second reason for assertive discipline's popularity relates to the point we just made about considering discipline consequences *before* problems occur. Assertive discipline not only considers these alternatives (listed in Table 11.1), but structures the administration of discipline through a system of three infractions and the student is out (e.g., of the classroom or a parent is called in). A bit simplistic, perhaps, but teachers who feel overwhelmed by the management task do find comfort in this structured approach.

The consequences you choose depend on your professional judgment. Our purpose is not to tell you what consequences you should specify, but rather to remind you to plan for what you will do when a student breaks a rule. We discuss the issue of breaking rules and consequences further in the section on implementing management plans.

**TABLE 11.1**   Alternative Consequences

Reprimands
Initial warnings
Isolation (same classroom)
Time out (another classroom)
Loss of privileges (e.g., recess or gym)
After-school detention
Principal's office
Parental involvement
In-school suspension
Suspension from school

## Procedures

**Procedures** (or procedural rules) are systems for dealing with routine classroom tasks that help structure student activities during the course of the day. They help students understand what is expected of them during different activities and at different times. As opposed to rules, which are few in number, the typical classroom will have a number of procedures, encompassing activities such as entering the classroom, putting materials in folders, passing in work, bathroom passes, changing activities, going to lunch, and many others. With high school students who have learned the game of school, the teaching of procedures is often quite simple, and planning for them is easy. In contrast, planning the procedures for a kindergarten or first-grade class requires careful consideration.

As procedures become established, they become routines. This is your goal. Routines are invaluable to both teacher and students for several reasons. They provide teachers with a framework within which instructional activities are embedded. If students know they are to come in and get out their homework while the teacher checks attendance, the class is ready to begin when the teacher is ready to teach. Conversely, routine procedures provide students with concrete structures that communicate expectations (e.g., Friday is quiz day, after we discuss and hand in our homework). As this procedure becomes a routine, it frees both students and teacher to concentrate their energies on learning and teaching.

Routines occur at many levels and across many time frames. We have school-level routines that govern comings and goings from assemblies and cafeterias. Within the classroom, we have annual routines that open and close the school year as well as quarterly routines, within which are embedded grading and report card routines. On the daily level, routines influence students' passage from class to class as well as their activities within the classroom. In addition, research reveals that many effective teachers use weekly routines to structure basic skill areas (Good et al., 1983).

Some general areas where procedures need to be considered are listed in Table 11.2. These procedures provide direction for students from the time they enter the

**TABLE 11.2**   General Classroom Procedural Areas

| Procedural Area | Concerns |
| --- | --- |
| 1. Entering classroom/beginning of period | What should students do when they enter the classroom? |
| 2. Large-group instruction | What are the rules for participation (e.g., should students raise their hands to respond)? |
| 3. Individual/small-group instruction | What should students do when they need help? when they're done? |
| 4. Materials and equipment | How are papers handed in and back? What about tape and scissors? |
| 5. End of period | How do students leave the classroom (e.g., does the bell or the teacher signal permission to leave)? |
| 6. Out-of-room policies | How do children receive permission to use the bathroom or go to the main office? |

**TABLE 11.3**  Specific Procedural Concerns at the Beginning of a Class

| Area | Questions |
| --- | --- |
| 1. Entering class | Should students go directly to their seat when they enter the class? Can they talk? Can they walk around the room? Is there an assignment on the board? |
| 2. Attendance | How will the teacher take attendance? What about tardies (e.g., do they go to the office to remove their names from the absent list)? |
| 3. Previous absences | Is a note from parents required? What about missed work (e.g., homework and quizzes)? |
| 4. Logistics | What about lunch count? Milk money? Special schedule for the day (e.g., assemblies, PE, etc.)? |

classroom until they leave. Your consideration of these *before* students arrive in your class and the teaching and explanation of these to your students is crucial to the smooth functioning of your classroom.

To give you an idea of the kind of detail needed in considering these procedures, we've broken down one area—Entering Classroom/Beginning of Period—into subareas of concern (see Table 11.3). While the amount of detail may seem overwhelming, it is important to think these through, considering the age of your students and the school you teach in. Talking to other teachers can be invaluable here. Find out what procedures teachers in earlier grades and other classrooms use and build on this foundation. Don't feel obligated to follow other teachers' procedures, but when you deviate from those regularly used in your school, make sure you take the time to teach and explain these differences to your students.

# IMPLEMENTING MANAGEMENT PLANS

It is September 3, Sarah's first day of kindergarten. She has been to the school before to see her brother in a play and to attend the fall carnival. She has heard about school from her brother and parents, but still she is not sure what to expect. Her dad walks her to school, and she feels good. The sun is warm, and she is excited. As she gets closer to school, she notices all the people and cars. Her dad helps her thread her way through the crowds to her classroom. She sees some familiar faces of neighborhood playmates, but most of the people are strangers. The teacher approaches her, smiles, welcomes her, and takes her to her desk just as the bell rings. She apprehensively wonders, "What next?"

Jim, too, is excited about his first day of school. He is in sixth grade and is looking forward to playing on the playground before school and seeing all of his old friends. When he arrives at school, the playground is just as he expected—chaos. He goes over to the baseball diamond where some of his friends are playing catch and half-heartedly trying to get a game going.

Soon, the bell rings, and the students funnel into the school. Jim knows the name of his teacher and the location of the classroom. Reputation has it that he is strict but good. The teacher stands at the door and directs each student to find the desk with his or her name on it. As the teacher moves to the front of the room, Jim thinks, "I wonder what this year will be like."

Sandra is beginning her junior year of high school. In addition to the rest of her schedule, she is taking advanced placement American history, even though she was in standard world history as a tenth grader. She is excited to be in school this first morning but somewhat anxious about the honors class. After the perfunctory homeroom-period discussions of pep rallies and homeroom representatives, the bell sends her to first period, where Mrs. Houson waits. As she enters the class, she notes a sign on the board: "Seat yourself and fill out the card on your desk." For better or for worse, she is in advanced placement American history.

These examples have a key feature in common. They each involve students who are beginning the first day of school with both expectations and apprehensions. The apprehension results from uncertainty about what to expect and what is expected of them. It exists to some degree in each of the students. Apprehension in response to uncertainty is universal; it spans cultures and age groups. We all feel more comfortable when we know what is expected of us. Teachers address this need when they plan for classroom management and communicate these plans to students.

That the vignettes all illustrated the beginning of the school year is also significant. This crucial period sets the stage for the remainder of the school year.

## Implementation: The First Ten Days

The beginning of the year is critical for classroom management. It sets the tone and lays the foundation for the rest of the year. A confused and uncertain first 2 weeks communicates to students that this is what to expect from this classroom, and it also drains the energy and resolve of the teacher.

Suggestions from a number of large-scale studies of the beginning of the school years can be summarized in one word—*simplify!* (Emmer et al., 1980; Emmer and Evertson, 1980). Treat the first day as distinctly different from the others, and view it as the beginning of a long-term effort to teach the rules and procedures of the classroom. Resist the intuitive urge to jump into immediate immersion in the content itself; instead, spend the necessary time organizing the class for the rest of the year.

Some guidelines for the first days of class distilled from research include the following (Vasa, 1984):

**1.** Plan initial meetings for maximum contact and control. Plan instructional activities during the first 2 weeks of class with management concerns a high priority

(Doyle, 1986). Plan to use large-group instruction rather than small-group work, minimize work with individual students, and keep the number of transitions from one activity to another low (Arlin, 1979). Stay in the classroom and don't allow yourself to become distracted by parents or new students (Evertson et al., 1989).

**2.** Make explicit positive statements about expectations for students' behavior (e.g., "We have some general guidelines for behavior in this class, and I think they're important because they'll help us learn."). In Chapter 4 we discussed the impact of teacher expectations on student achievement, and they are no less important in helping establish appropriate behavior patterns.

**3.** Begin by teaching, explaining, and modeling your rules and procedures the very first day of school. For example, a second-grade teacher began her first day of class by having the students write their full name on a card and taping the name tag to their shoulder with masking tape. Her instructions to her class were as follows:

*Teacher:* Now, everyone, when I teach I have some rules that are important to me. My first rule is that when we're having a discussion, it is very important that you wait and stay completely quiet until I call on you. I will call on each of you as we go along, so you must wait your turn. Now, what is the first rule, Sidney?

*Sidney:* We don't talk until you call on us.

*Teacher:* Yes, exactly, Sidney. So, if I call on Sharon and she is having a hard time answering the question, what do you do? Steve?

*Steve:* I wait. I don't say anything.

*Teacher:* Yes, excellent, Steve. And why do you suppose this rule is so important? Kim?

*Kim:* Well, if we all shout out answers, no one will be able to hear.

*Teacher:* That's right, Kim. That's very important. And it's also important that we all get a chance to answer and practice on the ideas we're learning. So, we must wait our turn.

The teacher in this case actually "taught" the students the rule, much in the same way she would teach any concept. She presented and explained it, followed with an illustration, and explained why the rule is important. Time and effort is well spent on this process. It eliminates problems before they begin and results in more smoothly functioning classrooms throughout the year.

Some teachers choose to display the rules in a prominent place in the classroom, such as on a front bulletin board or a portion of the chalkboard. Others, who think prominent display of rules detracts from a positive classroom climate, prefer merely to discuss the rules or hand them out on a sheet of paper. Whether the rules are displayed is not the critical issue; the critical factor is that they are carefully taught, communicated, explained, reviewed, and reinforced. The goal is for all students to be aware of all the rules at all times.

Some procedures that should be considered the first day are

   **a.** Entering and exiting the classroom
   **b.** Classroom facilities and material use
   **c.** Student emergencies (e.g., sickness or having to use the bathroom)
   **d.** Turning in assignments.

Researchers have found that effective primary teachers actually have young children practice "dry runs" on procedures like putting papers in folders at the front of the room and using and returning materials such as scissors (McGreal, 1985). They do two or three dry runs each day for the first few days; students quickly adapt to the procedure, and a positive pattern is established in a matter of 2 or 3 days.

   **4.** Monitor and enforce rules with complete consistency during this period. Your goal during this period is to make the management environment completely predictable. You want all students to know that you will intervene immediately when a rule is broken. For instance, consider the following episode:

> The second day of class, Mr. Stancil began reviewing problems for finding the area of rectangles with his sixth graders. He knew that they had covered the topic in fifth grade, but he was not sure of their mastery of it. He displayed a problem and began, "What is the first step in the solution? Toni?"
>
> Toni did not respond.
>
> "We multiply," Susan jumped in.
>
> Mr. Stancil turned directly to Susan and asked firmly but evenly, "Susan, what was the first rule we discussed?"
>
> "We don't talk until you call on us."
>
> "Yes, exactly. Very good, thanks, Susan. Now, what should we do first, Toni?"

Despite a teacher's careful effort to teach the rules, students will still break them, particularly during the first few days, and often because they simply forget or "slip up." Each time this happens, successful teachers take the time to stop and immediately remind the students of the rule and why it is important before continuing. This is what Mr. Stancil did.

   While most students comply with the rules when they are carefully taught and reviewed, some students "test" us; in these cases, it is even more important that the rules are monitored thoroughly and consistently. We "pass the test" by dealing with the infraction before continuing.

   Classroom instruction may be disrupted by these management interventions during the first few days of the year. However, we cannot state too strongly how important it is to establish during this period the patterns you expect for the remainder of the year. Unfortunately, we have seen too many examples of teachers near the end of the first or second grading period who are still trying to teach over the top of students who are visiting with each other in the back of the room, goofing off, or even sitting with their backs to the teacher. Learning cannot take place under these conditions. Time spent during the first 2 weeks to establish desired patterns will pay enormous dividends during the rest of the year.

**5.** Communicate openly and congruently with your students. Notice, for example, that Mr. Stancil faced Susan directly and firmly when she broke the rule. In Chapter 4, we discussed the need for congruent verbal and nonverbal behavior in communication. This congruence is particularly important in dealing with management issues. Telling students to be quiet as we glance over our shoulders at them in the back of the room communicates a much different message than moving close, facing them directly, looking in their eyes, and then telling them to stop talking. There is, however, no place in the classroom for threats and ultimatums. They detract from a positive climate and reduce the teacher's credibility. Open and honest communication makes the teacher accessible and human without reducing authority. It enhances the dignity of both the students and the teacher.

**6.** Open lines of communication with parents early. For example, a teacher sent the following letter home:

September 30, 1992

Dear Parents and Students,

It was a pleasure meeting so many of you during our Open House. Thank you for your cooperation and help in making this year the best one ever for your youngster.

I am looking forward to an exciting year in geography, and I hope you are too! In order for us to work together most effectively, some guidelines are necessary. They are listed below. Please read through the information carefully and sign at the bottom of the page. If you have any questions or comments, please feel free to call Lakeside Junior High School (272-8160). I will return your call promptly. This sheet must be kept in your student's notebook and/or folder all year.

Sincerely,

*Survival Guidelines*
1. Follow directions the first time they are given.
2. Be in class, seated, and quiet when the bell rings.
3. Bring covered textbooks, notebook and/or folder, paper, pen, and pencils to class every day.
4. Raise your hand for permission to speak or to leave your seat.
5. Keep hands, feet, and objects to yourself.

*Homework Guidelines*
1. Motto—I will always TRY, and I will NEVER give up!
2. I will complete all assignments. If the assignment is not finished or is not ready when called for, a zero will be given.
3. Head your paper properly—directions were given in class. Use pen/pencil—no red, orange, or pink ink. If you have questions, see Mrs. Barnhart.
4. Whenever you are absent, it is your responsibility to come in early in the morning (8:15–8:50) and make arrangements for makeup work. Class

time will not be used for this activity. Tests are always assigned three to five days in advance—if you are absent the day before the test, you should come prepared to take the test as announced.

5. No extra credit work will be given. If you do all the required work and study for the tests, there should be no need for extra credit.

_____ (student)   _____ (parent)

(V. L. Barnhart, personal communication, October 15, 1992)

This communication serves three functions. First, the students' parents are made aware of important rules and procedures. As a result, when students leave the house in the morning, parents will be more inclined to say, "Do you have your homework with you?" or "Do you have paper?" Unfortunately, not all parents will be helpful or cooperative, but if the letter induces assistance in only a few, you are ahead of where you would have been.

Second, the letter communicates that the teacher is accessible to parents. It also paves the way for further communication should the teacher need to call parents about some issue later in the year.

Finally, the signature at the bottom symbolizes a form of commitment to the rules and procedures on the part of both students and their parents. As a result, serious infractions are less likely to take place.

Communication can be enhanced in other ways. A simple handwritten note sent home with a child that has been doing particularly well takes only a minute and can do much to promote a positive home–school partnership. Periodic phone calls, while admittedly time-consuming, can help with both management and achievement problems. This pattern can be established in the first 2 weeks. How do parents feel when they get a phone call from the teacher the second week of class? Our experience has been that more often than not it communicates that the teacher is "on top of things" and that he or she cares about the particular student. The most common parental complaint we hear is, "Why weren't we told that he was misbehaving?" or "We never knew he was having trouble in history." You are much more likely to have problems with parents by not communicating than you are by being a little overzealous the first 2 weeks.

## Implementation: The Rest of the Year

By establishing expectations, rules, and procedures early in the school year, we can devote more of the remaining time to instruction and to monitoring the rules and procedures we have established. This is the case with effective teachers. In fact, one criterion to use in judging the success of a teacher's classroom management is the extent to which it allows instruction to take place with as little disruption as possible. This again illustrates the close relationship between management and instruction. If management is effective, it will be unobtrusive; if instruction is effective, it will actively involve students in learning, minimizing the need for management interventions. Three factors help us maintain the patterns we have established those first 10 days: orchestration, momentum, and smoothness. We turn to these topics now.

**Orchestration** *Orchestration* refers to the teacher's ability to function as ringmaster, keeping the lesson going while addressing the human ("Can I go to the bathroom?") and management ("Sarah, turn around, please.") concerns in the classroom. On one level, it can be thought of as keeping routines in motion. If the lesson format is familiar to students, and if there are established procedures for using bathrooms, then a quick nod of the head to the one student and a quiet "Sarah, turn around, please" can be integrated smoothly into the instructional flow of the class.

Orchestration can also be analyzed using the concept of entropy. All systems in the universe require energy for their creation and maintenance. Our bodies are a case in point; we need to eat food to grow and to maintain the various systems that are essential for life. Without energy input, the body declines. Classrooms are also complex systems that require continual doses of energy to maintain them. In the absence of this strategically placed energy, chaos ensues. Orchestration is the application of energy to maintain the flow of classroom activities.

At the classroom level, orchestration can be thought of as coordinating and sustaining all the activities that occur within it. In second grade, it might involve conducting a reading group while the rest of the class is doing seatwork; at the secondary level, it might involve monitoring a laboratory activity for the whole class while simultaneously helping one small group.

At the micro, or lesson level, orchestration can be thought of as movement management. This involves initiating an activity so that all students understand the goals of the lesson and become involved in the activity, sustaining the activity through monitoring and continued input, and ending the activity cleanly so another one can begin. These tasks seem simple enough, but accomplishing them with large groups of students can sometimes verge on crowd control.

A variable closely related to orchestration is overlapping (Kounin, 1970). **Overlapping** involves the ability to monitor more than one activity at a time. It is especially important in elementary classrooms, where many of the students do seatwork while the teacher works with a small reading group. At the secondary level, inexperienced teachers sometimes become so involved dealing with individual students who were late or absent the day before that the behavior of the rest of the class disintegrates into bedlam. Experienced teachers deal with these problems by giving the class a task and handling the individuals quickly and efficiently while simultaneously scanning the room. In short, they can do two things at one time. While this is not easy, it can be learned with practice. We turn now to two other concepts based on Kounin's work—momentum and smoothness—that influence classroom management.

**Momentum** In Chapter Five, we discussed effective questioning strategies that involve all students in the lesson. We talked about the necessity of maintaining pace; the content to be learned had to be presented at a pace sufficient to challenge most of the students while not losing too many others. Momentum and smoothness are additional dimensions of a lesson that provides the lesson direction with strength and continuity.

Central to the concept of momentum is the idea of activity vector. A vector is a line that indicates the strength and direction of a force. Just as forces have direction and strength, so do lessons. Some lesson vectors are weak, barely maintaining the teacher's interest, much less the students'. Successful lessons actively involve the students in the lesson vector; in a sense, they are swept along by their interest in a lesson. Here we can again see the interconnectedness of management and instruction. High-interest lessons that build on students' backgrounds and interests help to minimize disruptions. One characteristic of these lessons is momentum, which carries both content and students along. Lessons with strong vectors pull the class along, much like a fast-paced mystery novel. An observer can almost feel the intellectual excitement in the air. Other lessons plod on, and both teacher and student are glad when they are completed.

The vector for an activity results from the unique interaction of the content, the students, and the type of instructional activity taking place. This interaction is important; a potentially dead topic can be made to come alive if the content is framed in the right way. For instance, consider the following example illustrating one teacher's approach to the play *Julius Caesar*. Many of us have labored through this fine play by Shakespeare, lost in the Elizabethan English and wondering what it was all about. One teacher attacked the problem in this way:

*Julius Caesar* is basically a play about internal conflicts, a moral decision for which there is really no wrong or right answer. If I kill this man, we might save our republic but we endanger ourselves. If we don't kill him, we could be endangered. It focuses on one man's struggle with a moral decision, the consequences of his actions and how people turn against him. And so what I had them do was . . . I gave them an artificial scenario. I said, "You are the first officer on the Starship Enterprise. Captain Kirk has been getting out of hand. He's a good captain, he's been made Commander of the Fleet. But you, his closest friend, and your fellow officers have been noticing that he's been getting too risky, a little big-headed. You're afraid that he's going to endanger the Federation Fleet and might just seek glory in some farcical campaign." And they really took off on that . . . they said they found out that there really wasn't a right answer. They argued back and forth. You couldn't just kill him because the whole fleet likes him. If you kill him, it's your head on the chopping block, too. But you also have a moral obligation to your country and you can't let him go on. What they finally came up with was that it's a pretty tough decision to make. (Wilson et al., 1987, p. 112)

By involving students in the content and relating the content to students' own backgrounds and concerns, the teacher created a powerful lesson vector that carried through the whole unit. Lessons with these characteristics minimize management problems.

Obstacles to momentum are teacher (and student) actions that drain energy away from the thrust of a lesson. A fire bell during a class in which the book *Old Yeller* is being read orally and is coming to heart-rending conclusion is an example of an out-of-class obstacle to momentum. Teacher-generated sources are found in Table 11.4.

**TABLE 11.4**    Obstacles to Momentum

| Behavior | Example |
|---|---|
| Behavior overdwelling | Nagging or preaching. Continuing to talk about a misbehavior after it stopped. For example, "How many times do I have to tell you to stop that talking?" or "This is the third time today that I've told you to stop playing with your pencils." |
| Content overdwelling | Staying on a task well after students had mastered it. For example, teaching the concept of odd numbers by having the class name *all* odd numbers up to 100. |
| Fragmentation | Having single students or small groups do work that the whole group could do. (If this is the case, why not do the activity as a whole and save time and effort?) |

*Source:* Adapted from Kounin, 1970

**Smoothness**    Smoothness is related to lesson continuity and means not interrupting an instructional sequence with irrelevant information, and not becoming diverted by behaviors and events that detract from the main thrust of the lesson. Problems with lesson smoothness occur when teachers allow the lesson focus to wander, or when they spend an inordinate amount of time interrupting the lesson to reprimand students. Smoothness relates closely to the concept *academic focus*, or the conceptual focus of the lesson. Some obstacles to smoothness are shown in Table 11.5. Partial solutions here are well-planned lessons with a clear content focus and unobtrusive management strategies that minimize classroom interruptions.

## Classroom Management: Situational Variables

In our discussion of starting the school year, we suggested that one way to simplify the management task was to employ whole-group instruction versus other, more complicated, instructional patterns. This makes sense from a teacher perspective because it simplifies the orchestration process. Empirically, it also makes sense; research has shown that student engagement rates are highest during large-group

**TABLE 11.5**    Obstacles to Smoothness

| Behavior | Example |
|---|---|
| Distractions | Calling attention to a piece of paper on the floor in the middle of explaining a math problem. (This *may* be important, but should it occur now?) |
| Intrusions | In the middle of a reading lesson, the teacher says, "I just noticed that Sally isn't here. Does anybody know why she's absent?" (The teacher should write a note to himself or herself and find out later.) |
| Flip-flops | Returning to an activity after it is done. After science books are put away and social studies has begun, the teacher says, "Oh, yeah, I just remembered one more thing about arthropods." |

*Source:* Adapted from Kounin, 1970

instruction and lowest during individual seatwork (Atwood, 1983; Gump, 1967; Kounin, 1970). There are a number of factors involved here, and an understanding of these factors should help you design instructional activities with a management perspective.

In Chapter 5, we discussed the concept of *pacing*, and we want to return to it again here because it also affects management (Doyle, 1986). Active pacing occurs when the teacher, through interactive teaching techniques, involves the students in brisk question and answer or interactive lecture-recitation activities. The questioning skills we discussed in Chapter Six are powerful aids in helping maintain a brisk lesson pace. Passive pacing occurs when the student's own motivation and work habits in individual assignments, such as seatwork and independent projects, establish the work rate. Passively paced activities, particularly when used with students who need high structure, carry with them the potential for management problems.

The continuity and insulation of the lesson's signal also influences management in the classroom (Kounin and Gump, 1974). When students are receiving information regularly—such as a teacher presentation, reading a book, or teacher-student interaction—self-management is easier for them. When the continuity is low, such as during group projects or group discussions, there is more opportunity for students' thoughts to drift off. The same is true when they are insulated from distraction. When the number of potential distractions is high, as in lab activities and group construction projects in which students share materials, the potential for off-task behaviors increases. An extreme example of coping with this problem with highly distractible special education students is to have them work in individual carrels where the high walls insulate the student against signal distractions.

From this discussion we can see that certain types of activities are intrinsically harder to manage than others. Gump's 1967 study of third-grade classrooms found that engagement rates were highest for teacher-led small groups and lowest for pupil presentations. In addition, Gump found that engagement rates for whole-class activities—such as recitations, tests, and presentations—were around 80 percent and higher than engagement rates during seatwork (75 percent).

Other studies (Kounin and Sherman, 1979; Rosenshine, 1980) have found similar patterns in favor of teacher-led work. Engagement rates during teacher-led presentations averaged around 85 percent, while those for seatwork averaged around 66 percent. Burns (1984) found that the frequency of seatwork was also a variable; the more often it was used, the lower were student-engagement rates.

Implications for practice? Use nothing but teacher-led presentations? We hope this is not the conclusion you have drawn. Ideally, you will use a variety of instructional strategies varying in scope from large-group presentations to individualized work. But, as you plan for these, be aware that different instructional approaches put different management demands on teachers and different self-control requirements on students.

Beginning teachers are continually amazed to discover that different groups of students react to instructional activities differently. One junior high teacher shared this experience with us.

We had been studying this play and I thought that reading it out loud might be fun. I tried it in my first-period class and it went beautifully. I assigned different parts to different students and the play really came alive. Then my second period class. I should have guessed. Before I knew it things got out of hand and I had to stop the lesson and talk to them about it. Same lesson! I can't believe the difference!

As we saw earlier, students differ in their ability to manage their own behavior. Sensitive teachers match task demands to students' abilities, both in terms of cognitive and emotional development. Much of this comes from experience. Expert teachers are more adept at reading a classroom situation and diagnosing trouble spots; beginning teachers need to plan their instructional lessons with a third eye to management.

Also, be aware that events outside the regular instructional task also provide management challenges. Transitions between activities provide ambiguities for students about what they should be doing and opportunities for minor classroom disturbances to occur (Arlin, 1979). Part of this is due to teachers' own lack of clarity about when one activity ends and another begins. Arlin called this *boundary indeterminacy*. Analysis of classroom transcripts reveals that approximately 30 major transitions occur daily in a typical elementary classroom, and they occupy approximately 15 percent of class time. Although the figures are less for secondary classrooms, unnecessary transitions pose a dual problem at both levels — wasted instructional time and the potential for management problems (Doyle, 1984; Evertson, 1982).

Interruptions are another management problem not directly related to instruction (Behnke, 1979). Most interruptions (90 percent) come from the classroom itself and last only 10 seconds or less, while external interruptions (e.g., the loudspeaker) are infrequent in number (10 percent) but often disrupt lesson flow for several minutes. The way a teacher deals with interruptions, both internal and external, has a large influence on the momentum and smoothness of a lesson.

# MANAGEMENT INTERVENTIONS

*The best laid plans of mice and men often go awry.*

Robert Burns

In our discussion of management during the first 10 days of school, we briefly discussed the need for interventions when rule breaking occurs. The purpose in those interventions is to establish the desired behavior patterns early in the school year to reduce problems later on. This strategy works. However, despite the teacher's best effort, and regardless of the level of planning and the approach used, management incidents will inevitably recur. When this happens, the teacher needs to intervene to prevent a student from disrupting the classroom. These interventions are often as brief as "Jerry, pay attention, please" and occur as frequently as 16 times per hour in the typical classroom (White, 1975). However, in problem classrooms, frequent interventions can chew up valuable class time, interrupt momentum, bother students, and completely wear out the teacher. In a reanalysis of his 1970 data, Kounin (1983) found that one teacher had task involvement rates of only 25 percent and accumulated 986 interventions in one day. Whew!

## Defining Misbehavior

Interventions occur as a result of misbehavior and the teacher's (and students') interpretation of that misbehavior. To understand the complex relationship between misbehavior and teachers' reactions, we must first come to some understanding of what constitutes misbehavior. This is not an easy task because what is misbehavior in one classroom falls well within the range of acceptable behavior in another. We all remember this from our own experience in classrooms. Compounding our problem is the fact that even within the same classroom behaviors are reacted to differently when performed by different students at different times in different contexts (Doyle, 1986). For example, not paying attention is much more likely to be accepted at the end of a lesson than at the beginning or middle. Also, quiet talking between students is generally acceptable during transitions but not during the main part of a lesson. So how are teachers (much less students) to come to any understanding of the concept of misbehavior? Doyle (1986) helps us out here.

Misbehavior should be thought of as action in context and in terms of its resultant effects on the ongoing program of action. The idea of vectors is once again valuable here. An action is considered misbehavior when the consequences of that action, a vector of energy, compete with the instructional vector. Here the dimensions of *public* and *contagious* are important. If a student's actions compete for attention (public) with the main instructional program and have the potential for drawing other students away from the learning task at hand (contagious), the behavior is *mis*behavior. The consequences of the behavior are central here; certain behaviors (quiet talking) are quite acceptable under certain circumstances (e.g., a class discussion) while unacceptable in others (e.g., a movie). The difference is not in the action itself but its potential for disrupting the flow of the classroom.

## Causes of Misbehavior

Why do students misbehave? If a teacher understood the causes of misbehavior, he or she would be in a much better position to deal with it when it occurred. Reasons vary from boredom to testing the teacher and the classroom system of order (Doyle, 1986). The boredom argument is a variation on the old dictum "Idle minds are the workshop of the Devil." Without wanting to seem moralistic, there is a good deal of legitimacy to the boredom argument. Although we do not know the specifics of the situation, it is hard to believe that the teacher with 986 interventions in one day was implementing a stimulating program of instruction.

Another explanation for misbehavior has to do with the custodial nature of much of schooling, in which 30 students are asked to remain relatively quiet (and busy) for extended periods of time. The temptations to talk (or send notes or communicate nonverbally) are just too great. The teacher attempts to minimize these social excursions with looks and frequent "Shhhs."

Two other more subtle possible explanations for misbehavior are testing and negotiating. Both center around the image of students as actors in hierarchical social organizations. The testing hypothesis is more informational in flavor; it contends that students attempt to clarify limits in the classroom by experimenting with misbehavior. As the teacher clarifies the boundaries between appropriate and inappropriate behavior with his or her reactions, the student learns limits through this feedback. Our earlier discussions about the need for clear expectations and rules are relevant here. The clearer the rules and expectations for behavior, the less likely students will be to test areas of ambiguity.

The negotiation argument centers on the idea that student misbehavior is in reaction to boring content or tasks that are too demanding or ambiguous. This view of misbehavior acknowledges that all management is not top to bottom and that students exert a considerable influence on the climate in a classroom.

In an empirical study of the motives behind classroom behavior, Allen (1986) observed 100 high school students. These students had two major classroom goals, to socialize and to pass the course. To achieve these goals, they all employed the strategy of figuring out the teacher; that is, what did the teacher want and what would he permit? In classes where there were few academic demands, students reverted to the dual goals of having fun and reducing boredom to pass the time. In faster paced classes, the students attempted to give the teacher what he wanted, but would also attempt to minimize work and reduce boredom if the content of the class was dry. In addition, all students attempted to "stay out of trouble."

It is probable that research with younger students, especially early primary, would yield slightly different orientations, but we believe the overall pattern would be the same. Students try to figure out what the teacher expects of them, and they want to learn something and enjoy the company of their classmates. Most of us did (and continue to do) something like this when we found ourselves in classroom situations.

What, then, should a teacher do when an intervention becomes necessary? This is the topic of the next section.

## Crime and Punishment: The Crucial Match

In a previous section of this chapter, we said that one of the essential dimensions of withitness was matching the intervention to the misbehavior. This is essential because it not only communicates to students that the teacher is aware but also helps students understand limits and consequences. The link between behavior and disruptiveness is also important here. Students should be helped to understand that the *consequence* of behavior on the instructional program is an important variable. Research suggests that high-ability students may understand this link better than do low-ability students and strategically time their misbehaviors (e.g., transitions and end of lessons) better than lower achieving classmates (Rusnock and Brandler, 1979). Developmental differences also operate here; older students are better at integrating their transgressions into the class flow.

Teachers can assist in helping students understand the consequences of their misbehavior by clearly communicating when misbehavior occurs. For example, "Ken, turn around and stop bothering Anne" is preferable to "Ken, shh!" if our intent is to help Ken understand that his behavior is interfering with Anne's learning.

Another consideration in deciding on an appropriate desist strategy is the effect of the intervention on the instructional flow of the classroom. If the lesson is proceeding smoothly and the misbehavior is fleeting and private, the teacher is ill advised to interrupt the routine. However, if the misbehavior is lengthy and obtrusive, the teacher must intervene to prevent a "ripple effect" (Kounin, 1970) from spilling over onto other students. But even here the teacher must use judgment; too long an intervention can generate problems of its own. Students become bored and fidgety, and other potential problems arise.

Research on ineffective classroom managers revealed two major problems with their intervention strategies (Erickson and Mohatt, 1982; Kounin, 1970). Ineffective managers persisted in their interventions beyond the point necessary to stop a behavior. Related to this problem, ineffective teachers used classroom incidents as opportunities to establish rules inductively. In contrast, more effective managers had already established classroom rules and procedures deductively during the first part of the year and steered lessons through management roadblocks. In short, they remembered that their primary goal was instruction and digressed into management only when necessary and returned to instruction as quickly as possible while still stopping the misbehavior.

What options does the teacher have to prevent misbehavior and how should they be matched with the misbehavior? As Figure 11.1 illustrates, teacher actions can be ordered along a continuum of disruptiveness, and these teacher actions can be matched with the obtrusiveness and severity of the student's behavior.

The easiest teacher response to temporary misbehavior is to ignore it. This is appropriate when the inappropriate behavior (1) is short and not likely to persist or spread; (2) is a minor deviation; and (3) intervening would interrupt the lesson or reinforce the behavior (Evertson et al., 1989).

Next on the continuum of disruptiveness is nonverbal cues. Nonverbal behavior is a very effective nondisruptive intervention technique, and expert teachers are versatile in the range of emotions they can project with a gesture or facial expression (Woolfolk and Brooks, 1985). Eye contact along with a piercing glare can communi-

**FIGURE 11.1**   The Match Between Student Misbehavior and Teacher Actions

| Student actions | | |
|---|---|---|
| Nondisruptive | | More disruptive |
| Temporary and private misbehavior | Temporary but potentially disruptive | Persistent and intentional misbehavior |

Teacher interventions

| Ignore | Nonverbal | Short squelch | Extended response |
|---|---|---|---|

Increasingly Disruptive

cate clearly, as does a simple finger over the lips. Another effective nonverbal technique for both prevention *and* intervention is movement around the room. This, combined with a touch on the shoulder to the nonattending student, communicates intent clearly without the loss of a single word. Our guess is that nonverbal interventions become increasingly important in secondary classrooms as students become more sensitive to nonverbal cues, but they are still a major tool of elementary teachers.

The most commonly used verbal technique is the simple squelch (Humphrey, 1979) or reprimand. Simple verbal reprimands comprise 58 percent of the interventions in first- and fifth-grade classrooms (Sieber, 1979, 1981). In a similar study in kindergarten and third-grade classrooms, Humphrey (1979) reported that 47 percent of the interventions were simple reminders consisting of *shhs*, *nos*, or *stops* and that quite frequently (28 percent of the time) these would be extended into slightly longer but still economical short phrases such as "Take turns" or "Class, it's too noisy."

An extended response to student misconduct lies at the far end of the teacher continuum. We have already discussed the problems involved with a prolonged response — they center around a loss of lesson momentum and the fact that the rest of the class, ostensibly not involved in the problem, have to listen to an extended diatribe. Apart from the cathartic function that it might serve, a direct and explicit response to student misbehavior can also serve an informational function in further clarifying limits. For example, "Class, I need your attention for a minute. We said that quiet talk was okay during art period. But I'm hearing too many loud voices and too much giggling. Each of you has your own project to complete. If we can't work on these while we talk quietly, we'll have to put them away." This intervention was direct and to the point, and it clearly identified the problem and the consequences if the problem did not clear up.

As teachers analyze and evaluate their classroom management strategies, two factors should be considered. One is how widespread the management problems are. If they seem to be widespread, encompassing virtually the whole class, two factors may be operating. One is that the classroom rules and procedures may not be functioning effectively. They may be insufficient in number or detail or may not be clearly understood by students. Another possible explanation is that the instructional activities might not be geared to the right level of difficulty or be motivating or interesting enough. If students are bored and confused, a lot more energy needs to be expended to keep the management program going.

## Management Interventions: Planned Consequences

Jim Harris had a lively fourth-grade class that liked to talk during seatwork. The better students would get their work done in spite of the noise, but other students would get distracted and forget to do their work. Jim felt he was fighting a losing battle just to keep the lid on during seatwork.

This type of problem is not unusual. Talking and minor misbehavior comprises the vast majority of management problems and can literally drive a teacher crazy.

Often the problem is so pervasive that individual intervention just doesn't work. Assuming that the seatwork is appropriate and that students do know the rules and procedures for seatwork, then a planned management system may be called for. A management system makes the consequences for behavior (and misbehavior) concrete and specific. In planning consequences, two decisions have to be made:

1. Will positive behaviors be reinforced or negative behaviors punished?
2. Should the consequences be individual or group oriented?

Let's see how Jim Harris wrestled with these questions.

> In thinking about his problem, Jim tried to decide whether the problem was the talking or not doing the seatwork. Actually it was both, but he decided to focus on the work, hoping the talking would take care of itself. Group or individual rewards? Hmm, why not both? The next day he began math seatwork by displaying several new math games. He showed the class how they worked and announced that students could play with them as soon as their seatwork was done. That would take care of the fast workers, but what about the slow starters? He also announced a token reward system that would allow the class to have a class party when they had accumulated 50 tokens. It worked like this. Jim would circulate around the room during seatwork, and if students were working he would put a ticket on their desk. At the end of the morning session, the class would put their tokens in a fishbowl and Jim would tally them during lunch hour. The talking wasn't completely eliminated, but the change in the atmosphere of the room was dramatic. The class was actually trying.

In analyzing Jim's system, let's return to the question asked earlier. Will positive behaviors be reinforced or negative behaviors punished? In general, reinforcing positive behaviors is preferable to punishing negative ones, for several reasons. The first has to do with the dynamics of punishment—punishment doesn't teach new behaviors, it only suppresses old ones. In addition, the affective consequences of punishment make the classroom unpleasant and place the teacher in a policing role. Jim wisely attacked his problem by positively reinforcing work behaviors in two ways—games and tokens.

In deciding whether consequences should be individual or group oriented, the teacher has to decide whether the problem is limited to one or two students or involves the class as a whole. In Jim's case the talking was pervasive, so he instituted a system aimed at the whole class. In doing this, he was able to use group cooperation and peer pressure to accomplish his goals.

Another type of management problem that is equally taxing is the single student who does not seem to want to cooperate. This kind of problem can be frustrating in terms of the time and energies it requires of the teacher and the potential it has for disrupting the whole management system. When teachers deal with problem students, their primary concerns are to minimize disruptions to the rest of the class and to integrate the student into the classroom (Brophy, 1985). We discuss this type of problem in the next section.

## Dealing with Individual Problems

So far in this chapter, we have approached classroom management from a group perspective. This approach is consistent with the realities of most classrooms, where the major problem is arranging the flow of classroom life so that student energies can be channeled into learning. However, one of the weaknesses of this group-oriented approach is that it ignores that we teach individual human beings with unique needs and interests. These unique needs may take precedence over the management system that exists, and when this happens, the problem must be dealt with individually.

Every class seems to have one or more students who do not seem to respond like the rest of the students. Whereas most of the class seem to be following the plan of action (more or less), one or two students sometimes fight against the system. If this problem is singular, or at least isolated, concentrated individual action is warranted.

The approach we recommend is both humanistic and informational, based on the works of Gordon (1974) and Glasser (1969, 1977). Each of these authors stressed the importance of clear and open communication between teacher and students. Gordon emphasized active listening in which both teachers and students acknowledge one another's message by restating it to communicate understanding. Glasser emphasized helping students understand the realities of the roles and obligations of various members of the classroom. Glasser's (1977) 10 sequential steps to dealing with exceptional problems are especially valuable here. This procedure is labor intensive, and each step escalates the seriousness of the problem, so the procedure should be used judiciously.

1. Identify a student for concentrated attention and list typical reactions to his or her past behavior.
2. Analyze this list and identify those that do not seem to work. In the future, focus on the ones that are more productive.
3. Make a concerted effort to make the student feel accepted in the classroom. Talk to the student, give him or her extra special responsibilities, and use extra encouragement.
4. If progress is not being made, talk to the student and discuss the problem. Here, active listening on both sides is important. Make sure that the student understands the problem. Require the student to describe the behavior in his or her own words; when the description is sufficiently clear, ask that he or she stop doing it.
5. Again, confer with the student and have the student restate the behavior and whether it is against the rules. Also, ask the student what he or she should be doing instead.

6. Repeat step five but call attention to the fact that previous attempts have not been successful. Require that a plan of action be drawn up that will solve the problem. This plan must include the student's overt commitment to the plan.

7. Nonadherence to the plan requires action by the teacher. Isolate the student or use time-out procedures. During this time, the *student* is responsible for devising a reinstatement plan that encompasses the problem behavior. This plan must be approved by the teacher and must have the commitment of the student to follow it.

8. The next step is in-school suspension. Because the student has not been able to deal effectively with the problem in the classroom with the teacher, the principal is called in. Previous steps followed in defining the problem and working out a plan of action should be followed, and it should be made clear that return to the classroom is contingent on following the rules.

9. If a student cannot be integrated back into the classroom, the parents are called in to discuss the problem and made aware that the student will be sent home. One-day home suspensions are used when students continue to ignore the rules.

10. If the student still does not respond, it may be necessary to refer him or her to another agency.

As you can see, this process can be terribly time-consuming, which is one of the major problems with this type of approach to management. But, when other approaches fail, the teacher should actively seek solutions to a situation that not only is stressful but also detracts from the learning environment of the classroom. The cooperation and participation of the principal is essential here. Talk the problem over with the principal, and if his or her intervention is necessary, alert him or her in advance. Also, actively recruit the assistance of parents; most are eager to work with the teacher in creating a growth environment for their child.

## Serious Management Problems: Violence and Aggression

Class is disrupted by a scuffle. You look up to see that Ron has left his seat and gone to Phil's desk, where he is punching and shouting at Phil. Phil is not so much fighting back as trying to protect himself. You don't know how this started but you do know that Phil gets along well with other students and that Ron often starts fights and arguments without provocation. (Brophy and Rohrkemper, 1987, p. 60)

This morning, several students excitedly tell you that on the way to school they saw Tom beating up Sam and taking his lunch money. Tom is the class bully and has done things like this many times. (Brophy and Rohrkemper, 1987, p. 53)

How would you handle these problems? What would you do immediately? What long-term strategies would you employ to ensure that these problems would not reoccur? The answers to these questions are the focus of this section.

Before we attempt to answer these questions, let's put violence and aggression in perspective. In our experience, the vast majority of management problems are minor. Some will require additional time and attention working with individual students, but these, too, are usually solvable. However, in virtually every school and at every grade level you will probably encounter more serious problems at some point in your teaching career. Your understanding of these problems and alternatives available to you will help you deal with them effectively.

When expert teachers were asked to respond to the situations cited at the beginning of this section, they had both short- and long-term suggestions (Brophy and Rohrkemper, 1987). Short term, these experts recommended an immediate and assertive response to these aggressive acts. Students should be confronted immediately and told clearly that violence will not be tolerated in either the classroom or the school. In the classroom incident, students should be separated immediately. In the problem involving lunch money, Tom should be made aware that his actions did not go unnoticed, that they are unacceptable, and that they will not be tolerated.

In both instances, students should be confronted with the problem and asked to explain their actions (e.g., "Ron, you were out of your seat and hitting Phil. Can you tell me why you did this?"). In the lunch money incident, the teacher might say, "Tom, tell me what happened on the way to school this morning." In both cases it is important that students know that the problem is serious, that it won't be tolerated, and that they are being held accountable for their actions.

Longer term, teachers recommended dealing with the problem from a problem-solving perspective. First, concern should be with protecting the victim from any long-term retaliation. Then, aggressors should be pressured to exert better control over their behavior (e.g., "Ron, I know you and Phil had an argument, but hitting is no way to settle a disagreement."). If punishment is used, it should be viewed not as retribution but as consequences designed to bring about desired behavior. Offending students should also be taught more effective ways to handle frustration and control their temper. These include teaching them to solve conflicts through communication and negotiation rather than aggression and expressing anger verbally rather than physically.

What if the problem reoccurs? If the teacher has tried all of these suggestions with no positive results, then other people should be involved. Parents should be made aware of the problem and asked to contribute to a solution. Within the school, counselors, social workers, and principals can provide additional advice and assistance. Persistent or serious problems of violence and aggression should not be faced alone by the teacher.

Throughout this chapter as well as the book as a whole, we've stressed the importance of creating a learning environment that is safe, secure, and conducive to learning. This can't occur if students fear for their own safety. To place this problem in perspective, remember that problems such as these are, fortunately, the exception rather than the rule. However, teachers should be aware of the possibility of such problems and be mentally prepared to deal with them quickly and assertively when they occur.

If violence is a possibility at your school, talk to other professionals about the problem. Principals and counselors are trained to deal with these problems; get their advice. Talk to experienced teachers and find out how they deal with this problem.

As with the problem of defiance, have a plan of action in mind before the problem occurs.

Now take a moment to read the chapter summary before completing the exercises that follow.

## SUMMARY

Research has revealed several important ideas about successful classroom management. First, there is a close relationship between classroom management and instruction; this relationship is synergistic, with effectiveness in one area influencing and building on effectiveness in the other. Second, effective teachers prevent classroom management fires from occurring rather than simply putting them out once they have started. Related to this is a third important idea—effective classroom management is often hard to analyze because smoothly run classrooms mask the considerable time and effort needed to produce them.

Planning for management is as essential as planning for instruction. Developmental differences in students are powerful influences in the shape and structure of a management system. The physical environment is also important in management planning, influencing these plans and also contributing to the effectiveness of these plans.

Rules and procedures are the threads that provide structure to the social fabric of the classroom. Rules should be relatively few in number and provide general guidelines for behavior. Procedures are greater in number and specificity and describe efficient ways of completing a myriad of classroom tasks. As procedures become established, they develop into routines that shape and structure the classroom environment.

The beginning of the school year is crucial for classroom management. Rules, procedures, and general outlines for behavior are framed during this time. Teachers need to communicate clearly and positively their expectations for the school year, helping students understand how to succeed in the classroom. These expectations often need to be taught to younger students; older students, who have been socialized in terms of the classroom, often need only to be reminded.

Effective managers orchestrate their classrooms so that routines and procedures complement, rather than detract from, instruction. Lesson momentum creates a positive instructional vector that pulls students in and actively involves them in learning. Another dimension of effective lessons, smoothness, maintains the direction of the lesson while minimizing internal and external distractions.

Misbehavior is an elusive concept, dependent on both context and the amount of disruption it causes. Teachers need to help students understand this concept through their words and actions.

In dealing with misbehavior, the match between the problem and its consequences is important. Minor problems that inevitably occur must be dealt with quickly and efficiently, minimizing their effects on the lesson itself.

More serious or persistent breaches of conduct need to be dealt with firmly and directly. In dealing with problem students, expectations should be clearly defined and operationalized in terms of a contract. If this approach does not work, other adults, including principals and parents, need to be called in to ensure that the problem does not detract from learning in the classroom.

# ADDITIONAL READINGS FOR PROFESSIONAL GROWTH

Charles, C. (1989). *Building classroom discipline. From models to practice* (3rd ed.). New York: Longman. Charles discusses management in terms of different strategies or models.

Doyle, W. (1986). Classroom organization and management. In M. Wittrock (Ed.), *Handbook of research on teaching* (3rd ed., pp. 392–431). New York: Macmillan. This chapter provides an excellent overview of the research on classroom management.

Emmer, E., Evertson, C., Sanford, J., Clements, B., & Worsham, M. (1989). *Classroom management for secondary teachers* (2nd ed.). Englewood Cliffs, NJ: Prentice Hall. A comprehensive and thorough treatment of management issues at the secondary level.

Evertson, C., Emmer, E., Clements, B., Sanford, J., & Worsham, M. (1989). *Classroom management for elementary teachers* (2nd ed.). Englewood Cliffs, NJ: Prentice Hall. This book docs an excellent job of describing how to manage an elementary classroom.

# EXERCISES

1. *Rules and Procedures.* Examine the following list of rules and procedures and determine which are rules (R) and which are procedures (P).

    _____ **a.** Keep your hands to yourself.

    _____ **b.** When finished with assignments, you may read or do a free-choice activity.

    _____ **c.** No running in school.

    _____ **d.** Homework is due the first part of each class.

    _____ **e.** No pencil sharpening during large-group activities.

    _____ **f.** No snowball throwing on the playground.

    _____ **g.** No smoking on school grounds.

2. *Classroom Management: Implementation.* The following scenario describes a teacher beginning the school year. Read it and answer the questions that follow.

    Nick Giardo was excited about the beginning of his first year of teaching at Sandalwood Junior High. Student teaching had been a little rocky, but he was sure that most of his problems were due to his taking over another teacher's class in mid-year.

As students filed into his first-period class, he was in the back of the room putting the final touches on his bulletin board. After the bell rang, he walked to the front of the room and said, "Welcome to U.S. History 202. I'm Mr. Giardo, and I'll be your teacher for the year. I see you've all found seats, so why don't we begin."

At that point, two confused students straggled in, looking for their classrooms. One of these students belonged there, the other did not. Mr. Giardo directed the one to sit down while he escorted the other into the hallway to help him find his class. As he returned to the room, there was a general buzz of student talk. Beginning again, he said, "Okay, class, let's get started. This is American History, and I'm really excited about the year. Since you've all been in school before, I'm not going to waste a lot of time with rules. You all know how to play the game. Instead, I'd like to jump right into the content. I want this course to be important to you, so I'd like to get some idea of the kinds of things you'd like to learn about in here. I'd like you to break up into groups of four or five, and make a list of the kinds of things you'd like to learn this year. Then we'll come back together and discuss our lists."

As the students began to talk in their groups, one student raised his hand. Mr. Giardo pulled up a chair and sat down to talk with the student. As he did so, students in back of him started throwing spitballs and erasers.

The year was off to a rocky start.

Mr. Giardo made a number of mistakes as he began his school year. Identify these errors in terms of the following categories and describe an alternative course of action.

**a.** Establishing rules and procedures

**b.** Seating

**c.** Instructional activities

**d.** Withitness (identify two errors here)

3. *Momentum and Smoothness.* Certain teacher actions not only detract from instruction but also contribute to management problems. In the following case studies, determine whether the problem is behavior overdwelling (B), content overdwelling (C), intrusion (I), or flip-flop (F).

_____ **a.** Mr. Henley was leading a review of the major concepts in the chapter for a test on Friday. Janice raised her hand to answer a question when Mr. Henley said, "Go ahead, Janice. But before I forget—make sure you see Mrs. Carter, the counselor, before lunch."

_____ **b.** The class was getting out paper and pencil to take their spelling test when Mr. Johnston said, "Class, before we actually take the test, I forgot to say one more thing about plural endings."

_____ **c.** Mrs. Stern was discussing the presidential election of 1988. She turned to Jim and said, "Who was the loser in that lopsided election? Jim?

Speaking of lopsided victories, Jim, what happened to our basketball team last week?"

_____ **d.** Mr. Henson was leading a discussion on the Great Depression when he saw Jill turn around to whisper something to Tom. "Jill, turn around, or is it that important that it can't wait? Do you want to share it with the whole class? No, well, then, turn around and stay turned around. Now, where were we?"

_____ **e.** Miss Stover was discussing a topic near and dear to her heart, the symbolism of Herman Melville, which had been the focus of her master's thesis in English. As she brought the topic up in reviewing for the exam on the book, one of her students was overheard whispering to another, "Why couldn't the whale have been grey like the rest of them?"

_____ **f.** Mr. Christian, an avid bird-watcher, was explaining how DNA transmits its code to RNA. In the middle of a sentence he said, "Class, look out the window! That's a cedar waxwing. We don't get many of them in this part of the state."

## DISCUSSION QUESTIONS

**1.** The topic of classroom management used to be called _classroom discipline._ Why did the term change?

**2.** How are rules different from procedures? To what extent can rules be generalized across grade levels and schools? procedures?

**3.** What classroom rules and procedures were made explicit at the beginning of the course for which this text is being used? Which rules and procedures were left implicit? How important are explicit and implicit rules and procedures in public school classrooms? How important are explicit and implicit rules and procedures at different levels?

**4.** Examine the alternative consequences for not following rules found in Table 11.1. What are the advantages and disadvantages of each? Which are more appropriate for younger students? Older?

**5.** How do the following factors influence the number of procedures that operate in a classroom?

  **a.** Grade level

  **b.** Subject matter

  **c.** Type of student (e.g., high versus low achiever)

  **d.** Type of instruction (e.g., large group versus small group)

**6.** If you were a substitute teacher (or a student teacher) and were going to take over a class mid-year for the rest of the year, what kinds of things would you need to know and do in terms of classroom management?

7. How are the following concepts related: engagement rates, pace, momentum, activity vector, accountability?

8. Four explanations were offered in this chapter for misbehavior: boredom, the custodial nature of schools, student teaching, and negotiating. Do these behaviors vary with grade level? subject matter? What can teachers do in terms of each of these?

9. Explain the statement "Misbehavior is contextual." Give a concrete example.

10. What are the advantages and disadvantages of the following interventions?

    a. Ignoring

    b. Nonverbal cues

    c. Simple squelch

    d. Extended response

    e. Punishment

11. Research suggests that high-ability students are smarter about breaking classroom rules. Some have interpreted this finding to mean that teachers should spend some time with low-ability students to help them become better at playing the classroom game. Discuss the pros and cons of this position.

## APPLYING IT IN THE SCHOOLS

1. *School Rules.* Observe students as they move and interact in the halls. Infer what the rules are in regards to dress, appropriate hall behavior, and tardiness and the bell. Discuss these topics with a teacher and compare your conclusions.

2. *Classroom Rules.* Interview two high- and two low-ability students in a class and record their answers to the following questions:

    a. What rules do you have in your class?

    b. Which ones are most important?

    c. Why do you have them?

    d. What happens if they are not followed?

    Compare the responses of the two groups of students.

3. *Classroom Procedures.* Observe a class for several sessions and try to identify the procedural rules which are functioning for the following actions:

    a. Entering the class

    b. Taking attendance

    c. Handing in papers

    d. Sharpening pencils

    e. Volunteering to answer a question

    f. Exiting class

Discuss your findings with a student (or teacher) to check the accuracy of your findings.

4. *Classroom Rules and Procedures.* One teacher suggested that if you wanted to find out the invisible rules and procedures operating in a classroom, you should observe a new student in the class. If possible, do this. Observe a student who has just transferred to the class and see what aspects of the rules and procedures are familiar to him or her. Ask him or her to describe the dimensions of procedural rules listed in question 3. Also, determine which of the school and class rules he knows and how he learned them.

5. *Interactive Management.* Tape and observe a classroom lesson. Identify places in the lesson where the teacher either verbally or nonverbally exhibited the following behaviors/characteristics:

   **a.** Withitness

   **b.** Overlapping

   **c.** Accountability

   **d.** Momentum

   **e.** Smoothness

6. *Management Interventions.* What types of management interventions does a teacher use? Observe a teacher (or tape yourself) teaching a lesson and note the kinds of desists used. Then answer these questions:

   **a.** When and how often does a teacher use desists?

   **b.** What is the most common intervention used?

   **c.** Is there any pattern to these interventions (e.g., time of lesson or group of students)?

   **d.** Is there any relationship between the type of intervention and the type of student misbehavior?

7. *Individual Management Problems.* How are the following management interventions handled in your class/school?

   **a.** In-class time out

   **b.** Trip to the principal's office

   **c.** In-school suspension

   **d.** Home suspension

   What kinds of behaviors warrant each of these? How often are they used? What are the advantages and disadvantages of each?

# CHAPTER 12
# Effective Classroom Assessment

## OVERVIEW

The previous chapter focused on instructional strategies. Effective teachers help students learn by employing research-based strategies together with considered professional judgment, which has been termed the science and art of teaching. However, one question remains unanswered: How do we know if students have actually learned what we intended? We will never know if our instruction is truly effective until we can answer that question. Classroom assessment attempts to answer that question in an effective and efficient fashion. In this chapter, we examine the role of assessment, assessment patterns, testing, grading, homework, and communication with parents, all of which make up the topic of classroom assessment.

## MAIN IDEAS

### Classroom Assessment

Gathered information, together with decisions based on the information, is called *classroom assessment*.

Assessment allows for *instructional decisions* and *feedback to parents*, while permitting *instructional goals* to be met.

Effective assessment is *valid*, *systematic*, and *practical*.

### Assessment Patterns

*Performance assessments*, commonly used in elementary schools, examine actual samples of work.

Elementary teachers rely heavily on *commercially prepared* tests.

*Affective assessments* are weighted heavily in lower elementary grades.

*Objective tests* occur much more commonly than do *subjective tests* at all levels.

### Effective Testing

Learning is *significantly enhanced* by testing.

*Frequent* testing improves learning more than does infrequent testing.

Effective test preparation includes *specifying precisely* what the test will cover, providing for *practice*, and establishing *positive expectations*.

Tests are administered effectively when *clear directions* are given and tests are carefully *monitored*.

Effective teachers *return tests promptly*, *discuss results*, and *comment positively* about the outcomes.

### Assessment Systems

An *assessment system* includes grading practices, provisions for absences and tardies, homework, and all other factors in the assessment process.

Teachers commonly grade on either a *percentage* or *point* system.

*Open houses, parent–teacher conferences*, and *written descriptions of expectations* help communicate with parents.

*Interim progress reports* and *report cards* are the most common forms of communicating assessment results.

. . . . . . . . . . . . . . . . . . . . . . . . . . . . . . . . . . . .

Steve Vockel's second graders were working on the application of rules for adding *ing* to words. After putting several words on the board, Steve circulated among the students, making periodic comments.

"Check this one again, Nancy," he said when he saw that she had written *jumpping* on her paper. He continued this process for 10 minutes before he moved on to another activity.

Later he commented at lunch, "My kids just can't seem to get the rule straight. Either they forget about the long vowel so they double the consonant on a word like *blow* or they forget about two consonants at the end of a word like *jump* and they double the *p*. What do you do about it? If I spend much more time on it, we won't get all the objectives covered."

Terry Graham gives her chemistry class a one- or two-problem quiz every other day. She was scoring the students' answers to a problem in which the mass of an element in grams was converted to moles and number of atoms. "I need to do some more of these," she thought. "They can convert moles to grams, but they can't go the other way."

Marianne Generette's class was passing their prealgebra homework in to her. They had exchanged papers, scored the homework, and gone over the problems causing most difficulty.

"How many got all the problems right?" she asked the class.

"Good!" she responded to their show of hands. "You get this stuff. Remember that we have a test on this whole chapter on Friday, but now we're going to move on to subtraction of integers."

In each of the examples, the teacher was trying to gather information about his or her students' achievement and progress. A seatwork assignment for Steve, a quiz for Terry, and homework in Marianne's case provided the information they used to make instructional decisions, such as giving the students more practice in Terry's case or moving to a new topic in Marianne's. Periodically, even the conscientious gathering of data results in uncertainty, which was Steve's problem. He was caught in the dilemma of concluding that his students didn't understand the rule, but at the same time feeling the need to move on. There are no easy answers in these situations.

The information-gathering and decision-making processes these three teachers were involved in, called *classroom assessment*, is the focus of this chapter. These topics are covered in courses on measurement and evaluation, where students of education study test construction and analysis, item specifications, standardized testing, and a variety of other topics. Research examining classroom assessment, however, reveals that these courses have not met the real-world needs of classroom teachers (Stiggins and Bridgeford, 1985). For example, teachers — particularly those in elementary schools — rarely write their own test items, obtaining them instead from their textbooks, teachers' guides, or other supplementary materials. They are even less likely to prepare item specifications. Further, when using standardized tests, teachers tend to rely almost exclusively on the most common concepts related to testing, such as stanines, grade equivalents, and percentiles.

On the other hand, all teachers, regardless of grade level or subject matter area, make assessment decisions about their students and must be able to defend these decisions based on information. The purpose of this chapter is to help teachers design effective classroom assessment systems that are compatible with the realities of classroom practice.

## FUNCTIONS OF AN ASSESSMENT SYSTEM

Before we deal with the specifics of assessment, we must understand the functions that an assessment system performs. These can be divided into two broad categories — instructional and institutional.

We assess students to promote learning, the most important instructional function (Dempster, 1991). As we have seen earlier, practice and feedback are essential components of effective teaching, and assignments, quizzes, and tests provide opportunities for students to use the information and skills they have acquired. In this process, they not only practice but also receive feedback about how much they are learning. This feedback is helpful both to them and to other interested parties. As we saw in the introductory anecdotes, test results provide feedback to teachers and allow them to assess the effectiveness of their instruction. If students are not learning, the teacher needs to do something differently; if they are learning, the teacher can use this information to move forward, building on this knowledge base.

Student performance also provides valuable information for parents, allowing them to make decisions about homework, television, and a host of other school-related issues. Research documents what teachers have known all along — that a supportive home environment including a commitment to homework and a restriction on unlimited television contribute to learning (Walberg, 1984). An effective classroom assessment system helps parents gauge the academic progress of their children and make appropriate home-based decisions.

In addition to instructional functions, a classroom assessment system also fulfills institutional needs. Teachers work within school systems that give grades, send report cards to parents, promote students, and ultimately grant diplomas. Teachers' individual classroom assessment systems are an integral part of the overall system. In this respect, teachers need to be aware of the larger context in which they operate. Grades (e.g., *A, B, C, D*), one component of a classroom assessment system, are an example here. Teachers who give grades that are radically higher or lower than their peers give will hear about it, either from peers, students, parents, or the principal. As teachers design and implement their own assessment systems, they need to be aware of the context in which they are working.

# CHARACTERISTICS OF EFFECTIVE ASSESSMENT

Effective assessment in the real world of the classroom teacher has three interrelated features: It must be valid, systematic, and practical. To be valuable while remaining professionally sound, the assessment system must possess all three features.

## Validity

**Validity** means that the assessment measures what it is supposed to measure. It includes "the appropriateness of the interpretations made from test scores and other evaluation results" (Gronlund and Linn, 1990, p. 47).

One way of thinking about validity is to ask, "Is the assessment consistent with the specific goals being assessed?" The opposite is surprisingly common. We have all had teachers who taught one thing and then tested something else. This not only upsets students but also makes the test invalid. Another way of thinking of validity is in terms of *curricular alignment* (Cohen, 1987). This means that instruction is congruent with curricular goals and tests are congruent with both. In the case studies at the beginning of the chapter, Steve's assignment would be valid if one of his language arts goals was for students to learn how to add *ing* endings to words. In a similar way, the quizzes and assignments of the other two teachers would be valid if they matched their goals and instruction. When a logical match exists between measurement procedures and what was intended and taught, we have validity.

Validity can be compromised by the way we administer our assessment procedures. For example, suppose we are teaching a concept and we ask students to give us some examples as we apply the concept to a new situation. A volunteer raises her hand and supplies an excellent example. We repeat the process with the same result. We do it once more, and again we get a very good example. What is our tendency? Naturally, we conclude that the class understands the concept. However, we have heard from only three students, and further, they were volunteers. We have little idea about the class's overall understanding and particularly that of the less able or more reluctant responders. Our conclusion easily could be invalid.

How common is this tendency? Research indicates that it is more common than we would like to believe. As teachers make the routine decisions necessary to keep a class or lesson moving, they tend to gather group data; that is, they tend to rely on the responses and nonverbal behavior of a subset of the class for feedback as the basis for deciding to repeat instruction or to move on to the next topic (Dahlof and Lundgren, 1970). A systematic attempt to gather assessment data from *all* students, and not just volunteers, would make the process more valid.

Other, more dangerous factors can detract from validity. In Chapter 3, we saw that the way teachers plan is partially in response to their need for simplification.

The same thing occurs in assessment. Teachers tend to assess students on the basis of characteristics that are easily measured, such as their behavior and the number of assignments they complete rather than the quality of the work, the difficulty of the assignment, or the appropriate weight of one assignment compared to another (Whitmer, 1983). Research indicates that teachers further simplify the assessment process by forming impressions of student ability early in the year; once formed, the impression is not likely to change (Calderhead, 1983). Teachers also tend to fix on initial impressions of students that are often based on inaccurate information and then use subsequent information to corroborate their initial impressions (Peterson and Barger, 1985). One way to guard against these tendencies is to design and implement a systematic assessment system.

## Systematic Assessment

An effective assessment system gathers information frequently and systematically. In our example with the three students volunteering responses, the measurements were not systematic, and conclusions based on them would be suspect. Informal measurements such as these are valuable but should be combined with more formal measures, such as a quiz or a verbal item directing *each student* to write one or two examples on a piece of paper and turn it in. This form of assessment would be more systematic and therefore more effective. Of our three introductory case studies, Terry's was the most systematic, and Steve's observations of the children doing their seatwork was the least. We certainly do not suggest that Steve abandon his practice of monitoring students' work, but we do suggest that he gather some additional information through the frequent and systematic monitoring of *all* students' assignments.

To be useful, assessments need to be administered frequently. The longer the delay between teaching and testing, the less useful are the test results (Glaser, 1987). For example, a short quiz given and graded at the end of a presentation provides immediate feedback about learning. The teacher can use this information to plan for the next day. This is why classroom questions are an invaluable assessment source. In contrast, one test at the end of a unit comes too late to adjust instructional procedures.

This has important implications for teachers. Students need ample opportunities for practice, and both teachers and students benefit from the feedback. This is true for all students, and especially those who are younger or of lower ability. Effective assessment involves frequently graded homework assignments and regular quizzes. In contrast, a course with only a final exam or one end-of-the-quarter term paper, with little or no feedback, fails to meet the instructional needs of either students or the teacher.

## Practical Assessment

A practical assessment system needs to be efficient. Assessment is one component of effective teaching, but it cannot take so much time and energy that other components are compromised. Elementary teachers are responsible for reading, math, science, social studies, spelling, language arts, and sometimes art, music, and physical education. Middle, junior high, and secondary teachers have five sections of 25 to 35 students a day, often with two or three preparations. Teachers have no time for assessment procedures that are not usable.

The assessments that each of the teachers in our introductory case studies made were economical. Steve quickly wrote the words on the board, and he easily scored the responses. Terry only took minutes to prepare her chemistry problem, and Marianne had the students score their own papers. In each case, the assessment took little instructional time, and it took little teacher energy.

# TEACHERS' ASSESSMENT PATTERNS: DEVELOPMENTAL CONSIDERATIONS

To begin this section, we ask the question, "Is effective assessment the same for all classrooms?" Research says no and identifies grade level and subject-matter area as two key variables that affect the form assessment takes (Stiggins and Bridgeford, 1985).

In the elementary schools, three assessment characteristics are predominant:

1. Performance assessment, where the teacher evaluates an actual sample of students' work, is very important at the lower levels, but its use declines later. Examples of performance assessments include writing essays in English, using a map in social studies, and performing a lab experiment with equipment in science.
2. Elementary teachers depend heavily on commercially prepared and published tests (Herman and Dorr–Bremme, 1982).
3. Affective goals, such as "Works and plays well with others," are weighted heavily in the elementary schools (Salmon–Cox, 1981). Our experience confirms these findings. In examining a sample of kindergarten progress reports sent home to parents, we found that over one third of the categories were devoted to personal or social factors.

As students progress through the grades, assessment patterns change, and the following patterns become dominant.

1. Teachers do not rely on published tests to the extent that elementary teachers do, choosing instead to prepare their own.
2. Teachers depend more heavily on tests than on performance measures for their assessments.
3. Objective tests, such as multiple choice and fill-in-the-blanks, become more popular than subjective measures, such as essay tests.
4. The emphasis on grades for cognitive performance increases, with correspondingly less emphasis given to affective goals.

Let's examine these characteristics in more detail.

The lower elementary grades are characterized by considerable agreement about essential content and skills. Commercially prepared tests are useful here because a high degree of consensus about the curriculum exists. Later, the curriculum becomes more diverse, and teaching becomes more unique. One eighth-grade American history teacher's approach and emphasis will be different from another's, and consequently, commercially prepared tests no longer meet each teacher's individual needs. As a result, teachers tend to personalize the assessment process by preparing their own tests.

The press for simplification remains, however. Teachers tend to prepare and use tests in the least time-consuming way. Fleming and Chambers (1983) reached the following conclusions based on an analysis of nearly 400 teachermade tests encompassing thousands of test items:

1. Just over one percent of all teacher-made test items are essay questions.
2. The most frequently used item format is short answer, such as:

   Which two planets in our solar system have orbits that overlap?

   _____

3. Matching items are the next most commonly used by teachers. For example:

   Put the correct letter in the blank in front of each numbered item.

   | | |
   |---|---|
   | _____ **1.** Collapse of the Byzantine Empire | **A.** Conducted to retake the Holy Land from the Moslems. |
   | _____ **2.** Crusades | **B.** Marked the first and last time England was conquered. |
   | _____ **3.** The Great Schism | **C.** The church was split into the Roman Catholic and Greek Orthodox units. |
   | _____ **4.** The Battle of Hastings | **D.** Constantinople fell to the Ottoman Turks. |
   | | **E.** The Spanish fleet was completely destroyed, ending Spain's expansion into the new world. |
   | | **F.** Laid a foundation for human and civil rights. |

4. Nearly eighty percent of all test items measure *knowledge* of facts, terms, rules, or principles with few items measuring students' ability to make applications. Junior high school teachers are the worst offenders. Nearly ninety-four percent of their items were written at the knowledge level compared to sixty-nine percent for both elementary and senior high teachers.
5. Further, once items are constructed, teachers tend to reuse them without analysis and revision (Gullickson and Ellwein, 1985).

Why do these patterns exist? There are two primary reasons. The first is the need for efficiency and simplicity that we discussed earlier, and the second is a feeling of inadequacy (which may also explain why elementary teachers depend so heavily on commercially prepared tests). Teachers are insecure about their test-constructing abilities (Carter, 1984), and their tests have been criticized for being ambiguous and written at a low intellectual level (Carter, 1984; Fleming and Chambers, 1983).

With these factors in mind, the research findings are not surprising. Teachers write recall questions because it is easiest to write and grade items at this level. When the efforts of constructing and scoring items are combined, the easiest formats to use are short answer and matching. Essay questions, while easy to construct, are extremely difficult to score, and teachers are notoriously inconsistent in comparing one student to another. Some evidence indicates that even the physical attractiveness of the writer and penmanship can have an impact on the scoring of an essay (Bull and Stevens, 1979).

In contrast, multiple-choice items are easy to score, but good ones are very difficult to construct; true–false questions, while appearing easy to prepare on the surface, are actually very demanding if they are prepared well. This, in combination with the widespread criticism of the format (i.e., the ease of guessing), explains why true–false is not widely used.

In addition to greater use of teachermade tests, there is also greater emphasis on grades, accountability, and quality control at the upper levels. Often at the lower levels, formal grades (e.g., *A*, *B*, *C*) are replaced with descriptive statements (e.g., "Can print all the letters of the alphabet clearly," or "Can count from one to ten orally"). Later, more emphasis is placed on the accountability aspects of grading. For example, in the late 1980s the state of Texas instituted a "no-pass, no-play" provision for high school football. Football fans were incensed and critics argued that the marginal students affected by the provision are the very ones who needed success experiences in areas like sports. Their arguments were not heeded. Other states have pushed the accountability issue further by requiring state competency tests before promotion to higher levels or graduation. Teachers need to be aware of these pressures as they design their own assessment systems.

As we said earlier, measurement and evaluation differences also exist across subject-matter areas. Teachers in science and social studies tend to use more objective assessments, while those in the language arts—including reading, writing, and speaking—make greater use of performance assessments. These differences have more to do with the subject matter and how teachers teach them than anything else. It is easier to make up objective items in more content-oriented areas, whereas skill areas lend themselves better to performance assessments.

# CLASSROOM ASSESSMENT: TESTING

Before we examine effective testing practice, let us consider what the research literature tells us about the relationship between testing and achievement.

## Testing, Achievement, and Motivation

The effects of testing as it relates to student achievement have been controversial for years. In spite of the controversy, however, the movement toward greater teacher and school accountability has resulted in more rather than less testing. Students in some states are now faced with a national standardized test such as the Stanford Achievement Test; statewide assessments exist in some areas, such as math, science, reading, writing, and computer literacy, with a trend toward testing in all the content areas; and district-designed minimum-level skills tests are also in use. The federal government is even getting into the act. *America 2000: An Education Strategy* (1991), a policy initiative addressing the issue of an increased federal role for education, proposes national standards in core curricula and a new (voluntary) nationwide examination system (Sewall, 1991). Extensive testing is with us, and it is likely to remain so in the foreseeable future. Further, rigorous academic testing is the norm in industrialized countries other than the United States (Cheney, 1988).

But what does research say about the impact of testing on learning? The relationship is strong and robust; students learn more in classes where they're tested thoroughly and often (Bangert–Drowns, Kulik, and Kulik, 1988; Dempster, 1991). In fact, the relationship is so strong that Elton and Laurillard (1979) were moved to state, "Here is something approaching a law of learning behavior for students; namely that the quickest way to change learning is to change the assessment system" (p. 100).

Linking assessment to motivation is even more controversial, since ideally students should be motivated to learn for learning's own sake. Some critics even argue that testing actually detracts from motivation. In the real world, however, the evidence runs counter to those arguments. Students study harder and are more motivated in classes in which they're frequently and thoroughly tested (Crooks, 1988).

The type of test is important, however. If tests are arbitrary or invalid, the positive effect they can have on motivation is eliminated. If students know that the tests focus on the mere recall of factual information, they will study the same way. Assessment affects not only how much students study but also the way they study (Crooks, 1988).

## Effective Testing

In this section, we look at how teachers can make testing more effective by the way they prepare their students for tests, administer the tests, and analyze the results. As we will see, these strategies apply to any item format and content area, and to most grade levels. To begin, let us look at a teacher preparing his class for a unit test. His goals for the unit were for students to understand the concept of culture, to apply it to various groups in Central America and Mexico, and to know basic facts about these countries.

Andrew Robinson is a seventh-grade social studies teacher who is finishing his cultural unit on Mexico and Central America. He teaches five sections of geography. We join him with his first-period class.

"Okay, everyone," Andrew began, "listen carefully, now. We are finished with our study of Central America and its cultural traditions. I've reminded you every day since last Wednesday that we're having a test tomorrow."

"Oh, Mr. Robinson, do we have to?" Sheila groaned in mock protest.

"Too bad. Mean Mr. Robinson gives a test every week," Andrew smiled back at Sheila. "Just think. We have it tomorrow, I'll give it back to you on Friday, and I'll even give you the weekend off."

"ALL RIGHT!" the class shouted.

Andrew held up his hand to settle them down and went on, "Now, let's think about the test. First, let's talk about some individual items; then, I'll give you an overview of the test. I'm going to challenge you on some of the questions, but you've all been working hard, and I know you'll do well. Every time you've had a tough test, you've tried harder and done better."

He continued, "We've been comparing cultures, and I want you to get more practice in making those comparisons, plus I want you to keep working on expressing yourselves in writing. Take a look at this."

Andrew displayed the following paragraphs for the students on the overhead projector:

> Read the description, and identify (in the example) the characteristics of culture that were discussed in class.
>
> Jorgé (pronounced Horhay) is a small Mexican boy who is growing up on a farm in the mountains outside Mexico City. He rises early, goes to the small chapel in his home for his morning prayers, and then breakfasts on a large meal of beans and tortillas made from the products of the family farm. His mother always asks him if the Virgin Mary gave him her blessings, and Jorgé always says "yes" with a smile. Jorgé walks to school a mile down the dusty road. He leaves as his father goes out to cultivate the corn that is the primary source of income for the family. Jorgé's mother then milks the goats and turns the rich cream into delicious butter and cheese.
>
> In the early afternoon, Jorgé comes home from school, and the family talks quietly in their dialect, which is Spanish with some influence from the Aztecs. As the day cools, Jorgé often plays soccer with boys in the nearby village while his father strums his guitar and his mother hums the rhythmic Latin melodies they all love. They go to bed shortly after sunset to prepare for the next day.

"Read the example carefully," Andrew directed his students.

"Now, take out a piece of paper, and answer the question that is given in the directions," he continued after waiting for a few moments.

Andrew watched as the students studied the screen and worked silently for about 10 minutes. Finally, he began, "Someone tell me what they wrote as a response."

"It says in the example that they eat beans and tortillas, and we discussed the food a group eats as part of their culture," Judy responded.

"Yes, very good, Judy," Andrew praised. "Notice, everyone, that Judy didn't just say 'food,' but instead, identified the food they eat in the example. This indicates that she is relating the information in the example to what we discussed in class."

The class went on with students identifying the religion, type of work, and recreation in Jorgé's family.

"They're in good shape," Andrew thought as he listened to their analysis. He went on, "That's all very good. Now, on the test tomorrow, you're going to have to do something like this with another example. Remember, when you write your responses, you're going to have to relate the example to what we have discussed in class, just as we did with Jorgé and his family."

He continued, "You're also going to need to know the countries' climates, natural resources, and physical features, as well as be able to locate them on a map and identify their capitals. For example, what country is this?" he asked, displaying an outline map on the overhead projector and pointing to Nicaragua. "Mike?"

"Nicaragua!" Mike responded instantly.

"Give us another example," the class requested.

"Okay," Andrew smiled and displayed the following on the overhead:

We are about 17 degrees north of the equator and are about in the middle of this country. We are in the most populous country in Central America. Most of the people here are of Indian or mixed European and Indian descent. This description best fits:

a. Belize
b. Guatemala
c. Honduras
d. Mexico

"What is the answer? Mary?" Andrew asked.

"It's Guatemala," Mary said nervously after some hesitation.

"Yes, excellent, Mary!" Andrew encouraged, knowing that Mary appeared to be genuinely nervous in anticipating tests and frequently missed them, the following day producing a note saying she had been sick. "Now, tell us why it's Guatemala," Andrew continued. "Sue?"

"First, 17 degrees only goes through sort of the middle of Guatemala and Belize," Sue responded.

"Also, Guatemala is the most populous country in Central America, and they are of Indian descent," Marsha added.

"Now, I'd like to share with you an outline that I used in preparing the test. It should give you a clear picture of how to spend your study time." With that, he displayed Figure 12.1 on an overhead.

"Will the essay question be like the one we practiced on, Mr. Robinson?" asked Tony.

"Good question. Yes, the same format, but I'll give you different information to work with." With that, he concluded his review.

We joined him the next morning before school. He came in the classroom before the students arrived, and, even though his room is quite crowded, he moved the desks as far apart as possible and had them ready when the students walked in. He opened a window and then changed his mind, reacting to the noise of a lawn mower outside.

**FIGURE 12.1** Test Breakdown Matrix

| | Type of Item |
|---|---|
| Facts about Countries:<br>  Capitals<br>  Climate<br>  Natural resources<br>  Physical features | Fill-in-the-Blank<br>Multiple Choice<br>25 Questions × 1 = 25 Points |
| Cultures of Countries | Short Answer<br>3 Questions × 5 = 15 Points |
| Cultures of Countries | Essay<br>10 Points |

As the class filed into the room, he directed them to their seats, asking for their attention. When everyone was looking at him, he instructed them to clear everything off their desks.

He then said, "Tear the last sheet off the back of the test and write your name on it. Do that right now. Now, as you take the test, put all your answers on this sheet. When you're finished, turn the test over, and I'll come around and pick it up. Then, begin the assignment on the board. I've written that it's due on Tuesday to remind you. If anyone gets too warm as you're working, raise your hand, and I'll turn on the fan," he continued, referring to the large floor fan at the front of the room.

"Work carefully on the test, now," he said with a smile. "You're all well prepared, and I know you will do your best. You have the whole period, so you should have plenty of time."

Andrew stood in the front corner of the room, scanning the class as the students worked. As he watched, he noticed Mary periodically looking out the window for several seconds at a time. Finally, he went over to her desk, looked at her paper, and whispered as he touched her shoulder, "It looks like you're moving along very well. Try and concentrate on the test a little harder now, and I'll bet you do fine." He moved quietly back to the front of the room.

Suddenly, the intercom broke into the silence. "Mr. Robinson," the voice said, "Mrs. Brown [the principal] needs to see you for a moment. Could you come down to the office?"

"I'll come down at the end of the period," Andrew said back to the box. "I'm in the middle of a test right now."

"Thank you," the voice responded, and the intercom was then silent.

As the students finished their papers, Andrew moved to their desks, picking up the tests, and stacking them on a table in front of the room. The students then began the assignment Andrew had referred to just before they began taking the test.

Friday morning, the students filed into the room and asked as they came in, "Do you have our tests finished yet?"

"Yes, I do," Andrew responded. "I was up half the night scoring them."

"How did we do?"

"Mostly, very well, but there were some problem areas, and I want to go over them this morning, so when you have another test you won't run into the same problems," and he quickly handed the students back their tests.

"What does this mean that you wrote on my paper, 'You identified the cultural feature *recreation*, but you didn't say what it was in the example'?" Sondra asked from the back of the room.

"Remember on Wednesday we said that you needed to identify both the cultural characteristic and the example of it from the description, like soccer and music from the example with Jorgé that we analyzed," Andrew responded. "Antonio swam, dived, and fished, and you needed to say that in your essay. We'll discuss the essay question in a bit, but let's start from the beginning of the test."

"A number of you had trouble with item 15," he continued. "Many of you took choice *c*. What is the correct answer? Ann?"

Andrew then discussed several of the items, in each case describing what was wrong with the incorrect choices. He discussed the essay question in detail and finally said, "I have placed two exceptionally good essay responses on the board for everyone to examine. We'll discuss these tomorrow. I will be here after school today and tomorrow morning before class. If you have any other questions, come and see me either time."

With that, he picked up the tests, putting his original copy with notes for revising several of the items in a special file folder, and he began his lesson for the day.

Let's look now at what Andrew did and relate this to what the research literature tells us about effective testing.

## Preparing the Students

As he prepared his students for the test, Andrew did three things that helped his students achieve at their best: (1) He specified precisely what the test would cover; (2) he gave them a chance to practice the kinds of behaviors they would be expected to demonstrate when they took the actual test; and (3) he tried to establish positive expectations in the students as they anticipated the test. These factors work in combination with each other to ensure the best possible results. Let us look at each now.

Specifying the test content offers security for students by providing a structured set of content and skills to be mastered, which in turn leads to higher achievement (Carrier and Titus, 1981). Further, it can help reduce test anxiety (Everson, Tobias, Hartman, and Gourgey, 1991). Andrew specified skills students would have to demonstrate when he said he wanted them to have more practice in making comparisons, and he reinforced the description when he said they would "need to know the climate, natural resources, physical features. . . ."

In addition, he shared with them an overview of the test, including major content to be covered and the types of items to be expected. This outline, called a **table of specifications**, serves two functions. First, it helps teachers systematically plan their tests. A cross grid with content on one axis and item type or level (e.g., high versus low or knowledge versus application) on the other ensures that the test accurately reflects the teacher's goals and instruction. Aligning the test with instruction ensures validity.

A table of specifications also serves an informational function. Once constructed, this outline can be shared with students to help them allocate their study efforts.

Just describing what students would need to know may not provide sufficient guidance for some students (particularly those in middle school or younger), so Andrew did not stop at that point. Instead, he immediately illustrated the description with a sample exercise that paralleled those they would experience on the test. He offered a practice essay item and provided practice with a multiple-choice format. Doing this is very important. When students take a test, two things are always being measured — their understanding of the content being covered on the test *and* their ability to respond to the format being used. If the second feature interferes with the first, the validity of the test is reduced. Practice with the anticipated format can increase students' test-taking skills, which in turn reduces the impact of the format on the students' performances. These effects have been confirmed experimentally with young children (Kalechstein, Kalechstein, and Doctor, 1981) and with cross-cultural groups (Dreisbach and Keogh, 1982). As students mature, their test-taking skills tend to increase (Slakter, Koehler, and Hampton, 1970). Andrew then followed through by presenting items that were consistent with the content he taught and the sample items he presented as review.

Andrew established high expectations for his students when he said, "I know you'll do well. Every time you've had a tough test, you've tried harder and done better." Good (1987), in a review of 2 decades of studies examining the relationship between expectations and performance, concluded that positive expectations can influence student test performance.

## Administering the Test

Now, look at Andrew's behavior the day he administered the test. He got to the room early and arranged the seating in advance to ensure as much distance as possible between the desks, and he arranged the overall physical environment to minimize distractions, such as the lawn mower outside. Distractions can affect test performance, especially for younger and low-ability students (Trentham, 1975). Teachers administering standardized tests often deal with this problem by hanging a sign on the closed door.

When the students got into the room and were seated, Andrew waited until he had everyone's attention and then gave clear and precise directions for taking the test, collecting the papers, and doing the assigned work after the test was finished.

As the students progressed with the test, Andrew carefully monitored their behavior. When he noticed that Mary seemed distracted, he went to her, provided encouragement, and urged her to increase her concentration. Test-anxious people tend to lose their focus on the task at hand, and to become preoccupied with factors not relevant to the test (Nottelman and Hill, 1977). Mary's behavior fit this pattern, so Andrew intervened as soon as he noticed her not attending to the test.

As the test progressed, he maintained his presence in the room and refused to go to the main office until after the students were finished. Unfortunately, cheating is part of classroom reality, and some students will cheat if the opportunity presents itself. Interestingly, external factors such as the teacher's leaving the room and the emotional climate of the class contribute more to student cheating than the inherent characteristics of the students themselves. Further, outright appeals to honesty do not seem to help. In one study involving fourth, fifth, and sixth graders, researchers made what they called an informative appeal to honesty, stressing the importance of doing their own work so the test results would be accurate; still, nearly two thirds cheated. In the same study, two alternatives seemed to work — threats of punishment and a classroom discussion about cheating (Bushway and Nash, 1977). The latter, combined with physical support from the teacher, appears to be the most promising solution to this problem.

## Examining the Results

Turn now to Andrew's actions after he administered the test. First, he scored and returned the test the following day; second, he discussed the test results; and finally, he made generally positive comments about the students' performance. All of these behaviors have positive effects on achievement. Students need to receive feedback on their work, whether it be a quiz or homework, and this feedback should occur as soon as possible. Graded homework has an effect on learning that is almost three times as powerful as ungraded homework (Walberg, 1984). It is not clear whether this effect is due to students' working harder when being held accountable or to the added information connected to feedback.

We know that students need frequent opportunities for practice and feedback and that this feedback should occur as quickly as possible. But given the time demands of other instructional activities, how can teachers do this? Some possible solutions include the following:

1. Students grading papers in class as a whole-class exercise
2. Student aides (e.g., older or advanced students)
3. Parent volunteers.

None of these is as good as the teacher's grading and providing direct feedback on every sample of student work, but when combined with careful monitoring by the teacher, these alternatives offer one way to avoid mountains of paperwork *and* can provide essential feedback to students.

In discussing the test, Andrew carefully reviewed the items the students had most commonly missed, providing corrective feedback in each case. In discussing objective items, feedback should be strategic, and incorrect answers, if missed by a large number of students, should be explained. Correct items can be skipped over unless the information is important for later study (Barringer and Gholson, 1979). This targets valuable classroom time on trouble spots.

For the essay questions, Andrew provided specific corrective feedback in the cases of incorrect or incomplete answers. In addition, he supplied examples of excellent responses for students to read and the class to discuss. The combination of providing model answers and discussing them is a good way to teach students to improve their essay responses.

Finally, Andrew made positive comments about the general performance of the class on the test. In a study of seventh-grade classrooms, students who were told they did well on a test performed better on a subsequent measure than did those who were told they did poorly, even though the two groups did equally well on the first test (Bridgeman, 1974).

## Classroom Testing: Implications for Teachers

Where does all this leave us as teachers? Based on our study of the literature and experience with teachers in classrooms, we make the following recommendations:

**1.** Test thoroughly and often. Be certain that abundant objective information is gathered about *each student*. Contrary to some authors who decry the use of paper and pencil measurements, we believe that when they are used properly, they are an invaluable source of information for teachers. While they should not be the sole form of measurement, not using them on the grounds of potential damage to students simply has no support in the research literature. Much of the content taught in our schools is amenable to paper and pencil tests, so take advantage of the efficiency in this form of measurement.

Also, the literature indicates that teachers tend to form expectations of students, retain the initial impressions, and act on them. Individual students have a greater chance of a "fair shake" on a test than on any other form of assessment.

**2.** Be certain that instruction and testing are aligned; the topics and content emphasized in class should be the same ones emphasized on the test. This call for validity may be self-evident, but interestingly, teachers will conduct learning activities and then later create a test with only a general thought to the content that was covered, so instruction and testing do not receive consistent emphasis. A table of specifications outlining test content can be invaluable here.

**3.** During instruction and review sessions, give students a chance to practice the kinds of behaviors they will be expected to perform on the test. Andrew did an excellent job in this respect. He gave the students sample items, reviewed the items, and then gave similar items on the actual test.

**4.** After you give a test, hand it back to the students, carefully review commonly missed items, and then collect the copies again. You do not have time to create new test items continually. The learning derived from review of the test comes primarily from the discussion and not from the students' having the tests available for further review. The discussion, if properly focused, also can help students improve their test-taking skills.

**5.** To be efficient, follow the procedure Andrew used in our introductory case: File a master copy, write notes on the copy, and revise the items for further use when student feedback indicates the item is misleading. This may seem like a laborious and time-consuming process, but help is on the way. With the increasing use of computers, the ability to store, modify, and retrieve test items quickly is now a reality (Bluhm, 1987). Even without a computer, items can be efficiently modified and improved for later use if teachers make the initial effort. The primary problem is that teachers often fail to collect tests or write notes on the master copy and then store it so they cannot find it again. Our experience with teachers indicates that this simple organization-and-storage system is the primary reason teachers do not revise their tests.

**6.** Also, in the interest of efficiency, choose the objective format for outcomes that can be measured with either essay or objective items. Use essay items when you want to measure student ability to organize and present information or make and defend an argument. Keep essay items relatively short and describe clearly what the essay is to contain. When Andrew used his essay item on the test, he first prepared his students by practicing on a sample item and then specified precisely what they would be required to do on the essay. This helped them develop their essay-writing skills while ensuring that their answers on the tests would be valid indicators of what they knew.

**7.** Establish positive expectations for students as they anticipate the test. This requires sensitivity and careful judgment. As with praise, continually using the same phrase or exhortation with the students will soon become hollow and empty if it is insincere or if their performance is not good. Tests need to be constructed so that students have an opportunity to demonstrate what they have learned. The key is to establish the expectation and then manage to have the class meet it, which, in turn, serves to reinforce a similar expectation for the next experience.

This concludes our discussion of tests and testing, important components of many classroom assessment systems. But, as we saw earlier, a total system is more than just tests or quizzes. Integrating tests and quizzes into a total system is discussed in the next section.

# DESIGNING AN ASSESSMENT SYSTEM

Let us return to an idea that we introduced earlier. A classroom assessment system has multiple audiences. In addition to your own need to know how much students are learning, the students themselves, parents, and principals need information about achievement. Designing a comprehensive system that gathers information and communicates this information to the various audiences is the topic of this section.

Where should we start? There are so many decisions to make, such as the number of tests and quizzes, the kinds of assignments, the weight of each, and grading, that it is hard to know where to begin.

One way to begin the planning process is to analyze the context in which you are working. What kinds of evaluation information will be expected of you and when will it be due? A starting point is to examine a report card that you will be expected to use. (We look at several kinds of report cards later in this chapter.) In analyzing a report card, the following questions apply:

What areas are evaluated?

How is student performance described (e.g., letter grade, percentage, or descriptive statement)?

How frequently do grades need to be given?

How are affective dimensions like cooperation and following rules reported?

What about tardiness and absence?

These may seem like mundane concerns, but we know first-year teachers who were only weeks away from their first report cards and conferences with parents when they realized they were expected to give grades in penmanship and citizenship. They scurried to gather the necessary information!

After you have inspected a report card, it is helpful to talk with other teachers to learn about prevailing attitudes and patterns. Are there any pitfalls to avoid? How do the grade distributions of other teachers vary? What is the policy on tardiness and absence? What if these are unexcused? (Some districts include unexcused absences as an integral part of the grading system; others specifically prohibit the practice.) Although the legal basis for this practice is unclear, teachers should understand the evaluation policies and procedures in their district (Hills, 1985).

Your principal is another valuable resource. He or she can tell you the district's expectations. Are there any district guidelines to help you in the design of your system? Are you expected to administer any state or district instruments? Are there restrictions or requirements in grading practices? Does the principal want to see your report cards before you hand them out to students? How are grades recorded in permanent folders? Answers to these questions help frame later decisions as you evaluate your students.

Now you know what is expected of you, but you still have not clarified your own ideas about assessment and the realities of putting these ideas into practice. At this stage, we recommend the "blank-page-and-calendar" approach. The calendar helps frame your decisions in terms of real-life constraints — when the first grading period ends. This is also a good time to consult any long-term plans that you have made. You will recall from the chapter on planning that these often occur in the form of topics and dates. These topics help frame your evaluation decisions in terms of unit dimensions. Keeping in mind the essential characteristics of valid, systematic, frequent, and economical, you need to address these questions about your evaluation instruments:

What kinds?
How many?
How often?

Measurement routines can be helpful in structuring your assessment system. We have already discussed one effective routine in elementary math:

Mon.: Review last week's work; introduce new concepts

Tues., Weds., Thurs.: Development of major ideas with daily seatwork and homework

Fri.: Review and quiz.

One teacher we interviewed who used this type of system had this to say:

The children like it and the parents like it. They all know exactly what to expect. I grade all their homework, and send it home with them in a packet every Friday. I have very little problem with the children not doing their homework. Their parents get on them to be sure the homework is done.

She went on to say that she believed that the amount of time she spent in looking at their homework papers was well spent because she knew what problems each child was having. She also commented that her kids' achievement test scores were consistently the highest in the school for their ability level. Research supports her practice; when homework and quizzes are integrated into a systematic instructional system, students benefit (Rosenshine, 1987).

## Grades and Grading

An essential part of the planning process is the consideration of grades. You already know the form that these will take on report cards; your job now is to translate the various assignments, quizzes, projects, and tests into a comprehensive system. Two major ways of doing this are summarized in Table 12.1.

**TABLE 12.1**  Weighted Scores and Point Grading Systems

| *Point System* | | *Weighted Scores* | |
|---|---|---|---|
| Every graded assignment or quiz is given a point value. These are then added up to provide a total score. | | Every assignment is given a letter grade and all grades are then weighted. | |
| *Example:* | | *Example:* | |
| Assignments (20 × 10 pts.) | 200 | Assignments (20) | 25% |
| Quizzes (8 × 25 pts.) | 200 | Quizzes (8) | 25% |
| Tests (4 × 100 pts.) | 400 | Tests (4) | 50% |
| Total possible points = | 800 | Total = | 100% |
| Grade Range | | | |
| A  750–800 | | | |
| B  700–750 | | | |
| C  650–700 | | | |
| D  600–650 | | | |

A **point system** is fairly straightforward; the importance of each assignment and quiz is reflected in the points allocated. Then, these are added up and grades are given. Weighted scores are slightly more complex. Let us see how one system might work. We will use Steve Vockel's exercises on the board as the illustration. Suppose he wrote 10 words on the board and then scored the students' papers. Now imagine that he gave another short exercise of five items and a third of eight items. In scoring these items, teachers typically convert the raw scores to a percentage. A student who got 8 of 10 correct in the first case would have a score of 80 written in the grade book; 2 of 5 in the second case would be a score of 40; and 7 of 8 in the third case would be a score of 88. Teachers then typically find an average to arrive at the final score on which the student's grade is based. In this case, the student's average would be a 69, which in most grading systems is a *D*. However, in reality, the student responded to a total of 23 items, 17 of which he answered correctly. His actual percentage is 74—five points higher and a *C* in most grading systems. The problem with the system as we have just illustrated it is that each of the exercises is given the same weight, even though the number of items is markedly different—10, 5, and 8, respectively.

If this system seems flawed, why is it so common? Two reasons are often cited. First, it is simple, and as we have noted repeatedly, the need to simplify is very powerful. Second, both students and parents tend to prefer the percentage system because it is simpler for them also. We have talked to teachers who have used the raw scores, converting to a percentage only at the end of a marking period, and later went back to the percentage system throughout because of pressure from students.

In assigning grades within either system, teachers have two options. One, called *criterion based*, uses preestablished percentages or number totals for grades (e.g., 90–100, *A*; 80–90, *B*; 70–80, *C*; etc.). The advantage of this approach is that it communicates grading standards clearly and is noncompetitive; students strive against the criteria rather than each other. The difficulty with this approach is that it requires accurate calibration of the difficulty level of assignments and tests. If this does not occur, most students in the class can end up with *A*s or with *F*s, depending on whether the difficulty level was too low or too high. The alternative, called *norm referenced*, compares a student's score on a quiz with other students' performance. Grading "on the curve" is an example here. Many beginning teachers use a flexible curve system, assigning grades at each quiz or test and then adjusting totals at the end of the grading period. This has the advantage of letting students know where they stand throughout the grading period while still providing the teacher with the flexibility to use professional decision making at the end.

## Seatwork and Homework

Another major grading decision to make is how to handle homework in the assessment process. The research literature clearly indicates that use of seatwork and homework has a positive impact on learning (McGreal, 1985; Walberg, 1984), but it provides little guidance about how to integrate it into an assessment system.

A major issue here is accountability, a concept we have discussed in other contexts. Students need to feel responsible for doing the homework and need to understand that homework is crucial to learning. They also need to be rewarded by words and actions for their efforts on the homework. Implementing a viable system that does not bury you under mounds of paperwork is the problem. You have a series of available options:

1. Assign homework, grade it yourself, and record the scores. This is the best option, because it gives you the most insight into the students' work. However, it is demanding. Many teachers don't have the time to go through all the students' papers on a regular basis. This option is more viable if you have a teacher aide or a parent volunteer who can help you with some of the routine work.

2. Assign homework, select one or two samples from the assignment, have the students turn in those problems, and record the score on those problems. This is a compromise. The teacher scores the homework, but the amount is reduced.

3. Have the students exchange papers in class, and score all the homework as a group. This saves time and gives students immediate feedback. However, it can be time consuming, and if the teacher discusses the material as the homework is scored, the students don't get feedback, because they aren't looking at their own papers.

4. Assign homework, give the students credit for having done the homework, whether or not it is correct, and then use class time to cover material the students found difficult. This option has the advantage of allowing the students to check their own work and correct their own mistakes. On the other hand, some teachers argue that students do not try as hard in this system, because there is no penalty for incorrect answers. Others argue that they perform better, because success is guaranteed.

5. Assign homework, collect it at random intervals, and score and mark it. This option reduces the teacher's workload, but the homework must be collected regularly or students tend to stop doing it.

6. Do not grade homework, but give frequent short quizzes based on the material covered in the homework. This was the option Terry Graham chose for her chemistry class. This option is more viable with older students who understand the relationship between doing the homework and doing well on the quizzes.

Which system should you adopt? We recommend that you talk to other teachers and experiment to find out what works best for you.

# COMMUNICATION

Communication is an integral part of an effective assessment system. At the beginning of the school year, you need to explain to students what is expected of them and share this information with parents. As information is gathered throughout the school year, it needs to be shared with both students and parents. Ways of doing this are the focus of this section.

## Communication: Expectations

We have seen earlier how positive and negative teacher expectations can influence learning. For positive expectations to affect learning, both students and parents must know what these expectations are; effective communication is critical. Further, researchers have documented the importance of the home–school partnership, and effective communication with parents is a critical dimension of this partnership (Brookover et al., 1982). Teachers use a variety of ways to communicate their expectations to parents and students.

**Written Communication**   In the primary grades, because the children are young, the communication may be aimed more directly at the parents than at the students. As children get older, the communication is directed to both the parents and children. The following information is used each year by a fifth-grade teacher to communicate expectations.

Dear Parents and Students,

   I am looking forward to an exciting year in fifth grade, and I hope you are too! In order for us to work together most effectively, some guidelines are necessary. They are listed below. Please read through the information carefully and sign at the bottom of the page. Thank you for your cooperation and help in making this year the best one ever for your youngster.

Sincerely,<br>Mrs. Kathy Mease

**Survival Guidelines**

1. Follow directions the first time they are given.
2. Be in class, seated, and quiet when the bell rings.
3. Bring covered textbooks, notebook and/or folder, paper, pen, and pencils to class daily.
4. Raise your hand for permission to speak or to leave your seat.
5. Keep hands, feet, and objects to yourself.

**Homework Guidelines**

1. Motto—I will always TRY, and I will NEVER give up!
2. I will complete all assignments. If the assignment is not finished or is not ready when called for, a zero will be given.
3. Head your paper properly—directions were given in class. Use pen/pencil—no red, orange, or pink ink. If you have questions, see Mrs. Mease.
4. Whenever you are absent, it is your responsibility to come in early in the morning (7:30–8:00) and make arrangements for makeup work. Class time will not be used for this activity. Tests are always assigned three to five days in advance—if you are absent the day before the test, you should come prepared to take the test because you will be expected to take it.
5. No extra credit work will be given. If you do all the required work and study for the tests, there should be no need for extra credit.
6. A packet of papers is sent home with the children each Tuesday. Please look them over carefully. If you have any questions or comments, please

feel free to call Lone Trail Elementary School (272-8160). I will return your call promptly.

Again, my best wishes for a terrific year.

_____ (student)    _____ (parent)

At the junior high and high school levels, parents and students often are interested in the content of the course and how student work will be graded. One algebra teacher sent this document home at the beginning of the school year.

**Course Expectations**
- I. Course Title: Algebra I
- II. Course Description: This course explores basic algebraic concepts and applications, including a complete review of the number system. The main emphasis of the course is on solving linear and quadratic equations.
- III. Course Objectives
  - A. To understand the basic terms and symbols used in the study of algebra.
  - B. To perform the basic operations with signed numbers.
  - C. To solve simple linear equations and inequalities in one unknown.
  - D. To understand the graphical properties of linear equations.
  - E. To perform basic operations with polynomials.
  - F. To solve quadratic equations using factoring.
  - G. To perform fundamental operations with algebraic fractions.
  - H. To solve quadratic equations using the quadratic formula.
  - I. To apply equation solving techniques to story problems.
- IV. Learning Activities
  - A. Daily assignments
  - B. Teacher demonstration
  - C. Class discussion
  - D. Note taking and writing projects
  - E. Peer tutoring
  - F. Reviews
  - G. Student demonstration
- V. Grading Procedure: Grades will be based on test performance, notebooks, daily assignments, and quizzes. Grades will be weighted as follows:
  - Tests—40%
  - Quizzes—40%
  - Daily Assignments—20%
  - Final Grades will be determined on the following scale:

  | | |
  |---|---|
  | 93–100% | A |
  | 85– 92% | B |
  | 73– 84% | C |
  | 65– 72% | D |
  | 0– 64% | F |

**VI.** Materials
    **A.** Text: *Holt Algebra One*, Holt, Rinehart and Winston Publishers, 1992.
    **B.** Calculator: It is recommended that each student obtain a scientific calculator.
    **C.** Paper, pencil, and pen.
    **D.** Learning log.
**VII.** Student Expectations
    **A.** Students must come prepared to class each day with their book, notebook, pencil and paper, and assignments.
    **B.** School policy states that four unexcused absences will result in failure. Make-up tests must be taken within three days of return from absence. Make-up assignments must be turned in on the second day of return from absence. No make-up quizzes will be given. The low quiz in each grading period will be dropped.
    **C.** To facilitate roll taking and grading, students are expected to sit in the seats that will be assigned to them.
    **D.** Cheating will not be tolerated. Anyone guilty of cheating will receive a failure for the grading period. Talking during tests will result in a zero and makeup will not be allowed.
    **E.** Courtesy and respect are expected to be shown at all times. This includes not eating during class, listening to the lecture, and staying on task. Stereos and headsets are to be left in students' lockers.

I have read this disclosure statement and understand the grading procedure and classroom management rules.

_____ Student _____ Parent

Note how the teacher described (1) the content of the course, (2) instructional activities, (3) grading procedures and student requirements. These were addressed in a positive, businesslike manner and set the stage for a productive school year. We recommend a document like this at the beginning of the year. It is straightforward and informative and communicates not only positive expectations but also competence.

**Open House**   Most school systems have a scheduled Open House at a specified date early in the school year. Parents are invited to attend, and they move through an abbreviated schedule of a typical day's activities. Teachers describe their policies and expectations and invite input from parents. The written expectations teachers have are often distributed in these sessions.

The image you project as a teacher is critical at this time. Because Open House is often the only time you will see a parent during the year, the impression you make will be lasting. Proper dress, careful use of language and grammar, clear and neatly written communications, and a warm and pleasant but professional manner are all important in creating a good impression.

**Parent–Teacher Conferences**   An additional opportunity to communicate expectations, grading policies, and student progress is through conferences where the parents and teachers meet face to face. At the elementary level, regularly scheduled parent–teacher conferences occur at least once a year and sometimes twice; they are much less common at the secondary level. Some teachers have experimented with inviting students to these conferences and have noted the benefits of students' being informed of and rewarded for their efforts in class. Some suggestions for conducting successful parent–teacher conferences are as follows:

1. Organize and prepare before the meeting. The files and records of each of your students should be readily available during the meeting.
2. Begin with a positive statement (e.g., "Mary is such a lively, energetic second grader" – despite the fact that she is about to drive you crazy.) This puts the parent at ease and sets the stage for later comments.
3. Be factual in your statements and use supporting documentation. At the elementary level, this might consist of samples of the student's work; at the secondary level, it could include scores and averages on assignments and tests.
4. Listen carefully to parents' questions and concerns. This is important because it shows you care, and it gives you information about the student.
5. To end the session, summarize the discussion and end on an optimistic note (e.g., "Jim *can* learn math, and if we both encourage him on his homework, I'm sure we'll see a difference next report card").

## Communication: Report Cards

We have all had experience with report cards. While the form varies, report cards at a given level generally communicate similar information. An excerpt from a report sent to the parents of kindergarten children is shown in Figure 12.2.

Notice that this report (1) includes affective and personal growth goals; (2) is based primarily on performance measures; and (3) uses an *O, S, I, N* scale versus an *A, B, C, D* scale for reporting. On a form like this, there also would be space for some short written comments.

Compare this kindergarten report to one used in the intermediate grades (Figure 12.3).

We can see from this example that affective goals such as social behaviors and attitudes are still evaluated at the junior high level, but a separate scale is used. In addition, comparative information is provided in basic skills in the areas of absolute achievement, progress made during the quarter, and effort.

As students progress into high school, less emphasis is placed on affective considerations, and grades are often quantified in terms of percentages (see Figure 12.4). This latter point has strong implications for the kind of grading system the teacher designs, a point we made earlier.

**Interim Progress Reports**  In examining these report cards, we see that they are sent home every 9 or 10 weeks. Typically, schools also report progress at midterm as well. In some cases, students get interim progress reports only when a student is experiencing difficulty, while in others, all students receive them. The purpose of the

**FIGURE 12.2** Kindergarten Progress Report

## KINDERGARTEN PROGRESS REPORT

19_____ - 19_____

**MARKING KEY**

O - Outstanding
S - Satisfactory
I - Improvement Shown
N - Needs Improvement
Ø - Not Evaluated

Name _____

Teacher _____

School _____

| Attendance | 1 | 2 | 3 | 4 | Total |
|---|---|---|---|---|---|
| Days Present | | | | | |
| Days Absent | | | | | |
| Days Tardy | | | | | |

| SOCIAL DEVELOPMENT AND WORK HABITS | 1 | 2 | 3 | 4 |
|---|---|---|---|---|
| Works and plays well with others | | | | |
| Is kind and courteous | | | | |
| Listens attentively | | | | |
| Uses socially acceptable language | | | | |
| Respects ruler | | | | |
| Accepts correction graciously | | | | |
| Respects rights of others | | | | |

| LANGUAGE READINESS | 1 | 2 | 3 | 4 |
|---|---|---|---|---|
| Recognizes colors: R O GR Y BL P BR BK WH | | | | |
| Reads color words: R O GR Y BL P BR BK WH | | | | |
| Identifies and uses opposites | | | | |
| Knows rhyming sounds | | | | |
| Know directions (up,down, left, right) | | | | |
| | | | | |
| | | | | |

| MATHEMATICS | 1 | 2 | 3 | 4 |
|---|---|---|---|---|
| Recognizes shapes ○△□ ◇ | | | | |
| Counts objects 1,2,3,4,5,6,7,8,9,10, 11,12,13,14,15,16,17,18,19,20 | | | | |
| Correctly writes 0,1,2,3,4,5,6,7,8,9,10 | | | | |
| Recognizes 0,1,2,3,4,5,6,7,8,9,10 11,12,13,14,15,16,17,18,19,20 | | | | |
| Counts to _____ | | | | |

| MOTOR SKILLS | 1 | 2 | 3 | 4 |
|---|---|---|---|---|
| Demonstrates large muscle control (hop, skip, jump, throw, catch, run, balance) | | | | |
| Demonstrates fine motor control: Forms letters and numbers correctly | | | | |
| Holds pencil and crayon correctly | | | | |
| Traces over lines | | | | |
| Can cut out | | | | |

**FIGURE 12.3** Intermediate Grade Report Card

STUDENT _____

| BEHAVIOR AND ATTITUDES | Report period | | | |
|---|---|---|---|---|
| | 1 | 2 | 3 | 4 |
| 1. Accepts responsibility | | | | |
| 2. Follows directions | | | | |
| 3. Completes assignments on time | | | | |
| 4. Shows judgement in use and care of materials | | | | |
| 5. Displays creativity | | | | |
| 6. Is courteous and considerate of others | | | | |
| 7. Uses time well | | | | |
| 8. Works well in groups | | | | |
| 9. Abides by school rules | | | | |

## BEHAVIOR AND ATTITUDES

These behaviors are important to success in school. These factors reflect attitude toward school, self, and others. They have a direct bearing on the progress being made in the basic skills.

E - Excellent

S - Satisfactory

NI- Needs Improvement

| ACHIEVEMENT, PROGRESS, AND EFFORT | 1 | | | 2 | | | 3 | | | 4 | | |
|---|---|---|---|---|---|---|---|---|---|---|---|---|
| | Achievement | Progress | Effort | Achievement | Progress | Effort | Achievement | Progress | Effort | Achievement | Progress | Effort |
| Reading | | | | | | | | | | | | |
| Language Arts | | | | | | | | | | | | |
| Handwriting | | | | | | | | | | | | |
| Spelling | | | | | | | | | | | | |
| Mathematics | | | | | | | | | | | | |
| Health | | | | | | | | | | | | |
| Science | | | | | | | | | | | | |
| Social Studies | | | | | | | | | | | | |
| Art* — Satisfactory Performance | | | | | | | | | | | | |
| Art* — Needs Improvement | | | | | | | | | | | | |
| Music* — Satisfactory Performance | | | | | | | | | | | | |
| Music* — Needs Improvement | | | | | | | | | | | | |
| Phys. Ed.* — Satisfactory Performance | | | | | | | | | | | | |
| Phys. Ed.* — Needs Improvement | | | | | | | | | | | | |

*Letter grades are not given in these subject areas due to the difficulty of precise measurement of acquired skills.

**FIGURE 12.4** High School Report Form

## • REPORT CARD •

| NAME | SCHOOL | STUDENT NUMBER | HOME ROOM | SCHOOL YEAR |
|---|---|---|---|---|
| ADDRESS | CITY | ZIP CODE | TELEPHONE | |

| PERIOD FROM-THRU | COURSE NAME | WGT | TEACHER NAME | TEA. NO. | 1ST GRD | 1ST C | 1ST ABS | 2ND GRD | 2ND C | 2ND ABS | 1ST SEM EXAM | 1ST SEM AVG | 3RD GRD | 3RD C | 3RD ABS | 4TH GRD | 4TH C | 4TH ABS | 2ND SEM EXAM | 2ND SEM AVG | YR AVG | CREDIT EARNED |
|---|---|---|---|---|---|---|---|---|---|---|---|---|---|---|---|---|---|---|---|---|---|---|
| 1 | M/J LIFE SCI ADV | | | 082 | 93A | 0 | | 90B | 0 | | 1 | 92B | 90B | 0 | 3 | 93A | 0 | 2 | | 92B | 92B | |
| 2 | M/J BAND 4 | | | 129 | 97A | 0 | | **A | 0 | | 2 | 99A | 97A | 0 | 3 | 95A | 0 | 3 | | 96A | 97A | |
| 3 | ALGEBRA | | | 029 | 96A | 0 | | 93A | 0 | | 1 | 95A | 91B | S | 3 | 91B | S | 2 | | 91B | 93A | |
| 4 | POL. SCIENCE | | | 053 | 92B | S | | 91B | 0 | | 1 | 92B | 93A | S | 2 | 94A | S | 2 | | 94A | 93A | |
| 5 | AM. LITERATURE | | | 004 | 93A | S | | 90B | 0 | | 1 | 92B | 89B | S | 2 | 93A | S | 2 | | 91B | 91B | |
| 6 | M/J PHYS ED 2 | | | 101 | 96A | S | | 97A | S | | 1 | 97A | 97A | S | 1 | 94A | S | 2 | | 96A | 96A | |

*PROMOTED*

**FIGURE 12.5**   Interim Certificate

THIS IS TO HEREBY CERTIFY

THAT

_____

has been doing outstanding work in

_____

for the past two weeks

report is to provide feedback to both students and parents regarding progress. These can be especially helpful if problems develop.

An effective way to supplement report cards is through the use of certificates, another form an interim progress report can take. Figure 12.5 shows an example of a certificate.

A simple certificate reporting good news or positive results can be a tremendous boost in promoting positive attitudes in students and parents. Information sent home to parents all too often communicates a problem. Parents are asked to attend a conference only when there is some difficulty, and reports to the parents often bear only bad news. A simple positive communication takes very little time and helps break the negative pattern.

## SUMMARY

Classroom assessment performs several functions. It provides practice and feedback for students, information about learning growth for teachers and parents, and academic progress data for other professionals.

Effective assessment is valid, systematic, and practical. Valid assessments are congruent with the goals being measured. Validity can be improved with frequent and systematic data gathering. A classroom assessment system must be practical and economical; the information it provides must augment instruction and must not consume inordinate amounts of instructional time.

The ways teachers assess learning depends on grade level and the subject matter being taught. In the lower grades, performance assessments are widespread and teachers' use of commercially prepared tests is common. Affective and social goals are emphasized. In later grades, greater stress is placed on accountability, and objective items are popular, with short answer and matching being the most common.

An effective assessment system takes into account tests, quizzes, homework, and any other sources of information about student progress. Talking to school leaders and other teachers can help in designing your system.

Communication needs to be an integral part of an effective assessment system. Positive and concrete expectations set the stage for future learning, and this information must be shared with both students and parents.

This brings us to the end of this chapter and to the end of the text. We hope that the information you have read and studied is useful and practical. As we have seen, research has much to offer the classroom teacher, but the teacher is essential in translating this research into practice. In addition, we have seen how teacher judgment is a critical element in all the decisions teachers make. This should not be a matter of concern, for it is one of the characteristics that makes teaching a profession. With sincere effort, you will make an important contribution to education—the most rewarding of professions. We hope this text has contributed to that effort.

## ADDITIONAL READINGS FOR PROFESSIONAL GROWTH

Airasian, P. (1991). *Classroom assessment*. New York: McGraw-Hill. An up-to-date and practical overview of the field of classroom assessment.

Crooks, T. (1988). The impact of classroom evaluation practices on students. *Review of Educational Research, 58*, 438–481. This excellent review documents the powerful effect evaluation has on learning.

Gronlund, N. (1988). *How to construct achievement tests* (4th ed.). Englewood Cliffs, NJ: Prentice Hall. An excellent guide to constructing your own evaluation items.

## EXERCISES

1. Read the following short case study. At least five important criticisms and two more minor criticisms can be directed at the teacher in it based on the content of this chapter. List those criticisms.

Al Leland is a physics teacher in a large metropolitan high school. He begins his class on Thursday by announcing a test to be given the following day.

"Be certain that you study for the test," he announced. "This one and your final each count a third of your 9 weeks' grade, and some of you have been slipping up on your homework." He went on, "You will need to solve all the forms of velocity and acceleration problems including the acceleration of gravity."

The next day, Al brought in the test and stated, "All right, everyone, spread out, and keep your eyes to yourself. You're juniors in high school now, and you should know enough not to be gazing around. You have 50 minute to finish the test." He waited a moment as the students rearranged themselves and then began passing out the test papers.

He watched for a few minutes as the students were busily working and then went into the storage room to gather some equipment for the following day's demonstration.

Glancing at his watch as he busied himself in the equipment room, he suddenly reacted to himself. "Yikes, the period is nearly over!" Returning to the class, he announced. "You have 10 minutes left."

On Monday, Al handed back the test and said, "I've included a dittoed sheet with the letter of the correct answer for the multiple-choice items and the answers to the problems. Take these home tonight and go over them. Bring the test back to class tomorrow. Now, I want to begin a discussion of force and motion."

2. Refer back to the case study at the beginning of the section, "Effective Testing." Describe what Andrew did to enhance the validity of his test in terms of *curricular alignment* as described in this chapter.

3. Consider Mary's behavior during the test, and suppose Andrew's expectations for her had been different. How might this have adversely affected his behavior as it was directed toward her?

## DISCUSSION QUESTIONS

1. One characteristic of an effective assessment system is that student evaluations should be frequent and systematic. How does this characteristic relate to the concept of pacing discussed earlier in this text?

2. What advantages are there to establishing measurement routines? Are there any disadvantages to these routines?

3. Some have suggested that grades act as motivators. Do they work that way for you? What about the students you teach? For what kinds of students will grades be the most motivating? the least motivating? How does age and grade level affect this factor?

4. How does your specific teaching focus (e.g., subject matter or grade level) influence the kind of assessment instruments you will use?

5. Identify the advantages and disadvantages of the following ways to assess student performance. How does the concept of validity affect the selection of one compared to the other?

   **a.** Essay

   **b.** Short answer

   **c.** Multiple choice

   **d.** True/false

   **e.** Performance assessment

6. Consider each of the options for collecting, scoring, and using homework that we presented in this chapter. What advantages and disadvantages does each have in addition to those we listed? How does the type of student (e.g., younger or older, high ability versus low ability) influence the effectiveness of any option? What other options for handling homework exist?

7. What kind of grading system, norm- or criterion-referenced, do you prefer? Why? Do you think your opinion is similar to the students you will be teaching?

8. What do you consider to be essential information on a beginning-of-the-year expectations statement? How does grade level or the type of student (e.g., high or low ability) influence your response?

## APPLYING IT IN THE SCHOOLS

1. Analyze the assessment system for the course in which you are using this book. Comment on the following dimensions:

   **a.** Type of evaluation instruments used (e.g., objective versus performance assessment)

   **b.** Validity

   **c.** Frequency

   **d.** Course expectations

   **e.** Norm- or criterion-referenced grading

2. Examine a report card.

   **a.** How are grades reported?

   **b.** How often are report cards given?

   **c.** In addition to content areas like social studies and science, what other areas (e.g., citizenship) are evaluated?

3. Is there a document summarizing your district's or school's evaluation policy? If so, examine it and answer the following questions:

   **a.** Is there a statement of philosophy? If so, summarize the major points.

   **b.** How are parents involved in the process?

   **c.** What are each teacher's individual responsibilities?

   **d.** How do *D*s and *F*s influence promotion?

   **e.** What is the relationship of grades to extracurricular activities?

   **f.** How are unexcused absences and tardiness treated?

**4.** Observe a teacher administering a test or quiz. How did the teacher deal with the following issues:

   **a.** Expectations

   **b.** Directions

   **c.** Feedback

   **d.** Grades

   **e.** Makeups

**5.** *Homework.* Interview a teacher to see how the following are handled:

   **a.** Correcting

   **b.** Grades

   **c.** Late or missing

   **d.** Makeups for absences

**6.** *Record Keeping.* Interview a teacher at your grade level or in your subject-matter area and find out what his or her responsibilities are in terms of the following:

   **a.** Individual attendance records

   **b.** Tardiness

   **c.** Report cards

   **d.** Cumulative folders

# Exercise Feedback

## Chapter 2: Student Diversity

1. **a.** *Emphasizing the importance of a topic.* Mary did this when she said, "This is an important skill that you will use again and again, not only this year but later on."

   **b.** *Communicating that all are expected to learn.* She did this by saying, "I'm sure that all of you will learn how to do this and we'll practice until we're all good at it."

   **c.** *Monitoring.* This was evidenced by Mary noticing that Will was poking Steve and by her circulating around the room while students worked.

   **d.** *Opportunities for practice and feedback.* Practice and feedback were provided when students practiced the new skill collectively with some at the board and individually at their seats.

   **e.** *Accountability.* Mary held all students accountable by requiring a completed assignment from each student.

2. **a.** *Samantha.* The description suggests that Samantha was mildly mentally retarded. The evidence here include the terms, *slow* and *struggled in every subject.* Mild mental retardation generally affects performance in most school subjects.

   **b.** *Jake.* The evidence here suggests that Jake has a learning disability. Characteristics of this condition that Jake displayed included fidgeting and hyperactivity and uneven performance in different school subjects (e.g., "Though he did all right in math, he struggled in any subject in which he had to read.")

   **c.** *Steven.* Steven is probably behaviorally disordered. Data to support this conclusion include, "Temper with a short fuse" and "Once Jim got him settled down again, he'd do fine but it took some doing."

   The classroom teacher would not normally be solely responsible for diagnosis. Instead, teachers would work in tandem with a professional team including special educators, school psychologists, and school counselors. Knowledge of these terms will help a classroom teacher contribute to this process.

3. **a.** *Teacher directed.* This lesson was clearly teacher directed. The teacher was the

major initiator and actor and controlled the direction and pace of the lesson through the questions she asked.

**b.** *Public questioning.* The lesson was driven by teacher questions that were asked to the whole class.

**c.** *Ordered turn-taking.* The teacher determined who answered next by surveying the raised hands and calling on a designated student.

**d.** *Competition for turns.* Since only one student can respond at a time, students must raise their hands and compete with each other for an opportunity to respond.

## Chapter 3: Teacher Planning

**1. a.** (When given a list of both facts and opinions,)<sup>C</sup> (students will label)<sup>P</sup> (90 percent of these correctly)<sup>Cr</sup>.

                                 C
**a.** (When given a list of both facts and opinions,) (students will label)
        Cr
(90 percent of these correctly).

                               C
**b.** (Given the names of composers of the Romantic period and their
                   P               Cr
major works,) (students will match) (all the works with their composers).

               C                   P
**c.** (Given a clock with hands,) (the student will be able to tell the time
          Cr
(within 1 minute of the correct time).

                               C
**d.** (Given a description of an experiment illustrating the basic steps of the
                P              Cr
scientific method,) (the student will label) (each step and explain the basis of his or her classification in writing).

             C                P
**e.** (Given a bar graph,) (the student will describe the information in
          Cr
the graph) (in factual terms).

            C                P
**f.** (Given a list of 10 words,) (the student will alphabetize these)
         Cr
(so that the whole list is alphabetized correctly).

             C
**g.** (Given the choice of topics and resources such as a dictionary,)

P                                    Cr

(the student will write) a (500-word expository essay that is grammatically correct, punctuated properly, corrected for spelling, and organized according to the format described in class).

2. *Gronlund's format.* As you compare your responses to ours, note that the exact wording may vary.

   **a.** Understands the difference between facts and opinions

   **b.** Knows the names of the major composers of the Romantic period and their works

   **c.** Knows how to tell time on a clock with hands

   **d.** Understands the steps of the scientific method

   **e.** Knows how to read a bar graph

   **f.** Understands principles of alphabetization

   **g.** Applies rules of grammar, punctuation, spelling, and organization to writing expository essays

3. **a.** Psychomotor

   **b.** Cognitive

   **c.** Cognitive

   **d.** Affective (Note how this has a cognitive component, knowing the rules.)

   **e.** Cognitive

   **f.** Affective

   **g.** Psychomotor (Note how this also has cognitive elements, such as knowing correct finger placement and function keys.)

   **h.** Psychomotor (Contrast this goal with *b.* Before students can print correctly, they must cognitively learn the correct shapes of letters.)

4. *Lesson planning.* Match the following components of the basic lesson plan model with their function.

   | | | |
   |---|---|---|
   | D  **a.** Unit title | **A.** | Reminds the teacher of the major concepts, skills, or topics |
   | E  **b.** Instructional goal | **B.** | Describes how student learning will be measured |
   | C  **c.** Performance objective | **C.** | Specifies what students will be able to do after the lesson |
   | F  **d.** Rationale | **D.** | Links the lesson to broader topics |
   | A  **e.** Content | **E.** | Describes the purpose of the lesson in general terms |
   | H  **f.** Instructional procedures | **F.** | Explains the importance or significance of the lesson |

  B   **g.** Evaluation procedures   **G.** Provides a quick reference for any supplies or equipment needed

  G   **h.** Materials and aids   **H.** Outlines teaching/learning strategies

5. *Lesson planning.* As with previous exercises, the specific wording may vary; what is important is that the intent of each component is congruent.

   **a.** Unit: Parts of speech

   **b.** Instructional goal: Students should understand proper nouns.

   **c.** Performance objective: When given a list of common and proper nouns, the student will circle all of the proper nouns; when given a list of sentences with proper nouns embedded in them, the student identifies by underlining all proper nouns.

   **d.** Rationale: Understanding proper nouns is essential to the writing skill of capitalization.

   **d.** Content: Nouns: person, place, or thing
Proper nouns: Specific person, place, or thing

       **Examples:**

          Specific person — Abraham Lincoln
                           Harriet Tubman
                           King George III
                           Mary Smith

          Specific place   — New York
                           Chicago
                           Prairieville

          Specific thing   — Empire State Building
                           Hope Diamond
                           Acme Corporation

   **f.** Instructional procedures:

     (1) Review definition of noun
     (2) Define proper noun
     (3) Explain why important in terms of capitalization
     (4) Illustrate definition with examples
     (5) Put sentences on board and have students identify proper nouns
     (6) Pass out worksheet for in-class work
     (7) Assign exercise 9.4, p. 137, in workbook

   **g.** Evaluation procedures: Check worksheet
                                       Grade homework
                                       Quiz on Friday — sentences in *Teacher's Guide*

   **h.** Materials and aids: Overhead transparency
                             Worksheets
                             Quiz (need by Friday)

## Chapter 4: Effective Teaching

1. The area of the band represents time lost to noninstructional activities, such as taking roll and other management routines. The area of the band would be greater for Dennis Orr, since he spent more of his time on noninstructional activities than did Steve Weiss.

2. Kathy got started at 11:02 and went to 11:28, which gave her 26 minutes of instructional time.

3. Her engaged time is slightly less than her instructional time. This is based on the example in the case study where she saw that Jim was being inattentive.

4. Kathy called on Ann Marie, and Ann Marie sat quietly. Instead of turning to another student, Kathy asked another question which helped Ann Marie to answer successfully.

5. Kathy displayed the following behaviors that Collins (1978) operationally defined as indicators of enthusiasm:

    "Yes, they're generally east of us," Kathy adds, as *she walks quickly* and points to the map at the side of the room. . . .

    "OK, good observation," Kathy nods *energetically.*

    "You have done very well, everyone," she smiles, *jabbing her finger in the air for emphasis.*

6. Kathy indicated her responsiveness by recognizing that Jim wasn't paying attention, and she intervened by calling on him. Also, Kathy recognized that Carol was uncertain in her response, so she gave Carol specific praise by saying, "Very good description, Carol, . . . You identified auto manufacturing as an important part of our economy, and that's a good example." She also was responsive when she helped Ann Marie through prompting.

7. This statement is also a form of emphasis.

8. Effective organization was evidenced in the following ways:

    a. She began her lesson within 2 minutes of the time it was scheduled to start.

    b. She had her chart prepared in advance.

    c. The statement, "At 11:02 the students have their social studies books on their desks . . ." indicated that Kathy had well-established routines for her class, since the students took out their books without having to be told to do so.

9. Kathy began her review by saying, "We began talking about the Northern and Southern Colonies yesterday. Let's see what we remember. Where are they compared to where we live? Jo?" and she continued through, "We also talked about some important ideas, like 'Economy,' . . . What do we mean by economy? Carol?"

10. She involved the students by questioning them, and she also had them work on their summary statements in pairs.

11. Her closure was evidenced by the description, "Kathy has several of the pairs offer their summary statements; they further develop the statements as a whole group; . . ."

12. Teacher organization most strongly affects instructional time.

13. Student involvement affects both engaged time and academic learning time. When students are active, they process information in more meaningful ways, which leads to higher levels of success, which in turn increases academic learning time.

14. Students tend to be more attentive when teachers are enthusiastic, which increases engaged time.

15. Opening and closing reviews help make information meaningful to students, which promotes success, which in turn increases academic learning time.

## Chapter 5: Involving Students in Learning

1. From your list of the students José called on, you can see that virtually every member of the class responded at least once in the lesson. He further involved his lowest achievers by calling on them more than he did the other students. As we saw in Chapter Two, teachers typically involve low achievers less than they do higher achievers. José was keenly aware of the need for equitable distribution and compensated—perhaps even overcompensated—by increasing his effort to involve Keith, Don, Gretchen, Ginny, and Jason. No rules exist to tell you exactly how much a teacher should call on a particular individual; the decision is a matter of teacher judgment. A critical feature of José's teaching was that all the students participated.

2. a. The sequence suggests that Ginny was momentarily inattentive. When she was "caught," he quickly offered to repeat the question to take her off the hook. A less responsive teacher might not have made the effort to reinvolve her in the lesson or, worse yet, would not even have noticed that she was not attending.

   b. Ginny was one of José's lowest achievers, and the fact that he first made an effort to regain her attention and then stayed with her until she gave an acceptable response indicates that he was aware of the need to involve all the students as equally as possible.

3. Jason answered the question without José's recognition. It illustrates a call-out.

4. José praised Jason for his response. This reinforced the behavior, making Jason more likely to repeat it in the future. However, because Jason was the only student who called out an answer, José apparently did not have a serious problem with this behavior. (A prime reason for accepting this call-out may have been the fact that Jason was one of José's low achievers. Knowing when to follow research

findings and when to ignore them is a true test of teacher judgment.) Other options would have been to ignore the response or remind the class that they had a rule prohibiting call-outs and then proceed.

5. José solicited a choral response when he said, "Everybody say *expand*." In this instance, he wanted all students to learn and use a specific term and specifically asked for the whole class to respond. Choral responding is appropriate under those conditions.

6. Mr. Walker called on Keith, but instead of asking the question first and identifying the student's name second, he first called on Keith by name, waited a few seconds, and then went on with the question.

   If this is the dominant questioning pattern, students might learn that as soon as one of them is identified the rest of the class is "off the hook," and they would be less attentive to the questions.

   If identifying the student before asking the question occurred infrequently, it might have indicated that Keith was not attending and perhaps was even disruptive. Mr. Walker might then have used this question to intervene. Because the question was open ended, it provided Keith with an easy opportunity to respond. The combination of being called on together with ensured success is a powerful invitation for continued student participation.

7. José called on Reginald to answer the question, and instead of prompting when he received no response, turned instead to another student. While not a serious problem if it happens periodically, a pattern of leaving the nonresponder in favor of another student is undesirable because it fails to reinforce attempting to respond and encourages passivity. Our discussion in this chapter would suggest that instead of leaving Reginald to call on Steve, the teacher should instead prompt Reginald to get an acceptable response from him.

8. A wide variety of prompting questions could be asked, so many more than three are possible. The following is a brief list:

   "How did Alice and Joe walk toward each other?"
   "What word describes the way Alice and Joe walked?"
   "How are Alice and Joe walking?"

   In addition, open-ended questions can be used as prompts, such as the following:

   "What is happening in the sentence?"
   "What is the sentence about?"
   "What can you tell us about the sentence?"
   "What do you notice about the sentence?"
   "What do you observe in the sentence?"

## Chapter 6: Facts, Concepts, and Generalizations: The Building Blocks of Learning

1. **a.** The superordinate concept was *mammal*; the coordinate concepts were *tiger* and *horse*.

**b.** Some facts mentioned in the passage include:

> There are two kinds of elephants.
> African elephants have bigger ears.
> Elephant babies may weigh 200 pounds.
> Hannibal used elephants to carry his troops.

**c.** Probably the clearest example of a generalization is that the length of the gestation period is related to the size of the animal.

**2. a.** This was a deductive lesson. The teacher defined the concept and then illustrated it with examples. She could have used the same examples in an inductive lesson by first displaying the plants, asking for observations, analyzing them for similarities and differences, and then having the class form a definition based on similarities among the positive examples.

**b.** This was an inductive lesson because it proceeded from data to abstraction. In a deductive sequence, the teacher would have first defined the generalization and then used the examples to illustrate it.

**3. a.** This was a deductive lesson because the teacher defined the concept (sources of protein) and illustrated it with examples.

**b.** The problem with this lesson was that the concept being taught was incomplete. This was partially due to the definition the teacher provided. Proteins, in addition to animal products, also include legumes like peas, beans, and peanuts. Also, all the examples selected were farm products, while some non-farm products like fish and venison are also sources of protein. When we teach content that is not terribly familiar to us, we need to consult alternate sources to make sure our content is accurate.

## Chapter 7: Organized Bodies of Knowledge

**1. a.** Several facts are listed in the passage. The best examples are

> "Our first person is a champion weight lifter and holds several U.S. records."

> "This other woman won the last state triathlon, which includes running, bicycling, and swimming."

The two most prominent concepts in the passage are *isometric exercise* and *isotonic exercise*. Several generalizations are listed in the passage. Some of them are

> "The specifics of the diet can help you gain or lose weight."

> "Exercise is the same way; you can use different kinds of exercise to do different things."

> "If you did isometrics over and over again for a long period of time, you might build up endurance."

> "If you planned them right, isotonics might also build up coordination."

We would describe Shirley's lesson as teaching an organized body of knowledge because the lesson didn't focus on any of the facts, concepts, or generalizations, per se. Rather it focused on the integration of them.

b. Her pictures and question were a form of introductory focus, designed to attract the students' attention and pull them into the lesson.

c. She organized the lesson with her hierarchy and matrix.

d. The *lesson presentation* phase of Shirley's lesson began approximately at the point when she said, "Okay, we've heard a number of different opinions about which person is more physically fit and each of you is partially right, depending on how we define fitness. Physical fitness actually has several dimensions. . . ." (Suggesting that the phase began when Shirley said, "Physical fitness actually has several dimensions . . ." would be an equally good answer.)

The *comprehension-monitoring* phase began approximately at the point when Shirley said, "Let's review some of the ideas we just talked about. Who can give me a definition of isometric exercise? . . ."

The line between *comprehension monitoring* and *integration* can be somewhat blurred, and this is the case in this example. Integration typically occurs after the second lecture recitation-cycle when the content of the second cycle is related to the content of the first cycle.

e. The effectiveness of this review and closure was enhanced by the teacher's use of the overhead which had been presented at the beginning of the lesson. This allowed students to see how the lesson had progressed and provided a visual image to take with them.

2. a. Information presentation. This phase occurred when Henry discussed the functions of the teeth and saliva.

b. Comprehension check. Henry checked for understanding when he asked Kerry to explain the importance of the conversion of starch to sugar.

c. Integration. The final phase in the cycle occurred when Henry asked, "What would happen if. . . ."

3. One possible matrix might look like this:

| | Early Life | Adult Life | Setting of Novels | Plots of Novels |
|---|---|---|---|---|
| Hemingway | | | | |
| Fitzgerald | | | | |

Other variations are possible; what is important is to present students with data that allows them to link the authors' lives with their works.

## Chapter 8: Skills Instruction

1. a. In the introduction, Mr. North related the new skill of composition writing to the previously learned skill of writing paragraphs. During this phase, he also

explained how and when the new skill would be used — to write book reports and describe science experiments.

**b.** The explanation phase consisted of Mr. North's modeling the skill with the topic "Getting Ready for Work in the Morning."

**c.** Teacher-directed practice occurred as Mr. North walked the class through the composition "This School Year at Brookwood." Note how he asked Mandy to think out loud while she went through the steps.

**d.** Independent practice consisted of the in-class writing project. During this phase, Mr. North circulated around the room fielding questions and problems as they arose.

**e.** Extended practice occurred in several ways. The first was the composition that students wrote later in the week. Students would get additional practice with this new skill when they used it to write their book reports and science lab descriptions.

**2. a.** *Possible lesson design.*

   **(1)** During the introduction, the following components ought to be covered:

      **(a)** Objective (e.g., "Today we're going to learn how to make contractions out of words.")

      **(b)** Content (e.g., "A contraction occurs when we combine two words and shorten them by dropping a letter. Like *did not* and *didn't*, or *do not* becomes *don't*. When we form a contraction we combine the two words and put an apostrophe where the vowel is missing. A negative contraction has *not* in it. Who remembers what a vowel and an apostrophe are?").

      **(c)** Procedures (e.g., "First, we're going to look at some different words that we can make contractions out of. Then, we're going to see how we do this on the board. Then, each of you is going to practice at your desk. If we get good enough, I'd like you to take some home and practice.")

      **(d)** Motivation (e.g., "We form contractions all the time when we talk. Once you know how to do this, you'll be able to make contractions in your writing and understand where they come from when we encounter them when we read.")

   **(2)** Teacher explanation. During this phase, the teacher would need a number of examples of word pairs that can be formed into contractions (see 2.b, below). Using the thinking-out-loud strategy discussed earlier, the teacher would take several of these examples and make them into contractions, explaining his or her thinking in the process.

   **(3)** Teacher-directed practice. Once students understand the skill, one or two might be asked to come to the board to make contractions out of additional words.

   **(4)** Independent practice. Here, the teacher wants to know if each individual student understands the skill. To find out, the teacher could put additional examples on the board or use a worksheet.

(5) Extended practice. Homework performs part of this function. This would need to be followed by later work incorporating this skill into additional reading and writing lessons.

**b.** *Examples.* Some possible examples to use in teaching this skill might include the following (Note how the conversion of the last two word pairs also requires the dropping of letters. These should be included at the end to help students see exceptions to the earlier, simpler rule.):

| *Original Word Pairs* | *Contractions* |
| --- | --- |
| do not | don't |
| did not | didn't |
| could not | couldn't |
| should not | shouldn't |
| cannot | can't |
| will not | won't |

## Chapter 9: Teaching Thinking Skills

1. **a.** During the introduction, Tanya defined the skill of classification by putting the definition on the board. She explained how and why it was important when she said, "This is an important skill we'll be using all year long, not only in science but in other areas as well. If you know how to classify, you'll be able to group things that are similar."

   **b.** Tanya explained the thinking skill through modeling and thinking out loud, using the items in her lunch bag to classify.

   **c.** Teacher-directed practice occurred when she had students classify the different vehicles under her supervision.

   **d.** Independent practice did *not* occur during the lesson. Tanya could have done this by assigning new lists of objects to classify and asking students to do this at their desks while she helped develop their metacognitive knowledge about thinking.

   **e.** Extended practice also did not occur. Tanya could encourage generalization and transfer by using the skill of classification later on in other subject-matter areas.

2. **a.** Carmen began her lesson on possessives by displaying the sentences and asking students to compare them.

   **b.** Through her questioning, she was able to help them conclude that the apostrophe came before the *s* in singular possessives and after in plural ones.

   **c.** Carmen encouraged students to apply the pattern when she displayed the sentence about the girls' new dresses on the board.

**d.** Carmen helped her class analyze their thinking when she asked them "And when you do that, what process will we be practicing?" Having students explicitly identify and talk about their thinking processes helps develop their metacognitive knowledge about thinking.

**3. a.** To make some of the observations and inferences that they did, David's students needed to have some background knowledge about geometric figures. This was evidenced in the use of concepts like *sides* and *interior angles* and by Toby's comments about "plane closed figures." Again, it's important that students have some background knowledge if we expect them to use their thinking skills.

**b.** Metacognition refers to students' understanding of their own cognitive processes. Metacognition was evidenced by Toby's comment, "We don't have to measure; we can infer it."

**c.** Positive attitudes and dispositions toward thinking skills were suggested by Deena's questions, "Hey, wait, how do we know that? We didn't measure them." Teachers often infer attitudes from the spontaneous comments and actions of students.

**4.** McTighe would say that Carmen least emphasized the teaching *of* thinking. Instead, she involved the students in thinking as they moved toward her content goal of understanding her rule, which McTighe called teaching *for* thinking. In the process, she made the students aware of the processes they were using, which McTighe called teaching *about* thinking.

**5. a.** The question or problem involves "factors that influence the shape and content of TV commercials." This problem will provide the focus for the remainder of the lesson.

**b.** Some possible hypotheses might include:

> The content of the commercial will correspond to the content of the program (e.g., toy commercials during cartoons and car commercials during sports programs).
> Commercials are more frequent at the end of a program.
> The length of commercials varies with the popularity of the program.

Ideally, these hypotheses would be ones that students generate and are interested in pursuing.

**c.** Students would gather data by actually watching TV and observing the length and content of commercials. This would probably best be done by assigning different tasks to different groups and having these report back to the class as a whole. The planning that goes into the data-gathering process provides valuable opportunities for students to practice their thinking skills.

**d.** Data analysis would be done on the information that students gathered. The teacher's role during this phase should be facilitative, helping students consider and process the information.

# Chapter 10: Alternatives to Direct Instruction

1. **a.** This was an example of group investigation. Each group of students focused on a specific topic that was of interest to them and reported their findings to the whole group.

   **b.** Marsha Anderson was using Jigsaw II to investigate the different American authors. A student in each group became an expert on a particular author and shared this expertise with other members of the group.

   **c.** This was an example of STAD. The content being taught was convergent rules. Students practiced applying these rules in their teams, and everyone took a common test at the end of the period.

2. **a.** This goal focuses on facts and would not be appropriate for discussion strategies.

   **b.** Exploring relationships is an important goal for discussions. Some basic facts and concepts about health and nutrition should precede this discussion.

   **c.** Analysis is also an important goal for discussions. With a goal like this, students would not only be using and reinforcing important information about the Vietnam War, but would also be improving their analysis skills.

   **d.** Understanding the concepts of *adjective* and *adverb* would not be an appropriate goal for discussions; this goal would be more appropriately taught using one of the direct instructional strategies discussed earlier.

   **e.** Analysis of motives is an appropriate goal for discussions.

   **f.** This goal asks students to examine different value positions and could be approached by asking students to take a personal position on these.

3. Ralph made a number of mistakes here; the most glaring were the following:

   **a.** *Timing.* Good discussions require a knowledge base and are best held at the end of a unit, not the beginning.

   **b.** *Focus.* Productive discussions begin with a specific focus; Ralph's was broad and nebulous. Alternatives might include these:

   1) Some people have said that the Civil Rights Movement was the most important event changing the course of twentieth-century America. Defend or disagree with this position.

   2) The Civil Rights Movement only affected blacks in the South. Do you agree or disagree with this position? Defend your answer with facts.

   **c.** *Monitoring.* He left the room during the discussion. This is not only unwise from a management perspective, it also poses special problems during discussions. Teachers need to monitor discussions actively to ensure that they keep on track and are productive.

   **d.** *Time.* In addition to being focused, discussions need to be bound by shorter and more realistic time frames.

**e.** *Nonproduct oriented.* Each small group should have been given a specific task to perform and have been held accountable for it.

## Chapter 11: Classroom Management

1. **a.** *Rule.* This is a general principle of behavior that applies to a broad spectrum of situations.

   **b.** *Procedure.*

   **c.** *Rule.*

   **d.** *Procedure.* This procedure prevents students from coming to class without their homework and rushing through it or copying it from neighbors.

   **e.** *Procedure.* (A good one—it helps retain sanity in the classroom.)

   **f.** *Rule.*

   **g.** *Rule.*

2. **a.** *Establishing rules and procedures.* The problem here is that Mr. Giardo did not take the time to discuss rules and procedures in terms of his own classroom. Even though students have operated under similar rules and procedures before, Mr. Giardo needs to take the time to clarify and reinforce them and adjust them to his own classroom.

   **b.** *Seating.* Students like to sit by their friends, and friends like to talk to each other. At the beginning of the school year, it is advisable to assign students to seats. This is especially important if management problems was anticipated.

   **c.** *Instructional activities.* Teacher-led, large-group activities provide more structure than small-group activities, and the teacher can adapt the pace and momentum of the former to maintain the lesson vector if problems arise. Mr. Giardo should save small-group activities for later in the year when management is not a major concern.

   **d.** *Withitness.* A withit teacher is aware of what is going on in the classroom and communicates this awareness to students. There were several lapses in the scenario:

   **(1)** Mr. Giardo was at the back of the room as students entered the class. Make your presence known as students come in by positioning yourself at the front of the room and communicating withitness both verbally (e.g., "Hi Mary! Nice shirt, Bob.") and nonverbally.

   **(2)** Mr. Giardo left the room to assist the lost student to his class. Leaving the room at this critical point in the class and the school year is a mistake; if a student needs help, ask another student to assist.

   **(3)** As he answered a student question, Mr. Giardo sat down with his back to the class. Instead, he could have leaned down and discussed the question with the group while still monitoring the rest of the class.

3. **a.** *Intrusion.* What else could Mr. Henley have done? He might have written a short note to Janice or whispered the message to her while listening to another student's response.

   **b.** *Flip-flop.* Teachers have a million things on their minds, and flip-flops are a natural part of the classroom environment. Thorough planning helps, but teacher judgment (i.e., how important is this bit of information right now?) may be the best prevention.

   **c.** *Intrusion.* Teachers are human beings, and one way that they show this is through interest in their students' lives. But, as intrusions become excessive, they detract from learning.

   **d.** *Behavior overdwelling.* A simple "Jill, turn around" probably would have been sufficient. If Jill needs more of a reminder than that, it should probably be done after class.

   **e.** *Content overdwelling.* Each of us has topics that are exciting to us; this interest is one of the basic ingredients of teacher enthusiasm. When this basic teacher enthusiasm fails to ignite student enthusiasm, we have a problem.

   **f.** *Intrusion.* The line is fine between a scattered teacher whose lessons are peppered with intrusions and a human teacher who shares his or her life and loves with students. What else would you need to know about this teacher and this class to make a hard-and-fast decision on whether this intrusion was warranted?

# Chapter 12: Assessment

1. Al can be criticized for the following:

   **a.** He announced the test for the first time on Thursday and planned to give it on Friday. This gave the students only 1 day to prepare and study for the test. Test scheduling should be an integral part of the instructional process.

   **b.** The fact that his test counted one third of the students' 9 weeks' grade indicated that he tested infrequently. This, plus the lack of advance notice of the test, detracts from achievement.

   **c.** His description of the test content was general and rather vague. This could have been easily remedied by either giving the class some sample problems or identifying problems from their homework that would serve as prototypes for the test.

   **d.** He did not monitor the test as the students were taking it. Not only does this provide students with the temptation to cheat, it also eliminates the chance to intervene in the case of student confusion.

   **e.** After turning back the test, he only identified the correct answers for the students in his feedback and did not discuss the test or any of the problem items with the students.

   Al could also have arranged his room and materials in advance, so the test could have been handed out as soon as the class period started. However, with juniors in high school, the arranging of the desks could be done quickly, so this is not a serious criticism.

Al also did little to establish positive expectations in the students. His statements, "some of you have been slipping on your homework," and "you should know enough to not be gazing around," do little to enhance either motivation or achievement. At best, statements of this form are neutral, and at worst they are negative. Even if they are true, they are better left unsaid.

2. Curricular alignment refers to the match between goals, instructional procedures, and assessment. Andrew's goals for the unit were for students to understand the concept of culture, to be able to apply the concept to different cultures, and to have a basic understanding of facts about Mexico and Central America. Because the description did not include details about the teaching that occurred, we can only infer whether the instruction was aligned with his goals. We do know, however, that on the test students were asked to apply the concept of culture to a case study and that students were responsible for facts about climate, natural resources, physical features, and capitals. From this, we can conclude that curricular alignment did occur.

3. Mary's behavior could easily create the impression, particularly if it represents a pattern, that she is a marginal student. Andrew, acting on this impression, could easily conclude subconsciously that it would not be worth the effort to take extra time with her. Unfortunately, this is a common pattern. However, Andrew instead carefully monitored his class and responded positively and with encouragement to her. His effort and personal communication over time can produce positive changes in student efforts and achievement. At the very worst, it will do no harm.

# References

Adams, R. S. (1969). Location as a feature of instructional interaction. *Merrill Parker Quarterly*, *15*(4), 309–321.

Adams, R. S., & Biddle, B. (1970). *Realities of teaching: Exploration with videotape*. New York, NY: Holt, Rinehart & Winston.

Alexander, K., & McDill, E. (1976). Selection and allocation within schools: Some causes and consequences of curriculum placement. *American Sociological Review*, *41*, 963–980.

Allen, J. (1986). Classroom management: Students' perspectives, goals and strategies. *American Educational Research Journal*, *23*, 437–459.

Alvermann, D., Dillan, D., & O'Brien, D. (1987). *Using discussion to promote reading comprehension*. Newark, DE: IRA.

*America 2000: An educational strategy*. (1991). Washington, DC: United States Department of Education.

Ames, C. (1990). Motivation: What teachers need to know. *Teachers College Record*, *90*(3), 409–421.

Ames, R. (1982). Teacher attributions for their own testing. In J. Levine & M. Wang (Eds.), *Teacher and student perceptions*. Hillsdale, NJ: Lawrence Erlbaum.

Anastasi, A. (1988). *Psychological testing* (6th ed.). New York: Macmillan.

Anderson, B. (1978). The effects of long wait-time on high school physics pupils' response length, classroom attitudes and achievement. *Dissertation Abstracts International*, *39*, 349A (University Microfilms No. 78-23-871).

Anderson, C. (1983). Computer literacy: Changes for teacher education. *Journal of Teacher Education*, *34*, 6–9.

Anderson, L. (1989). Learners and learning. In M. Reynolds (Ed.), *Knowledge base for the beginning teacher* (pp. 85–100). Elmsford, NY: Pergamon.

Anderson, L., Brubaker, N., Alleman–Brooks, J., & Duffy, G. (1985). A qualitative study of seatwork in first-grade classrooms. *The Elementary School Journal*, *86*, 123–140.

Anderson, L., Evertson, C., & Brophy, J. (1979). An experimental study of effective teaching in first grade reading groups. *Elementary School Journal*, *79*, 193–223.

Anderson, T., & Armbruster, B. (1984). Studying. In D. Pearson (Ed.), *Handbook of reading research* (pp. 657–679). New York: Longman.

Arends, R. (1991). *Learning to teach* (2nd ed.). New York: McGraw-Hill.

Arlin, M. (1979). Teacher transitions can disrupt time flow in classrooms. *American Educational Research Journal*, *16*, 42–56.

Atwood, R. (1983). *The interacting effects of task form and activity structure on students' task involvement and teacher evaluations*. Montreal: AERA.

Ausubel, D. (1963). *The psychology of meaningful verbal learning*. New York: Grune and Stratton.

Ausubel, D. (1968). *Educational psychology: A cognitive view*. New York: Holt, Rinehart and Winston.

Ausubel, D. (1978). In defense of advance organizers: A reply to the critics. *Review of Educational Research*, *48*, 251–259.

Babad, E., Bernieri, F., & Rosenthal, R. (1991). Students as judges of teachers' verbal and nonverbal behavior. *American Educational Research Journal*, *28*(1), 211–234.

Ballantine, J. (1989). *The sociology of education*. Englewood Cliffs, NJ: Prentice Hall.

Bangert-Drowns, R., Kulik, J. & Kulik, C. (1988). *Effects of frequent classroom testing*. Unpublished manuscript, The University of Michigan, Ann Arbor.

Barrett, E., & Paradis, J. (1988). Teaching writing in an on-line classroom. *Harvard Educational Review*, *58*(2), 154–165.

Barringer, C., & Gholson, B. (1979). Effects of type and combination of feedback upon conceptual learning by children: Implications for research in academic learning. *Review of Educational Research*, *49*, 459–478.

Becker, W. (1977). Teaching reading and language to the disadvantaged — what we have learned from field research. *Harvard Educational Review*, *47*, 518–543.

Behnke, G. (1979). *Coping with classroom distractions: The formal research study* (Report 79-2). San Francisco, CA: Far West Laboratory.

Bennett, N., & Blundell, D. (1983). Quantity and quality of work in rows of classroom groups. *Educational Psychology*, *3*, 93–105.

Berliner, D. (1979). Tempus educare. In P. Peterson and H. Walberg (Eds.), *Research on teaching* (pp. 120–135). Berkeley, CA: McCutchon.

Berliner, D. (1984). Research and teacher effectiveness. In *Making our schools more effective: Proceedings of three state conferences*. San Francisco, CA: Far West Laboratory.

Berliner, D. (1985, April). *Effective teaching*. Pensacola, FL: Florida Educational Research and Development Council.

Berliner, D. (1987). Simple views of effective teaching and a simple theory of classroom instruction. In D. Berliner & B. Rosenshine (Eds.), *Talks to teachers* (pp. 93–110). New York: Random House.

Berliner, D. (1988). *The development of expertise in pedagogy*. New Orleans: American Association of Colleges for Teacher Education.

Berman, P., & McLaughlin, M. (1978). *Federal programs supporting educational change, Vol. III: Implementing and sustaining innovations*. Santa Monica, CA: Rand Corporation.

Bettencourt, E., Gillett, M., Gall, M., & Hull, R. (1983). Effects of teacher enthusiasm on student on-task behavior and achievement. *American Educational Research Journal*, *20*, 435–450.

Beyer, B. (1984). Improving thinking skills — defining the problem. *Phi Delta Kappan*, *41*, 486–490.

Beyer, B. (1987). *Practical strategies for the teaching of thinking*. Needham Heights, MA: Allyn & Bacon.

Beyer, B. (1988). Developing a scope and sequence for thinking skills instruction. *Educational Leadership*, *47*(5), 26–30.

Bloom, B. (Ed.). (1956). *Taxonomy of educational objectives. Handbook I: Cognitive domain*. New York: David McKay.

Bloom, A. (1987). *The closing of the American mind*. New York: Simon and Schuster.

Bloom, B. (1981). *All our children learning*. New York: McGraw-Hill.

Bluhm, H. (1987). *Administrative uses of computers in the schools*. Englewood Cliffs, NJ: Prentice Hall.

Borich, G. (1988). *Effective teaching methods*. Columbus, OH: Merrill.

Bridgeman, B. (1974). Effects of test score feedback on immediately subsequent test performance. *Journal of Educational Psychology*, *66*, 62–66.

Brookover, W., Beamer, L., Efthim, H., Hathaway, D., Lezotte, L., Miller, S., Passalacqua, J., & Tornatzky, L. (1982). Effective instruction. In E. Erickson & L. Carl (Eds.), *Creating effective schools: An inservice program for enhancing school learning climate and achievement* (pp. 128–148). Holmes Beach, FL: Learning Publications.

Brophy, J. (1980). *Teachers' cognitive activities and overt behaviors*. East Lansing, MI: Michigan State University, College of Education.

Brophy, J. (1981a). On praising effectively. *The Elementary School Journal*, *81*(5), 269.

Brophy, J. (1981b). Teacher praise: A functional analysis. *Review of Educational Research*, *51*(1), 5–32.

Brophy, J. (1982a). *Fostering student learning and motivation in the elementary school classroom*. East Lansing, MI: Michigan State University Institute for Research on Teaching.

Brophy, J. (1982b). Successful teaching strategies for the inner-city child. *Phi Delta Kappan*, *63*, 527–530.

Brophy, J. (1983). Classroom organization and management. *Elementary School Journal*, *83*, 265–268.

Brophy, J. (1985). Teachers' expectations, motives and goals for working with problem students. In C. Ames & R. Ames (Eds.), *Research on motivation in education* (Vol. II, pp. 175–216). New York: Academic Press.

Brophy, J. (1986). Research linking teacher behavior to student achievement: Potential implications for instruction of Chapter 1 students. In B. Williams, P. Richmond, & B. Mason (Eds.), *Designs for compensatory education conference proceedings and papers* (pp. IV-121–IV-179). Washington, DC: Evaluation Associates.

Brophy, J., & Evertson, C. (1974). *Process–product correlation in the Texas teacher effectiveness study. Final report* (*research report no. 74-4*). Austin, TX: University of Texas Research and Development Center for Teacher Education.

Brophy, J., & Evertson, C. (1976). *Learning from teaching: A developmental perspective.* Boston, MA: Allyn & Bacon.

Brophy, J., & Good, T. (1986). Teacher behavior and student achievement. In M. Wittrock (Ed.), *Third handbook of research on teaching* (3rd ed., pp. 328–375). New York: Macmillan.

Brophy, J., & Rohrkemper, M. (1987). *Teachers' strategies for coping with hostile-aggressive students.* Institute for Research on Teaching, Michigan State University, East Lansing, MI: ERIC 286–881.

Brophy, J. E., & Evertson, C. M. (1978). Context variables in teaching. *Educational Psychologist, 12,* 310–316.

Brown, A. (1982). Learning and development: The problems of compatibility, access and induction. *Human Development, 25,* 89–115.

Brown, A., & Palincsar, A. (1985). *Reciprocal teaching of comprehension strategies: A natural history of one program of enhancing learning* (*tech report no. 334*). Champaign-Urbana: University of Illinois Center for Study of Reading.

Bruner, J. (1966). *Toward a theory of instruction.* New York: Norton.

Bryan, J., & Walbeck, N. (1970). Preaching and practicing generosity: Children's actions and reactions. *Child Development, 41,* 329–353.

Bull, R., & Stevens, J. (1979). The effects of attractiveness of writer and penmanship on essay grades. *Journal of Occupational Psychology, 52,* 53–59.

Bullough, B., Goldstein, S., & Holt, L. (1984). *Human interests in the curriculum.* Columbia: Teachers College Press.

Bullough, R. (1989). *First year teacher.* New York: Teachers College Press.

Burns, R. (1984). How time is used in elementary schools: The activity structure of classrooms. In L. W. Anderson (Ed.), *Time and school learning: Theory, research, and practice.* London, England: Croom & Helm.

Bushway, A., & Nash, W. (1977). School cheating behavior. *Review of Educational Research, 147,* 623–632.

Calfee, R. C. (1986). *Those who can explain teach.* San Francisco: AERA.

Canter, L., & Canter, M. (1976). *Assertive discipline.* Los Angeles: Lee Canter and Associates.

Calderhead, T. (1983). A psychological approach to research on teachers' classroom decision making. *British Educational Research Journal, 7*(1), 51–57.

Carlsen, W. (1987). *Why do you ask? The effects of science teacher subject-matter knowledge on teacher questionings and classroom discourse.* Washington, DC: AERA.

Carnegie Task Force on Teaching as a Profession. (1986). *A nation prepared: Teachers for the 21st century.* New York: Carnegie Foundation.

Carnine, D. (1990). New research on the brain: Implications for instruction. *Phi Delta Kappan, 71,* 372–377.

Carrier, C., & Titus, A. (1981). Effects of notetaking pretraining and text mode expectations on learning from lectures. *American Educational Research Journal, 18,* 385–397.

Carter, K. (1984). Do teachers understand the principles for writing tests? *Journal of Teacher Education, 35*(6), 57–60.

Carter, K. (1986). Test-wiseness for teachers and students. *Educational Measurement: Issues and Practice, 5,* 20–23.

Carter, K., & Doyle, W. (1987). Teachers' knowledge structures and comprehension processes. In J. Calderhead (Ed.), *Exploring teachers' thinking.* London: Holt, Rinehart & Winston, pp. 147–160.

Cazden, C. (1986). Classroom discourse. In M. Wittrock (Ed.), *Handbook of research on teaching* (3rd ed., pp. 432–464). New York: Macmillan.

Chapman, J. (1988). Learning disabled children's self concept. *Review of Educational Research, 58,* 347–371.

Cheney, L. (1988). *Humanities in America: A preport to the President, the Congress, and the American people.* Washington, DC: National Endowment for the Humanities.

Chewprecha, T., Gardner, M., & Sapianchai, X. (1980). Comparison of training methods in modifying questioning and wait-time behaviors of Thai high school chemistry teachers. *Journal of Research in Science Teaching, 17,* 191–200.

Clark, C., & Elmore, J. (1981). *Transforming curriculum in mathematics, science, and writing: A case study of teacher yearly planning (research series no. 99).* East Lansing, MI: Michigan State University Institute for Research on Teaching.

Clark, C., & Peterson, P. (1986). Teacher's thought processes. In M. Wittrock (Ed.), *Handbook of research on teaching* (3rd ed., pp. 255–296). New York: Macmillan.

Clark, C., & Yinger, R. (1979). *Three studies of teacher planning (research series no. 55).* East Lansing, MI: Michigan State University Institute for Research on Teaching.

Cohen, E. (1986). *Designing groupwork: Strategies for the heterogeneous classroom.* New York: Teachers College Press.

Cohen, E. (1991). Strategies for creating a multi-ability classroom. *Cooperative Learning, 12*(1), 4–7.

Cohen, S. (1987). Instructional alignment: Searching for a magic bullet. *Educational Researcher,* Nov., 16–20.

Coleman, J., Campbell, E., Hobson, D., McPortland, J., Mood, A., Weinfield, F., & York, R. (1966). *Equality of educational opportunity.* Washington, DC: U.S. Office of Health, Education and Welfare.

Collins, M. (1978). Effects of enthusiasm training on preservice elementary teachers. *Journal of Teacher Education, 24,* 53–57.

Corno, L. (1987). Teaching and self-regulated learning. In D. Berliner & B. Rosenshine (Eds.), *Talks to teachers* (pp. 249–266). New York: Random House.

Crooks, T. (1988). The impact of classroom evaluation practices on students. *Review of Educational Research, 58,* 438–481.

Cruickshank, D. (1985). Applying research on teacher clarity. *Journal of Teacher Education, 35*(2), 44–48.

Cuban, L. (1984). *How teachers taught: Constancy and change in American classrooms: 1890–1980.* New York, NY: Longman.

Cuban, L. (1986). *Teachers & machine.* New York: Teachers College Press.

Dahlof, U., & Lundgren, V. (1970). *Macro and micro approaches combined for curriculum process evaluation: A Swedish field project* (research report). Gotenberg, Sweden: University of Gotenberg, Institute of Education.

deBono, E. (1983). The cognitive research trust (CoRT) thinking program. In W. Maxwell (Ed.), *Thinking: The expanding frontier.* Philadelphia: The Franklin Institute Press.

Dembo, M., & Gibson, S. (1985). Teachers' sense of efficacy: An important factor in school improvement. *Elementary School Journal, 86,* 173–184.

Dempster, F. (1988). The spacing effect. *American Psychologist, 43*(8), 627–634.

Dempster, F. (1991). Synthesis of research on reviews and tests. *Educational Leadership, 48*(7), 71–76.

Devin-Sheehan, L., Feldman, R., & Allen, V. (1976). Research on children tutoring children: A critical review. *Review of Educational Research, 46,* 355–385.

Dillon, D. (1989). Showing them that I want them to learn & that I care about who they are: A microethnography of the social organization of a secondary low-track English reading classroom. *American Educational Research Journal, 26*(2), 227–259.

Dillon, J. (1981). To question and not to question during discussions II. Non-questioning techniques. *Journal of Teacher Education, 32,* 15–20.

Dillon, J. (1982). Cognitive correspondence between question/statement response. *American Educational Research Journal, 19,* 540–551.

Dillon, J. (1987). *Classroom questions and discussions.* Norwood, NJ: Ablex.

Doyle, W. (1984). How order is achieved in classrooms: An interim report. *Journal of Curriculum Studies, 15*(3), 259–277.

Doyle, W. (1986). Classroom organization and management. In M. Wittrock (Ed.), *Handbook of research on teaching,* 3rd ed. (pp. 392–431). New York: Macmillan.

Dreisbach, M., & Keogh, B. (1982). Testwiseness as a factor in readiness test performance of young Mexican-American children. *Journal of Educational Psychology, 74,* 224–229.

Driscoll, J. (1978). *The effects of a teacher's eye contact, gestures, and voice intonation on student retention of factual material.* Unpublished doctoral dissertation. Hattiesburg, MS: University of Southern Mississippi.

Duffy, G., & Roehler, L. R. (1985). *Constraints on teacher change.* East Lansing, MI: Michigan State University Institute for Research on Teaching.

Duffy, G., Roehler, L., Meloth, M., & Vavrus, L. (1985). *Conceptualizing instructional explanation.* Chicago: AERA.

Duffy, G., Roehler, L., & Rackliffe, G. (1985). *Qualitative differences in teacher's instructional talk as they influence student awareness of lesson content.* Chicago: AERA.

Duffy, G., Roehler, L., & Rackliffe, G. (1986). How teachers' instructional talk influences students' understanding of lesson content. *Elementary School Journal, 87*, 3–16.

Dunkin, M., & Biddle, B. (1974). *The study of teaching.* New York, NY: Holt, Rinehart & Winston.

Dunn, R., & Dunn, K. (1978). *Teaching students through their individual learning styles.* Reston, VA: Reston Publishing.

Eggen, P., & Kauchak, D. (1988). *Strategies for teachers: Information processing models in the classroom* (2nd ed.). Englewood Cliffs, NJ: Prentice Hall.

Eggen, P., & Kauchak, D. (1992). *Educational psychology: Classroom connections.* Columbus, OH: Merrill.

Eggen, P., Kauchak, D., & Kirk, S. (1978). Hierarchial cues and the learning of concepts from prose materials. *Journal of Experimental Education, 46*(4), 7–10.

Eisner, E. (1969). Instructional and expressive educational objectives: Their formulation and use in curriculum. In W. Popham, E. Eisner, H. Sullivan, & L. Tyler (Eds.), *Monograph series on curriculum evaluation, no. 3.* Chicago, IL: Rand McNally.

Elam, S., Rose, L., & Gallup, A. (1991). The 23rd Annual Gallup Poll of the public's attitudes toward the public schools. *Phi Delta Kappan, 3*(1), 41–56.

Ellis, E., & Sabornie, E. (1986). Effective instruction with microcomputers: Promises, practices and preliminary findings. *Focus on Exceptional Children, 19*(4), 1–16.

Elton, L., & Laurillard, D. (1979). Trends in research on student learning. *Studies in Higher Education, 4*, 87–102.

Elwall, E., & Shanher, J. (1989). *Teaching reading in the elementary school* (2nd ed.). Columbus, OH: Merrill.

Emmer, E., & Evertson, C. (1980). *Effective management at the beginning of the school year in junior high classes (report no. 6107).* Austin: University of Texas Research and Development Center for Teacher Education.

Emmer, E., & Evertson, C. (1981). Synthesis of research on classroom management. *Educational Leadership, 38*, 342–349.

Emmer, E., Evertson, C., & Anderson, L. (1980). Effective classroom management at the beginning of the school year. *Elementary School Journal, 80*(5), 219–231.

Emmer, E., Evertson, C., Sanford, J., Clements, B., & Worsham, M. (1989). *Classroom management for secondary teachers* (2nd ed.). Englewood Cliffs, NJ: Prentice Hall.

Ennis, R. (1987). A taxonomy of critical thinking dispositions and abilities. In J. Baron & R. Sternberg (Eds.), *Teaching thinking skills* (pp. 9–26). New York: Freeman.

Erickson, F. (1986). Qualitative methods in research on teaching. In M. Wittrock (Ed.), *Handbook of research on teaching* (3rd ed.). New York: Macmillan, 119–162.

Erickson, F., & Mohatt, G. (1982). Cultural organization of participation structures in two classrooms of Indian students. In G. Spindler (Ed.), *Doing the ethnography of schooling.* New York: Holt, Rinehart & Winston.

Everson, H., Tobias, S., Hartman, H., & Gourgey, A. (1991, April). *Text anxiety in different curricular areas: An exploratory analysis of the role of subject matter.* Paper presented at the annual meeting of the American Educational Research Association, Chicago.

Evertson, C. (1980, April). *Differences in instructional activities in high and low achieving junior high classes.* Boston: AERA.

Evertson, C. (1982). Differences in instructional activities in higher- and lower-achieving junior high English and math classes. *Elementary School Journal, 82*, 329–350.

Evertson, C., Emmer, E., Clements, B., Sanford, J., & Worsham, M. (1989). *Classroom management for elementary teachers* (2nd ed.). Englewood Cliffs, NJ: Prentice Hall.

Fisher, C., Berliner, D., Filby, N., Marliave, R., Cahen, L., & Dishaw, M. (1980). Teaching behaviors, academic learning time, and student achievement: An overview. In C. Denham & A. Lieberman (Eds.), *Time to learn* (pp. 7–32). Washington, DC: National Institute of Education.

Fleming, M., & Chambers, B. (1983). Teacher-made tests: Windows on the classroom. In W. Hathaway (Ed.), *Testing in the schools: New directions for testing and measurement, no. 19* (pp. 29–38). San Francisco, CA: Jossey-Bass.

Floden, R., Porter, A., Schmidt, W., Freeman, D., & Schuille, J. (1981). Responses to curriculum pressures: A policy-capturing study of teacher decisions about content. *Journal of Educational Psychology, 73*, 129–141.

Florida State Office of Education (1985). *Minimum standards, science.* Tallahassee: Author.

Floyd, W. (1960). *An analysis of the oral questioning activity in selected Colorado primary classrooms.* (Doctoral dissertation, Colorado State College). Ann Arbor, MI: University Microfilms No. 60-6253.

Frederick, W. (1977). The use of classroom time in high schools above or below the median reading score. *Urban Education, 11*, 459–464.

French, P., & MacLure, M. (1981). Teacher questions, pupils' answers: An investigation of questions and answers in the infant classroom. *First Language, 2*, 31–45.

Fuchs, D., Fuchs, L., Bahr, M., Reeder, P., Gilman, S., Fernstrom, P., & Roberts, H. (1990). Prereferral intervention to increase attention and work productivity among difficult-to-teach pupils. *Focus on Exceptional Children, 22*(6), 1–7.

Gage, N. (1960). *Address appearing in "proceedings" research resume, Vol. 16.* Burlingame, CA: California Teachers Association.

Gage, N. (1978). *The scientific basis of the art of teaching.* New York: Teachers College Press.

Gage, N. L. (1985). *Hard gains in the soft sciences: The case of pedagogy.* Bloomington, IN: Center on Evaluation, Development and Research.

Gage, N., & Berliner, D. (1992). *Educational psychology* (5th ed.). Boston: Houghton Mifflin.

Gage, N., & Giaconia, R. (1981, Spring). Teaching practices and student achievement: Causal connections. *New York University Education Quarterly*, 2–9, 11–12.

Gall, M. (1987). Discussion methods. In M. Dunkin (Ed.), *International encyclopedia of teaching & teacher education* (pp. 232–236). Elmsford, NY: Pergamon Press.

Gall, M., & Gall, R. (1976). The discussion method. In N. Gage (Ed.), *The psychology of teaching methods* (pp. 166–216). Chicago: University of Chicago Press.

Gall, M. D. (1984, November). Synthesis of research on teachers' questioning. *Educational Leadership*, 40–47.

Gallup, A., & Clark, D. (1987). The 19th Annual Gallup Poll of the Public's Attitude Toward the Public School. *Phi Delta Kappan*, Sept., 17–30.

Gardner, H. (1983). *Frames of mind: The theory of multiple intelligences.* New York: Basic Books.

Gavelek, J., & Raphael, T. (1985). Metacognition, instruction, and their role of questioning activities. In D. Forrest-Pressley, G. MacKinnon, & T. Waller (Eds.), *Metacognition, cognition, and human performance: Vol. 2. Instructional practices* (pp. 103–136). New York: Academic Press.

Glaser, R. (1987). The integration of instruction and testing: Implications from the study of human cognition. In D. Berliner & B. Rosenshine (Eds.), *Talks to teachers.* New York: Random.

Glasser, W. (1969). *Schools without failure.* New York: Harper & Row.

Glasser, W. (1977). Ten steps in good discipline. *Today's Education, 66*, 61–63.

Glickman, C. (1990). *Supervision of instruction* (2nd ed.). Boston: Allyn & Bacon.

Glickman, C., & Bey, T. (1990). Supervision. In R. Houston (Ed.), *Handbook of research on teacher education* (pp. 549–568). New York: Macmillan.

Glover, J., Ronning, R., & Bruning, R. (1990). *Cognitive psychology for teachers.* New York: Macmillan.

Golden, N., Gersten, R., & Woodward, J. (1990). Effectiveness of guided practice during remedial reading instruction: An application of computer-managed instruction. *Elementary School Journal, 90*(3), 291–304.

Good, T. (1979). Teacher effectiveness in the elementary school. *Journal of Teacher Education, 30*(2), 52–64.

Good, T. (1983, April). *Classroom research.* New York: AERA.

Good, T. (1987). Two decades of research on teacher expectations: Findings and future directions. *Journal of Teacher Education*, July–August, 32–47.

Good, T., Biddle, B., & Brophy, J. (1975). *Teachers make a difference.* New York: Holt, Rinehart and Winston.

Good, T., & Brophy, J. (1991). *Looking in classrooms* (5th ed.). New York: Harper & Row.

Good, T., Grouws, D., & Ebmeier, J. (1983). *Active mathematics teaching.* New York: Longman.

Goodlad, J. (1984). *A place called school.* New York: McGraw-Hill.

Gordon, T. (1974). *Teacher effectiveness training.* New York: Peter H. Wyden.

Graham, S., & Harris, K. (1989). Components analysis of cognitive strategy instruction: Effects on learning disabled students' compositions and self-efficacy. *Journal of Educational Psychology, 81*(3), 353–361.

Graham, S., & Johnson, L. (1989). Teaching reading to learning disabled students: A review of research-supported procedures. *Focus on Exceptional Children, 21*(6), 1–9.

Gronlund, N. (1985a). *Measurement and evaluation in education* (6th ed.). New York: Macmillan.

Gronlund, N. (1985b). *Stating objectives for classroom instruction* (2nd ed.). New York: Macmillan.

Gronlund, N., & Linn, R. (1990). *Measurement and evaluation in teaching* (6th ed.). New York: Macmillan.

Gullickson, A., & Ellwein, M. (1985). Post hoc analysis of teacher-made tests: The goodness-of-fit between prescription and practice. *Educational Measurement: Issues and Practice, 4*(1), 15–18.

Gump, P. (1967). *The classroom behavior setting: Its nature and relation to student behavior* (Final Report). Washington, DC: U.S. Office of Education, Bureau of Research (ED 015 515).

Hallihan, M. (1984). Summary and implications. In P. Peterson, L. Wilkinson, & M. Hallinan (Eds.), *The social content of instruction: Group organization and group processes* (pp. 229–240). New York: Academic Press.

Hamachek, D. (1987). Humanistic psychology: Theory, postulates and implications for educational processes. In J. Glover & R. Ronning (Eds.), *Historical foundations of educational psychology* (pp. 159–182). New York: Plenum.

Hamilton, R., & Brady, M. (1991). Individual and classwide patterns of teachers' questioning in mainstreamed social studies and science classes. *Teaching & Teacher Education, 7*(3), 253–262.

Hardman, M., Drew, C., Egan, M., & Wolf, B. (1990). *Human exceptionality: Society, school and family* (3rd ed.). Boston, MA: Allyn & Bacon.

Harrow, A. (1972). *A taxonomy of the psychomotor domain: A guide for developing behavioral objectives.* New York: David McKay.

Harvard University Press. (1985). Homework. *Harvard Education Letter, 1,* 1.

Harvey, G., Kell, D., & Gadzuk–Drexler, N. (1990). *Implementing technology in the classroom: Paths to success and failure.* Boston, MA: AERA.

Hasselbring, T., Goin, L., & Bransford, J. (1988). Developing math automaticity in learning handicapped children: The role of computerized drill and practice. *Focus on Exceptional Children, 20*(6), 1–70.

Hassett, J. (1986). *Computer technology in the classroom.* New York: Horizon Technologies.

Heath, S. (1983). *Ways with words: Language, life, and work in communities and classrooms.* New York: Cambridge University Press.

Hersh, R., Miller, J., & Fielding, G. (1980). *Models of moral education.* New York: Longman.

Herman, J., & Dorr–Bremme, D. (1982). *Assessing students: Teachers routine practices and reasoning.* New York: AERA.

Hill, J., Yinger, R., & Robbins, D. (1981, April). *Instructional planning in a developmental preschool.* Los Angeles: AERA.

Hills, J. (1985). *Measurement and evaluation with classrooms* (2nd ed.). Columbus, OH: Melville.

Hines, C., Cruickshank, D., & Kennedy, J. (1985). Teacher clarity and its relationship to student achievement and satisfaction. *American Educational Research Journal, 22,* 87–99.

Hirsch, E. (1987). *Cultural literacy.* Boston: Houghton Mifflin.

Hodgkinson, H. (1991). Reform versus reality. *Phi Delta Kappan, 73*(1), 8–16.

Holley, C., & Dansereau, D. (1984). *Spatial learning strategies.* New York: Academic Press.

Humphrey, F. (1979). *"Shh!": A sociolinguistic study of teachers' turn-taking sanctions in primary school lessons.* Unpublished doctoral dissertation, Georgetown University, Washington, DC.

Hunter, M. (1984). Knowing, teaching and supervising. In P. Hosford (Ed.), *Using what we know about teaching* (pp. 169–192). Alexandria, VA: Association for Supervision and Curriculum Development.

Institute of Research on Teaching. (1978). Teacher planning studied and described. *Communication Quarterly, 1.* East Lansing, MI: Michigan State University Institute on Research on Teaching.

Jackson, P. (1968). *Life in classrooms.* New York: Holt, Rinehart & Winston.

Jackson, P. (1977). Looking into education's crystal ball. *Instructor, 87*(38), 38.

Jacobson, D., Eggen, P., & Kauchak, D. (1993). *Methods for teaching: A skills approach* (4th ed.). Columbus, OH: Merrill.

James, W. (1914). *Talks to teachers.* New York: Henry Holt.

Jarolimek, J. (1990). *Social studies in elementary education* (8th ed.). New York: Macmillan.

Jensen, A. (1987). Individual differences in mental ability. In J. Glover & R. Ronning (Eds.), *Historical foundations of educational psychology* (pp. 61–88). New York: Plenum.

Johnson, D., & Johnson, R. (1991). *Learning together & alone* (3rd ed.). Englewood Cliffs, NJ: Prentice Hall.

Jones, T., Sowell, V., Jones, J., & Butler, L. (1981). Changing children's perceptions of handicapped people. *Exceptional Children, 47,* 365–368.

Jones, V., & Jones, L. (1990). *Comprehensive classroom management: Motivating and managing students* (3rd ed.). Boston: Allyn & Bacon.

Jones, W., Jones, B., Bowyer, K., & Ray, M. (1983). *Computer literacy.* Reston, VA: Reston Publishing Co.

Julyan, C. (1989). National Geographic kids network: Real science in the elementary classroom. *Classroom Computer Learning, 10*(2), 30–41.

Kagan, S. (1989). *Cooperative learning: Resources for teachers.* San Juan Capistrano, CA: Resources for Teachers.

Kalechstein, P., Kalechstein, M., & Doctor, R. (1981). The effects of instruction on test-taking skills in second grade black children. *Measurement and Evaluation in Guidance, 13,* 198–202.

Karweit, N. (1984). Time on task reconsidered: Synthesis of research on time and learning. *Educational Leadership,* May, 32–35.

Karweit, N. (1985). Time scales, learning events, and productive instruction. In C. Fisher & D. Berliner (Eds.), *Perspectives in instructional time.* New York: Longman, 169–185.

Kauchak, D., & Peterson, K. (1987). *Teachers' thoughts on the assessment of their teaching.* Washington, DC: AERA.

Kellogg, J. (1988). Forces of change. *Phi Delta Kappan, 70,* 199–204.

Kerman, S. (1979). Teacher expectations and student achievement. *Phi Delta Kappan, 60*(10), 70–72.

Kim, E., & Kellough, R. (1983). *A resource guide for secondary school teaching* (3rd ed.). New York: Macmillan.

Kohlberg, L. (1976). Moral stages and moralization. In T. Lickona (Ed.), *Moral development and behavior* (pp. 2–15). New York: Holt, Rinehart and Winston.

Korinek, L. (1985). *Teacher questioning strategies used with elementary level mildly handicapped students.* Unpublished doctoral dissertation, University of Florida, Gainesville, FL.

Kounin, J. (1970). *Discipline and group management in the classroom.* New York: Holt, Rinehart & Winston.

Kounin, J. (1983). *Classrooms: Individuals or behavior settings?* (Monographs in Teaching and Learning, No. 1). Bloomington, IN: Indiana University School of Education.

Kounin, J., & Gump, P. (1974). Signal systems of lesson settings and the task-related behavior of preschool children. *Journal of Educational Psychology, 66,* 554–562.

Kounin, J., & Sherman, L. (1979). School environments as behavior settings. *Theory into Practice, 18,* 145–151.

Krathwohl, D., Bloom, B., & Masia, B. (1964). *Taxonomy of educational objectives. Handbook II: Affective domain.* New York: David McKay.

Kuhara–Kojima, K., & Hatana, G. (1991). Contribution of content knowledge and learning ability to the learning of facts. *Journal of Educational Psychology, 83*(2), 253–263.

Langer, J., Bartolome, L., Vasquez, O., & Lucas, T. (1990). Meaning construction in school literacy tasks: A study of bilingual students. *American Educational Research Journal, 27*(3), 427–471.

Larivee, B. (1985). *Effective teaching for successful mainstreaming.* New York: Longman.

Lee, J. (1985). *Teacher wait-time: Task performance of developmentally delayed and non-delayed young children.* Unpublished doctoral dissertation, University of Florida, Gainesville, FL.

Leinhardt, G. (1987). *Situated knowledge: An example from teaching.* Washington, DC: AERA.

Leinhardt, G., & Greeno, J. (1986). The cognitive skill of teaching. *Journal of Educational Psychology*, *78*(2), 75–95.

Leinhardt, G., Zigmond, N., & Cooley, W. (1981). Reading instruction and its effect. *American Education Research Journal*, *81*, 343–361.

Lemke, J. (1982). *Classroom communication of science*. Final report to NSF/RISF, April (Ed 222 346).

Levin, T., Libman, Z., & Amiad, R. (1980). Behavior patterns of students under an individualized learning strategy. *Instructional Science*, *5*, 391–401.

Lipman, M. (1987). Some thoughts on the foundations of reflective education. In J. Baron & R. Sternberg (Eds.), *Teaching thinking skills: Theory and practice* (pp. 151–161). New York: Freeman.

Logan, G. (1988). Automaticity, resources, and memory: Theoretical controversies and practical implications. *Human Factors*, *30*(5), 583–598.

Maddox, H., & Hoole, E. (1975). Performance decrement in the lecture. *Educational Review*, *28*, 17–30.

Mager, R. (1962). *Preparing instructional objectives*. Palo Alto, CA: Fearon.

Marsh, C. (1978). Socio-psychological influences upon expression and inhibition of curiosity. *Dissertation Abstracts International*, *39*, 445–B.

Marzano, R., Brandt, R., Hughes, C., Jones, B., Presseisen, B., Rankin, S., & Suhor, C. (1989). *Dimensions of thinking: A framework for curriculum and instruction*. Alexandria, VA: Association for Supervision and Curriculum Development.

Mayer, R. (1983). Can you repeat this? Qualitative effects of repetition and advance organizers from science prose. *Journal of Educational Psychology*, *75*, 40–49.

Mayer, R. (1987). *Educational psychology*. Boston: Little Brown.

McAshan, H. (1974). *The goals approach to performance objectives*. Philadelphia, PA: W. B. Saunders.

McCutcheon, G. (1982). How do elementary school teachers plan? The nature of planning and influences on it. In W. Doyle & T. Good (Eds.), *Focus on teaching* (pp. 260–279). Chicago, IL: University of Chicago Press.

McDaniel-Hine, L., & Willower, D. (1988). Elementary school teachers' work behavior. *Journal of Educational Research*, *81*, 274–281.

McGreal, T. (1985, November). *Characteristics of effective teaching*. Paper presented at the first annual Intensive Training Symposium, Clearwater, FL.

McTighe, J. (1987). Teaching for thinking, of thinking, and about thinking. In M. Heiman & J. Slomianko (Eds.), *Thinking skills instruction: Concepts and techniques*. Washington, DC: National Education Association.

Medly, D. M. (1979). The effectiveness of teachers. In P. Peterson & H. Walbert (Eds.), *Research on teaching: Concepts, findings, and interpretations*. Berkeley, CA: McCutchan, pp. 11–27.

Mehrabian, A., & Ferris, S. (1967). Inference of attitude from nonverbal behavior in two channels. *Journal of Consulting Psychology*, *31*, 248–252.

Mercer, J. (1973). *Labeling the mentally retarded*. Berkeley, CA: University of California Press.

Miller, P. (1985). Metacognition and attention. In D. Forrest-Pressley, G. MacKinnon, & T. Waller (Eds.), *Metacognition, cognition, and human performance: Vol. 2. Instructional practices* (pp. 181–222). New York: Academic Press.

Mills, S., Rice, C., Berliner, D., & Rousseau, E. (1980). The correspondence between teacher questions and student answers in classroom discourse. *Journal of Experimental Education*, *48*, 194–204.

Morine-Dershimer, G. (1979). *Teacher plans and classroom reality: The South Bay study: Part 4* (Research Series No. 60). East Lansing: Michigan State University Institute for Research on Teaching.

Morine-Dershimer, G., & Vallance, C. (1976). *Teacher planning*. Beginning Teacher Evaluation Study, Special Report C. San Francisco: Far West Laboratory.

Moyer, J. *An exploratory study of questioning in the instructional processes in selected elementary schools*. Doctoral dissertation, Columbia University. Ann Arbor, MI: University Microfilms, 1966. No. 66-2661.

Murphy, J., Weil, M., & McGreal, T. (1986). The basic practice model of instruction. *The Elementary School Journal*, *87*, 83–93.

Murray, F. (1986, May). *Necessity: The developmental component in reasoning*. Paper presented at the sixteenth annual meeting, Jean Piaget Society, Philadelphia.

Nazario, S. (1989). Failing in 81 languages. *Wall Street Journal*, *213*(63), B21.

Neale, D., Pace, A., & Case, A. (1983, April). *The influence of training, experience, and organizational environment on teachers' use of the systematic planning model.* New Orleans: AERA.

Neale, D., Smith, D., & Johnson, V. (1990). Implementing conceptual change teaching in primary science. *Elementary School Journal, 91*(2), 109–132.

Neudecker, T. (1989). Computer intensive classroom. *Technical Horizons in Education Journal, 16*(9), 61–65.

Nickerson, R. (1984). Kinds of thinking taught in current programs. *Educational Leadership, 42*(1), 26–36.

Nickerson, R. (1985). Understanding understanding. *American Journal of Education, 93,* 201–239.

Nickerson, R. (1988). On improving thinking through instruction. In E. Rothkopf (Ed.), *Review of research in education.* Washington, DC: American Educational Research Association.

Nickerson, R., Perkins, D., & Smith, E. (1985). *The teaching of thinking.* Hillsdale, NJ: Erlbaum.

Nosofsky, R. (1988). Similarity, frequency, and category representations. *Journal of Experimental Psychology: Learning, Memory and Cognition, 14,* 54–65.

Nottelman, E., & Hill, K. (1977). Test anxiety and off-task behavior in evaluative situations. *Child Development, 48,* 225–231.

Novak, J., & Gowin, B. (1984). *Learning how to learn.* New York: Cambridge University Press.

O'Keefe, P., & Johnston, M. (1987). *Teachers' abilities to understand the perspectives of students: A case study of two teachers.* Washington, DC: AERA.

Orlich, D., Harder, R., Callahan, C., Kravas, C., Kauchak, C., Pendergrass, R., & Keough, A. (1989). *Teaching strategies* (3rd ed.). Lexington, MA: D. C. Heath.

Oser, F. (1986). Moral education and values education: The discourse perspective. In M. Wittrock (Ed.), *Handbook of research on teaching,* 3rd ed., (pp. 917–941). New York: Macmillan.

Otteson, J., & Otteson, C. (1980). Effects of teacher gaze on children's story recall. *Perceptual and Motor Skill, 50,* 35–42.

Paivio, A. (1971). *Imagery and verbal processes.* New York: Holt, Rinehart & Winston.

Palincsar, A. (1991). Scaffolded instruction of listening comprehension with first graders at risk for academic difficulty. In A. McKeough & J. Lupart (Eds.), *Toward the practice of theory-based instruction* (pp. 50–65). Hillsdale, NJ: Erlbaum.

Palincsar, A., & Brown, A. (1987). Advances in improving the cognitive performance of handicapped students. In M. Wang, M. Reynolds, & H. Walberg (Eds.), *Handbook of special education, research and practice. Vol. I: Learner characteristics and adaptive education* (pp. 93–112). New York: Pergamon.

Palincsar, A., & Brown, A. (1989). Classroom dialogues to promote self-regulated comprehension. In J. Brophy (Ed.), *Advances in research in teaching* (Vol. 1). Greenwich, CT: JAI Press.

Papert, S. (1984). Trying to predict the future. *Popular Computing, 3*(12), 38.

Paul, R. (1984). Critical thinking: Fundamental to education for a free society. *Educational Leadership, 42,* 4–14.

Paul, R., Binker, A., & Charbonneau, M. (1987). *Critical thinking handbook: K–3.* Rohnert Park, CA: Center for Critical Thinking & Moral Critique.

Pearson, P., & Dole, J. (1985, April). *Explicit comprehension instruction: The model, the research, and the concerns.* Chicago: AERA.

Peterson, D. (1984). Nine issues. *Popular Computing, 3*(12), 11.

Peterson, P. (1986). Selecting students and services for compensatory education: Lessons from aptitude-treatment interaction research. In B. Williams, P. Richmond, & B. Mason (Eds.), *Designs for compensatory education: Conference proceedings and papers* (pp. II-1–II-62). Washington, DC: Research & Evaluation Associates.

Peterson, P., & Barger, S. (1985). Attribution theory and teacher expectancy. In J. Dasek, V. Hall, & W. Meyer (Eds.), *Teacher expectancies* (pp. 159–184). Hillsdale, NJ: Lawrence Erlbaum.

Peterson, P., Marx, A., & Clark, C. (1978). Teacher planning, teacher behavior, and student achievement. *American Educational Research Journal, 15,* 417–432.

Philips, S. (1972). Participant structures and communicative competence: Warm Springs children in community and classroom. In C. Cazden, V. John, & D. Hymes (Eds.), *Functions of language in the classroom* (pp. 370–394). New York: Teachers College Press.

Popham, J., & Baker, E. (1970). *Establishing instructional goals.* Englewood Cliffs, NJ: Prentice Hall.

Pratton, J., & Hales, L. W. (1986). The effects of active participation on student learning. *Journal of Educational Research, 79,* 210–215.

Prawat, R. (1989). Promoting access to knowledge, strategy, and disposition in students: A research synthesis. *Review of Educational Research, 59,* 1–41.

Presseisen, B. (1986). *Thinking skills: Research and practice.* Washington, DC: National Educational Association.

Presseisen, B. (1987). *Teaching thinking throughout the curriculum: A conceptual design.* Bloomington, IN: Pi Lambda Theta.

Pressley, M., Burkell, J., Cariglia-Bull, T., Lysynchuk, L., McGoldrick, Jr., Schneider, B., Snyder, B., Symons, S., & Woloshyn, V. (1990). *Cognitive strategy instruction.* Cambridge, MA: Brookline Books.

Pressley, M., Woloshyn, V., Lysynchuk, L., Martin, V., Wood, E., & Wiloughby, T. (1990). A primer of research on cognitive strategy instruction: The important issues and how to address them. *Educational Psychology Review, 2*(1), 1–58.

Purkey, S., & Smith, M. (1983). School reform: The district policy implications of the effective school literature. *Elementary School Journal, 85,* 353–389.

Ranzijn, F. (1991). The number of video examples and the dispersion of examples as instructional design variables in teaching concepts. *Journal of Experimental Education, 59*(4), 320–330.

Ravitch, D., & Finn, C. (1987). *What do our 17-year-olds know?* New York: Harper.

Redfield, D., & Rousseau, E. (1981). A meta-analysis of experimental research on teacher questioning behavior. *Review of Educational Research, 51*(2), 237–245.

Resnick, L. (1987a). *Education and learning to think.* Washington, DC: National Academy Press.

Resnick, L. (1987b). Learning in school and out. *Educational Researcher, 16*(4), 13–20.

Resnick, L., & Klopfer, L. (1989). Toward the thinking curriculum: An overview. In L. Resnick & L. Klopfer (Eds.), *Toward the thinking curriculum: Current cognitive research* (pp. 1–18). Alexandria, VA: Association for Supervision & Curriculum Development.

Reynolds, R., & Shirey, L. (1988). The role of attention in studying and learning. In C. Weinstein, E. Goetz, & P. Alexander (Eds.), *Learning and study strategies* (pp. 77–110). New York: Academic Press.

Rist, R. (1970). Student social class and teacher expectations: The self-fulfilling prophecy in ghetto education. *The Harvard Educational Review, 40,* 411–451.

Rock Kane, P. (1991). *The first year of teaching: Real world stories from American teachers.* New York: Walker.

Roehler, L., & Duffy, G. (1984). Direct explanation of comprehension processes. In G. Duffy, L. Roehler, & J. Mason (Eds.), *Comprehension instruction: Perspectives and suggestions* (pp. 265–279). New York: Longman.

Rogers, J., Moursund, D., & Engel, G. (1986). "Preparing precollege teachers for the computer age." In S. Toffe, *Computer applications in education.* New York: Random House.

Rokeach, M. (1973). *The nature of human values.* New York: Free Press.

Rosenfield, P., Lambert, N., & Black, A. (1985). Desk arrangement effects on pupil classroom behavior. *Journal of Educational Psychology, 77,* 101–108.

Rosenshine, B. (1971). *Teaching behaviors and student achievement.* London: National Foundation for Educational Research.

Rosenshine, B. (1979). Content, time, and direct instruction. In P. Peterson and H. Walberg (Eds.), *Research on teaching* (pp. 28–55). Berkeley, CA: McCutchan.

Rosenshine, B. (1980). How time is spent in elementary classrooms. In C. Denham & A. Lieberman (Eds.), *Time to learn.* Washington, DC: National Institute of Education.

Rosenshine, B. (1983). Teaching functions in instructional programs. *The Elementary School Journal, 83,* 335–351.

Rosenshine, B. (1986). *Unsolved issues in teaching content: A critique of a lesson on federalist paper no. 10 (1,2).* San Francisco: AERA.

Rosenshine, B. (1987). Explicit teaching. In D. Berliner & B. Rosenshine (Eds.), *Talks to teachers.* New York: Random House.

Rosenshine, B., & Furst, N. (1973). The use of direct observation to study teaching. In R. Travers (Ed.), *Second handbook of research on teaching* (pp. 122–183). Chicago: Rand McNally.

Rosenshine, B., & Stevens, R. (1986). Teaching functions. In M. Wittrock (Ed.), *Third handbook of research on teaching* (pp. 376–391). New York: Macmillan.

Rowe, M. (1974). Relation of wait-time and rewards to the development of language, logic, and fate control: Part one—wait time. *Journal of Research in Science Teaching, 11*(2), 81–94.

Rowe, M. (1975). Help denied to those in need. *Science and Children, 12*(6), 23–25.

Rowe, M. (1986). Wait time: Slowing down may be a way of speeding up. *Journal of Teacher Education*, Jan.–Feb., 43–50.

Rumelhart, D. (1981). Schemata: The building blocks of cognition. In J. Guthric (Ed.), *Comprehension and teaching: Research reviews*. Newark, DE: International Reading Association.

Rusnock, M., & Brandler, N. (1979, April). *Time off-task: Implications for learning*. San Francisco: AERA.

Rutter, M., Maughan, B., Mortimore, P., Ouston, J., & Smith, A. (1979). *Fifteen thousand hours*. Cambridge, MA: Harvard University Press.

Sabers, D., Cushing, K., & Berliner, D. (1991). Differences among teachers in a task characterized by simultaneity, multidimensionality and immediacy. *American Educational Research Journal, 28*(1), 63–88.

Salmon–Cox, L. (1981). Teachers and standardized achievement tests: What's really happening? *Phi Delta Kappan, 62*, 631–634.

Sanford, J., & Evertson, C. (1981). Classroom management in a low SES junior high: Three case studies. *Journal of Teacher Education, 32*, 34–38.

Sardo, D. (1982, October). *Teacher planning styles in the middle school*. Paper presented at the annual meeting of the Eastern Educational Research Association, Ellenville, NY.

Schreiber, J. (1967). *Teachers' question-asking techniques in social studies*. (Doctoral dissertation, University of Iowa.) Ann Arbor, MI: University Microfilms, No. 67-9099.

Schunk, D., & Swartz, C. (1991). *Process goals & progress feedback: Effects on children's self-efficiency & skills*. Chicago, IL: AERA.

Schwartz, B., & Reisberg, D. (1991). *Learning and memory*. New York: Norton.

Sewall, G. (1991). American 2000: An appraisal. *Phi Delta Kappan, 73*, 204–209.

Shields, P., & Shaver, D. (1990, April). *The mismatch between the school and home cultures of academically at-risk students*. Paper presented at the annual meeting of the American Educational Research Association, Boston.

Shimron, J. (1976). Learning activities in individually prescribed instruction. *Instructional Science, 5*, 391–401.

Shulman, L. (1986). Those who understand: Knowledge growth in teaching. *Educational Researcher*, February, 11–14.

Shulman, L. (1987). Knowledge and teaching: Foundations of the new reform. *Harvard Educational Review, 57*, 1–22.

Sieber, R. (1979). Schoolrooms, pupils, and rules. The role of informality in bureaucratic socialization. *Human Organizations, 38*(3), 273–283.

Sieber, R. (1981). Socialization implications of school discipline, or how first-graders are taught to "listen." In R. T. Sieber & A. J. Gordon (Eds.), *Children and their organizations: Investigations in American culture* (pp. 18–43). Boston: G. K. Hall.

Siegel, M., & Davis, D. (1986). *Understanding computer-based education*. New York: Random House.

Slakter, M., Koehler, R., & Hampton, S. (1970). Grade level, sex and related aspects of testwiseness. *Journal of Educational Measurement, 7*, 119–122.

Slavin, R. (1988). *Educational psychology* (2nd ed.). Englewood Cliffs, NJ: Prentice Hall.

Slavin, R. (1989). PET and the pendulum: Faddism in education & how to stop it. *Phi Delta Kappan, 70*(10), 252–258.

Slavin, R. (1990). *Cooperative learning: Theory, research and practice*. Englewood Cliffs, NJ: Prentice Hall.

Slavin, R., Karweit, N., & Madden, N. (Eds.). (1989). *Effective programs for students at risk*. Boston: Allyn & Bacon.

Smith, D., & Luckason, R. (1992). *Introduction to special education.* Boston, MA: Allyn & Bacon.

Smith, L., & Cotten, M. (1980). Effect of lesson vagueness and discontinuity on student achievement and attitude. *Journal of Educational Psychology, 72,* 670–675.

Smith, L., & Land, M. (1981). Low-inference verbal behaviors related to teacher clarity. *Journal of Classroom Interaction, 17,* 37–41.

Smith, R. (1987, March). *Multicultural considerations: Working with families of developmentally disabled and high-risk children: The Hispanic perspective.* Paper presented at the conference of the National Center of Clinical Infant Programs, Los Angeles.

Smyth, J. (1979). *An ecological analysis of pupil use of academic learning time.* Unpublished doctoral dissertation, University of Alberta.

Snyder, S., Bushur, L., Hoeksema, P., Olson, M., Clark, S., & Snyder, J. (1991, April). *The effect on instructional clarity and concept structure on students' achievement and perception.* Paper presented at the annual meeting of the American Educational Research Association, Chicago.

Snyderman, M., & Rothman, S. (1987). Survey of expert opinion on intelligence and aptitude testing. *American Psychologist, 42,* 137–144.

Stallings, J. (1975). Implementation and child effects of teaching practices in follow through classrooms. *Monographs of the Society for Research in Child Development, 40,* 7–8.

Stallings, J. (1980). Allocated academic learning time revisited or, beyond time on task. *Educational Researcher, 9,* 11–16.

Stallings, J. (1983). *Findings from the research on teaching: What we have learned.* Nashville: Peabody Center for Effective Teaching.

Stallings, J., Needels, M., & Staybrook, N. (1979). *How to change the process of teaching basic reading skills in secondary schools.* Menlo Park, CA: SRI International.

Sternberg, R. (1986). *Intelligence applied: Understanding and increasing your intellectual skills.* San Diego: Harcourt, Brace, Jovanovich.

Sternberg, R. (1987). Teaching intelligence: The application of cognitive psychology to the improvement of intellectual skills. In J. Baron & R. Sternberg (Eds.), *Teaching thinking skills: Theory and practice* (pp. 182–281). New York: Freeman.

Stevens, R. (1912). The question as a measure of efficiency in instruction: A critical study as a measure of classroom practice. *Teachers College Contributions to Education,* No. 48.

Stiggins, R., & Bridgeford, N. (1985). The ecology of classroom assessment. *Journal of Educational Measurement, 22,* 271–286.

Stipek, D. (1988). *Motivation to learn.* Englewood Cliffs, NJ: Prentice Hall.

Sund, R., Adams, D., Hackett, J., & Moyer, R. (1985). *Accent on science, level 3.* Columbus, OH: Merrill.

Swartz, R. (1987). Critical thinking, the curriculum, and the problem of transfer. In D. Perkins, J. Lochhead, & J. Bishop (Eds.), *Thinking: Progress in research and teaching.* Hillsdale, NJ: Erlbaum.

Taylor, P. (1970). *How teachers plan their courses.* Slough, Berkshire, England: National Foundation for Educational Research.

Tennyson, R., & Cocciarella, M. (1986). An empirically based instructional design theory for teaching concepts. *Review of Educational Research, 56,* 40–71.

Tobin, K. (1983). Management of time in classrooms. In B. Fraser (Ed.), *Classroom management* (pp. 22–35). Perth, Australia: WAIT Press.

Tobin, K. (1987). Role of wait time in higher cognitive level learning. *Review of Educational Research, 57*(1), 69–95.

Tobin, K., & Capie, W. (1982). Relationships between classroom process variables and middle school science achievement. *Journal of Educational Psychology, 14,* 441–454.

Top, B., & Osguthorpe, R. (1987). Reverse role tutoring: The effects of handicapped students tutoring regular class students. *Elementary School Journal, 87*(4), 413–425.

Trentham, L. (1975). The effect of distractions on sixth-grade students in a testing situation. *Psychology in the Schools, 16,* 439–443.

Tyler, R. (1949). *Basic principles of curriculum and instruction.* Chicago: University of Chicago Press.

United States Department of Education. (1990). *Twelfth annual report to congress on the implementation of the Education of the Handicapped Act.* Washington, DC: U.S. Government Printing Office.

Vasa, S. (1984). Classroom management: A selected review of the literature. In R. Egbert & M. Kluender (Eds.), *Using research to improve education* (pp. 64–73). Washington, DC: AACTE.

Vaughn, J. (1984). Concept structuring: The technique and empirical evidence. In C. Holley and D. Dansereau (Eds.), *Spatial learning strategies*. New York, NY: Academic Press.

Veenman, S. (1984). Perceived problems of beginning teachers. *Review of Educational Research, 54*(2), 143–178.

Villegas, A. (1991a). *Culturally responsive pedagogy for the 1990's & beyond*. Princeton, NJ: Educational Testing Service.

Villegas, A. (1991b). *Culturally responsive teaching*. Princeton, NJ: Educational Testing Service.

Vito, R., & Connell, J. (1988, April). *A longitudinal study of at-risk high school students: A theory-based description and intervention*. Paper presented at the annual meeting of the American Educational Research Association, New Orleans.

Vygotsky, L. (1978). *Mind in society: The development of higher psychological processes*. Cambridge, MA: Harvard University Press.

Walberg, H. J. (1984). Improving the productivity of America's schools. *Educational Leadership, 41*, 19–27.

Walberg, H., Paschal, R., & Weinstein, T. (1985). Homework's powerful effects on learning. *Educational Leadership*, April, 76–79.

White, M. (1975). Natural rates of teacher approval and disapproval in the classroom. *Journal of Applied Behavior Analysis, 8*, 367–372.

Whitmer, S. (1983). *A descriptive multimethod study of teacher judgment during the marking process (research series no. 122)*. East Lansing: Michigan State University Institute for Research on Teaching (ED 234-052).

Wiley, D., & Harnishefeger, A. (1974). Explosion of a myth: Quantity of schooling and exposure to instruction, major education vehicles. *Educational Researcher, 3*, 7–12.

Wilson, S., Shulman, L., & Richert, A. (1987). "100 different ways" of knowing: Representations of knowledge in teaching. In J. Calderhead (Ed.), *Exploring teacher thinking* (pp. 104–125). London: Cassel.

Wilson, Z. (1991). Answers and questions. In P. Kane (Ed.), *The first year of teaching: Real world stories from America's teachers* (pp. 45–50). New York: Walker & Co.

Winitzky, N. (1991). Multicultural and mainstreamed classrooms. In R. Arends, *Learning to teach* (2nd ed., pp. 125–158). New York: McGraw-Hill.

Winne, P. (1979). Experiments relating teachers' use of higher cognitive questions to student achievement. *Review of Educational Research, 49*, 13–50.

Wittrock, M. (Ed.). (1986). *Third handbook of research on teaching*. New York: Macmillan.

Wlodkowski, R. (1984). *Motivation and teaching: A practical guide*. Washington, DC: The National Education Association.

Wlodkowski, R. (1987, October). The relationship between teacher motivation and student motivation—a dynamic relationship. Paper presented at the Near East South Asia Council for Overseas Schools, Nairobi, Kenya.

Wlodkowski, R., & Jaynes, J. (1990). *Eager to learn: Helping children become motivated and love learning*. San Francisco: Jossey-Bass.

Woolfolk, A., & Brooks, D. (1985). The influence of teachers' nonverbal behaviors on student's perceptions and performance. *The Elementary School Journal, 85*, 513–528.

Yinger, R. (1977). *A study of teacher planning: Description and theory development using ethnographic and information processing methods*. Unpublished doctoral dissertation, Michigan State University, East Lansing, MI.

Young, R., & O'Shea, T. (1981). Errors in children's subtraction. *Cognitive Science, 5*, 153–177.

Zahorik, J. (1968). Classroom behavior of teachers. *Journal of Educational Research, 62*, 147–150.

Zahorik, J. (1975). Teachers' planning models. *Educational Leadership, 33*, 134–139.

Zellermayer, M., Salomon, G., Glaberson, T., & Givon, H. (1991). Enhancing writing-related metacognitions through a computerized writing partner. *American Educational Research Journal, 28*(2), 373–391.

Zimmerman, B., & Blotner, R. (1979). Effects of model persistence and success on children's problem solving. *Journal of Educational Psychology, 71*, 508–513.

Zimmerman, B., & Ringle, J. (1981). Effects of model persistence and statements of confidence on children's self-efficacy and problem solving. *Journal of Educational Psychology, 73*, 485–493.

# Author Index

# Subject Index

MAY 0 7 2021

WITHDRAWN

MAY 0 7 2024

DAVID O. McKAY LIBRARY
BYU-IDAHO